The *CCNA Exam Certification Guide* uses real-world scenarios with exercises, challenging questions, detailed explanation of exam objectives, and a test simulation on the accompanying CD-ROM to help you master the CCNA exam objectives. All exam objectives are covered and are pointed out like this:

Objective 44: Configure standard and extended access lists to filter IP traffic

You'll be tested with challenging questions before and after the chapters:

Q&A: How would a user who does not have the enable password find out what access lists have been configured, and where they are enabled?

Scenario-based exercises at the end of each chapter test your knowledge and ability:

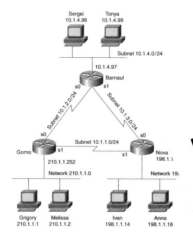

Scenarios: Given the network setup in the accompanying diagram, configure a correct access list for the routers, and enable the access list assuming the f llowing set of requirements for filterir

ot connect to hosts in

sts on Nova's

er communications are allowed

In addition, the CD provides a simulation of the CCNA exam with multiple-choice questions to help ensure your mastery of the exam objectives. For example:

Q. How would you apply access list 101 to the Ethernet interface of a 2501 Cisco router for outbound traffic?

a. ip access group 101 out

b. ip access class 101 out

c. access list 101 out

d. None of the above

The book's chapters are organized by topic area: OSI Reference, WAN Protocols, IOS, Network Protocols, Routing, Network Security, and LAN Switching. By working through the information, exercises, and questions, you should feel confident as you prepare to take the exam and acquire your CCNA certification.

Feedback Information

At Cisco Press, our goal is to create in-depth technical books of the highest quality and value. Each book is crafted with care and precision, undergoing rigorous development that involves the unique expertise of members from the professional technical community.

Readers' feedback is a natural continuation of this process. If you have any comments regarding how we could improve the quality of this book, or otherwise alter it to better suit your needs, you can contact us through e-mail at ciscopress@mcp.com. Please make sure to include the book title and ISBN in your message.

We greatly appreciate your assistance.

Associate Publisher	Jim LeValley
Executive Editor	John Kane
Cisco Systems Program Manager	H. Kim Lew
Managing Editor	Patrick Kanouse
Development Editors	Christopher Cleveland
	Andrew Cupp
Project Editor	Dayna Isley
Copy Editor	Sydney Jones
Technical Editors	Thomas M. Thomas II
	Henry Benjamin
	Jeff Doyle
	Kevin Downes
Team Coordinator	Amy Lewis
CD Questions	Thomas M. Thomas II
	Jeffrey King
Book Designer	Scott Cook
Cover Designer	Karen Ruggles
Proofreaders	John Rahm
	Megan Wade
Layout Technician	Brad Lenser
Indexer	Tim Wright

About the Author

Wendell Odom, CCIE, is the Technology Director of Lacidar Unlimited, Inc., a networking consulting and training company in Atlanta, Georgia. In this role, Wendell provides both expert advice about many aspects of building networks, and full design and implementation assistance for large projects. Wendell is CCIE #1624 and a Certified Cisco Systems Instructor and has taught various Cisco certification courses including Introduction to Cisco Router Configuration (ICRC), Advanced Cisco Router Configuration (ACRC), Cisco SNA for Multiprotocol Administrators (SNAM), Cisco Channel Interface Processor (CIP), and Cisco ATM (CATM). Wendell is one of the first Cisco instructors certified without a probationary testing period and is the first non-Cisco instructor in the United States to teach Cisco's SNAM, CIP, and DLSw courses.

About the Technical Reviewers

Thomas M. Thomas II, a member of the OSPF Working Group, is Cisco Certified and a Course Designer in Cisco Systems' Worldwide Training Division. Prior to his duties at Cisco, Tom was a Senior Network Engineer and Group Leader of the Advanced Systems Solutions Engineering Team for MCI's Managed Network Services. His responsibilities included network support and design consulting. Tom has also worked as a technical team leader at AT&T Solutions, for which he provided technical support and network management for Cisco routers over ATM and Frame Relay, configured various networking protocols, and developed custom training programs. He has also performed network management and troubleshooting duties for many years as a member of the United States Air Force. Tom is the author of *OSPF Network Design Solutions*, published by Cisco Press.

Henry Benjamin, CCNA, is a Senior Network Consultant for a large organization specializing in IP routing protocols and SNA. He is a Cisco Certified Network Associate and has planned, designed, and implemented large networks including IGRP, EIGRP, and OSPF. Over the past two years he has focused on large SNA networks including the largest Cisco DLSw+ network in the world. Henry also holds a Bachelor of Engineering degree from Sydney University.

Jeff Doyle is a Senior Network Systems Consultant with International Network Services (INS) in Denver, Colorado. He is a Cisco Certified Internetwork Expert (CCIE #1919) and a Certified Cisco Systems Instructor. He has developed and taught a variety of networking and internetworking courses. Jeff is the author of *CCIE Professional Development: Routing TCP/IP, Volume I*, published by Cisco Press

Kevin Downes is a Senior Network Systems Consultant with International Network Services (INS). His network certifications include the Cisco CCIE, Bay Networks CRS, Certified Network Expert (CNX) Ethernet, Novell CNE, and Banyan Systems CBE. He has published several articles on the subjects of network infrastructure design, network operating systems (NOS), and Internet Protocol (IP). He completed his B.S. in Computer Information Systems from Strayer University in 1993. Kevin is the coauthor of *Internetworking Troubleshooting Handbook* and *Internetworking Technologies Handbook, Second Edition*, both published by Cisco Press.

Dedications

First, to my loving wife, Kris, whose support and tolerance during our first year of marriage allowed me to write this book. Also, to Kris's now deceased, longtime companion, Sterling the cat, who kept Kris company for 17 years before we met, and who kept me company during my first month of writing this book at home.

Acknowledgments

Chris Cleveland, development editor for Cisco Press, deserves a great deal of credit for making this book much better. When one person tells you someone is the best at what he does, you might at least pay attention. When everyone does, it's impressive. All the accolades are true—great job!

John Kane of Cisco Press was a great help as we set the tone for the Cisco Press Certification series. John, our many talks together, refining what the books should and should not be, were of great help. Your infinite patience working with a first-time author helped as well.

Amy Lewis of Cisco Press helped greatly by taking care of many details. Amy, in five years of running a business, I have never had business transactions taken care of with such ease and professionalism. And thanks for getting those advance checks to me in a timely fashion!

Tom Thomas and Henry Benjamin provided excellent technical review for the book chapters. Tom, your insight and interest in all aspects of Cisco certification helped beyond the call of duty, and your thoroughness absolutely made the book better. Henry, your specific suggestions for how to fix problematic parts of the book were particularly helpful, as well as your Aussie sense of humor! I saw from your comments that you have what it takes to succeed as a writer, as Tom has already shown with his OSPF book.

Clare Gough was also very helpful with technical discussions, as was Margo Lindenmayer of Network Associates. James Deoglaer of Convergent Communications was generous enough to give me the keys to their lab, which was very helpful for some of the lab scenarios. And Mike Zanotto of Skyline Computer provided some timely but flexible business, so I could write and pay my bills. Thanks!

To my good friends Greg and Lance, whose prayers in the midst of several nagging illnesses helped get me through the process. And to my wife, Kris, who has been a blessing beyond compare, both by doing more of my share of the work at home, and with emotional support. And finally, and most important, to Jesus Christ, my savior, whose joy gives me strength.

Contents at a Glance

Table of Contents

Introduction: Overview of Certification and How to Succeed

Professional certifications have been an important part of the computing industry for many years and will continue to become more and more important. Many reasons exist for these certifications, but the most popularly cited reason is that of credibility. All other considerations held equal, the certified employee/consultant/job candidate is considered more valuable than one who is not.

Cisco Certifications: Training Paths and Exams

The *Cisco Certified Internetwork Expert (CCIE)* certification program has been available since the early '90s. This long-standing certification has maintained a high degree of credibility and is recognized as a certification that lives up to the name "expert." The CCIE certification process requires passing a computer based test and then a two-day hands-on lab. Recertification is required every two years to ensure that the individual has kept skills up-to-date.

Many problems were created by having one highly credible, but difficult to pass, certification. One problem was that there was no way to distinguish between someone who is almost ready to pass CCIE and a novice. The CCIE lab test is meant to prove that the individual not only has mastery of many topics, but the ability to learn and unravel situations quickly and under pressure. Many highly respected engineers have failed the CCIE lab on the first try. Employers wanting to reward employees based on certification, employers looking at prospective new employees, and network managers trying to choose between competing consulting companies have had too few Cisco-related certifications on which they could base their decisions.

In an effort to solve these problems, Cisco Systems has created several new "Cisco Career Certifications." Included in these new certifications is a series of certifications related to routing and switching. The *Cisco Certified Network Associate (CCNA)* certification, accomplished by passing a computer-based exam, is one of these new certifications oriented toward routing and switching. CCNA is the first certification in this series. If you understand the protocols listed in the table of contents, plus how they apply to the network diagramed in Figure I–1, then you are a candidate who should be ready for the CCNA exam.

Figure I–1   *Typical Network Used for the CCNA Exam*

The WAN links in the Figure I-1 are Frame Relay, point-to-point serial, and ISDN links. The LANs are typically Ethernet, with LAN switches in some cases.

The CCNA exam is used to prove mastery of the features used in typical small networks. CCNA certification is required before attempting CCNA and CCDP certifications. Figure I–2 lists the various Cisco certifications relating to routing and switching, along with the exams required.

Some reasons for taking the CCNA exam are as follows:

1. To prove your mastery of basic internetwork concepts.

2. To create a more impressive entry in your résumé.

3. To prove that beyond simply taking a Cisco certified course, you understand the topics in the class.

4. To demonstrate that you have equivalent experience and expertise to those who have taken the Cisco certified courses.

5. To obtain a Cisco certification while you gain the experience needed to pass the CCIE Routing and Switching or CCIE ISP Dial certifications. (Unless you want to shoot for the stars and take a CCIE test now, **CCNA is the only first step** toward certification involving routing and LAN switching.)

6. To encourage self-discipline in your study as you try to become CCIE certified.

7. As a stepping stone to the CCNP and CCDP certifications.

8. For consultants, to provide a marketing edge compared to your competitors by asserting that a Cisco certified individual will be working with a particular prospective client.

Two suggested training paths are outlined on Cisco's Web site and include suggested courses that will prepare you to pass the exam. These paths are also described later in this chapter, along with two other training paths.

Figure I–2 *Cisco Certifications and Exams on the Routing and Switching Career Path*

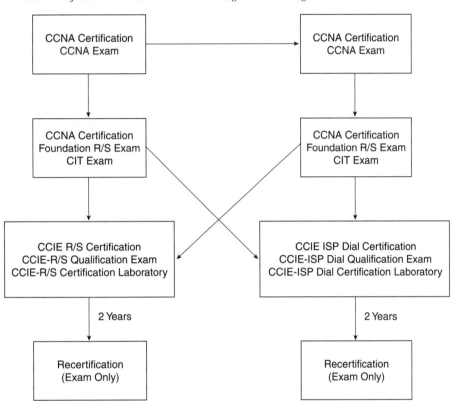

The *Cisco Certified Networking Professional (CCNP)* exam is used to prove mastery of more complex networks. In this case, complex means topics covered in the prerequisite courses. Like CCNA, the CCNP certification is oriented toward proving the skills needed to implement internetworks. Most of the same reasons for wanting to become CCNA certified are also true for CCNP. **CCNA certification is a prerequisite to taking the CCNP exam.**

When this book went to press, the courses suggested in the training path defined by Cisco for CCNP were as follows:

1. A training path leading to CCNA certification

2. The Advanced Cisco Router Configuration (ACRC) course

3. The Cisco LAN Switching Course (CLSC) course

4. The Configuring, Monitoring, and Troubleshooting Dial-up Services (CMTD) course

5. The Cisco Internetwork Troubleshooting (CIT) course

The *Cisco Certified Design Associate (CCDA)* exam is used to prove mastery over network design issues for basic networks. It is similar to CCNA but is focused on design issues. This certification is particularly important for those with presales oriented jobs.

When this book went to press, the courses suggested in the training path defined by Cisco for CCDA were as follows:

1. The Internetworking Technology Multimedia (ITM) CD-based course

2. The Designing Cisco Networks (DCN) course

The *Cisco Certified Design Professional (CCDP)* exam is used to prove mastery over design issues for more advanced networks. This certification proves mastery of design issues in complex networks. In this case, complex means topics covered in the prerequisite courses. This certification is particularly important for those with presales oriented jobs. **CCDA and CCNA certification are prerequisites to taking the CCDP exam.**

When this book went to press, the courses suggested in the training path defined by Cisco for CCDP were as follows:

1. A training path leading to CCDA and CCNA certification

2. The Advanced Cisco Router Configuration (ACRC) course

3. The Cisco LAN Switching Course (CLSC) course

4. The Configuring, Monitoring, and Troubleshooting Dial-up Services (CMTD) course

5. The Cisco Internetwork Design (CID) course

A Few Words on the Various Cisco Certifications

You should note the following when considering CCNA, CCNP, CCDA, and CCDP Cisco routing and switching certifications:

Most people will not pursue all four of these certifications: CCNA, CCNP, CCDA, and CCDP—Most people will follow a track of getting CCNA and then either focus on the design certifications or the implementation certifications.

Certification exams cover the content taught in Cisco Systems Certified Courses—There is a definite benefit to taking the courses suggested by Cisco before taking the exam. The courses are not required for certification, however.

The old CCIE is now CCIE-R/S—Cisco added the designation R/S for "routing and switching," which includes both LAN and ATM switching. This is the CCIE of old. CCIE-ISP covers dial issues in more depth, as well as exterior routing protocols. CCIE-WAN, which entails a separate career path of recommended courses and exams, covers WAN switching and voice.

Only the CCIE certifications require a hands-on lab exam—CCIE-R/S, CCIE-ISP, and CCIE-WAN all require passing a hands-on lab exam after passing a written (computer-based) exam. Recertification for CCIE of any kind currently does not require a hands-on lab, but rather a more detailed written test on an area of specialization.

Recertification is not (yet) required for CCNA, CCNP, CCDA, and CCDP—Because these certifications were announced in early 1998, there is not yet a need for recertification rules. In my opinion, Cisco will eventually require recertification for these, probably with a written (computer-based) test.

In the future, CCNA might be required before taking CCIE—Today, you can take the CCIE written exam at any time. In my opinion, the reason these new certifications are not required before taking the CCIE exam today is that there would be complaints from people who have prepared for CCIE, but would have then to back up and take other tests. If my theory is true, it seems reasonable to assume that one day Cisco will require CCDP or CCNP certification before taking the CCIE written and lab exams. Of course, the CCNP and CCDP certifications require CCNA certification first. It will be interesting to see if my predictions come true!

There is also a WAN Switching Career Certifications path—There is a whole other set of certifications with the acronym WAN in the title, which refer to the WAN switching topics and the functions of what was once the Stratacom product line (which was bought by Cisco). CCNA-WAN, CCNP-WAN, CCDP-WAN, and CCIE-WAN are the certifications; only a CCDA-WAN is missing as compared to the routing/switching certifications. These certifications are similar in concept to the others, but because the technology concerned is WAN switching, there are different exams and courses for the Career Certification levels. Please see Cisco's Web site for more details.

Objectives

The objective of this book is to help you fully understand, remember, and recall all the details of the topics covered on the CCNA exam. When that objective is reached, passing the CCNA exam should follow. The CCNA exam will be a foundation for most people as they progress through the other Cisco certifications; passing the exam because of a thorough understanding and recall of the topics will be incredibly valuable at the next steps.

This book will help you **pass the CCNA exam**, by doing the following:

- Helping you discover which test topics you have not mastered

- Providing explanations and information to fill in your knowledge gaps

- Supplying exercises and scenarios which enhance your ability to recall and deduce the answers to test questions

- Providing practice exercises on the topics and the testing process via online test questions (delivered on the CD)

Who Should Read This Book?

This book is not designed to be a general networking topics book, although it can be used for that purpose. This book is intended to tremendously increase your chances of passing the CCNA exam. Although others may benefit from using this book, the book is written assuming you want to pass the exam.

So why should you want to pass CCNA? To get a raise. To show your manager you are working hard to increase your skills. As a requirement from your manager before he will spend money on another course. As a résumé enhancer. Because you work in a presales job at a reseller and want to become CCDA and CCDP certified. To prove you know the topic, if you learned via on-the-job training (OJT) rather than from taking the prerequisite classes. Or one of many other reasons.

Others who may want to use this book are those considering moving beyond Cisco's ICRC (Introduction to Cisco Router Configuration) course to take Cisco's ACRC (Advanced Cisco Router Configuration) or CLSC (Cisco LAN Switch Configuration) courses. If you can answer a high percentage of the questions in this book, you are ready for those courses!

Have You Mastered All the Exam Objectives?

The exam will test you on a wide variety of topics; most people will not remember all the topics on the exam. Because some study will be required, this book focuses on helping you obtain the maximum benefit from the time you spend preparing for the exam. There are many sources for the information covered in the exam; for example, you could read the Cisco Documentation CD. However, this book is the most effective way to prepare for the exam.

You should begin your exam preparation by reading Chapter 1 and spending ample time reviewing the exam objectives listed there. Check out Cisco's "Cisco Connection Online" Web Site (http://www.cisco.com) for any future changes to the list of objectives.

Preparation Before Using This Book

This book assumes that you fit into one of four general categories relating to your preparation before using this book. These categories, or training paths, are outlined in Table I–1.

Table I–1 *Four Possible CCNA Training Paths*

Training Path	What Is Involved
1. CCNA Path 1	As defined by Cisco Systems, this involves taking two courses:
	Internetworking Technology Multimedia (ITM) (CD-based).
	Cisco Routing and LAN Switching (CRLS) (instructor led).
2. CCNA Path 2	As defined by Cisco Systems, this involves taking three courses:
	Internetworking Technology Multimedia (ITM) (CD-based).
	Intro to Cisco Router Configuration (ICRC) (instructor led).
	High Performance Solutions for Desktop Connectivity (HPSDC) (CD-based).
3. Cisco Networking Academy	Cisco's Networking Academies are designed for high school and university students, with a goal of providing a learning path that provides the students with valuable Cisco skills, ready to use in the marketplace.
4. "OJT"	As defined by this book, on-the-job training, without the previous courses.

If you fall into Training Path 1, you happened to have taken the path that most closely matches what is covered on the exam. Many, however, have already taken Training Path 2, or at least the ICRC part of it. If that is the case, you will need to learn about LAN switching. The HPSDC CD course, and/or this book, can fill the gap. If you are in Training Path 3, this book will help you decide what pieces are missing from your skill set, and direct you in how to prepare. If you followed Training Path 4, you probably have lots of knowledge, but possibly not all the knowledge about the topics that are covered on the exam. This book will help you find the additional topics you need to study before taking the exam.

This book is designed with features that help CCNA candidates from each of these four preparation tracks complete their mastery of basic networks and pass the exam. Figure I–3 outlines the basic approach that you should use, depending on which training path you have followed. The details about which topics you should pay attention to during your preparation time are contained in Chapter 1.

Figure I–3 *Achieving Mastery through the Training Paths*

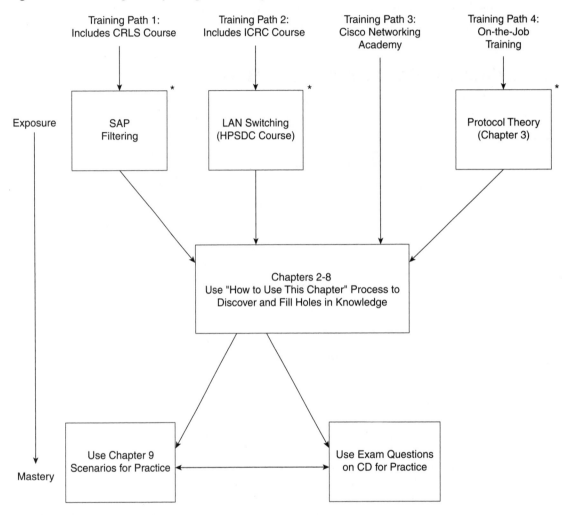

How This Book Is Organized

The book begins with a chapter definition of the topics that will be covered by the CCNA exam. Before studying for any exam, knowing the topics that could be covered is vitally important. With the CCNA exam, knowing what is on the exam is seemingly straightforward; Cisco publishes a list of 60 CCNA objectives. However, the objectives are certainly open to interpretation. Many topics may be considered on the fringe of what an objective implies; Chapter 1 attempts to clarify what is definitely on the exam, what is not, and it also lists which topics may be on the exam.

Chapters 2–8 match directly to Cisco's CCNA exam objectives. Each chapter begins with a quiz so that you can quickly determine your current level of readiness. The chapters are as follows:

2. Understanding Cisco's Internetwork Operating System (IOS) Software

3. Understanding the OSI Reference Model

4. Understanding LANs and LAN Switching

5. Network Protocols: Understanding the TCP/IP Suite and Novell NetWare Protocols

6. Understanding Routing

7. Understanding Network Security

8. WAN Protocols: Understanding Point-to-Point, Frame Relay, and ISDN

Additional scenarios in Chapter 9, "Scenarios for Final Preparation," provide a method of final preparation with more questions and exercises. Also, example test questions and the testing engine on the CD allow simulated exams for final practice.

Approach

Retention and recall are the two features of human memory most closely related to performance on tests. This exam preparation guide focuses on increasing both the retention and recall of the topics on the exam. The other human characteristic involved in successfully passing the exam is intelligence; this book does not address that issue!

Adult retention is typically less than that of children. It is common for four year olds to pick up basic language skills in a new country faster than their parents. Children retain facts as an end unto itself; adults typically need either a stronger reason to remember a fact, or must have a reason to think about that fact several times to retain that fact in memory. For these reasons, a student who attends a typical Cisco course, and retains 50 percent of the material, is actually quite an amazing student!

Memory recall is based on connectors to the information that needs to be recalled. For example, if the exam asks what ARP stands for, we automatically add information to the question. We know the topic is networking, because of the test. We may recall the term "ARP Broadcast," which implies it is the name of something that flows in a network. Maybe we do not recall all three words in the acronym, but we recall that it has something to do with Addressing. Of course, because the test is multiple choice, if only one answer begins with Address, we have a pretty good guess. Having read the answer "Address Resolution Protocol," then we may even have the infamous "aha" experience, in which we are then sure that our answer is correct (and possibly a brightly lit light bulb is hovering over our head). All these added facts and assumptions are the connectors that eventually lead our brains to the fact needed to be recalled.

Of course, recall and retention work together. If you do not retain the knowledge, it will be difficult to recall it!

This book is designed with features to help you increase retention and recall. It does this in the following ways:

- Providing succinct and complete methods of helping you decide what you already know and what you do not know.

- Giving references to the exact passages in this book that review those concepts you did not recall, so you can quickly be reminded about a fact or concept.

- Including exercise questions that supply fewer "connectors" than multiple choice questions. This helps you exercise recall and avoids giving you a false sense of confidence, as a multiple-choice only exercise might do. For example, fill-in-the-blank questions require you to have better recall than a multiple choice question.

- Pulling the entire breadth of subject matter together. A separate, larger chapter (Chapter 9) containing scenarios and several related questions, covering every topic on the exam, gives you the chance to prove that you have gained a mastery over the subject matter. This reduces the "connectors" implied by questions residing in a particular chapter and requires you to exercise other connectors to remember the details!

- Finally, accompanying this book is a CD-ROM that has exam-like, multiple-choice questions. These are useful for you to practice taking the exam and to get accustomed to the time restrictions imposed during the exam.

Features and Conventions of This Book

The various features of this book are listed as follows:

Cross Reference to CCNA Objectives—Cisco lists the objectives of the CCNA exam on their Web site. That list is included in Chapter 1, "What Is CCNA?" of this book. A section of each core chapter will include a reference to the CCNA objectives discussed in that chapter.

"Do I Know This Already?" Quiz—This beginning section of each chapter is designed to thoroughly quiz you on all topics in that chapter. Use your score on these questions to determine your relative need to study this topic further.

Foundation Topics—This section in each chapter explains and reviews topics that will be covered in the exam. If you feel the need for some review of the topics listed in that chapter, read through the explanations in this section. If you do not feel as much need to review these topics, review the charts and lists in each chapter and then proceed directly to the exercises at the end of the chapter.

Charts and Tables—Most of the facts learned in the prerequisite courses are summarized in tables and charts in each chapter. This enables you to review a chapter quickly, focusing on these charts and tables, without having to read the text. If you want to learn more, pause, and read the paragraphs leading up to the chart or paragraph. This is just one of the methods used in this book to enable you to make maximum use of you preparation time!

Q&A— Thinking about the same fact in many different ways increases recall; during a timed test, recall is a very important factor. During study time, increasing retention is most important, so there is something in memory you can recall in the future. These end-of-the-chapter questions focus on recall, covering topics in the Foundation Topics section by using several types of questions. And because the "Do I Know This Already?" quiz questions can help increase your recall as well, they are restated in the Q&A sections. Restating these questions, along with new questions, provides a larger set of practice questions for when you finish a chapter and for final review when your exam date is approaching.

Scenarios—Chapter 9, "Scenarios for Final Preparation," presents several scenarios with a battery of questions on each scenario. These scenarios are intended for use after you have reviewed the chapters and are ready to validate your mastery of all CCNA topics. If you get a high percentage of these questions correct, you should feel very confident about the CCNA exam!

Test Questions—Using the test engine on the CD, you can take simulated exams, as well as choose to be presented with several questions on a topic you need to work on more. The online testing tool will provide you with practice that will make you more comfortable when you actually take the CCNA exam.

Guidance Through Using Each Chapter—Chapters 2–8 can be used to discover gaps in your knowledge, fill those gaps, and practice recalling the new information. Figure I-4 describes how to use each of these chapters best.

Figure I-4   *How To Use Each Chapter*

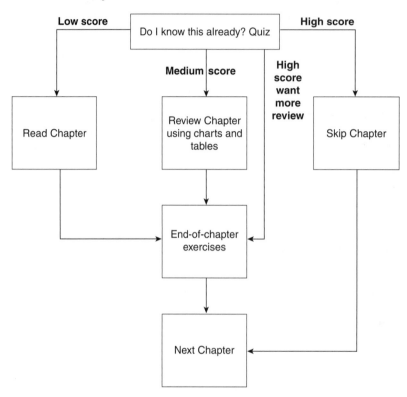

By following this process, you can gain confidence, fill the holes in your knowledge, and know when you are ready to take the exam.

Knowing Cisco is not enough. Knowing Cisco, and being able to prove that you know it, both at your job and with credentials, is vitally important in the job markets of the 21st century. The days of working an entire career at one firm are most likely gone; your skills, both professional and technical, will be invaluable as your career evolves. Being certified is a key to getting the right opportunities inside your company, with your clients, and with your next job move!

CHAPTER 1

What Is CCNA?

The growth of Cisco Systems since its inception has been phenomenal and consistent. This growth has occurred in part due to market dominance in their core product lines, as well as through adding breadth of products through acquisition of other companies. The stock price has grown to the point that many Cisco employees who get stock options as part of their compensation packages cannot afford to leave Cisco and leave such a large sum of money behind!

The Cisco Certified Internetwork Expert (CCIE) certification program was introduced in 1994 as the only Cisco certification. The entire breadth of the then-current product line was allowed to be covered on the exam, and it was intended to be a truly difficult certification to obtain. Certification required an exam (computer-based) and then a hands-on, two-day lab. The failure rate on each portion was high.

NOTE Cisco does not publish the success rate for passing the CCIE exam or lab. I did some informal surveys, none of which I am allowed to quote. Consistently, the feedback was more than a 50 percent failure rate on CCIE lab candidates, with about an 80 percent failure rate for first-time candidates!

The breadth of Cisco's product line has been growing and will continue to grow. Inside the Cisco sales arena, Systems Engineers and Account Managers sometimes long for the days of a one-volume, thin product manual. In those days, the entire product line could be memorized. Today, the product line is too broad for any one person to remember and to understand how all the products work.

So two problems evolved for Cisco relating to certification: one relating to the breadth of topics, the other to the depth of knowledge required. The CCIE exam could no longer cover the breadth of products. One solution was to create types of CCIE certifications, of which there are now three:

- **CCIE**—Routing/Switching
- **CCIE**—ISP
- **CCIE**—WAN

This helped address the problems that the breadth of product line created for the CCIE program.

The other solution was to create certifications in addition to the CCIE that did not require the same depth of skills and knowledge. The Cisco Certified Networking Associate (CCNA) certification is the first and most basic of these certifications. (The rest of these new certifications are described in the Introduction to this book.)

The CCNA exam is basic, but not necessarily easy. The purpose of the exam could be best summarized as follows:

> **To prove the candidate has mastered the topics covered on the CCNA exam, to the technical depth required for basic networks.**

Of course, that objective is open to considerable interpretation. What is a basic network? What breadth of topics are covered? Does basic mean small?

This chapter provides a complete interpretation of what the CCNA exam actually covers and the depth of knowledge needed. It also compares these objectives with the typical training you would have taken before attempting the exam. Cisco publishes a detailed list of CCNA objectives; each will be described. Finally, a "game plan" of how to complete your preparations with this study guide is included.

CCNA Exam Philosophy

This book defines the objective of the CCNA exam as "proving mastery of the basics." Mastery, in this case, means recalling all the facts and concepts relating to the subject. The only two questions that remain are as follows:

- What are the subjects?

- How deeply do I need to know each subject?

We begin by examining all that Cisco has published about the exam.

What Cisco Says about CCNA

After sifting through the materials currently available from Cisco, the following is what we **know** about the exam:

- There are 60 published exam objectives that can be covered on the exam.

- A basic network (the exam covers "basic" networks) has two or three routers, LAN switches, leased lines or Frame Relay for WAN access, and ISDN for dial backup.

- Cisco's certification Web page is URL http://www.cisco.com/warp/public/10/wwtraining/ certprog.

Figure 1-1 illustrates a basic network.

Figure 1-1   *Typical Basic CCNA Network*

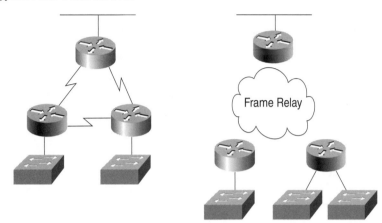

The objectives create a great tool for preparation. If you are going to prepare only slightly, making sure you can answer all 60 objectives is an obvious thing to do. However, **what each objective means, and the breadth of questions that could be asked based on an individual objective, is open to interpretation**. This book gives an interpretation of the objectives and makes suggestions to you about topics that you need to be ready for, and topics that are unlikely to be covered on the exam.

The definition of "basic network" is in a diagram on Cisco's Web site, with Figure 1-1 being essentially identical. However, the network diagram does not necessarily define the list of topics that this test covers. Is DECNET covered? Is AppleTalk? IPX? X.25? ATM? The list goes on. So, from what Cisco tells us, we cannot define what is on the test exactly. But, you can get a pretty good idea, based on the objectives.

What We Can Infer from What Cisco States

A full definition of exactly what topics are on the exam will probably never be stated by Cisco. Cisco does want candidates to succeed at passing the CCNA exam, but not at the expense of making CCNA a "paper certification." Paper certification refers to the process through which someone can just buy a test study guide, read it, memorize portions, take the test, and pass. Cisco's goal is that passing CCNA should reflect the fact that you have internalized and mastered these basic concepts, not that you can read a book and memorize well. To protect you against having the CCNA slowly lose credibility due to people just reading a book and passing the test, Cisco will probably always avoid an exact definition of the topics on the exam. By giving a general definition only, those who understand networks are rewarded. Those who prefer to memorize will be less likely to pass the test.

An exact definition of what is covered on the CCNA exam is difficult to construct. Cisco's 60 stated CCNA objectives should describe all the topics that will be on your exam. However, the objectives are subject to interpretation. To address this potential problem, this book directly refers to the CCNA objectives whenever possible. In this chapter, an interpretation of the objectives is offered. A chart containing many of the borderline topics is included, with an opinion about how likely it is for each topic to be on the exam.

The objectives will change as time goes on. As this happens, a higher percentage of the test questions will not be in the list of objectives found in this book. Of course, Cisco will change or add to the objective list at their discretion, so pulling the latest CCNA objectives list from Cisco's Web site is worth the effort. In an effort to make any changed objective lists more usable, Cisco Press will include my comments on its Web site (http://www.ciscopress.com/) with an explanation of each new objective.

The CCNA exam topics will closely match what is covered in the recommended prerequisite training. Cisco Worldwide Training (WWT) is the Cisco organization responsible for the certifications. Many of the certification exams, including CCNA, were an evolution from exams covering a particular course. It is reasonable to expect, with good benefits to us, that CCNA and the other certifications will cover the topics in the prerequisite classes. Knowing that, we can make better choices on which topics to focus upon, and which to ignore.

These suggested prerequisite classes are listed by Cisco as key parts of the *Training Paths* you can take to prepare for the CCNA and other certifications. Because I am inferring that the CCNA exam will only cover topics in these courses, knowing what these topics are and the depth to which the courses cover each topic will be important to your preparation. An entire section of this chapter, titled "Analysis of Training Paths," is devoted to an examination of the CCNA recommended prerequisite training.

Summary of the CCNA Exam Philosophy

The following list encapsulates the basic philosophy behind preparing for the CCNA exam based on what Cisco is willing to disclose to CCNA candidates.

- While open to interpretation, the CCNA objectives define the main topics covered on the exam. At a minimum, you should know about each subject covered in these objectives.

- The depth of knowledge on each topic is comparable to what is covered in the prerequisite courses. The book attempts to cover the topics at a slightly deeper level to make sure you know more than enough.

- Getting the latest copy of Cisco's CCNA objectives from their Web site is very useful. Comparing that list to the one used for this book will let you know the topics you will need to spend additional time studying.

- Do not expect to pass the exam if your only preparation has been to read this book. One of the suggested training paths should be used. You should also work with routers and switches for the best chance at success.

CCNA Exam Preparation Philosophy

When I was a child, I loved basketball. Almost all my relatives played. My favorite uncle was the all-time leading scorer at the local high school, and my first recollections about my childhood involve a basketball. I loved to play, but I also loved to practice. So I practiced. A lot. (Of course, I am not a well-known NBA star; so you know how good I really was.) Anyway, I always practiced with my left hand a lot more because I was right-handed. I hoped to overcome my weakness in the left hand and gain an advantage over others. Ironically, by the time I reached college, I had lost some of my skills using my right hand, and players would anticipate that I would go to the left!

I digress only to make a point. Preparing for the exam by reading many exam-like questions is like practicing a sport only by playing games; you will never fully learn the fundamentals. So this book attempts to enforce some self-discipline for practicing and learning, outside the context of a multiple-choice question. This book helps you learn what your weaknesses are, so you can practice more with those. But to keep you from forgetting what you are best at, the scenarios in the last chapter remind you of all the topics so that you can feel sure you have not focused too much on just your weaknesses.

This book attacks the process of your preparation for the CCNA exam in a manner similar to training for sporting events. Some of the key features to help you prepare are outlined in the next few sections.

Core Chapters Match the Major Topics in the CCNA Objectives

Cisco organizes the 60 CCNA exam objectives into seven major categories. Not coincidentally, the chapter titles for the next seven chapters happen to match the general topical areas of these major categories. Some objectives may need to be covered in two chapters because of the related topics in each chapter, but most of the coverage in each chapter pertains to the objectives in that major category. In a couple of cases, an objective listed in one major category is better covered in a different chapter, but cross references have been inserted so that you can quickly and easily find material on a particular objective. Also, a complete cross-reference table of objectives and chapters is included in this introductory chapter.

Determining Your Strengths and Weaknesses

You may feel confident about one topic, and less confident about another. However, that may be a confidence problem, not a knowledge problem! One key to using your time well is to determine if you truly need more study or not, and if so, how much?

The chapters are designed to guide you through the process of determining what you need to study. Suggestions are made as to how to study a topic based on your personal strength on the topics of that chapter. Just as listed in the Introduction to this book, Figure 1-2 presents a more granular view of how to attack a major topical area (chapter). This same information is reiterated in each core chapter, immediately after the "Do I Know This Already?" quiz for that chapter.

Figure 1-2 *How to Use This Chapter*

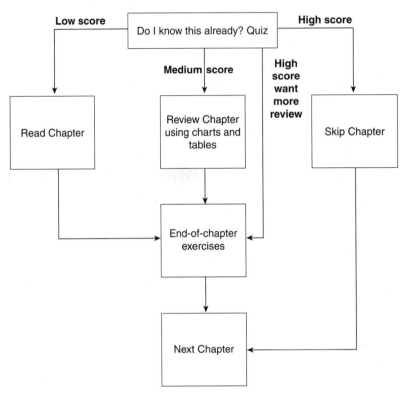

Each chapter begins with a quiz that helps you decide how well you recall the topics in that chapter. From there, you choose a path of fully reading the entire chapter, ignoring that chapter because you know it already, or something in between. Much of the factual information is summarized into lists and charts, so a review of the chapter is easy. Also, exercises at the end of the chapter provide an excellent tool for practice and for quick review.

Questions and Exercises That Are Harder Than the Actual Exam

Teams practicing to play against the University of Kentucky's teams when Rick Pitino was their coach would sometimes practice with seven players on defense and five on offense. The only way to truly feel the pressure of Kentucky's great defense, as implemented by lots of great athletes, was to put a couple of extra practice players on the court. The theory was, if you could beat seven average players, you had a chance to beat a great team of five Kentucky players.

Likewise, the exercises in this book are intended to make you stretch beyond what the exam requires. Do not be discouraged as you take the quizzes and exercises in the book; they are intended to be harder than the exam. If, by the end of your study time, you are getting 70–80 percent of these harder non-multiple choice questions correct, the CCNA exam should be easier to handle. You will probably want to validate your readiness by using the testing engine included on the CD with this book, as suggested in Figure 1-3 later in this chapter.

The main method of making this book's exams harder than the CCNA exam is not by asking for facts or concepts you will never see on the CCNA exam; it is by asking for information in ways that will not imply the correct answer. You will get some questions correct on the CCNA exam just because the multiple choice answers will trigger your memory to the correct information. By asking questions that are not multiple choice, and by asking for the same information in different ways, you will exercise your memory so that the multiple-choice exam is easy!

Scenarios for Final Preparation

If all you do is focus on your weaknesses, your strengths may suffer. Chapter 9, "Scenarios for Final Preparation," provides exercises that can cover any topic in this book. As a side effect, it gives you an opportunity to exercise all your knowledge and skills, both strong and weak. These scenarios also give you one last reminder of some facts you may have forgotten.

Simulated Testing on the CD

Of course, if you never practice using actual exams, you will not be fully prepared. The test engine on the CD can be used in two ways to help you prepare for the actual test. First, it gives you a timed test of the same length as the actual CCNA exam and score the exam for you. Secondly, you can tell the tool to feed you questions on a particular subject, so you can do some intensive review.

Summary of the CCNA Exam Preparation Philosophy

The following list encapsulates the basic philosophy behind preparing for the CCNA exam based on the features that this book provides for you as a CCNA candidate:

- This book has tools to help you prepare for the exam.

- If you use the book, you should be confidently prepared for the exam.

- Look to the section titled "Game Plan" in this chapter for a synopsis of how to use this book best.

Analysis of CCNA Training Paths

Training Paths is the term Cisco uses to describe the training that will help you gain the knowledge you need to pass a certification exam. As mentioned before, Cisco World Wide Training (WWT) owns the responsibility for certifications inside Cisco. Not surprisingly, of the two Training Paths suggested by Cisco for preparation for the CCNA exam, both include WWT courses.

Another training path is implied by Cisco, although not called a training path on their Web site. That training path is via the Cisco Networking Academies, a program in which high school and university students take a four-semester series of courses. The knowledge and skills learned in these courses probably exceeds what is required for CCNA; however, a disadvantage of being a typically younger candidate is that you may not have learned as much information "accidentally," by simply working in the industry for some years. This book treats the Cisco Networking Academies as simply a third *training path* for CCNA preparation.

Finally, I am adding a fourth training path, which Cisco does not mention, to the mix. The On-the-Job-Training (OJT) Training Path, which includes no formal preparation, has an obvious meaning. There is no required training for the CCNA exam; just like there is no required training for the CCIE exam and lab. If you have had no formal training, but plenty of experience, then this training path describes where you are coming from.

NOTE   A very common occurrence for networking personnel leads them toward the OJT path for CCNA preparation. Many learn the basics about routing and switching before taking a Cisco class, possibly due to budget constraints, or possibly due to learning another vendor's routers before learning about Cisco. From a training perspective, many students skip the Introduction to Cisco Router Configuration (ICRC) course and attend the Advanced Cisco Router Configuration (ACRC) course. The theory is that if only one class fits into the budget, most people would rather be lost in portions of the ACRC class than be bored silly in portions of the ICRC course. These same people may prefer to take the CCNA exam before taking a class. Passing CCNA, which proves mastery of the subjects in ICRC (plus a few other topics), validates their choice to go directly to the ACRC class.

Table 1-1 summarizes the training paths for CCNA certification.

Table 1-1   *CCNA Training Path*

Training Path	What Is Involved
CCNA Path 1	As defined by Cisco Systems, this involves taking courses:
	Internetworking Technology Multimedia (ITM) (CD-based)
	Cisco Routing and LAN Switching (CRLS) (instructor led)
CCNA Path 2	As defined by Cisco Systems, this involves taking courses:
	Internetworking Technology Multimedia (ITM) (CD-based)
	Introduction to Cisco Router Configuration (ICRC) (instructor led)
	High-Performance Solutions for Desktop Connectivity (HPSDC)
Cisco Networking Academy	Cisco's Networking Academies are designed for high school and university students, with a goal of providing a learning path that provides the students with valuable Cisco skills, ready to use in the marketplace
OJT	As defined by this book, on-the-job training, without the courses above

Cisco's Recommended Courses

Knowing what is covered in Cisco's recommended prerequisite courses is important to anyone wanting to pass the CCNA exam. This importance is due to the following **opinions**:

- The CCNA exam covers topics to the depth they are covered in the recommended courses.

- The CCNA exam includes topics covered in the recommended prerequisite courses.

- The objectives are tied to the course content of the prerequisite courses and, in some cases, use terminology specifically from the courses.

So if you are in Training Paths 1 or 2 and have a really good memory, then you know exactly what's on the exam. If you took Training Paths 1 or 2, but have an imperfect memory, or you are part of Cisco's Networking Academies or OJT Training Paths, you have a small problem, which this book can help solve. The problem is knowing what is in each of these prerequisite courses and how deeply the topics are covered. This book will help solve these problems by attempting to do the following:

- Listing the prerequisite course topics in detail in this section

- Providing a depth of coverage slightly deeper than in the courses

What follows is a detailed description of the core prerequisite training courses, with analysis of what could be inferred about the CCNA exam from a close examination of these courses.

Introduction to Cisco Router Configuration

Cisco's Introduction to Cisco Router Configuration (ICRC) class has been the key introductory course for several years. ICRC traditionally covered only topics related to routing. A new introductory level course, Cisco Routing and LAN Switching (CRLS), is an alternative to ICRC that includes coverage of LAN switching concepts. Eventually, the ICRC course may be phased out in deference to CRLS.

A rating system devised specifically for this book is referenced in some soon-to-follow tables. The rating is an opinion (mine) about how likely it is that a particular topic will be covered on the CCNA exam. I examined the prerequisite courses in detail, examined the objectives in detail, took the exam, and e-mailed all over Cisco for some verification. Tables 1-2, 1-3, and 1-4 represent the results of these efforts.

The ratings are based mainly on three assessments. First, whether or not the topic is covered by a narrow interpretation of the objectives, a broad interpretation of the objectives, or is not covered by an objective at all is considered. Next, whether the topic is covered by both, only one, or neither of the suggested Training Paths is considered. Finally, informal feedback from Cisco, watching certification mailing lists, whether course topics are likely to be dropped in the next course releases, and other intangibles are all considered. After consideration, I chose a rating for each topic based on the following four-point scale:

1. Likely

2. Somewhat likely

3. Somewhat unlikely

4. Unlikely

Table 1-2 is a paraphrased version of the ICRC Version 11.3 course. Included with the references are the ratings and a few comments about the content.

Table 1-2 *ICRC Version 11.3 Course Summary*

Chapter Title	Rating	Topics in This Chapter
Layered Models	1 (Likely)	OSI model, layered protocol concepts, encapsulation
Application and Upper Layers	1 (Likely)	Describes the 4 upper layers of OSI, defines "segment," describes connection-oriented protocols
Physical and Data Link Layers	1 (Likely)	Lists common physical and data link specifications; defines MAC address; describes Ethernet, Token Ring, and FDDI operation; brief explanation of WAN data links
Network Layer and Path Determination	1 (Likely)	Concepts behind routing tables and routed and routing protocols; IP, IPX, AppleTalk, and X.25 addressing concepts; routing protocol concepts (metrics, distance vector, split-horizon, holddown, link state, hybrid routing)

Table 1-2 *ICRC Version 11.3 Course Summary (Continued)*

Chapter Title	Rating	Topics in This Chapter
Basic Router Operations	1 (Likely)	Logging in, initialization, modes of operation, passwords, help, command editing, various **show** commands
Configuring a Router	1 (Likely)	Manipulating configuration files; configuration modes; saving configurations; configuring passwords and interfaces; choosing which IOS to load; IOS image management; "setup" mode
Accessing Other Routers	1 (Likely)	CDP
TCP/IP Overview: Basics, ARP	1 (Likely)	Protocol stack versus OSI; application layer examples; TCP error recovery; TCP and UDP ports; TCP, UDP, and IP Headers; ICMP
IP Address Configuration	1 (Likely)	Class A, B, and C networks: IP addresses, mask subnetting, and planning; configuring IP addresses; configuring host names; configuring DNS; verifying operation with **ping**, **trace**, and **show** commands
IP Routing Configuration	1 (Likely)	Configuring static routes; configuring default routes; Interior versus Exterior routing protocols; configuring RIP; debugging RIP; IGRP configuration; IGRP **debug** and **show** commands
Configuring Novell IPX	1 (Likely)	Protocol versus OSI; IPX addresses; Novell encapsulation options; RIP; SAP; GNS; configuring IPX; displaying IPX; debugging IPX
Configuring AppleTalk	4 (Unlikely)	Protocol versus OSI; addressing; extended networks; address acquisition; Zones; AppleTalk routing protocols; configuring AppleTalk; configuring discovery mode; monitoring AppleTalk
Basic Traffic Management with Access Lists	1 (Likely)	Why use access lists, logic diagrams, standard and extended access lists, TCP/IP access lists; wildcard masks; configuring standard IP access lists; configuring extended access lists; monitoring IP access lists; configuring IPX standard access lists; configuring IPX extended access lists; SAP access lists; monitoring IPX access lists; AppleTalk packet access lists; AppleTalk zone access lists; monitoring AppleTalk access lists
Introduction to Serial Connections	1 (Likely)	Telephone company service basics, survey of data-link protocols for WANs, SDLC/HDLC/PPP/LAPB framing, PPP functions, PAP and CHAP authentication, PAP and CHAP configuration

continues

Table 1-2 *ICRC Version 11.3 Course Summary (Continued)*

Chapter Title	Rating	Topics in This Chapter
Configuring X.25	4 (Unlikely)	Protocol stack versus OSI, addressing, terminology, framing, PVCs and SVCs, configuring X.25, adjusting windows and packet sizes, monitoring X.25, X.25 switching by a router
Configuring Frame Relay	1 (Likely)	Terminology, LMI messages, Inverse ARP, addressing, configuration, monitoring, configuration using subinterfaces, NBMA, full and partial mesh issues

High-Performance Solutions for Desktop Connectivity

High-Performance Solutions for Desktop Connectivity (HPSDC) could be renamed "LAN Switching Basics: All about FastHub 300s and 2820 and 1900 Switches." It is a particularly good reference for those wanting CCDA and CCDP certification because this course focuses more on design tradeoffs than some other courses. Several of the CCNA objectives not covered in ICRC are covered in this course, particularly those relating to comparisons of bridges, routers, and switches.

Table 1-3 is a paraphrase of what is covered in the HPSDC course.

Table 1-3 *HPSDC Course Summary*

Chapter Title	Rating	Topics in This Chapter
Introduction to Fast Ethernet and Switching Concepts	1 (Likely)	Bridging versus routing versus switching comparisons, benefits of switching and fast Ethernet
FastHub 300 Series Repeaters	3 (Somewhat Unlikely)	Features and functions
Positioning and Applications of FastHub Series Repeaters	3 (Somewhat Unlikely)	Basic design alternatives
Installation and Configuration of FastHub 300 Series Repeaters	3 (Somewhat Unlikely)	Configuration, user interface
Maintenance and Troubleshooting of FastHub 300 Series Repeaters	4 (Unlikely)	LED interpretation, management reporting

Table 1-3 *HPSDC Course Summary (Continued)*

Chapter Title	Rating	Topics in This Chapter
The Catalyst 2820 and 1900 Switches	3 (Somewhat Unlikely)	Features and functions
Positioning and Applications of Catalyst 2820 and 1900 Switches	3 (Somewhat Unlikely)	Basic design alternatives
Installation and Configuration of Catalyst 2820 and 1900 Switches	4 (Unlikely)	Cabling and configuration
Maintenance and Troubleshooting of Catalyst 2820 and 1900 Switches	4 (Unlikely)	LED interpretation, examining status from the console

Cisco Routers and LAN Switches (CRLS)

Cisco's CRLS course was previously called "Cisco SupportPro" and was geared toward presale engineers. The current version of this course is more focused on the technical portions of the earlier class. There is significant overlap with ICRC, both in topics and identical course materials.

Table 1-4 shows a paraphrased outline of CRLS, along with some analysis.

Table 1-4 *CRLS Course Summary*

Chapter Title	Rating	Topics in This Chapter
Cisco Overview	2 (Somewhat Likely)	Short product overview (one page on routers, for example)
Cisco Networking Solutions	3 (Somewhat Unlikely)	Product positioning, telecommuting, access routers, 25xx routers, 36xx routers, SOHO routers, IOS features sets, high performance LANs, 1900 and 2820 switches, FastHub 300 series
Cisco IOS Overview	3 (Somewhat Unlikely)	What is IOS, WAN services, compression, TACACs, management, ClickStart, each topic just shows basic concept (no configuration)
(IOS) User Interface	1 (Likely)	Login, passwords, command help, command editing

continues

Table 1-4 *CRLS Course Summary (Continued)*

Chapter Title	Rating	Topics in This Chapter
Router Basics	1 (Likely)	RAM, NVRAM, Flash, ROM, popular **show** commands, command modes, showing configurations, CDP, Telnet, **ping**, **trace**, **debug**, log messages
Configuration Methods and Modes	1 (Likely)	Initialization, setup mode, manipulating configuration files, using TFTP for configurations, configuration modes, configuring banner, passwords, interfaces, hostname
Managing Cisco IOS Files	1 (Likely)	Choosing the IOS to load, configuration register, boot system command, flash, loading from TFTP, upgrading IOS
Network Layer Basics and IP Address Configuration	1 (Likely)	OSI Layer 3 concepts, IP and IPX as examples, routed versus routing protocols, static and dynamic routes, routing protocol metrics, distance vector logic, split-horizon, holddown timer, IP addresses, Classes A, B, and C, subnet masks, subnetting, subnet planning, address configuration, hostname configuration, DNS configuration, **ping**, **trace**
Routing Protocol Configuration	1 (Likely)	Static route configuration, default route configuration, IP RIP configuration, monitoring RIP and routing, IGRP configuration, **debug** commands
Configuring Novell IPX	1 (Likely)	NetWare versus OSI, IPX addressing, IPX encapsulations, RIP, SAP, GNS, configuration, monitoring IPX, debugs
Basic Traffic Management with Standard and Extended Access Lists	1 (Likely)	What they are, where to locate access lists, access list logic, standard IP access list configuration, extended IP access list configuration. This course does not cover IPX SAP filtering, which is likely to be on the exam!
Network Address Translation	4 (Unlikely)	Concepts, terminology, translating, overloading, TCP load distribution, configuration, monitoring, debugs
Introduction to Wide-Area Network Services	1 (Likely)	Service provider basic services, framing for PPP, HDLC, SDLC, LAPB, ISDN concepts, Frame Relay concepts, X.25 concepts
Configuring Frame Relay	1 (Likely)	Concepts and terminology, LMI messages, Inverse ARP, basic configuration, monitoring Frame Relay, configuration using subinterfaces, NBMA issues, full-mesh and partial-mesh issues

Table 1-4 *CRLS Course Summary (Continued)*

Chapter Title	Rating	Topics in This Chapter
Configuring DDR, PPP, and ISDN	1 (Likely) for PPP configuration. 2 (Somewhat Likely) for ISDN configuration. 4 (Unlikely) for DDR configuration	DDR concepts, basic DDR configuration, DDR logic, DDR with ISDN, PPP concepts, PAP and CHAP authentication, monitoring PPP, ISDN protocols and reference points, DDR with ISDN, simple ISDN BRI configuration, monitoring ISDN, BRI access lists, S-Bus and subaddresses, multilink PPP, advanced configuration
Configuring the Cisco 760 Series (Router)	4 (Unlikely)	Features and functions, configuration, IP routing, bridging, IPX routing, spoofing, caller-id
Introduction to Switching Concepts	1 (Likely)	Collisions and broadcasts, segmenting with bridges, segmenting with routers, segmenting with switches, switching modes, half- and full-duplex Ethernet
Catalyst 1900/ 2800 Switch Configuration	4 (Unlikely)	Features and functions, menus, learning and flooding, switching modes, VLANs, SNMP, monitoring, NO CONFIGURATION SAMPLES
Fasthub 300 Installation and Configuration	4 (Unlikely)	Features and functions, stacking, LEDs, no configuration required, sample menu, statistic report samples, NO CONFIGURATION SAMPLES
Network Management Solutions	4 (Unlikely)	Management theory, Cisco Fast Step™ for 700 series, Config Maker, Autoinstall, CiscoWorks for Windows

Internetworking Technology Multimedia (ITM)

ITM is a CD with basic technology self-study material that is accessed with your favorite Web browser. It covers all the basics that will be on the CCNA exam, plus a few extra topics. It does not cover these topics to the depth needed to pass the CCNA exam, however. (ITM is actually intended as a prerequisite course to the CRLS and ICRC courses.) An outline is not given because ITM is essentially prerequisite material. However, it is a good study tool and ends each section with multiple-choice questions.

Analysis of Prerequisite Courses

Many topics will obviously be covered by the exam: IP and IPX addressing, routing, router and switch configuration mode, the OSI model, filtering, Frame Relay configuration, LAN-switching concepts, and the list goes on. These topics are found in the prerequisite course outlines in Tables 1-2 through 1-4, for both Cisco-defined CCNA Training Paths.

Some topics will certainly not be on the CCNA exam. DECNET, Banyan Vines, Novell NLSP, OSPF, and other advanced topics are not covered on CCNA. Of course, because Cisco provides no absolutely definitive list of topics on the CCNA exam, this is an opinion, but these topics are far beyond what is implied by Cisco's 60 listed objectives.

As with any test, deciding whether a fringe topic is or is not going to be on the test is always a difficult part of choosing what to study. Table 1-5 lists some descriptions of fringe topics, and my opinion as to whether they are covered on the exam. This table uses the four-point rating scale described earlier. This is my opinion, but I will also list my reasons, so you can decide if you agree or not.

Table 1-5 *CCNA Fringe Topics That Might (or Might Not) Appear on the Exam*

Topic	Rating	Reasons
AppleTalk	4 (Unlikely)	It is not covered at all in Training Path 1.
X.25 concepts	3 (Somewhat Unlikely)	Concepts are covered in both Training Path 1 and 2. X.25 was deleted from the original CCNA objectives by Cisco when the objectives were changed in November 1998.
X.25 Configuration	4 (Unlikely)	Configuration is not covered at all in Training Path 1. Also, the topic of X.25 protocol concepts was deleted from the original CCNA objectives by Cisco when the objectives were changed in November 1998; so without the concepts, configuration would be difficult to test.
FastHub 300 Features and Functions	3 (Somewhat Unlikely)	Covered in both Training Path 1 and 2; relatively low importance. Not specifically mentioned in any objective.
FastHub 300 User Interface	4 (Unlikely)	Covered in both Training Path 1 and 2; easy user interface, so testing is not vital. The only user interface covered by even a broad interpretation of the CCNA objectives is the IOS; the 300 does not use IOS.
Cisco 760 Series	4 (Unlikely)	Not covered in training path 2. Also, the only user interface covered by even a broad interpretation of the CCNA objectives is the IOS; the 760 does not use IOS.
Cisco 1900 and 2820 Switches—Features and Functions	4 (Unlikely)	Covered in both Training Paths, but topic of relatively low importance on this exam. Also, the only user interface covered by even a broad interpretation of the CCNA objectives is the IOS; the 1920 and 2800 do not use IOS.

Table 1-5   *CCNA Fringe Topics That Might (or Might Not) Appear on the Exam (Continued)*

Cisco 1900 and 2820 Switches—Configuration and Troubleshooting	4 (Unlikely)	Not covered by Training Path 1; covered in Training Path 2 only in HPSDC. Also, the only user interface covered by even a broad interpretation of the CCNA objectives is the IOS; the 300 does not use IOS.
ISDN Protocols	1 (Likely)	Not covered in ICRC, but is part of ITM; it is specifically mentioned as a CCNA objective.
ISDN Configuration	2 (Somewhat Likely)	Not covered in ICRC, but is part of ITM; it is not specifically mentioned as a CCNA objective, but the protocols are specifically mentioned in an objective.
DDR Concepts and Configuration	3 (Somewhat Unlikely)	Not covered in ICRC, but is part of ITM; it was originally mentioned in the original CCNA objectives, but with the changes made to the objectives by Cisco in November 1998, DDR coverage was deleted from the objectives.
IPX Packet and SAP Filtering	1 (Likely)	Not covered in Training Path 1, but is listed as an objective.

This book covers topics that are considered likely or somewhat likely to be on the CCNA exam.

The 60 Stated CCNA Objectives

The most definitive description of what is required on the CCNA exam is the list of 60 CCNA objectives on Cisco's Web site. This book will ensure that each of the 60 objectives are covered in enough detail to answer the questions on the exam. Taking the exam before becoming comfortable with the meanings of these objectives will put you at a severe disadvantage.

Other topics besides those listed in these objectives will be covered on the CCNA exam. For instance, ISDN configuration is not mentioned in any objective, but ISDN protocols are mentioned; a question could list an ISDN configuration and ask a question about the ISDN protocols that router is using. The most likely of these topics are those covered in the Training Paths 1 and 2, as listed in the previous section. However, knowing the following topics is a must.

In this section, the 60 objectives are listed, verbatim, from Cisco's Web site along with notes of my interpretation of each objective. Finally, two cross references are listed: one referring to the chapter of this book that each objective is discussed in, and the other listing all the objectives covered in an individual book chapter.

List and Interpretation of the 60 Stated CCNA Objectives

These objectives were collected in November 1998, during the initial writing of this book. The CCNA exam will consist of a combination of the objectives listed in Table 1-6. Many of the objectives are clearly worded and have no hidden meaning. Some of the objectives, in my opinion, either contain hidden nuances or are unclear. The interpretation found in column three of Table 1-6 is not an attempt to describe in detail an "answer" for each objective, but rather is here both to clarify and to provide a brief reminder of the topic that each objective covers.

Table 1-6 *CCNA Objectives*

Objective	Description	Interpretation
1	Identify and describe the functions of each of the seven layers of the OSI reference model.	Self-explanatory. You will be well prepared if you can recall this material from class, or if you can recall the material on OSI in Chapter 3 of this book.
2	Describe connection-oriented network service and connectionless network service, and identify the key differences between them.	The term "connection oriented" sometimes has ambiguous meaning, which is covered in Chapter 3.
3	Describe data link addresses and network addresses, and identify the key differences between them.	The key difference is that Layer 3 addresses are media independent and are assigned without the need to be concerned about the type of media. Data-link addresses are, by definition, addressing a networking entity for which the type of media is important.
4	Identify at least 3 reasons why the industry uses a layered model.	This objective's "answer" is an opinion. The objective is gathered from Chapter 1 in ICRC. The list of answers from the course is: "Reduces complexity, standardizes interfaces, facilitates modular engineering, ensures interoperable technology, accelerates evolution, and simplifies teaching and learning."

Table 1-6 *CCNA Objectives (Continued)*

Objective	Description	Interpretation
5	Define and explain the 5 conversion steps of data encapsulation.	This objective is unclear unless you have taken ICRC and remember a particular page. The concept, however, is vitally important, and will most likely be on your exam. The idea is that each layer of a stack is responsible for creation of some of the bits that are sent. For TCP/IP, from which Cisco based the "5 conversion steps of data encapsulation," the application creates some bits, called the "data" (Step 1). The transport layer (TCP or UDP typically) creates a header with the data inside it, called a *segment* (Step 2). The IP layer adds an IP header, with the segment after it, with the entire set of bits called a *packet* (Step 3). The appropriate data-link header and trailer are wrapped around the packet, creating a *frame* (Step 4). Finally, the physical layer applies appropriate energy to the medium, transmitting some energy that will be interpreted as the correct *bit stream* (Step 5).
6	Define flow control and describe the three basic methods used in networking.	Flow control is an easily defined subject, and is covered in Chapter 3. The three basic methods refer to the three basic models of flow control, but this phrase is not a well-accepted term that I could uncover. Chapter 3 provides an explanation of flow control, three categorizations or methods of flow control, and some hints about other names that the exam may include when asking about this objective.
7	List the key internetworking functions of the OSI Network layer and how they are performed in a router.	The term *internetworking* in this objective is unneeded, but it is otherwise clear. This is a duplicate, practically speaking, of objective 1.

continues

Table 1-6 *CCNA Objectives (Continued)*

Objective	Description	Interpretation
8	Differentiate between the following WAN services: Frame Relay, ISDN/LAPD, HDLC, & PPP.	The objective is clear, but the depth needed to answer exam questions is not. All that is needed is to consider these differences between the terms: is it point-to-point or not; multiprotocol or not; data-link protocol with headers and trailers or not; and whether it is typically leased or dial. If you have the ITM CD, the depth covered for each of these topics on the CD is more than enough to address this question.
9	Recognize key Frame Relay terms and features.	Frame Relay concepts and configuration will be covered on the exam.
10	List commands to configure Frame Relay LMIs, maps, and subinterfaces.	Self-explanatory.
11	List commands to monitor Frame Relay operation in the router.	Self-explanatory. Because most people use online help to remember many of these options, reviewing the different options so they will be recognizable in the answers on the exam is useful.
12	Identify PPP operations to encapsulate WAN data on Cisco routers.	This objective may be clear to some, but unclear to others. An alternate phrasing might be, "Identify PPP header and trailer fields, its use of control protocols, and describe how a router uses PPP to encapsulate a packet." Practically speaking, you need to understand PPP better than simply thinking of it as having a header and trailer. You should understand the need for the protocol field, and the purpose of Layer 3-specific control protocols.
13	State a relevant use and context for ISDN networking.	This objective mainly refers to ISDN's use as a switched WAN media.

Table 1-6 *CCNA Objectives (Continued)*

Objective	Description	Interpretation
14	Identify ISDN protocols, function groups, reference points, and channels.	The objective is clear, but the depth is not. The protocols specified by ISDN, particularly the reference points, are likely to be on the exam. Knowing ISDN protocols to the depth of the ITM course should be enough; this depth is covered in Chapter 8.
15	Describe Cisco's implementation of ISDN BRI.	Self-explanatory.
16	Log into a router in both user and privileged modes.	Self-explanatory.
17	Use the context-sensitive help facility.	"Context-sensitive" simply means that help in one mode gives you help about commands particular to that user interface mode.
18	Use the command history and editing features.	"Editing" refers to the ability to change the text in a command after retrieving an old command with command history.
19	Examine router elements (RAM, ROM, CDP, show).	Self-explanatory.
20	Manage configuration files from the privileged exec mode.	This objective refers to how to move configuration files out of a router, or back into a router. By comparing this objective to the prerequisite courses, focusing on copying configurations with TFTP should cover all that is needed. No knowledge of moving configuration files with CiscoWorks or another management tool is necessary.
21	Control router passwords, identification, and banner.	Self-explanatory. Know the different passwords; TACACS is unlikely to be covered.
22	Identify the main Cisco IOS commands for router startup.	This really refers to the **boot** command, the configuration register and how they affect which IOS a router will load.

continues

Table 1-6   *CCNA Objectives (Continued)*

Objective	Description	Interpretation
23	Enter an initial configuration using the setup command.	Setup is also called the "Initial Configuration Dialogue" and is most typically used when a router is booted with no configuration in NVRAM. Practicing this once will be useful if you have a spare router. Also, this process is the only process that writes the same configuration to NVRAM and RAM based on one action by the user of the router.
24	Copy and manipulate configuration files.	Self-explanatory, and the same objective in practice as objective 20.
25	List the commands to load Cisco IOS software from: flash memory, a TFTP server, or ROM.	Self-explanatory, and the same objective in practice as objective 22.
26	Prepare to backup, upgrade, and load a backup Cisco IOS software image.	A nuance to this objective is that some routers do not load the entire IOS into RAM, but instead leave portions of the IOS in Flash memory to be read as needed. The IOS disallows writing into Flash memory if this is the case. In older IOS releases, you had to manually boot an IOS from ROM and then copy files into Flash memory. Chapter 2 covers all these details, and shows a sample automated version of this process in later IOS releases. The nuance is that this objective is focused on the process, and in particular, the process when Flash memory is not "writable" when you type the **copy** command.
27	Prepare the initial configuration of your router and enable IP.	The objective does not imply whether setup mode or configuration mode would be used in this case. Regardless, you should be able to use either for the purposes of passing this exam. For the purposes of succeeding in building router networks, setup mode is relatively useless after you have hands-on skills in configuration mode.

Table 1-6 *CCNA Objectives (Continued)*

Objective	Description	Interpretation
28	Monitor Novell IPX operation on the router.	Like objective 32, but for IPX.
29	Describe the two parts of network addressing, then identify the parts in specific protocol address examples.	This concept is not only important to the CCNA exam, but is knowledge you will need for the other exams as well. Chapter 3 contains a discussion of Layer 3 routing and the role that Layer 3 address groupings play in the process of routing.
30	Create the different classes of IP addresses [and subnetting].	Self-explanatory.
31	Configure IP addresses.	Self-explanatory.
32	Verify IP addresses.	Verify in this case is one way of saying log in to the router, and use commands to verify that it configured and is working correctly. This is mainly an outgrowth of Cisco's courses tending to have three main topics in an implementation chapter: concepts, configuration, and commands to show if it worked. Objectives 30–32 cover those three aspects of IP addresses in a Cisco router.
33	List the required IPX address and encapsulation type.	I do not know what this one really means. There is no required IPX address. There are multiple encapsulation types for IPX on Ethernet, FDDI, and Token Ring. So, in this book I will treat this objective instead to mean, "Describe how to configure IPX addressing, IPX routing, and explain the meaning and purpose of the different IPX encapsulation types on LANs." That is most of what is covered, except for access lists, in the Novell chapters in ICRC and CRLS courses.

continues

Table 1-6 *CCNA Objectives (Continued)*

Objective	Description	Interpretation
34	Enable the Novell IPX protocol and configure interfaces.	Self-explanatory, and very similar to my interpretation of objective 33.
35	Identify the functions of the TCP/IP transport-layer protocols.	Self-explanatory, and could be learned from many documents and books besides Cisco courses or this book.
36	Identify the functions of the TCP/IP network-layer protocols.	See analysis for objective 35.
37	Identify the functions performed by ICMP.	See analysis for objective 35.
38	Configure IPX access lists and SAP filters to control basic Novell traffic.	Self-explanatory. SAP filters are more likely to be covered than packet filters.
39	Add the RIP routing protocol to your configuration.	This objective, as well as objective 40, could be taken as the objectives of two labs from the ICRC and CRLS courses. After configuring IP addresses, without a routing protocol, the student is asked to add RIP and then IGRP. You should know how to remove either, as well as know what running both would imply.
40	Add the IGRP routing protocol to your configuration.	See interpretation for objective 39.
41	Explain the services of separate and integrated multiprotocol routing.	This objective can be particularly confusing if you come from a non-Cisco shop or from the OJT Training Path. Separate multiprotocol routing is what normal routing protocols do—that is, exchange routing information for a single routable protocol. Integrated multiprotocol routing refers to the function of EIGRP that exchanges routing information for IP, IPX, and AppleTalk, all as one set of protocol flows.

Table 1-6 *CCNA Objectives (Continued)*

Objective	Description	Interpretation
42	List problems that each routing type encounters when dealing with topology changes and describe techniques to reduce the number of these problems.	This objective is unclear due to the term *routing type*, which is not used in the prerequisite courses. Routing type might be better termed *routing protocol*, for instance, RIP, IGRP, EIGRP, OSPF, NLSP, and so on. An even better phrase might be *type of routing protocol* because the objective is really referring to distance vector and link-state routing protocol logic. This objective actually opens up what is one of the more advanced topics covered on this exam. If you understand the distance vector and link-state logic covered in this book, you should be well prepared. The DUAL algorithm used by EIGRP should not be on the exam, nor should the link state algorithm be covered.
43	Describe the benefits of network segmentation with routers.	Self-explanatory.
44	Configure standard and extended access lists to filter IP traffic.	Self-explanatory. The depth of your understanding should include recalling all parts of an IP packet that can be examined by the access list to make a match, as well as the nuances of where the access list is enabled, compared to the flow of the packets you are interested in filtering.
45	Monitor and verify selected access list operations on the router.	"Monitor and verify," in this and other objectives, means you should know the commands, most typically **show** and **debug**, that help you learn if you configured correctly.
46	Describe the advantages of LAN segmentation.	Objectives 46–49 make the most sense when compared with one another. Consider them all at one time. These topics are mainly covered in Chapter 4.

continues

Table 1-6 *CCNA Objectives (Continued)*

Objective	Description	Interpretation
47	Describe LAN segmentation using bridges.	See interpretation for objective 46.
48	Describe LAN segmentation using routers.	See interpretation for objective 46.
49	Describe LAN segmentation using switches.	See interpretation for objective 46.
50	Name and describe two switching methods.	Because there is no industry standard name for what this objective calls switching methods, this objective may be a bit ambiguous. The objective refers to internal processing and whether the FCS is checked before the frame is forwarded. The two methods, cut-through and store-and-forward, are covered in Chapter 4.
51	Describe full- and half-duplex Ethernet operation.	Self-explanatory.
52	Describe network congestion problem in Ethernet networks.	This objective might be better stated as, "Describe collisions, broadcasts, and their affect on shared Ethernet performance." Without understanding this objective, you cannot fully explain the next several objectives.
53	Describe the benefits of network segmentation with bridges.	Self-explanatory, and identical to objective 47.
54	Describe the benefits of network segmentation with switches.	Self-explanatory, and identical to objective 49.
55	Describe the features and benefits of Fast Ethernet.	Self-explanatory.
56	Describe the guidelines and distance limitations of Fast Ethernet.	Self-explanatory. Just memorize it!
57	Distinguish between cut-through and store-and-forward LAN switching.	Self-explanatory. This objective is practically identical to objective 50.

Table 1-6 *CCNA Objectives (Continued)*

Objective	Description	Interpretation
58	Describe the operation of Spanning-Tree Protocol and its benefits.	This objective is barely covered in the prerequisite courses. ICRC and CRLS do not address spanning tree; only the HPSDC covers spanning tree, with two paragraphs. As time goes on, and CRLS gains more focus on LAN switching, I believe more in-depth questions on spanning tree will be on the CCNA exam. For our purposes, if you understand spanning trees to the depth covered in this book, you should be ready for the exam.
59	Describe the benefits of virtual LANs.	Self-explanatory.
60	Define and describe the function of a MAC address.	Media Access Control addresses identify LAN interface cards. Using and understanding MAC addresses is a key part of the logic behind routers, bridges, and switches.

Cross Reference to Book Chapters Covering an Objective

Table 1-7 lists the objectives found at Cisco's Web page and the corresponding chapter this book that covers the topic.

Table 1-7 *Chapter Roadmap of CCNA Objectives as Covered in the Book*

Objective	Chapter
1	3
2	3
3	3
4	3
5	3
6	3
7	3
8	8

continues

Table 1-7 *Chapter Roadmap of CCNA Objectives as Covered in the Book (Continued)*

Objective	Chapter
9	8
10	8
11	8
12	8
13	8
14	8
15	8
16	2
17	2
18	2
19	2
20	2
21	2
22	2
23	2
24	2
25	2
26	2
27	2
28	5, 6
29	3, 5
30	5
31	5
32	5
33	5
34	5, 6
35	5
36	5
37	5
38	5, 7

Table 1-7 *Chapter Roadmap of CCNA Objectives as Covered in the Book (Continued)*

Objective	Chapter
39	6
40	6
41	6
42	6
43	4
44	7
45	7
46	4
47	4
48	4
49	4
50	4
51	4
52	4
53	4
54	4
55	4
56	4
57	4
58	4
59	4
60	3, 4

Cross Reference to Objectives Covered in Each Chapter

Table 1-8 lists the chapters in this book and the corresponding CCNA objectives that each chapter covers:

Table 1-8 *Chapter Roadmap of CCNA Objectives as Covered in Individual Chapters*

Chapter	Objective
2	16–27
3	1–7, 29, 60
4	43, 46–60
5	28–38
6	28, 34, 39–42
7	38, 44–45
8	8–15

A Game Plan for CCNA Success

You will not have as much time to prepare for the CCNA exam as you would like. The goal of this game plan is to streamline the process, so the time you do invest will be well spent.

There are seven major categories of objectives covered by the exam. The general flow of how you should attack these topics is as follows:

1. Find out how much review you need for that objective category.

2. Review, whether in this book or other resources.

3. Perform the exercises at the end of the chapter.

4. Move on to another chapter.

The chapters are ordered to make sense to a novice. However, because you have been exposed to most if not all of these topics, you can skip around in these chapters as much as you like.

Although this book is designed to be used by itself, using your Cisco Certified coursebooks, or the Cisco Press book *Introduction to Cisco Router Configuration*, will be useful as well. If you choose to do that, you will want to refer to this chapter's section on analyzing the courses, so you can easily find the topics that are worth reviewing in those books and ignore those that are unimportant. Refer back to Figure 1-2 to review how to attack a major topic area (chapter) as documented in this book.

Your Final Preparation for the Exam

After you have completed the seven major objective categories, what remains is your final preparation. This includes review of all topics, as well as simulated tests, so you can practice taking an exam.

Your final preparation does not need to follow a particular order. Figure 1-3 outlines how to do your final preparations.

Figure 1-3 *Strategy for Approaching Final Preparations for Taking the CCNA Exam*

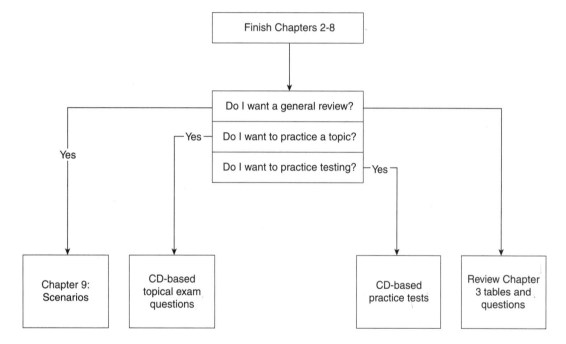

Summary

You should walk away from this chapter with the following things in mind:

- The CCNA exam is a test to prove your mastery of basic internetworking concepts.

- The CCNA exam objectives outline topics that will definitely be on the exam.

- The training paths provide clues to other topics on the exam.

- Cisco will most likely never completely define the scope or depth of what will be covered on this or other certification exams.

- The game plan will help you maximize the productivity of your preparation time.

The following CCNA exam objectives are reviewed in this chapter. The numbers shown correspond to the master list of objectives found in Chapter 1, "What Is CCNA?"

Objective	Description
16	Log into a router in both user and privileged modes.
17	Use the context-sensitive help facility.
18	Use the command history and editing features.
19	Examine router elements (RAM, ROM, CDP, show).
20	Manage configuration files from the privileged exec mode.
21	Control router passwords, identification, and banner.
22	Identify the main Cisco IOS commands for router startup.
23	Enter an initial configuration using the setup command.
24	Copy and manipulate configuration files.
25	List the commands to load Cisco IOS software from: flash memory, a TFTP server, or ROM.
26	Prepare to backup, upgrade, and load a backup Cisco IOS software image.
27	Prepare the initial configuration of your router and enable IP.

CHAPTER 2

Understanding Cisco's Internetwork Operating System (IOS) Software

This chapter focuses on the CCNA objectives falling under Cisco's CCNA exam objective heading *IOS*. IOS is important because no headings or individual objectives mention any other operating system or any other user interface that appears on the CCNA exam. In other words, with the current exam objectives, the IOS user interface is the only user interface you need to know, and IOS commands are the only commands you need to know for the exam.

The IOS user interface is integral to these objectives; the best way to refresh your memory about any user interface is to use it! If you can get time using a Cisco router, the learning and recall from your practice will be of significant value. This chapter is designed to remind you of details you may not notice when practicing and provide a reference for those of you who do not have access to routers for practice.

The other focus of this chapter's CCNA objectives is a myriad of basic command functions in the IOS. The set of commands and features covered in this chapter closely matches those implied by the objectives and covered in the Cisco CCNA Training Paths. However, knowing more about commands than what is covered in the courses may be helpful on other exams. Therefore, you may want to take a little extra router practice time to examine other commands.

How to Best Use This Chapter

By taking the following steps, you can make better use of your study time:

- Keep your notes and answers for all your work with this book in one place for easy reference.

- Take the quiz and write down your answers. Studies show retention is significantly increased through writing facts and concepts down, even if you never look at the information again.

- Use the diagram in Figure 2-1 to guide you to the next step.

Figure 2-1 *How To Use This Chapter*

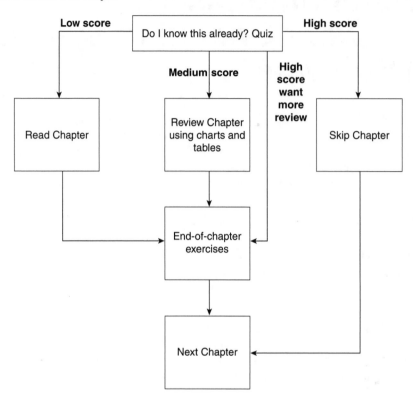

"Do I Know This Already?" Quiz

1. What are the two different names for the router's mode of operation that when accessed enable you to issue commands that could be disruptive to router operations?

_____

_____

_____

2. What command would you use to receive command help if you knew the **show** command option you cannot recall begins with a "C"?

_____

_____

_____

3. Instead of **show ip route**, which is the only command you typed since logging in to the router, you now want to issue a **show ip arp** command. What steps would you take to do so, without simply typing **show ip arp**?

   _____

   _____

   _____

4. What configuration command causes the router to demand a password from the console? What configuration mode "context" must you be in; that is, what command(s) must be typed before this command after entering configuration mode?

   _____

   _____

   _____

5. What is the purpose of Flash memory in a Cisco router?

   _____

   _____

   _____

6. What is the purpose of ROM in a Cisco router?

   _____

   _____

   _____

7. What configuration command would be needed to cause a router to use an IOS image named *c2500-j-l.112-14.bin* on TFTP server 128.1.1.1 when the router is reloaded? If you forgot the first parameter of this command, what steps must you take to learn the correct parameters and add the command to the configuration? (Assume you are not logged in to the router when you start.)

   _____

   _____

   _____

8. When using setup mode, you are prompted at the end of the process as to whether you want to use the configuration parameters you just typed in. Which type of memory is this configuration stored into if you type **yes**?

   _____

   _____

   _____

9. What two methods could a router administrator use to cause a router to load the IOS stored in ROM?

_____

_____

_____

10. What is the process used to update the contents of Flash memory so that a new IOS in a file called *c2500-j-l.112-14.bin* on TFTP server 128.1.1.1 is copied into Flash memory?

_____

_____

_____

11. Two different IOS files are in a router's flash memory, one called *c2500-j-l.111-3.bin* and one called *c2500-j-l.112-14.bin*. Which one does the router use when it boots up? How could you force the other IOS file to be used? Without looking at the router configuration, what command could be used to discover which file was used for the latest boot of the router?

_____

_____

_____

12. What does CDP stand for?

_____

_____

_____

The answers to the quiz are found in Appendix B on page 541. Review the answers, grade your quiz, and choose an appropriate next step in this chapter based on the suggestions in Figure 2-1. Your choices for the next step are as follows:

- **5 or fewer correct**—Read this chapter.

- **6, 7, or 8 correct**—Review this chapter, looking at the charts and diagrams that summarize most of the concepts and facts in this chapter.

- **9 or more correct**—If you want more review on these topics, skip to the exercises at the end of this chapter. If you do not want more review on these topics, skip this chapter.

Foundation Topics

Routers: The IOS and Its User Interface

CCNA Objectives Covered in This Section

16	Log into a router in both user and privileged modes.
17	Use the context-sensitive help facility.
18	Use the command history and editing features.
19	Examine router elements (RAM, ROM, CDP, show).

Hardware Review

Before examining the IOS, a review of hardware and hardware terminology is useful. This section of the book reviews common hardware details.

Most Cisco routers have a console and an auxiliary port. All Cisco routers have a console port, which is meant for local administrative access, from an ASCII terminal or computer using a terminal emulator. The auxiliary port, missing on a few models of Cisco routers, is intended for asynchronous dial access from an ASCII terminal or terminal emulator; the auxiliary port is often used for dial backup.

Each router has different types of memory as follows:

- **RAM**—Sometimes called DRAM for *dynamic* random-access memory, RAM is used by the router just like it is used by any other computer—for working storage.

- **ROM**—This type of memory stores a bootable IOS image, which is not typically used for normal operation. ROM does contain the code that is used to boot the router until the router knows where to get the full IOS image.

- **Flash memory**—Either an EEPROM or a PCMCIA card. Flash memory stores full function IOS images and is the IOS default for where the router gets its IOS at boot time. Flash memory may also be used to store configuration files on Cisco 7500 series platforms (**copy config flash**).

- **NVRAM**—Nonvolatile RAM stores the initial or *startup* configuration file.

All of these types of memory are permanent memory except RAM. There is no hard disk or diskette storage on Cisco routers. Figure 2-2 summarizes the use of memory in Cisco routers.

Figure 2-2 *Cisco Router Memory Types*

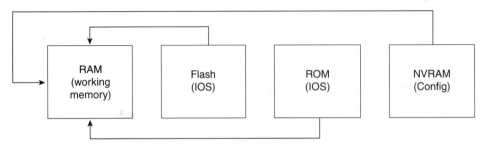

The processors in the routers vary from model to model. Although they are not specifically listed as requirements for the CCNA exam, some reference to terminology is useful. In most routers, the model number you order or own implies the processor speed; you would not then order a specific processor type or card. The exception to this is the 7000, 7200, and 7500 series of routers, for which you choose either a Route Switch Processor 1 (RSP-1), RSP-2, or RSP-4. In any case, the 2500 series, 3600 series, 4000 series, and 7xxx series all run the IOS. This commonality allows Cisco to have exams, such as CCNA, that cover the IOS features without having to cover many hardware details.

Interfaces are used by a router for routing/bridging packets/frames through a router. The types of interfaces available change over time due to new technology. For example, packet-over-SONET and voice interfaces are relatively recent additions to the product line. However, some confusion exists about what to call the actual cards that house the physical interfaces. Table 2-1 summarizes the terminology that may be referred to on the test.

Table 2-1 *Router Interface Terminology*

Model Series	What the IOS Calls Interfaces	What the Product Catalog Calls the Cards with the Interfaces on Them
2500	interface	Module
3600	interface	Network Module
4500	interface	Network Processor Module
7200	interface	Port Adapters and Service Adapters
7500	interface	Interface Processors

Physical interfaces are referred to as *interfaces* by the IOS commands, as opposed to *ports* or *plugs*. IOS commands familiar on one platform will be familiar on another. There are some nuances to numbering the interfaces, however. In all routers except the 7xxx routers, the interface number is a single number. However, with the 7xxx series routers, the interface is numbered first with the slot in which the card resides, followed by a slash, and then the port number on that card. For example, port 3 on the card in slot 2 would be interface 2/3. Numbering starts with 0 for card slots and 0 for ports on any card.

If you want to dig deeper, reading about processors and interfaces in the Cisco Product Manual would be useful.

Internetwork Operating System (IOS)

IOS, a registered trademark of Cisco Systems, is the name for the operating system found in most of Cisco's routers. Cisco's products have evolved to the point that routing functions are performed by cards inside larger multifunction routing/switching devices; these more complex devices use the IOS for the routing and related services. For example, the Route/Switch Module (RSM) card for the Catalyst 5000 series LAN switches performs routing functions and executes the IOS.

Fixes and code updates to the IOS can include new features and functions. To learn more about the code release process, features added at particular IOS revision levels, and other terminology that will help you talk to the Cisco Technical Assistance Center (TAC), check out a current Cisco Product Bulletin describing the "Software Release Process." One such example is Product Bulletin #537 (http://www.cisco.com/warp/public/732/General/537_pp.htm).

The Command-Line Interface (CLI)

CLI is the acronym used by Cisco for the terminal user command-line interface to the IOS. The CLI implies that the user is using a terminal, terminal emulator, or telnet connection, at which commands are typed. While you can pass the CCNA exam without ever having used the CLI, actually using the CLI will greatly enhance your chances of passing the exam.

To access the CLI, use one of three methods, as illustrated in Figure 2-3.

Regardless of which method is used, the CLI is placed in user mode, or user EXEC mode. *EXEC* refers to the fact that the commands typed here are executed, as some response messages are displayed on the screen. The alternative to an EXEC mode is *configuration mode*, which is covered in the next section.

Passwords can be required when accessing the CLI. Table 2-2 reviews the different types of passwords and the configuration for each type.

Figure 2-3   *LI Access*

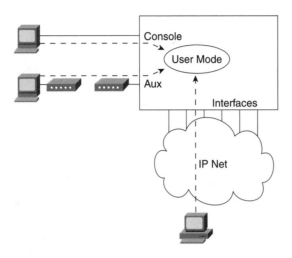

Table 2-2   *CLI Password Configuration*

Access From...	Password Type	Configuration
Console	Console password	**line console** *0* **login** **password** *faith*
Auxiliary	Auxiliary password	**line aux** *0* **login** **password** *hope*
Telnet	VTY password	**line vty** *0 4* **login** **password** *love*

The **login** command actually tells the router to display a prompt. The **password** commands specify the text password to be typed by the user to gain access. The first command in each configuration is a **context-setting** command, as described later in the chapter.

It is typical for all three passwords to have the same value.

Several concurrent Telnet connections to a router are allowed. The **line vty** *0 4* command signifies that this configuration applies to vty's (virtual teletypes—terminals) 0 through 4. Only these five vtys are allowed on the IOS if the router is not also a dial access-server. In this case, all five vtys have the same password, which is handy because users connecting to the router via a Telnet cannot choose which vty they get!

User EXEC mode is one of two command EXEC modes in the IOS user interface. Enable mode (also known as privileged mode or privileged EXEC mode) is the other. It is called enable mode because of the command used to reach enable mode, as shown in Figure 2-4; it is called privileged mode because only powerful, or privileged, commands can be executed there.

Figure 2-4   *User and Privileged Modes*

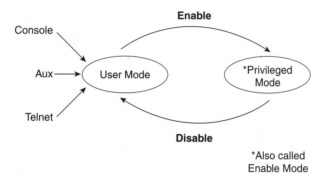

Commands Made Easier on the CLI

Because the user has access to the CLI, one might presume that commands should be typed there. One way to know what those commands are is to get one of several references. The IOS documentation is available on CD and is free if you own one router or switch that has a current maintenance agreement. The documentation is also available from Cisco on paper. If you prefer tangible reference material, Cisco Press offers *Cisco documentation,* which can probably be found at the same bookstore where you found this CCNA exam guide. Also, all Cisco documentation is available online at Cisco's web site (http://www.cisco.com/univercd/home/home.htm).

No matter which documentation you use, it is incredibly unlikely that you will remember all IOS commands. (The command reference manuals stack 14" high!) Therefore, tools and tricks to recall commands are particularly useful. Table 2-3 summarizes command recall help options available at the CLI.

Table 2-3 *IOS Command Help*

What You Type	The Help You Get
?	Help for all commands available in this mode.
Help	Text describing the details listed in this chart; no actual command help is given.
Command ?	Text help describing all the first parameter options for the command "command."
Com?	A list of commands that start with the letters "com."
Command parm?	This style of help lists all parameters beginning with the letters "parm." (Notice, no spaces are between the letters **parm** and the **?**.)
Command parm\<TAB>	If the user presses the TAB key midword, the CLI will either (a) spell the rest of this keyword on the command line for the user, or (b) do nothing. If the CLI does nothing, it means that this string of characters represents more than one possible next parameter, so the CLI does not know which to spell out.
Command parm1 ?	With a space before the question mark, the CLI lists all next parameters and gives a brief explanation of each.

*When you type the ?, the IOS's CLI reacts immediately; that is, you don't need to press the Return key or any other keys. The router also redisplays what you had typed before the ? to save you some keystrokes.

The context in which help is requested is also important. For example, when ? is typed in user mode, the commands allowed only in privileged mode are not displayed. Also, help is available in configuration mode; only configuration commands are displayed in that mode of operation.

Commands you use at the CLI are stored in a command history buffer. The buffer retains the last ten commands you typed. You can change the history size with the **terminal history size** *x* command, where *x* is the number of commands for the CLI to recall.

Of course, most people want to use a previously typed command (perhaps with a different parameter). Commands you have previously used during the current console/aux/Telnet connection can be retrieved and then edited to save you some time and effort. This is particularly useful when you are typing long configuration commands. Table 2-4 lists the commands used to manipulate previously typed commands.

Table 2-4 *Key Sequences for Command Edit and Recall*

Keyboard Command	What the User Gets
Up-arrow or Ctrl-P	The most recently used command. If pressed again, the next most recent command appears, until the history buffer is exhausted. (P is for *Previous.*)
Down-arrow or Ctrl-N	If you have gone too far back into the history buffer, these keys will go forward, in order, to the more recently typed commands.
Left-arrow or Ctrl-B	Moves cursor backward in the command without deleting characters.
Right-arrow or Ctrl-F	Moves cursor forward in the command without deleting characters.
Backspace	Moves cursor backward in the command, deleting characters.
Ctrl-A	Moves the cursor directly to the first character of the command.
Ctrl-E	Moves the cursor directly to the end of the command.
Esc-B	Moves the cursor back one word.
Esc-F	Moves the cursor forward one word.

Cisco Discovery Protocol (CDP)

CDP is used by Cisco routers and switches to ascertain basic information about neighboring routers and switches. You can use this information to learn addresses quickly for easier Simple Network Management Protocol (SNMP) management, as well as learn the addresses of other devices when you do not have passwords to log in to them.

The **show cdp neighbors detail** command provides a window into the most telling parts of what the CDP can show you. Example 2-1 provides one sample **show cdp neighbors detail** command output:

Example 2-1 *show cdp neighbors detail* Output

```
fred>show cdp neighbor detail
------------------------
Device ID: dino
Entry address(es):
  IP address: 199.1.1.66
Platform: Cisco 2500,  Capabilities: Router
Interface: Serial0,  Port ID (outgoing port): Serial0
Holdtime : 148 sec

Version :
Cisco Internetwork Operating System Software
IOS (tm) 2500 Software (C2500-AINR-L), Version 11.2(11), RELEASE SOFTWARE (fc1)
Copyright (c) 1986-1997 by Cisco Systems, Inc.
Compiled Mon 29-Dec-97 18:47 by ckralik


------------------------
Device ID: Barney
Entry address(es):
  IP address: 199.1.1.98
Platform: Cisco 2500,  Capabilities: Router
Interface: Serial1,  Port ID (outgoing port): Serial0
Holdtime : 155 sec

Version :
Cisco Internetwork Operating System Software
IOS (tm) 2500 Software (C2500-AINR-L), Version 11.2(11), RELEASE SOFTWARE (fc1)
Copyright (c) 1986-1997 by Cisco Systems, Inc.
Compiled Mon 29-Dec-97 18:47 by ckralik
```

Routers: Configuration Processes and the Configuration File

CCNA Objectives Covered in This Section

20	Manage configuration files from the privileged exec mode.
21	Control router passwords, identification, and banner.
23	Enter an initial configuration using the setup command.
24	Copy and manipulate configuration files.
27	Prepare the initial configuration of your router and enable IP.

As mentioned in Chapter 1, configuration mode is another mode for the Cisco CLI. Changing the configuration of the router by typing various configuration commands is the purpose of configuration mode. Figure 2-5 illustrates the relationships between configuration mode and the other modes.

Figure 2-5   *CLI Configuration Mode Versus EXEC Modes*

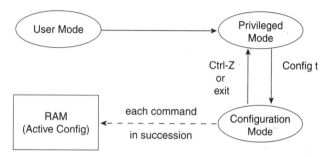

Notice that RAM is shown, but not NVRAM. Configuration mode updates the active configuration file, adding the configuration the user types in configuration mode. Changes are moved into the active configuration file each time the user presses the Return key at the end of the line and are acted upon immediately by the router.

In configuration mode, context setting commands are used before most configuration commands. These context setting commands tell the router what the topic is that you are about to type commands about. More importantly, it tells the router what commands to list when you ask for help! The reason for these contexts in the first place is to make online help more convenient and clear for you.

NOTE   *Context setting* is not a Cisco term—it's just a term I use to help make sense of configuration mode.

The most often used context setting configuration command is the **interface** command. As an example, the CLI user enters interface configuration mode after typing the **interface ethernet 0** configuration command. Command help in interface configuration mode displays only commands specifically about configuring Ethernet interfaces. Commands used in this context are called *subcommands*, or in this specific case, *interface subcommands*. Figure 2-6 shows several different configuration mode contexts, including *interface configuration mode*, with the relationships and methods of moving between each.

Figure 2-6 *Relationships among Context Setting Commands*

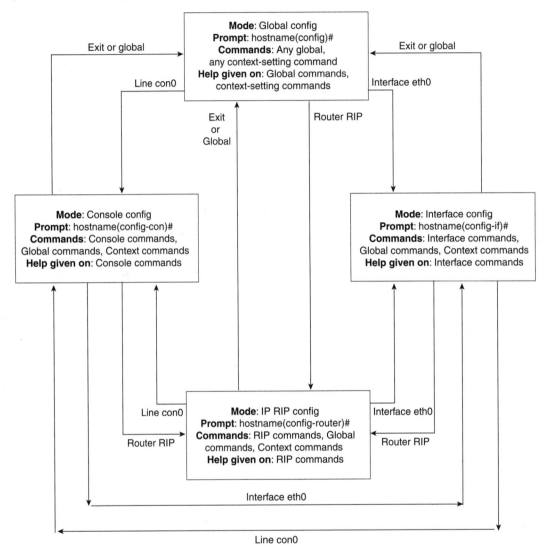

Note that not all line transitions between modes are shown in Figure 2-6. For example, from console configuration mode, the **interface ethernet 0** command could move you to the box to the right, which represents interface configuration mode.

If you have significant experience using the CLI in configuration mode, much of this will be second nature. From a CCNA exam perspective, recalling whether popular commands are global commands or subcommands to a particular configuration mode will be useful.

Use Ctrl-Z to exit configuration mode back to privileged mode.

Example Configuration Process

Example 2-2 illustrates the console password being defined, along with banner, hostname, prompt, and interface descriptions. The finished configuration is also shown.

Example 2-2 *Configuration Process Example*

```
This Here's the Rootin-est Tootin-est Router in these here Parts!

User Access Verification

Password:
Yosemite>enable
Password:
Yosemite#configure terminal
Yosemite(config)#line console 0
Yosemite(config-line)#login
Yosemite(config-line)#password cisco
Yosemite(config-line)#hostname Critter
Critter(config)#prompt Emma
Emma(config)#interface serial 1
Emma(config-if)#description this is the link to Albuquerque
Emma(config-if)#exit
Emma(config)#exit
Emma#
 Emma#show running-config
Building configuration...

Current configuration:
!
version 11.2
! Version of IOS on router, automatic command
!


no service udp-small-servers
no service tcp-small-servers
!
hostname Critter
prompt Emma
! Prompt overrides the use of the hostname as the prompt
!
enable password lu
```

continues

Example 2-2 *Configuration Process Example (Continued)*

```
! This sets the priviledge exec mode password
!
no ip domain-lookup
! Ignores all names resolutions unless locally defined on the router.
!
ipx routing 0000.3089.b170
! Enables IPX rip routing
!
interface Serial0
 ip address 137.11.12.2 255.255.255.0
 ipx network 12
!
interface Serial1
 description this is the link to Albuquerque
 ip address 137.11.23.2 255.255.255.0
 ipx network 23
!
interface TokenRing0
 ip address 137.11.2.2 255.255.255.0
 ipx network CAFE
 ring-speed 16
!
router rip
 network 137.11.0.0
!
no ip classless
!
!
!
banner motd ^C This Here's the Rootin-est Tootin-est Router in these here Parts! ^C
! Any text between the Ctl-C keystroke is considered part of the banner, including
!the return key.!


line con 0
 password cisco
 login
! login tells the router to supply a prompt; password defines what the user must
!type!
!
line aux 0
line vty 0 4
 password cisco
 login
!
end
```

Managing Configuration Files

There are two configuration files internally on all router platforms (except in the 7xxx series of routers). One file is in NVRAM; the other file, which is in RAM, is the one the router uses during operation. The router copies the file from NVRAM into RAM as part of the boot process. Exterior to the router, configuration files can be stored as ASCII text files anywhere.

Several methods of manipulating configuration files are provided by Cisco. CiscoWorks and other management products let you create configurations for one or many routers without logging on to those routers. NetSys Connectivity Tools actually check all the configuration files in your network, make suggestions for improvements, and uncover errors. But the most basic method for manipulating configuration files and moving them into and out of a router is by using a TFTP server. This method is the one covered in the CCNA exam.

The **copy** command is used to move configuration files between RAM, NVRAM, and a TFTP server. The files can be copied between any pair, as Figure 2-7 illustrates.

Figure 2-7   *Locations for Copying and Results from Copy Operations*

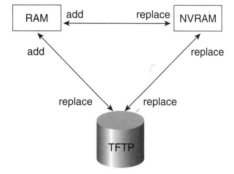

The commands can be summarized as follows:

```
copy {tftp|running-config|startup-config} {tftp|running-config|startup-config}
```

The first parameter is the "from" location; the next one is the "to" location. (Of course, choosing the same option for both parameters is not allowed.)

Confusion about what these commands actually do is pervasive. Any **copy** command option moving a file into NVRAM or a TFTP server replaces the existing file. Any copy command option moving the file into RAM, however, is effectively an add or merge operation. For example, only one **hostname** *Siberia* configuration command is allowed. Therefore, a file copied into RAM, with **hostname** *Siberia* in it, will replace the previous hostname command (if any). However, if the file being copied has the **access-list** *1* **permit host** *1.1.1.1* command in it, and an access list number 1 already exists in the RAM configuration file, **access-list** *1* **permit host** *1.1.1.1* is placed on the end of that existing access list. The old entries in access-list 1 are not deleted. This is because many **access-list** *1* commands are allowed in the same access list.

So why did Cisco not include a replace action, similar to the action used to copy to NVRAM or TFTP? Who knows. A replace action would probably require that you empty all routing tables, which might cause you to be outraged. Possibly this particular nuance is a result of some Cisco programmer, years ago, deciding to take the loaded gun out of users' hands. However, advanced users can accomplish the effect of a replace action by entering configuration mode and issuing commands. This requires that the user know whether a particular command will replace another that is like it in the RAM configuration file, or whether a command would simply be added to the configuration, like an **access-list** command.

7000, 7200, and 7500 Series Routers' Configuration Files

The larger routers happen to have several options for additional Flash memory. Each Route-Switch Processor (RSP) has two slots that can be used for Flash PCMCIA cards, as well as an on-board EEPROM Flash memory. Because Flash memory contains a basic file system, any file can be stored there including configuration files.

The configuration file used at router initialization time is traditionally stored in NVRAM, and with only one such file in NVRAM, there was no need to name the file. The IOS supports storing configuration files in Flash memory, whereas NVRAM can still store only one file. The router knows which configuration file to use at initialization, or when the **startup-config** keyword is used, based on a global variable setting. This variable can refer to any file in any Flash memory, and NVRAM. Because there can be many files in Flash memory, this variable must specify the particular Flash memory and the name of the file. Figure 2-8 illustrates this point.

Figure 2-8   *The Configuration File Environment Variable*

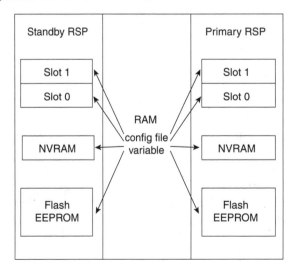

The term **startup-config** then is ambiguous on a 7xxx router because the configuration file can be located in several places. The command **boot config** is used to set an environment variable so that the router knows what file is meant when it encounters any command using the term **startup-config**. For example, **boot config slot0:***fred* means the file called fred in the Flash card in slot0 is used any time a command uses the term **startup**. Table 2-5 provides a list of Flash types, their meanings, and the format of the associated filename.

Table 2-5 *Types of Flash Memory*

Name	Description	Format of Filename
flash	Flash on RP in 7000 series	flash:name
bootflash	Flash on RP in 72xx and 75xx series	bootflash:name
slot0	PCMCIA Flash card in slot 0 of RSP	slot0:name
slot1	PCMCIA Flash card in slot 1 of RSP	slot1:name

The **copy** command can be used with the keyword **startup-config**, or it can simply be used with parameters that use Flash filenames.

Viewing the Configuration and Old-Style Configuration Commands

Once upon a time, commands that were used to move configuration files between RAM, NVRAM, and TFTP did not use easy-to-recall parameters like **startup-config** and **running-config**. In fact, most people could not remember the commands or got the different ones confused.

Figure 2-9 shows both the old and new commands used to view configurations.

Figure 2-9 *Configuration **show** Commands*

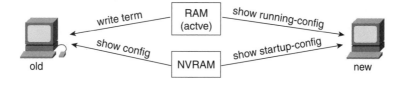

Initial Configuration (Setup Mode)

Setup mode is a router configuration mode that prompts the user for basic configuration parameters. A Cisco router can be configured using the CLI in configuration mode without using setup mode. However, some users like to use setup mode, particularly until they become more familiar with the CLI.

NOTE   If you plan to work with Cisco routers much at all, you should become accustomed to the CLI
configuration mode discussed earlier. Setup only allows very basic configuration.

Setup mode is a topic covered on the CCNA exam. So whether or not you plan to use it,
remembering how it works is important! Figure 2-10 and Example 2-2 describe the process.

Figure 2-10 *Getting into Setup Mode*

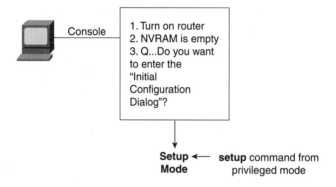

Example 2-3 shows a screen capture of setup mode.

Example 2-3 *Router Setup Configuration Mode*

```
Notice: NVRAM invalid, possibly due to write erase.
          --- System Configuration Dialog ---

At any point you may enter a question mark '?' for help.
Use Ctrl-C to abort configuration dialog at any prompt.
Default settings are in square brackets '[]'.Would you
like to enter the initial configuration dialog? [yes]:
First, would you like to see the current interface summary? [yes]:
Any interface listed with OK? value "NO" does not have a valid configuration

Interface            IP-Address      OK? Method Status                Protocol
Serial0              unassigned      NO  unset  down                  down
Serial1              unassigned      NO  unset  down                  down
TokenRing0           unassigned      NO  unset  reset                 down
TokenRing1           unassigned      NO  unset  reset                 down

Configuring global parameters:

  Enter host name [Router]: fred
The enable secret is a one-way cryptographic secret used
instead of the enable password when it exists.
  Enter enable secret: cisco
The enable password is used when there is no enable secret
```

Example 2-3 *Router Setup Configuration Mode (Continued)*

```
and when using older software and some boot images.
  Enter enable password: cisco2

Enter virtual terminal password: cisco
Configure SNMP Network Management? [yes]: n
Configure IP? [yes]:
Configure IGRP routing? [yes]: n
Configure RIP routing? [no]: n
Configuring interface parameters:
Configuring interface Serial0:
  Is this interface in use? [yes]:
Configure IP on this interface? [yes]:
IP address for this interface: 163.4.8.3
Number of bits in subnet field [0]: 0
Class B network is 163.4.0.0, 0 subnet bits; mask is /16

Configuring interface Serial1:
  Is this interface in use? [yes]: n
Configuring interface TokenRing0:
  Is this interface in use? [yes]: y
Tokenring ring speed (4 or 16) ? [0]: 16
Configure IP on this interface? [yes]:
IP address for this interface: 163.5.8.3
Number of bits in subnet field [0]: 0
Class B network is 163.5.0.0, 0 subnet bits; mask is /16

Configuring interface TokenRing1:
  Is this interface in use? [yes]: n
The following configuration command script was created:

hostname fred
enable secret 5 $1$aMyk$eUxp9JmrPgK.vQ.nA5Tge.
enable password cisco
line vty 0 4
password cisco
no snmp-server
!
ip routing
!
interface Serial0
ip address 163.4.8.3 255.255.0.0
!
interface Serial1
shutdown
no ip address
!
interface TokenRing0
ring-speed 16
```

continues

Example 2-3 *Router Setup Configuration Mode (Continued)*

```
ip address 163.5.8.3 255.255.0.0
!
interface TokenRing1
shutdown
no ip address
!
end

Use this configuration? [yes/no]: y


Building configuration...[OK]
Use the enabled mode 'configure' command to modify this configuration.


Press RETURN to get started!
```

As Example 2-3 illustrates, you can use two methods to get into setup mode. First, if you are at the console and you power up the router, and there is no configuration file in NVRAM, the router asks you if you want to enter the "initial configuration dialog." Answering **y** or **yes** puts you into setup mode. Alternatively, the **setup** privileged EXEC command puts you in setup mode.

When you are finished with setup, you are asked whether you want to use this configuration. If you answer **yes**, the configuration you created is placed in RAM and NVRAM. This is the only operation in the IOS that changes both files to include the same contents based on a single action by you.

Routers: Managing IOS Images

CCNA Objectives Covered in This Section

22	Identify the main Cisco IOS commands for router startup.
25	List the commands to load Cisco IOS software from: flash memory, a TFTP server, or ROM.
26	Prepare to backup, upgrade, and load a backup Cisco IOS software image.

IOS image is simply a term referring to the file containing the IOS. Managing those files entails getting new IOS images from Cisco, backing up the currently used, older version from your routers, updating your routers with the new image, and testing. Also included in IOS image management is how to tell a router to use a particular IOS the next time it boots.

Flash memory is the typical location for the IOS used by a router. It is writable, permanent storage, which is ideal for storing files that need to be retained when the router loses power. Also, because there are no moving parts, there is a smaller chance of failure, which provides better availability.

Upgrading an IOS Image into Flash Memory

As Figure 2-11 illustrates, to upgrade an IOS image into Flash memory, first you obtain the IOS image from Cisco. Then you must place the IOS image into the default directory of the TFTP server. Finally, the **copy** command is issued from the router, copying the file into Flash memory.

Figure 2-11 *Complete IOS Upgrade Process*

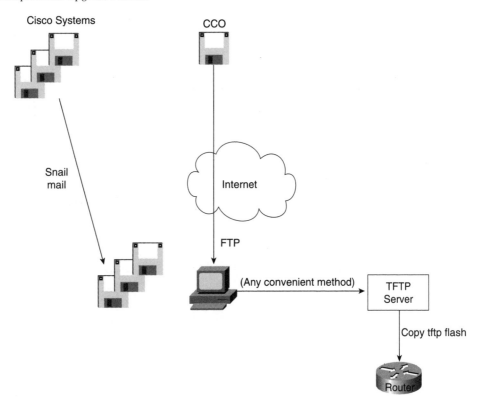

Example 2-4 provides an example of the final step, copying the IOS image into Flash memory.

Example 2-4 *copy tftp flash* Command

```
R1#copy tftp flash

System flash directory:
File  Length    Name/status
  1   7530760   c2500-ainr-l_112-31.bin
[7530824 bytes used, 857784 available, 8388608 total]
Address or name of remote host [255.255.255.255]? 134.141.3.33
Source file name? c2500-ainr-l_112-11.bin
Destination file name [c2500-ainr-l_112-11.bin]?
Accessing file 'c2500-ainr-l_112-11.bin' on 134.141.3.33...
Loading c2500-ainr-l_112-11.bin from 134.141.3.33 (via TokenRing0): ! [OK]

Erase flash device before writing? [confirm]
Flash contains files. Are you sure you want to erase? [confirm]

Copy 'c2500-ainr-l_112-11.bin' from server
  as 'c2500-ainr-l_112-11.bin' into Flash WITH erase? [yes/no]y
Erasing device... eeeeeeeeeeeeeeeeeeeeeeeeeeeeeeee ...erased
Loading c2500-ainr-l_112-11.bin from 134.141.3.33 (via TokenRing0):
!!!!!!!!!!!!!!!!!!!!!!!!!!!!!!!!!!!!!!!!!!!!!!!!!!!!!!!!!!!!!!!!!!!!!!!!!!!!!!!!!
!!!!!!!!!!!!!!!!!!!!!!!!!!!!!!!!!!!!!!!!!!!!!!!!!!!!!!!!!!!!!!!!!!!!!!!!!!!!!!!!!
!!!!!!!!!!!!!!!!!!!!!!!!!!!!!!!!!!!!!!!!!!!!!!!!!!!!!!!!!!!!!!!!!!!!!!!!!!!!!!!!!
!!!!!!!!!!!!!!!!!!!!!!!!!!!!!!!!!!!!!!!!!!!!!!!!!!!!!!!!!!!!!!!!!!!!!!!!!!!!!!!!!
!!!!!!!!!!!!!!!!!!!!!!!!!!!!!!!!!!!!!!!!!!!!!!!!!!!!!!!!!!!!!!!!!!!!!!!!!!!!!!!!!
!!!!!!!!!!!!!!!!!!!!!!!!!!!!!!!!!!!!!!!!!!!!!!!!!!!!!!!!!!!!!!!!!!!!!!!!!!!!!!!!!
!!!!!!!!!!!!!!!!!!!!!!!!!!!!!!!!!!!!!!!!!!!!!!!!!!!!!!!!!!!!!!!!!!!!!!!!!!!!!!!!!
!!!!!!!!!!!!!!!!!!!!!!!!!!!!!!!!!!!!!!!!!!!!!!!!!!!!!!!!!!!!!!!!!!!!!!!!!!!!!!!!!
!!!!!!!!!!!!!!!!!!!!!!!!!!!!!!!!!!!!!!!!!!!!!!!!!!!!!!!!!!!!!!!!!!!!!!!!!!!!!!!!!
!!!!!!!!!!!!!!!!!!!!!!!!!!!!!!!!!!!!!!!!!!!!!!!!!!!!!!!!!!!!!!!!!!!!!!!!!!!!!!!!!
!!!!!!!!!!!!!!!!!!!!!!!!!!!!!!!!!!!!!!!!!!!!!!!!!!!!!!!!!!!!!!!!!!!!!!!!!!!!!!!!!
!!!!!!!!!!!!!!!!!!!!!!!!!!!!!!!!!!!!!!!!!!!!!!!!!!!!!!!!!!!!!!!!!!!!!!!!!!!!!!!!!
!!!!!!!!!!!!!!!!!!!!!!!!!!!!!!!!!!!!!!!!!!!!!!!!!!!!!!!!!!!!!!!!!!!!!!!!!!!!!!!!!
!!!!!!!!!!!!!!!!!!!!!!!!!!!!!!!!!!!!!!!!!!!!!!!!!!!!!!!!!!!!!!!!!!!!!!!!!!!!!!!!!
!!!!!!!!!!!!!!!!!!!!!!!!!!!!!!!!!!!!!!!!!!!!!!!!!!!!!!!!!!!!!!!!!!!!!!!!!!!!!!!!!
!!!!!!!!!!!!!!!!!!!!!!!!!!!!!!!!!!!!!!!!!!!!!!!!!!!!!!!!!!!!!!!!!!!!!!!!!!!!!!!!!
!!!!!!!!!!!!!!!!!!!!!!!!!!!!!!!!!!!!!!!!
[OK - 7530760/8388608 bytes]

Verifying checksum...  OK (0xA93E)
Flash copy took 0:04:26 [hh:mm:ss]
R1#
```

During this process of copying the IOS image into Flash memory, the router will need to discover several important facts:

1. What is the IP address or hostname of the TFTP server?

2. What is the name of the file?

3. Is there space available for this file in Flash memory?

4. If not, will you let the router erase the old files?

The router will prompt you for answers, as necessary. After that is completed, the router erases Flash memory if necessary, copies the file, and then verifies that the checksum for the file shows no errors occurred in transmission. After that, the **show flash** command can be used to verify the contents of Flash memory (see Example 2-5). Before the new IOS is used, however, the router must be reloaded.

Example 2-5 *Verifying Flash Memory Contents with the **show flash** Command*

```
fred#show flash

System flash directory:
File  Length    Name/status
  1   4181132   c2500-i-1.112-7a
[4181196 bytes used, 4207412 available, 8388608 total]
8192K bytes of processor board System flash (Read ONLY)
```

In some cases, Flash memory may be in read-only mode. That is the case when a router, to conserve RAM, loads only part of the IOS into RAM. Other parts, which are not referenced often, are kept in Flash memory. (Flash memory access time is much slower than RAM.) In this case, if Flash memory is erased to make room for a new image, the IOS could not continue to run.

If the router is using a portion of the IOS in Flash memory to run from, the router must first be booted using the IOS in ROM. Then, the Flash memory will be in read/write mode, and the erase and copy can be accomplished. The **copy tftp flash** command in later releases of the IOS actually performs the entire process for you. In earlier releases, you had to boot the router from ROM and then issue the **copy tftp flash** command.

Choosing Which IOS Image to Load

Two methods are used to determine where the router tries to obtain an IOS to execute. The first is based on the value of the configuration register, which is a 16-bit software register in Cisco's more recently developed routers. (Some older routers had a hardware configuration register, with jumpers on the processor card, to set bits to a value of 0 or 1.) The second method used to determine where the router tries to obtain an IOS to execute is through the use of the **boot**

system configuration command. Figure 2-12 shows an example binary breakdown of the default value for the configuration register.

Figure 2-12 *Binary Version of Configuration Register, Value Hex 2102*

15	14	13	12	11	10	9	8	7	6	5	4	3	2	1	0
0	0	1	0	0	0	0	1	0	0	0	0	0	0	1	0

The boot field is the name of the low-order four bits of the configuration register. This field can be considered a four-bit value, represented as a hexadecimal digit. Cisco represents hexadecimal values by preceding the hex digit(s) with a *0x*, for example, *0xA* would mean a single hex digit *A*.

Table 2-6 summarizes the use of the configuration register and the **boot system** command at initialization time.

Table 2-6 *boot system Command*

Value of Boot Field	Boot System Commands	Result
0x0	Ignored if present	ROM monitor mode, a low-level problem determination mode, is entered.
0x1	Ignored if present	IOS from ROM is loaded.
0x2-0xF	**boot system ROM**	IOS from ROM is loaded.
0x2-0xF	**boot system flash**	First file from Flash is loaded.
0x2-0xF	**boot system flash** *filename*	IOS with name *filename* is loaded from Flash.
0x2-0xF	**boot system tftp 10.1.1.1** *filename*	IOS with name *filename* is loaded from TFTP server.
0x2-0xF	Multiple boot system commands, any variety	Attempt to load IOS based on first boot command in configuration. If that fails, second boot command is used, etc., until one is successful.

Q&A

As mentioned in Chapter 1, the questions and scenarios are more difficult than what you should experience on the actual exam. The questions do not attempt to cover more breadth or depth than the exam; however, the questions are designed to make sure you know the answer. Rather than allowing you to derive the answer from clues hidden inside the question itself, your understanding and recall of the subject will be challenged. Questions from the "Do I Know This Already?" quiz from the beginning of the chapter are repeated here to ensure that you have mastered the chapter's topic areas. Hopefully, these questions will help limit the number of exam questions on which you narrow your choices to two options, and then guess!

1. What are the two different names for the router's mode of operation that when accessed allow you to issue commands that could be disruptive to router operations?

2. What are three methods of logging on to a router?

3. What is the name of the user interface mode of operation used when you cannot issue disruptive commands?

4. Can the auxiliary port be used for anything besides remote modem user access to a router? If so, what other purpose can it serve?

5. How many console ports can be installed on a Cisco 7500 router?

6. What command would you use to receive command help if you know the **show** command option that you cannot recall begins with a "C"?

7. While you are logged in to a router, you issue the command **copy ?** and get a response of "Unknown command, computer name, or host." Offer an explanation as to why this error message appears.

8. Is the number of retrievable commands based on the number of characters in each command, or is it simply a number of commands, regardless of their size?

9. How can you retrieve a previously used command? (Name two ways.)

10. Instead of **show ip route**, which is the only command you typed since logging into the router, you now want to issue a **show ip arp** command. What steps would you take to do so, without simply typing **show ip arp**?

11. After typing **show ip route** *128.1.1.0*, you now want to issue the command **show ip route** *218.1.4.0*. What steps would you take to do so, without simply typing **show ip route** *218.1.4.0*?

12. What configuration command causes the router to demand a password from the console? What configuration mode "context" must you be in; that is, what command(s) must you type before this command?

13. What configuration command is used to tell the router the password that is required at the console? What configuration mode "context" must you be in; that is, what command(s) must you type before this command?

14. What is the purpose of Flash memory in a Cisco router?

15. What is the intended purpose of NVRAM memory in a Cisco router?

16. What does the NV stand for in NVRAM?

17. What is the intended purpose of RAM in a Cisco router?

18. What is the purpose of ROM in a Cisco router?

19. What configuration command would be needed to cause a router to use IOS an image named *c2500-j-l.112-14.bin* on TFTP server 128.1.1.1 when the router is reloaded? If you forgot the first parameter of this command, what steps must you take to learn the correct parameters and add the command to the configuration? (Assume you are not logged in to the router when you start.)

20. What command sets the password that would be required after typing the **enable** command? Is that password encrypted by default?

21. What is missing from the configuration command **banner** *This is Ivan Denisovich's Gorno Router—Do Not Use* for it to have the correct syntax?

22. Name two commands that affect the text used as the command prompt.

23. When using setup mode, you are prompted at the end of the process as to whether you want to use the configuration parameters you just typed in. Which type of memory is this configuration stored into if you type **yes**?

24. What two methods could a router administrator use to cause a router to load the IOS stored in ROM?

25. What could a router administrator do to cause a router to load file *xyz123.bin* from TFTP server 128.1.1.1 upon the next reload? Is there more than one way to accomplish this?

26. What is the process used to update the contents of Flash memory so that a new IOS in a file called *c2500-j-l.112-14.bin* on TFTP server 128.1.1.1 is copied into Flash memory?

27. Name three possible problems that could prevent the command **boot net** c2500-j-l.112-14.bin *128.1.1.1* from succeeding.

28. Two different IOS files are in a router's Flash memory, one called *c2500-j-l.111-3.bin* and one called *c2500-j-l.112-14.bin*. Which one does the router use when it boots up? How could you force the other IOS file to be used? Without looking at the router configuration, what command would you use to discover which file was used for the latest boot of the router?

29. What does CDP stand for?

30. What type of interfaces is CDP enabled on by default? (Assume IOS 11.0 and beyond.)

31. What command can be used to provide as much detailed information as is possible with CDP?

32. Is the password required at the console the same one that is required when Telnet is used to access a router?

33. How could a router administrator disable CDP? What command(s) would be required on a Cisco 2501 (2 serial, 1 Ethernet) router?

34. Which IP routing protocols could be enabled using **setup**?

35. Name two commands used to view the configuration to be used at the next reload of the router. Which one is a more recent addition to the IOS?

36. Name two commands used to view the configuration that is currently used in a router. Which one is a more recent addition to the IOS?

37. The **copy startup-config running-config** command always changes the currently used configuration for this router to exactly match what is in the startup configuration file. (T/F). Why?

Scenarios

Scenario 2-1

Compare the following output from router commands. The first screen capture was gathered at 11:00 a.m., 30 minutes earlier than the second screen capture. What can you definitively say happened to this router during the intervening half hour?

Example 2-6   *11:00 a.m.* ***show running-config***

```
hostname Gorno
!
enable password cisco
!
interface Serial0
 ip address 134.141.12.1 255.255.255.0
!
interface Serial1
 ip address 134.141.13.1 255.255.255.0
!
interface Ethernet0
 ip address 134.141.1.1 255.255.255.0
!
router rip
 network 134.141.0.0
!
line con 0
 password cisco
 login
line aux 0
line vty 0 4
 password cisco
 login
```

Example 2-7   *11:30 a.m.* ***show running-config***

```
hostname SouthernSiberia
prompt Gorno
!
enable-secret $8df003j56ske92
enable password cisco
!
interface Serial0
 ip address 134.141.12.1 255.255.255.0
!
interface Serial1
 ip address 134.141.13.1 255.255.255.0
!
interface Ethernet0
```

Example 2-7 *11:30 a.m. show running-config (Continued)*

```
ip address 134.141.1.1 255.255.255.0
no cdp enable
!
router rip
network 134.141.0.0
!
line con 0
 password cisco
 login
line aux 0
line vty 0 4
 password cisco
 login
```

Questions on Scenario 2-1

1. During the process of changing these two configurations in Scenario 2-1, the command prompt temporarily was **SouthernSiberia(config)#**. What configuration commands, and in what order, could have changed the configuration as shown and allowed the prompt to temporarily be **SouthernSiberia(config)#**?

2. Assuming that Figure 2-13 is complete, what effect does the **no cdp enable** command have?

Figure 2-13 *Siberian Enterprises Sample Network*

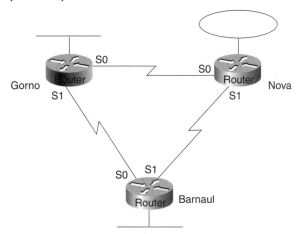

3. What effect would the **no enable secret cisco** command have at this point?

Scenario 2-2

Example 2-8 shows that the **running-config** command was executed on the Nova router at 11:30 a.m. as well.

Example 2-8   *Configuration of Router Nova*

```
hostname Nova
banner # This is the router in Nova Sibiersk; Dress warmly before entering! #
!
boot system tftp 134.141.88.3 c2500-js-113.bin
boot system flash c2500-j-1.111-9.bin
boot system rom
!
enable password cisco
!
interface Serial0
 ip address 134.141.12.2 255.255.255.0
!
interface Serial1
 ip address 134.141.23.2 255.255.255.0
!
interface Ethernet0
 ip address 134.141.2.2 255.255.255.0
!
router rip
 network 134.141.0.0
!
line con 0
 password cisco
 login
line aux 0
line vty 0 4
 password cisco
 login
```

Questions on Scenario 2-2

1. If this is all the information that you have, what IOS do you expect will be loaded when the user reloads Nova?

2. Examine the following command outputs taken immediately before the user is going to type the **reload** command (see Example 2-9). What IOS do you expect will be loaded?

Example 2-9 *show ip route* on *Nova*

```
Nova#show ip route
Codes: C - connected, S - static, I - IGRP, R - RIP, M - mobile, B - BGP
       D - EIGRP, EX - EIGRP external, O - OSPF, IA - OSPF inter area
       N1 - OSPF NSSA external type 1, N2 - OSPF NSSA external type 2
       E1 - OSPF external type 1, E2 - OSPF external type 2, E - EGP
       i - IS-IS, L1 - IS-IS level-1, L2 - IS-IS level-2, * - candidate default
       U - per-user static route, o - ODR

Gateway of last resort is not set

     134.141.0.0/24 is subnetted, 6 subnets
C       134.141.2.0 is directly connected, TokenRing0
R       134.141.3.0 [120/1] via 134.141.23.3, 00:00:15, Serial1
R       134.141.1.0 [120/1] via 134.141.12.1, 00:00:20, Serial0
C       134.141.12.0 is directly connected, Serial0
R       134.141.13.0 [120/1] via 134.141.12.1, 00:00:20, Serial0
                     [120/1] via 134.141.23.3, 00:00:15, Serial1
C       134.141.23.0 is directly connected, Serial1
```

3. Now examine the following **show flash** command, which was issued immediately after the **show ip route** command in Example 2-9, but before the user issued the **reload** command (see Example 2-10). What IOS do you think would be loaded in this case?

Example 2-10 *show flash* on *Router Nova*

```
Nova# show flash
4096K bytes of flash memory sized on embedded flash.
File   name/status
 0 c2500-j-l.111-3.bin
[682680/4194304 bytes free/total]
```

4. Now examine the configuration in Example 2-11. Assume that there is now a route to 134.141.88.0, and that the file c2500-j-l.112-14.bin is an IOS image in Flash memory. What IOS do you expect will be loaded now?

Example 2-11 *show running-config on Router Nova*

```
 hostname Nova
banner # This is the router in Nova Sibiersk; Dress warmly before entering! #
!
boot system flash c2500-j-1.112-14.bin
boot system rom
!
enable password cisco
!
interface Serial0
 ip address 134.141.12.2 255.255.255.0
!
interface Serial1
 ip address 134.141.23.2 255.255.255.0
!
interface Ethernet0
 ip address 134.141.2.2 255.255.255.0
!
router rip
 network 134.141.0.0
!
line con 0
 password cisco
 login
line aux 0
line vty 0 4
 password cisco
 login
!
config-register 0x2101
```

Answers to Scenarios

Scenario 2-1 Answers

In Scenario 2-1, the following commands were added to the configuration:

- **enable-secret** as a global command
- **prompt** as a global command
- **no cdp enable** as an Ethernet0 subcommand
- The **hostname** command also was changed

The scenario question's answers are as follows:

1. If the hostname was changed to *SouthSiberia* first and then the **prompt** command added during the intervening time, the prompt would have been SouthSiberia. Configuration commands are added to the RAM configuration file immediately and used. In this case, when the **prompt** command was added, it caused the router to use that text and not the hostname as the prompt.

2. No practical effect. Because no other Cisco CDP enabled devices are on that Ethernet, CDP messages from Gorno are useless. So, the only effect is to lessen the overhead on that Ethernet is a very small way.

3. No effect other than cleaning up the configuration file. The **enable password** is not used if an **enable secret** is in use.

Scenario 2-2 Answers

The answers to the questions in Scenario 2-2 are as follows:

1. The first boot system statement would be used: **boot system tftp** *134.141.88.3 c2500-js-113.bin*.

2. The **boot system flash** command would be used. The TFTP boot would presumably fail because there is not currently a route to the subnet the TFTP server is part of. It is reasonable to assume that a route would not be learned two minutes later when the router had reloaded. So, the next boot system command (**flash**) would be used.

3. The **boot system ROM** command would be used. Because there is no file in Flash called c2500-j-l.111-9.bin, the boot from Flash would fail as well, leaving only one boot command.

4. The IOS from ROM would be loaded due to the configuration register. If the configuration register boot field is set to 0x1, boot system commands are ignored. So, having a route to the 134.141.88.0/24 subnet, and having c2500-j-l.111-9.bin in Flash, does not help.

The following table outlines the CCNA exam objectives that are reviewed in this chapter. The numbers shown correspond to the master list of objectives found in Chapter 1, "What Is CCNA?"

Objective	Description
1	Identify and describe the functions of each of the seven layers of the OSI reference model.
2	Describe connection-oriented network service and connectionless network service, and identify the key differences between them.
3	Describe data link addresses and network addresses, and identify the key differences between them.
4	Identify at least 3 reasons why the industry uses a layered model.
5	Define and explain the 5 conversion steps of data encapsulation.
6	Define flow control and describe the three basic models used in networking.
7	List the key internetworking functions of the OSI Network layer and how they are performed in a router.
29	Describe the two parts of network addressing, then identify the parts in specific protocol address examples.
60	Define and describe the function of a MAC address.

CHAPTER 3

Understanding the OSI Reference Model

In years past, the need to understand the Open Systems Interconnection (OSI) reference model for networking grew rapidly. The U.S. government passed laws requiring vendors to support OSI software on their systems or they would no longer buy the systems. Several vendors even predicted that the global Internet would evolve towards using OSI as the protocol instead of TCP/IP. As we near the turn of the century, however, OSI has been implemented on a much smaller scale than predicted. Few vendors push their OSI software solutions, if they have them. Several components of the OSI model are popularly implemented today. For example, OSI NSAP network layer addresses are often used for signaling in Asynchronous Transfer Mode (ATM) networks. However, full seven-layer OSI implementations are relatively rare today.

So why have a whole chapter on OSI? The biggest reason is that the OSI seven-layer reference model is an excellent point of reference for describing the concepts and functions behind other network protocol implementations. References to Layer 2 switching and Layer 3 switching, which are popular topics today, refer to the comparison to Layers 2 and 3 of the OSI model. Cisco courses make generous use of the OSI model as reference for comparison of other network protocol implementations. So, this chapter will not actually help you understand OSI fully, but rather it will discuss OSI functions in comparison with popularly implemented protocols.

How to Best Use This Chapter

By taking the following steps, you can make better use of your study time:

- Keep your notes and answers for all your work with this book in one place for easy reference.

- Take the quiz and write down your answers. Studies show retention is significantly increased through writing facts and concepts down, even if you never look at the information again!

- Use the diagram in Figure 3-1 to guide you to the next step in preparation for this topic area on the CCNA exam.

Figure 3-1 *How To Best Use This Chapter*

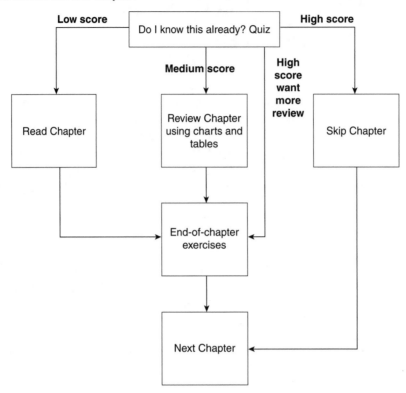

"Do I Know This Already?" Quiz

1. Name the seven layers of the OSI model.

_____

_____

_____

2. What is the main purpose of Layer 3?

_____

_____

_____

3. What is the main purpose of Layer 2?

_____

_____

_____

4. Describe the process of data encapsulation as data is processed from creation until it exits a physical interface to a network. Use the OSI model as an example.

_____

_____

_____

5. Describe the services provided in most connection-oriented protocol services.

_____

_____

_____

6. Name three terms popularly used as a synonym for MAC addresses.

_____

_____

_____

7. What portion of a MAC address encodes an identifier representing the manufacturer of the card?

_____

_____

_____

8. Name two differences between Layer 3 addresses and Layer 2 addresses.

_____

_____

_____

   9. How many bits in an IP address?

   _____

   _____

   _____

   10. Name the two main parts of an IP address. Which part identifies which "group" this
        address is a member of?

   _____

   _____

   _____

   11. Name at least three benefits to layering networking protocol specifications.

   _____

   _____

   _____

   12. Describe the differences between a routed protocol and a routing protocol.

   _____

   _____

   _____

The answers to the quiz are found in Appendix B, on page 549. Review the answers, grade your
quiz, and choose an appropriate next step in this chapter based on the suggestions diagrammed
in Figure 3-1. Your choices for the next step are as follows:

- **5 or fewer correct**—Read this chapter.

- **6, 7, or 8 correct**—Review this chapter, looking at the charts and diagrams that
  summarize most of the concepts and facts in this chapter.

- **9 or more correct**—If you want more review on these topics, skip to the exercises at the
  end of this chapter. If you do not want more review on these topics, skip this chapter.

Foundation Topics

The OSI, TCP/IP, and Novell NetWare Network Protocol Architectures

CCNA Objectives Covered in This Section

1	Identify and describe the functions of each of the seven layers of the OSI reference model.
2	Describe connection-oriented network service and connectionless network service, and identify the key differences between them.
4	Indentify at least 3 reasons why the industry uses a layered model.
5	Define and explain the 5 conversion steps of data encapsulation.
7	List the key internetworking functions of the OSI Network layer and how they are performed in a router.

This chapter deals with many of the theoretical concepts and procedures defined as portions of networking protocols. Four topics of particular importance for the CCNA exam are covered in this chapter. The OSI model is described. (Expect questions on the functions of each layer.) Data-link protocols and network layer protocols, the protocols most important to switching and routing, are reviewed. Plus, an anecdote from the classroom that helps you remember what routing and routing protocols are!

Three topics of particular importance for the CCNA exam are covered in this chapter:

- **The OSI model**—Expect questions on the functions of each layer and examples at each layer in the CCNA exam.

- **Data-link protocols**—This section is important to properly understand LAN switching.

- **Network layer protocols**—This section is important to properly understand routing.

If you come from the OJT or college training track (see Chapter 1), a full reading of this chapter is probably in your best interest. If you have taken the ICRC training track, the data-link (Layer 2) details might be of the most interest to you. Finally, as usual, if you took the CRLS training track, these concepts should have been fully covered in class, and you are more likely to be able to pick and choose topics from this chapter.

OSI: Origin and Evolution

The difficulty in these last years of the century, when using the OSI protocol specifications as a point of reference, is that almost no one uses them. You cannot typically walk down the hall and see a computer whose main, or even optional, networking protocols are defined by OSI.

So what is OSI? It is the Open Systems Interconnection model for communications. It is a rather well-defined set of protocol specifications with many options for accomplishing similar tasks. Some participants in OSI's creation and development wanted it to become *the* networking protocol and have all applications use OSI. The United States government went so far as to require OSI support on every computer it would buy as of a certain date in the early '90s via an edict called the Government OSI Profile (GOSIP), which certainly gave vendors some incentive to write OSI code. In fact, in my old IBM days, we even had charts showing how the TCP/IP installed base would start declining by 1994, OSI installations would take off, and OSI would be the protocol that the twenty-first century Internet was built from. (In IBM's defense, moving the world to OSI may have been yet another case of "You just can't get there from here.")

What is OSI today? Well, the protocols are still in existence and are used around the world to some degree. The United States government reversed its GOSIP directive officially in May 1994, which was probably the final blow to the possibility of pervasive OSI implementations. Cisco routers will route OSI. OSI Network Service Access Point (NSAP) addresses are used in Cisco ATM devices for signaling. Digital Equipment's DECnet Phase V uses several portions of OSI, including the networking layer (Layer 3) addressing and routing concepts. But more often than not, in 1998 (at the writing of this book), the OSI model is mainly used as a point of reference for discussing other protocol specifications.

OSI Layers

The OSI model consists of seven layers each of which can, and typically does, have several sublayers. The CCNA exam should not cover any sublayers with the exception of the sublayers for Local Area Network (LAN) Data Links; the names of the OSI model layers and their main functions are simply good things to memorize. And frankly, if you want to pursue your Cisco certifications beyond CCNA, these names and functional areas will come up continually. Table 3-1 diagrams the seven OSI layers.

Table 3-1 *OSI Reference Model*

Layer Name	Functional Description	Examples
Application (Layer 7)	An application that communicates with other computers is implementing OSI application layer concepts. The application layer refers to communications services to applications. For example, a word processor that lacks communications capabilities would not implement code for communications, and word processor programmers would not be concerned about OSI Layer 7. However, if an option for transferring a file were added, then the word processor would need to implement OSI Layer 7 (or the equivalent layer in another protocol specification).	FTP, WWW browsers, Telnet, NFS, SMTP gateways (Eudora, CC:mail), SNMP, X.400 mail, FTAM

Table 3-1 *OSI Reference Model (Continued)*

Layer Name	Functional Description	Examples
Presentation (Layer 6)	This layer's main purpose is defining data formats, such as ASCII text, EBCDIC text, binary, BCD, and JPEG. Encryption is also defined by OSI as a presentation layer service. For example, FTP allows you to choose binary or ASCII transfer. If binary, the sender and receiver do not modify the contents of the file. If ASCII is chosen, the sender translates the text from the sender's character set to a standard ASCII and sends the data. The receiver translates back from the standard ASCII to the character set used on the receiving computer.	TIFF, GIF, JPEG, PICT, ASCII, EBCDIC, encryption, MPEG, MIDI, HTML
Session (Layer 5)	The session layer defines how to start, control, and end conversations (called *sessions*). This includes the control and management of multiple bidirectional messages so that the application can be notified if only some of a series of messages are completed. For example, an Automated Teller Machine transaction in which you get cash out of your checking account should not debit your account and fail before handing you the cash, and then record the transaction even though you did not receive money. The session layer creates ways to imply which flows are part of the same session and which flows must complete before any is considered complete.	RPC, SQL, NFS, NetBios names, AppleTalk ASP, DECnet SCP
Transport (Layer 4)	Layer 4 includes the choice of protocols that either do or do not provide error recovery. Reordering of the incoming data stream, when packets arrive out of order is included, as well as reassembly of the data if the packets fragmented during transmission. For example, TCP may give a 4200 byte segment of data to IP for delivery. IP will fragment the data into smaller sizes if a 4000 byte packet could not be delivered across some media. So, the receiving TCP might get three different segments or 1400 bytes apiece. The receiving TCP might receive these in a different order as well, so it reorders the received segments, compiles them into the original 4200 byte segment, and then is able to move on to acknowledging the data.	TCP, UDP, SPX

continues

Table 3-1 *OSI Reference Model (Continued)*

Layer Name	Functional Description	Examples
Network (Layer 3)	This layer defines end-to-end delivery of packets. To accomplish this, the network layer defines logical addressing so that any endpoint can be identified. It also defines how routing works and how routes are learned so the packets can be delivered. The network layer also defines how to fragment a packet into smaller packets to accommodate media with smaller maximum transmission unit sizes. The network layer of OSI defines most of the details that a Cisco router considers when routing OSI. For example, IP running in a Cisco router is responsible for examining the destination IP address of a packet, comparing that address to the IP routing table, fragmenting the packet if the outgoing interface requires smaller packets, and queuing the packet to be sent out to the interface.	IP, IPX, AppleTalk DDP
Data link (Layer 2)	The data link (Layer 2) specifications are concerned with getting data across one particular link or medium. The data-link protocols define delivery across an individual link. These protocols are necessarily concerned with the type of media in question; for example, 802.3 and 802.2 are specifications from the IEEE, which are referenced by OSI as valid data-link (Layer 2) protocols. These specifications define how Ethernet works. Other protocols, like High-Level Data Link Control (HDLC) for a point-to-point WAN link, deal with the different physical details of a WAN link. OSI, like other protocol specifications, often does not create any original specification for the data link layer but instead relies on other standards bodies such as IEEE to create new data link and physical layer standards.	Frame Relay, HDLC, PPP, IEEE 802.3/802.2, FDDI, ATM, IEE 802.5/802.2

Table 3-1   *OSI Reference Model (Continued)*

Layer Name	Functional Description	Examples
Physical (Layer 1)	These physical layer (Layer 1) specifications, which are also typically standards from other organizations that are referred to by OSI, deal with the physical characteristics of the physical medium. Connectors, pins, use of pins, electrical currents, encoding, and light modulation are all part of different physical layer specifications. Multiple specifications are sometimes used to complete all details of the physical layer. For example, RJ45 defines the shape of the connector and number of wires/pins in the cable. Ethernet and 802.3 define the use of wires/pins 1,2,3, and 6. So to use a category 5 cable, with an RJ-45 connector for an Ethernet connection, Ethernet and RJ-45 physical layer specifications are used.	EIA/TIA-232, EIA/TIA-449, V.35, V.24, RJ45, Ethernet, 802.3, 802.5, FDDI, NRZI, NRZ, B8ZS

Some protocols define details of multiple layers. For example, because the TCP/IP application layer correlates to OSI Layers 5 to 7, the Network File System (NFS) implements elements matching all three layers. NFS is specifically pointed out here because the ICRC course mentions NFS under the topic "session layer." Likewise, 802.3, 802.5, and Ethernet define data link and physical layer details.

Layering Benefits and Concepts

The layering of protocol specifications has many benefits. One obvious benefit is that the protocols, while not individually complex, are very detailed. Simply thinking about the concepts in layers helps us! The following list summarizes the benefits of layering protocol specifications:

- Easier for humans to discuss and learn about the many details of a protocol specification.

- Standardizes interfaces between layers, which allows different products to provide only functions of some layers (such as a router with Layers 1 to 3) or allows different products to supply parts of the functions of the protocol (such as Microsoft TCP/IP built into Win95, or the Eudora Email application providing TCP/IP application layer support). The reference in the ICRC course to this capability to allow a package to implement only some layers of the protocol is called *Facilitates Modular Engineering*. The term is mentioned here because the exact term is possibly one of the choices in exam questions about CCNA objective 4.

- Creates better environment for interoperability.

- Reduces complexity, allowing easy programming changes and faster product evolution.

- Each layer creates headers and trailers around the user data when sending and interprets them when receiving. Anyone examining these headers or trailers for troubleshooting can find the header or trailer for Layer X and know what type of information should be found.

- The layer below another layer provides services to the higher layer. Therefore, remembering what each layer does is easier. (For example, the network layer needs to deliver data end-to-end. To do this, it uses data links to forward data to the next successive device along that end-to-end path.)

Layer Interactions

The software and/or hardware products implementing the logic of some of the OSI protocol layers provide two general functions:

- Each layer provides a service to the layer above it in the protocol specification.

- Each layer communicates some information with the same layer's software or hardware on other computers, in particular with the other endpoint computer.

In the coming pages, you will learn more about each of these two functions.

Interactions Between Adjacent Layers on the Same Computer

To provide services to the next higher layer, a layer must know about the standard interfaces defined between layers. These interfaces include definitions of what Layer N+1 must provide to Layer N to get services, as well as what information Layer N must provide back to Layer N+1.

Figure 3-2 presents a graphical representation of two computers and provides an excellent backdrop for a discussion of interactions between layers on the same computer.

Figure 3-2 *Example for Discussion of Adjacent Layer Interactions*

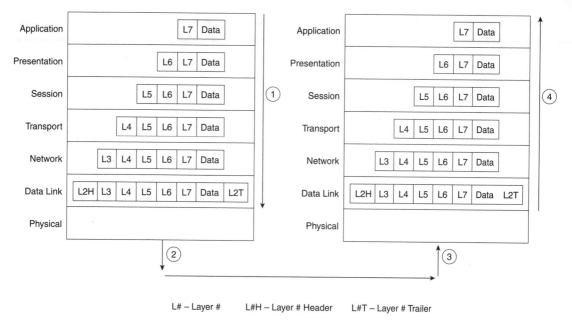

L# – Layer #   L#H – Layer # Header   L#T – Layer # Trailer

The data is created by some application on Host A. For example, an e-mail is typed by the user. Each layer creates a header and passes the data down to the next layer. (The arrows in Figure 3-2, Step 1, denote the passing of data between layers.) Passing the data down to the next layer implies that the lower layer needs to perform some services for the higher layer; to perform these services, the lower layer adds some information in a header or trailer. For example, the transport layer hands off its data and header; the network layer adds a header with the correct destination network-layer address so the packet can be delivered to the other computer.

After the application creates the data, the software and hardware implementing each layer performs its work, adding the appropriate header and trailer. The physical layer can use the media to send a signal for physical transmission as shown in Step 2 in Figure 3-2.

Host B, upon receipt (Step 3), will begin the adjacent layer interactions on Host B. The right side of Figure 3-2 shows an arrow pointing next to the computer (Step 4), signifying that the received data is being processed as it goes up the protocol stack. In fact, thinking about what each layer does in the OSI model can help you decide what information could be in each header. The following sequence outlines the basics of processing at each layer and how each lower layer is providing a service to the next higher layer:

1. The physical layer (Layer 1) ensures bit synchronization and places the received binary pattern into a buffer (transfer across a medium). It notifies the data link layer that a frame has been received after decoding the incoming signal into a bit stream.

ata-link layer examines the frame check sequence (FCS) in the trailer to determine whether errors occurred in transmission (error detection). If an error has occurred, the frame is discarded. (Some data-link protocols perform error recovery, and some do not.) The data-link address(es) are examined so Host B can decide whether to process the data further. The data between the Layer 2 header and trailer is given to the Layer 3 software on Host B. The data link delivers the data across that link.

3. The network layer (Layer 3) destination address is examined. If the address is Host B's address, processing continues (logical addressing), the data after the Layer 3 header is given to the transport layer (Layer 4) software, having provided the service of end-to-end delivery.

4. If error recovery was an option chosen for the transport layer (Layer 4), the counters identifying this piece of data are encoded in the Layer 4 header along with acknow-ledgment information (error recovery). After error recovery and reordering the incoming data, the data is given to the session layer.

5. The session layer (Layer 5) can be used to ensure that a series of messages is completed. For example, this data may be meaningless if the next four exchanges are not completed. The Layer 5 header would include fields that signify that this is a middle flow, not an ending flow, in a session (session control). After the session layer ensures that all flows are completed, it passes the data after the Layer 5 header to the Layer 6 software.

6. The presentation layer (Layer 6) defines and manipulates data formats. For example, if the data is binary, instead of character data, the header will state that fact. The receiver will not attempt to convert the data using the default ASCII character set of Host B. Typically, this type of header is included only for initialization flows and not with every message being transmitted (data formats). After the data formats have been converted, the data (after the Layer 6 header) is then passed to the application layer (Layer 7) software.

7. The application layer (Layer 7) processes the final header and then can examine the true end-user data. This header signifies agreement to operating parameters by the applications on Host A and Host B; the headers are used to signal the values for all parameters; therefore, the header is typically sent and received at application initialization time only. For example, the screen size, colors supported, special characters, buffer sizes, and other parameters for terminal emulation would be included in this header (application parameters).

Interactions between the Same Layers on Different Computers

Layer N must interact with Layer N on another computer to successfully implement its functions. For example, the transport layer (Layer 4) can send data, but if another computer does not acknowledge that the data was received, the sender will not know when to perform error recovery. Likewise, the sending computer encodes a destination network layer (Layer 3) address in the network layer header. If the intervening routers do not cooperate by performing their network layer tasks, the packet will not be delivered to the true destination.

To interact with the same layer on another computer, each layer defines a header and in some cases a trailer. Headers and trailers are additional data bits, created by the sending computer's software or hardware that are placed before or after the data given to Layer N by Layer N+1. The information needed for the layer to communicate with the same layer process on the other computer is encoded in the header and trailer. The receiving computer's Layer N software or hardware interprets the headers and trailers created by the other computer's Layer N, learning how Layer N's processing is being handled in this case.

Figure 3-3 provides a conceptual perspective on the concept of same-layer interactions. The application layer on Host A communicates with the application layer on Host B. Likewise, the transport, session, and presentation layers on Host A and Host B also communicate. The bottom three layers of the OSI model have to do with delivery of the data; Router 1 is involved in that process. Host A's network, physical, and data link layers communicate with Router 1, and likewise, Router 1 communicates with Host B's physical, data link, and network layers. Figure 3-3 provides a visual representation of the same-layer interaction concepts.

Figure 3-3 *Same Layer Interactions on Different Computers*

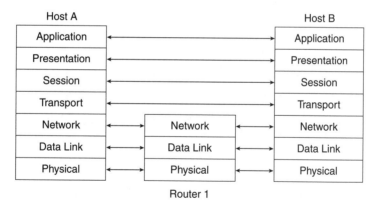

Data Encapsulation

The concept of placing data behind headers (and before trailers) for each layer is typically called *encapsulation* by Cisco documentation. As seen previously in Figure 3-2, when each layer creates its header, it places the data given to it by the next higher layer behind its own header, thereby encapsulating the higher layer's data. In the case of a data-link (Layer 2) protocol, the Layer 3 data is placed between the Layer 2 header and Layer 2 trailer. The physical layer does not use encapsulation because it does not use headers or trailers.

Again referring to Figure 3-2, Step 1, the following list describes the encapsulation process from user creation of the data, until the physical signal is encoded at Step 2:

1. The applications create the data.

2. The application layer creates the application header and places the data behind it.

3. The presentation layer creates the presentation header and places the data behind it.

4. The session layer creates the session header and places the data behind it.

5. The transport layer creates the transport header and places the data behind it.

6. The network layer creates the network header and places the data behind it.

7. The data-link layer creates the data-link header and places the data behind it.

8. The physical layer encodes a signal onto the medium to transmit the frame.

The previous eight-step process is accurate and meaningful for the seven-layer OSI model. However, CCNA exam objective 5 uses a slightly different view of the process. (This different view is based on the ICRC course.) The "five steps of data encapsulation" from the previous objective are in the following list:

1. Create the data.

2. Package the data for transport. In other words, the transport layer creates the transport header and places the data behind it.

3. Add the destination network layer address to the data. In other words, the network layer creates the network header and places the data behind it.

4. Add the destination data-link address to the data. In other words, the data-link layer creates the data-link header and places the data behind it.

5. Transmit the bits. In other words, the physical layer encodes a signal onto the medium to transmit the frame.

CCNA exam objective 5 basically modifies the steps of encapsulation to match with TCP/IP. With the TCP/IP model, after the application negotiated parameters, the headers used will be a TCP or UDP header, an IP header, and then an appropriate data-link header or trailer. The addition of those three headers makes up the middle three steps in the five-step process according to the course. The first step is the application handing the data to the transport layer (TCP or UDP). The final (fifth) step is the physical layer encoding the signal onto the media. Figure 3-4 depicts the concept; the numbers shown represent each of the five steps.

Figure 3-4 *TCP/IP Headers and Trailers*

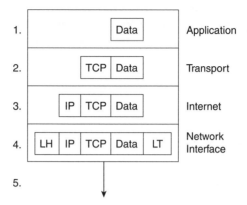

Some common terminology is needed to discuss the data that a particular layer is processing. *Layer N PDU* (protocol data unit) is a term used to describe a set of bytes that includes the Layer N header and trailer, all headers encapsulated, and the user data. From Layer N's perspective, the higher layer headers and the user data forms one large *data* or *information* field. A few other terms also describe some of these PDUs. The Layer 2 PDU (including the data-link header and trailer) is called a *frame*. Similarly, the Layer 3 PDU is called a *packet*, or sometimes a *datagram*. Finally, the Layer 4 PDU is called a *segment*. Figure 3-5 illustrates the construction of frames, packets, and segments and the different layers' perspectives on what is considered to be the *data*.

Figure 3-5 *Frames, Packets, and Segments*

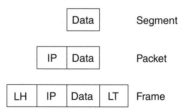

The TCP/IP and NetWare Protocols

Two of the most pervasively deployed protocols are TCP/IP and NetWare. Not coincidentally, they are the two most important protocols you need to know to pass the CCNA exam. Each of these are covered in detail in Chapters 5, "Network Protocols: Understanding the TCP/IP Suite and Novell NetWare Protocols;" 6, "Understanding Routing;" and 7, "Understanding Network Security."

In this short section, TCP/IP, Novell, and OSI are compared. The goal is to provide some insights into what some popularly used terminology really means. In particular, routing is defined as a *Layer 3 process*; in this section, we will review how that term relates to TCP/IP and NetWare.

For perspective, Figure 3-6 shows the layers of these two protocols as compared with OSI.

Figure 3-6   *OSI, TCP/IP, and NetWare Protocols*

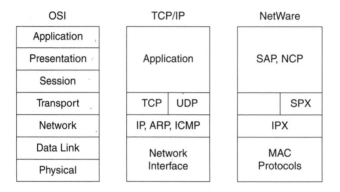

As Figure 3-6 illustrates, the IP and IPX protocols most closely match the OSI transport layer—Layer 3. Many times, even on the CCNA exam, IP and IPX will be called *Layer 3 protocols*. Clearly, IP is in TCP/IP's Layer 2, but for consistent use of terminology, it is commonly called a Layer 3 protocol. Both IP and IPX define logical addressing, routing, the learning of routing information, and end-to-end delivery rules.

The lower layers of each stack, as with OSI Layers 1 and 2 (physical and data link, respectively), simply refer to other well-known specifications. For example, the lower layers all support the IEEE standards to Ethernet and Token Ring, the ANSI standard for FDDI, the ITU standard for ISDN, and the Frame Relay protocols that are specified by the Frame Relay Forum, ANSI, and the ITU.

Connection-Oriented Protocols, Connectionless Protocols, and Flow Control

CCNA Objectives Covered in This Section

2	Describe connection-oriented network service and connectionless network service, and identify the key differences between them.
6	Define flow control and describe the three basic models used in networking.

This section addresses two interrelated CCNA objectives. Definitions are needed for all the terms. Also, a solid understanding of how connection-oriented protocols work is necessary to understand flow control fully. Finally, in objective 6, the "three basic models used in networking" needs some clarification.

Connection-Oriented Versus Connectionless Protocols

The terms *connection-oriented* and *connectionless* have some relatively well-known connotations inside the world of networking protocols. Table 3-2 summarizes what is meant by each.

Table 3-2 *Connection-Oriented Versus Connectionless Protocols*

Type	Functions	Examples
Connection-oriented	Error Recovery (reliability)	LLC type 2 (802.2), TCP (TCP/IP), SPX (NetWare), X.25
Connection-oriented	Pre-established pathing	X.25 Virtual Circuits (X.25), Frame Relay Virtual Circuits (no error recovery), ATM Virtual connections
Connectionless	Simple delivery of data; no overhead for error recovery or set-up flows to establish a path. No error recovery, no pre-established connections	IPX (NetWare), UDP (TCP/IP), IP (TCP/IP), LLC type 1 (802.2)

As you might have noticed, two characteristics cause a protocol to be considered connection-oriented: error recovery and a pre-established path through a network. A particular protocol need only have one or the other characteristic to be called a connection-oriented protocol.

Many people confuse error detection with error recovery. Any header or trailer with a Frame Check Sequence (FCS) or similar field can be used to detect bit errors in the PDU (that is error detection that results in discarding the PDU). However, error recovery implies that the protocol reacts to the lost data and somehow causes the data to be retransmitted. An example of error recovery is shown later in this section.

NOTE   Some documentation refers to the terms *connected* or *connection-oriented*. These terms are used synonymously. You will most likely see the use of the term *connection-oriented* in Cisco documentation.

In the context of the Cisco official courses, connection-oriented protocols are typically discussed in the same context as *reliable* protocols or *error recovery* protocols. The following litany describes the attitude of the course books on error recovery, which of course is a good perspective to remember for the exam.

The following list describes the general process used for error recovery. The list is followed by an example.

1. Protocols providing error recovery are by definition connection oriented and use some initialization flows to create an agreement for a connection.

2. The protocol implementing the connection defines headers; for example, TCP provides error recovery and defines a TCP header. The headers used by that protocol have some numbering and acknowledgment fields to both acknowledge data and notice when it has been lost in transmission. The endpoints that are sending and receiving data use the fields in this header to identify that data was sent and signify that data was received.

3. A sender of data will want an acknowledgment of the data. When an error occurs, many error recovery algorithms require the sender of data to send all data, starting with the lost data. To limit the negative effect of having to resend lots of data, a window of unacknowledged data, which can be dynamic in size, is defined. This window defines the maximum amount of data that can be sent without getting an acknowledgment.

The translation of the preceding litany is that reliable error recovering protocols are connection oriented; however, not all connection-oriented protocols are error recovering. For example, TCP is connection oriented, and provides error recovery. Frame Relay is connection oriented because of the pre-established virtual circuit, but it does no error recovery.

How Error Recovery Is Accomplished

Regardless of which protocol specification performs the error recovery, they all work in basically the same way. Generically, the transmitted data is labeled or numbered. After receipt, the receiver will signal back to the sender that the data was received, using the same label or number to identify the data. Figure 3-7 summarizes the operation.

Figure 3-7 *Forward Acknowledgment*

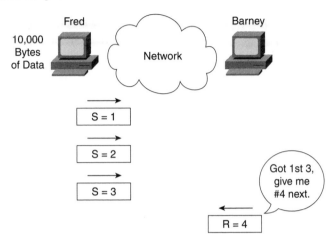

As Figure 3-7 illustrates, the data is numbered, as shown with the numbers 1, 2, and 3. These numbers are placed into the header used by that particular protocol; for example, the TCP header contains such numbering fields. When Barney sends his next frame to Fred, Barney acknowledges that all three frames were received by setting his acknowledgment field to 4. The number 4 refers to the next data to be received, which is called *forward acknowledgment*. This means that the acknowledgment number in the header states the next data that is to be received, not the last one received. (In this case, 4 is next to be received.)

In some protocols, such as LLC2, the numbering always starts with zero. In other protocols, such as TCP, the number is stated during initialization by the sending machine. Some protocols count the frame/packet/segment as "1"; others count the number of bytes sent. In any case, the basic idea is the same.

Of course, error recovery has not been covered yet. Take the case of Fred and Barney again, but notice Barney's reply in Figure 3-8.

Figure 3-8 *Recovery Example*

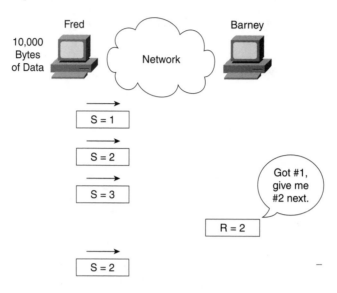

Because Barney is expecting packet number 2 next, what could Fred do? Two choices exist. Fred could send 2 and 3 again, or Fred could send 2, and wait, hoping Barney's next acknowledgment will say "4," meaning Barney just got 2 and already had 3 from earlier.

Finally, it is typical that error recovery uses two sets of counters, one to count data in one direction, and one to count data in the opposite direction. So, when Barney acknowledges packet number 2 with the *number acknowledged* field in the header, the header would also have a *number sent* field that identifies the data in Barney's packet.

Table 3-3 summarizes the concepts behind error recovery and lists the behavior of three popular error-recovery protocols.

Table 3-3 *Examples of Error Recovery Protocols and Their Features*

Feature	TCP	SPX	LLC2
Acknowledges data in both directions?	Yes	Yes	Yes
Forward acknowledgment?	Yes	Yes	Yes
Counts bytes or frame/packets?	Bytes	Packets	Frames
Resend all, or just one and wait, when resending?	One and wait	Resend all	Resend all

Flow Control

Flow Control is the process of controlling the rate at which a computer sends data. Depending on the particular protocol, both the sender and receiver of the data, as well as any intermediate routers, bridges, or switches, might participate in the process of controlling the flow from sender to receiver.

The reason flow control is needed is that any computer sending data can send it faster than it can receive the data, or faster than the intermediate devices can forward the data. This happens in every network, sometimes temporarily, and sometimes regularly, depending on the network and the traffic patterns. The receiving computer can be out of buffer space to receive the next incoming frame, or possibly the CPU is too busy to process the incoming frame. Intermediate routers might need to discard the packets based on temporary lack of buffers or processing as well.

Comparing what happens when flow control is used, versus when it is not used, is helpful for understanding why flow control could be useful. Without flow control, some PDUs are discarded. If there is some connection-oriented protocol in use that happens to implement error recovery, then the data is resent. The sender can send as fast as possible. With flow control, the sender can be slowed down enough so that the original PDU can be forwarded to the receiving computer, and the receiving computer can process the PDU. Flow control protocols do not prevent all loss of data; they simply reduce the amount, which hopefully reduces overall congestion. However, with flow control, the sender was artificially slowed or throttled, so that it sends data less quickly than it could without flow control.

Three methods of implementing flow control relate directly to CCNA objective 6. The phrase "three basic models" in that objective relates to the three examples about to be shown.

Buffering is the first method of implementing flow control. It simply means that the computers reserve enough buffer space so bursts of incoming data can be held until processed. No attempt is made to actually slow down the rate of the sender of the data.

Congestion avoidance is the second method of flow control covered here. The computer receiving the data will notice that its buffers are filling. This causes a PDU or field in a header to be sent toward the sender, signaling the sender to stop transmitting. Figure 3-9 shows an example.

Figure 3-9 *Congestion Avoidance Flow Control*

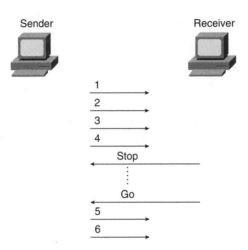

"Hurry up and wait" is a popular expression used to describe the process used in this congestion avoidance example. This process is used by Synchronous Data Link Control (SDLC) and Link Access Procedure, Balanced (LAPB) serial data link protocols.

A preferred method might be to get the sender to simply slow down, instead of stopping altogether. This method would still be considered congestion avoidance, but instead of signaling the sender to stop, the signal would mean to slow down. One example is the TCP/IP Internet Control Message Protocol (ICMP) message "Source Quench." This message is sent by the receiver or some intermediate router to slow the sender. The sender can slow down gradually until Source Quench messages are no longer received.

The third category of flow control methods is called *Windowing*. A Window is the maximum amount of data the sender can send without getting an acknowledgment. If no acknowledgment is received by the time the window is filled, then the sender must wait for acknowledgment. Figure 3-10 shows an example. The slanted lines indicate the time difference between sending a PDU and its receipt.

Figure 3-10 *Windowing Flow Control*

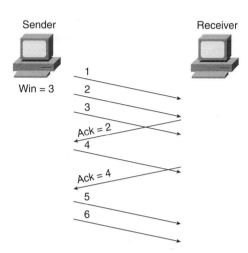

In this example, the sender has a window of three frames. After the frame acknowledges the receipt of frame 1, frame 4 can be sent. After a time lapse, the acknowledgment for frame 2 and 3 are received, which is signified by the frame sent by the receiver with the acknowledgment field equal to 4. So, the sender is free to send 2 more frames—frames 5 and 6—before another acknowledgment is received.

The terms used to describe flow control are not all well defined in the objectives; nor are they well defined in Training Paths 1 and 2. Focusing on understanding the concepts, as always, gives you a chance to get the exam questions correct. Table 3-4 summarizes the flow control terms and provides examples of each type.

Table 3-4   *Flow Control Methods—Summary*

Name Used in This Book	Other Names	Example Protocols[1]
Buffering		N/A
Congestion Avoidance	Stop/Start, RNR, Source Quench	SDLC, LAPB, LLC2
Windowing		TCP, SPX, LLC2

1. Protocol can implement more than one flow control method; for example, LLC2 uses Congestion Avoidance and Windowing.

A Close Examination of OSI Data-Link (Layer 2) Functions

CCNA Objectives Covered in This Section

1	Identify and describe the functions of each of the seven layers of the OSI reference model.
3	Describe data link addresses and network addresses, and identify the key differences between them.
60	Define and describe the function of a MAC address.

Three objectives are covered in this section. Most of the text of this section relates specifically to objective 1 with a detailed discussion of data-link (Layer 2) protocols. Objective 3 is covered partially because data-link addresses are described here. The rest of objective 3 is covered in the next section. Finally, objective 60 is covered in this chapter and in Chapter 4, "Understanding LANs and LAN Switching." It is covered more briefly here, mainly to allow the related discussion of data link layer processing to be complete.

Many different data link (Layer 2) protocols exist. In this section, four different protocols are examined: Ethernet, Token Ring, HDLC, and Frame Relay. A generalized definition of the function on a data-link protocol will be used to guide us through the comparison of these four data-link protocols. This definition could be used to examine any other data-link protocol. The four components of this definition of the functions of data-link (Layer 2) protocols are as follows:

- Arbitration, which determines when it is appropriate to use the physical medium.

- Addressing, so that the correct recipient(s) receive and process the data that is sent.

- Error detection, which determines whether the data made the trip across the medium successfully.

- Notification, which determines the type of header that follows the data-link header. This feature is optional.

Ethernet and Token Ring are two popular LAN Layer 2 protocols. These protocols are defined by the IEEE in specifications 802.3 and 802.5, respectively. Also, each protocol also uses the 802.2 protocol—a subpolar of these LAN data-link protocols purposefully designed to provide functions common to both Ethernet and Token Ring.

HDLC is the default data-link protocol (encapsulation) on Cisco routers. Frame Relay headers are based on the HDLC specification, but for a multi-access (more than 2 device) network, these provide enough differences to highlight the important parts of the functions of the data-link layer (Layer 2).

Data-Link Function 1: Arbitration

Arbitration is only needed when there are times that it is appropriate to send data and other times that it is not appropriate to send data across the media. LANs were originally defined as a shared media, on which each device must wait until the appropriate time to send data. The specifications for these data-link protocols define how to arbitrate.

Ethernet uses the carrier sense multiple access collision detect (CSMA/CD) algorithm for arbitration. The basic algorithm for using an Ethernet when there is data to be sent consists of the following steps:

1. Listen to find out if a frame is currently being received.

2. If no other frame is on the Ethernet, send!

3. If another frame is on the Ethernet, wait, and then listen again.

4. While sending, if a collision occurs, stop, wait, and listen again.

With Token Ring, a totally different mechanism is used. A free-token frame rotates around the ring when no device has data to send. When sending, a device "claims" the free token, which really means changing bits in the 802.5 header to signify "token busy." The data is then placed onto the ring after the Token Ring header. The basic algorithm for using a Token Ring when there is data to be sent consists of the following steps:

1. Listen for the passing token.

2. If token is *busy*, listen for the next token.

3. If the token is *free*, mark the token as a *busy* token, append the data, and send the data onto the ring.

4. When the header with the busy token returns to the sender of that frame after completing a full revolution around the ring, remove the data from the ring.

5. The device can send another busy frame with more data or send a free token frame.

The algorithm for Token Ring does have other rules and variations, but these are beyond the depth of what is needed for the CCNA exam. Network Associates (the "Sniffer" people!) have an excellent class covering Token Ring in detail. To find out more about their classes, use URL www.nai.com.

With HDLC, arbitration is a nonissue today. HDLC is used on point-to-point links, which are typically full-duplex (four-wire) circuits. In other words, either endpoint can send at any time.

Frame Relay, from a physical perspective, is comprised of leased line between a router and the Frame Relay switch. These links are also typically full duplex links, so no arbitration is needed. The Frame Relay network is shared amongst many data terminal equipment (DTE) devices, whereas the Access Link is not shared, so arbitration of the medium is not an issue.

A Word About Frames *Frame*, as used in this book and in the ICRC and CRLS courses, refers to particular parts of the data as sent on a link. In particular, *frame* implies that the data-link header and trailer are part of the bits being examined and discussed. Figure 3-11 shows frames for the four data-link protocols.

Figure 3-11 *Popular Frame Formats*

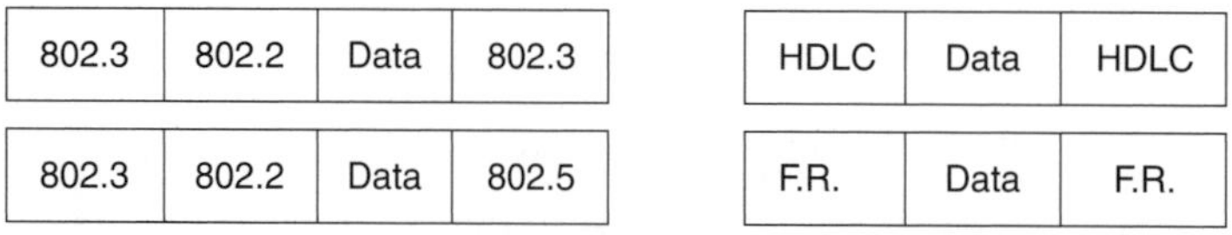

802.3	802.2	Data	802.3

802.3	802.2	Data	802.5

HDLC	Data	HDLC

F.R.	Data	F.R.

Data-Link Function 2: LAN Addressing

Addressing is needed on LANs because there can be many possible recipients of data; that is, there could be more than two devices on the link. Because LANs are *broadcast media*—a term signifying that all devices on the media receive the same data—each recipient must ask the question, "Is this frame meant for me?"

With Ethernet and Token Ring, the addresses are very similar. Each use Media Access Control (MAC) addresses, which are six bytes long and are represented as hexadecimal numbers. Table 3-5 summarizes most of the details about MAC addresses.

Table 3-5 *LAN MAC Address Terminology and Features*

LAN Addressing Terms and Features	Description
MAC	Media Access Control. 802.3 (Ethernet) and 802.5 (Token Ring) are the MAC sublayers of these two LAN data-link protocols.
Ethernet Address, NIC address, LAN address, Token Ring address, card address	Other names often used for the same address that this book refers to as a MAC address.
Burned-in-address	The address assigned by the vendor making the card. It is usually burned in to a ROM or EEPROM on the LAN card.
Locally administered address	Via configuration, an address that is used instead of the burned-in address.
Unicast Address	Fancy term for a MAC that represents a single LAN interface.

Table 3-5   *LAN MAC Address Terminology and Features (Continued)*

LAN Addressing Terms and Features	Description
Broadcast Address	An address that means "All devices that reside on this LAN right now."
Multicast Address	Not valid on Token Ring. On Ethernet, a multicast address implied some subset of all devices currently on the LAN.
Functional Address	Not valid on Ethernet. On Token Ring, these addresses are reserved to represent the device(s) on the ring performing a particular function, such as all source-route bridges supply the ring number to other devices, so they each listen for the Ring Parameter Server (RPS) functional address.

HDLC includes a meaningless address field, since it is only used on point-to-point serial links. The recipient is implied; if one device sent a frame, the other device is the only possible intended recipient.

With Frame Relay, there is one physical link that has many logical circuits called *virtual circuits* (*VCs*). (See Chapter 8, "WAN Protocols: Understanding Point-To-Point, Frame Relay, and ISDN," for more background on Frame Relay.) The address field in Frame Relay defines a data-link connection identifier (DLCI), which identifies each VC. For example, in Figure 3-12 the Frame Relay switch that router Timbuktu is connected to will receive frames; it will forward the frame to either Kalamazoo or East Egypt based on the DLCI, which identifies each VC.

Figure 3-12 *Frame Relay Network*

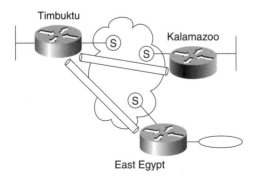

Data-Link Function 3: Error Detection

Error detection is simply the process of learning if bit errors occurred during the transmission of the frame. To do this, most data links include a *frame check sequence* (*FCS*) or *cyclical redundancy check* (*CRC*) field in the data-link trailer. This field contains a value which, when plugged into a mathematical formula along with the frame contents, can determine if the frame had bit errors. All four data links discussed in this section contain a FCS field in the frame trailer.

Error detection does not imply recovery; most data links, including 802.5 Token Ring and 802.3 Ethernet, do not provide error recovery. In these two cases, however, there is an option in the 802.2 protocol, called LLC type 2, that does perform error recovery. SNA and NetBIOS are the typical higher-layer protocols in use that request the services of LLC2.

Data-Link Function 4: What's in the "Data"?

Finally, the fourth, but optional part of a data link is that of identifying the contents of the data field of the frame. Figure 3-13 helps make the usefulness of this feature apparent.

Figure 3-13 *Multiplexing Using Data-Link Type and Protocol Fields*

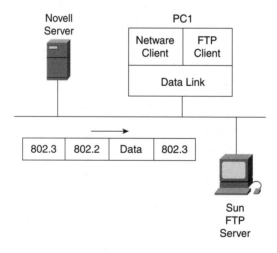

When PC1 receives data, does it give the data to the TCP/IP software or the NetWare client software? Of course, it depends on what is inside the data field. If the data came from the Novell Server, then PC1 will hand the data off to the NetWare client code. If the data comes from the Sun FTP server, PC1 will hand it off to the TCP/IP code.

Ethernet and Token Ring provide a field in their headers to identify the type of data that is in the data field.

PC1 will receive frames that basically look like the two shown in Figure 3-14. Each data link header will have a field with a code that means IP, or IPX, or some other designation defining the type of protocol header that follows. In the first frame in the Figure 3-14 the destination service access point (DSAP) field has a value of E0, which means the next header is a Novell IPX header. In the second frame, the type field in the Subnetwork Access Protocol (SNAP) header has a value of 0800, signifying that the next header is an IP header.

Figure 3-14 *802.2 SAP and SNAP Type Fields*

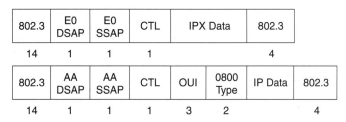

Similarly, HDLC and Frame Relay need to identify the contents of the data field. Of course, it is atypical to have end-user devices attached to either of these types of data links. In this case, routers provide an example more typically found in most WAN environments, as shown in Figure 3-15.

Figure 3-15 *Typical WAN Environment*

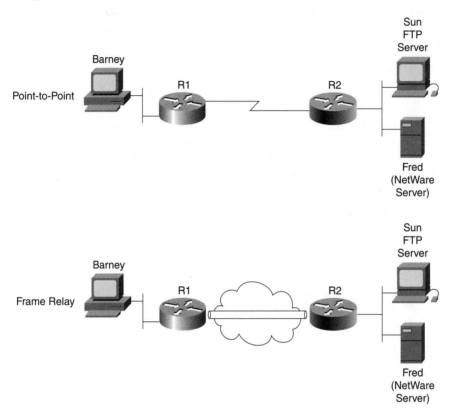

Referring to Figure 3-15, if Barney is using FTP to transfer files to the Sun system and is also connected to the NetWare server (Fred) using IPX, then Barney will generate both TCP/IP and NetWare IPX traffic. As this traffic passes over the HDLC controlled link, R2 will need to know if an IP or IPX packet follows the HDLC header. Mainly, this is so the router can find the Layer 3 destination address, assume its length (32 bits or 80 bits), perform table lookup into the correct routing table, and make the correct routing decision.

HDLC does not provide a mechanism to identify the type of packet in the data field. The Cisco IOS adds a two-byte field immediately after the HDLC header that identifies the contents of the data.

With Frame Relay, the intervening switches do not care what is inside the data field. The receiving router, R2, does care for the same reasons that the HDLC link attached R2 router cares. Frame Relay headers originally did not address this issue either because the headers were based on HDLC. However, the IETF created a specification called RFC 1490 that defined additional headers that followed the standard Frame Relay header. These headers include several fields that can be used to identify the "data" so the receiving device knows what type of data is hidden inside.

The ITU and ANSI picked up the specifications of RFC 1490, and added it to their official Frame Relay standards, ITU T1.617 Annex F, and ANSI Q.933 Annex E, respectively.

Figure 3-16 shows the fields that identify the type of protocol found in the data field.

Figure 3-16 *HDLC and Frame Relay Protocol Type Fields*

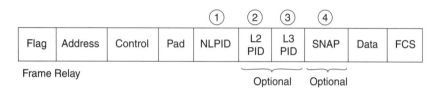

As seen in the Figure 3-16, there is a protocol type field after the HDLC control field. In the Frame Relay example, four different options exist for identifying the type of data inside the frame. The details of those fields are not needed for the depth required on the CCNA exam; RFC 1490 provides a complete reference.

Table 3-6 summarizes the different choices for encoding protocol types for each of the four data link protocols. Notice that the length of some of these fields is only one byte, which historically has led to the addition of other headers. For example, the SNAP header contains a longer type field because one byte is not big enough to number all the available options for what is inside the data.

Table 3-6 *Different Choices for Encoding Protocol Types for Each of the Four Data Link Protocols*

Data-Link Protocol	Field	Header It Is Found In	Size
Ethernet and Token Ring	DSAP	802.2 Header	1 byte
Ethernet and Token Ring	SSAP	802.2 Header	1 byte
Ethernet and Token Ring	Protocol Type	SNAP header	2 bytes
Ethernet (DIX)	EtherType	Ethernet header	2 bytes
HDLC	Cisco proprietary protocol id field	Extra Cisco header	2 bytes
Frame Relay RFC 1490	NLPID	RFC1490	1 byte
Frame Relay RFC 1490	L2 or L3 Protocol ID	Q.933	2 bytes each
Frame Relay RFC 1490	SNAP Protocol Type	SNAP Header	2 bytes

Summary: Data-Link Functions

Table 3-7 summarizes the basic functions of data-link protocols:

Table 3-7   *Data-Link Protocol Functions*

Function	Ethernet	Token Ring	HDLC	Frame Relay
Arbitration	CSMA/CD Algorithm	Token passing	N/A	N/A
Addressing	Source and Destination MAC addresses	Source and Destination MAC addresses	Single one byte address; unimportant on point-to-point links	DLCI used to identify Virtual Circuits.
Error Detection	FCS in trailer	FCS in trailer	FCS in trailer	FCS in trailer
Identifying contents of "data"	802.2 DSAP, SNAP header, or Ethertype, as needed	802.2 DSAP, or SNAP header, as needed	Proprietary Type field	RFC 1490 headers, with NLPID, L2 and L3 protocol ID's, or SNAP header

A Close Examination of OSI Layer 3 Functions

CCNA Objectives Covered in This Section

1	Identify and describe the functions of each of the seven layers of the OSI reference model.
3	Describe data link addresses and network addresses, and identify the key differences between them.
7	List the key internetworking functions of the OSI Network layer and how they are performed in a router.
29	Describe the two parts of network addressing, then identify the parts in specific protocol address examples.

The two key functions for any Layer 3 protocol are end-to-end routing and addressing. These two functions are intertwined and are not truly understood by most people unless considered at the same time. So, this chapter will cover routing and addressing. By doing so, objectives 1 and 7 will be covered.

Network layer (Layer 3) addressing will be covered in enough depth to describe IP, IPX, and AppleTalk addresses, as mentioned in objective 29. Also, now that data link and network layer addresses have been covered in this chapter, a comparison of the two can be made, as suggested in objective 3.

Routing

Routing can be thought of as a three-step process, as seen in Figure 3-17.

Figure 3-17 *Three Steps of Routing*

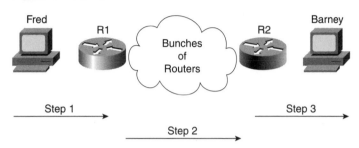

As illustrated in Figure 3-17, the three steps of routing include the following.

1. Sending the data from the source computer to some nearby router

2. Delivering the data from the router near the source to a router near the destination

3. Delivering the data from the router near the destination to the end destination computer

Step 1: Sending Data to a Nearby Router

The creator of the data, who is also the sender of the data, decides to send data to a device in another group. A mechanism must be in place so the sender knows of some router on a *common data link with the sender* so data can be sent to the router. The sender sends a data link frame across the medium; this frame includes the packet in the data portion of the frame. That frame uses data link (Layer 2) addressing in the data link header to ensure that the nearby router receives the frame.

Step 2: Routing Data Across the Network

The routing table for the network layer protocol type of that particular packet is nothing more than a list of network layer address groupings. As shown in Table 3-8 later in this section, these groupings vary based on the network layer protocol type. The router compares the destination network layer address to the routing table, and a match is made. This matching entry in the routing table tells this router where to forward the packet next.

Any intervening routers repeat the same process. The destination network layer (Layer 3) address identifies the group that the destination is a member of. The routing table is searched for a matching entry, which tells this router where to forward the packet next. Eventually, the packet is delivered to the router nearby the destination host, as previously shown in Figure 3-17.

Step 3: Delivering Data to the End Destination

When the packet arrives at a router sharing a data link with the true destination, the router and the destination of the packet are in the same L3 grouping. That router can forward the data to the destination. As usual, a new data link header and trailer are created before a frame, which contains the packet that made the trip across the entire network, can be sent onto the media. This matches the final step (Step 3) as previously shown in Figure 3-17.

A Comment About Data Links

Because the routers build new data-link headers and the new headers contain data-link addresses, the routers must have some way to decide what data-link addresses to use. An example of how the router figures out which DL address to use is the IP Address Resolution Protocol (ARP) protocol. ARP is used to dynamically learn the data link address of some IP host. Another example is that the IPX address includes the MAC address as its last 48 bits, so the MAC address is implied.

An example specific to TCP/IP will be useful to solidify the concepts behind routing. (If you do not understand the basics of IP addressing already, you may want to bookmark this page, and refer to it after you have reviewed Chapter 5, "Network Protocols: Understanding the TCP/IP Suite and Novell NetWare Protocols," which covers IP addressing.) Figure 3-18 provides an example network with which we can review the routing process.

Figure 3-18 *Routing Logic*

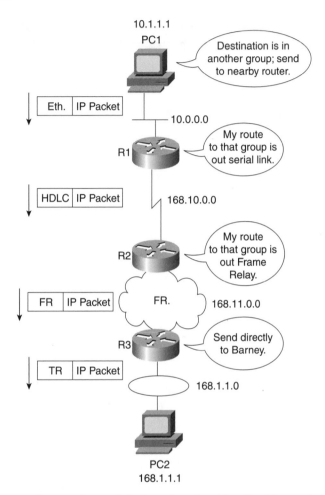

The logic at each step of our original routing algorithm for this case is in the following list:

1. PC1 needs to know its nearby router. PC1 first knows of R1's IP address by either having a *default router* or *default gateway* configured. Alternatively, PC1 can learn of R1's IP address using dynamic Host Configuration Protocol (DHCP). Because DHCP is not mentioned for the CCNA exam, I will assume that a default router of 10.1.1.100 is configured on PC1, and that it is R1's Ethernet IP address.

2. PC1 needs to know R1's Ethernet MAC address before PC1 can complete building the Ethernet header (see Figure 3-18). In the case of TCP/IP, the ARP process is used to dynamically learn R1's MAC address. (See Chapter 5 for a discussion of ARP.) Once the address is known, PC1 completes the Ethernet header with the destination MAC address being R1's MAC address.

3. At Step 2 of the routing process, the router has many items to consider. First, the incoming frame (Ethernet interface) is processed only if the Ethernet FCS is passed and the router's MAC address is in the destination address field. Then, the appropriate type field is examined, so that R1 knows what type of packet is in the data portion of the frame. At this point, R1 discards the Ethernet header and trailer; routers route the packet and use each data link to deliver the packet to the next router or host.

4. The next part of Step 2 is to find an entry in the routing table for network 168.1.0.0, the network that PC2 is a member of. In this case, the route references 168.1.0.0 and lists R1's serial interface as the interface to which to forward the packet. Also, the IP address of R2's HDLC serial interface is listed as the next router to which the packet should be sent.

5. Finally in Step 2, R2 builds an HDLC header and trailer to place around the IP packet. Because HDLC data link uses the same address field every time, there is no process like ARP needed to allow R1 to build the HDLC header.

6. Step 2 is repeated by R2 when it receives the HDLC frame. The HDLC FCS is checked; the type field is examined to learn that the packet inside the frame is an IP packet, and then the HDLC header and trailer are discarded. The IP routing table in R2 is examined for network 168.1.0.0, and a match is made. The entry directs R2 to forward the packet to its Frame Relay serial interface. The routing entry also identifies the next router's IP address, namely R3's IP address on the other end of the Frame Relay VC.

7. Before R2 can complete its Step 2 of our end-to-end routing algorithm, R2 must build a Frame Relay header and trailer. Before it can complete the task, the correct DLCI for the VC to R3 must be decided. In most cases today, the dynamic Inverse ARP process will have associated R3's IP address with the DLCI R2 uses to send frames to R3. (See Chapter 8, "WAN Protocols: Understanding Point-to-Point, Frame Relay, and ISDN," for more details on Inverse ARP and Frame Relay mapping.) With that mapping information R2 can complete the Frame Relay header and send the frame to R3.

8. Step 3 of our original algorithm is performed by R3. Like R1 and R2 before it, it checks the FCS in the data link trailer, looks at the type field to decide the packet inside the frame is an IP packet, and then R3 discards the Frame Relay header and trailer. The routing table entry for 168.1.0.0 shows that the outgoing interface is R3's Token Ring interface. However, there is no next router IP address because there is no need to forward the packet to another router. R3 simply needs to build a Token Ring header and trailer and forward the frame that contains the original packet to PC2. Before R3 can finish building the Token Ring header, an IP ARP must be used to find PC2's MAC address (assuming R3 doesn't already have that information in its IP ARP cache).

Network Layer (Layer 3) Addressing

Network layer addresses are created to allow logical grouping of addresses. In other words, something about the numeric value of an address implies a group or set of addresses, all of which are considered to be in the same grouping. In TCP/IP, this group is called a *network* or *subnet*. In IPX, it is called a *network*. In AppleTalk, the grouping is called a *cable range*.

Network layer addresses are also grouped based on physical location in a network. The rules differ for some network layer protocols, but the grouping concept is identical for IP, IPX, and AppleTalk. In each of these network layer protocols, all devices with addresses in the same group cannot be separated from each other by a router. Or stated differently, all devices in the same group (subnet/network/cable-range) must be connected to the same data link; for example, all devices must be connected to the same Ethernet.

Routing relies on the fact that Layer 3 addresses are grouped together. The routing tables for each network layer protocol can reference the group, not each individual address. Imagine an Ethernet with 100 Novell Clients. A router needing to forward packets to any of those clients needs only one entry in its IPX routing table. If those clients were not required to be attached to the same data link, and if there was no way to encode the IPX network number in the IPX address of the client, routing would not be able to have just one entry in the table. This basic fact is one of the key reasons that routers, using routing as defined by a network layer (Layer 3), can scale to allow tens and hundreds of thousands of devices.

With that in mind, most network layer (Layer 3) addressing schemes were created with the following goals:

- The address should be large enough to accommodate the largest network the designers imagined the protocol would be used for.

- The addresses need to allow for unique assignment, so there is little or no chance of address duplication.

- The address structure needs to have some grouping implied, so that many addresses are considered to be in the same group.

- In some cases, dynamic address assignment is desired.

A great analogy for this concept of network addressing is the addressing scheme used by the U.S. Postal Service. Instead of getting involved with every small community's plans for what to name new streets, the Post Office simply has a nearby office with a ZIP code. The rest of the post offices in the country are already prepared to send mail to new businesses and residences on the new streets; they only care about the ZIP code, which they already know! It is the local postmaster's job to assign a mail carrier to deliver and pick up mail on those new streets. There may be hundreds of Main streets in different ZIP codes, but as long as there is just one per ZIP code, the address is unique; and with an amazing amount of success, the U.S. Postal Service delivers the mail to the correct address.

Example Address Structures

Each Layer 3 address structure contains at least two parts. One (or more) parts at the beginning of the address works like the ZIP code and essentially identifies the grouping. All instances of addresses with the same value in these first bits of the address are considered to be in the same group, for example, the same IP subnet or IPX network or AppleTalk cable-range. The last part of the address acts as a local address, uniquely identifying that device in that particular group. Table 3-8 outlines several Layer 3 address structures.

Table 3-8   *Layer 3 Address Structures*

Protocol	Size of Address (Bits)	Name and Size of Grouping Field	Name and Size of Local Address Field
IP	32	Network or subnet (variable, between 8–30 bits)	Host (variable, between 2–24 bits)
IPX	80	Network (32)	Node (48)
AppleTalk	24	Network (16) (Consecutively numbered values in this field can be combined into one group, called a "cable range.")	Node (8)
OSI	Variable	Many formats, many sizes	DSP (typically 56, including NSAP)

For more information about IP and IPX addresses, please refer to Chapter 5.

Routing Protocols

Conveniently, the routing tables in the example based on Figure 3-18 all had the correct routing information already in the tables. These entries, in most cases, are built dynamically by use of a routing protocol. Routing protocols define message formats and procedures just like any other protocol, but the end goal is to fill the routing table with all known destination groups and the best route to reach each group.

A technical description of the logic behind two underlying routing protocol algorithms, distance vector and link state, is found in Chapter 5. Specific routing protocols for TCP/IP and IPX are listed in Chapter 6, "Understanding Routing."

This section, however, presents an anecdote that may help you remember the difference between the terms *routing, routed protocols,* and *routing protocols.*

NOTE   This somewhat silly story is the result of the Cisco World Wide Training division's proctors for the instructor certification process emphasizing that the instructors should be creative in the use of tools to help students remember important details. After trying this story during certification, it has been propagated by other instructors. I am curious—if you have heard this story or a variation before reading it here, please let me know when you heard it and from whom (wendell@lacidar.com)!

The Story of Ted and Ting

Ted and Ting both work for the same company at a facility in Snellville, Georgia. They work in the same department; their job is to make lots of widgets. (Widgets are imaginary products, and the term widget is used in the United States often to represent a product, when the actual product is not the topic of discussion.)

Ted was very fast and worked hard. In fact, because he was a very intense person, Ted tended to make more widgets than anyone else in Snellville, including Ting. Ted liked to have everything he needed instantly available when and where he wanted it.

Ting, on the other hand, worked very hard but was much more of a planner. He tended to think first and then act. Ting planned very well and had all supplies well stocked, including all the instructions needed to make the different kinds of widgets. In fact, all the information about how to build each type of widget was on a table by his door. He had a problem with the table getting "reallocated" (that is, stolen); so he put a nonremovable label on the table, with the words, "Ting's Table," so he could find the table in case someone stole it.

It turns out that Ted's productivity was in part a result of sitting next to Ting. In fact, Ted often was ready to make the next widget but needed something, like the instruction sheet for a particular unique widget. By swinging into Ting's office, Ted could be back at it in just a few seconds. In fact, part of the reason Ting kept the instruction sheets on "Ting's Table" by the door was that he was tired of Ted always interrupting him looking for something.

Well, Ted got lots of bonuses for being the most productive worker, and Ting did not. But being fair, Ted realized that he would not be as successful without Ting.

Then one day the president decided to franchise the company because they were the best widget making company in the world. The president, Dr. Rou, decided he wanted to make a manual to be used by all the franchisees to build their business. So, Dr. Rou went to the most productive widget maker, Ted, and asked him what he did every day. Along the way, Dr. Rou noticed that Ted went next door a lot. So being the bright guy that he was, Dr. Rou visited Ting next and asked him what he did.

The next day Dr. Rou emerged with the franchise manual. Being an ex-computer networking professional, he had called the manual, "Protocols for Making Widgets." One part of the protocol defined how Ted made widgets very fast. Another part described how Ting kept everything needed by Ted at arm's length, including all the instructions Ted needed. It even mentioned "Ting's Table" as the place to store the instruction sheets. To give credit where credit was due, but not too much credit, the names of these protocols were:

- The "Rou-Ted Protocol"—How to make widgets really fast

- The "Rou-Ting Protocol"—How to plan so the other guy can make widgets fast

- The "Rou-Ting Table"—The place to store your widget making instruction sheets

Similarly, with networking, the *routed protocol* is the one being routed, such as IP, IPX, OSI, DECnet, and so forth. The *routing protocol* is the one preparing the information needed to perform the routing process quickly, such as RIP, IGRP, OSPF, NLSP, and so forth. The *routing table* is where the information needed to perform routing is held, as built by the routing protocol, and used by the routing process to forward the packets of the routed protocol.

That's all just to distinguish between the terms *routed protocol*, *routing protocol*, and *routing table*.

Q&A

As mentioned in Chapter 1, these questions and scenarios are more difficult than what you should experience on the actual exam. The questions do not attempt to cover more breadth or depth than the exam; however, the questions are designed to make sure you know the answer. Rather than allowing you to derive the answer from clues hidden inside the question itself, your understanding and recall of the subject will be challenged. Questions from the "Do I Know This Already?" Quiz from the beginning of the chapter are repeated here to ensure that you have mastered the chapter's topic areas. Hopefully, these questions will help limit the number of exam questions on which you narrow your choices to two options and guess!

The answers to these questions can be found in Appendix B, on page 550.

1. Name the seven layers of the OSI model.

2. What is the main purpose of Layer 7?

3. What is the main purpose of Layer 6?

4. What is the main purpose of Layer 5?

5. What is the main purpose of Layer 4?

6. What is the main purpose of Layer 3?

7. What is the main purpose of Layer 2?

8. What is the main purpose of Layer 1?

9. Describe the process of data encapsulation as data is processed from creation until it exits a physical interface to a network. Use the OSI model as an example.

10. Describe the services provided in most connectionless protocol services.

11. Name at least three connectionless protocols.

12. Describe the services provided in most connection-oriented protocol services.

13. In a particular error recovering protocol, the sender sends three frames that are labeled 2, 3, and 4. The receiver of these frames, on its next sent frame, sets an acknowledgment field to "4." What does this typically imply?

14. Name three connection-oriented protocols.

15. What does MAC stand for?

16. Name three terms popularly used as a synonym for MAC address.

17. Are IP addresses defined by a Layer 2 or Layer 3 protocol?

18. Are IPX addresses defined by a Layer 2 or Layer 3 protocol?

19. Are OSI NSAP addresses defined by a Layer 2 or a Layer 3 protocol?

20. What portion of a MAC address encodes an identifier representing the manufacturer of the card?

21. Are MAC addresses defined by a Layer 2 or a Layer 3 protocol?

22. Are DLCI addresses defined by a Layer 2 or a Layer 3 protocol?

23. Name two differences between Layer 3 addresses and Layer 2 addresses.

24. How many bits in an IP address?

25. How many bits in an IPX address?

26. How many bits in a MAC address?

27. How many bits in a DLCI address?

28. Name the two main parts of an IPX address. Which part identifies which "group" this address is a member of?

29. Name the two main parts of an IP address. Which part identifies which "group" this address is a member of?

30. Name the two main parts of a MAC address. Which part identifies which "group" this address is a member of?

31. Name three benefits to layering networking protocol specifications.

32. What header and/or trailer does a router discard as a side effect of routing?

33. Describe the differences between a routed protocol and a routing protocol.

34. Name at least three routed protocols.

35. Name at least three routing protocols.

36. How does an IP host know what router to send a packet to? In which cases does an IP host choose to send a packet to this router instead of directly to the destination host?

37. How does an IPX host know which router to send a packet to? In which cases does an IPX host choose to send a packet to this router instead of directly to the destination host?

38. Name three items in an entry in any routing table.

Scenarios

Scenario 3-1

Given the network in Figure 3-19, and the design criteria in Table 3-9, perform the tasks that follow.

Figure 3-19 *Musketeer Network for Scenario*

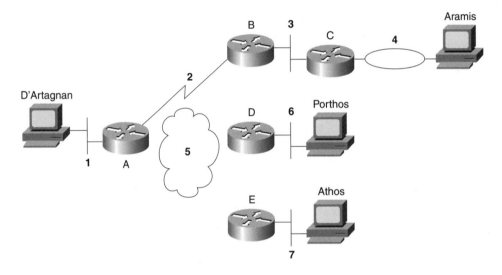

Table 3-9 provides the routing table for the network setup in Figure 3-19.

Table 3-9 *Routing Table for Network in Figure 3-19*

Router	Interface	Address
A	E0	group-1.local-A
A	s0	group-2.local-A
A	s1	group-5.local-A
B	S0	group-2.local-B
B	E0	group-3.local-B
C	E0	group-3.local-C
C	T0	group-4.local-C
D	S0	group-5.local-D
D	E0	group-6.local-D

Table 3-9 *Routing Table for Network in Figure 3-19 (Continued)*

Router	Interface	Address
E	S0	group-5.local-E
E	E0	group-7.local-E
D'Artagnan		group-1.local-M
Aramis		group-4.local-M
Porthos		group-6.local-M
Athos		group-7.local-M

Task 1 for Scenario 3-1

Create the routing table in Router A; assume that all parts of the network are up and working properly.

Task 2 for Scenario 3-1

D'Artagnan sends a packet to Aramis (source group-1.local-M, destination group-4.local-M). D'Artagnan sends this packet inside an Ethernet frame to Router A. Given this information, determine the following:

1. What two methods discussed in this chapter could be used by D'Artagnan to determine that Router A is the router to send this packet to?

2. List the routing table entries in each router that are necessary for the packet to be delivered to Aramis.

3. What type of data link header or trailer is discarded by each router in that route?

4. What destination-only data-link address is placed into the new data-link headers by each router?

5. What routes must be in which routers to ensure that Aramis can send a return packet to D'Artagnan?

Task 3 for Scenario 3-1

D'Artagnan sends a packet to Porthos (source group-1.local-M, destination group-6.local-M). D'Artagnan sends this packet inside an Ethernet frame to Router A. Given this information, determine the following:

1. What two methods discussed in this chapter could be used by D'Artagnan to determine that Router A is the router to send this packet to?

2. List the routing table entries in each router that are necessary for the packet to be delivered to Aramis.

3. What type of data-link header or trailer is discarded by each router in that route?

4. What destination-only data link address is placed into the new data-link headers by each router?

5. What routes must be in which routers to ensure that Aramis can send a return packet to D'Artagnan?

Scenario Answers

Answers to Task 1 for Scenario 3-1

Based on the network design illustrated in Figure 3-19, Task 1 for Scenario 3-1 asks you to create the routing table in Router A; assume that all parts of the network are up and working properly. The routing table for Router A is as follows:

Group	Outgoing Interface	Next Router
group-1	Ethernet 0	N/A
group-2	serial 0	N/A
group-3	serial 0	group-2.local-B
group-4	serial 0	group-2.local-B
group-5	serial 1	N/A
group-6	serial 1	group-5.local-D
group-7	serial 1	group-5.local-E

Answers to Task 2 for Scenario 3-1

Based on the network design illustrated in Figure 3-19, Task 2 for Scenario 3-1 states that D'Artagnan sends a packet to Porthos (source group-1.local-M, destination group-6.local-M). D'Artagnan sends this packet inside an Ethernet frame to Router A. The following are the solutions to exercises 1 through 5 for Task 2.

1. Either the use of a default route or the use of a RIP request to broadcast asking for a router to reply.

2. The routes to the attached groups used in the routes to group-4 must also be included. The routing tables are as follows:

In Router A:

Group	Outgoing Interface	Next Router
group-2	serial 0	N/A
group-4	serial 0	group-2.local-B

In Router B:

Group	Outgoing Interface	Next Router
group-3	Ethernet 0	N/A
group-4	Ethernet 0	group-3.local-C

In Router C:

Group	Outgoing Interface	Next Router
group-4	Token ring 0	N/A

3. Router A discards the Ethernet and adds an HDLC header. Router B discards the HDLC header and adds an Ethernet header. Router C discards the Ethernet and adds a Token Ring header.

4. Router A places the never changing HDLC address (Hex 03) into the header. Router B places Router C's Ethernet MAC address into the destination address field. Router C places Aramis's Token Ring MAC address into the destination address field.

5. This is all noise if Aramis cannot get a packet back to D'Artagnan. The following routing tables show the routes needed for both directions:

In Router A:

Group	Outgoing Interface	Next Router
group-1	Ethernet 0	N/A
group-2	serial 0	N/A
group-4	serial 0	group-2.local-B

In Router B:

Group	Outgoing Interface	Next Router
group-1	serial 0	group-2.local-A
group-2	serial 0	N/A
group-3	Ethernet 0	N/A
group-4	Ethernet 0	group-3.local-C

In Router C:

Group	Outgoing Interface	Next Router
group-1	Ethernet 0	group-3.local-B
group-3	Ethernet 0	N/A
group-4	Token ring 0	N/A

Answers to Task 3 for Scenario 3-1

Based on the network design illustrated in Figure 3-19, Task 3 for Scenario 3-1 states that D'Artagnan sends a packet to Porthos (source group-1.local-M, destination group-6.local-M). D'Artagnan sends this packet, inside an Ethernet frame, to Router A. The following are the solutions to exercises 1 through 5 for Task 3.

1. Either the use of a default route or the use of a RIP request to broadcast asking for a router to reply.

2. The routes to the attached groups used in the routes to group-6 must also be included. The routing tables are as follows:

In Router A:

Group	Outgoing Interface	Next Router
group-5	serial 1	N/A
group-6	serial 1	group-5.local-D

In Router D:

Group	Outgoing Interface	Next Router
group-6	Ethernet 0	N/A

3. Router A discards the Ethernet and adds a Frame Relay header. Router D discards the Frame Relay header and adds an Ethernet header.

4. Router A places the Frame Relay DLCI for the VC connecting it to router D into the address field in the header. Router D places Porthos's Ethernet MAC address into the destination address field.

5. This is all noise if Porthos cannot get a packet back to D'Artagnan. The following routing tables show the routes needed for both directions:

In Router A:

Group	Outgoing Interface	Next Router
group-1	Ethernet 0	N/A
group-5	serial 1	N/A
group-6	serial 1	group-5.local-D

In Router D:

Group	Outgoing Interface	Next Router
group-1	serial 0	group-5.local-A
group-5	serial 0	N/A
group-6	Ethernet 0	N/A

The following table outlines the CCNA exam objectives that are reviewed in this chapter. The numbers shown correspond to the master list of objectives found in Chapter 1, "What Is CCNA?"

Objective	Description
46	Describe the advantages of LAN segmentation.
47	Describe LAN segmentation using bridges.
48	Describe LAN segmentation using routers.
49	Describe LAN segmentation using switches.
50	Name and describe two switching methods.
51	Describe full- and half-duplex Ethernet operation.
52	Describe network congestion problem in Ethernet networks.
53	Describe the benefits of network segmentation with bridges.
43	Describe the benefits of network segmentation with routers.
54	Describe the benefits of network segmentation with switches.
55	Describe the features and benefits of Fast Ethernet.
56	Describe the guidelines and distance limitations of Fast Ethernet.
57	Distinguish between cut-through and store-and-forward LAN switching.
58	Describe the operation of the Spanning-Tree Protocol and its benefits.
59	Describe the benefits of virtual LANs.
60	Define and describe the function of a MAC address.

CHAPTER 4

Understanding LANs and LAN Switching

The depth of coverage of LAN-oriented topics on the CCNA exam is an elusive target to hit. From the sheer volume of CCNA objectives, it might seem that these topics are the most important on the entire exam. Of course, a closer examination shows that several of these objectives overlap. The LAN switching topics are not covered in Training Path 2, and an informal survey I did while writing this chapter showed about eight ICRC courses (Training Path 2) being offered for every one CRLS course (Training Path 1) by the largest Training Partners. However, LAN switching is very important in real networks, which is more evidence that preparing yourself on those topics for the CCNA exam is important.

Products that do not use the IOS are unlikely to be covered on the CCNA exam. The Training Paths cover several products that are not mentioned at all in the exam objectives, namely, FastHub 300 and the 1900 and 2820 LAN switches. These products use a different user interface than the command-line interface (CLI) of the IOS. However, these three products are not likely to be the key products in typical Cisco installations. The LAN topics that could be included in the future CCNA exam objectives include Catalyst 5000 series product details and user interface details. Of course, predicting the future is not easy! If any other user interface will be covered on the CCNA exam, in my opinion, it will be Catalyst 5000. However, the CCNP exams include detailed coverage of LAN switching and Catalyst 5000 series features. Therefore, Cisco has a dilemma of whether to overlap CCNA with CCNP if they ever consider adding Catalyst 5000 to the CCNA exam.

So, are you wondering why I have diverged into these opposing opinions about what is on the test? Well, for this simple reason: You need to make the best decision about what topics to spend your time studying. My suggestion for how to treat LAN and LAN switching topics for the CCNA exam are as follows:

1. Concentrate on the tables in this chapter, which summarize the information relating to all the CCNA objectives listed at the start of this chapter.

2. Concentrate on objectives 47-49, 53, 54, 43, and 59. These are the most likely objectives to be subject to interpretation, so I will take care to reflect the attitudes from the courses from which these objectives were directly extracted.

3. Get the CCNA objectives from Cisco's Web site (http://www.cisco.com) and search for the word "Catalyst". If it has been added, go to this book's Web site at Cisco Press Online (http://www.ciscopress.com/catalog/title_list.html). I will be posting some additional materials on this topic, free of charge, if the CCNA covers Catalyst switches in the future.

How to Best Use This Chapter

By taking the following steps, you can make better use of your study time:

- Keep your notes and answers for all your work with this book in one place for easy reference.

- Take the "Do I Know This Already?" quiz and write down your answers. Studies show retention is significantly increased through writing facts and concepts down, even if you never look at the information again!

- Figure 4-1 helps guide you to the next step in preparation for this topic area on the CCNA exam.

Figure 4-1 *How to Use This Chapter*

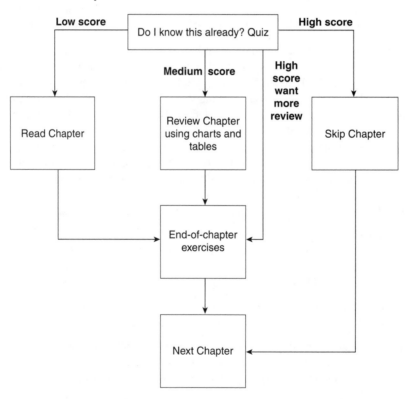

"Do I Know This Already?" Quiz

1. Name two benefits of LAN segmentation using transparent bridges.

_____

_____

_____

2. What settings are examined by a bridge or switch to determine which bridge or switch should be elected as root of the spanning tree?

_____

_____

_____

3. Assume a building has 100 devices that are attached to the same Ethernet. These devices are migrated to two different shared Ethernet segments, each with 50 devices. The two segments are connected to a Cisco LAN switch to allow communication between the two sets of users. List two benefits that would be derived for a typical user.

_____

_____

_____

4. Name the two methods of internal switching on typical switches today. Which provides less latency for an individual frame?

_____

_____

_____

5. Describe how a transparent bridge decides whether it should forward a frame and how it chooses the interface out of which to forward the frame.

_____

_____

_____

6. Describe the benefits of the Spanning-Tree Protocol as used by transparent bridges and switches.

_____

_____

_____

7. Does a bridge/switch examine just the incoming frame's source MAC address, destination MAC address, or both? Why?

_____

_____

_____

8. When a bridge or switch using the Spanning-Tree Protocol first initializes, who does it claim should be the root of the tree?

_____

_____

_____

9. Define the difference between broadcast and multicast MAC addresses.

_____

_____

_____

10. Define the term _broadcast domain_.

_____

_____

_____

11. Explain the function of the loopback and collision detection features of an Ethernet NIC in relation to half-duplex and full-duplex operation.

_____

_____

_____

12. Name the three interface states that the Spanning-Tree Protocol uses, other than _forwarding_. Which of these states is transitory?

_____

_____

_____

You can find the answers to the "Do I Know This Already?" quiz in Appendix B on page 555. Review the answers, grade your quiz, and choose an appropriate next step in this chapter based on the suggestions in the "How to Best Use this Chapter" topic earlier in this chapter. Your choices for the next step are as follows:

- **5 or fewer correct**—Read this chapter.

- **6, 7, or 8 correct**—Review this chapter, looking at the charts and diagrams that summarize most of the concepts and facts in this chapter.

- **9 or more correct**—If you want more review on these topics, skip to the exercises at the end of this chapter. If you do not want more review on these topics, skip this chapter.

Foundation Topics

LAN Overview

CCNA Objectives Covered in This Section

51	Describe full- and half- duplex Ethernet operation.
52	Describe network congestion problem in Ethernet networks.
55	Describe the features and benefits of Fast Ethernet.
56	Describe the guidelines and distance limitations of Fast Ethernet.
60	Define and describe the function of a MAC address.

This section provides some tables with important LAN details that you should memorize for the exam. The section continues with details on Ethernet related to objectives 51, 52, 55, and 56.

The three main types of LANs that the CCNA exam covers are Ethernet, Token Ring, and FDDI. There is a bias toward questions about Ethernet, which I think is reasonable given the installed base in the marketplace. However, be prepared for questions on all three types.

The IEEE defines most of the standards for these three types of LANs. The summary Table 4-1 lists the specification that defines the Media Access Control (MAC) and Logical Link Control (LLC) sublayers.

Table 4-1 *LAN Standards on the CCNA Exam*

Name	MAC Sublayer Spec	LLC Sublayer Spec	Other Comments
Ethernet Version 2 (DIX Ethernet)	Ethernet	Not applicable	This spec is owned by Digital, Intel, and Xerox.
IEEE Ethernet	IEEE 802.3	IEEE 802.2	Also popularly called 802.3 Ethernet.
Token Ring	IEEE 802.5	IEEE 802.2	IBM helped development before the IEEE took over.
FDDI	ANSI X3T9.5	IEEE 802.2	ANSI liked 802.2, so they just refer to the IEEE spec.

The details of the LAN frames are shown in Figure 4-2. You should remember some details of the contents of the headers and trailers for each LAN type—in particular, the addresses and their location in the headers. Also, the name of the field that identifies the type of header that follows the LAN headers is important. Finally, the fact that a frame check sequence (FCS) is in the trailer for each protocol is also vital. Figure 4-2 summarizes the various header formats.

Figure 4-2   *LAN Header Formats*

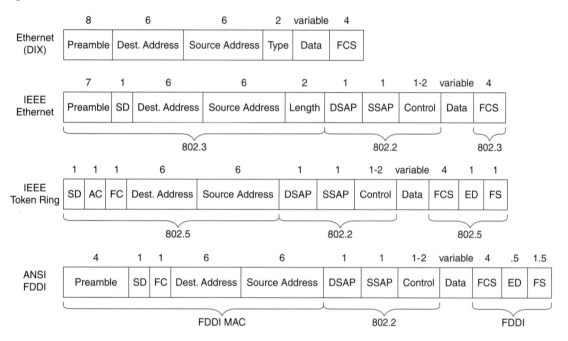

The function of identifying the header that follows the LAN header is covered rather extensively in Chapter 3, "Understanding the OSI Reference Model." Any computer receiving a LAN frame needs to know what is in the "data" portion of the frame. (Refer to Figure 4-2 for the data field.) Table 4-2 summarizes the fields that are used for identifying the types of data contained in a frame.

Table 4-2 *Protocol Type Fields in LAN Headers*

Field Name	Length	LAN Type	Comments
Ethernet Type	2 bytes	Ethernet	RFC 1700 (assigned Numbers RFC) lists the values. Xerox owns the assignment process.
802.2 DSAP and SSAP	1 byte each	IEEE Ethernet, IEEE Token Ring, ANSI FDDI	The IEEE Registration Authority controls the assignment of valid values. The source SAP and destination SAP do not have to be equal, so 802.2 calls for the sender's protocol type (SAP) and the destination's type.
SNAP Protocol	2 bytes	IEEE Ethernet, IEEE Token Ring, ANSI FDDI	Uses EtherType values. Used only when DSAP is hex AA. It is needed because the DSAP and SSAP fields are only 1 byte in length.

MAC Addresses

One important and obvious function of MAC addresses is to identify or address the LAN interface cards on Ethernet, Token Ring, and FDDI LANs. These addresses are called *unicast addresses* or *individual addresses* because they identify an individual LAN interface card. The term *unicast* was chosen mainly for a contrast with the terms *broadcast*, *multicast*, and *group addresses*. Frames between a pair of LAN stations use a source and destination address field to identify each other.

Having globally unique Unicast MAC addresses on all LAN cards is a goal of the IEEE, so they administer a program in which manufacturers encode the MAC address onto the LAN card, usually in a ROM chip. The first half of the address is a code that identifies the vendor; the second part is simply a unique number common to all cards that vendor has manufactured. These addresses are called *burned-in addresses (BIAs)*, and sometimes called *Universally Administered Addresses (UAA)*. The value used by the card can be overridden via configuration; the overriding address is called a *Locally Administered Address (LAA)*.

Another important function of IEEE MAC addresses is to address more than one LAN card. Group addresses (as opposed to unicast or individual addresses) can address more than one device on a LAN. This function is satisfied by three types of IEEE group MAC addresses:

- **Broadcast addresses**—The most popular type of IEEE MAC address, the broadcast address has a value of FFFF.FFFF.FFFF (Hex). The broadcast address implies that all devices on the LAN should process the frame.

- **Multicast addresses**—Used by Ethernet and FDDI, multicast addresses fulfill the requirement to address a subset of all the devices on a LAN. Multicast addresses address some subset of all the stations on the LAN. A station processes a frame to a particular multicast address only if configured to do so. An example of multicast addresses is a range of addresses—1000.5exx.xxxx—where different values are assigned in the last three bytes. Multicast addresses are also used in networks that implement IP multicast.

- **Functional addresses**—Valid only on Token Ring, functional addresses identify one or more interfaces that provide a particular function, for example, the Ring Error Monitor function. An example is c000.0000.0001, which is used by the Token Ring Active Monitor.

Finally, the order of bits in each byte of the addresses is different between Ethernet and the other LAN types. As Figure 4-3 illustrates, the bytes are listed in the same order; however, the bit order in each byte is opposite.

Figure 4-3   *MAC Address Format*

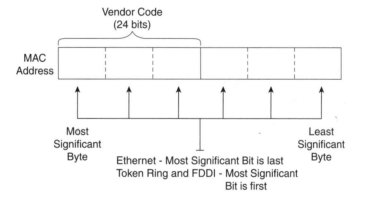

The bit order in Ethernet is called little-endian and on FDDI and Token Ring it is called big-endian. The meaning of these terms is that on Ethernet, the most significant bit in a byte is listed last in the byte. For example, assume the binary string 01010101 is the value in a byte of an Ethernet address. The right-most bit is considered to be the most-significant bit in this byte. The hexadecimal equivalent is 55. However, if writing the same value in a byte of a Token Ring address, the value written would be 10101010, so that the most significant bit is on the left, and the hexadecimal equivalent would be AA. For example, the Token Ring address 4000.3745.0001 would be converted to 0200.ECA2.0080.

The following list summarizes many of the key features of MAC addresses:

- Unicast MAC addresses address an individual LAN interface card.

- Broadcast MAC addresses address all devices on a LAN.

- Multicast MAC addresses address a subset of the devices on an Ethernet or FDDI LAN.

- Functional MAC addresses identify devices performing a specific IEEE defined function, on Token Ring only.

- Ethernet orders the bits in each byte of the MAC address with the least significant bit first; this convention is called *little-endian*.

- Token Ring and FDDI order the bits in each byte of the MAC address with the most significant bit first; this convention is called *big-endian*.

- The most significant bit on the first byte of an address must have a value of binary 0 for unicast addresses, and 1 for broadcast, multicast, and functional addresses. This bit is called the *broadcast bit*.

- The second most significant bit in the first byte of the MAC address is called the local/universal bit. A binary value of 0 implies that a burned-in or Universally Administered Address (UAA) is being used; a binary 1 implies that a Locally Administered Address (LAA) is being used.

Ethernet Standards and Operation

Several of the CCNA objectives (51, 52, 55, and 56) refer specifically to details of Ethernet operation. This section covers the details relating to the CCNA objectives, as well as some additional background. Equivalent details on Token Ring and FDDI are not covered here. Many good sources exist for more information on Token Ring and FDDI, but you may want to refer to your Cisco coursebooks or to Cisco Press's *Introduction to Cisco Router Configuration*.

Table 4-3 lists the key Ethernet specifications and several related details about the operation of each.

Table 4-3 *Ethernet Standards*

Standard	Maximum Cable Length	Type of Cable	MAC Sublayer Specification	Device Connects to a Hub or Directly to a Bus
10B5	500 m[1]	50 Ohm thick coaxial cable	802.3	Bus
10B2	185 m[1]	50 Ohm thin coaxial cable	802.3	Bus
10BT	100 m[2]	UTP	802.3	Hub
10BFL	2000 m[2]	Fiber	802.3	Hub
100BTx	100 m[2]	UTP/STP	802.3	Hub
100BT4	100 m[2]	UTP, 4 pair	802.3	Hub
100BFx	400 m[2]	Fiber	802.3	Hub

1. For entire bus
2. From device to hub/switch

Ethernet congestion is most obvious when considering the 10B5 and 10B2 specifications. The bus is shared between all devices on the Ethernet, using the carrier sense multiple access with collision detection (CSMA/CD) algorithm for accessing the bus. (The bus also allows transmission at 10 Mbps.) Basically, the following three features contribute to Ethernet congestion:

- Collisions could occur with normal use of the CSMA/CD algorithm if stations send frames at (practically) the same instant in time. All collided frames sent are not received correctly, so each station has to resend the frames. This wastes time on the bus.

- Devices might have to wait before sending a frame if another frame is being received at the same time that the device is ready to send. This increases latency while waiting for the incoming frame to complete.

- There is a limit to the amount of bits that can be sent. The theoretical maximum throughput for the LAN segment is 10 Mbps. For example, if the average frame is 1250 bytes, then 1000 frames per second would fill the Ethernet to its complete 10 Mbps capacity.

NOTE   As a reminder, the CSMA/CD algorithm works like this: The sender is ready to send a frame. The device listens to hear if any frame is currently being received. When the Ethernet is silent, the device begins sending the frame. During this time, the device listens (on the receiving pair) because the frame it is sending is looped back onto its receive path. If no collisions occur, the bits of the sent frame are received back successfully. If a collision has occurred, the collision is detected because the received signal does not match the transmitted signal. In that case, the device sends a jam signal then waits a random amount of time and repeats the process, beginning with listening to hear if another frame is currently being received.

Full- and Half-Duplex Ethernet Operation

The use of full-duplex Ethernet can relieve some of the congestion. Half- and full-duplex Ethernet imply the use of 10BT or some other hub-based topology.

Ethernet hubs were created with the advent of 10BT. These hubs are essentially multiport repeaters; repeaters extend the bus concept of 10B2 and 10B5 by regenerating the same electrical signal sent by the original sender of the frame. Therefore, collisions can still occur, so CSMA/CD access rules continue to be used. Knowledge of the operation of Ethernet cards and the attached hub is important to a complete understanding of the congestion problems and a need for full-duplex Ethernet. Figure 4-4 outlines the operation of half-duplex 10BT with hubs.

Figure 4-4 *10BT Half-Duplex Operation*

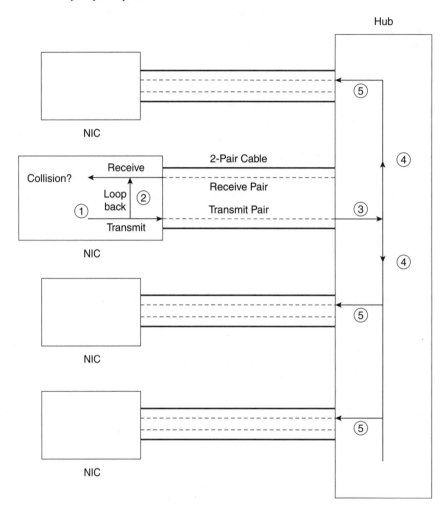

The chronological steps illustrated in Figure 4-4 are as follows:

1. The network interface card (NIC) sends a frame.

2. The NIC loops the sent frame onto its receive pair.

3. The hub receives the frame.

4. The hub sends the frame across an internal bus so all *other* NICs can receive the electrical signal.

5. The hub repeats the signal out of each receive pair to all other devices.

Because CSMA/CD rules are used when collisions could occur, full-duplex operation would not be useful. If a card is receiving a frame, it would not choose to also start sending another frame. Half-duplex operation is a side effect of the original design choice of retaining the CSMA/CD media access for 10BT networks.

Full-duplex operation creates a situation whereby frames that are sent cannot collide with frames being received. Imagine the use of Ethernet between a pair of NICs instead of cabling the NIC to a hub. Figure 4-5 shows the full-duplex circuitry.

Figure 4-5   *10BT Full-Duplex Operation*

Because no collisions are possible, the sender does not need to loop frames onto the receive pair, as shown in Figure 4-5. Both ends can send and receive simultaneously. This reduces Ethernet congestion related to all three points previously listed:

- Collisions do not occur; therefore, time is not wasted retransmitting frames.

- Waiting for others to send their frames is not necessary because there is only one sender for each twisted pair.

- There are 10 Mbps in each direction, increasing the available capacity (bandwidth).

Fast Ethernet

Fast Ethernet relieves congestion in some fairly obvious ways. Collisions and wait time are decreased when compared to 10 Mbps Ethernet, simply because it takes 90 percent less time to transmit the same frames. Capacity is greatly increased as well—with 1250 byte frames, a one million frames per second theoretical maximum can be reached.

The two main features of Fast Ethernet are faster speed and autonegotiation. Autonegotiation allows an Ethernet card, hub, or switch to determine which type of 100 Mbps Ethernet is supported by the device/hub/switch on the other end of the cable. Also, support for half-duplex or full-duplex is negotiated. And if the other device, such as a 10BT NIC, does not support autonegotiation, autonegotiation will settle for half-duplex 10BT, assuming no overriding configuration was added.

Table 4-4 outlines the Fast Ethernet specifications and a few details about cabling restrictions.

Table 4-4 *Fast Ethernet Standards*

Standard	What It Defines	Type of Cable	Maximum Length to Hub	Maximum Distance between Devices
802.3	MAC framing and CSMA/CD rules	N/A	N/A	N/A
802.3	10BT	Cat 3,4,5 UTP (2 pair)	100m	100m
	10B2	50 Ohm thin coaxial cable	N/A	185m
	10B5	50 Ohm thick coaxial cable	N/A	500m
802.3u	100BTX	CAT 5 UTP (2 pair)	100m	412m
	100BFX	MM Fiber (2 strands)	100m	412m, 2km w/ FDX
	100BT4	CAT 3,4,5 UTP (4 pair)	100m	412m
	autonegotiation			
802.3x	full-duplex operation	N/A	N/A	N/A

For more information on Fast Ethernet, try the following Web pages:

http://www.ots.utexas.edu/ethernet/descript-100quickref.html
http://www.iol.unh.edu/training
http://www.cisco.com/Mkt/cc/cisco/mkt/switch/fasteth/feth_tc.htm

Ethernet LAN Segmentation

CCNA Objectives Covered in This Section

46	Describe the advantages of LAN segmentation.
47	Describe LAN segmentation using bridges.
48	Describe LAN segmentation using routers.
49	Describe LAN segmentation using switches.
52	Describe network congestion problem in Ethernet networks.
53	Describe the benefits of network segmentation with bridges.
43	Describe the benefits of network segmentation with routers.
54	Describe the benefits of network segmentation with switches.

The CCNA exam questions about the objectives for this section can be a little more subjective than some other topics. The terms "benefits" and "advantages" are the first clues to the danger—they allow one person to see a benefit that another person may think is unimportant.

This section directly lists answers to these more subjective objectives. The Training Path 1 and 2 courses have been examined, and the opinions of those course writers are included in the lists here. Also, I will include my opinion in a few cases.

LAN segmentation is explained in the context of Ethernet LANs in this section; Token Ring and FDDI are not mentioned. The reason is that courses address only Ethernet segmentation, and comments from other sources imply that Ethernet is indeed the focus. However, if you want to consider this section to include concepts about Token Ring and FDDI, any benefit or advantage listed that does not pertain to collisions, for example, longer LAN length, would apply to these other LAN types.

LAN Segmentation Advantages (CCNA Objective 46)

Ethernet LAN segmentation has the following attributes:

- Overcomes distance limitations.

- Decreases or eliminates collisions, which should decrease latency and improve throughput.

- Reduces the impact of broadcasts and multicasts, which should decrease latency and improve throughput.

- Increases the amount of total bandwidth per user.

- Confines user traffic to different LAN segments.

Transparent Bridging

Transparent bridging is the first of the three segmentation methods covered in this section. This section begins by reviewing transparent bridging behavior. The discussion continues with a review of the advantages of LAN segmentation listed in the preceding section in the context of using transparent bridging as the method of segmentation. The discussion on transparent bridging concludes with a list of other considerations unique to segmentation using bridges.

Transparent bridges perform three key functions:

- Learning MAC addresses by examining the source MAC addresses of each frame received by the bridge

- Deciding when to forward a frame and when to filter a frame, based on the destination MAC address

- Creating a loop-free environment with other bridges using the Spanning-Tree Protocol

To appreciate the use of bridges for segmentation, consider Figure 4-6. A client first asks for a DNS name resolution, followed by connecting to a web server. All three devices are on the same LAN segment. ARP requests are used to find the MAC addresses of the DNS and the web server.

Figure 4-6 *Example Protocol Flows—Single Ethernet Segment*

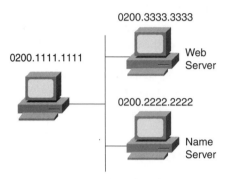

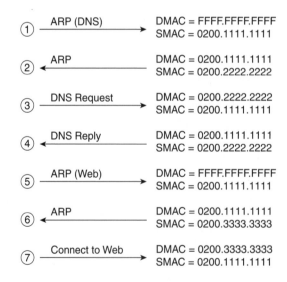

The following list provides some additional text relating the steps shown in Figure 4-6:

1. The PC is preconfigured with the IP address of the DNS; it must ARP to find the DNS's MAC address.

2. The DNS replies to the ARP request with its MAC address, 0200.2222.2222.

3. The PC requests name resolution for the web server.

4. The DNS returns the IP address of the web server to the PC.

5. The PC does not know the web server's MAC address, so it sends an ARP broadcast to learn the MAC address.

6. The web server replies to the ARP, stating that its MAC address is 0200.3333.3333.

7. The PC can now connect to the web server.

Now consider the same protocol flow, but with the DNS on a separate segment and a transparent bridge separating the segments as shown in Figure 4-7. The computers act no differently, sending the same frames/packets. The transparent bridge forwards all broadcasts, all unicast destination frames not in its bridge table, and multicasts.

Figure 4-7 illustrates several important ideas related to segmentation. The ARP requests in Steps 1 and 5 are forwarded by the bridge because they are broadcasts. However, the rest of the frames from the client to the web server and back will not be forwarded by the bridge because the bridge knows that both MAC addresses are on the same Ethernet as its E0 interface. Also, because there is no redundant path through other bridges, there is no need to use the Spanning-Tree Protocol to block interfaces and limit the flow of frames.

The following list provides the key features of transparent bridging, relating to objective 47:

- Broadcasts and multicast frames are forwarded by a bridge.

- Transparent bridges perform switching of frames using Layer 2 headers and Layer 2 logic and are Layer 3 protocol independent. This means that installation is simple because no Layer 3 address group planning or address changes are necessary. For example, because the bridge retains a single broadcast domain, all devices on all segments attached to the bridge look like a single subnet. Cisco might consider this *plug-and-play*.

- Store-and-forward operation is typical in transparent bridging devices. Because an entire frame is received before being forwarded, additional latency is introduced (as compared to a single LAN segment).

- The transparent bridge must perform processing on the frame, which also can increase latency (as compared to a single LAN segment).

The following list addresses the concepts raised by objective 53 of the CCNA exam and provides the benefits of Ethernet LAN segmentation in light of transparent bridging. The comments in this list compare a single LAN segment versus multiple LAN segments separated by a transparent bridge:

- Distance limitations are overcome because each segment can be built with the maximum distance for that type of Ethernet.

- Collisions are decreased because some frames are filtered by the bridge.

- Bridges do not reduce the impact of broadcasts/multicasts.

- Total bandwidth is increased because each segment runs at 10 or 100 Mbps instead of a single 10 or 100 Mbps segment.

- User traffic is confined to individual LAN segments for frames whose source and destination are on the same LAN segment. Bridges often allow administrative filters (for example, Cisco access-lists) to limit the flow of frames as well.

Figure 4-7   *Example Protocol Flows—Using a Transparent Bridge*

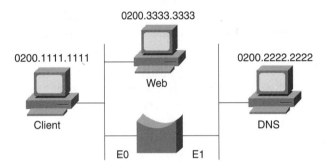

		Address Table After Step 1
①	ARP (DNS) DMAC = FFFF.FFFF.FFFF SMAC = 0200.1111.1111	0200.1111.1111 E0

Address Table After Step 2

②	ARP DMAC = 0200.1111.1111 SMAC = 0200.2222.2222	0200.1111.1111 E0 0200.2222.2222 E1

Address Table After Step 3

③	DNS Request DMAC = 0200.2222.2222 SMAC = 0200.1111.1111	0200.1111.1111 E0 0200.2222.2222 E1

④	DNS Reply DMAC = 0200.1111.1111 SMAC = 0200.2222.2222	

⑤	ARP (Web) DMAC = FFFF.FFFF.FFFF SMAC = 0200.1111.1111	

Address Table After Step 6

⑥	ARP DMAC = 0200.1111.1111 SMAC = 0200.3333.3333	0200.1111.1111 E0 0200.2222.2222 E1 0200.3333.3333 E0

⑦	Connect to Web DMAC = 0200.3333.3333 SMAC = 0200.1111.1111	

LAN Segmentation Using Routers

Segmenting LANs using routers is the second segmentation method covered in this section on Ethernet LAN segmentation. This section relates directly to CCNA objectives 43 and 48. Because the concepts behind routing are covered extensively in Chapters 3 and 5 of this book, not much detail on the process is included here. However, Figure 4-8 illustrates a couple of key features.

Figure 4-8 *Example Protocol Flows—Using a Router*

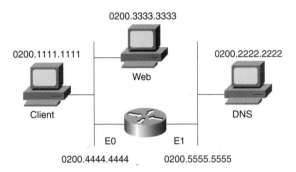

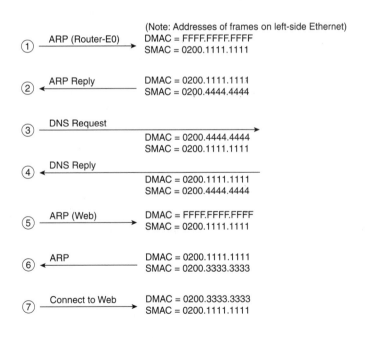

The following list provides some additional text relating the steps shown in Figure 4-8:

1. The PC is preconfigured with the IP address of the DNS. It first notices that the IP address is on a different subnet, so the PC will want to forward the packet to its default router first. However, the PC does not know its default router's MAC address yet, so it must ARP to find that router's MAC address.

2. The router replies to the ARP request with its MAC address, 0200.4444.4444.

3. The PC requests name resolution for the web server by sending a packet with the destination IP address of the DNS but the destination MAC address of the router.

4. The DNS returns the IP address of the web server to the PC in the DNS reply.

5. The PC does not know the web server's MAC address, so it sends an ARP broadcast to learn the MAC address. The router has no need to forward the ARP broadcast.

6. The web server replies to the ARP, stating that its MAC address is 0200.3333.3333.

7. The PC can now connect to the web server.

The ARP broadcasts are not forwarded by the router. In fact, the logic in Step 1 begins with an ARP looking for the MAC of the client's default router, namely the router's E0 MAC address. This broadcast was not forwarded by the router, a fact that causes a router to be called a *broadcast firewall*. Comparing this to a transparent bridge, this difference in broadcast treatment is the biggest advantage of routers. The following list summarizes the features of routing relating to Ethernet LAN segmentation (objective 48):

- Broadcasts and multicast frames are not forwarded by a router (by default).

- Routers perform switching of packets using Layer 3 headers and logic and are Layer 3 protocol dependent. This means that migration from a single LAN requires planning because Layer 3 address changes are necessary. For example, in Figure 4-8, two IP subnets are used, one on each LAN attached to the router. If migrating from the network in Figure 4-6, where one subnet was in use, a new subnet would need to be allocated and new addresses assigned to some interfaces.

- Routers use the store-and-forward process like a transparent bridge, although it is unusual to see the term used to describe a router. Because an entire packet is received before being forwarded, additional latency is introduced, as compared to a single LAN segment.

- The router must process more portions of the received frames and possibly apply many additional logic steps before a packet is routed, which can add latency.

The following list summarizes the benefits of Ethernet LAN segmentation with routers (objective 43):

- Distance limitations are overcome because each segment can be built with the maximum distance for that type of Ethernet.

- Collisions are decreased because frames between devices on the same segment are not forwarded by the router.

- Routers reduce the impact of broadcasts/multicasts because routers do not forward broadcasts/multicasts.

- Total bandwidth is increased because each segment runs at 10 or 100 Mbps instead of a single 10 or 100 Mbps segment.

- Routers provide better manageability, particularly because the routing process has knowledge of more details of the packet flows than does a transparent bridge.

- Routers provide more functionality compared to transparent bridge devices, for example, packet fragmentation and reassembly, plus packet lifetime control.

- Multiple active paths (routes) are possible with routers (unlike transparent bridges).

- The extra workload of routing can introduce more latency than bridges. However, faster internal processing can make up the difference. Faster internal processing methods, like fast switching, autonomous switching, Silicon switching, optimum switching, and NetFlow switching can speed the internal processes and greatly decrease latency of each packet. (For more information, get Cisco's Networkers conference presentation called "Router Architecture and Performance," URL http://www.cisco.com/networkers/presentation/layer3/index.html.)

LAN Segmentation Using Switches

The next section of this chapter reviews the concepts of Ethernet switching in more detail. However, to maintain continuity within this section on Ethernet LAN Segmentation, I decided to keep the topic "LAN Segmentation Using Switches" with the similar topics on transparent bridging and routing. If you have little knowledge of LAN switching, you may want to skip ahead and then come back to this short section.

The best description of Ethernet switching I personally have heard is this: A switch is a transparent bridge on steroids. Ethernet switching does the same thing as a transparent bridge, but with more strength and speed. So the advantages of switching will sound familiar, but with some additions based on the extra functions typically found in LAN switches.

First, look at Figure 4-9, which shows the same protocol flows as Figure 4-7 and 4-8, with only a LAN switch in use.

Figure 4-9 *Example Protocol Flows—Using a Switch*

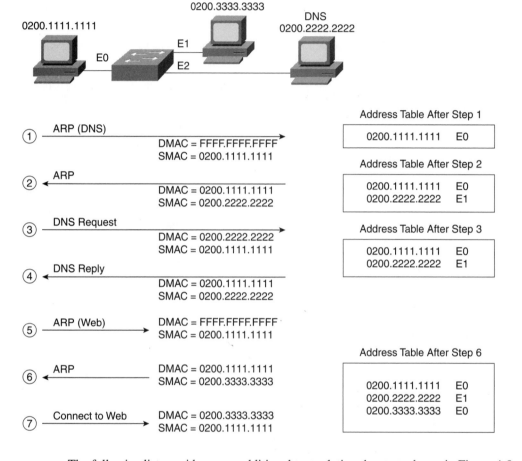

The following list provides some additional text relating the steps shown in Figure 4-9:

1. The PC is preconfigured with the IP address of the DNS. The PC notices that the DNS IP address is in the same subnet as its own IP address; therefore, the PC sends an ARP broadcast hoping to learn the DNS's MAC address.

2. The DNS replies to the ARP request with its MAC address, 0200.2222.2222.

3. The PC requests name resolution for the web server by sending a packet with the destination IP address of the DNS.

4. The DNS returns the IP address of the web server to the PC in the DNS reply.

5. The PC does not know the web server's MAC address, so it sends an ARP broadcast to learn the MAC address. Because it is a MAC broadcast, the switch forwards the frame on all ports.

6. The web server replies to the ARP, stating that its MAC address is 0200.3333.3333.

7. The PC can now connect to the web server.

The two ARP broadcasts (Steps 1 and 5) are sent out all switch ports because switches and bridges do not perform the *broadcast firewall* function that a router performs. After the switching table (often called the address table) is built, the switch forwards unicasts only out of the appropriate ports.

The switch network has created three separate Ethernet segments, as compared to the transparent bridge network in Figure 4-7, which creates two LAN segments. Each segment is called a *collision domain* because frames sent by any device on that segment could collide with other frames on the segment. Switches can be used to create many collision domains, each with 10 or 100 Mbps capacity.

Frames can be forwarded concurrently through a switch. Consider Figure 4-10, with Fred sending a frame to Wilma and Barney sending a frame to Betty.

Figure 4-10 *Concurrently Switching Frames in a Switch*

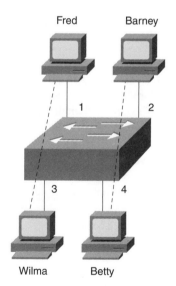

Because the switch forwards the frame coming in port 1 out onto port 3, and likewise the frame coming in port 2 out port 4, and because these are all in four different collision domains, no collision occurs. A 4-port transparent bridge would behave the same way, but switches are optimized for concurrent frame forwarding, so latency is likely to be less with a switch.

Full-duplex Ethernet, in conjunction with switches, can add other benefits. Figure 4-11 shows a server (Pebbles) that is both sending and receiving a frame at the same time. Betty and Wilma are in different collision domains, and Pebbles cannot have a collision due to the nature of full-duplex Ethernet.

Figure 4-11 *Full-Duplex Ethernet and Switches*

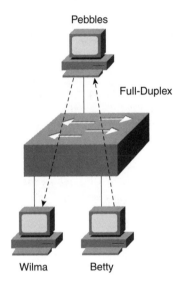

Finally, the internal processing on the switch can decrease latency for frames. Transparent bridges use store-and-forward processing, meaning that the entire frame is received before the first bit of the frame is forwarded. Switches can use store-and-forward, as well as cut-through, processing logic. Cut-through means that the first bits of the frame are sent out the outbound port before the last bit of the incoming frame is received, instead of waiting for the entire frame to be received. In other words, as soon as the switching port receives enough of the frame to see the destination MAC address, the frame is transmitted out the appropriate outgoing port to the destination device. The unfortunate side effect is that, because the frame check sequence (FCS) is in the Ethernet trailer, the forwarded frame may have bit errors that the switch would have noticed with store-and-forward logic.

The following list summarizes the features of switching relating to Ethernet LAN segmentation (objective 49):

● Broadcasts and multicast frames are forwarded by a switch.

- Switches perform switching of frames using Layer 2 headers and logic and are Layer 3 protocol independent. This means that installation is simple because no Layer 3 address group planning or address changes are necessary. For example, because the switch retains a single broadcast domain, all devices on all segments attached to the bridge look like a single subnet. Cisco might consider this *plug-and-play.*

- Store-and-forward and cut-through operations are typical in switches. Both types introduce latency; cut-through reduces latency compared to store-and-forward, at the risk of forwarding errored frames.

- Switches must perform processing on the frame, which also can increase latency.

The following list summarizes the benefits of Ethernet LAN segmentation with switches (objective 54):

- Distance limitations are overcome because each segment can be built with the maximum distance for that type of Ethernet.

- Collisions are decreased because unicast frames are forwarded only out of the correct port.

- Switches do not reduce the impact of broadcasts. However, Cisco uses the Cisco Group Message Protocol (CGMP) to allow switches to help reduce the impact of multicasts.

- Total bandwidth is increased because each segment runs at 10 or 100 Mbps instead of a single 10 or 100 Mbps segment.

- User traffic is confined to individual LAN segments for frames whose source and destination is on the same LAN segment. Switches often allow administrative filters, such as Cisco access lists, to limit the flow of frames as well.

- Concurrent frame forwarding is allowed, with switches using specialized processors to optimize the process.

- Switches are typically hardware-optimized for speedy switching, which reduces latency as compared to a transparent bridge, which typically uses a single processor.

LAN Switching and Virtual LANs

CCNA Objectives Covered in This Section

50	Name and describe two switching methods.
57	Distinguish between cut-through and store-and-forward LAN switching.
59	Describe the benefits of virtual LANs.

Externally, it seems that an Ethernet switch uses the same logic as a transparent bridge. Internally, the switch is optimized for performing the basic function of choosing when to forward and when to filter a frame. The basic logic is performed as follows:

1. A frame is received.

2. If the destination is a broadcast or multicast, forward on all ports.

3. If the destination is a unicast and the address is not in the address table, forward on all ports.

4. If the destination is a unicast and the address is in the address table, forward the frame out the associated port, unless the MAC address is associated with the incoming port.

Three general methods of switching are used internally. The details of internal processing varies among models of switches and switch vendors; regardless, the internal processing can be categorized as one of the methods listed in Table 4-5. The first two methods listed in the table are specifically mentioned in the Training Paths and are implied by objectives 50 and 57. The third method is covered in the HPSDC course.

Table 4-5 *Switch Internal Processing*

Switching Method	Description
Store-and-forward	The switch fully receives all bits in the frame (store) before forwarding the frame. This allows the switch to discard frames that fail the FCS check. (FCS is in the Ethernet trailer.)
Cut-through	The switch performs the address table lookup as soon as the destination address field in the header is received. The first bits in the frame can be sent out the outbound port before the final bits in the incoming frame are received. This does not allow the switch to discard frames that fail the FCS check. (FCS is in the Ethernet trailer.)
FragmentFree	This performs like cut-through, but the switch waits for 64 bytes to be received before forwarding the first bytes of the outgoing frame. Because collisions should be detected during the first 64 bytes of the frame according to Ethernet specifications, frames in error due to collision will not be forwarded. The FCS still cannot be checked.

Another feature of switches is that they forward broadcasts and multicasts on all ports. However, they reduce the impact of collisions because devices on separate switch ports are on separate Ethernet segments (which are separate collision domains). This behavior of switches resulted in the creation of the terms *collision domain* and *broadcast domain*. Figure 4-12 shows a network with six collision domains—six sets of interface cards for which CSMA/CD logic is used to share the LAN segment.

Figure 4-12 *Collision Domains*

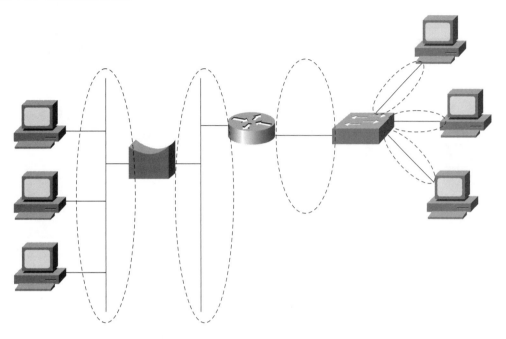

Each collision domain is separated by either a transparent bridge, a switch, or a router. There may be a shared hub (not pictured) attached to the switch, or simply a single device. In either case, if a bridge (transparent bridge or switch) or routing function separates devices, the devices are in separate collision domains.

NOTE   Many vendors, including Cisco, sell cards in switches that do not switch on all ports. In other words, the equivalent of a shared hub with several ports is built into a card rather than each port being treated as its own collision domain. Frames destined for a MAC address off one of these ports are sent out all ports. The switch ports in the figures in this chapter are all switched unless otherwise specified.

The broadcast domain concept is similar to the concept of collision domains; however, only routers stop the flow of broadcasts. Figure 4-13 provides the broadcast domains for the same network depicted in Figure 4-12.

Figure 4-13 *Broadcast Domains*

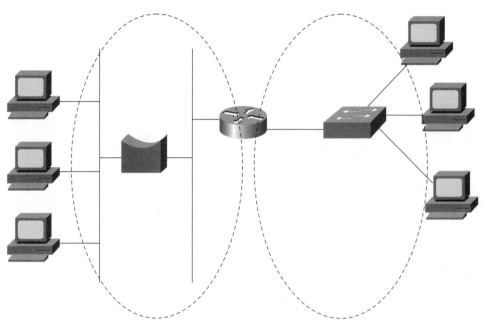

The broadcast domain is not affected by the inclusion or exclusion of switches or bridges. The router creates its own broadcasts (RIP, IGRP, SAP, and so on), but the router does not forward broadcasts received in the left-side interface out the right-side interface. In other words, broadcasts created and sent by a device in one domain are not sent to devices in another broadcast domain.

Layer 3 addressing is affected any time a router is added to a network. For example, if only bridges and switches had existed in the network in Figure 4-13, and the router was later added, Layer 3 IP and IPX addresses would have been changed. To use the terminology in Chapter 3, two separate address groupings (for example, IP subnets) would be used for IP—one for the devices to the left of the router and another for devices to the right of the router. A definition of Layer 3 address groupings on LANs, which will help us understand VLANs better, is as follows:

> All devices in the same broadcast domain (Layer 2) will be in the same Layer 3 address grouping—in other words, the same IP subnet or same IPX network.

Virtual LANs

A virtual LAN (VLAN) is a broadcast domain created by one or more switches. The VLAN is created via configuration in the switch, or possibly configuration referred to by the switch but residing in some external server. A VLAN is effectively what could have been created by attaching the devices in a broadcast domain to one switch, devices in a second broadcast domain to a second switch, and so on. With VLANs, a single switch can perform the same task, with some ports in one broadcast domain, and other ports in another broadcast domain.

Separate VLANs imply separate broadcast domains, which imply separate Layer 3 groups. A router is needed for forwarding traffic between the different Layer 3 groups. Figure 4-14 depicts a network with three VLANs, each with five ports.

Figure 4-14 *Example with Three VLANs*

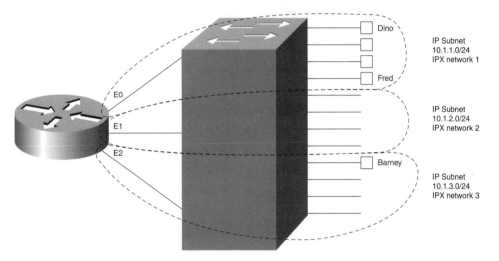

The switch forwards frames to the router interfaces only if the frame is a broadcast or is destined for one of the MAC addresses of the router. For example, Fred sends frames to the router's E0 MAC address when trying to communicate with Barney; this is because Fred's default router should be the E0 interface's IP address. However, when Fred sends frames to Dino, the destination MAC address is Dino's MAC address, and there is no need to get the router involved.

VLANs allow easy moves, additions, and changes. For example, if Barney moved to a different office, which was cabled to a different port on the switch, he can still be considered to be in VLAN 3. No Layer 3 address changes are necessary, which means no changes need be made on Barney.

To implement VLANs in one switch, a separate address (bridging) table is needed for each VLAN. If a frame is received on a port in VLAN 2, the VLAN 2 address table will be searched, both for adding new addresses learned by examining the source MAC address, and for choosing the right port for forwarding the frame, based on the destination address.

Implementing VLANs with multiple switches adds more complexity that is not necessarily obvious. Consider Figure 4-15, which uses two switches connected with a Fast Ethernet. Two VLANs are configured.

Figure 4-15 *Two Switches, Two VLANs*

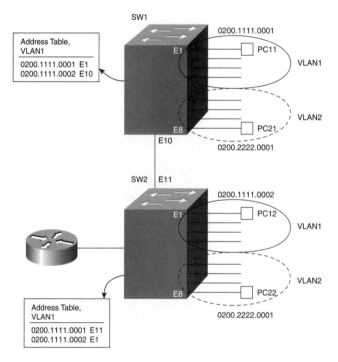

The address table for VLAN1 lists the only two MAC addresses being used in VLAN1. However, consider a frame sent from PC11 to PC12:

Step 1: PC11 generates the frame, with destination MAC 0200.1111.0002.

Step 2: Switch 1 receives the frame on port E1.

Step 3: Switch 1 performs address table lookup in VLAN1's address table because port E1 is in VLAN1.

Step 4: Switch 1 forwards the frame out its E10 port.

Step 5: Switch 2 receives the frame in its E11 port.

At this point in the logic, everything seems straightforward. In the next step, however, several choices could have been made by our counterparts who created the protocols used for LAN switching. The choices for how Switch 2 could react to the incoming frame are as follows:

Step 6: Switch 2 considers port E11 to be in VLAN1, so it performs table lookup for 0200.1111.0002 in that address table.

Or...

Step 6: Switch 2 does not consider port E11 to be in any particular VLAN, so it does table lookup in all tables and forwards out all ports matched.

Or...

Step 6: Before Switch 1 forwarded the frame in Step 4, it added a header that identifies the VLAN. Then, Switch 2 can do table lookup just in that address table.

The third option for Step 6 is the one that is actually implemented. The first option would work fine for one VLAN, and in fact is used when connecting multiple switches without using VLANs. However, the logic in this first option fails when devices in VLAN2 send frames because their addresses would never be found in VLAN1's address table. The second option would actually work well for unicasts, particularly because a unicast address is typically found in only a single address table. However, broadcasts would be sent on all interfaces, regardless of VLAN, which would cause horrendous side effects for OSI Layer 3 processes. So, the third option, called *VLAN trunking* or *tagging*, is used.

Tagging can also be used to reduce the number of router ports that are needed. Figure 4-15 shows the router with a single interface and a single connection to Switch 2. The same tagging method used between switches is used for frames sent to the router, so it knows from which VLAN the frame originated. For frames that the router routes between the two VLANs, the incoming frame is tagged with one VLAN ID, and the outgoing frame is tagged with the other VLAN ID by the router before sending the frame back to the switch.

Table 4-6 lists the various types of tagging used by Cisco and the types of interfaces on which they are used:

Table 4-6   *Frame Trunking/Tagging Protocols*

Tagging Method	Media
Inter-Switch Link (ISL)	Fast Ethernet
802.10	FDDI
LAN Emulation (LANE)	ATM

The first two options in Table 4-6 are much easier to conceptualize. The frame headers are modified in each case to reflect a VLAN ID before the frame is sent onto the link between switches. Before forwarding to the endpoint device, the frame header is changed back to the original format. With LANE, there is an ATM network between switches. (LANE is a way to make the ATM network behave like an Ethernet in some ways.) There is no tagging in LANE, but instead, the result is a different ATM virtual connection used between the switches for each VLAN. The virtual connection used implies the VLAN ID.

There are many benefits of VLANs, but frankly, the benefits are subjective. CCNA objective 59 specifically states that these benefits are covered on the exam. The following list provides the benefits culled from the Training Path courses:

- With VLANs, moves, additions, and changes to device connections are easier.

- By forcing a Layer 3 routing device to be involved between VLANs, greater administrative control can be used (better accounting, access lists, and so on).

- Compared to a single broadcast domain, the use of multiple VLANs (creating multiple broadcast domains) reduces the percentage of the LAN bandwidth consumed by broadcasts.

- Broadcast reduction by using multiple VLANs reduces the CPU utilization on all the connected devices because all devices must process broadcasts.

Spanning-Tree Protocol

CCNA Objectives Covered in This Section

58	Describe the operation of Spanning-Tree Protocol and its benefits.

The Spanning-Tree Protocol is an important topic for a true understanding of bridged and switched networks. Ironically, neither Training Path 1 or 2 explains the Spanning-Tree Protocol or even lists its benefits. At one point in the history of the ICRC course, a chapter on transparent bridging briefly covered the concept of spanning tree, but that chapter was eventually moved to the ACRC course.

So why cover the Spanning-Tree Protocol in this book? First, there are questions about it on the exam, with varying degrees of coverage in the courses in the Training Paths. Second, one of the goals of this book is to help you master the materials covered by the CCNA exam so that you have a firm foundation for CCNP exam preparation. Finally, this section is reasonably short and worth reading.

NOTE   A wonderful source of information about the Spanning-Tree Protocol is a book by Radia Perlman called *Interconnections: Bridges and Routers*. For the last 5 years of teaching Cisco courses, I have always told students that if you have space for just three networking books on your shelf, Radia's should be one of them.

The purpose of the Spanning-Tree Protocol is to dynamically create a bridged/switched network in which only one path exists between any pair of LAN segments (collision domains). To accomplish this task, all bridging devices, including switches, use a dynamic protocol. The result of the protocol is that each interface on a bridging device will settle into a *blocking* state or a *forwarding* state. Blocking means that the interface cannot forward or receive data frames, but they can send and receive Configuration Bridge Protocol Data Units (CBPDUs); forwarding means the interface can send and receive data frames. By having a correct subset of the interfaces block, a single currently active logical path will exist between each pair of LANs.

NOTE   For the rest of this chapter, when using the term *bridge* or *bridging device*, the device can be a transparent bridge or a LAN switch. If a distinction between the two needs to be made, transparent bridge or switch will be used.

Figure 4-16 demonstrates the obvious need for a loop-free path between segments. Frames destined for unknown MAC addresses, or broadcasts, will be forwarded infinitely by the bridges.

Figure 4-16   *Looping without the Spanning-Tree Protocol*

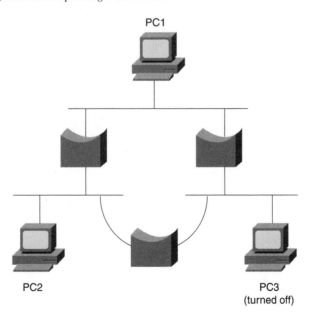

Frames addressed to PC3's MAC address will loop forever (or at least until the millennium or when time is no more, depending on your beliefs)! There is no mechanism defined in Ethernet to mark the frame to be thrown away by a bridge; this is similar to the way an IP router uses time-to-live fields. The frame destined to PC3 would be forwarded because the bridges do not have PC3's MAC address in their bridge tables. Similarly, bridges forward broadcasts on all interfaces, so if PC1 or PC2 sent a broadcast, the broadcast would loop for a long time.

Of course, having only one physical path between segments is a poor design for availability. If any part of that one path failed, the network would be broken into separate parts, whose devices could not communicate. So there is a need for physical redundancy with only one active path because transparent bridging logic will not tolerate multiple active paths. The solution is to build bridged networks with physical redundancy and use spanning tree to dynamically block some interface(s) so that only one active path exists at any instant in time.

Finally, any possibility of loops occurring during the process of converging to a new spanning tree must be avoided. Consider Figure 4-17, particularly bridges 4 and 5. If a loop occurred in this network, frames would rotate forever, and the number of frames would grow. A frame on either segment that both bridges 4 and 5 are attached to would be forwarded by both bridges, duplicating the frames. In a few short seconds, all LAN segments would be filled with copies of the one frame that occurred during the loop, possibly preventing the Spanning-Tree Protocol from completing its task of recreating the loop-free environment.

Figure 4-17 *Looping and Frame Replication*

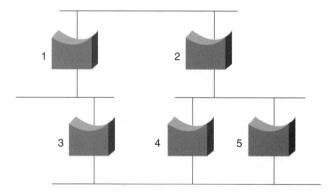

To sum up, the benefits of the Spanning-Tree Protocol are as follows:

- Physically redundant paths in the network are allowed to exist and be used when other paths fail.

- Bridging logic is confused by multiple active paths to the same MAC address; Spanning-Tree Protocol avoids this by creating only one path.

- Loops in the bridged network are avoided.

How the Spanning-Tree Protocol Works

The spanning-tree algorithm results in each bridge interface being placed into either a forwarding state or a blocking state. Interfaces in forwarding state are considered to be in the current spanning tree; those in blocking state are not considered to be in the tree. The algorithm is elegant but basic. Figure 4-18 illustrates the basic concept behind the Spanning-Tree Protocol and the processes of creating the spanning tree.

Figure 4-18 *Spanning Tree Sample Diagram*

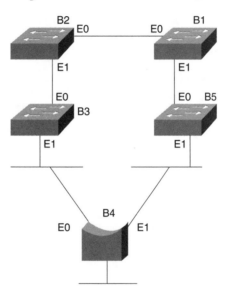

The setup in Figure 4-18 uses four switches (bridges 1, 2, 3, and 5) and one transparent bridge. A variety of bridges and switches are shown to make the point that both switches and transparent bridges use spanning tree.

The key to the algorithm is that the set of all forwarding interfaces (those in the tree) form one path through the LAN segments (collision domains), assuming at least one physical path is available. Three methods are used to place an interface into forwarding mode:

- All interfaces on the root bridge are in forwarding state.

- Each nonroot bridge considers one of its ports to have the least administrative cost between itself and the root bridge. This interface, called that bridge's *root port*, is placed into a forwarding state.

- Many bridges can attach to the same segment, and many of these can be forwarding CBPDUs declaring their administrative cost to the root bridge. The bridge with the lowest such cost is called the *designated bridge* on that segment. The interface on the *designated bridge* on that segment is placed into forwarding state.

All other interfaces are placed into a blocking state.

Building an Initial Spanning Tree

Each bridge begins by claiming to be the root bridge. The Spanning-Tree Protocol defines messages used to exchange information with other bridges. These messages are called *Configuration Bridge Protocol Data Units (CBPDUs)*. Each bridge begins by sending a CBPDU stating the following:

- The root bridge's bridge ID. This is typically a MAC address on one of the bridge's interfaces. Each bridge sets this value to its own bridge ID.

- An administratively set priority.

- Cost between the bridge sending this CBPDU and the root. At the beginning of the process, each bridge is claiming to be root, so the value is set to 0.

- The bridge ID of the sender of this CBDPU. At the beginning of the process, each bridge is claiming to be root, so this ID is the same as the root bridge's ID.

The root bridge will be the bridge with the lowest priority value. If there is a tie based on priority, the lowest root bridge ID will be the root. The bridge IDs should be unique because MAC addresses are supposed to be unique.

The process of choosing the root begins with all bridges claiming to be the root by sending CBPDUs with their bridge IDs and priorities. If a bridge hears of a better candidate, it stops advertising itself as root and starts forwarding the CBPDUs sent by the better candidate. Before forwarding that CBPDU, the bridge increments the cost by a value based on a cost setting of the interface on which the better candidate's CBPDU was received. It's almost like a political race, with candidates dropping out once they cannot win and throwing their support behind the best candidate. At the end of the election, the best candidate will win. Figure 4-19 outlines what the bridges are doing after the process has settled. Table 4-7 lists the different costs used on each interface.

Given the scenario in Figure 4-19, Bridge 2 adds its E0 cost (100) to the cost of the CBPDU from Bridge 1 (root=Bridge 1, cost=0), so Bridge 2 considers its cost to the root to be 100. But Bridge 2 does not send a CBPDU out its E0 port because that is the port in which the CBPDU about the best root candidate entered. Instead, Bridge 2 only advertises a CBPDU out its other ports. Bridge 3 receives the CBPDU from Bridge 2 and adds the port cost of the incoming port, its E0 port, to the cost. Bridge 3 considers its cost to the root to be 200, as reflected in its CBPDU.

Figure 4-19 *Root Bridge Election—Bridge 1 Wins!*

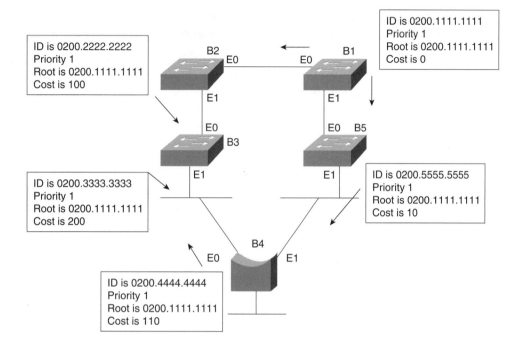

ID is 0200.2222.2222
Priority 1
Root is 0200.1111.1111
Cost is 100

ID is 0200.1111.1111
Priority 1
Root is 0200.1111.1111
Cost is 0

ID is 0200.3333.3333
Priority 1
Root is 0200.1111.1111
Cost is 200

ID is 0200.5555.5555
Priority 1
Root is 0200.1111.1111
Cost is 10

ID is 0200.4444.4444
Priority 1
Root is 0200.1111.1111
Cost is 110

Table 4-7 *Bridge Cost Values*

Bridge Interface	Cost
Bridge 1, E0	100
Bridge 1, E1	10
Bridge 2, E0 *	100
Bridge 2, E1	100
Bridge 3, E0 *	100
Bridge 3, E1	10
Bridge 4, E0	10
Bridge 4, E1 *	100
Bridge 5, E0 *	10
Bridge 5, E1	100

* signifies the values that affected the cost values in the CBPDUs.

Consider the steady-state CBPDU messages from Bridge 4's perspective. It receives a CBPDU about Bridge 1 as root from both Bridge 3 and Bridge 5. The cost in the CBPDU from Bridge 5 is lower; therefore, that is the message that Bridge 4 reacts to. Following the same logic, Bridge 4 adds its E1 port cost to the cost learned from Bridge 5, leaving a total of 110. Bridge 4 sends a CBPDU out all other ports besides its E1 port.

Of course, the creation of the spanning tree, causing some interfaces to forward and others to block is the goal. Both ports on Bridge 1 will be in a forwarding state. The interface in which the other bridges receive their lowest cost CBPDU about the root is considered to be their *root port*. Figure 4-20 shows the root ports with a simple designation of *RP*.

Figure 4-20 *Root Ports*

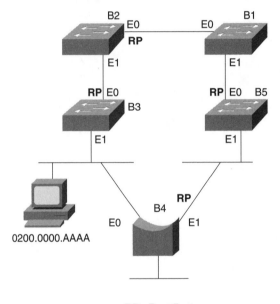

RP= Root Port

The final step in the process is for each bridge to decide whether to forward or block on its nonroot ports. Each LAN has one bridge that is sending the CBPDU about the root with the least cost. Referring to Figure 4-19, the segment that Bridge 3 and Bridge 4 are attached to shows Bridge 4 advertising the lower cost (110). Bridge 4 is then considered to be the *designated bridge* on that LAN segment, so Bridge 4 places its E0 port into forwarding state. On the other LAN segments, only one bridge is sending CBPDUs, so it is obvious which bridge will be designated bridge on each of those segments—Bridge 2's E1 port and Bridge 5's E1 port will be placed into forwarding state as well.

The process is now complete, with all ports in forwarding state except for Bridge 3's E1 interface. Table 4-8 outlines the state of each port and why it is in that state.

Table 4-8 *The State of Each Interface*

Bridge Interface	State	Reason Interface Is in Forwarding State
Bridge 1, E0	Forwarding	Interface is on root bridge
Bridge 1, E1	Forwarding	Interface is on root bridge
Bridge 2, E0	Forwarding	Root Port
Bridge 2, E1	Forwarding	Designated Bridge
Bridge 3, E0	Forwarding	Root Port
Bridge 3, E1	Blocking	Not applicable
Bridge 4, E0	Forwarding	Designated Bridge
Bridge 4, E1	Forwarding	Root Port
Bridge 5, E0	Forwarding	Root Port
Bridge 5, E1	Forwarding	Designated Bridge

Noticing and Reacting to Changes in Network Topology

A periodic notice is sent to tell all bridges that nothing has changed in the network. The protocol mechanism begins when the root sends CBPDUs on all its interfaces with the same information in it as before: its bridge ID, priority, cost (0), and the root bridge ID, which is itself. And as seen in Figure 4-19, the bridges receive the CBPDUs, adjust the cost, and send the CBPDUs on all interfaces that accept their root port.

The CBPDU created by the root also includes some important timers:

- **Hello time**—The time that the root waits before resending the periodic CBPDUs, which are then forwarded by successive bridges.

- **MaxAge**—The time any bridge should wait before deciding that the topology has changed.

- **Forward Delay**—Affects the time between when an interface changes from a blocking state to a forwarding state; this timer will be covered in more depth shortly.

The MaxAge timer is typically a multiple of Hello. This allows some CBPDUs to be lost, without the bridges reacting and changing the spanning tree. The MaxAge setting should also consider the variations in how long it takes the CBPDUs to traverse the network. In a local environment, these variations should be minimal unless severe congestion causes a large number of frames to be discarded.

When the network is up and no problems are occurring, the process works like this:

1. The root sends a CBPDU, cost 0, out all its interfaces.

2. The neighboring bridges send CBPDUs out their nonroot-port interfaces referring to the root, but with their cost added.

3. Step 2 is repeated by each bridge in the network as it receives these CBPDUs, as long as the CBPDU is received on a bridge's root port.

4. The root repeats Step 1 every Hello time.

5. If a bridge does not get a CBPDU in Hello time, it continues as normal, unless the larger MaxAge timer is passed.

Reacting to Changes in the Spanning Tree

The process used to react to changes in topology varies depending on the instance. This section describes two instances, one briefly, and the other in detail. Other variations than the two instances covered here do occur. Regardless of the details, the process always begins as a result of a bridge not receiving a CBPDU on its root port in MaxAge time.

No CBPDUs Received on Any Ports

If the bridge whose MaxAge parameter expires is also not receiving any other CBPDUs on ports that are not the root port, that bridge reacts by claiming to be the root bridge and begins sending CBPDUs describing itself. This process reduces to the same logic as described earlier in the section "Building an Initial Spanning Tree."

For instance, imagine that the root bridge failed in the network in Figure 4-19. Each bridge would have MaxAge expire at about the same time. Each would claim to be the root; one would be elected. A different spanning tree would result, but the process is the same as described earlier.

CBPDUs Received on Some Ports

The process of recalculating the spanning tree only occurs if CBPDUs are no longer received on the root port. But a bridge can still be receiving CBPDUs on other ports. Consider the familiar diagram shown in Figure 4-21. Bridge 5's E1 port has failed, preventing Bridge 4 from receiving CBPDUs on its root port, namely Bridge 4's E1 interface.

Figure 4-21 *CBPDUs While Bridge 4's MaxAge Expires*

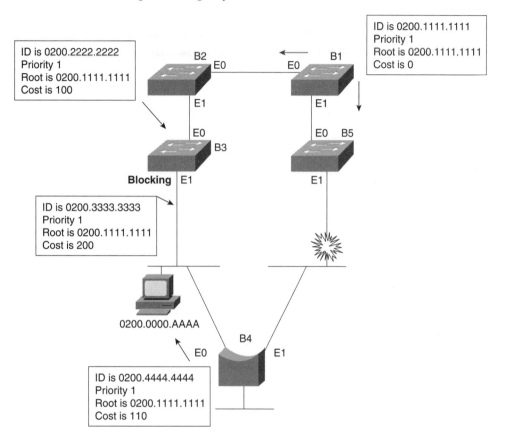

ID is 0200.1111.1111
Priority 1
Root is 0200.1111.1111
Cost is 0

ID is 0200.2222.2222
Priority 1
Root is 0200.1111.1111
Cost is 100

ID is 0200.3333.3333
Priority 1
Root is 0200.1111.1111
Cost is 200

ID is 0200.4444.4444
Priority 1
Root is 0200.1111.1111
Cost is 110

0200.0000.AAAA

A review of the behavior of this network is useful before seeing how it is about to change. For example, for MAC addresses residing on the Ethernet between Bridges 3 and 4, the traffic cannot be forwarded by Bridge 3 because it is blocking on its E1 interface. The instant Bridge 5's E1 port fails, so frames can no longer be forwarded or received on that interface. So during the period that MaxAge is expiring on Bridge 4, frames are sent, but may not be delivered. If the endpoints are on opposite sides of Bridge 5, the frames are not delivered.

Only Bridge 4's MaxAge expires. The other bridges are still receiving CBPDUs on their root ports. After MaxAge expires, Bridge 4 will decide the following:

1. My E1 port is no longer my root port.

2. The same root bridge is being advertised in a CBPDU on my E0 port.

3. There are no other CBPDUs being received.

4. My best (only in this case!) path to the root is out my E0 port; therefore, my root port is now E0.

5. Because no other CBPDUs are entering my E1 port, I must be the designated bridge on that segment. So, I will start sending CBPDUs on E1, adding my E0 port cost (10) to the cost of the CBPDU received in the CBPDU entering E0 (200), for a total cost of 210.

6. I will no longer send CBPDUs out E0 because it is my root port.

Figure 4-22 illustrates the result of Bridge 4's reaction.

Figure 4-22 *CBPDUs After Bridge 4's MaxAge Expires*

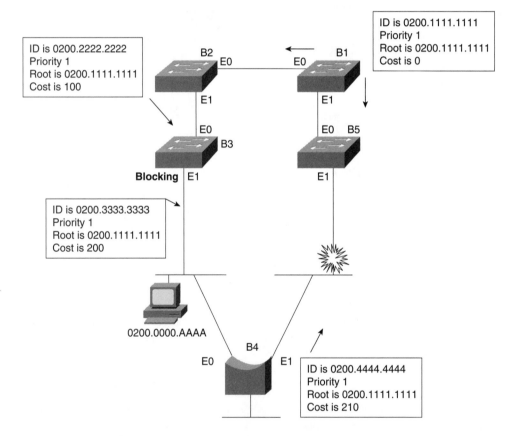

The logic used by Bridge 4 seems relatively straightforward, albeit detailed. There is a subtle but important occurrence in this case: both of Bridge 4's interfaces were forwarding before the change, and both are still forwarding. In other words, neither interface has changed state. But the process is not finished because some change to the spanning tree must take place for new paths to be available. In this case, Bridge 3's E1 will need to change from blocking to forwarding state, which has not occurred yet. The key part of the upcoming logic is based on this corollary of spanning tree:

> A change that affects the spanning tree results in at least one bridge interface changing from blocking to forwarding, or vice-versa.

At this point in the process, no changes to the spanning tree have been made, and many address table entries refer to the path that has failed. Table 4-9 refers to the address table entries for 0200.0000.AAAA in all 5 bridges, showing that 4 of the 5 bridge address tables refer to the failed path. Use Table 4-10 in comparison with Figure 4-22 to verify the path to this MAC address is still invalid.

Table 4-9   *Address Table Entries for 0200.0000.AAAA, Before Spanning Tree Has Been Changed*

Bridge	MAC	Outgoing Interface
Bridge 1	0200.0000.AAAA	E1
Bridge 2	0200.0000.AAAA	E0
Bridge 3	0200.0000.AAAA	E0
Bridge 4	0200.0000.AAAA	E0
Bridge 5	0200.0000.AAAA	E1

The spanning tree change that is needed is for Bridge 3 to change from blocking state to forwarding state on its E1 interface. Bridge 3's reaction to the lack of CBPDUs from Bridge 4 causes this change to occur. Consider the logic that Bridge 3 uses in this case:

1. I am no longer receiving any CBPDUs on my E1 interface.

2. After Step 1 has occurred for MaxAge time, I assume the designated bridge has failed. I will assume the status of designated bridge on the LAN segment to which E1 is attached because no other bridges are forwarding CBPDUs onto that segment.

3. I will immediately change E1's status from blocking to *listening*. That means I will not learn addresses based on frames entering E1. I will not forward frames entering E1, nor will I forward frames out E1.

4. I will clear entries in my address table using a short timer (typically a few seconds).

5. I will send a message out my root port signifying that a topology change is being made. (The root will eventually receive the message.)

6. A Forward Delay timer is started at Step 3. When it expires, I will change my E1 status to *learning* and begin to add address table entries learned from frames entering my E1 interface. I will not forward frames out my E1 interface yet, nor will I forward frames that enter E1 yet.

7. Another Forward Delay timer was started after Step 6. When the timer expires, I will change my E1 status to *forwarding*.

The spanning tree has now changed so that a single active path exists between all LAN segments. The intermediate states are used in an effort to reduce the possibility of temporary loops. Table 4-10 summarizes the intermediate states of the spanning tree.

Table 4-10 *Spanning Tree Interface States*

State	Forward Data Frames?	Learn MACs Based on Received Frames?	Transitory or Stable State?
Blocking	no	no	stable
Listening	no	no	transitory
Learning	no	yes	transitory
Forwarding	yes	yes	stable

The listening and learning states are intermediate states as a bridge makes a new choice about which bridge is root. In listening state, all that matters is listening for CBPDUs, so a new choice for root can be made. In learning state, MAC addresses can be learned based on incoming frames.

One last step is necessary to complete the logic. The address table entries may not have timed out yet (see Table 4-9). The Spanning-Tree Protocol includes the concept of notifying all bridges that a tree change has occurred, allowing the bridges to quickly time out address table entries. By doing so, the new path can be used very quickly.

The notification of a changing spanning tree is begun by Bridge 3 in Figure 4-22, in Step 5 of its logic (shown in the list following Figure 4-22). The topology change message is received by the root because each intervening bridge is tasked with forwarding the message. The root reacts by setting a topology change flag in its CBPDUs for a period of time. Because all bridges propagate these messages, all bridges will notice the *topology change flag* in the CBPDU. Each bridge can then choose to use a shorter time (for example, 2 seconds) to time out address table entries.

Spanning-Tree Protocol Summary

Spanning trees accomplish the goals of allowing physical redundancy but with only one concurrently active path through a bridged network. Spanning trees use the following features to accomplish the goal:

- All bridge interfaces eventually stabilize at either a forwarding state or a blocking state. The forwarding interfaces are considered to be a part of the "spanning" tree.

- One of the bridges is elected as root. The process includes all bridges claiming to be root, until one is considered best by all. All root bridge interfaces are in forwarding state.

- Each bridge receives CBPDUs from the root, either directly or forwarded by some other bridge. Each bridge may receive more than one such message on its interfaces, but the port in which the least cost CBPDU is received is called the root port of a bridge, and that port is placed into forwarding state.

- For each LAN segment, one bridge will be sending the forwarded CBPDU with the lowest cost. That bridge is the designated bridge for that segment. That bridge's interface on that segment is placed into a forwarding state.

- All other interfaces are placed into a blocking state.

- The root sends CBPDUs every Hello time seconds. The other bridges expect to receive forwarding copies of these CBPDUs, so they know that nothing has changed. Hello time is defined in the CBPDU itself, so all bridges use the same value.

- If a bridge does not receive a CBPDU for MaxAge time, it begins the process of causing the spanning tree to change. The reaction can vary from topology to topology. (MaxAge is defined in the CBPDU itself, so all bridges use the same value.)

- One or more bridges decide to change interfaces from blocking for forwarding or vice-versa, depending on the change in the network. If moving from blocking to forwarding, the interim listening state is entered first. After Forward Delay time (another timer defined in the root CBPDU), the state is changed to learning. After another Forward Delay time, the interface is placed in forwarding state.

- The Spanning-Tree Protocol includes these delays to help ensure no temporary loops occur.

Q&A

As mentioned in Chapter 1, the questions and scenarios are more difficult than what you should experience on the actual exam. The questions do not attempt to cover more breadth or depth than the exam; however, the questions are designed to make sure you know the answer. Rather than allowing you to derive the answer from clues hidden inside the question itself, your understanding and recall of the subject will be challenged. Questions from the "Do I Know This Already?" quiz from the beginning of the chapter are repeated here to ensure that you have mastered the chapter's topic areas. Hopefully, these questions will help limit the number of exam questions on which you narrow your choices to two options, and then guess!

1. What do the letters MAC stand for? What other terms have you heard to describe the same or similar concept?

2. Name two benefits of LAN segmentation using transparent bridges.

3. What routing protocol does a transparent bridge use to learn about Layer 3 addressing groupings?

4. What settings are examined by a bridge or switch to determine which should be elected as root of the spanning tree?

5. Define the term *VLAN*.

6. Assume a building has 100 devices that are attached to the same Ethernet. These users were then migrated onto two separate shared Ethernet segments, each with 50 devices, with a transparent bridge in between. List two benefits that would be derived for a typical user.

7. What standards body owns the process of ensuring unique MAC addresses worldwide?

8. Assume a building has 100 devices that are attached to the same Ethernet. These devices are migrated to two different shared Ethernet segments, each with 50 devices. The two segments are connected to a Cisco LAN switch to allow communication between the two sets of users. List two benefits that would be derived for a typical user.

9. Name the two methods of internal switching on typical switches today. Which provides less latency for an individual frame?

10. What is the distance limitation of 10BT? 100BTX?

11. Describe how a transparent bridge decides if it should forward a frame, and how it chooses the interface out which to forward the frame.

12. How fast is Fast Ethernet?

13. Describe the benefit of Spanning-Tree Protocol as used by transparent bridges and switches.

14. If a switch hears three different configuration BPDUs from three different neighbors on three different interfaces, and all three specify that Bridge 1 is the root, how does it choose which interface is its root port?

15. How does a transparent bridge build its address table?

16. How many bytes long is a MAC address?

17. Assume a building has 100 devices that are attached to the same Ethernet. These users are then migrated onto two separate Ethernet segments, each with 50 devices, and separated by a router. List two benefits that would be derived for a typical user.

18. Does a bridge/switch examine just the incoming frame's source MAC, destination MAC, or both? Why does it examine the one(s) it examines?

19. Define the term *collision domain*.

20. When a bridge or switch using Spanning-Tree Protocol first initializes, who does it assert should be the root of the tree?

21. Name the three reasons why a port is placed into a forwarding state as a result of spanning tree.

22. Define the difference between broadcast and multicast MAC addresses.

23. Excluding the preamble and starting delimiter fields, but including all other Ethernet headers and trailers, what is the maximum number of bytes in an Ethernet frame?

24. Define the term *broadcast domain*.

25. Describe the benefits of creating three VLANs of 25 ports each versus a single VLAN of 75 ports, in each case using a single switch. Assume all ports are switched ports (each port is a different collision domain).

26. If two Cisco LAN switches are connected using Fast Ethernet, what VLAN trunking protocols could be used? If only one VLAN spanned both switches, is a VLAN trunking protocol needed?

27. Explain the function of the loopback and collision detection features of an Ethernet NIC in relation to half-duplex and full-duplex operation.

28. Name the three interface states that Spanning-Tree uses, other than *forwarding*. Which of these states is transitory?

The following table outlines the CCNA exam objectives that are reviewed in this chapter. The numbers shown correspond to the master list of objectives found in Chapter 1, "What Is CCNA?"

Objective	Description
28	Monitor Novell IPX operation on the router.
29	Describe the two parts of network addressing, then identify the parts in specific protocol address examples.
30	Create the different classes of IP addresses [and subnetting].
31	Configure IP addresses.
32	Verify IP addresses.
33	List the required IPX address and encapsulation type.
34	Enable the Novell IPX protocol and configure interfaces.
35	Identify the functions of the TCP/IP transport-layer protocols.
36	Identify the functions of the TCP/IP network-layer protocols.
37	Identify the functions performed by ICMP.
38	Configure IPX access lists and SAP filters to control basic Novell traffic.

CHAPTER 5

Network Protocols: Understanding the TCP/IP Suite and Novell NetWare Protocols

TCP/IP is the most important protocol covered on the CCNA exam and is the most often used protocol in networks today. This chapter covers the TCP/IP protocols as well as IP addressing and subnetting. Cisco will require you to continually prove your understanding of IP subnetting on the CCNA exam and almost all other Cisco exams.

This chapter also covers Novell's NetWare protocols. NetWare protocols have been well established and widely implemented for a decade. Very few changes that affect the router's role in forwarding NetWare traffic were made during that time. Routing is straightforward; if you understand IP routing, then IPX routing should be easy to grasp. And, of course, this book assumes that you have been through one of the Training Paths and that NetWare protocols are not new to you. This chapter briefly reviews the main concepts, clarifies the trickiest details, and helps you refine your retention and recall with questions and scenarios.

Routing protocols for IP and IPX are covered in Chapter 6, "Understanding Routing," in an effort to match the chapter headings to Cisco's CCNA exam objectives organization. Chapter 7, "Understanding Network Security," covers IP and IPX access lists. However, the CCNA objective 38 mentioning IPX access lists is not listed under the Network Security category in the CCNA exam objectives, but under the heading Network Protocols, which is the category covered in this chapter. Objective 38 is better covered in Chapter 7 of this book; it is listed here so you can find where the topic is covered.

How to Best Use This Chapter

By taking the following steps, you can make better use of your study time:

- Keep your notes and answers for all your work with this book in one place for easy reference.

- Take the "Do I Know This Already?" quiz and write down your answers. Studies show retention is significantly increased through writing down facts and concepts, even if you never look at the information again!

- Figure 5-1 helps guide you to the next step in preparation for this topic area on the CCNA exam.

Figure 5-1 *How To Use This Chapter*

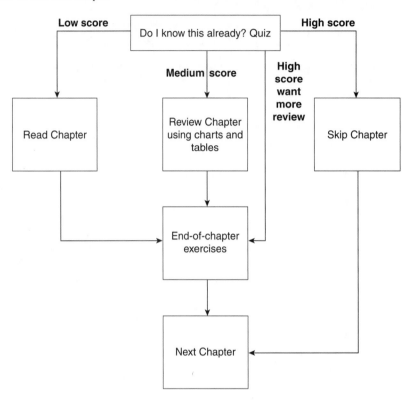

"Do I Know This Already?" Quiz

    1. Name the parts of an IP address.

    _____

    _____

    _____

    2. Write down the subnet number, broadcast address, and range of valid IP addresses for the following address and mask: 134.141.7.11 255.255.255.0

    _____

    _____

    _____

3. How many IP addresses could be assigned in the following subnet:
155.166.44.64 255.255.255.192

_____

_____

_____

4. How many valid subnets exist if the same mask (255.255.255.0) is used on all subnets of
network 134.141.0.0, with mask ?

_____

_____

_____

5. Create a minimal configuration enabling IP on each interface on a 2501 router (2 serial, 1
Ethernet). The NIC assigned you network 8.0.0.0. Your boss says you need at most 200
hosts per subnet. You decide against using VLSM. Your boss says to plan your subnets so
you can have as many subnets as possible, rather than allow for larger subnets later. You
decide to start with the lowest numerical values for subnets. Assume point-to-point serial
links will be attached to this router and that RIP is the routing protocol.

_____

_____

_____

6. Name the three classes of unicast IP addresses and list their default masks, respectively.
How many of each type could be assigned to companies and organizations by the NIC?

_____

_____

_____

7. Define the purpose of an ICMP redirect message.

_____

_____

_____

8. Describe the headers used for two examples of Ethernet encapsulation when using IPX.

_____

_____

_____

9. Create a configuration enabling IPX on each interface, with RIP and SAP enabled on each as well, for a 2501 (2 serial, 1 Ethernet) router. Use networks 100, 200, and 300 for interfaces S0, S1, and E0, respectively. Choose any node values.

_____

_____

_____

10. How many Novell encapsulation types are valid in the IOS for Ethernet interfaces? FDDI? Token Ring?

_____

_____

_____

11. A router is attached to an Ethernet LAN. Some clients on the LAN use Novell's Ethernet_II encapsulation, and some others use Ethernet_802.3. If the only subcommand on Ethernet0 reads **ipx network 1**, which of the clients are working? (all, Ethernet_II, or Ethernet_802.3?)

_____

_____

_____

12. In the **ipx network 11** command, does the IOS assume 11 is binary, octal, decimal, or hexadecimal? What is the largest valid value that could be configured instead of 11?

_____

_____

_____

You can find the answers to the "Do I Know This Already?" quiz in Appendix B on page 562. Review the answers, grade your quiz, and choose an appropriate next step in this chapter based on the suggestions in the "How to Best Use This Chapter" topic earlier in this chapter. Your choices for the next step are as follows:

- **5 or fewer correct**—Read this chapter.

- **6, 7, or 8 correct**—Review this chapter, looking at the charts and diagrams that summarize most of the concepts and facts in this chapter.

- **9 or more correct**—If you want more review on these topics, skip to the exercises at the end of this chapter. If you do not want more review on these topics, skip this chapter.

Foundation Topics

Functions at Each Layer

CCNA Objectives Covered in This Section

35	Identify the functions of the TCP/IP transport-layer protocols.
36	Identify the functions of the TCP/IP network-layer protocols.
37	Identify the functions performed by ICMP.

This section examines the TCP, UDP, ICMP, and ARP protocols in detail. TCP and UDP are the two transport-layer (Layer 4) protocols most often used by applications in a TCP/IP network. ICMP and ARP are actually parts of the network layer (Layer 3) of TCP/IP. All of these protocols are integral to a complete understanding of TCP/IP and are very likely to be covered on the CCNA exam.

Transmission Control Protocol

The Transmission Control Protocol (TCP), as defined in RFC 793 and referenced in objective 35, defines the following functions:

- Data transfer
- Multiplexing
- Reliable transfer
- Flow control
- Connections

TCP is focused on accomplishing these goals via mechanisms at the endpoint computers. End-to-end deliveries of the data, including routing issues, are not functions of TCP, but are instead functions of the IP protocol. In other words, TCP performs only part of the functions necessary to deliver the data between applications.

Data Transfer

Like other functions in any protocol stack, TCP provides service for the next higher layer. Because TCP's next higher layer is the application layer, TCP data transfer implies delivering data from one application to another. Applications use TCP services by issuing programmatic calls to TCP, supplying the data to be sent, the destination IP address, and a port number that identifies the application that should receive the data. The port number, along with the destination IP address, and the name of the transport-layer protocol (TCP) form a *socket*. TCP accomplishes data transfer by establishing a connection between a socket on each of the endpoint computers. *Applications use TCP services by opening a socket; TCP manages the delivery of the data to the other socket.* Put another way, an IP source/destination pair uniquely identifies a relationship between two devices in a network; a socket source/destination pair uniquely identifies a relationship between two applications in a network.

Multiplexing

Larry is a multi-user system in which two users have Telnetted to Curly. The socket used by the Telnet server on Curly consists of an IP address, the transport-layer protocol in use, and a port number, in this case, (10.1.1.3, TCP, 23). Because data coming from both Telnet clients is sent to that socket, Curly cannot distinguish which client has sent data to the Telnet server based on only Curly's socket. For the Telnet server to know which connection the data is coming over, the combination of the socket at the server and the socket at the client is used to uniquely identify connection. For example, Client #1 uses socket 10.1.1.1, TCP, 1027, and Client #2 uses socket 10.1.1.1, TCP, 1028. Now Curly can distinguish between the two clients.

Well-known port numbers are used by servers; other port numbers are used by clients. Applications that provide a service, such as FTP, Telnet, and web servers, open a socket and listen for connection requests. Because these connection requests from clients are required to include both the source and destination port numbers, the port numbers used by the servers must be well known. Therefore, each server has a hard coded well-known port number, as defined in the well-known numbers RFC. On client machines, where the requests originate, any unused port number can be allocated. The result is that each client on the same host uses a different port number, but a server uses the same port number for all connections. For example, 100 Telnet clients on the same host would each use a different port number, but the Telnet server, with 100 clients connected to it, would have only one socket and therefore only one port number. The combination of source and destination sockets allows all participating hosts to distinguish data.

Table 5-1 summarizes the socket connections as shown in Figure 5-2.

Table 5-1 *TCP Connections from Figure 5-2*

Connection	Client Socket	Server Socket
Telnet Client #1 to Server	(10.1.1.1, TCP, 1027)	(10.1.1.3, TCP, 23)
Telnet Client #2 to Server	(10.1.1.1, TCP, 1028)	(10.1.1.3, TCP, 23)
FTP Client to FTP Server	(10.1.1.2, TCP, 1027)	(10.1.1.3, TCP, 21)
Web Client to Web Server	(10.1.1.2, TCP, 1029)	(10.1.1.3, TCP, 80)

Figure 5-2 *Connections Between Sockets*

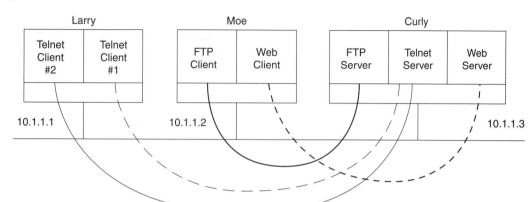

Multiplexing in this context is defined as the process of choosing which application receives the data after it is received. Consider that definition with the four socket connections in Table 5-1, for packets destined to the server (Curly). All destination socket information is for 10.1.1.3, with TCP, but the use of different port numbers allows Curly to choose the correct server to which to pass the data. Also notice that the port numbers do not have to be unique. The FTP client on Moe and the Telnet Client #1 on Larry both use port 1027, but their sockets are unique because each uses a different IP address. Also, when the Telnet servers send data back to Clients #1 and #2, Larry knows how to multiplex to the correct client because each uses a unique port number on Larry.

Reliable Data Transfer

Reliable data transfer is one of the most important and most typically remembered features of TCP. To accomplish reliability, data bytes are numbered via the sequence and acknowledgment fields in the TCP header. TCP achieves reliability in both directions, using the sequence number field of one direction combined with the acknowledgment field in the opposite direction. Figure 5-3 shows the basic operation.

In Figure 5-3, the acknowledgment field in the TCP header sent by the web server implies the next byte to be received; this is called *forward acknowledgment*. If the second TCP segment had been lost, the web server's reply should have had an ack field equal to 2000. The TCP function at the web client could then recover lost data by resending the second TCP segment. The TCP protocol allows for resending just that segment, and waiting, hoping the web server will reply with acknowledgment equals 4000. TCP also allows for the resending host to begin with a segment in error and resend all TCP segments.

Figure 5-3 *TCP Acknowledgment*

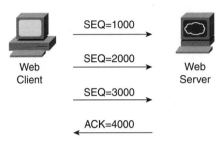

Flow Control

TCP implements flow control by taking advantage of the sequence and acknowledgment fields, along with a new field called the window field. This window field implies the maximum number of unacknowledged bytes outstanding at any instant in time. The window will grow over time as long as few errors are detected. The window starts small and then grows until errors occur. The window then "slides" based on network performance.

Connection Establishment

Connection establishment is the last TCP function reviewed in this section, but it occurs before any of the other TCP features can begin their work. Connection establishment refers to the process of initializing sequence and acknowledgment fields and agreeing to the port numbers used. Figure 5-4 shows an example of connection establishment flow.

Figure 5-4 *TCP Connection Establishment*

This three-way connection establishment flow must complete before data transfer can begin. The connection exists between the two sockets, although there is no single "socket" field in the TCP header. Of the three parts of a socket, the IP addresses are implied based on the source and destination IP address in the IP header; TCP is implied because a TCP header is in use; therefore, the only parts of the socket that need to be encoded are the port numbers. The sequence and acknowledgment fields are initialized to any number that fits into the four-byte fields.

TCP Function Summary

Table 5-2 summarizes TCP functions.

Table 5-2 *TCP Function Summary*

Function	Description
Data transfer	Continuous stream of ordered data.
Multiplexing	Allows receiving hosts to decide, based on the port number, the correct application for which the data is destined.
Reliable transfer	Data is numbered and acknowledged with sequence and acknowledgment header fields.
Flow control	Window sizes are used to protect buffer space and routing devices.
Connections	Used to initialize port numbers and other TCP header fields.

User Datagram Protocol

The User Datagram Protocol (UDP) was designed to provide a service for applications in which messages could be exchanged. (UDP is mentioned in objective 35.) Unlike TCP, UDP provides no reliability, no windowing, but it requires less overhead than TCP. Some functions of TCP, such as data transfer and multiplexing, are provided as functions of UDP.

UDP multiplexes using port numbers in an identical fashion to TCP. The only difference in UDP (compared to TCP) sockets is that instead of designating TCP as the transport protocol, the transport protocol is UDP. Because a UDP socket and TCP socket are considered to be different (although similar), an application could open identical port numbers on the same host, but use TCP in one case and UDP in the other. This is not typical, but certainly allowed. Servers that allow use of TCP and UDP reserve the use of the same port number for each, as shown in the well-known numbers RFC (currently RFC 1700).

UDP data transfer differs from TCP in that no reordering or recovery is accomplished. Applications using UDP are tolerant of the lost data, or they have some application mechanism to recover lost data. For example, Simple Network Management Protocol (SNMP) is tolerant of lost packets, thinking that the user of the management software will retry an operation. The Network File System (NFS) performs recovery with application layer code, so UDP features are acceptable to NFS.

Table 5-3 contrasts typical transport layer functions as performed (or not performed) by UDP or TCP.

Table 5-3 *TCP and UDP Functional Comparison*

Function	Description (TCP)	Description (UDP)
Data transfer	Continuous stream of ordered data	Message (datagram) delivery
Multiplexing	Allows receiving hosts to decide the correct application the data is destined for, based on port number	Allows receiving hosts to decide the correct application the data is destined for, based on port number
Reliable transfer	Data is acknowledged using the sequence and acknowledge-ment fields in the TCP header	Not a feature of UDP
Flow control	Used to protect buffer space and routing devices	Not a feature of UDP
Connections	Used to initialize port numbers and other TCP header fields	Not needed for UDP

Figure 5-5 shows TCP and UDP header formats. Note the existence of both source and destination port number fields in the TCP and UDP headers, but the absence of sequence acknowledgment fields in the UDP header, as in Figure 5-4. UDP does not need these fields because it makes no attempt to number the data for acknowledgments or resequencing.

Figure 5-5 *TCP and UDP Headers*

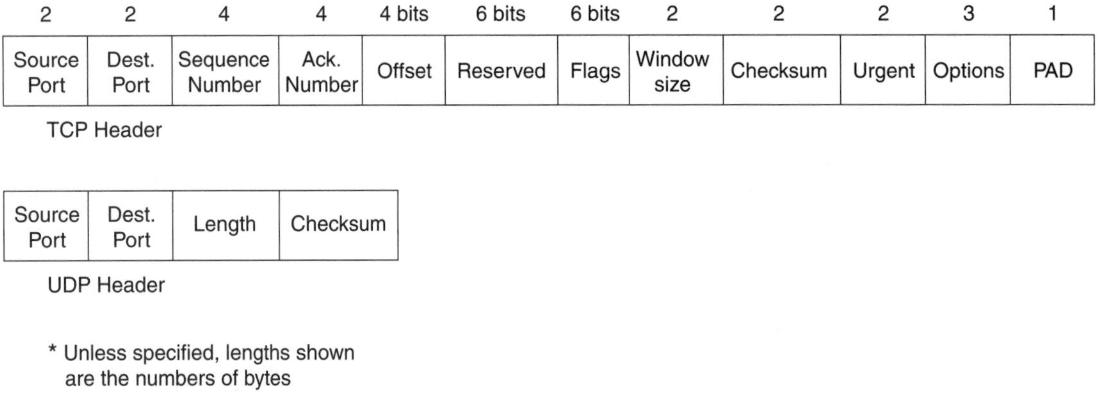

TCP Header

UDP Header

* Unless specified, lengths shown
  are the numbers of bytes

UDP gains some advantages over TCP by not using the sequence and acknowledgment fields. The most obvious is that there are fewer bytes of overhead. Not as obvious is the fact that UDP does not require waiting on acknowledgments, or holding the data in memory until it is acknowledged. This means UDP applications are not artificially slowed by the acknowledg-ment process and memory is freed more quickly.

Address Resolution Protocol

ARP is the process by which an IP host learns the LAN address of some other host. ARP is needed because to send an IP packet across some LAN, the data link header and trailer must first be created, with the IP packet placed between the data link header and trailer. And, ARP is part of the network layer of TCP/IP, as mentioned in CCNA objective 36. Figure 5-6 shows an example.

Figure 5-6 *The ARP Process*

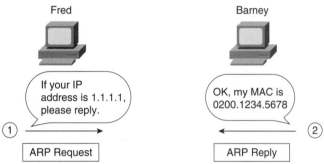

Considering both the protocol and programming perspectives can help your understanding of ARP. From an architecture perspective, ARP is a Layer 3 function, and is defined in RFC 826. From a programming perspective, IP calls the LAN data-link layer code, and supplies the destination MAC address. IP is counting on the data-link layer code to deliver the packet, inside a frame, across the LAN. Note the location of ARP in the architectural model in Figure 5-7.

Figure 5-7 *TCP/IP Architectural Model*

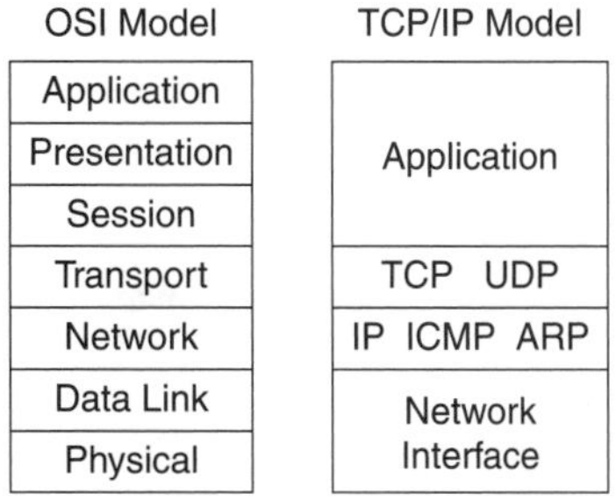

OSI Model	TCP/IP Model
Application	Application
Presentation	Application
Session	Application
Transport	TCP UDP
Network	IP ICMP ARP
Data Link	Network Interface
Physical	Network Interface

Note that ARP is in the lower part of the Internet layer in the diagram. ARP actually does not use an IP header, but an ARP header. ICMP, discussed next, uses IP services; an ICMP message is included after the IP header, instead of one of the transport layer protocols.

Internet Control Message Protocol

The Internet Control Message Protocol (ICMP) is a Layer 3 protocol used in conjunction with IP. *Control Message* is the most descriptive part of the name—ICMP helps control and manage the work of IP. Expect ICMP to be on your exam, as it is specifically mentioned in objective 36. RFC 792 defines ICMP, and it includes the following excerpt, which describes the protocol well:

> "Occasionally a gateway or destination host will communicate with a source host, for example, to report an error in datagram processing. For such purposes this protocol, the Internet Control Message Protocol (ICMP), is used. ICMP uses the basic support of IP as if it were a higher level protocol, however, ICMP is actually an integral part of IP, and must be implemented by every IP module."

Table 5-4 lists the ICMP messages. The messages denoted with asterisks are the messages most likely to be covered on the exam. The Destination Unreachable, Time Exceeded, and Redirect messages will be described in more detail following Table 5-4.

Table 5-4 *ICMP Message Types*

Message	Purpose
*Destination Unreachable	Tells the source host that there is a problem delivering a packet.
*Time Exceeded	The time it takes a packet to be delivered has become too long; the packet has been discarded.
Source Quench	The source is sending data faster than it can be forwarded; this message requests that the sender slow down!
*Redirect	The router sending this message has received some packet for which another router would have had a better route; the message tells the sender to use the better router.
*Echo	Used by the **ping** command to verify connectivity.
Parameter Problem	Used to identify a parameter that is incorrect.
Timestamp	Used to measure roundtrip time to particular hosts.
Address Mask request/ reply	Used to inquire and learn the correct subnet mask to be used.
Router Advertisement and Selection	Used to allow hosts to dynamically learn the IP addresses of the routers attached to the same subnet.

Each ICMP message contains a Type field and a Code field, as shown in Figure 5-8. The Type field implies the message types from Table 5-4. The Code field implies a subtype.

Figure 5-8 *ICMP Header Formats*

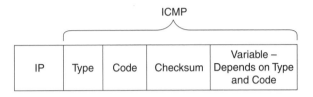

ICMP

| IP | Type | Code | Checksum | Variable – Depends on Type and Code |

ICMP Destination Unreachable Message

Five separate functions (codes) are accomplished using this ICMP message. The five functions are better described with the following Figure 5-9.

Figure 5-9 *Sample Network for Discussing ICMP Unreachable*

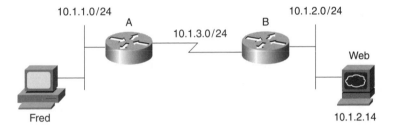

Assume that Fred is trying to connect to the web server, which uses TCP protocols. Three of the ICMP unreachable codes would possibly be used by Routers A and B. The other two codes would be used by the web server.

A code meaning *network unreachable* would be used by Router A if Router A did not have a route to 10.1.2.0/24. The message would be sent by Router A to Fred. If A had a route to 10.1.2.0/24, the packet would get to Router B. However, if the web server is down, Router B will not get an ARP reply from Web; B will send an unreachable with the *host unreachable* code field.

If Router A or Router B needed to fragment the packet, but the *do not fragment* bit was set in the IP header, it would send an unreachable with the *can't fragment* value in the code field.

If the packet successfully arrives at the web server, two other unreachable codes are possible. One implies that the protocol above IP, typically TCP or UDP, is not running. This is highly unlikely today. If true, the web server would reply with an unreachable with the code field value implying *protocol unavailable*. The final code field value is highly likely. If the computer was up, but the web server had been taken down, the web server would reply with an unreachable with the code field implying *port unavailable*.

Cisco IOS documentation and configuration commands sometime treat each different code value as a separate message. For example, it may state something like, An ICMP host unreachable message.... I would be surprised if the exam bothered being so picky as to expect you to know that there is no *host unreachable* message, but instead an *unreachable* message with code host.

Time Exceeded ICMP Message

One of the two codes for Time Exceeded will be described here—namely, the Time To Live (TTL) code option. This message is used with the IP header TTL field.

In the 1970s, a science fiction movie called *Logan's Run* was created. When turning 30, citizens on this planet participated in a religious ceremony that boiled down to their being cremated; the reason was for population control. Logan turned 30 and decided he did not like the rules...so he ran.

The TTL field in the IP header is like the counter used for citizens in *Logan's Run*. When the counter expires, so does the packet. Each router decrements the TTL field in each packet header. (The router does not actually calculate a time that should be decremented; it just decrements by one!) However, if TTL decrements to 0, the packet is discarded. (For those who remember *Logan's Run*, you can think of TTL as the Logan's Run field.)

The TTL exceeded option is used in a message from the router that discards the packet. The router sends the Time Exceeded, code Time To Live Exceeded message to the sending host. TTL is used to ensure that packets which are looping do not do so forever. TTL exceeded lets the host know that a routing loop may be occurring, so the human can choose to wait a few minutes before trying again.

The **trace** command uses the TTL exceeded message to its advantage. By purposefully sending IP packets (with a UDP transport layer) with TTL set to 1, an ICMP Time Exceeded message will be returned by the first router in the route. That's because that router will decrement TTL to 0, causing it to discard the packet, as well as sending the TTL exceeded message. Another IP packet with TTL=2 is routed by the first router but then discarded by the second router—which sends TTL exceeded messages as well. Eventually, the packet is delivered to the destination, which sends back an ICMP port unreachable message. The original packet sent by the host command uses a destination port number that is very unlikely to be used, expecting the destination host to return the port unreachable message. The ICMP port unreachable message signifies the packets reached the other host without having TTL being exceeded. Example 5-1 shows a **trace** command from a router (Router A) that is one hop away from a host; another router (Router B) has **debug ip icmp** enabled, which shows the resulting TTL exceeded messages. The commands were performed in the network in Figure 5-9.

Example 5-1 *ICMP **debug** on Router B, When Running **trace** Command on Router A*

```
RouterA#trace 10.1.3.1

Type escape sequence to abort.
Tracing the route to 10.1.3.1

  1 10.1.6.253 8 msec 4 msec 4 msec
  2 10.1.3.1 12 msec 8 msec 4 msec
RouterA#
```
```
RouterB#
ICMP: time exceeded (time to live) sent to 10.1.6.251 (dest was 10.1.3.1)
ICMP: time exceeded (time to live) sent to 10.1.6.251 (dest was 10.1.3.1)
ICMP: time exceeded (time to live) sent to 10.1.6.251 (dest was 10.1.3.1)
```

ICMP Redirect Message

ICMP redirect messages provide a very important element in routed IP networks. Many hosts are preconfigured with a default router IP address. These hosts, when sending packets destined to subnets other than the one they are directly connected to, send the packets to their default router. If there is a better local router to which the host should send the packets, an ICMP redirect can be used to tell the host to send the packets to another, different router.

For example, in Figure 5-10, the PC uses Router B as its default router. However, Router A's route to subnet 10.1.4.0 is a better route. (Assume use of mask 255.255.255.0 in each subnet in Figure 5-10.) The PC sends a packet to Router B (step 1 in Figure 5-10). Router B then forwards the packet based on its own routing table (Step 2); that route points through A, which has a better route. Finally, Router B sends the ICMP redirect message to the PC (Step 3), telling it to forward future packets destined for 10.1.4.0 to Router A instead.

Figure 5-10 *Example of an ICMP Redirect*

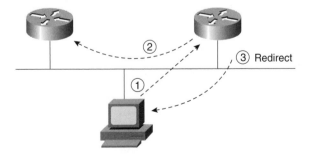

In summary, ICMP defines several message types and several subtypes, called codes. Popular use of terminology treats each differing code as a different message. Pay particular attention to the messages denoted with asterisks in Table 5-4. Finally, RFC 792 is a short and straightforward RFC to read if you want more information.

IP Addressing and Subnetting

CCNA Objectives Covered in This Section

29	Describe the two parts of network addressing, then identify the parts in specific protocol address examples.
30	Create the different classes of IP addresses [and subnetting].

A comfortable, confident understanding of IP addressing and subnetting is required for success with any Cisco certification. For CCNA, questions will directly ask for your interpretation of an address, its network number, subnet number, the other IP addresses in the same subnet, the broadcast address, and the other subnets that could be used if the same mask were in use. For the CCNP and CCIE tests, the questions will presume that you can interpret such details so that you can understand a question related to a more advanced topic. In other words, you had better know subnetting!

This section of the book summarizes the definitions and provides you with an opportunity for some practice to help you verify that your understanding is complete.

IP Addressing Basics: Terminology and Concepts

RFC 791, which defines IP addressing, does not claim to predict the future or anticipate private networks with thousands and tens-of-thousands of hosts, and a global Internet with hundreds-of-millions of hosts. With some literary license, one might imagine the original IP address structure was designed with the following criteria in mind:

- Each host should have a unique IP address.

- The IP address structure should be logical, not physical, to allow for future growth into new technologies.

- The address is assigned to the interface of the computer, not the computer itself.

- Addresses are grouped (both numerically) and based on where the interfaces are physically attached.

- The numeric grouping is the set of all addresses that have the same numeric value in the first part of the address, called the *network part* of the address.

- The interfaces in the same group must be attached to the same medium and must not be separated by an IP router.

- One address in each grouping is reserved as the number representing the entire group; this is called the *network number* or *network address*.

- By assigning each organization a unique network number, globally unique addresses can be accomplished. This allows for creation of a global Internet without confusing routers with duplicate groups or duplicate individual addresses.

- Some networks need to be large, others need to be small, so create networks of different sizes.

- Use a 32-bit address so that we will never run out.

IP Networks

Class A, B, and C networks provide three network sizes. By definition, all addresses in the same network have the same numeric value network portion of the addresses. The rest of the address is called the *host* portion of the address. Individual addresses in the same network all have a different value in the host parts of the addresses.

For example, Class A networks have a 1–byte–long network part. That leaves 24 bits for the "rest" of the address, or the host part. That means that 2^{24} addresses are numerically possible in a Class A network. Similarly, Class B networks have a 2–byte–long network part, leaving 16 bits for the host portion of the address. So, 2^{16} possible addresses exist in a single Class B network. Finally, Class C networks have a 3–byte–long network part, leaving only 8 bits for the host part, which implies only 2^{8} addresses in a Class C network. Table 5-5 summarizes the characteristics of Class A, B, and C networks.

Table 5-5   *Sizes of Network and Host Parts of IP Addresses with No Subnetting*

Any Network of This Class	Number of Network Bytes (Bits)	Number of Host Bytes (Bits)	Number of Addresses per Network*
A	1 (8)	3 (24)	2^{24}
B	2 (16)	2 (16)	2^{16}
C	3 (24)	1 (8)	2^{8}

*There are two reserved host addresses per network. The numbers above do not reflect the two unusable reserved addresses.

For example, Figure 5-11 is a small network with addresses filled in. Network 8.0.0.0 is a Class A network; Network 130.4.0.0 is a Class B network; 199.1.1.0 is a Class C network.

Figure 5-11 *Sample Network Using Class A, B, and C Network Numbers*

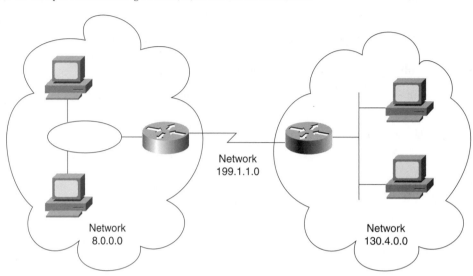

Network numbers look like addresses (canonical decimal format), but they are not assignable to any interface as an IP address. Conceptually, network numbers represent the group of all IP addresses in the network. Numerically, the network number is built with the actual value of the network number in the network part, but all binary 0s in the host part of the address. Given the three examples from Figure 5-11, Table 5-6 provides a closer look at the numerical version of the three network numbers: 8.0.0.0, 199.1.1.0, and 130.4.0.0.

Table 5-6 *Example Network Numbers, Decimal and Binary*

Network Number	Binary Representation, with Host Part Bold
8.0.0.0	0000 1000 **0000 0000 0000 0000 0000 0000**
130.4.0.0	1000 0010 0000 0100 **0000 0000 0000 0000**
199.1.1.0	1100 0111 0000 0001 0000 0001 **0000 0000**

There are many different Class A, B, and C networks. One goal of the writers of RFC 791 was to ensure that an individual IP address would be, by definition, in only one IP network. (In other words, the IP networks defined did not overlap.) So a strategy was used to take half of the address "space" and assign those numbers to the large (Class A) networks. Then, half of the remaining address space (25 percent of the total) was used to create medium sized (Class B) networks. Finally, 50 percent of the remaining space (12.5 percent of the total) was used to define small (Class C) networks. For other address types, for example, Class D multicast addresses, half of the then-remaining addresses were allocated for use. Table 5-7 summarizes the possible network numbers, the total number of each type, and the number of hosts in each Class A, B, and C network.

NOTE   The goal of non-overlapping networks was used to define the valid subnet numbers and is independent from the process of assigning network numbers to different organizations to ensure unique addressing in the Internet.

Table 5-7   *List of All Possible Valid Network Numbers**

Class	Valid Network Numbers	Total Number of This Class of Network	Number of Hosts per Network
A	1.0.0.0 through 126.0.0.0	126	2^{24}, with two reserved
B	128.1.0.0 through 191.254.0.0	2^{14}, minus two special cases	2^{16}, minus two special cases
C	192.0.1.0 through 223.255.254.0	2^{21}, minus two special cases	2^{8}, minus two special cases

* The numeric range just shows the range of mathematically possible addresses. This range includes several reserved values; for example, network 0.0.0.0 (available for use as a broadcast address) and 127.0.0.0 (available for use as the loopback address) are reserved.

The third column in Table 5-7 is sometimes confusing, but it is accurate. The number of networks of a particular class is equal to 2 to the power of the number of bits in the network part of the address. Normally, we think of the network part of a Class A address as 8 bits long, Class B as 16 bits long, and Class C as 24 bits long, and in most cases, that perspective is reasonable. However, when considering the true total number of Class A, B, and C networks, it is useful to consider the nit-picky but accurate fact that a Class A network's first byte always begins with binary 0. Therefore only seven bits are actually considered to comprise the network part of the address. Likewise, Class B networks always begin with binary 10; therefore only 14 bits of the 16 in the first two bytes are considered part of the network number. Similarly, Class C networks always begin with binary 110, and so only 21 bits of the 24 in the first three bytes are considered part of the network number.

NOTE   Perplexed? Examine the binary chart in Appendix A. Look at the binary versions of 1-127 decimal, 128-191, and then 192-223. Notice the ranges begin with 0, 10, and 110, respectively, and that these ranges match the values in the first byte of the three classes of IP networks!

Table 5-8 summarizes the valid values in the first byte of IP addresses and the class of network that is implied by each:

Table 5-8   *Range of First Bytes of Addresses, Class A, B, and C*

Range of First Byte Values, Decimal	Class
1–126	A
128–191	B
192–223	C
224–255	Reserved for other purposes not covered by CCNA; multicast and experimental addresses are in this range.

NOTE   The detail about the true size of the network portions of Class A, B, and C networks is trivia that is highly unlikely to be on the exam; it is included here to make sure you understand Table 5-7.

Masks

The address mask is used for several purposes. One key purpose is to define the number of host bits in an address; when subnetting is not being used, this then implies that the rest of the bits in the address are in the network part of the address. We already know the size of the network and host parts of addresses in each of the three classes of networks. Table 5-9 summarizes those details and adds a reference to the default network masks for each type of network.

Table 5-9   *Class A, B, and C Networks—Network and Host Parts and Default Masks*

Class of Address	Size of Network Part of Address in Bits*	Size of Host Part of Address in Bits	Default Mask for Each Class of Network
A	8	24	255.0.0.0
B	16	16	255.255.0.0
C	24	8	255.255.255.0

* We will treat the network part as is popularly viewed, with 1, 2, and 3 bytes, rather than with the exact but not typically useful view of 7 bits, 14 bits, and 21 bits.

The mask implies the number of host bits in an address. If a bit position in the binary version of the mask has a value of 0, that corresponding bit position in the address is in the host portion of the address. For example, a mask of 255.255.0.0, which has 16 bits of value 1, followed by 16 bits of value 0, implies that there are 16 host bits in the address, which is true of Class B addresses.

Determining Individual Address/Network Associations

Both people and computers need to think about the question, "which network is a particular address a member of?" Humans care because it is useful in troubleshooting, planning, and address assignment; computers need to know because the answer to this question is a vital part of routing. When a computer needs to answer the question, it performs a Boolean math operation called AND between the address in question and the mask. The result of the AND is that the host bits are *masked* out, that is, changed to binary 0s. Look at Table 5-10 for example.

Table 5-10 *Example Dissections of IP Addresses, No Subnetting*

IP Address	Network Part	Host Part	Network Number
8.1.4.5	8	1.4.5	8.0.0.0
130.4.100.1	130.4	100.1	130.4.0.0
199.1.1.4	199.1.1	.4	199.1.1.0
172.100.2.2	172.100	2.2	172.100.0.0

The Boolean AND is performed between the IP address and mask, in binary. Each bit is examined in the address and compared to the corresponding bit in the mask. The AND operation results in a binary 1 if both the address and mask bits are also 1; otherwise, the result is 0. The Boolean AND for the addresses in Table 5-10 is shown in the following examples.

Address	8.1.4.5	0000 1000 0000 0001 0000 0100 0000 0101
Mask	255.0.0.0	1111 1111 **0000 0000 0000 0000 0000 0000**
Result	8.0.0.0	0000 1000 0000 0000 0000 0000 0000 0000

Address	130.4.100.1	1000 0010 0000 0100 0110 0100 0000 0001
Mask	255.255.0.0	1111 1111 1111 1111 **0000 0000 0000 0000**
Result	130.4.0.0	1000 0010 0000 0100 0000 0000 0000 0000

Address	199.1.1.4	1100 0111 0000 0001 0000 0001 0000 0100
Mask	255.255.255.0	1111 1111 1111 1111 1111 1111 **0000 0000**
Result	199.1.1.0	1100 0111 0000 0001 0000 0001 0000 0000

Address	172.100.2.2	1010 1100 0110 0100 0000 0010 0000 0010
Mask	255.255.0.0	1111 1111 1111 1111 **0000 0000 0000 0000**
Result	172.100.0.0	1010 1100 0110 0100 0000 0000 0000 0000

Consider the second example using address 130.4.100.1, mask 255.255.0.0. The binary mask shows 16 binary 1s; any other binary value ANDed with binary 1 yields the original binary value. In other words, any 16-bit number ANDed with 16 binary 1s yields the same number you started with. So, the result shows **1000 0010 0000 0100** for the first 16 bits, which literally could be copied from the binary version of the address. The last 16 bits of the mask are all binary 0s; any value ANDed with a binary 0 yields a 0. So, no matter what value is in the last 16 bits of the address, once ANDed with the mask, the result will be all binary 0s, as shown in the example result. The result is called the *network number* when no subnetting is used; the result is the *subnet number* when subnetting is used.

Broadcast Addresses

As mentioned earlier, there are two reserved numbers in each network. One number is the *network number*, which is used to represent the entire network. The other reserved number is called the *broadcast address*. This number is used to represent all IP addresses in the network. The broadcast address is used when a packet needs to be sent to all hosts in a network. All hosts receiving the packet should notice that the packet is destined for their own network's broadcast address, and process the packet.

The broadcast address for a network is important when planning an IP addressing structure for a network. The reason for that is the following definition:

The network number is the lowest value numerically in that network. The broadcast address is the *largest* value numerically in that network. The valid, assignable addresses in that network are the numbers between the network number and broadcast address.

To derive the broadcast address for a network, use the following list:

1. Write down the network number, in binary.

2. If using a mask of 255.0.0.0, write down the first byte of the network number in binary, underneath the network number.

3. If using a mask of 255.255.0.0, write down the first two bytes of the network number in binary, underneath the network number.

4. If using a mask of 255.255.255.0, write down the first three bytes of the network number in binary, underneath the network number.

5. Complete the broadcast address by writing down all binary 1s in the remaining bits in the number created in Steps 2, 3, or 4.

Any number between the first number (network number) and second number (broadcast address) is an assignable IP address in this network. Each binary number will need to be converted to a decimal eight bits at a time, to show the addresses in decimal form.

Table 5-11 shows an example for the binary view.

Table 5-11 *Process for Deriving the Network Broadcast Address, in Binary.*

Step Number	What Is Written on the Paper After This Step
1	1000 0110 1000 1101 0000 0000 0000 0000 (network 134.141.0.0)
	xxxx xxxx xxxx xxxx xxxx xxxx xxxx xxxx (broadcast)
3 (steps 2 and 4 not applicable)	1000 0110 1000 1101 0000 0000 0000 0000 (network)
	1000 0110 1000 1101 *xxxx xxxx xxxx xxxx* (broadcast)
5	1000 0110 1000 1101 0000 0000 0000 0000 (network)
	1000 0110 1000 1101 *1111 1111 1111 1111* (broadcast) (134.141.255.255)

IP Subnetting

Almost every organization with a network uses IP, and almost every one of these organizations uses subnetting. Subnetting is simply the process of treating subdivisions of a single Class A, B, or C network as if it were a network itself. By doing so, a single Class A, B, or C network can be subdivided into many nonoverlapping subnets. There are two main reasons why organizations choose to use subnets, rather than just using lots of Class A, B, and C networks:

- The grouping concept in IP required that hosts in the same group not be separated by a router.

- Conversely, IP routing requires that hosts separated by a router must be in a different group (subnet). Without subnetting, that means each group would need to be a different Class A, B, or C network, which would be impractical if the organization is directly connected to the Internet, considering the lack of currently unassigned networks the NIC has available.

Consider all network interfaces in Figure 5-12 and note which ones are not separated by a router.

Figure 5-12 *Backdrop for Discussing Numbers of Different Networks/Subnets*

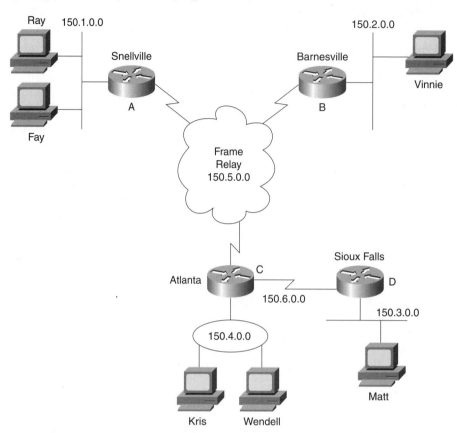

In Figure 5-12, six groupings exist. Four groups are more obvious, those being the set of all interfaces attached to each of the four LANs. In other words, the LANs attached to Routers A, B, C, and D are each a separate subnet. Additionally, the two serial interfaces composing the point-to-point serial link between Routers C and D are both in the same group because they are not separated by a router. Finally, the three router interfaces composing the Frame relay network between Routers A, B, and C would not be separated by an IP router and would compose the sixth group.

If building this network today, the NIC would not assign six separate network numbers. Instead, you might get a couple of Class C networks assigned by the NIC, with the expectation that you would use subnetting.

Definition of Subnetting

There are probably about eight ways to explain subnetting, none of which makes sense to all people. I personally have probably explained subnetting over 100 times in classrooms and countless more sitting around a board with clients. So, in this text I will include one more intuitive perspective on subnetting, and one exact binary perspective on subnetting. The first should help those new to subnetting learn more quickly, and the second perspective will prepare anyone for more advanced subnetting topics.

Subnets are subdivisions of a Class A, B, or C network. These subdivisions take on the properties of a network in many ways:

- Members of one subnet have the same numeric value in the subnet parts of the addresses.

- Members of one subnet cannot be separated by a router.

- Members of a second subnet must be separated from the first subnet by a router.

Two of the more popular views of subnetting follow.

Pretending the Network Part of the Address is Longer Than When Not Subnetting

One method that is typically easier to understand for those less inclined to enjoy binary math is *to pretend that the network field is longer than the Class A, B, and C rules imply.* For example, network 8.0.0.0 might be assigned. The organization treats it like a Class C address, with 24 network bits, and 8 host bits. The real NIC could care less; it is assigned you network 8.0.0.0, and it is happy! But inside your organization, someone must assign the different subnet numbers, like the NIC would have done. For example, imagine your organization has Class B network 150.150.0.0, and you want to treat it as a Class C network for the purposes of subnetting. Figure 5-13 shows one way to implement that idea.

Continuing with the "pretending" view of subnetting, the subnet numbers shown behave like Class C networks. These subnets are actually subnets of a Class B network; do not fall into the trap of thinking they have magically become Class C networks! All hosts beginning with 150.150.1 must be on the Router A Ethernet; all Frame Relay interface addresses must begin 150.150.5, and so on.

The two examples shown here use *basic* subnetting. *Basic* is a term used for our purposes in this book, and it denotes subnetting examples for which the math is easy. (More advanced subnetting is covered later in this section.)

Figure 5-13 *Using Subnets*

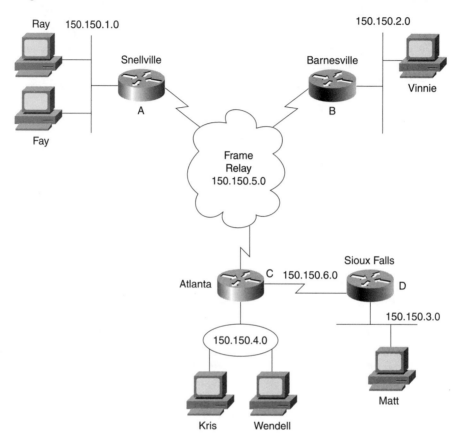

Binary View of Subnetting

The benefit of a binary definition of subnetting is that it is exact. For a full understanding of subnetting, particularly more advanced subnetting topics, as well as other IP addressing and routing topics beyond the scope of this book, an exact definition is required. If your job will include planning subnet number assignment, or troubleshooting, this binary understanding will be useful.

A review of some basic concepts used when not using subnetting can be used as a comparison to subnetting. When not subnetting, the default mask defined the number of host bits. The mask accomplished this by simply using binary 0 for each bit position in the mask that corresponded to the host part of the address in question. For example, the mask 255.255.0.0 (Class B) has a value of all binary 0s in the last 16 bits. This implies 16 network bits at the beginning of the address. The following list summarizes basic concepts when not using subnetting:

- The mask defines the number of host bits in the host part of an address.

- Class A, B, and C rules define the number of network bits in the network part of the address.

- Without subnetting, these two field (network and host) compose the entire 32-bit address.

- Each host address in the network has the same value in the network part of the address.

- Each host address in the network has a unique value in the host part of the address. (For example, 130.1.1.1 and 130.1.1.2 are in the same network, but can be assigned to two different network interfaces.)

Subnetting creates a third part of the address, called the *subnet field* or *subnet part*. For example, using network 150.150.0.0 again, assume that you want a third field called the subnet field. Several assertions are true in this case:

- The Class A, B, and C network field sizes cannot be changed; they remain as 8, 16, and 24 bits, respectively.

- The IP address must still be 32 bits in length.

- Therefore, to create a third field called the subnet part of the address, *some of the bits previously in the host part of the address are used.*

The subnet part of an address identifies the different subdivisions of this network. An address with a different value in the subnet field, as compared with a second address, is considered to be in a different subnet. For example, examine the following three IP addresses that would be part of Table 5-12.

Table 5-12 *Subnet Part of Sample Addresses*

Address in Decimal	Address in Binary
150.150.2.1	1001 0110 1001 0110 **0000 0010** 0000 0001
150.150.2.2	1001 0110 1001 0110 **0000 0010** 0000 0010
150.150.4.4	1001 0110 1001 0110 **0000 0100** 0000 0100

The example defines that the subnet field consists of bits 17–24 (the entire third byte). 150.150.2.1 and 150.150.2.2 are in the same subnet because they are in the same Class B network, and *their subnet fields have the same value* (0000 0010). 150.150.4.4 is in a different subnet of the same Class B network because the subnet field has a different value than the first two addresses (0000 0100). 150.150.4.4 must be physically located with at least one IP router between itself and 150.150.2.1 and 150.150.2.2.

The three different parts of an address need to be defined. Class A, B, or C rules are applied to define the size of the network part of the addresses. The subnet mask will be used for several purposes, including defining the number of host bits in the host part of an address. The remaining part of the address is the subnet part of the address. The following list summarizes these rules, along with a few other useful corollaries:

- The mask defines the number of host bits in the host part of an address, located at the end of the address.

- Class A, B, and C rules define the number of network bits in the network part of the address, located at the beginning of the address.

- With subnetting, the number of network and host fields total less than 32 bits. The remaining bit positions compose the subnet field and are located between the other two fields.

- Each host address in the network has the same value in the network part of the address.

- Each host address in the same subnet has a unique value in the host part of the address, but the same value in the network and subnet parts of the addresses.

In other words, the subnet mask does not define the size of the subnet field; it defines the size of the host field. The class rules define the size of the network part of the address. Finally, the bits left over between the network and host parts of the address compose the subnet part of the address.

Subnetting Terminology

The terminology used when subnetting is very similar to the terminology used when not subnetting. To ensure a full understanding of subnetting, review the terms defined in Table 5-13.

Table 5-13 *Subnetting Terminology*

Term	Definition
Network number	A number representing a group of hosts, whose network parts of their addresses are identical. Either 1, 2, or 3 bytes are identical, depending on whether the network is a Class A, B, or C network, respectively.
Subnet number	A number representing a group of hosts, whose network and subnet parts are identical. Many people in fact treat the network and subnet parts as one large part of the address because hosts in this same subnet have the same value in this large "subnet" part of the address.
Network address	Another term for network Number.
Subnet address	Another term for subnet Number

Table 5-13 *Subnetting Terminology (Continued)*

Term	Definition
Mask	32-bit binary number, usually written in canonical decimal form, used for two purposes. First, it defines the number of host bits in a particular address by having a value of binary 0 in the mask for each bit in the address that is considered to be in the host part of the address. The second feature is that the mask is used by computers using a Boolean AND operation to derive the network number of which an individual address is a member.
Default mask	The mask used by Class A, B, and C networks, that implies 24, 16, and 8 host bits, respectively.
Subnet mask	The subnet mask still defines the number of host bits in the addresses and is used by computers to compute the subnet number that an address is a member of, by performing a Boolean AND of the address and the subnet mask. This mask is used by an organization for a network, in which there are fewer host bits than the default mask. This creates a subnet part of the address.
Host address	IP address assigned to some interface. It cannot be the same number as any network number, and it cannot be the same number as any subnet number.
IP address	Another name for host address.

Dissecting IP Addresses: Deriving Subnet Numbers

In most organizations, a few people plan the subnetting scheme for the organization, but many others need to understand the subnetting scheme. Planning requires more abstract thought; however, for operating and troubleshooting an IP network, one particular skill relating to addressing is needed more than any other. That skill is the ability to quickly answer this question:

Given an IP address, what subnet is it a member of?

This section reviews the steps a computer uses to accomplish this goal. Table 5-14 lists several examples.

Table 5-14 *Subnetting Examples*

IP Address	Subnet Mask	Network and Subnet Part*	Full Subnet Number
8.1.4.5	255.255.0.0	8.1	8.1.0.0
130.4.100.1	255.255.255.0	130.4.100	130.4.100.0
199.1.1.4	255.255.255.0	199.1.1	199.1.1.0**
172.100.2.2	255.255.255.0	172.100.2	172.100.2.0
17.9.44.3	255.255.255.0	17.9.44	17.9.44.0

*The third column of Table 5-14 can be thought of as the second or third steps in the human algorithm that follows.
**This example shows a Class C address, with default mask. No subnetting is in use in this case!

Computers derive the subnet number by using a Boolean AND. When more difficult subnetting is addressed, understanding the process will be useful because the human algorithm is not so obvious in some cases. The process to derive the subnet numbers is as follows:

1. Convert the IP address and subnet mask to binary.

2. Perform a Boolean AND operation on each pair of bits (first bit in the address and mask, second bit in the address and mask, and so on).

3. Convert the resulting number back to canonical decimal.

Two of these steps require binary-to-decimal or decimal-to-binary conversion. Appendix A contains a binary-to-decimal conversion chart on page 531.

Repeating the same samples from Table 5-14, using the Boolean AND delivers the following results:

Address	8.1.4.5	0000 1000 0000 0001 0000 0100 0000 0101
Mask	255.255.0.0	1111 1111 1111 1111 **0000 0000 0000 0000**
Result	8.1.0.0	0000 1000 0000 0001 0000 0000 0000 0000

Address	130.4.100.1	1000 0010 0000 0100 0110 0100 0000 0001
Mask	255.255.255.0	1111 1111 1111 1111 1111 1111 **0000 0000**
Result	130.4.100.0	1000 0010 0000 0100 0110 0100 0000 0000

Address	199.1.1.4	1100 0111 0000 0001 0000 0001 0000 0100
Mask	255.255.255.0	1111 1111 1111 1111 1111 1111 **0000 0000**
Result	199.1.1.0	1100 0111 0000 0001 0000 0001 0000 0000

Address	172.100.2.2	1010 1100 0110 0100 0000 0010 0000 0010
Mask	255.255.255.0	1111 1111 1111 1111 1111 1111 **0000 0000**
Result	172.100.2.0	1010 1100 0110 0100 0000 0010 0000 0000

Address	17.9.44.3	0001 0001 0000 1001 0010 1100 0000 0011
Mask	255.255.255.0	1111 1111 1111 1111 1111 1111 **0000 0000**
Result	17.9.44.0	0001 0001 0000 1001 0010 1100 0000 0000

An example network will be used as a backdrop to discuss this binary of subnetting. Figure 5-14 illustrates six different subnets. Table 5-15 provides the list of subnet numbers.

Table 5-15 *Siberian Subnets*

Location of Subnet Geographically	Subnet Mask	Subnet Number
Ethernet off router in Barnaul	255.255.255.0	180.4.1.0
Ethernet off router in Nova	255.255.255.0	180.4.3.0
Token Ring off router in Gorno	255.255.0.0	8.7.0.0
Serial link between Barnaul and Nova	255.255.255.0	180.4.2.0
Serial link between Barnaul and Gorno	255.255.255.0	180.4.4.0
Serial link between Nova and Gorno	255.255.255.0	180.4.6.0

Figure 5-14 *Siberian CCNA Sample Network*

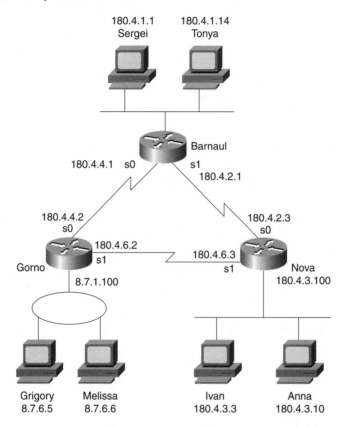

Keep in mind that all the addresses on the same data link must be in the same subnet. For example, Ivan and Anna must be in the same subnet, so performing either the easy human algorithm, or the more involved computer algorithm, on either address, will yield the same subnet number, 180.4.3.0. If the answers are unclear, do several of these using the algorithm used by computers. For example, using Ivan:

Address	180.4.3.3	1011 0100 0000 0100 0000 0011 0000 0011
Mask	255.255.255.0	1111 1111 1111 1111 1111 1111 **0000 0000**
Result	180.4.3.0	1011 0100 0000 0100 0000 0011 0000 0000

For additional practice, you may want to go to the scenarios section at the end of the chapter, specifically to Scenarios 5-2 and 5-3.

Subnet mask values can have something besides 255 or 0 in the decimal version of the mask. To speed up the process of examining these addresses (in case you are taking a timed test), memorizing the decimal and binary numbers in Table 5-16 will be useful.

Table 5-16   *Typical Mask Values*

Decimal	Binary
0	0000 0000
128	1000 0000
192	1100 0000
224	1110 0000
240	1111 0000
248	1111 1000
252	1111 1100
254	1111 1110
255	1111 1111

The biggest obstacle to understanding this step is failing to realize this one fact:

Binary-decimal-binary conversion is independent of the size of the network, subnet, and host fields. Conversion always is from one decimal number to 8 binary digits, and vice versa.

Typically, an example usually helps. Consider the following binary example:

Address	8.1.100.5	0000 1000 0000 0001 0110 0100 0000 0101
Mask	255.255.240.0	1111 1111 1111 1111 1111 0000 0000 0000
Result	8.1.96.0	0000 1000 0000 0001 0110 0000 0000 0000

Ignoring the decimal numbers on the left, a slow examination of the binary address, mask, and Boolean AND result shows that the conversion to binary and AND are correct as shown. The typical difficulty for those accustomed to thinking of IP addresses in decimal only is the last step, the step of conversion. Many want to convert the 12-bit host field to a decimal number and the 4-bit subnet field to a decimal number. Instead, for the last step (conversion to decimal), take the first 8-bit set and convert it to decimal (0000 1000 converted to decimal 8). Likewise, take the second 8-bit set (the second byte), and convert it to decimal (0000 0001 converted to decimal 1). Take the entire third byte, and convert to decimal (0110 0000 converted to decimal 96). Finally, take the entire last byte, and convert to decimal (0000 0000 converted to decimal 0). The third byte contains the entire subnet field and part of the host field; the conversion ignores these boundaries, always using byte boundaries.

The following examples are shown as additional examples of deriving the subnet number when a more difficult mask is used:

Address	130.4.100.1	1000 0010 0000 0100 0110 0100 0000 0001
Mask	255.255.255.128	1111 1111 1111 1111 1111 1111 1000 0000
Result	130.4.100.0	1000 0010 0000 0100 0110 0100 0000 0000

Address	199.1.1.4	1100 0111 0000 0001 0000 0001 0000 0100
Mask	255.255.255.224	1111 1111 1111 1111 1111 1111 1110 0000
Result	199.1.1.0	1100 0111 0000 0001 0000 0001 0000 0000

Address	172.100.201.2	1010 1100 0110 0100 1100 1001 0000 0010
Mask	255.255.254.0	1111 1111 1111 1111 1111 1110 0000 0000
Result	172.100.200.0	1010 1100 0110 0100 1100 1000 0000 0000

Address	17.9.44.70	0001 0001 0000 1001 0010 1100 0100 0110
Mask	255.255.255.192	1111 1111 1111 1111 1111 1111 1100 0000
Result	17.9.44.64	0001 0001 0000 1001 0010 1100 0100 0000

Dissecting IP Addresses: Deriving Broadcast Addresses

The broadcast address for a subnet is very similar to the broadcast address for a Class A, B, or C network. The subnet broadcast address is an address that implies all IP hosts in that subnet. The math used to derive the broadcast address is also very similar to the math used when no subnetting is in use.

A revised observation about broadcast addresses and their importance is as follows:

The subnet number is the lowest value numerically in that subnet. The subnet broadcast address is the largest value numerically in that subnet. The valid, assignable addresses in that subnet are the numbers between the subnet number and subnet broadcast address.

To derive the broadcast address for a subnet, use the following litany:

1. Write down the subnet number, in binary.

2. Immediately below the subnet number, transcribe the bits from the network and subnet portions of the subnet number. (In other words, copy the network and subnet parts, ignoring the host part.)

3. Complete the broadcast address by writing down all binary 1s in the remaining bits in the number created in Step 2. This places all binary 1s in the host part of the broadcast address, which is a required feature of every subnet broadcast address.

Any number between the first number (subnet number) and second number (subnet broadcast address) is an assignable IP address in this subnet. Each binary number will be converted to decimal, eight bits at a time, to show the addresses in decimal. Table 5-17 shows an example for the binary view.

Table 5-17 *Process for Deriving the Network Broadcast Address, in Binary, Mask 255.255.255.0*

Step Number	What Is Written on the Paper After This Step
1	1000 0110 1000 1101 0000 0101 0000 0000 (subnet 134.141.5.0)
	xxxx xxxx xxxx xxxx xxxx xxxx xxxx xxxx (broadcast)
2	1000 0110 1000 1101 0000 0101 0000 0000 (subnet)
	1000 0110 1000 1101 0000 0101 *xxxx xxxx* (broadcast)
3	1000 0110 1000 1101 0000 0101 0000 0000 (subnet)
	1000 0110 1000 1101 0000 0101 *1111 1111* (broadcast 134.141.5.255)

Several examples are listed next for practice.

Address	8.1.4.5	0000 1000 0000 0001 0000 0100 0000 0101
Mask	255.255.0.0	1111 1111 1111 1111 **0000 0000 0000 0000**
Subnet	8.1.0.0	0000 1000 0000 0001 0000 0000 0000 0000
Broadcast	8.1.255.255	0000 1000 0000 0001 **1111 1111 1111 1111**

Address	130.4.100.1	1000 0010 0000 0100 0110 0100 0000 0001
Mask	255.255.255.0	1111 1111 1111 1111 1111 1111 **0000 0000**
Subnet	130.4.100.0	1000 0010 0000 0100 0110 0100 0000 0000
Broadcast	130.4.100.255	1000 0010 0000 0100 0110 0100 **1111 1111**

Address	199.1.1.4	1100 0111 0000 0001 0000 0001 0000 0100
Mask	255.255.255.0	1111 1111 1111 1111 1111 1111 **0000 0000**
Subnet	199.1.1.0	1100 0111 0000 0001 0000 0001 0000 0000
Broadcast	199.1.1.255	1100 0111 0000 0001 0000 0001 **1111 1111**

Address	130.4.100.1	1000 0010 0000 0100 0110 0100 0000 0001
Mask	255.255.255.128	1111 1111 1111 1111 1111 1111 1000 0000
Subnet	130.4.100.0	1000 0010 0000 0100 0110 0100 0000 0000
Broadcast	130.4.100.127	1000 0010 0000 0100 0110 0100 **0111 1111**

Address	199.1.1.4	1100 0111 0000 0001 0000 0001 0000 0100
Mask	255.255.255.224	1111 1111 1111 1111 1111 1111 1110 0000
Subnet	199.1.1.0	1100 0111 0000 0001 0000 0001 0000 0000
Broadcast	199.1.1.31	1100 0111 0000 0001 0000 0001 000**1 1111**

Configuration of IP

CCNA Objectives Covered in This Section

31	Configure IP addresses.
32	Verify IP addresses.

Configuration of TCP/IP in a Cisco router is straightforward. Table 5-18 and Table 5-19 summarize the commands used in Training Paths 1 and 2 for IP configuration and verification. Two samples, with both configuration and EXEC command output, follow. The Cisco IOS documentation and the Cisco Press book, *Cisco IOS Configuration Fundamentals*, are excellent references for commands and options not covered here.

Table 5-18 *IP Configuration Commands in Training Paths 1 and 2*

Command	Configuration Mode
ip address *ip-address mask* [**secondary**]	Interface mode
ip host *name address*	Global
ip route *subnet mask* {*next-hop-router\output-interface*}	Global
ip name-server *ip-address* [*ip-address* [*ip-address* [*ip-address*…]]]	Global
ip domain-lookup	Global
ip routing	Global
ip netmask-format {**bitcount** I **decimal** I **hexadecimal**}	Interface mode

Table 5-19 *IP EXEC Commands in Training Paths 1 and 2*

Command	Function
show interfaces	Interface statistics, including IP address
show ip interface	Detailed view of IP parameter settings, per interface
show interfaces ip-brief	Summary of all interfaces and their IP addresses
show ip route [*subnet*]	Shows entire routing table, or one entry if subnet is entered
show ip arp	Displays IP ARP cache
debug ip packet	Issues log messages for each IP packet
terminal ip netmask-format {**bitcount** I **decimal** I **hexadecimal**}	Sets type of display for subnet masks in show commands
ping	Sends and receives ICMP echo messages to verify connectivity
trace	Sends series of ICMP echos with increasing TTL values, to verify the current route to a host

Collectively, Figure 5-15, along with Example 5-2, Example 5-3, and Example 5-4, show three sites, each with two serial links and one Ethernet. The following site guidelines were used when choosing configuration details:

- Use name servers at 10.1.1.100 and 10.1.2.100.

- Use host names from Figure 5-15.

- Router's IP addresses to be assigned from the last few valid IP addresses in their attached subnets.

Figure 5-15 *TCP/IP Configuration and Verifications*

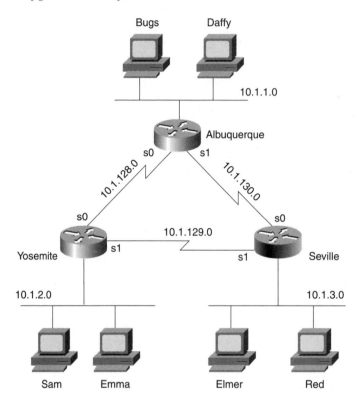

Example 5-2 *Albuquerque Router Configuration and EXEC Commands*

```
Albuquerque# show running-config
Building configuration...

Current configuration:
!
version 11.2

hostname Albuquerque
!
enable secret 5 $1$skrN$z4oq6OHfB6zu1WG4P/6ZY0
!
ip name-server 10.1.1.100
ip name-server 10.1.2.100
!
interface Serial0
 ip address 10.1.128.251 255.255.255.0
!
interface Serial1
 ip address 10.1.130.251 255.255.255.0
```

Example 5-2   *Albuquerque Router Configuration and EXEC Commands (Continued)*

```
 clockrate 1300000
!
interface Ethernet0
 ip address 10.1.1.251 255.255.255.0
!
no ip classless
banner motd ^C
  Should've taken a left turn here! This is Albuquerque...  ^C
!
line con 0
 password cisco
 login
line aux 0
line vty 0 4
 password cisco
 login
!
end

Albuquerque# show ip route
Codes: C - connected, S - static, I - IGRP, R - RIP, M - mobile, B - BGP
       D - EIGRP, EX - EIGRP external, O - OSPF, IA - OSPF inter area
       N1 - OSPF NSSA external type 1, N2 - OSPF NSSA external type 2
       E1 - OSPF external type 1, E2 - OSPF external type 2, E - EGP
       i - IS-IS, L1 - IS-IS level-1, L2 - IS-IS level-2, * - candidate default
       U - per-user static route, o - ODR

Gateway of last resort is not set

     10.0.0.0/24 is subnetted, 3 subnets
C       10.1.1.0 is directly connected, Ethernet0
C       10.1.130.0 is directly connected, Serial1
C       10.1.128.0 is directly connected, Serial0

Albuquerque#terminal ip netmask-format decimal
Albuquerque#show ip route
Codes: C - connected, S - static, I - IGRP, R - RIP, M - mobile, B - BGP
       D - EIGRP, EX - EIGRP external, O - OSPF, IA - OSPF inter area
       N1 - OSPF NSSA external type 1, N2 - OSPF NSSA external type 2
       E1 - OSPF external type 1, E2 - OSPF external type 2, E - EGP
       i - IS-IS, L1 - IS-IS level-1, L2 - IS-IS level-2, * - candidate default
       U - per-user static route, o - ODR

Gateway of last resort is not set

     10.0.0.0 255.255.255.0 is subnetted, 3 subnets
C       10.1.1.0 is directly connected, Ethernet0
C       10.1.130.0 is directly connected, Serial1C
 10.1.128.0 is directly connected, Serial0
Albuquerque#
```

Example 5-3 *Yosemite Router Configuration and EXEC Commands*

```
Yosemite# show running-config
Building configuration...

Current configuration:
!
version 11.2

hostname Yosemite
!
enable secret 5 $1$.Iud$7uHqWzDYgvJN09V7HSkLZ/
!
ip name-server 10.1.1.100
ip name-server 10.1.2.100
!
interface Serial0
 ip address 10.1.128.252 255.255.255.0
 no fair-queue
 clockrate 1300000
!
interface Serial1
 ip address 10.1.129.252 255.255.255.0
!
interface Ethernet0
 ip address 10.1.2.252 255.255.255.0
!
no ip classless
banner motd ^C
    This is the Rootin-est Tootin-est Router in these here parts!   ^C
!
line con 0
 password cisco
 login
line aux 0
line vty 0 4
 password cisco
 login
!
end

Yosemite#show ip interface brief
Interface              IP-Address      OK? Method Status                Protocol
Serial0                10.1.128.252    YES manual up                    up
Serial1                10.1.129.252    YES manual up                    up
Ethernet0              10.1.2.252      YES manual up                    up
Yosemite#
```

Example 5-4 *Seville Router Configuration and EXEC Commands*

```
Seville# show running-config
Building configuration...
```

Example 5-4 *Seville Router Configuration and EXEC Commands (Continued)*

```
Current configuration:
!
version 11.2
!
!
hostname Seville
!
enable secret 5 $1$ZvR/$Gpk5a5K5vTVpotd3KUygA1
!
ip name-server 10.1.1.100
ip name-server 10.1.2.100
!
interface Serial0
 ip address 10.1.130.253 255.255.255.0
 no fair-queue
!
interface Serial1
 ip address 10.1.129.253 255.255.255.0
clockrate 1300000
!
Ethernet0
 ip address 10.1.3.253 255.255.255.0
!
no ip classless
banner motd ^C
  Take a little off the top, Wabbit!  (Elmer)    ^C
!
line con 0
 password cisco
 login
line aux 0
line vty 0 4
 password cisco
 login
!
end

Seville#show ip route
Codes: C - connected, S - static, I - IGRP, R - RIP, M - mobile, B - BGP
       D - EIGRP, EX - EIGRP external, O - OSPF, IA - OSPF inter area
       N1 - OSPF NSSA external type 1, N2 - OSPF NSSA external type 2
       E1 - OSPF external type 1, E2 - OSPF external type 2, E - EGP
       i - IS-IS, L1 - IS-IS level-1, L2 - IS-IS level-2, * - candidate default
       U - per-user static route, o - ODR

Gateway of last resort is not set
```

continues

Example 5-4 *Seville Router Configuration and EXEC Commands (Continued)*

```
       10.0.0.0/24 is subnetted, 3 subnets
C       10.1.3.0 is directly connected, Ethernet0
C       10.1.130.0 is directly connected, Serial0
C       10.1.129.0 is directly connected, Serial1
Seville#show ip interface brief
Interface             IP-Address      OK? Method Status           Protocol
Serial0               10.1.130.253    YES manual up               up
Serial1               10.1.129.253    YES manual up               up
Ethernet0             10.1.3.253      YES manual up               up
Seville#show interface serial 0
Serial0 is up, line protocol is up
  Hardware is HD64570
  Internet address is 10.1.130.253/24
  MTU 1500 bytes, BW 1544 Kbit, DLY 20000 usec, rely 255/255, load 1/255
  Encapsulation HDLC, loopback not set, keepalive set (10 sec)
  Last input 00:00:05, output 00:00:04, output hang never
  Last clearing of "show interface" counters never
  Queueing strategy: fifo
  Output queue 0/40, 0 drops; input queue 0/75, 0 drops
  5 minute input rate 0 bits/sec, 0 packets/sec
  5 minute output rate 0 bits/sec, 0 packets/sec
     273 packets input, 18621 bytes, 0 no buffer
     Received 215 broadcasts, 0 runts, 0 giants, 0 throttles
     0 input errors, 0 CRC, 0 frame, 0 overrun, 0 ignored, 0 abort
     309 packets output, 20175 bytes, 0 underruns
     0 output errors, 0 collisions, 23 interface resets
     0 output buffer failures, 0 output buffers swapped out
     0 carrier transitions
     DCD=up  DSR=up  DTR=up  RTS=up  CTS=up
Seville#
```

Notice that the configuration matches the output of the **show interface**, **show ip interface**, and **show interface ip brief** commands. If these details did not match, one common oversight is that you are looking at the configuration in NVRAM, not in RAM. Make sure to use the **show running-config** or **write terminal** commands to see the active configuration.

The subnet mask in the output of **show** commands is encoded by numbering the network and subnet bits, for example, 10.1.4.0/24 meaning 24 network and subnet bits, leaving eight host bits with this subnetting scheme. The **terminal ip netmask** command can be used to change this formatting.

The routing table does not list all subnets because the routing protocol configuration has not been added. Notice the **show ip route** commands list routes to the directly attached subnets, but no others. The **ip route** commands in the following example (Example 5-5) have been added to Albuquerque. Example 5-6 and Example 5-7 contain **show** commands executed after the new configuration was added.

Example 5-5 *Static Routes Added to Albuquerque*

```
ip route 10.1.2.0 255.255.255.0 10.1.128.252
ip route 10.1.3.0 255.255.255.0 10.1.130.253
```

Example 5-6 *Albuquerque Router EXEC Commands, After Adding Static Routes for 10.1.2.0 and 10.1.3.0*

```
Albuquerque#show ip route
Codes: C - connected, S - static, I - IGRP, R - RIP, M - mobile, B - BGP
       D - EIGRP, EX - EIGRP external, O - OSPF, IA - OSPF inter area
       N1 - OSPF NSSA external type 1, N2 - OSPF NSSA external type 2
       E1 - OSPF external type 1, E2 - OSPF external type 2, E - EGP
       i - IS-IS, L1 - IS-IS level-1, L2 - IS-IS level-2, * - candidate default
       U - per-user static route, o - ODR

Gateway of last resort is not set

     10.0.0.0/24 is subnetted, 5 subnets
S       10.1.3.0 [1/0] via 10.1.128.253
S       10.1.2.0 [1/0] via 10.1.128.252
C       10.1.1.0 is directly connected, Ethernet0
C       10.1.130.0 is directly connected, Serial1
C       10.1.128.0 is directly connected, Serial0
Albuquerque#ping 10.1.128.252

Type escape sequence to abort.
Sending 5, 100-byte ICMP Echos to 10.1.128.252, timeout is 2 seconds:
!!!!!
Success rate is 100 percent (5/5), round-trip min/avg/max = 4/4/8 ms

! Note: the following extended ping command will result in some debug messages
! on Yosemite in Example 5-7.

Albuquerque#ping
Protocol [ip]:
Target IP address: 10.1.2.252
Repeat count [5]:
Datagram size [100]:
Timeout in seconds [2]:
Extended commands [n]: y
Source address or interface: 10.1.1.251
Type of service [0]:
Set DF bit in IP header? [no]:
Validate reply data? [no]:
Data pattern [0xABCD]:
Loose, Strict, Record, Timestamp, Verbose[none]:
Sweep range of sizes [n]:
Type escape sequence to abort.
Sending 5, 100-byte ICMP Echos to 10.1.2.252, timeout is 2 seconds:
. . . . .
Success rate is 0 percent (0/5)
Albuquerque#
```

Example 5-7 *show ip route on Yosemite, After Adding Static Routes to Albuquerque*

```
Yosemite#show ip route
Codes: C - connected, S - static, I - IGRP, R - RIP, M - mobile, B - BGP
       D - EIGRP, EX - EIGRP external, O - OSPF, IA - OSPF inter area
       N1 - OSPF NSSA external type 1, N2 - OSPF NSSA external type 2
       E1 - OSPF external type 1, E2 - OSPF external type 2, E - EGP
       i - IS-IS, L1 - IS-IS level-1, L2 - IS-IS level-2, * - candidate default
       U - per-user static route, o - ODR

Gateway of last resort is not set

     10.0.0.0/24 is subnetted, 3 subnets
C       10.1.2.0 is directly connected, Ethernet0
C       10.1.129.0 is directly connected, Serial1
C       10.1.128.0 is directly connected, Serial0
Yosemite#ping 10.1.128.251

Type escape sequence to abort.
Sending 5, 100-byte ICMP Echos to 10.1.128.251, timeout is 2 seconds:
!!!!!
Success rate is 100 percent (5/5), round-trip min/avg/max = 4/4/8 ms
Yosemite#ping 10.1.1.251

Type escape sequence to abort.
Sending 5, 100-byte ICMP Echos to 10.1.1.251, timeout is 2 seconds:
.....
Success rate is 0 percent (0/5)
Yosemite#debug ip icmp
ICMP packet debugging is on
Yosemite#
Yosemite#show debug
Generic IP:
  ICMP packet debugging is on
Yosemite#

!NOTE: the following debug messages are a result of the extended ping
!command issued on Albuquerque in example 5-6 above;
!these messages are generated by Yosemite!

ICMP: echo reply sent, src 10.1.2.252, dst 10.1.1.251
ICMP: echo reply sent, src 10.1.2.252, dst 10.1.1.251
ICMP: echo reply sent, src 10.1.2.252, dst 10.1.1.251
ICMP: echo reply sent, src 10.1.2.252, dst 10.1.1.251
ICMP: echo reply sent, src 10.1.2.252, dst 10.1.1.251
```

Two subtleties of the **ping** command are used in these two example console dialogs:

- Cisco **ping** commands use the output interface's IP address as the source address of the packet, unless otherwise specified in an extended ping. The first ping in Example 5-7 uses a source of 10.1.128.251; the extended **ping** uses the source address shown.

- ICMP echo reply messages (ping responses) reverse the IP addresses used in the ICMP echo request it is responding to.

A common oversight made more obvious by this last example is that a **ping** from a router may work when a **ping** from a host may not. The extended **ping** command on Albuquerque sent an echo request from 10.1.1.251 to 10.1.2.252; no response was received by Albuquerque. However, it appears that the ICMP echo requests were received by Yosemite because the debug messages on Yosemite imply that it sent ICMP echo replies back to 10.1.1.251, which is Albuquerque's Ethernet IP address. Somewhere between Yosemite's creating the ICMP echo replies and Albuquerque's receiving them, a problem occurred.

An examination of the steps after the echo replies are created by Yosemite is needed to understand the problem. ICMP will ask the IP code in Yosemite to deliver the packets. The IP code will perform IP routing table look-up to find the correct route for these packets, whose destination is 10.1.1.251. However, the **show ip route** command output in Example 5-7 shows that Yosemite has not routed to subnet 10.1.1.0. It seems that Yosemite created the echo reply messages, but failed to send them because it has no route to 10.1.1.0/24. This is just one example where the route in one direction is working fine, but the route in the reverse direction is not!

One key to troubleshooting with the **ping** command is an understanding of the various codes the command uses to signify the various responses it can receive. Table 5-20 lists the various codes that the Cisco IOS **ping** command can supply.

Table 5-20 *Explanation of the Codes the **ping** Command Receives in Response to Its ICMP Echo Request*

ping Command Code	Explanation
!	ICMP Echo reply received.
.	Nothing received.
U	ICMP unreachable (destination) received.
N	ICMP unreachable (network) received.
P	ICMP unreachable (port) received.
Q	ICMP Source Quench received.
M	ICMP Can't fragment message received.
?	Unknown packet received.

Using Secondary Addresses

Multiple subnets can be allowed to exist on the same data link; to support this type of design, Cisco uses secondary addressing. Secondary addressing is useful in some cases, but can be particularly confusing to people troubleshooting the network.

When most or all IP addresses in a subnet have been assigned, several solutions for continuing growth exist; the use of secondary addressing is one solution. One alternative solution is to change the mask used on that subnet, making the existing subnet larger. However, changing the mask may cause an overlap. For example, if 10.1.4.0/24 is running out of addresses, and a change to mask 255.255.254.0 (9 host bits, 23 network/subnet bits) is chosen, an overlap occurs. 10.1.4.0/23 includes addresses 10.1.4.0–10.1.5.255; this is indeed an overlap with the currently existing 10.1.5.0/24. Another alternative for continued growth is to change all the existing addresses in the mostly full subnet to be in another larger subnet. There must be a valid larger subnet number that is unassigned and does not create an overlap. However, this solution causes administrative effort. In either case, both solutions that do not use secondary addressing imply a strategy of using variable-length subnet masks (VLSMs), which brings up another set of complex routing protocol issues.

Secondary IP addressing is simple for the degree needed to succeed on the CCNA exam. The protocol flows for hosts on the same media but in different subnets are more involved, and may require that a router forward packets between such hosts. (These flows are not considered in the Training Paths, and are not covered here.) Because more than one subnet is used on the same medium, the router needs to have more than one IP address on the interface attached to that medium. For example, the most recent Figure (5-15) has subnet 10.1.2.0/24; assume that subnet has all IP addresses assigned. Assuming secondary addressing to be the solution, subnet 10.1.7.0/24 could also be used on the same Ethernet. The configuration is in Example 5-8.

Example 5-8 *Secondary IP Addressing Configuration and **show ip route** Command on Yosemite*

```
! Excerpt from show running-config follows…
Hostname Yosemite
ip domain-lookup
ip name-server 150.150.1.1 150.150.1.2
interface ethernet 0
ip address 10.1.2.252   255.255.255.0
ip address 10.1.7.252   255.255.255.0 secondary
interface serial 0
ip address 10.1.128.252   255.255.255.0
interface serial 1
ip address 10.1.129.252   255.255.255.0

Yosemite#show ip route
Codes: C - connected, S - static, I - IGRP, R - RIP, M - mobile, B - BGP
        D - EIGRP, EX - EIGRP external, O - OSPF, IA - OSPF inter area
        N1 - OSPF NSSA external type 1, N2 - OSPF NSSA external type 2
        E1 - OSPF external type 1, E2 - OSPF external type 2, E - EGP
        i - IS-IS, L1 - IS-IS level-1, L2 - IS-IS level-2, * - candidate default
        U - per-user static route, o - ODR

Gateway of last resort is not set

      10.0.0.0/24 is subnetted, 4 subnets
            Secondary IP Addressing Configuration and show ip route Command on
C         10.1.2.0 is directly connected, Ethernet0
```

Example 5-8   *Secondary IP Addressing Configuration and **show ip route** Command on Yosemite (Continued)*

```
C       10.1.7.0 is directly connected, Ethernet0
C       10.1.129.0 is directly connected, Serial1
C       10.1.128.0 is directly connected, Serial0
Yosemite#
```

IP Addressing with Frame Relay Subinterfaces

Frame Relay configuration can be accomplished with or without the use of subinterfaces. If subinterfaces are not used, then all router interfaces attached to this same Frame Relay cloud should be configured with IP addresses in the same subnet. In other words, treat the Frame Relay cloud as any other "multi-access" medium (that is, a LAN).

Subinterfaces are used for several reasons. The key reason is that the use of subinterfaces allows distance vector routing protocols to work well and maintain the split-horizon feature to defeat routing loops.

The use of subinterfaces, and the type of subinterface, implies the number of subnets used for Frame Relay. A point-to-point subinterface terminates one virtual circuit (VC), and has an IP address assigned to it; the router on the other end of the VC uses an IP address in the same subnet. Multipoint subinterfaces are used when multiple VCs terminate at the subinterface; subinterfaces on other routers are configured to be in the same subnet.

Most often, point-to-point subinterfaces are used when a partial mesh of VCs is used. Conversely, multipoint VCs are used when a full mesh is used. However, both are allowed in the same router. Figure 5-16 shows the need for three different subnets over a Frame Relay cloud. Example 5-9, Example 5-10, and Example 5-11 show the configurations on Routers A, B, and E, respectively.

Example 5-9   *Router A Configuration*

```
hostname routerA
interface serial 0
encapsulation frame-relay
!
interface serial 0.1 point-to-point
ip address 150.10.1.250   255.255.255.0
frame-relay interface-dlci 40
description this is for the VC to site B
!
interface serial 0.2 point-to-point
ip address 150.10.2.250   255.255.255.0
frame-relay interface-dlci 41
description this is for the VC to site C
!
interface serial 0.3 multipoint
ip address 150.10.3.250   255.255.255.0
interface-dlci 42
interface-dlci 43
description this is for the VC's to sites D and E
```

Figure 5-16 *Frame Relay Subnets with Point-To-Point and Multipoint Subinterfaces*

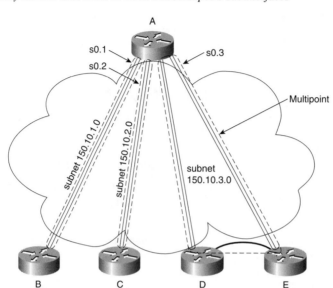

Example 5-10 *Router B Configuration*

```
hostname routerB
!
interface serial 0
encapsulation frame-relay
!
interface serial 0.1 point-to-point
ip address 150.10.1.251    255.255.255.0
frame-relay interface-dlci 44
description this is for the VC to site A
```

Example 5-11 *Router E Configuration*

```
hostname routerE
!
interface serial 0
encapsulation frame-relay
!
interface serial 0.3 multipoint
ip address 150.10.3.254    255.255.255.0
frame-relay interface-dlci 44
description this is for the VC to site A
```

For a more complete review of the concepts behind IP addressing over Frame Relay, refer to Chapter 8, "WAN Protocols: Understanding Point-to-Point, Frame Relay, and ISDN."

IPX Addressing and Routing

CCNA Objectives Covered in This Section

29	Describe the two parts of network addressing, then identify the parts in specific protocol address examples.
33	List the required IPX address and encapsulation type.

Novell's NetWare protocol stack defines Internetwork Packet Exchange (IPX) as a network layer equivalent protocol, as seen in Figure 5-17. IPX will be the focus of this initial section.

Figure 5-17 *Novell NetWare Protocols*

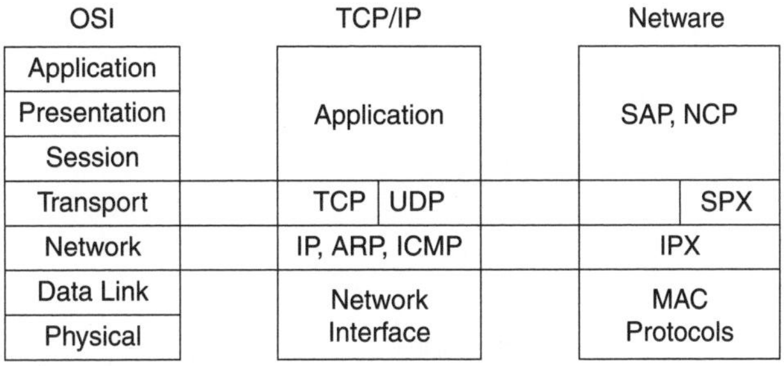

IPX defines the 80-bit address structure, which uses a 32-bit network part and 48-bit node part. Like IP and AppleTalk, all interfaces attached to the same data link use addresses in the same network. Table 5-21 lists four features of IPX addressing. The features listed in Table 5-21 are the same features used to generically describe a well-designed Layer 3 addressing scheme in Chapter 3, "Understanding the OSI Reference Model."

Table 5-21 *IPX Addressing Details*

Feature	Description
Size of a group	IPX addresses use a 48-bit node part of the address, giving 2^{48} possible addresses per network, which should be big enough!
Unique addresses	IPX calls for the LAN MAC address to be used as the node part of the IPX address. This allows for easy assignment, and little chance of duplication. Ensuring that no duplicates of the network numbers are made is the biggest concern because the network numbers are configured.
Grouping	The grouping concept is identical to IP, with all interfaces attached to the same medium using the same network number. There is no equivalent of IP subnetting.
Dynamic Address Assignment	Client IPX addresses are dynamically assigned as part of the protocol specifications. Servers and routers are configured with the network number(s) on their interfaces. Servers can choose to automatically generate an internal network number.

IPX routing works just like routing as described in Chapter 3 of this book. Steps 6 and 7 of the generalized routing algorithm from Chapter 3 are repeated here in Figure 5-18 for reference, with changes made to reflect IPX terminology.

Figure 5-18 *IPX Routing Algorithm*

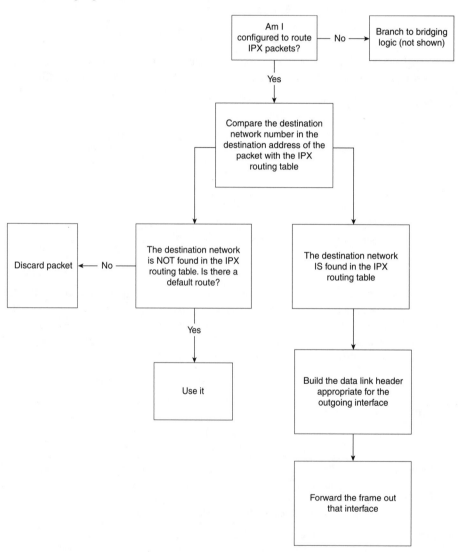

Internal Networks and Encapsulation Types

Two additional and important concepts related to routing are reviewed using Figure 5-19. NetWare servers use internal network numbers at the most recent versions. Also, clients, servers, and routers all must be configured to use the correct encapsulation. Routing will also be reviewed using the same figure.

Figure 5-19 *Sample IPX Network #1*

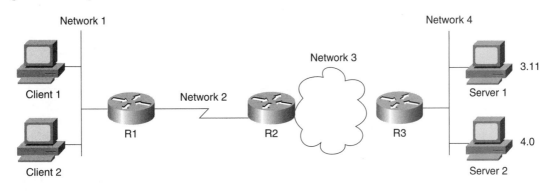

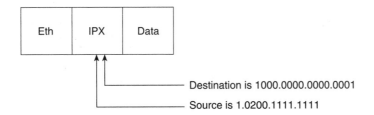

Destination is 1000.0000.0000.0001
Source is 1.0200.1111.1111

Server 1 internal net 1000
Server 2 internal net 1001
Server 1 MAC 0200.AAAA.AAAA
Server 2 MAC 0200.BBBB.BBBB

Client 1 has already logged in to Server 1 and is busily sending packets. Because NetWare servers use an internal network number, the destination of packets from Client 1 to Server 1 is 1000.0000.0000.0001. The source address of these packets is Client 1's IPX address (1.0200.1111.1111 in this case). The routers, of course, need network 1000 in their IPX routing tables. For example, Table 5-22 shows the contents of the IPX routing table of R3:

Table 5-22 *IPX Routing Table, R3*

Network	Outgoing Interface	Next Router
1	s0	3.0200.0000.2222
2	s0	3.0200.0000.2222
3	s0	N/A
4	E0	N/A
1000	E0	4.0200.AAAA.AAAA
1001	E0	4.0200.BBBB.BBBB

R3 learned the routes to networks 3 and 4 because they are directly attached. The other three routes were learned via a routing protocol, which can be RIP, EIGRP, or NLSP. (NLSP is not covered on the CCNA exam.) Server 1 and Server 2 send RIP updates advertising networks 1000 and 1001, respectively. That is one reason why NetWare servers send RIP updates even if they have only one interface, as is the case with Server 1.

Encapsulation is the term used by Cisco to describe the type of data-link header built in the routing algorithm illustrated by Figure 5-18. Encapsulation is also the source of confusion for many people when considering IPX, particularly when Ethernet is in use. Consider the IPX packet sent by Client 1 to Server 1 in Figure 5-19. Each successive router discards the data-link header of the incoming frame and builds a new data-link header according to the type of interface. However, there are four different styles of Ethernet header that can be built at R3 that are supported by Novell. The types of encapsulating Ethernet headers are shown in Figure 5-20 and are listed in Table 5-23. But first, a brief summary of encapsulation:

> Data Link Encapsulation defines the details of data-link headers and trailers created by a router and placed around a packet, before completing the routing process by forwarding the frame out an interface.

Figure 5-20 *IPX Ethernet Encapsulations*

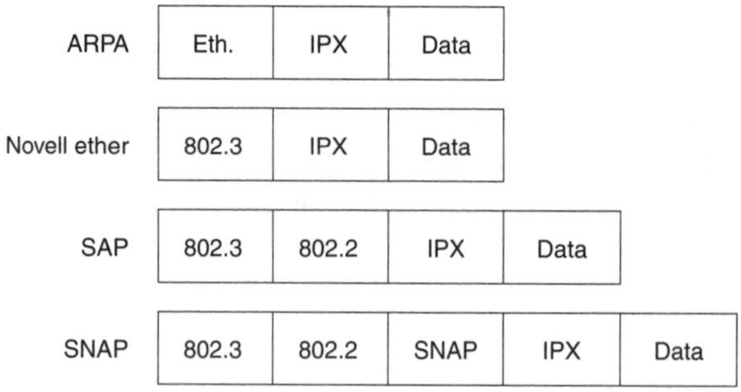

Table 5-23 *IPX Ethernet Encapsulations*

Novell's Name	Cisco IOS's Name	Hints for Remembering the Names and Meanings
Ethernet_II	ARPA	One way to help remember and correlate the two names is that ARPA was the original agency that created TCP/IP, and that Ethernet_II is the older version of Ethernet; remember that the "old" names go together.
Ethernet_802.3	Novell-ether	Novell's name refers to the final header before the IPX header in this case. No suggestions on easier ways to recall the IOS name Novell-ether! This setting is Novell's default on NetWare 3.11 and prior releases.
Ethernet_802.2	SAP	Novell's name refers to the final header before the IPX header in this case. Novell's name refers to the committee and complete header that defines the SAP field; Cisco's name refers to the SAP part of the 802.2 header. (The SAP field denotes that an IPX packet follows the 802.2 header.) This setting is Novell's default on NetWare 3.12 and later releases.
Ethernet_SNAP	SNAP	Novell's name refers to the final header before the IPX header in this case. Cisco's name refers to this same header.

The key for remembering the Novell encapsulation names is that each name refers to the header that directly precedes the IPX packet. This can help you recall header formats as well. Remembering the names in the order in this book can also help, because the size of the headers increases with the third and fourth options (see Figure 5-20).

The same encapsulation issue exists on Token Ring and FDDI interfaces. Table 5-24 outlines the options.

Table 5-24 *IPX Token Ring and FDDI Encapsulations*

Novell's Name	Cisco IOS's Name	Description and Hints for Remembering
FDDI_Raw	Novell-fddi	The IPX packet follows directly after the FDDI header. No Type field of any kind is used.
FDDI_802.2	SAP	The IPX packet follows the 802.2 header. Novell's name refers to the committee and complete header that defines the SAP field; Cisco's name refers to the SAP part of the 802.2 header.
FDDI_SNAP	SNAP	Novell's name refers to the final header before the IPX header in this case. Cisco's name refers to this same header.

continues

Table 5-24 *IPX Token Ring and FDDI Encapsulations (Continued)*

Novell's Name	Cisco IOS's Name	Description and Hints for Remembering
Token-ring	SAP	The IPX packet follows the 802.2 header. Novell's name refers to the committee and complete header that defines the SAP field; Cisco's name refers to the SAP part of the 802.2 header.
Token-ring_SNAP	SNAP	Novell's name refers to the final header before the IPX header. Cisco's name refers to this same header.

One or more encapsulations are needed per Ethernet interface. If all NetWare clients/servers on the Ethernet use the same encapsulation, just that single encapsulation is needed. However, if more than one is used, then multiple encapsulations are needed. To configure multiple encapsulations in the IOS, multiple IPX networks must be used on the same Ethernet.

Two methods of configuration can be used to create two IPX networks on the same link. The first method uses IPX secondary addresses, and is the method covered in the Training Paths and in this book. The IOS11.3 documentation mentions that IPX secondary addresses will not be supported in future releases and that subinterfaces will be required.

Figure 5-21 illustrates the concept of IPX secondary addressing. Server 1 uses Novell-ether, and Server 2 uses SAP encapsulation. Network 4 devices use Novell-ether, and Network 5 devices use SAP.

Figure 5-21 *Multiple IPX Encapsulations on One Ethernet*

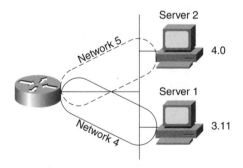

The router's choice of encapsulation for forwarding packets is relatively straightforward. If the route refers to a next router in Network 4, the router uses Novell-ether encapsulation. If the route refers to a next router in Network 5, the router uses SAP encapsulation. For RIP and SAP updates, the router sends updates on to both IPX networks, using the two different encapsulations, respectively. Troubleshooting can be more challenging because clients or servers using only a single encapsulation cannot communicate directly. Also, clients and servers on the same LAN that happen to use different encapsulations will require their packets to be routed by the router, so that the encapsulation is changed. Therefore, there are many advantages to not using multiple encapsulations.

Configuration of IPX

CCNA Objectives Covered in This Section	
28	Monitor Novell IPX operation on the router.
34	Enable the Novell IPX protocol and configure interfaces.
38	Configure IPX access lists and SAP filters to control basic Novell traffic.

Configuration of IPX and IPX RIP in a Cisco router is relatively straightforward. Table 5-25 and Table 5-26 summarize the commands used in Training Paths 1 and 2 for IPX configuration and verification, in addition to a few other commands. Two configuration samples follow. The Cisco IOS documentation and the Cisco Press book, Cisco IOS Configuration Fundamentals are excellent references for commands and options not covered here.

CCNA objective 38 is listed as covered in this section, but it is not actually covered. Objective 38 is listed by Cisco on its Web site as part of the "Network Protocols" general heading, so it is listed in this chapter, which corresponds to that heading. However, the concepts more closely match the CCNA objectives heading of "Network Security," which is covered in Chapter 7, "Understanding Network Security," of this book. Refer to Chapter 7 for coverage of IPX access lists and SAP filters.

Table 5-25 *IPX and IPX RIP Configuration Commands in Training Paths 1 and 2*

Command	Configuration mode
ipx routing [*node*]	Global
ipx maximum-paths *paths*	Global
ipx network *network* [**encapsulation** *type*] [**secondary**]	Interface mode

Table 5-26 *IPX EXEC Commands in Training Paths 1 and 2*

Command	Function
show ipx interface	Detailed view of IP parameter settings, per interface
show ipx route [*network*]	Shows entire routing table, or one entry if network is entered
show ipx servers	Shows SAP table
show ipx traffic	Shows IPX traffic statistics
debug ipx routing [*events\activity*]	Gives messages describing each routing update
debug ipx sap [*events\activity*]	Gives messages describing each SAP update
ping *ipx-address*	Sends IPX packets to verify connectivity

The first sample is a basic configuration for the network in Figure 5-22. Example 5-12, Example 5-13, and Example 5-14 provide the configuration.

NOTE
The IPX samples also contain IP configuration. This is not required for correct operation of IPX. However, to telnet to the routers in order to issue commands, IP needs to be configured. And in almost every network with Cisco routers, IP is indeed configured. Therefore, the IPX examples will generally include IP configuration.

Example 5-12 *Albuquerque Configuration for IPX, Sample 1*

```
ipx routing
!
interface serial0
ip address 10.1.12.1 255.255.255.0
ipx network 1012
bandwidth 56
!
interface serial1
ip address 10.1.13.1 255.255.255.0
ipx network 1013
!
interface ethernet 0
ip address 10.1.1.1 255.255.255.0
ipx network 1
```

Figure 5-22 *IPX Network with Point-to-Point Serial Links*

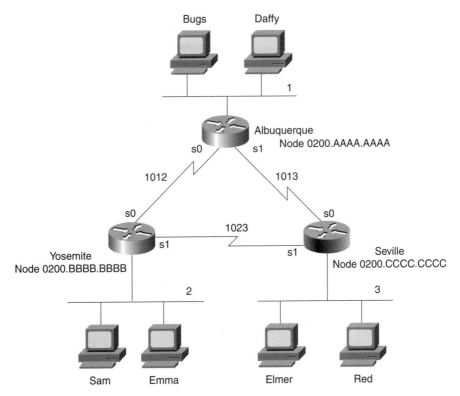

Example 5-13 *Yosemite Configuration for IPX, Sample 1*

```
ipx routing 0200.bbbb.bbbb
!
interface serial0
ip address 10.1.12.2 255.255.255.0
ipx network 1012
bandwidth 56
!
interface serial1
ip address 10.1.23.2 255.255.255.0
ipx network 1023
!
interface ethernet 0
ip address 10.1.2.2 255.255.255.0
ipx network 2
```

Example 5-14 *Seville Configuration for IPX, Sample 1*

```
ipx routing 0200.cccc.cccc
!
interface serial0
ip address 10.1.13.3 255.255.255.0
ipx network 1013
!
interface serial1
ip address 10.1.23.3 255.255.255.0
ipx network 1023
!
interface ethernet 0
ip address 10.1.3.3 255.255.255.0
ipx network 3
```

Enabling IPX routing globally, as well as on each interface, is all that is required to route IPX in a Cisco router. The **ipx routing** command enables IPX in this router and initializes the RIP and SAP processes. The individual **IPX network** statements on each interface enable IPX routing into and out of each interface and enable RIP and SAP on each interface, respectively.

The IPX addresses are not completely defined, however. Only the network number is configured. The full IPX network number is created by adding the MAC address of each interface to the configured IPX network number. For non-LAN interfaces, the MAC address of a LAN interface is used. However, for easier troubleshooting, a MAC address to be used as the node part of the IPX address on non-LAN interfaces can be configured. Notice the difference in the two commands in Example 5-15. The first is on Albuquerque, and the second is on Seville:

Example 5-15 *show ipx interface serial 0 on Albuquerque and Seville*

```
Albuquerque#show ipx interface serial 0
Serial0 is up, line protocol is up
  IPX address is 1012.0000.0ccf.21cd [up]
  Delay of this IPX network, in ticks is 6 throughput 0 link delay 0
  IPXWAN processing not enabled on this interface.
  IPX SAP update interval is 1 minute(s)
  IPX type 20 propagation packet forwarding is disabled
  Incoming access list is not set
  Outgoing access list is not set
  IPX helper access list is not set
  SAP GNS processing enabled, delay 0 ms, output filter list is not set
  SAP Input filter list is not set
  SAP Output filter list is not set
  SAP Router filter list is not set
  Input filter list is not set
  Output filter list is not set
  Router filter list is not set
  Netbios Input host access list is not set
  Netbios Input bytes access list is not set
  Netbios Output host access list is not set
  Netbios Output bytes access list is not set
```

Example 5-15 *show ipx interface serial 0 on Albuquerque and Seville (Continued)*

```
   Updates each 60 seconds, aging multiples RIP: 3 SAP: 3
   SAP interpacket delay is 55 ms, maximum size is 480 bytes
   RIP interpacket delay is 55 ms, maximum size is 432 bytes
   Watchdog processing is disabled, SPX spoofing is disabled, idle time 60
   IPX accounting is disabled
   IPX fast switching is configured (enabled)
   RIP packets received 39, RIP packets sent 44
   SAP packets received 27, SAP packets sent 29
Albuquerque#


Seville#show ipx interface serial 0
Serial0 is up, line protocol is up
  IPX address is 1013.0200.cccc.cccc [up]
  Delay of this IPX network, in ticks is 6 throughput 0 link delay 0
  IPXWAN processing not enabled on this interface.
  IPX SAP update interval is 1 minute(s)
  IPX type 20 propagation packet forwarding is disabled
  Incoming access list is not set
  Outgoing access list is not set
  IPX helper access list is not set
  SAP GNS processing enabled, delay 0 ms, output filter list is not set
  SAP Input filter list is not set
  SAP Output filter list is not set
  SAP Router filter list is not set
  Input filter list is not set
  Output filter list is not set
  Router filter list is not set
  Netbios Input host access list is not set
  Netbios Input bytes access list is not set
  Netbios Output host access list is not set
  Netbios Output bytes access list is not set
  Updates each 60 seconds, aging multiples RIP: 3 SAP: 3
  SAP interpacket delay is 55 ms, maximum size is 480 bytes
  RIP interpacket delay is 55 ms, maximum size is 432 bytes
  Watchdog processing is disabled, SPX spoofing is disabled, idle time 60
  IPX accounting is disabled
  IPX fast switching is configured (enabled)
  RIP packets received 51, RIP packets sent 51
  SAP packets received 2, SAP packets sent 28
Seville#
```

The **show ipx interface** command provides a lot of information about IPX, including the
complete IPX address. In this case, we see that the node part of Seville's IPX address is easily
recognizable, whereas Albuquerque's is not. Seville's node address is 0200.cccc.cccc based
on its **ipx routing 0200.cccc.cccc** configuration command (refer to Example 5-14). However,
because the node parameter was omitted from the IPX routing command on Albuquerque

(refer to Example 5-12), the router chooses a MAC on one of the LAN interfaces to use as the node portion of the IPX addresses on non-LAN interfaces.

NOTE   After the IPX routing command is entered, the router saves the command with the node value. In other words, even if Yosemite's configuration were typed as in Figure 5-13, the node number chosen from a LAN interface would be shown in the configuration.

There are several nuances to how the node parts of the addresses are assigned. The first nuance is that if the node part of the IPX address on WAN interfaces is derived from the MAC of a LAN interface and there is more than one LAN interface, then the IOS must choose one MAC address to use. The algorithm uses the MAC address of the "first" Ethernet interface, or first Token Ring interface if no Ethernet exists, or the first FDDI interface if no Ethernet or Token Ring exists. The lowest numbered interface number is considered to be "first." The next nuance is that if there are no LAN interfaces, the node parameter on the **ipx routing** command must be configured, or IPX routing will not work. The final nuance is that the node part of IPX addresses on router LAN interfaces ignore the node parameter of the **ipx routing** command, and use their specific MAC address as the node part of the address.

The second sample network (illustrated in Figure 5-23) uses Frame Relay with point-to-point subinterfaces. Example 5-16, Example 5-17, Example 5-18, and Example 5-19 show the configuration for this network.

Example 5-16 *Atlanta Configuration*

```
ipx routing 0200.aaaa.aaaa
!
interface serial0
encapsulation frame-relay
!
interface serial 0.1 point-to-point
ip address 140.1.1.1  255.255.255.0
ipx network 1
frame-relay interface-dlci 52
!
interface serial 0.2 point-to-point
ip address 140.1.2.1 255.255.255.0
ipx network 2
frame-relay interface-dlci 53
!
interface serial 0.3 point-to-point
ip address 140.1.3.1 255.255.255.0
ipx network 3
frame-relay interface-dlci 54
!
interface ethernet 0
ip address 140.1.11.1 255.255.255.0
ipx network 11
```

Figure 5-23 *IPX Network with Frame Relay and Point-To-Point Subinterfaces*

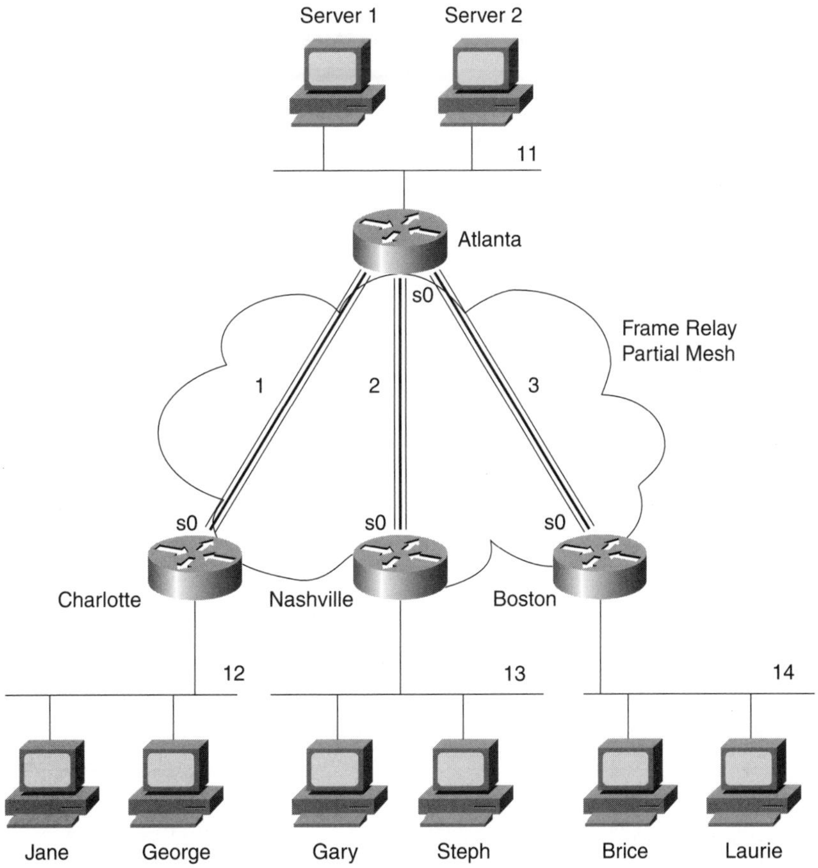

Example 5-17 *Charlotte Configuration*

```
ipx routing 0200.bbbb.bbbb
!
interface serial0
encapsulation frame-relay
!
interface serial 0.1 point-to-point
ip address 140.1.1.2  255.255.255.0
ipx network 1
frame-relay interface-dlci 51
!
interface ethernet 0
ip address 140.1.12.2 255.255.255.0
ipx network 12
```

Example 5-18 *Nashville Configuration*

```
ipx routing 0200.cccc.cccc
!
interface serial0
encapsulation frame-relay
!
interface serial 0.2 point-to-point
ip address 140.1.2.3 255.255.255.0
ipx network 2
frame-relay interface-dlci 51
!
interface ethernet 0
ip address 140.1.13.3 255.255.255.0
ipx network 13
```

Example 5-19 *Boston Configuration*

```
ipx routing 0200.dddd.dddd
!
interface serial0
encapsulation frame-relay
!
interface serial 0.3 point-to-point
ip address 140.1.3.4 255.255.255.0
ipx network 3
frame-relay interface-dlci 51
!
interface ethernet 0
ip address 140.1.14.4  255.255.255.0
ipx network 14
```

The configuration is very similar to the point-to-point network of Figure 5-22. The biggest difference is that each point-to-point subinterface is a different IPX network, as seen in Figure 5-23. Otherwise, SAP and RIP are enabled globally with the **ipx routing** command; each is allowed to be broadcast on interfaces with the **ipx network** interface subcommand. SAP and RIP updates are sent out each *subinterface*—this means that Atlanta will replicate and send three copies of the RIP update and three copies of the SAP update on its serial0 interface every 60 seconds.

Configuration when using multiple Ethernet encapsulations is the final configuration option to be reviewed. Assume Gary is an old NetWare client, running 3.11 code and using the Ethernet_802.3 Novell encapsulation. Stephanie is newer and uses the Ethernet_802.2 encapsulation. Two IPX networks are used on Nashville's Ethernet 0 interface in this case. Gary will be in Network 13, and Stephanie will be in Network 23. Example 5-20 shows the configuration for the Nashville network with a secondary IPX network on Ethernet 0.

Example 5-20 *Nashville Configuration with Secondary IPX Network on Ethernet 0*

```
ipx routing 0200.cccc.cccc
!
interface serial0
encapsulation frame-relay
!
interface serial 0.2 point-to-point
ip address 140.1.2.3 255.255.255.0
ipx network 2
frame-relay interface-dlci 51
!
interface ethernet 0
ip address 140.1.13.3 255.255.255.0
ipx network 13 encapsulation novell-ether
ipx network 23 encapsulation sap secondary
```

NOTE   IOS 11.3 documentation mentions that IPX secondary addresses will no longer be supported in future releases. Use of subinterfaces will be required to use multiple encapsulations. Multiple networks per physical interface will still be required. This change is in part due to the fact that NLSP does not support IPX secondary addresses.

Q&A

As mentioned in Chapter 1, the questions and scenarios are more difficult than what you should experience on the actual exam. The questions do not attempt to cover more breadth or depth than the exam; however, the questions are designed to make sure you know the answer. Rather than allowing you to derive the answer from clues hidden inside the question itself, your understanding and recall of the subject will be challenged. Questions from the "Do I Know This Already?" quiz from the beginning of the chapter are repeated here to ensure that you have mastered the chapter's topic areas. Hopefully, these questions will help limit the number of exam questions on which you narrow your choices to two options, and then guess!

1. What do TCP, UDP, IP, and ICMP stand for? Which protocol is considered to be *Layer 3 equivalent* when comparing TCP/IP to the OSI protocols?

2. Name the parts of an IP address.

3. Define the term *subnet mask*. What do the bits in the mask, whose values are binary 0, tell you about the corresponding IP address(es)?

4. Write down the subnet numbers, broadcast addresses, and range of valid IP addresses for the following addresses and masks:

   134.141.7.11   255.255.255.0

   10.5.118.3   255.255.0.0

   193.193.7.7   255.255.255.0

   167.88.99.66   255.255.255.192

5. How many IP addresses could be assigned in each of the following subnets?

   134.141.7.0   255.255.255.0

   155.166.44.64   255.255.255.192

   10.7.8.0   255.255.255.0

   128.5.0.0   255.255.0.0

6. Given the list of Class A, B, and C networks, how many valid subnets exist in each case, if the subnet mask shown beside each network number is used on all subnets of that network?

   Network 134.141.0.0   255.255.255.0

   Network 155.166.0.0   255.255.255.192

   Network 10.0.0.0   255.255.255.0

   Network 199.5.0.0   255.255.255.224

7. Create a minimal configuration enabling IP on each interface on a 2501 router (2 serial, 1 Ethernet). The NIC assigned you network 8.0.0.0. Your boss says you need at most 200 hosts per subnet. You decide against using VLSM. Your boss says to plan your subnets so you can have as many subnets as possible, rather than allow for larger subnets later. You decide to start with the lowest numerical values for subnets. Assume that point-to-point serial links will be attached to this router, and that RIP is the routing protocol.

8. In question 7, what would the IP subnet of the link attached to serial0 be? If another user came along and wanted to answer the same question, but he or she did not have the enable password, what command(s) might tell him or her this IP's addresses and subnets?

9. Describe the question and possible responses in setup mode when a router wants to know the mask used on an interface. How can the router derive the correct mask from the information supplied by the user?

10. Name the three classes of unicast IP addresses, and list their default masks, respectively. How many of each type could be assigned to companies and organizations by the NIC?

11. Describe how TCP performs error recovery. What role do the routers play?

12. Define the purpose of an ICMP redirect message.

13. Define the purpose of the **trace** command. What type of messages is it sending, and what type of ICMP messages is it receiving?

14. What does IP stand for? ICMP? Which protocol is considered to be *Layer 3 equivalent* when comparing TCP/IP to the OSI protocols?

15. What causes the output from an IOS **ping** command to display "UUUUU"?

16. Describe how to view the IP ARP cache in a Cisco router. Also describe the three key elements of each entry.

17. What dynamic process replaces ARP on Frame Relay networks? What command shows the equivalent of the ARP cache for Frame Relay networks? What are the three key parts to an entry in this table?

18. How many hosts are allowed per subnet if the subnet mask used is 255.255.255.192? 255.255.255.252?

19. How many subnets could be created, if using static length masks in a Class B network, when the mask is 255.255.255.224? When the mask is 255.255.252.0?

20. How many bytes compose an IPX address?

21. What do IPX and SPX stand for?

22. Define encapsulation in the context of Cisco routers and Novell IPX.

23. Give an example of an IPX network mask used when subnetting.

24. Describe the headers used for two examples of Ethernet encapsulation when using IPX.

25. Name the part of the NetWare protocol specifications that, like TCP, provides end-to-end guaranteed delivery of data.

26. Name the command that lists all of the SAP entries in a Cisco router.

27. How many different values are possible for IPX network numbers?

28. Create a configuration enabling IPX on each interface, with RIP and SAP enabled on each as well, for a 2501 (2 serial, 1 Ethernet) router. Use networks 100, 200, and 300 for interfaces S0, S1, and E0, respectively. Choose any node values.

29. In the previous question, what would the IPX address of the serial 0 interface be? If another user came along and wanted to know, but he or she did not have the enable password, what command(s) might tell him or her this IPX address?

30. What **show** command lists the IPX address(s) of interfaces in a Cisco router?

31. How many Novell encapsulation types are valid in the IOS for Ethernet interfaces? FDDI? Token Ring?

32. A router is attached to an Ethernet LAN. Some clients on the LAN use Novell's Ethernet_II encapsulation, and some others use Ethernet_802.3. If the only subcommand on Ethernet0 reads **ipx network 1**, which of the clients are working? (all, Ethernet_II, or Ethernet_802.3?)

33. A router is attached to an Ethernet LAN. Some clients on the LAN use Novell's Ethernet_802.2 encapsulation, and some others use Ethernet_snap. Create a configuration that allows both types of clients to send and receive packets through this router.

34. Up to 64 IPX networks can be used on the same Ethernet by using the IPX secondary address feature. (True/False). If true, describe the largest number that is practically needed. If false, what is the maximum number that is legal on an Ethernet?

35. In the **ipx network 11** command, does the IOS assume 11 is binary, octal, decimal, or hexadecimal? What is the largest valid value that could be configured instead of 11?

36. What IOS IPX encapsulation keyword implies use of an 802.2 header, but no SNAP header? On what types of interfaces is type of encapsulation valid?

Scenarios

Scenario 5-1: IP Addressing and Subnet Calculation

Assume you just took a new job. No one trusts you yet, so they will not give you any passwords to the router. Your "mentor" at your new company has left you at his desk while he goes to a meeting. He has left a Telnet window up, logged in to one router in user mode. In other words, you can only issue user mode commands.

Assuming you had issued the following commands (see Example 5-21), draw the most specific network diagram that you can.

Example 5-21 *Command Output on Router Fred*

```
fred>show interface
Serial0 is up, line protocol is up
  Hardware is HD64570
  Internet address is 199.1.1.65/27
  MTU 1500 bytes, BW 1544 Kbit, DLY 20000 usec, rely 255/255, load 1/255
  Encapsulation HDLC, loopback not set, keepalive set (10 sec)
  Last input 00:00:07, output 00:00:10, output hang never
  Last clearing of "show interface" counters never
  Input queue: 0/75/0 (size/max/drops); Total output drops: 0
  Queueing strategy: weighted fair
  Output queue: 0/1000/0 (size/max total/drops)
     Conversations  0/1/64 (active/max active/threshold)
     Reserved Conversations 0/0 (allocated/max allocated)
  5 minute input rate 0 bits/sec, 0 packets/sec
  5 minute output rate 0 bits/sec, 0 packets/sec
     27 packets input, 2452 bytes, 0 no buffer
     Received 27 broadcasts, 0 runts, 0 giants, 0 throttles
     0 input errors, 0 CRC, 0 frame, 0 overrun, 0 ignored, 0 abort
     29 packets output, 2044 bytes, 0 underruns
     0 output errors, 0 collisions, 28 interface resets
     0 output buffer failures, 0 output buffers swapped out
     7 carrier transitions
     DCD=up  DSR=up  DTR=up  RTS=up  CTS=up
Serial1 is up, line protocol is up
  Hardware is HD64570
  Internet address is 199.1.1.97/27
  MTU 1500 bytes, BW 1544 Kbit, DLY 20000 usec, rely 255/255, load 1/255
  Encapsulation HDLC, loopback not set, keepalive set (10 sec)
  Last input 00:00:01, output 00:00:01, output hang never
  Last clearing of "show interface" counters never
  Input queue: 0/75/0 (size/max/drops); Total output drops: 0
  Queueing strategy: weighted fair
  Output queue: 0/1000/0 (size/max total/drops)
     Conversations  0/1/64 (active/max active/threshold)
```

continues

Example 5-21 *Command Output on Router Fred (Continued)*

```
          Reserved Conversations 0/0 (allocated/max allocated)
     5 minute input rate 0 bits/sec, 0 packets/sec
     5 minute output rate 0 bits/sec, 0 packets/sec
        125 packets input, 7634 bytes, 0 no buffer
        Received 124 broadcasts, 0 runts, 0 giants, 0 throttles
        0 input errors, 0 CRC, 0 frame, 0 overrun, 0 ignored, 0 abort
        161 packets output, 9575 bytes, 0 underruns
        0 output errors, 0 collisions, 1 interface resets
        0 output buffer failures, 0 output buffers swapped out
        4 carrier transitions
        DCD=up  DSR=up  DTR=up  RTS=up  CTS=up
Ethernet0 is up, line protocol is up
Hardware is MCI Ethernet, address is 0000.0c55.AB44 (bia 0000.0c55.AB44)
   Internet address is 199.1.1.33/27
        MTU 1500 bytes, BW 10000 Kbit, DLY 1000 usec, rely 255/255, load 1/255
        Encapsulation ARPA, loopback not set, keepalive set (10 sec)
        ARP type: ARPA, PROBE, ARP Timeout 4:00:00

        Last input 0:00:00, output 0:00:00, output hang never
        Output queue 0/40, 0 drops; input queue 0/75, 0 drops
        Five minute input rate 4000 bits/sec, 4 packets/sec
        Five minute output rate 6000 bits/sec, 6 packets/sec
              22197 packets input, 309992 bytes, 0 no buffer
              Received 2343 broadcasts, 0 runts, 0 giants
              0 input errors, 0 CRC, 0 frame, 0 overrun, 0 ignored, 0 abort
              4456 packets output, 145765 bytes, 0 underruns
              3 output errors, 10 collisions, 2 interface resets, 0 restarts


fred>show ip route
Codes: C - connected, S - static, I - IGRP, R - RIP, M - mobile, B - BGP
       D - EIGRP, EX - EIGRP external, O - OSPF, IA - OSPF inter area
       N1 - OSPF NSSA external type 1, N2 - OSPF NSSA external type 2
       E1 - OSPF external type 1, E2 - OSPF external type 2, E - EGP
       i - IS-IS, L1 - IS-IS level-1, L2 - IS-IS level-2, * - candidate default
       U - per-user static route, o - ODR

Gateway of last resort is not set

     199.1.1.0/27 is subnetted, 6 subnets
R       199.1.1.192 [120/1] via 199.1.1.98, 00:00:01, Serial1
R       199.1.1.128 [120/1] via 199.1.1.98, 00:00:01, Serial1
                    [120/1] via 199.1.1.66, 00:00:20, Serial0
R       199.1.1.160 [120/1] via 199.1.1.66, 00:00:20, Serial0
C       199.1.1.64 is directly connected, Serial0
C       199.1.1.96 is directly connected, Serial1
C       199.1.1.32 is directly connected, Ethernet0

fred>show ip protocol
```

Example 5-21 *Command Output on Router Fred (Continued)*

```
Routing Protocol is "rip"
  Sending updates every 30 seconds, next due in 23 seconds
  Invalid after 180 seconds, hold down 180, flushed after 240
 Outgoing update filter list for all interfaces is not set
  Incoming update filter list for all interfaces is not set
  Redistributing: rip
  Default version control: send version 1, receive any version
    Interface       Send  Recv   Key-chain
    Serial0          1     1 2
    Serial1          1     1 2
    Ethernet0        1     1 2
  Routing for Networks:
    180.3.0.0
    199.1.1.0
  Routing Information Sources:
    Gateway         Distance      Last Update
    199.1.1.66           120      00:00:04
    199.1.1.98           120      00:00:14
  Distance: (default is 120)


fred>show cdp neighbor detail
-----------------------
Device ID: dino
Entry address(es):
  IP address: 199.1.1.66
Platform: Cisco 2500,  Capabilities: Router
Interface: Serial0,  Port ID (outgoing port): Serial0
Holdtime : 148 sec

Version :
Cisco Internetwork Operating System Software
IOS (tm) 2500 Software (C2500-AINR-L), Version 11.2(11), RELEASE SOFTWARE (fc1)
Copyright (c) 1986-1997 by Cisco Systems, Inc.
Compiled Mon 29-Dec-97 18:47 by ckralik


-----------------------
Device ID: Barney
Entry address(es):
  IP address: 199.1.1.98
Platform: Cisco 2500,  Capabilities: Router
Interface: Serial1,  Port ID (outgoing port): Serial0
Holdtime : 155 sec

Version :
Cisco Internetwork Operating System Software
IOS (tm) 2500 Software (C2500-AINR-L), Version 11.2(11), RELEASE SOFTWARE (fc1)
Copyright (c) 1986-1997 by Cisco Systems, Inc.
Compiled Mon 29-Dec-97 18:47 by ckralik
```

Scenario 5-2: IP Subnet Design with a Class B Network

Your job is to plan a new network. The topology required includes three sites, one Ethernet at each site, with point-to-point serial links for connectivity, as shown in Figure 5-24. The network may grow to need at most 100 subnets, with 200 hosts per subnet maximum. Use network 172.16.0.0. Use Table 5-27 to record your choices, or use a separate piece of paper.

Figure 5-24 *Scenario 5-2 Network Diagram*

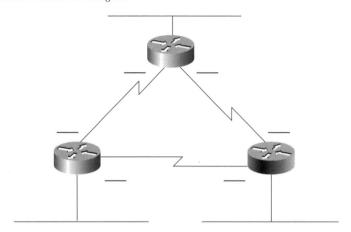

Table 5-27 *Scenario 5-2 Planning Chart*

Location of Subnet Geographically	Subnet Mask	Subnet Number	Router's IP Address
Ethernet off Router A			
Ethernet off Router B			
Ethernet off Router C			
Serial between A and B			
Serial between A and C			
Serial between B and C			

Given the information in Figure 5-24 and Table 5-27, perform the following activities:

1. Determine all subnet masks that meet the criteria in the introduction to this scenario.

2. Choose a mask and pick enough subnets to use for the original topology (refer to Figure 5-24).

3. Create IP-related configuration commands for each router.

Scenario 5-3: IP Subnet Design with a Class C Network

Your job is to plan yet another network. The topology required includes four sites, one Ethernet at each site, with partially-meshed Frame Relay for connectivity, as shown in Figure 5-25. The number of subnets will never grow. Choose a mask that will maximize the number of hosts per subnet. Use network 200.1.1.0. Use Table 5-28 to record your choices, or use a separate piece of paper.

Figure 5-25 *Scenario 5-3 Network Diagram*

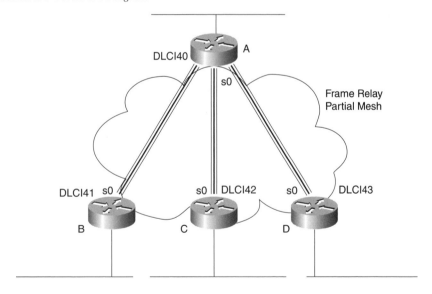

Table 5-28 *Scenario 5-3 Planning Chart*

Location of Subnet	Subnet Mask	Subnet Number	Router's IP Address
Ethernet off Router A			
Ethernet off Router B			
Ethernet off Router C			
Ethernet off Router D			
VC between A and B			
VC between A and C			
VC between A and D			

Given the network setup in Figure 5-25, perform the following activities:

1. Choose the best subnet mask meeting the criteria.

2. Use Table 5-28 to plan which subnet numbers will be used.

3. Create IP-related configuration commands for each router. Use the DLCIs from Figure 5-25.

Scenario 5-4: IPX Examination

Given the network in Figure 5-26 and the command output in Example 5-22, Example 5-23, and Example 5-24, answer the questions and perform the tasks listed after Example 5-24.

Figure 5-26 *Scenario 5-4 Network Diagram*

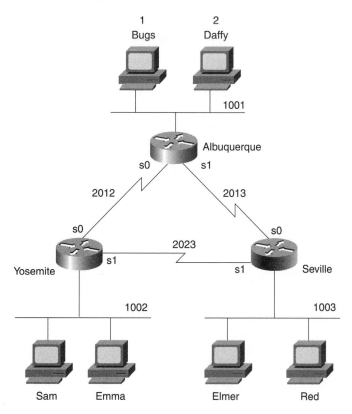

Example 5-22 *Albuquerque Command Output, Scenario 5-4*

```
Albuquerque#show ipx interface brief
Interface          IPX Network Encapsulation Status          IPX State
Serial0            2012        HDLC          up              [up]
Serial1            2013        HDLC          up              [up]
Ethernet0          1001        SAP           up              [up]

Albuquerque#show cdp neighbor detail
-----------------------
Device ID: Yosemite
Entry address(es):
  IP address: 10.1.12.2
  Novell address: 2012.0200.2222.2222
Platform: cisco 2500,  Capabilities: Router
Interface: Serial0,  Port ID (outgoing port): Serial0
Holdtime : 167 sec

Version :
Cisco Internetwork Operating System Software
IOS (tm) 2500 Software (C2500-AINR-L), Version 11.2(11), RELEASE SOFTWARE (fc1)
Copyright (c) 1986-1997 by Cisco Systems, Inc.
Compiled Mon 29-Dec-97 18:47 by ckralik

-----------------------
Device ID: Seville
Entry address(es):
  IP address: 10.1.13.3
  Novell address: 2013.0200.3333.3333
Platform: cisco 2500,  Capabilities: Router
Interface: Serial1,  Port ID (outgoing port): Serial0
Holdtime : 164 sec

Version :
Cisco Internetwork Operating System Software
IOS (tm) 2500 Software (C2500-AINR-L), Version 11.2(11), RELEASE SOFTWARE (fc1)
Copyright (c) 1986-1997 by Cisco Systems, Inc.
Compiled Mon 29-Dec-97 18:47 by ckralik
```

Example 5-23 *Yosemite Command Output, Scenario 5-4*

```
Yosemite#show ipx route
Codes: C - Connected primary network,    c - Connected secondary network
       S - Static, F - Floating static, L - Local (internal), W - IPXWAN
       R - RIP, E - EIGRP, N - NLSP, X - External, A - Aggregate
       s - seconds, u - uses

8 Total IPX routes. Up to 1 parallel paths and 16 hops allowed.

No default route known.

C      1002 (SAP),        To0
C      2012 (HDLC),       Se0
C      2023 (HDLC),       Se1
```

Example 5-23 *Yosemite Command Output, Scenario 5-4 (Continued)*

```
R          1 [08/03] via       2012.0200.1111.1111,    32s, Se0
R          2 [08/03] via       2012.0200.1111.1111,    33s, Se0
R       1001 [07/01] via       2012.0200.1111.1111,    33s, Se0
R       1003 [07/01] via       2023.0200.3333.3333,    32s, Se1
R       2013 [07/01] via       2012.0200.1111.1111,    33s, Se0

Yosemite#show ipx traffic
System Traffic for 0.0000.0000.0001 System-Name: Yosemite
Rcvd:   169 total, 0 format errors, 0 checksum errors, 0 bad hop count,
        8 packets pitched, 161 local destination, 0 multicast
Bcast:  160 received, 242 sent
Sent:   243 generated, 0 forwarded
        0 encapsulation failed, 0 no route
SAP:    2 SAP requests, 0 SAP replies, 2 servers
        0 SAP Nearest Name requests, 0 replies
        0 SAP General Name requests, 0 replies
        60 SAP advertisements received, 57 sent
        6 SAP flash updates sent, 0 SAP format errors
RIP:    1 RIP requests, 0 RIP replies, 9 routes
        98 RIP advertisements received, 120 sent
        45 RIP flash updates sent, 0 RIP format errors
Echo:   Rcvd 0 requests, 0 replies
        Sent 0 requests, 0 replies
        0 unknown: 0 no socket, 0 filtered, 0 no helper
        0 SAPs throttled, freed NDB len 0
Watchdog:
        0 packets received, 0 replies spoofed
Queue lengths:
        IPX input: 0, SAP 0, RIP 0, GNS 0
        SAP throttling length: 0/(no limit), 0 nets pending lost route reply
        Delayed process creation: 0
EIGRP:  Total received 0, sent 0
        Updates received 0, sent 0
        Queries received 0, sent 0
        Replies received 0, sent 0
        SAPs received 0, sent 0
NLSP:   Level-1 Hellos received 0, sent 0
        PTP Hello received 0, sent 0
        Level-1 LSPs received 0, sent 0
        LSP Retransmissions: 0
        LSP checksum errors received: 0
        LSP HT=0 checksum errors received: 0
        Level-1 CSNPs received 0, sent 0
        Level-1 PSNPs received 0, sent 0
        Level-1 DR Elections: 0
        Level-1 SPF Calculations: 0
        Level-1 Partial Route Calculations: 0
```

Example 5-24 *Seville Command Output, Scenario 5-4*

```
Seville#show ipx interface
Serial0 is up, line protocol is up
  IPX address is 2013.0200.3333.3333 [up]
  Delay of this IPX network, in ticks is 6 throughput 0 link delay 0
  IPXWAN processing not enabled on this interface.
  IPX SAP update interval is 1 minute(s)
  IPX type 20 propagation packet forwarding is disabled
  Incoming access list is not set
  Outgoing access list is not set
  IPX helper access list is not set
  SAP GNS processing enabled, delay 0 ms, output filter list is not set
  SAP Input filter list is not set
  SAP Output filter list is not set
  SAP Router filter list is not set
  Input filter list is not set
  Output filter list is not set
  Router filter list is not set
  Netbios Input host access list is not set
  Netbios Input bytes access list is not set
  Netbios Output host access list is not set
  Netbios Output bytes access list is not set
  Updates each 60 seconds, aging multiples RIP: 3 SAP: 3
  SAP interpacket delay is 55 ms, maximum size is 480 bytes
  RIP interpacket delay is 55 ms, maximum size is 432 bytes
  Watchdog processing is disabled, SPX spoofing is disabled, idle time 60
  IPX accounting is disabled
  IPX fast switching is configured (enabled)
  RIP packets received 53, RIP packets sent 55
  SAP packets received 14, SAP packets sent 25
Serial1 is up, line protocol is up
  IPX address is 2023.0200.3333.3333 [up]
  Delay of this IPX network, in ticks is 6 throughput 0 link delay 0
  IPXWAN processing not enabled on this interface.
  IPX SAP update interval is 1 minute(s)
  IPX type 20 propagation packet forwarding is disabled
  Incoming access list is not set
  Outgoing access list is not set
  IPX helper access list is not set
  SAP GNS processing enabled, delay 0 ms, output filter list is not set
  SAP Input filter list is not set
  SAP Output filter list is not set
  SAP Router filter list is not set
  Input filter list is not set
  Output filter list is not set
  Router filter list is not set
  Netbios Input host access list is not set
  Netbios Input bytes access list is not set
  Netbios Output host access list is not set
  Netbios Output bytes access list is not set
  Updates each 60 seconds, aging multiples RIP: 3 SAP: 3
 SAP interpacket delay is 55 ms, maximum size is 480 bytes
```

Example 5-24 *Seville Command Output, Scenario 5-4 (Continued)*

```
  RIP interpacket delay is 55 ms, maximum size is 432 bytes
 Watchdog processing is disabled, SPX spoofing is disabled, idle time 60
  IPX accounting is disabled
  IPX fast switching is configured (enabled)
  RIP packets received 53, RIP packets sent 62
  SAP packets received 13, SAP packets sent 37
Ethernet0 is up, line protocol is up
  IPX address is 1003. 0000.0cac.ab41, SAP [up]
  Delay of this IPX network, in ticks is 1 throughput 0 link delay 0
  IPXWAN processing not enabled on this interface.
  IPX SAP update interval is 1 minute(s)
  IPX type 20 propagation packet forwarding is disabled
  Incoming access list is not set
  Outgoing access list is not set
  IPX helper access list is not set
  SAP GNS processing enabled, delay 0 ms, output filter list is not set
  SAP Input filter list is not set
  SAP Output filter list is not set
  SAP Router filter list is not set
  Input filter list is not set
  Output filter list is not set
  Router filter list is not set
  Netbios Input host access list is not set
  Netbios Input bytes access list is not set
  Netbios Output host access list is not set
  Netbios Output bytes access list is not set
  Updates each 60 seconds, aging multiples RIP: 3 SAP: 3
  SAP interpacket delay is 55 ms, maximum size is 480 bytes
  RIP interpacket delay is 55 ms, maximum size is 432 bytes
  IPX accounting is disabled
  IPX fast switching is configured (enabled)
  RIP packets received 20, RIP packets sent 62
  SAP packets received 18, SAP packets sent 15

Seville#show ipx servers
Codes: S - Static, P - Periodic, E - EIGRP, N - NLSP, H - Holddown, + = detail
2 Total IPX Servers

Table ordering is based on routing and server info

    Type Name                     Net      Address    Port    Route Hops Itf
P      4 Bugs                      1.0000.0000.0001:0451      8/03   3  Se0
P      4 Daffy                     2.0000.0000.0001:0451      8/03   3  Se0
```

Assuming the details established in Figure 5-26 and the command output in Example 5-22, Example 5-23, and Example 5-24 for Scenario 5-4, complete or answer the following:

1. Complete Table 5-29 with all IPX network numbers. List the command(s) you use to find these network numbers. List all commands that helped you find the network numbers.

2. Complete as much of Table 5-30 as possible.

Table 5-29 *IPX Networks in Scenario 5-4*

IPX Network	Location (Such as "Between Albuquerque and Seville")	Command Used to Find This Information

Table 5-30 *IPX Addresses on Routers in Scenario 5-4*

Router	Interface	IPX Network	IPX Node
Albuquerque	E0		
	S0		
	S1		
Yosemite	E0		
	S0		

Table 5-30 *IPX Addresses on Routers in Scenario 5-4 (Continued)*

Router	Interface	IPX Network	IPX Node
	S1		
Seville	E0		
	S0		
	S1		

Scenario 5-5: IPX Configuration

Assume the network setup in Figure 5-27.

Figure 5-27 *Scenario 5-5 Network Diagram*

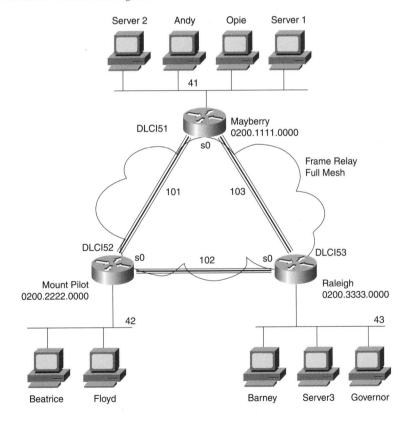

1. Assuming the details established in Figure 5-27 for Scenario 5-5, complete or answer the following: Configure IPX on all three routers. Use the network numbers listed in the figure. (Do not bother with IP.) Use point-to-point subinterfaces and use the IPX node addresses shown in the diagram on the serial interfaces.

2. You later find out that Beatrice is using NetWare's Ethernet_II encapsulation; Floyd is using Ethernet_802.3; Barney is using Ethernet_802.2, and Governor is using Ethernet_SNAP. Configure the changes necessary to support each client.

3. Assume Inverse ARP is disabled in Raleigh. Configure **frame-relay map** statements to allow IPX traffic to flow to all sites. (Yes, in real life you would fix the problem and use Inverse ARP—this scenario is contrived to make you think through IPX mapping and routing.)

Scenario Answers

Answers to Scenario 5-1: IP Addressing and Subnet Calculation

Assuming you had issued the commands in Example 5-21, the most specific network diagram would look like Figure 5-28.

Figure 5-28 *Scenario 5-1 Answer—Network with Router Fred*

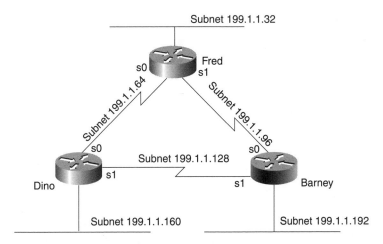

The clues that you should have found in the **show** commands are as follows:

- The types and IP addresses of the interfaces on Fred were in the **show interface** and **show ip interface brief** command output.

- The subnets could be learned form the **show ip route** command.

- The neighboring router's IP addresses could be learned from the **show ip protocol** command.

- The neighboring router's IP addresses and their hostnames could be learned for the **show cdp neighbor detail** command.

- The metric for subnet 199.1.1.128/27 in RIP updates imply that either both neighbors are attached to the same subnet, or they are attached to two separate physical media which both think they are the same subnet.

- If completely bored, the **telnet 199.1.1.x** command could be issued for all IP addresses in subnets not directly connected to Fred, hoping to get a router login prompt. That would identify the IP addresses of other router interfaces.

There is no way to know what physical media are beyond the neighboring routers. However, because CDP claims that both routers are 2500 series routers, the possible interfaces on these neighboring routers are limited. Figure 5-28 shows the other subnets generically.

Also, Figure 5-28 shows that the two neighboring routers are connected to the same subnet. If they were connected to two separate media, there would be two data links that have the same subnet number in use, which is illegal. Therefore, the figure shows the two neighboring routers attached to the same medium.

Answers to Scenario 5-2: IP Subnet Design with a Class B Network

Figure 5-29 shows the correct subnets for the network skeleton presented in Figure 5-24.

Figure 5-29 *Scenario 5-2 Diagram Scratch Pad*

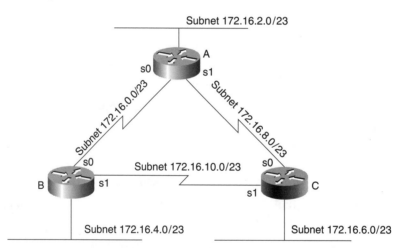

Answers to Task 1 for Scenario 5-2

Given the details in Figure 5-30 and Table 5-27 for Scenario 5-2, the subnet mask criteria are as follows:

- 200 hosts in a subnet maximum

- 100 subnets maximum

- Uses static size masks all over this network

So, the mask must have at least eight host bits because $2^7=128$ is not enough and $2^8=256$ is more than enough for numbering 200 hosts in a subnet. The mask must have at least seven subnet bits, likewise because 2^7 is the smallest power of 2 that is larger than 100, which is the required number of subnets. The first 16 bits in the mask must be binary 1, because we are using a Class B network (172.16.0.0). Figure 5-30 diagrams the possibilities.

Figure 5-30 *Subnet Mask Options for Scenario 5-2*

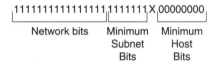

The only bit position in which a decision can be made is the 24th bit, shown with an x in Figure 5-30. That leaves two mask possibilities: 255.255.254.0 and 255.255.255.0. This sample will show the 255.255.254.0 mask because 255.255.255.0 is more intuitive.

Answers to Task 2 for Scenario 5-2

To choose a mask and pick enough subnets to use for the original topology illustrated in Figure 5-24, a review of the longer binary algorithm and shortcut algorithm for deriving subnet numbers is required. Reviewing, subnet numbers have the network number binary value in the network portion of the subnet numbers, and all binary 0s in the host bits. The bits that vary from subnet to subnet are the subnet bits—in other words, we are numbering different subnets in the subnet field.

Valid subnets with mask 255.255.254.0 are as follows:

172.16.0.0 (zero subnet)

172.16.2.0

172.16.4.0

172.16.6.0

.

.

.

172.16.252.0

172.16.254.0 (broadcast subnet)

The first six subnets, including the zero subnet, were chosen for this example, as listed in Table 5-31.

Table 5-31 *Scenario 5-2 Subnets and Addresses*

Location of Subnet Geographically	Subnet Mask	Subnet Number	Router's IP Address
Ethernet off Router A	255.255.254.0	172.16.2.0	172.16.2.1
Ethernet off Router B	255.255.254.0	172.16.4.0	172.16.4.2
Ethernet off Router C	255.255.254.0	172.16.6.0	172.16.6.3
Serial between A and B	255.255.254.0	172.16.0.0	172.16.0.1 (A) and .2 (B)
Serial between A and C	255.255.254.0	172.16.8.0	172.16.8.1 (A) and .3 (C)
Serial between B and C	255.255.254.0	172.16.10.0	172.16.10.2 (B) and .3 (C)

Answers to Task 3 for Scenario 5-2

Given the details in Figure 5-24 and Table 5-27 for Scenario 5-2, the configurations in Example 5-25, Example 5-26, and Example 5-27 satisfy the exercise of creating IP-related configuration commands for each router. These Examples include only the IP-related commands.

Example 5-25 *Router A Configuration, Scenario 5-2*

```
ip subnet-zero
no ip domain-lookup
!
interface serial0
ip address 172.16.0.1 255.255.254.0
interface serial 1
ip address 172.16.8.1 255.255.254.0
interface ethernet 0
ip address 172.16.2.1 255.255.254.0
!
router igrp 6
network 172.16.0.0
```

Example 5-26 *Router B Configuration, Scenario 5-2*

```
ip subnet-zero
no ip domain-lookup
!
interface serial0
ip address 172.16.0.2 255.255.254.0
interface serial 1
ip address 172.16.8.2 255.255.254.0
interface ethernet 0
ip address 172.16.4.2 255.255.254.0
!
router igrp 6
network 172.16.0.0
```

Example 5-27 *Router C Configuration, Scenario 5-2*

```
ip subnet-zero
no ip domain-lookup
!
interface serial0
ip address 172.16.10.3 255.255.254.0
interface serial 1
ip address 172.16.8.3  255.255.254.0
interface ethernet 0
ip address 172.16.6.3 255.255.254.0
!
router igrp 6
network 172.16.0.0
```

Answers to Scenario 5-3: IP Subnet Design with a Class C Network

Planning the network in this scenario requires a topology including four sites, one Ethernet at each site, with partially-meshed Frame Relay for connectivity, as shown previously in Figure 5-25. The number of subnets will never grow. You must choose a mask that will maximize the number of hosts per subnet and you must use network 200.1.1.0.

Answers to Task 1 for Scenario 5-3

Given the design criteria and the network setup illustrated in Figure 5-25, this scenario requires tricky subnet masks because a Class C network is used, and subnetting is needed. Using Frame Relay subinterfaces, there will be a need for seven different subnets—one for each Ethernet, and one for each Frame Relay VC.

If three subnet bits are used, eight mathematical possibilities exist for subnet numbers. However, one is the zero subnet, and the other is the broadcast subnet. In this case, use of one of the other is desired because the design called for maximizing the number of hosts per subnet. Deciding against use of the zero and broadcast subnets would then require four subnet bits, leaving only 14 hosts per subnet. So, three subnet bits, and five host bits, will be used in this solution (mask of 255.255.255.224). Figure 5-31 summarizes the subnets on the network diagram.

Figure 5-31 *Scenario 5-3 Network, with Subnets Written onto Diagram*

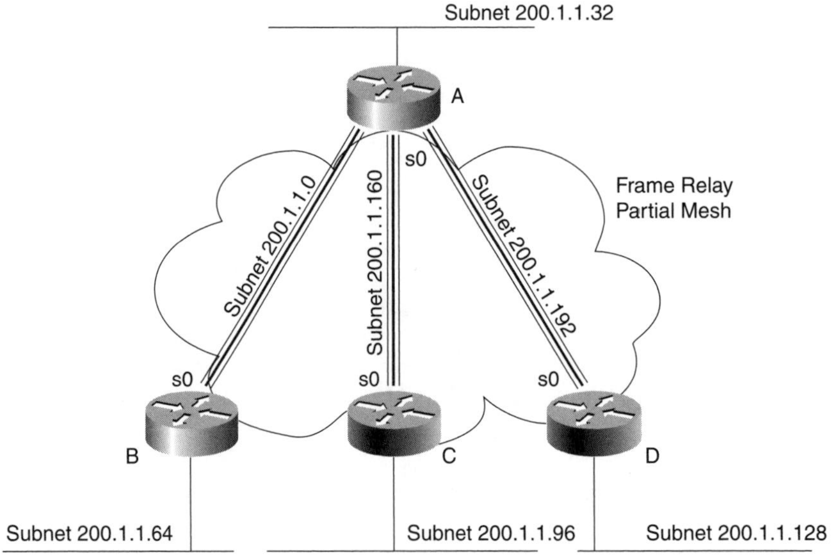

Answers to Task 2 for Scenario 5-3

Given the design criteria and the network setup illustrated in Figure 5-25 for Scenario 5-3, Table 5-32 shows the choices of subnets and addresses in this example. Only one subnet, 200.1.1.224, which is the broadcast subnet, is not used.

Table 5-32 *Scenario 5-3 Addresses and Subnets*

Location of Subnet	Subnet Mask	Subnet Number	Router's IP Address
Ethernet off Router A	255.255.255.224	200.1.1.32	200.1.1.33
Ethernet off Router B	255.255.255.224	200.1.1.64	200.1.1.65
Ethernet off Router C	255.255.255.224	200.1.1.96	200.1.1.97
Ethernet off Router D	255.255.255.224	200.1.1.128	200.1.1.129
VC between A and B	255.255.255.224	200.1.1.0	200.1.1.1 (A) and .2 (B)
VC between A and C	255.255.255.224	200.1.1.160	200.1.1.161 (A) and .162 (B)
VC between A and D	255.255.255.224	200.1.1.192	200.1.1.193 (A) and .194 (B)

Answers to Task 3 for Scenario 5-3

Using the DLCIs from Figure 5-25, Example 5-28, Example 5-29, Example 5-30, and Example 5-31 provide the IP-related configuration commands for each router.

Example 5-28 *Router A Configuration, Scenario 5-3*

```
ip subnet-zero
no ip domain-lookup
!
interface serial0
encapsulation frame-relay
interface serial 0.1
ip address 200.1.1.1 255.255.254.0
interface-dlci 41
!
interface serial 0.2
ip address 200.1.1.161 255.255.254.0
interface-dlci 42
!
interface serial 0.3
ip address 200.1.1.193 255.255.254.0
interface-dlci 43
!
interface ethernet 0
ip address 200.1.1.33 255.255.254.0
!
router igrp 6
network 200.1.1.0
```

Example 5-29 *Router B Configuration, Scenario 5-3*

```
ip subnet-zero
no ip domain-lookup
!
interface serial0
encapsulation frame-relay
interface serial 0.1
ip address 200.1.1.2 255.255.254.0
interface-dlci 40
!
interface ethernet 0
ip address 200.1.1.65 255.255.254.0
!
router igrp 6
network 200.1.1.0
```

Example 5-30 *Router C Configuration, Scenario 5-3*

```
ip subnet-zero
no ip domain-lookup
!
interface serial0
encapsulation frame-relay
interface serial 0.1
ip address 200.1.1.162 255.255.254.0
interface-dlci 40
!
interface ethernet 0
ip address 200.1.1.97 255.255.254.0
!
router igrp 6
network 200.1.1.0
```

Example 5-31 *Router D Configuration, Scenario 5-3*

```
ip subnet-zero
no ip domain-lookup
!
interface serial0
encapsulation frame-relay
interface serial 0.1
ip address 200.1.1.194 255.255.254.0
interface-dlci 40
!
interface ethernet 0
ip address 200.1.1.129 255.255.254.0
!
router igrp 6
network 200.1.1.0
```

Answers to Scenario 5-4: IPX Examination

Assuming the details established in Figure 5-26, and the command output in Example 5-22, Example 5-23, and Example 5-24 for Scenario 5-4, the **show ipx interface brief** command and **show ipx route** commands are the best methods for learning the network numbers in Table 5-33 (Task 1 for this scenario).

Table 5-33 *IPX Networks in Scenario 5-4—Completed Chart*

IPX Network	Location (Such as "Between Albuquerque and Seville")	Command Used to Find This Information
1001	Albuquerque Ethernet0	**show ipx interface brief** on Albuquerque
		show ipx route on Yosemite
1002	Yosemite Ethernet0	**show ipx route** on Yosemite
1003	Seville Ethernet0	**show cdp neighbor detail** on Albuquerque
2012	Albuquerque–Yosemite	**show cdp neighbor detail** on Albuquerque
		show ipx route on Yosemite
2013	Albuquerque–Seville	**show cdp neighbor detail** on Albuquerque
		show ipx route on Yosemite
2023	Yosemite–Seville	**show ipx route** on Yosemite
		show ipx interface on Seville
1	Bugs' internal network	**show ipx servers** on Seville
		show ipx route on Yosemite
2	Daffy's internal network	**show ipx servers** on Seville
		show ipx route on Yosemite

Assuming the details established in Figure 5-26 and the command output in Example 5-22, Example 5-23, and Example 5-24 for Scenario 5-4, the network numbers are found from several sources as seen in Table 5-33. The additional requirement for Task 2 is to find the node part of the IPX addresses on each interface. The easy way to learn this information is through the **show ipx interface** command. Of course, only one such command was provided in Example 5-22, Example 5-23, and Example 5-24. The output of the RIP and SAP debugs show the source IPX addresses of the updates sent by each router, which supplies the rest of the answers to the question. The full answers are listed in Table 5-34.

Table 5-34 *IPX Addresses on Routers in Scenario 5-4—Completed Table*

Router	Interface	IPX Network	IPX node
Albuquerque	E0	1001	0000.0c35.ab12
	S0	2012	0200.1111.1111
	S1	2013	0200.1111.1111
Yosemite	E0	1002	0000.0c24.7841
	S0	2012	0200.2222.2222
	S1	2023	0200.2222.2222
Seville	E0	1003	0000.0cac.ab41
	S0	2013	0200.3333.3333
	S1	2023	0200.3333.3333

Answers to Scenario 5-5: IPX Configuration

Answers to Task 1 for Scenario 5-5

Assuming the details established in Figure 5-27 for Scenario 5-5, Example 5-32, Example 5-33, and Example 5-34 provide the IPX configurations on all three routers: Mayberry, Mount Pilot, and Raleigh, respectively.

Example 5-32 *Mayberry Configuration, Scenario 5-5, Task 1*

```
ipx routing 0200.1111.0000
!
interface serial0
encapsulation frame-relay
!
interface serial 0.2 point-to-point
ipx network 101
frame-relay interface-dlci 52
!
interface serial 0.3 point-to-point
ipx network 103
frame-relay interface-dlci 53

!
interface ethernet 0
ipx network 41
```

Example 5-33 *Mount Pilot Configuration, Scenario 5-5, Task 1*

```
ipx routing 0200.2222.0000
!
interface serial0
encapsulation frame-relay
!
interface serial 0.1 point-to-point
ipx network 101
frame-relay interface-dlci 51
!
interface serial 0.3 point-to-point
ipx network 102
frame-relay interface-dlci 53
!
interface ethernet 0
ipx network 42
```

Example 5-34 *Raleigh Configuration, Scenario 5-5, Task 1*

```
ipx routing 0200.3333.0000
!
interface serial0
encapsulation frame-relay
!
interface serial 0.1 point-to-point
ipx network 103
frame-relay interface-dlci 51
!
interface serial 0.2 point-to-point
ipx network 102
frame-relay interface-dlci 52
!
interface ethernet 0
ipx network 42
```

Your answer should match Examples 5-32–5-34, with a few minor exceptions. The book does not specify the serial interface, nor does it restrict the subinterface numbers chosen. Likewise, the Ethernet interface number was not specified. Otherwise, the configuration should identically match these examples.

Answers to Task 2 for Scenario 5-5

Assuming the details established in Figure 5-27 for Scenario 5-5, the second task for Scenario 5-5 calls for additional encapsulations. Beatrice is using NetWare's Ethernet_II encapsulation, Floyd is using Ethernet_802.3, Barney is using Ethernet_802.2, and Governor is using Ethernet_SNAP. Hopefully, you remembered the encapsulation names used in the IOS; the names supplied in the problem statement use the NetWare names. In real life, a simple question mark when typing the **ipx network** interface subcommand would remind you of the names, but the objective is to memorize things so you can pass the test! (Refer to Table 5-23 for reminders on how to remember the names.) Example 5-35 and Example 5-36 show just the configuration commands used to change the configuration on Mount Pilot and Raleigh necessary to support each client.

Example 5-35 *Mount Pilot Configuration, Scenario 5-5, Task 2—Changes Only*

```
interface ethernet 0
ipx network 42 encapsulation arpa
ipx network 142 secondary
```

Example 5-36 *Raleigh Configuration, Scenario 5-5, Task 2—Changes Only*

```
interface ethernet 0
ipx network 43 encapsulation sap
ipx network 143 encapsulation snap secondary
```

Two new network numbers are needed; 142 and 143 are used in this case. Any numbers you use are fine, unless they are duplicates of some other network. The **ipx network 142 secondary** command on Mount Pilot has no encapsulation type configured because the default encapsulation type is Novell-ether. The second IPX network command must be configured with the **secondary** keyword, or it will replace **ipx network** command that was configured first.

Answers to Task 3 for Scenario 5-5

Assuming Inverse ARP is disabled in Raleigh, as depicted in Figure 5-27, two **frame-relay map** commands are needed on Raleigh, and one each on the other two routers. For a full description of **frame-relay map** statements, refer to Chapter 8, "WAN Protocols: Understanding Point-to-Point, Frame Relay, and ISDN."

The key to **map** statements is knowing the IPX address of the neighboring router on the other side of the link—in this case, the IPX addresses associated with each subinterface. Figure 5-32 summarizes these addresses.

The key components of the **map** statements include the routed protocol (IPX), next-hop addresses, and associated DLCI. Example 5-37 lists all 4 **map** commands, with notations as to which command is configured on which router. If RIP and SAP updates are to be sent, the **broadcast** keyword must also be coded, as shown in the Example 5-37.

Figure 5-32 *IPX Addresses on Frame Relay, Scenario 5-5*

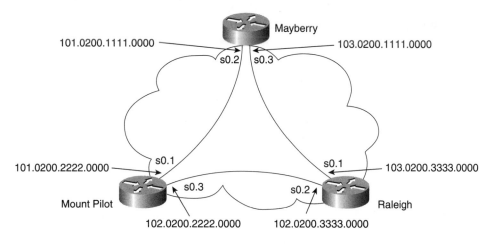

Example 5-37 *frame-relay map Commands—Scenario 5-5, Task 3*

```
Mayberry(config)#frame-relay map ipx 103.0200.3333.0000 53 broadcast

MountPilot(config)#frame-relay map ipx 102.0200.3333.0000 53 broadcast

Raleigh(config)#frame-relay map ipx 103.0200.1111.0000 51 broadcast
Raleigh(config)#frame-relay map ipx 102.0200.2222.0000 52 broadcast
```

The following table outlines the CCNA exam objectives that are reviewed in this chapter. The numbers shown correspond to the master list of objectives found in Chapter 1, "What Is CCNA?"

Objective	Description
28	Monitor Novell IPX operation on the router.
34	Enable the Novell IPX protocol and configure interfaces.
39	Add the RIP routing protocol to your configuration.
40	Add the IGRP routing protocol to your configuration.
41	Explain the services of separate and integrated multiprotocol routing.
42	List problems that each routing type encounters when dealing with topology changes and describe techniques to reduce the number of these problems.
43	Describe the benefits of network segmentation with routers. [1]

1. Although listed as an objective covered in this chapter, objective 43 is much better placed in this book with the discussion contrasting segmentation using bridges and switches, so that objective is covered in Chapter 4.

CHAPTER 6

Understanding Routing

This book is organized into chapters based on the organization of the CCNA objectives as defined by Cisco Systems. This chapter matches the CCNA objectives organization topic titled simply "Routing." The objectives in this topic are actually better described as *routing protocols*—the protocols used to create routes in a routing table. *Routing* generally refers to the work a router does when deciding how to forward an individual packet. For a more complete discussion of the terms *routing* and *routing protocol,* please refer to Chapter 3, "Understanding the OSI Reference Model."

This chapter starts with an examination of routing protocol concepts then reviews IGRP and IP RIP configuration. A discussion of IPX RIP, SAP, and GNS follows. SAP and GNS are not specifically mentioned in the objectives, other than for SAP filtering, but a review is needed; it is included in this chapter. Finally, the chapter concludes with an explanation of objective 41: the services of separate and integrated multiprotocol routing.

How to Best Use This Chapter

By taking the following steps, you can make better use of your study time:

- Keep your notes and answers for all your work with this book in one place for easy reference.

- Take the "Do I Know This Already?" quiz and write down your answers. Studies show retention is significantly increased through writing facts and concepts down, even if you never look at the information again!

- Figure 6-1 helps guide you to the next step in preparation for this topic area on the CCNA exam.

Figure 6-1   *How To Use This Chapter*

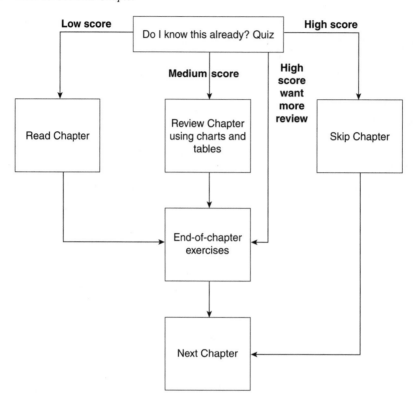

"Do I Know This Already?" Quiz

1. What type of routing protocol algorithm uses a holddown timer? What is its purpose?

   _____

   _____

   _____

2. Define what split-horizon means to the contents of a routing update. Does this apply to both the distance vector algorithm and link state algorithm?

   _____

   _____

   _____

3. How does the IOS designate a subnet in the routing table as a directly connected network? A route learned with IGRP? A route learned with RIP?

_____

_____

_____

4. Create a configuration for IGRP on a router with these interfaces and addresses: e0 using 10.1.1.1, e1 using 224.1.2.3, s0 using 10.1.2.1, and s1 using 199.1.1.1. Use process ID 5.

_____

_____

_____

5. How often does IPX RIP send routing updates by default?

_____

_____

_____

6. What does GNS stand for? Who creates GNS requests, and who creates GNS replies?

_____

_____

_____

7. Define the term Separate Multiprotocol Routing in the context of the Cisco IOS and Novell IPX.

_____

_____

_____

8. If Serial0 has a **bandwidth 1544** interface subcommand, and Serial1 has a **bandwidth 56** interface subcommand, what metric will IPX RIP associate with each interface?

_____

_____

_____

9. What **show** commands list IPX RIP metric values in a Cisco router?

_____

_____

_____

10. Define the term *Integrated Multiprotocol Routing* in the context of the Cisco IOS and Novell IPX.

_____

_____

_____

11. If the commands **router rip**, followed by **network 10.0.0.0**, with no other **network** commands were configured in a router that has an Ethernet0 interface with IP address 168.10.1.1, would RIP send updates out Ethernet0?

_____

_____

_____

12. What routing protocols support integrated multiprotocol routing?

_____

_____

_____

You can find the answers to the "Do I Know This Already?" quiz in Appendix B on page 573. Review the answers, grade your quiz, and choose an appropriate next step in this chapter based on the suggestions in the "How to Best Use This Chapter" topic earlier in this chapter. Your choices for the next step are as follows:

- **5 or fewer correct**—Read this chapter.

- **6, 7, or 8 correct**—Review this chapter, looking at the charts and diagrams that summarize most of the concepts and facts in this chapter.

- **9 or more correct**—If you want more review on these topics, skip to the exercises at the end of this chapter. If you do not want more review on these topics, skip this chapter.

Foundation Topics

How Distance Vector Routing Protocols Work

CCNA Objective Covered in This Section

42	List problems that each routing type encounters when dealing with topology changes and describe techniques to reduce the number of these problems.

This section explains distance vector routing protocols in detail. Two distance vector routing protocols, RIP and IGRP, will be used as examples. Configuration on a Cisco router is left until the next section.

Terminology relating to routing protocols is often misunderstood; this confusion is a direct result of inconsistent use of terminology by authors! The terminology relating to routing protocols and routing in this book is consistent with the courses in Training Path 1 and Training Path 2, as well as with most Cisco documentation. The first term that needs to be defined is *routing protocol*. This term can be contrasted with *routed protocol*. Chapter 3 provides a silly, but I hope a memorable, story (The "Ted and Ting" Story) that can help distinguish between the first two terms. Three definitions follow:

- A *routing protocol* fills the routing table with loop-free routing information. Examples include RIP and IGRP.

- A *routed protocol* describes a protocol that has a Layer 3 equivalent specification, which defines logical addressing and routing. The packets defined by the network layer (Layer 3) portion of these protocols can be routed. Examples of protocols include IP and IPX.

- *Routing type* is the term used in CCNA objective 42, which describes the underlying algorithms and logic of a routing protocol. Distance vector and link state are the two types of routing protocols covered by the CCNA exam.

IP routing protocols fill the IP routing table with valid, loop-free routes. Each route includes a subnet number, the interface out which to forward packets so they are delivered to that subnet, and the IP address of the next router that should receive packets destined to that subnet (if needed).

Before discussing the underlying logic, the goals of a routing protocol should be considered. The goals documented in the following list are common for any IP routing protocol, regardless of its underlying logic type:

- Dynamically learn and fill the routing table with a route to all subnets in the network.

- If more than one route to a subnet is available, place the best route in the routing table.

- Notice when routes in the table are no longer valid, and remove those routes from the routing table.

- If a route is removed from the routing table and another route through another neighboring router is available, add the route to the routing table. (Many people think of this goal and the previous one as a single goal.)

- Add new routes, or replace lost routes with the best currently available route, as quickly as possible. The time between losing the route and finding a working replacement route is called *convergence time*.

- Prevent routing loops.

Several routing protocols for TCP/IP exist. IP's long history and continued popularity have called for several different competing options to be specified and created. So, classifying IP routing protocols based on their differences is useful, as well as being a fair topic for exam questions!

One major classification of IP routing protocols is whether they are optimized for creating routes inside one organization, or routes for two or more interconnected organizations. Exterior routing protocols are optimized for use between routers from different organizations. Border Gateway Protocol (BGP) and Exterior Gateway Protocol (EGP) are the two options for exterior routing protocols; BGP is the most popular and more recently developed of the two. (EGP is not technically a routing protocol, but a "reachability" protocol; it is obsolete.)

This chapter concentrates only on interior routing protocols, simply because Training Path 1 and Training Path 2 focus on interior routing protocols. If you are interested in pursuing CCIE-ISP or CCIE-R/S certification, understanding exterior routing protocols is very important.

The type of underlying logic is the next classification of routing protocols. CCNA objective 42 calls this concept *routing type*. Others call it *routing algorithm*. Personally, I prefer *type of routing protocol*, yet a third term for the same concept. Terminology counts; for the CCNA exam, remember all three terms.

One type of routing protocol is *link state*. Link-state protocols cause a topological database to be built on each router; entries describing each router, each router's attached links, and each router's neighboring routers, are included in the database. An analogy is that each router builds a complete map of the network. The topology database is processed by an algorithm called the *Dijkstra shortest path first* (SPF) algorithm for choosing the best routes to place into the routing table. This detailed topology information along with the Dijkstra algorithm lets link-state protocols avoid loops and converge quickly.

Distance vector is the other type of routing protocol and will be discussed in much detail in the next subsection.

Several different implementations of distance vector and link-state routing protocols could be covered on the CCNA exam; only RIP version 1 and IGRP should be covered in-depth. RIP v1 and IGRP are similar in most details, with the big exception being that IGRP uses a much more robust metric. Both RIP v1 and IGRP are covered in more detail later in this chapter.

RIP v2 includes many improvements over RIP v1. Most notably, the subnet mask associated with each advertised route is included in the routing update. The mask allows routers to use features such as variable-length subnet masks (VLSM) and route summarization, which are features sure to be covered on the CCNP exams.

Enhanced IGRP (EIGRP) is another distance vector routing protocol, but it uses more advanced features to avoid loops and speed convergence. The underlying algorithm is called the *Diffusing Update Algorithm (DUAL)*. DUAL defines a method for each router to not only calculate the best current route to each subnet, but to also calculate alternative routes that could be used should the current route fail. An alternate route, using what DUAL defines as a neighboring *Feasible Successor router*, is guaranteed to be loop-free; so convergence can happen quickly. EIGRP also transmits the subnet mask for each routing entry. Therefore, features such as VLSM and route summarization are easily supported.

Open Shortest Path First (OSPF) is a link-state routing protocol used for IP. OSPF avoids routing loops by transmitting and keeping more detailed topology information, which allows it to use calculations that prevent loops. The subnet mask information is also transmitted, allowing features such as VLSM and route summarization.

A more detailed explanation of these routing protocols can be found in an excellent Cisco Press book titled *CCIE Professional Development: Routing TCP/IP, Volume 1*.

Table 6-1 lists interior IP routing protocols and their types. Also, a column referring to whether the routing protocol includes subnet mask information in the routing updates is listed for future reference.

Table 6-1 *Interior IP Routing Protocols and Types*

Routing Protocol	Type	Loop Prevention Mechanisms	Mask Sent in Updates?
RIP v1	Distance vector	Holddown timer, split-horizon	No
RIP v2	Distance vector	Holddown timer, split-horizon	Yes
IGRP	Distance vector	Holddown timer, split-horizon	No
EIGRP	Distance vector	DUAL and Feasible successors	Yes
OSPF	Link-state	Dijkstra SPF algorithm and full topology knowledge	Yes

Distance Vector Routing Protocols

To understand what distance vector routing means is to understand how a routing protocol accomplishes the following goals:

- Learning routing information

- Noticing failed routes

- Adding the current best route after one has failed

- Preventing loops

The following list summarizes the behavior of a router that uses the RIP v1 or IGRP distance vector routing protocols:

- *Directly connected subnets* are already known by the router; these routes are advertised.

- *Routing updates* are broadcast (or multicast) in many cases. This is so all neighboring routers can learn routes via the single broadcasted or multicasted update.

- *Routing updates* are listened for, so this router can learn new routes.

- A *metric* describes each route in the update. The metric describes how good the route is; if multiple routes to the same subnet are learned, the lower metric route is used.

- *Topology information* in routing updates include, at a minimum, the subnet and metric information.

- *Periodic updates* are expected to be received from neighboring routers at a specified interval. Failure to receive updates from a neighbor in a timely manner results in the removal of routes learned from that neighbor.

- A *route* learned from a neighboring router is assumed to be through that router.

- A *failed route* is advertised for a time, with a metric that implies the network is "infinite" distance. This route is considered unusable.

Figure 6-2 demonstrates how directly connected subnets are already known by the router through advertisement. In this case, Router A advertises two directly connected routes. Table 6-2 shows the resulting routing table on Router B.

Figure 6-2   *Router A Advertising Directly Connected Routes*

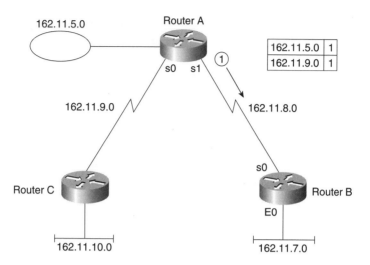

Table 6-2   *Router B Routing Table, After Receiving Update in Figure 6-2*

Group (Mask is 255.255.255.0)	Outgoing Interface	Next Router
162.11.5.0	S0	162.11.8.1
162.11.7.0	E0	
162.11.8.0	S0	
162.11.9.0	S0	162.11.8.1

The two directly connected routes on Router B do not have a *Next Router field* because packets to those subnets can be sent directly to hosts in those subnets. The Next Router field for the routes learned from Router A show Router A's IP address as the Next Router, as described previously. (A route learned from a neighboring router is assumed to be through that router.) Router B typically learns Router A's IP address for these routes by simply looking at the source IP address of the routing update.

Metric values are cumulative. A subnet learned via an update from a neighbor is advertised, but with a higher metric. For example, an update received on serial 1 lists a subnet with metric 5. Before advertising that subnet in an update sent out some other interface, the router adds to the metric, based on a value associated with serial 1. With RIP, because hop count is the metric, the advertised metric would be 6 in this case. Figure 6-3 and Table 6-3 illustrate the concept.

Figure 6-3 *Router A Advertising Routes Learned from Router C*

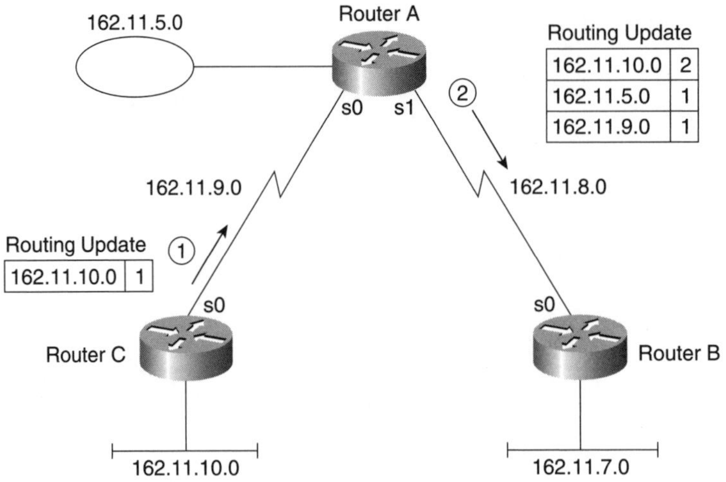

Table 6-3 *Router B Routing Table, After Receiving Update in Figure 6-3*

Group	Outgoing Interface	Next Router
162.11.5.0	S0	162.11.8.1
162.11.7.0	E0	
162.11.8.0	S0	
162.11.9.0	S0	162.11.8.1
162.11.10.0	S0	162.11.8.1

Figure 6-3 demonstrates the seven distance vector routing protocol behaviors previously listed with the exception of periodic updates and failed routes. The metric describing subnet 162.11.10.0, received from Router C, was incremented by one before advertising about that subnet to Router B. This metric value represents hop count, which is used by RIP. (IGRP uses a different metric, which will be discussed later.) The route to 162.11.10.0 that Router B adds to its routing table refers to Router A as the next router because Router B learned the route from Router A; Router B knows nothing about the network topology on the "other side" of Router A.

Periodic routing updates are sent by each router. A routing update timer determines how often the updates are sent; the timer is equal on all routers. The absence of routing updates for a preset number of routing timer intervals results in the removal of the routes previously learned from the router that has become silent.

Most of the issues with distance vector routing protocols arise when working with networks with redundant links. One issue is straightforward, whereas the other two are not as obvious. Table 6-4 summarizes these issues, and then each will be explained in succession.

Table 6-4 *Issues Relating to Distance Vector Routing Protocols in Networks with Redundant Links*

Issue	Solution
Multiple routes to same subnet, equal metric	Implementation options of either using the first route learned or putting all routes in the routing table
Routing loops occurring due to updates passing each other over a single link	Split-horizon
Routing loops occurring due to updates passing each other in networks with redundancy	Poison Reverse
Counting to infinity—side effect of propagating transient bad routing information	Holddown timer

Issues When Multiple Routes to the Same Subnet Exist

The first issue is straightforward and is described more easily with the example in Figure 6-4 and Table 6-5 and Table 6-6.

Figure 6-4 *Routers A and C Advertising to Router B*

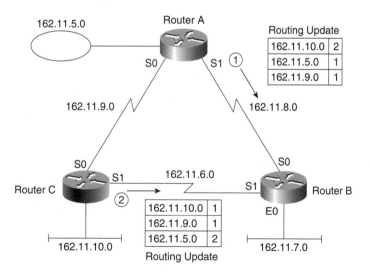

Table 6-5 *Router B Routing Table, with Two Routes to Same Subnet, While Router B Serial 1 Is Down*

Group	Outgoing Interface	Next Router	Metric
162.11.5.0	S0	162.11.8.1	1
162.11.7.0	E0		0
162.11.8.0	S0		0
162.11.9.0	S0	162.11.8.1	1
162.11.10.0	S0	162.11.8.1	2

Table 6-6 *Router B Routing Table, with Two Routes to Same Subnet, After Router B Serial 1 Is Up*

Group	Outgoing Interface	Next Router	Metric
162.11.5.0	S0	162.11.8.1	1
162.11.6.0	S1		0
162.11.7.0	E0		0
162.11.8.0	S0		0
162.11.9.0	S0	162.11.8.1	1
162.11.10.0	S1	162.11.6.2	1

One route was changed, one route was added, and one route that could have been changed was not. The route to 162.11.10.0 was changed because the metric for the route through Router C (metric 1) is smaller than the one from Router A (metric 2). The route to directly connected subnet 162.11.6.0 was added, but not because of this distance vector routing protocol; it was added by Router B because it is a directly connected subnet, and that interface is now up. Finally, the route to subnet 162.11.9.0 is advertised with metric 2 by both Routers A and C. In this case, the route that was already in the table is left in the table, which is a reasonable choice. The choice of just placing one of the two equal metric routes in the table is an implementation decision. Cisco routers can include up to six equal-cost routes in the routing table, instead of the choice shown in this example.

Split-Horizon, Holddown, and Poison Reverse

Routing loops can occur when using distance vector routing protocols because bad routing information can be propagated. Split-horizon is the popular solution to the problem and works very well in most topologies. Split-horizon with Poison Reverse tackles more robust topological cases. Figure 6-5 shows an example of this problem.

Figure 6-5 *Advertisements Passing on Serial Link for Subnet 162.11.7.0*

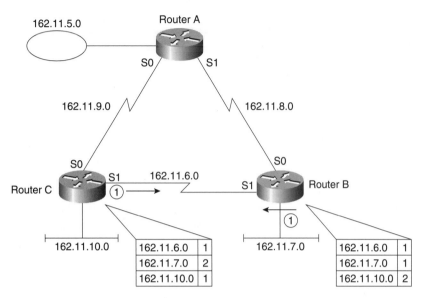

NOTE   The routing updates in Figure 6-5 show only the information needed for the point being made in this example; other routes that would normally be in the routing update are omitted.

In Figure 6-5, the routing updates are sent periodically. There is no requirement or effort to make the updates flow from C and B at the same time; however, in this case, B and C are sending updates at the same instant in time. This is not a problem until B advertises an infinite distance (metric) route to 162.11.7.0 because it just failed. However, the update from C passes the update from B on the serial link. Table 6-7 and Table 6-8 show the resulting routing table entries, with a reference to the metric values.

Table 6-7   *Router B Routing Table, After Subnet 162.11.7.0 Failed, and Update from Router C Is Received*

Group	Outgoing Interface	Next Router	Metric
162.11.6.0	S1		0
162.11.7.0	S1		2
162.11.10.0	S1	162.11.6.2	1

Table 6-8   *Router C Routing Table, After Subnet 162.11.7.0 Failed, and Update from Router B Is Received*

Group	Outgoing Interface	Next Router	Metric
162.11.6.0	S1		0
162.11.7.0	S1		999
162.11.10.0	E0		1

Now Router C has an infinite distance route, but Router B will send packets to 162.11.7.0 to Router C. Router C claimed to have a metric 2 route to 162.11.7.0, at the same time Router C was receiving the update that told it the route to 162.11.7.0 was no longer valid. The process repeats itself with the next routing update, except Router B advertises metric 3, and Router C will advertise an infinite (bad) metric for subnet 162.11.7.0. This will continue until both numbers reach infinity! For those less patient, each distance vector routing protocol implementation sets a metric value for which the number is considered to be infinite, for example, 16 is infinite for RIP.

But routes learned with an update entering an interface do not need to be advertised again out the same interface because the other routers sharing that link should already know about those routes from the original routing update.

Split-horizon is the solution to the counting to infinity problem in this case. Split-horizon simply means that routes learned via updates on interface x are not advertised on updates sent out interface x. Figure 6-6 shows the updated version of Figure 6-5, with split-horizon enabled. Subnet 162.11.10.0 is not advertised by Router B, and 162.11.7.0 is not advertised by Router C, on their S1 interfaces, respectively.

Figure 6-6   *Split-Horizon Enabled*

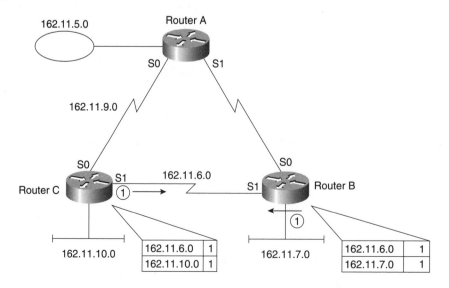

Split-horizon defeats a problem that is sometimes called *counting to infinity.* The holddown timer is part of a solution to the counting to infinity problem for more redundant networks. Split-horizon does not defeat the counting to infinity problem in all topologies. An additional solution is required, which includes a holddown timer and a routing update feature called Poison Reverse. Figure 6-7 shows an example topology showing counting to infinity.

Figure 6-7   *Counting to Infinity*

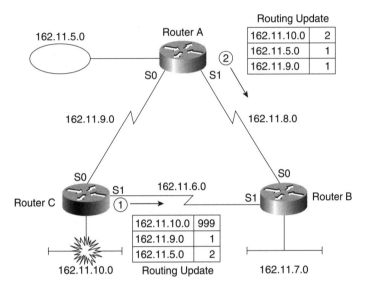

For the scenario in Figure 6-7, subnet 162.11.10.0 fails; Router C sends updates to Router B and Router A, as shown in Step 1 of Figure 6-7. Router A happens to send its next update out its S1 interface to Router B just before it hears the bad news about 162.11.10.0, as denoted as Step 2 in Figure 6-7. Table 6-9 shows the result of these two updates entering Router B.

Table 6-9   *Router B Routing Table, After Updates in Figure 6-7 Are Received*

Group	Outgoing Interface	Next Router	Metric
162.11.5.0	S0	162.11.8.1	1
162.11.6.0	S1		
162.11.7.0	E0		
162.11.8.0	S0		
162.11.9.0	S0	162.11.8.1	1
162.11.10.0	S0	162.11.8.1	2

Router B now thinks it has a valid route to 162.11.10.0, pointing back to Router A. On B's next updates, it will not advertise subnet 162.11.10.0 out S0 due to split-horizon rules, but Router B will advertise 162.11.10.0 to Router C.

The solution is to enable a holddown timer. In the example in Figure 6-7, Router B's original route pointed to Router C. It was then changed to point to Router A. Holddown would require Router B to wait for a period to learn new routes after an old one has failed, in this case ignoring the metric 2 route learned from Router A. Holddown is defined as:

> When learning about a failed route, ignore any new information about that subnet for a time equal to the holddown timer.

With holddown enabled, Router C would not process the metric 3 route learned in Step 1 of Figure 6-7. During the same time, Routers C and A would both be advertising infinite metric routes to 162.11.10.0 to Router B, which would also quickly only be receiving routing updates for 162.11.10.0 with an infinite metric.

(*Infinite* is a term used to signify the concept, not the actual value. Each routing protocol can, and typically does, define a maximum usable metric value with any number over that being considered infinite.)

Poison Reverse is another method to help avoid loops and speed convergence. When a distance vector routing protocol notices that a particular route is no longer valid, it has two choices. One is simply to quit advertising about that subnet; the other is to advertise that route, but with an infinite metric, signifying that the route is bad. Poison Reverse calls for the second of these options, which removes any ambiguity about whether the route is still valid. For example, in Figure 6-7 again, a metric of 999 is used to signify infinity. Router C is using Poison Reverse to ensure that Router A and Router B do not point routes for 162.11.10.0 back through Router C.

RIP and IGRP

RIP and IGRP use distance vector logic, so they are very similar in many respects. There are a couple of major differences, which will be explained in the upcoming text. Table 6-10 outlines the features of RIP and IGRP.

Table 6-10 *RIP and IGRP Feature Comparison*

Feature	RIP (Defaults)	IGRP (Defaults)
Update Timer	30 seconds	90 seconds
Metric	Hop Count	Function of bandwidth and delay (default); can include reliability, load, and MTU
Holddown timer	180	280
Flash updates?	Yes	Yes
Mask sent in update?	No for RIP v1, yes for RIP v2	No

The metric with IGRP is more robust than RIP's metric. The metric is calculated using an unpublished algorithm, which uses the bandwidth and delay settings on the interface on which the update was received. By setting bandwidth and delay, the metric is more meaningful; longer hop routes over faster links can be considered better routes. However, without the unpublished algorithm, you do not know which route would be chosen unless you try it!

The metric used by IP RIP is hop count. When an update is received, the metric for each subnet in the update signifies the number of routers between the router receiving the update and each subnet. Before sending an update, a router increments its metric for routes to each subnet by one.

Flash updates, also known as triggered updates, speed up convergence. When a router notices a directly connected subnet has failed, it immediately sends another routing update on its other interfaces rather than waiting on the routing update timer to expire. This causes the information about the failed route to be forwarded more quickly and starts the holddown timers more quickly as well on the neighboring routers, as seen in Figure 6-8.

Figure 6-8   *IGRP Flash Updates*

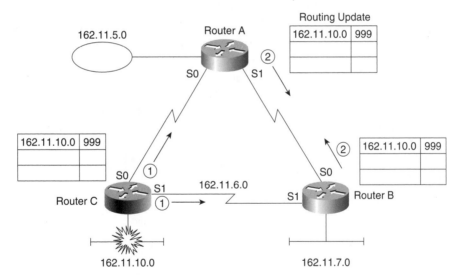

All routing updates in Figure 6-8 are sent immediately, without waiting for the next routing update timer. Because all the routers will ignore any new information about this subnet for holddown time, fast propagation of the fact that the route failed is not harmful. This mechanism quickly prevents packets from being unnecessarily routed.

Finally, the issue of whether the mask is sent is particularly important if VLSMs in the same network are desired. This topic is discussed in the section "Configuration of RIP and IGRP."

Distance Vector Routing Protocol Summary

Distance vector routing protocols learn and advertise routes. The routes placed into the routing table should be loop-free and the best known working route. Metrics are used to choose the best route. Mechanisms such as split-horizon and holddown timers are used to prevent routing loops.

Configuration of RIP and IGRP

CCNA Objectives Covered in This Section

39	Add the RIP routing protocol to your configuration.
40	Add the IGRP routing protocol to your configuration.

RIP and IGRP configuration requires an understanding of two subtle nuances, namely, what the **network** command really implies, and how the router interprets the **network** command. Other than these two details, configuration is relatively easy.

Verification of the configuration is Cisco Worldwide Training's choice of terms to describe the process of verifying that the router is doing what you expect, based on the configuration. The routing protocol is often assumed to be working, until some tricky problem occurs. Several key points about the **show** and **debug** commands that are useful when working with routing protocols will be covered in this section. Table 6-11 and Table 6-12 list the key commands for configuration and verification of IP routing protocols RIP and IGRP.

Table 6-11   *IP RIP and IGRP Configuration Commands in Training Path 1 and Training Path 2*

Command	Configuration mode
router rip	Global
router igrp *process-id*	Global
network *net-number*	Router subcommand
passive interface *type number*	Router subcommand
maximum-paths *x*	Router subcommand

Table 6-12   *IP RIP and IGRP EXEC Commands in Training Path 1 and Training Path 2*

Command	Function
show ip route [*subnet*]	Shows entire routing table, or one entry if subnet is entered
show ip protocol	Routing protocol parameters, current timer values
debug ip rip	Issues log messages for each RIP update
debug ip igrp transactions	Issues log messages with details of the IGRP updates

Table 6-12 *IP RIP and IGRP EXEC Commands in Training Path 1 and Training Path 2 (Continued)*

Command	Function
debug ip igrp events	Issues log messages for each IGRP packet
ping	Sends and receives ICMP echo messages to verify connectivity
trace	Sends series of ICMP echos with increasing TTL values to verify the current route to a host

The network **Command**

Each **network** command "enables" RIP or IGRP on a set of interfaces. However, what enables really means is not obvious from Cisco IOS documentation. Also, the parameters on the network command are not intuitive to many people new to Cisco IOS configuration commands; therefore, routing protocol configuration, including the **network** command, is a likely topic for tricky questions on the exam.

The **network** command causes implementation of the following three functions:

- RIP or IGRP updates are broadcast out an interface.

- RIP or IGRP updates are processed if they enter that same interface.

- The subnet directly connected to that interface is advertised.

The **network** command matches some of the interfaces on a router. The interfaces matched by the **network** command have the three functions previously mentioned performed on them. Examples provide a much easier understanding of the **network** command, as demonstrated in Figure 6-9 and Example 6-1.

Figure 6-9 *Sample Router with Five Interfaces*

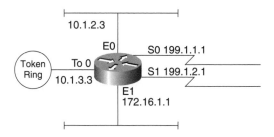

Example 6-1 *Sample Router Configuration with RIP Partially Enabled*

```
interface ethernet 0
ip address 10.1.2.3 255.255.255.0
interface ethernet 1
ip address 172.16.1.1 255.255.255.0
interface Tokenring 0
ip address 10.1.3.3 255.255.255.0
interface serial 0
ip address 199.1.1.1 255.255.255.0
interface serial 1
ip address 199.1.2.1 255.255.255.0
!
router rip
network 10.0.0.0
network 199.1.1.0
```

The router matches interfaces with the **network** command by asking this simple question:

> Which of my interfaces have IP addresses in the same network number referenced in this **network** subcommand?

For any interfaces that have IP addresses in the same network number referenced in this **network** subcommand, routing updates are broadcasted, listened for, and the connected subnet is advertised. A single **network** command will probably match more than one interface because the parameter to the **network** command is a Class A, B, or C network number, and most networks will be using multiple subnets of that same class A, B, or C network. Because many smaller networks will use subnets of a single network, a single **network** command will match all interfaces!

In Example 6-1, RIP broadcasts are being sent out serial 0, Ethernet 0, and Token Ring 0. Likewise, RIP updates entering those three interfaces alone are processed. Finally, each RIP update created by this router advertises only directly connected subnets 10.1.2.0, 199.1.1.0, and 10.1.3.0, plus any routes learned from other routers using RIP.

A common oversight is to forget to configure a **network** command to match interface Ethernet 1. Seemingly, if no other routers are attached to that same Ethernet, then there is no need to broadcast RIP/IGRP or listen for RIP/IGRP on the interface. However, three functions are enabled by matching an interface with the **network** command, as discussed earlier. If there is no **network** command matching the Ethernet 1 interface, no RIP/IGRP updates from this router will advertise about subnet 172.16.1.0.

The **passive-interface** command can be used to cause the router to listen for RIP/IGRP and advertise about the connected subnet, but not to send RIP/IGRP updates on the interface. In Example 6-2, a sample IGRP configuration causes the router to advertise about all connected subnets, listen on all interfaces for IGRP updates, but to not advertise on Ethernet 1.

Example 6-2 *Sample IGRP Configuration and* **show ip route** *Output*

```
interface ethernet 0
ip address 10.1.2.3 255.255.255.0
interface ethernet 1
ip address 172.16.1.1 255.255.255.0
interface tokenring 0
ip address 10.1.3.3 255.255.255.0
interface serial 0
ip address 199.1.1.1 255.255.255.0
interface serial 1
ip address 199.1.2.1 255.255.255.0
router igrp 1
 network 10.0.0.0
 network 199.1.1.0
 network 199.1.2.0
 network 172.16.0.0
 passive-interface ethernet 1

Mayberry#show ip route
Codes: C - connected, S - static, I - IGRP, R - RIP, M - mobile, B - BGP
       D - EIGRP, EX - EIGRP external, O - OSPF, IA - OSPF inter area
       N1 - OSPF NSSA external type 1, N2 - OSPF NSSA external type 2
       E1 - OSPF external type 1, E2 - OSPF external type 2, E - EGP
       i - IS-IS, L1 - IS-IS level-1, L2 - IS-IS level-2, * - candidate default
       U - per-user static route, o - ODR

Gateway of last resort is not set

     10.0.0.0/24 is subnetted, 3 subnets
C       10.1.2.0 is directly connected, TokenRing0
C       10.1.3.0 is directly connected, Ethernet0
I       10.1.4.0 [100/8539] via 10.1.2.14, 00:00:50, Ethernet0
     172.16.0.0/24 is subnetted, 2 subnets
C       172.16.1.0 is directly connected, Ethernet1
I       172.16.2.0 [100/6244] via 172.16.1.44, 00:00:20, Ethernet1
C     199.1.1.0/24 is directly connected, Serial0
C     199.1.2.0/24 is directly connected, Serial1
```

Notice that the four network commands match all interfaces on the router (refer to Figure 6-9). The **passive-interface** command causes the router to not send IGRP updates on interface E1. Also, notice the "1" on the **router igrp** command—all other routers using IGRP must use this same process-id, assuming all routers want to exchange routing information using IGRP.

IGRP uses a composite metric. The metric is calculated as a function of bandwidth, delay, load, and reliability. By default, only the bandwidth and delay are considered; the other parameters are considered only if enabled via configuration. Delay and bandwidth are not measured values but are set via the **delay** and **bandwidth** interface subcommands. (The same formula is used for calculating the metric for EIGRP, but with a scaling factor so that the actual metric values are larger, allowing more granularity in the metric.)

The **show ip route** command in Example 6-2 shows the IGRP metric values in brackets. For example, the route to 10.1.4.0 shows the value [100/8539] beside the subnet number. The metric 8539 is a single value, as calculated based on bandwidth and delay.

NOTE   Although unlikely to be on the exam, the other number in brackets in the **show ip route** output is interesting. If multiple IP routing protocols are in use in a single router, both can learn routes to the same subnets. Because their metric values are different (for example, hop count or a function of bandwidth and delay), there is no way to know which routing protocol's routes are better. So, Cisco supplies a method of stating the equivalent of, "IGRP-learned routes are always better than RIP-learned routes." The IOS implements this concept using something called *administrative distance*. Administrative distance is an integer value; a value is assigned to each source of routing information. The lower the administrative distance, the better the source of routing information. IGRP's default is 100, OSPF's is 110, RIP's is 120, and EIGRP's is 90. The value "100" in brackets in the **show ip route** output signifies that the administrative distance used for IGRP routes is 100—in other words, the default value is in use.

Split-Horizon and Infinity

Split-horizon effects and the advertising of infinite distance routes were covered in the section "Distance Vector Routing Protocols." RIP and IGRP are distance vector routing protocols, but split-horizon and infinite distance routes are features that can be better understood by examining debug messages. Figure 6-10 and Example 6-3 show a stable network, with split-horizon rules that affect the RIP updates. Then, Ethernet 0 on Yosemite is shut down, and Yosemite advertises an infinite distance route, as seen in Example 6-4.

Figure 6-10 *Split-Horizon and Infinite Distance Routes (Continued)*

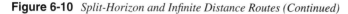
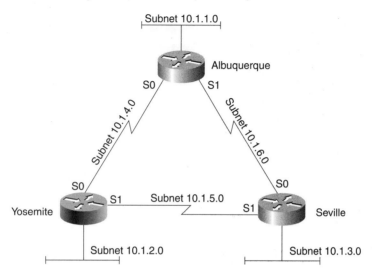

Example 6-3 *RIP Configuration and Debugs on Albuquerque*

```
interface ethernet 0
ip addr 10.1.1.251 255.255.255.0
interface serial 0
ip addr 10.1.4.251 255.255.255.0
interface serial 1
ip addr 10.1.6.251 255.255.255.0

router rip
network 10.0.0.0


Albuquerque#
RIP: received v1 update from 10.1.6.253 on Serial1
     10.1.3.0 in 1 hops
     10.1.2.0 in 2 hops
     10.1.5.0 in 1 hops
RIP: sending v1 update to 255.255.255.255 via Serial0 (10.1.4.251)
     subnet  10.1.3.0, metric 2
     subnet  10.1.1.0, metric 1
     subnet  10.1.6.0, metric 1
RIP: sending v1 update to 255.255.255.255 via Serial1 (10.1.6.251)
     subnet  10.1.2.0, metric 2
     subnet  10.1.1.0, metric 1
     subnet  10.1.4.0, metric 1
RIP: sending v1 update to 255.255.255.255 via Ethernet0 (10.1.1.251)
```

continues

Example 6-3 *RIP Configuration and Debugs on Albuquerque (Continued)*

```
        subnet  10.1.3.0, metric 2
        subnet  10.1.2.0, metric 2
        subnet  10.1.6.0, metric 1
        subnet  10.1.5.0, metric 2
        subnet  10.1.4.0, metric 1
RIP: received v1 update from 10.1.4.252 on Serial0
        10.1.3.0 in 2 hops
        10.1.2.0 in 1 hops
        10.1.5.0 in 1 hops
Albuquerque#
(Yosemite E0 shutdown at this time...)

RIP: received v1 update from 10.1.4.252 on Serial0
        10.1.3.0 in 2 hops
        10.1.2.0 in 16 hops (inaccessible)
        10.1.5.0 in 1 hops
RIP: sending v1 update to 255.255.255.255 via Serial0 (10.1.4.251)
        subnet  10.1.3.0, metric 2
        subnet  10.1.2.0, metric 16
        subnet  10.1.1.0, metric 1
        subnet  10.1.6.0, metric 1
RIP: sending v1 update to 255.255.255.255 via Serial1 (10.1.6.251)
        subnet  10.1.2.0, metric 16
        subnet  10.1.1.0, metric 1
        subnet  10.1.4.0, metric
RIP: sending v1 update to 255.255.255.255 via Ethernet0 (10.1.1.251)
        subnet  10.1.3.0, metric 2
        subnet  10.1.2.0, metric 16
        subnet  10.1.6.0, metric 1
        subnet  10.1.5.0, metric 2
        subnet  10.1.4.0, metric 1
RIP: received v1 update from 10.1.6.253 on Serial1
        10.1.3.0 in 1 hops
        10.1.2.0 in 16 hops (inaccessible)
        10.1.5.0 in 1 hops
```

Example 6-4 *RIP Configuration and Debugs on Yosemite*

```
interface ethernet 0
ip addr 10.1.2.252 255.255.255.0
interface serial 0
ip addr 10.1.4.252 255.255.255.0
interface serial 1
ip addr 10.1.5.252 255.255.255.0

router rip
network 10.0.0.0
```

Several interesting items can be seen in the configuration and debugs in Example 6-3 and Example 6-4. RIP is enabled on all interfaces and on all routers in this example. The RIP update sent out Albuquerque's Ethernet0 interface advertises five routes, but does not advertise the route to 10.1.1.0 because that is the subnet of that attached Ethernet. Albuquerque's update, sent on its Serial1 interface, advertises only three routes due to split-horizon rules. Finally, notice the update received on Albuquerque, entering Serial0 (from Yosemite) after Yosemite's Ethernet0 interface has failed. Yosemite has described subnet 10.1.2.0 with a metric 16 route, which is considered infinite by RIP.

RIP v1 and IGRP—No Subnet Masks

RIP version 1 and IGRP do not transmit the subnet mask in the routing updates, as seen in the debugs in this section. Several subtle actions are taken in light of the lack of mask information in the update:

- Updates sent out an interface in network *X*, when containing routes about subnets of network *X*, contain the subnet numbers but not the masks.

- Updates sent out an interface in network *X*, when containing routes about subnets of network *Y*, are summarized into one route about the entire network *Y*.

- When receiving a routing update containing routes referencing subnets of network *X*, the receiving router assumes the mask in use is the same mask it uses on an interface with an address in network *X*.

- When receiving an update about network *X*, if the receiving router has no interfaces in network *X*, it will treat the route as a route to the entire Class A, B, or C network *X*.

Figure 6-11 and Example 6-5, Example 6-6, and Example 6-7 contain **show** and **debug** command output on Albuquerque, Yosemite, and Seville with the effects described in the preceding list.

Figure 6-11 *Two Network Numbers, RIP, No Masks in Routing Updates*

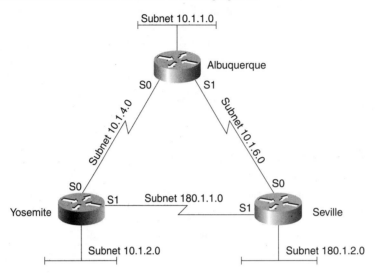

Example 6-5 *Configuration and Debug IP RIP on Albuquerque*

```
interface ethernet 0
ip addr 10.1.1.251 255.255.255.0
interface serial 0
ip addr 10.1.4.251 255.255.255.0
interface serial 1
ip addr 10.1.6.251 255.255.255.0
!
router rip
network 10.0.0.0


Albuquerque#
RIP: received v1 update from 10.1.4.252 on Serial0
      10.1.2.0 in 1 hops
      180.1.0.0 in 1 hops
RIP: received v1 update from 10.1.6.253 on Serial1
      180.1.0.0 in 1 hops
RIP: sending v1 update to 255.255.255.255 via Serial0 (10.1.4.251)
      subnet  10.1.1.0, metric 1
      subnet  10.1.6.0, metric 1
RIP: sending v1 update to 255.255.255.255 via Serial1 (10.1.6.251)
      subnet  10.1.2.0, metric 2
      subnet  10.1.1.0, metric 1
      subnet  10.1.4.0, metric 1
RIP: sending v1 update to 255.255.255.255 via Ethernet0 (10.1.1.251)
      subnet  10.1.2.0, metric 2
```

Example 6-5 *Configuration and Debug IP RIP on Albuquerque (Continued)*

```
           subnet  10.1.6.0, metric 1
           subnet  10.1.4.0, metric 1
           network 180.1.0.0, metric 2
Albuquerque#undebug all
All possible debugging has been turned off
Albuquerque#show ip route
Codes: C - connected, S - static, I - IGRP, R - RIP, M - mobile, B - BGP
       D - EIGRP, EX - EIGRP external, O - OSPF, IA - OSPF inter area
       N1 - OSPF NSSA external type 1, N2 - OSPF NSSA external type 2
       E1 - OSPF external type 1, E2 - OSPF external type 2, E - EGP
       i - IS-IS, L1 - IS-IS level-1, L2 - IS-IS level-2, * - candidate default
       U - per-user static route, o - ODR

Gateway of last resort is not set

       10.0.0.0/24 is subnetted, 4 subnets
R         10.1.2.0 [120/1] via 10.1.4.252, 00:00:00, Serial0
C         10.1.1.0 is directly connected, Ethernet0
C         10.1.6.0 is directly connected, Serial1
C         10.1.4.0 is directly connected, Serial0
R      180.1.0.0/16 [120/1] via 10.1.4.252, 00:00:01, Serial0
                    [120/1] via 10.1.6.253, 00:00:25, Serial1
Albuquerque#
```

Example 6-6 *Configuration on Yosemite*

```
interface ethernet 0
ip addr 10.1.2.252 255.255.255.0
interface serial 0
ip addr 10.1.4.252 255.255.255.0
interface serial 1
ip address 180.1.1.252 255.255.255.0

router rip
network 10.0.0.0
network 180.1.0.0
```

Example 6-7 *Configuration on Seville*

```
interface ethernet 0
ip addr 180.1.2.253  255.255.255.0
interface serial 0
ip addr 180.1.1.253  255.255.255.0
interface serial 1
ip address 10.1.6.253  255.255.255.0
!
router rip
network 10.0.0.0
network 180.1.0.0
```

By examining the RIP updates received at Albuquerque, both Seville and Yosemite are advertising a route to 180.1.0.0, with the same metric. Both routes are added to the routing table when using default configuration settings with RIP and IGRP. With Fast Switching enabled (default), packets to some destination IP addresses will use one route from Albuquerque, and packets to other destination IP addresses in 180.1.0.0 will use the other route. (For more information on fast switching, surf Cisco's Web site for the Networker's conference presentation titled, "Router Architecture and Performance," URL http://www.cisco.com/networkers/presentation/layer3/index.html.)

The assumptions made by RIP (or IGRP had it been used in this case) about the subnet mask creates a situation where some packets will be suboptimally routed. Using a routing protocol that transmits mask information (RIP v2, EIGRP, or OSPF) overcomes this problem. These types of nuances are typical of the issues that will be required in the CCNP exam and CCIE exam and lab.

NOTE   By default, the IOS supports four routes to the same IP subnet in the routing table at the same time. This number can be changed to between one and six using the **ip maximum-paths** x configuration command, where x is the maximum number of routes to any subnet. As mentioned earlier, the packets are balanced on a per-destination address basis by default; packets can also be balanced on a packet-by-packet basis, but at a performance penalty.

RIP v2 includes the subnet masks in routing updates, and authentication to confirm that the sender of a routing update is a valid source for routing information. In the following configuration, which would be on all three routers, RIP v2 is configured. Autosummary is turned off; this means that RIP will not summarize all subnets of network 180.1.0.0 as a single class B network when advertising into another network. For example, referring to Figure 6-11, Yosemite will advertise about subnets 180.1.1.0 and 180.1.2.0 in its updates sent out its serial0 interface. Example 6-8 shows the configuration on Seville, and Example 6-9 shows a sample RIP debug on Albuquerque.

Example 6-8 *RIP v2 Sample Configuration for Routers in Figure 6-11*

```
router rip
network 10.0.0.0
network 180.1.0.0
version 2
no auto-summary
```

Example 6-9 *RIP v2 Routing Updates, No Autosummary, on Albuquerque*

```
Albuquerque#
RIP: sending v2 update to 224.0.0.9 via Serial0 (10.1.4.251)
     10.1.1.0/24 -> 0.0.0.0, metric 1, tag 0
     10.1.6.0/24 -> 0.0.0.0, metric 1, tag 0
     180.1.2.0/24 -> 0.0.0.0, metric 2, tag 0
RIP: sending v2 update to 224.0.0.9 via Serial1 (10.1.6.251)
     10.1.2.0/24 -> 0.0.0.0, metric 2, tag 0
     10.1.1.0/24 -> 0.0.0.0, metric 1, tag 0
     10.1.4.0/24 -> 0.0.0.0, metric 1, tag 0
RIP: sending v2 update to 224.0.0.9 via Ethernet0 (10.1.1.251)
     10.1.2.0/24 -> 0.0.0.0, metric 2, tag 0
     10.1.6.0/24 -> 0.0.0.0, metric 1, tag 0
     10.1.4.0/24 -> 0.0.0.0, metric 1, tag 0
     180.1.1.0/24 -> 0.0.0.0, metric 2, tag 0
     180.1.2.0/24 -> 0.0.0.0, metric 2, tag 0
RIP: received v2 update from 10.1.6.253 on Serial1
     10.1.2.0/24 -> 0.0.0.0 in 2 hops
     180.1.1.0/24 -> 0.0.0.0 in 1 hops
     180.1.2.0/24 -> 0.0.0.0 in 1 hops
RIP: received v2 update from 10.1.4.252 on Serial0
     10.1.2.0/24 -> 0.0.0.0 in 1 hops
     180.1.1.0/24 -> 0.0.0.0 in 1 hops
     180.1.2.0/24 -> 0.0.0.0 in 2 hops
```

A couple of important items should be noted in the **debug** output of Example 6-9. The updates sent by Albuquerque are sent to multicast IP address 224.0.0.9, as opposed to a broadcast address; this allows the devices that are not using RIP v2 to ignore the updates and not waste processing cycles. Also, notice the update received on serial0 (from Yosemite). It includes routing information for both 180.1.1.0 and 180.1.2.0 because autosummarization is disabled on Yosemite.

IPX RIP, Plus SAP and GNS

CCNA Objectives Covered in This Section

28	Monitor Novell IPX operation on the router.
34	Enable the Novell IPX protocol and configure interfaces.

Chapter 5, "Network Protocols: Understanding the TCP/IP Suite and Novell NetWare Protocols," also covers the objectives discussed in this section. However, some coverage of objectives 28 and 34 is also provided in this chapter because this chapter is about routing protocols, and of course, IPX can use IPX RIP as a routing protocol. It also seemed more appropriate to review the IPX routing table and IPX RIP commands in the same chapter as the related distance vector routing protocol discussions.

RIP for IPX works in a similar manner to IP RIP. The most obvious difference is that IPX RIP advertises IPX network numbers, not IP subnet numbers. Table 6-13 lists the similarities and differences:

Table 6-13   *RIP for IPX and IP Compared*

Novell RIP	IP RIP
Distance vector	Distance vector
Based on XNS RIP	Based on XNS RIP
Uses 60 second update timer (default)	Uses 30 second update timer (default)
Uses timer ticks as primary metric, hop count as secondary metric	Uses hop count as only metric

IPX RIP uses two metrics: ticks and hops. Ticks are 1/18 of one second; the metric is an integer counter of the number of ticks delay for this route. By default, a Cisco router treats a link as having a certain number of ticks delay. LAN interfaces default to one tick, and WAN interfaces default to six ticks. The number of hops is considered only when the number of ticks is a tie. By using ticks as the primary metric, better routes can be chosen, as opposed to just using hop count. For example, a three-hop, three-tick route that uses three Ethernets will be chosen over a two-hop, eight-tick route that uses two Ethernets and a serial link.

Service Advertisement Protocol

Service Advertisement Protocol (SAP) is one of the more important parts of the NetWare protocol specification, but it is also one of the biggest challenges when trying to scale an IPX network. SAP is used by servers to propagate information that describes their services.

The SAP process is very much like the process used by a distance vector routing protocol. In fact, SAP uses a concept similar to split-horizon to stop a node from advertising SAP information it learned on an interface with updates sent out that same interface. Each server sends SAP updates that include its IPX address, server name, and service type. Every other server and router listens for these updates, but does not forward the SAP packet(s). Instead, the SAP information is added to a SAP table in the server or router; then the packets are discarded. When that router or server's SAP timer expires, then new SAP broadcasts are sent. As with IPX RIP for routing information, IPX SAP propagates service information until all servers and routers have learned the information.

Client initialization flows provide some insight into why routers need to learn SAP information. Consider Figure 6-12, which includes the use of the Get Nearest Server (GNS) request and shows a typical startup with a client configured with a preferred server of Server1.

Figure 6-12 *Client Initialization Flows*

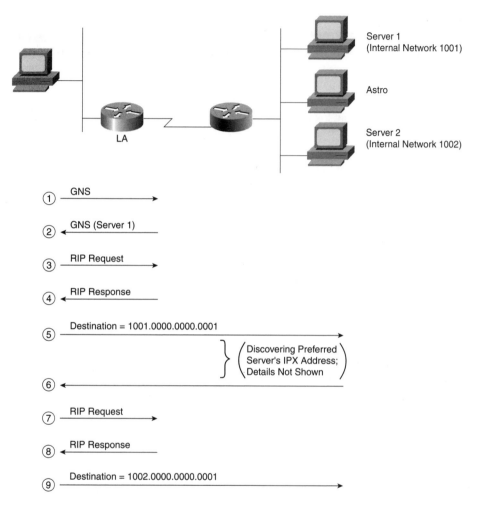

The overall goal of the client is to log in to its preferred server. The first step is to connect to some server that has a full SAP table, so the client can learn the IPX address of its preferred server. (The preferred server name is configured on the client, not the IPX address of the preferred server.) The router may know the preferred server's name and IPX address in its SAP table, but there is no IPX message defined that allows the client to query the router for "name resolution." However, an IPX broadcast message asking for any nearby server is defined by IPX—the GNS request. The router can supply the IPX address of some nearby server (Step 2 in Figure 6-12) because the router has a SAP table.

Next, the client needs to learn which router to use to forward packets to the server discovered by its GNS request. RIP requests and replies are used by the client to learn the route from any router (or server) on the same LAN, as seen in Steps 3 and 4 in Figure 6-12.

After connecting to Server1, the client learns the IPX address of Server2, its preferred server (Steps 5 and 6 in Figure 6-12). The client needs to know the best route to the preferred server's network; therefore, a RIP request and reply to learn the best next-hop router to network 1002 is shown in Steps 7 and 8 in Figure 6-12. Finally, packets are sent between the client and Server 2 so that the client can log in; the intervening routers are simply routing the packets.

NOTE   IPX clients create their own IPX address using the network number in the source address field of the GNS reply. The GNS reply is always sent by a router or server on the same network as the client. The client examines the source IPX address of the GNS reply to learn its own IPX network number. The complete client IPX address is formed by putting that network number with the MAC address of the client's LAN interface.

Configuration of IPX

As seen in Chapter 5, enabling RIP and SAP on a router is very straightforward. The **ipx routing** command enables both in a router, and the **ipx network** command on an interface implies that RIP and SAP updates should be sent and listened for on those interfaces. Router Yosemite has been configured for RIP and SAP (see Figure 6-13). The command output in Example 6-10 shows the result of some RIP and SAP **show** and **debug** commands. (Do not forget—the CCNA exam will ask questions about what commands can be used to view certain details!)

Figure 6-13 *IPX Network with Point-to-Point Serial Links*

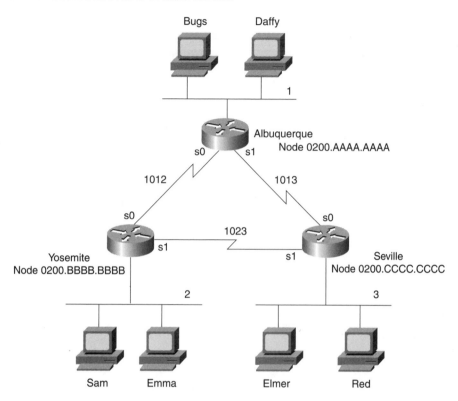

Example 6-10 *Routing and SAP Information on Yosemite*

```
Yosemite#show ipx route
Codes: C - Connected primary network,    c - Connected secondary network
       S - Static, F - Floating static, L - Local (internal), W - IPXWAN
       R - RIP, E - EIGRP, N - NLSP, X - External, A - Aggregate
       s - seconds, u - uses

8 Total IPX routes. Up to 1 parallel paths and 16 hops allowed.

No default route known.

C          2 (SAP),         E0_
C       1012 (HDLC),        Se0
C       1023 (HDLC),        Se1
R          1 [07/01] via    1012.0000.aaaa.aaaa,   14s, Se0
R          3 [07/01] via    1023.0200.cccc.cccc,    1s, Se1
R       1001 [08/03] via    1023.0200.cccc.cccc,    1s, Se1
R       1013 [12/01] via    1023.0200.cccc.cccc,    1s, Se1
```

continues

Example 6-10 *Routing and SAP Information on Yosemite (Continued)*

```
Yosemite#show ipx servers
Codes: S - Static, P - Periodic, E - EIGRP, N - NLSP, H - Holddown, + = detail
1 Total IPX Servers

Table ordering is based on routing and server info

    Type Name                     Net      Address     Port    Route Hops Itf
P      4 Server1                  1001.0000.0000.0001:0451    8/03    3  Se1

Yosemite#debug ipx routing activity
IPX routing debugging is on

Yosemite#
IPXRIP: positing full update to 2.ffff.ffff.ffff via Ethernet0 (broadcast)
IPXRIP: src=2.0200.bbbb.bbbb, dst=2.ffff.ffff.ffff, packet sent
    network 1, hops 2,  delay 8
    network 1001, hops 4,  delay 9
    network 1012, hops 1,  delay 2
    network 3, hops 2,  delay 8
    network 1013, hops 2,  delay 8
    network 1023, hops 1,  delay 2

IPXRIP: positing full update to 1012.ffff.ffff.ffff via Serial0 (broadcast)
IPXRIP: src=1012.0200.bbbb.bbbb, dst=1012.ffff.ffff.ffff, packet sent
    network 1001, hops 4,  delay 14
    network 3, hops 2,  delay 13
    network 1013, hops 2,  delay 13
    network 1023, hops 1,  delay 7
    network 2, hops 1,  delay 7

IPXRIP: update from 1012.0200.aaaa.aaaa
    1013 in 1 hops, delay 7
    1 in 1 hops, delay 7
    1001 in 4 hops, delay 14
    3 in 2 hops, delay 13
IPXRIP: 1023 FFFFFFFF not added, entry in table is static/connected/internal
    1023 in 2 hops, delay 13

IPXRIP: update from 1023.0200.cccc.cccc
    1 in 2 hops, delay 13
    1001 in 3 hops, delay 8
    3 in 1 hops, delay 7
    1013 in 1 hops, delay 7
IPXRIP: positing full update to 1023.ffff.ffff.ffff via Serial1 (broadcast)
IPXRIP: src=1023.0200.bbbb.bbbb, dst=1023.ffff.ffff.ffff, packet sent
    network 1, hops 2,  delay 13
    network 1012, hops 1,  delay 7
    network 2, hops 1,  delay 7

Yosemite#debug ipx sap activity
IPX service debugging is on
```

Example 6-10 *Routing and SAP Information on Yosemite (Continued)*

```
IPXSAP: positing update to 1012.ffff.ffff.ffff via Serial0 (broadcast) (full)
IPXSAP: Update type 0x2 len 96 src:1012.0200.bbbb.bbbb
➥dest:1012.ffff.ffff.ffff(452)
 type 0x4, "Server1", 1001.0000.0000.0001(451), 4 hops

IPXSAP: Response (in) type 0x2 len 96 src:1012.0200.aaaa.aaaa
➥dest:1012.ffff.ffff.ffff(452)
 type 0x4, "Server1", 1001.0000.0000.0001(451), 4 hops

IPXSAP: positing update to 1023.ffff.ffff.ffff via Serial1 (broadcast) (full)
IPXSAP: suppressing null update to 1023.ffff.ffff.ffff
IPXSAP: Response (in) type 0x2 len 96 src:1023.0200.cccc.cccc
➥dest:1023.ffff.ffff.ffff(452)
 type 0x4, "Server1", 1001.0000.0000.0001(451), 3 hops

IPXSAP: positing update to 2.ffff.ffff.ffff via Ethernet0 (broadcast) (full)
IPXSAP: Update type 0x2 len 96 src:2.0000.3089.b170 dest:2.ffff.ffff.ffff(452)
 type 0x4, "Server1", 1001.0000.0000.00011(451), 4 hops
```

The **show ipx route** command lists the metric values in brackets; the number of ticks is listed first and then the hop count. The number of seconds listed at the end of each line for RIP derived routes is the time since the routing information was heard; the ticks metric shows only as a number of ticks, never as a number of seconds. For example, in Example 6-10, Yosemite lists a route to network 3, with the numbers [7,1] shown beside the IPX network number. Seven is the number of ticks, which in this case is the sum of six ticks for the serial link to Seville, and one tick for the Ethernet in Seville. The one in brackets represents the hop count.

NOTE   The **show ip route** command also lists two numbers in brackets, but only the second number is the metric. The first number is called *administrative distance*. If multiple IP routing protocols are in use on a single router, both can learn routes to the same subnet. Administrative distance is a number that defines which source of routing information is more believable; the lower the number, the more believable.

The **show ipx servers** command was purposely kept small for this example; in many networks, there are thousands of SAP entries. The name of the server and the SAP type is listed; SAP type will be important for SAP filters. The IPX address and socket used by the server for this service is also listed; the socket may be important when filtering IPX packets. The metric values for the route to network 1001 are shown under the word "route." By having metric information handy, good choices for GNS replies can be made easily. In Example 6-10, Server1 is listed with SAP type 4, which is File Servers; its IPX address is 1001.0000.0000.0001, and it uses IPX port 0451. The route to network 1001 has a metric of eight ticks and three hops, and when packets are sent to Server1, they are sent out Yosemite's interface Serial1.

The **debug ipx routing activity** command enables output describing every RIP update sent and received. The number of ticks on LAN interfaces defaults to one and on WAN interfaces defaults to six. Although Albuquerque and Yosemite have coded a bandwidth parameter of 56 on the serial link between them, and the other links default to 1,544, the ticks are not affected. The **ipx delay** *ticks* interface subcommand can be used to change the metric for a particular interface.

Finally, the **debug ipx sap activity** command enables output describing every SAP update sent and received. Notice the update Yosemite wants to send out network 1023; it is time to send a SAP broadcast, but the SAP update is null. This is because the only SAP in the table (Server1, SAP type 4) was learned from Seville over network 1023, so Yosemite is using split-horizon rules to not send information about this SAP back to Albuquerque.

Only one route to each network is allowed in the routing table by default. Notice that the route to network 1013, metric [7/1], points to next hop 1023.0200.cccc.cccc (Seville), out Yosemite's Serial 1 interface. However, 1012.0200.aaaa.aaaa (Albuquerque) is sending RIP updates describing a route to network 1013 with seven ticks and one hop into Yosemite's S0 interface (see RIP debug output). Yosemite heard from Seville first; therefore, only that route is included. If the **ipx maximum-paths 2** global command had been configured on Yosemite, both routes would be included. Unlike IP, when two routes are in the IPX routing table, per packet load balancing across these paths occurs, even if fast switching is enabled.

NOTE   The default per-packet load balancing used for IPX when multiple routes to the same network are in the routing table may not be desired because packets can arrive out of order. By having the router send all packets to an individual IPX address over the same route every time, those packets should be received in order. The **ipx per-host-load-share** configuration command disables per-packet balancing and enables balancing based on the destination address. Of course, the penalty is that the traffic will not be completely balanced, based on the numbers of packets to each destination.

Integrated Routing Protocols

CCNA Objective Covered in This Section

41	Explain the services of separate and integrated multiprotocol routing.

The concepts behind CCNA objective 41 are very straightforward, but the terminology can confuse the meaning of the objective. The first key to understanding this objective is to separate the full terms:

Separate multiprotocol routing

Integrated multiprotocol routing

First, a reminder of some of the details of multiprotocol routing is in order. Consider Figure 6-14, which reminds us of one such concept.

Figure 6-14 *Multiprotocol Routing*

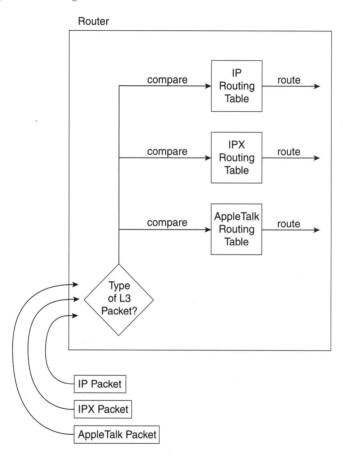

As discussed in Chapter 3, the router determines what type of Layer 3 packet is inside the received frame. There is a separate routing table for each routable or routed protocol. (If you previously skipped Chapter 3, you may want to review the generalized routing algorithm, or the "Ting and Ted" story.) The routing decision is therefore dependent on a routing table specific for that one Layer 3 protocol. This process is called *multiprotocol routing*.

Routing protocols fill the routing tables of the various Layer 3 protocols. Although not covered elsewhere in this book, AppleTalk uses yet another derivative of XNS RIP, called RTMP, as its routing protocol. Consider the following simple network in Figure 6-15 and the routing updates that are sent out S0 by Router1.

Figure 6-15 *IP-RIP, IPX-RIP, and RTMP Updates*

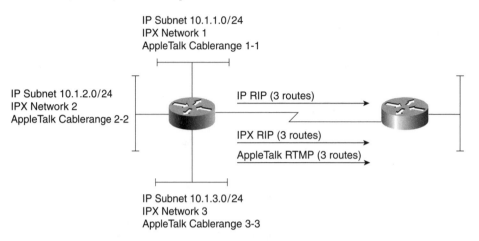

IP Subnet 10.1.1.0/24
IPX Network 1
AppleTalk Cablerange 1-1

IP Subnet 10.1.2.0/24
IPX Network 2
AppleTalk Cablerange 2-2

IP RIP (3 routes)

IPX RIP (3 routes)

AppleTalk RTMP (3 routes)

IP Subnet 10.1.3.0/24
IPX Network 3
AppleTalk Cablerange 3-3

Separate multiprotocol routing is described in the figure. The word *separate* refers to the separate routing updates sent by the respective routing protocols. Each separate routable protocol (IP, IPX, and AppleTalk) uses a separate routing protocol. (IP uses RIP, IPX uses RIP, and AppleTalk uses RTMP.)

Many similarities exist between IP, IPX, and AppleTalk; these similarities allow integrated multiprotocol routing to exist. In particular, if Router1's E0 interface failed, then IP subnet 10.1.1.0/24, IPX network 1, and AppleTalk Cable-range 1-1 would all be inaccessible. In fact, the key similarity is that all three Layer 3 protocols use the same concept of grouping devices; that is, all interfaces attach to the same medium. In fact, the following statement can be made about this similarity:

> Events that could cause a router's directly connected IP route to fail will often cause the directly connected IPX and AppleTalk routes associated with that same data link to fail.

A failure of Router1's E0 interface would cause IP RIP, IPX RIP, and AppleTalk RTMP to advertise that the associated subnet/network/cable-range was not accessible. Each routing protocol would send its own updates, as diagrammed in Figure 6-16.

Figure 6-16 *Multiple Routing Updates—Separate Multiprotocol Routing*

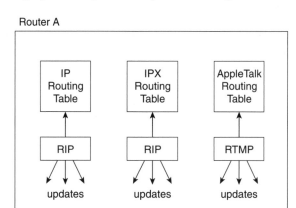

Integrated multiprotocol routing uses a single routing protocol to propagate routing information for multiple routable protocols. EIGRP is the only routing protocol covered in Training Path 1 and Training Path 2 that provides integrated multiprotocol routing; EIGRP does this for IP, IPX, and AppleTalk. (IGRP and Integrated IS-IS can also use Integrated Multiprotocol Routing for IP and OSI CLNS.) Figure 6-17 diagrams the basic idea behind Integrated Multiprotocol Routing.

Figure 6-17 *Single Routing Update—Integrated Multiprotocol Routing*

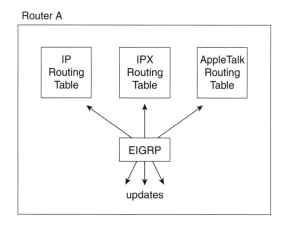

NOTE   EIGRP happens to have many additional features that are better than IP RIP, IPX RIP, and RTMP. For a full discussion of EIGRP features, refer to the Cisco Press book *CCIE Professional Development: Routing TCP/IP* for a great and detailed description of what and how EIGRP works.

Table 6-14 summarizes the key concept behind CCNA objective 41.

Table 6-14   *Separate and Integrated Multiprotocol Routing*

Separate Multiprotocol Routing	Integrated Multiprotocol Routing
Multiple routing tables; one each for IP, IPX, and AppleTalk	Multiple routing tables; one each for IP, IPX, and AppleTalk
Multiple routing updates, one per routing protocol	One routing update combined for all three routed protocols

Q&A

As mentioned in Chapter 1, the questions and scenarios are more difficult than what you should experience on the actual exam. The questions do not attempt to cover more breadth or depth than the exam; however, the questions are designed to make sure you know the answer. Rather than allowing you to derive the answer from clues hidden inside the question itself, your understanding and recall of the subject will be challenged. Questions from the "Do I Know This Already?" quiz from the beginning of the chapter are repeated here to ensure that you have mastered the chapter's topic areas. Hopefully, these questions will help limit the number of exam questions on which you narrow your choices to two options, and then guess!

1. What type of routing protocol algorithm uses a holddown timer? What is its purpose?

2. Define what split-horizon means to the contents of a routing update. Does this apply to both the distance vector algorithm and link state algorithm?

3. Write down the steps you would take to migrate from RIP to IGRP in a router whose current RIP configuration includes only **router rip**, followed by a **network 10.0.0.0** command.

4. How does the IOS designate a subnet in the routing table as a directly connected network? A route learned with IGRP? A route learned with RIP?

5. Create a configuration for IGRP on a router with these interfaces and addresses: e0 using 10.1.1.1, e1 using 224.1.2.3, s0 using 10.1.2.1, and s1 using 199.1.1.1. Use process ID 5.

6. Create a configuration for IGRP on a router with these interfaces and addresses: to0 using 200.1.1.1, e0 using 128.1.3.2, s0 using 192.0.1.1, and s1 using 223.254.254.1.

7. From a router's user mode, without using debugs or privileged mode, how can you determine what routers are sending you routing updates?

8. How often does IPX RIP send routing updates, by default?

9. Describe the metric(s) used by IPX RIP in a Cisco router.

10. Define **split-horizon**. Does IPX RIP use it?

11. RIP and SAP information is sent in the same packets. (T/F)

   If true, can only one of the two be enabled in a router? If false, what commands enable each protocol globally in a router?

12. What does GNS stand for? Who creates GNS requests, and who creates GNS replies?

13. Define the term *Separate Multiprotocol Routing* in the context of the Cisco IOS and Novell IPX.

14. How often does a router send SAP updates by default?

15. If Serial0 has a **bandwidth 1544** interface subcommand, and Serial1 has a **bandwidth 56** interface subcommand, what metric will IPX RIP associate with each interface?

16. Routers forward SAP packets as they arrive, but broadcast SAP packets on interfaces in which no SAP packets have been received in the last 60 seconds. (T/F)

17. What **show** commands list IPX RIP metric values in a Cisco router?

18. Define the term *Integrated Multiprotocol Routing* in the context of the Cisco IOS and Novell IPX.

19. If the commands **router rip** followed by **network 10.0.0.0** with no other **network** commands were configured in a router that has an Ethernet0 interface with IP address 168.10.1.1, would RIP send updates out Ethernet0?

20. If the commands **router igrp** 1 followed by **network 10.0.0.0** were configured in a router that has an Ethernet0 interface with IP address 168.10.1.1, would IGRP advertise about 168.10.0.0?

21. If the commands **router igrp** 1 followed by **network 10.0.0.0** were configured in a router that has an Ethernet0 interface with IP address 168.10.1.1, would this router have a route to 168.10.0.0?

22. What routing protocols support integrated multiprotocol routing?

Scenarios

Scenario 6-1: IP Configuration 1

Your job is to deploy a new network. The network engineering group has provided a list of addresses and a network diagram, as shown in Figure 6-18 and Table 6-15.

Figure 6-18 *Scenario 6-1 Network Diagram*

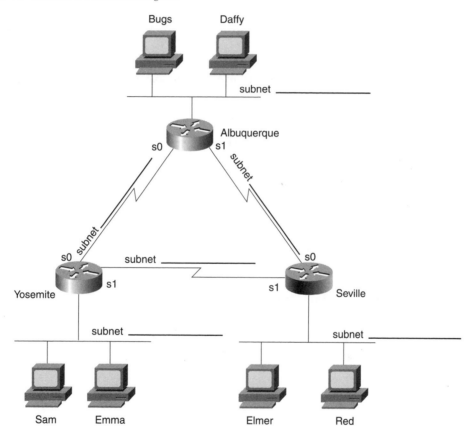

Table 6-15 *Scenario 6-1 IP Addresses*

Location of Subnet Geographically	Subnet Mask	Subnet Number	Subnet Broadcast
Ethernet off router in Albuquerque	255.255.255.0	148.14.1.0	
Ethernet off router in Yosemite	255.255.255.0	148.14.2.0	
Ethernet off router in Seville	255.255.255.0	148.14.3.0	
Serial between Albuquerque and Yosemite	255.255.255.0	148.14.4.0	
Serial between Albuquerque and Seville	255.255.255.0	148.14.5.0	
Serial between Seville and Yosemite	255.255.255.0	148.14.6.0	

Assuming the details established in Figure 6-18 and Table 6-15 for Scenario 6-1, complete or answer the following:

1. Create the configurations to enable IP as described in Table 6-15.

2. Describe the contents of the routing table on Seville after the routers are installed and all interfaces are up, but no routing protocols or static routes have been configured.

3. Configure static routes for each router so that any host in any subnet could communicate with other hosts in this network.

4. Configure IGRP to replace the static routes in Task 3.

5. Calculate the subnet broadcast address for each subnet.

Scenario 6-2: IP Configuration 2

Your job is to deploy another new network. The network engineering group has provided a list of addresses and a network diagram, with Frame Relay global DLCIs shown, as shown in Figure 6-19 and Table 6-16.

Figure 6-19 *Scenario 6-2 Network Diagram*

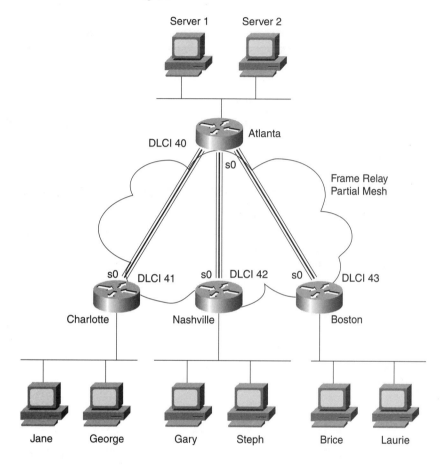

Table 6-16 *Scenario 6-2 IP Addresses*

Location of Subnet Geographically	Subnet Mask	Subnet Number	Subnet Broadcast
Ethernet off router in Atlanta	255.255.255.0	10.1.1.0	
Ethernet off router in Charlotte	255.255.255.0	10.1.2.0	
Ethernet off router in Nashville	255.255.255.0	10.1.3.0	
Ethernet off router in Boston	255.255.255.0	10.1.4.0	
VC between Atlanta and Charlotte	255.255.255.0	10.2.1.0	
VC between Atlanta and Nashville	255.255.255.0	10.2.2.0	
VC between Atlanta and Boston	255.255.255.0	10.2.3.0	

Assuming the details established in Figure 6-19 and Table 6-16 for Scenario 6-2, complete or answer the following:

1. Create the configurations to enable IP as described in Table 6-16. Do not enable a routing protocol.

2. Configure RIP.

3. Calculate the subnet broadcast address for each subnet.

4. Describe the contents of the RIP update from Boston sent to Atlanta; also the RIP update from Atlanta to Charlotte.

Scenario 6-3: IP Addressing and Subnet Derivation

Perform the tasks and answer the questions following several upcoming figures and examples. Figure 6-20 shows the network diagram for Scenario 6-3, and Example 6-11, Example 6-12, and Example 6-13 contain **show** command output from the three routers. Also, use Table 6-17 to record the subnet numbers and broadcast addresses as directed in the upcoming tasks.

Figure 6-20 *Scenario 6-3 Network Diagram*

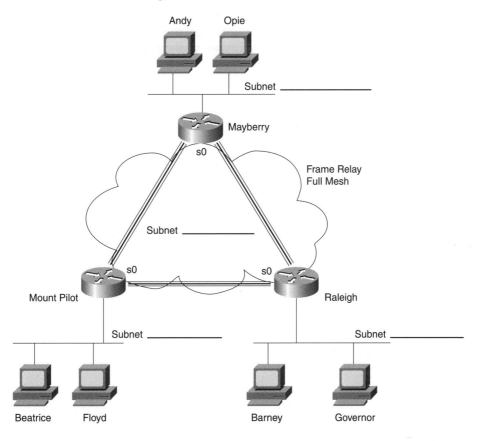

Table 6-17 *Subnets and Broadcast Addresses*

Location of Subnet Geographically	Subnet Mask	Subnet Number	Subnet Broadcast
Ethernet off router in Mayberry	255.255.255.0		
Ethernet off router in Mount Pilot	255.255.255.0		
Ethernet off router in Raleigh	255.255.255.0		
VC between Mayberry and Mount Pilot	255.255.255.0		
VC between Mayberry and Raleigh	255.255.255.0		
VC between Mount Pilot and Raleigh	255.255.255.0		

Example 6-11 *Scenario 6-3,* **show** *Commands on Router Mayberry*

```
Mayberry#show ip route
Codes: C - connected, S - static, I - IGRP, R - RIP, M - mobile, B - BGP
       D - EIGRP, EX - EIGRP external, O - OSPF, IA - OSPF inter area
       N1 - OSPF NSSA external type 1, N2 - OSPF NSSA external type 2
       E1 - OSPF external type 1, E2 - OSPF external type 2, E - EGP
       i - IS-IS, L1 - IS-IS level-1, L2 - IS-IS level-2, * - candidate default
       U - per-user static route, o - ODR

Gateway of last resort is not set

     170.1.0.0/24 is subnetted, 4 subnets
C       170.1.1.0 is directly connected, Serial0
I       170.1.103.0 [100/8539] via 170.1.1.3, 00:00:50, Serial0
I       170.1.102.0 [100/8539] via 170.1.1.2, 00:00:32, Serial0
C       170.1.101.0 is directly connected, Ethernet0

Mayberry#show ip interface brief
Interface           IP-Address      OK? Method Status               Protocol
Serial0             170.1.1.1       YES NVRAM  up                    up
Serial1             10.1.6.251      YES NVRAM  administratively down down
Ethernet0           170.1.101.1     YES NVRAM  up                    up

Mayberry#debug ip igrp transaction
IGRP protocol debugging is on
Mayberry#debug ip igrp events
IGRP event debugging is on
Mayberry#
IGRP: received update from 170.1.1.3 on Serial0
       subnet 170.1.1.0, metric 10476 (neighbor 8476)
       subnet 170.1.103.0, metric 8539 (neighbor 688)
       subnet 170.1.102.0, metric 10539 (neighbor 8539)
       subnet 170.1.101.0, metric 10539 (neighbor 8539)
IGRP: Update contains 4 interior, 0 system, and 0 exterior routes.
IGRP: Total routes in update: 4
IGRP: received update from 170.1.1.2 on Serial0
       subnet 170.1.1.0, metric 10476 (neighbor 8476)
       subnet 170.1.103.0, metric 10539 (neighbor 8539)
       subnet 170.1.102.0, metric 8539 (neighbor 688)
       subnet 170.1.101.0, metric 10539 (neighbor 8539)
IGRP: Update contains 4 interior, 0 system, and 0 exterior routes.
IGRP: Total routes in update: 4
IGRP: sending update to 255.255.255.255 via Serial0 (170.1.1.1)
       subnet 170.1.1.0, metric=8476
       subnet 170.1.103.0, metric=8539
       subnet 170.1.102.0, metric=8539
       subnet 170.1.101.0, metric=688
IGRP: Update contains 4 interior, 0 system, and 0 exterior routes.
IGRP: Total routes in update: 4
IGRP: sending update to 255.255.255.255 via Ethernet0 (170.1.101.1)
       subnet 170.1.1.0, metric=8476
       subnet 170.1.103.0, metric=8539
       subnet 170.1.102.0, metric=8539
IGRP: Update contains 3 interior, 0 system, and 0 exterior routes.
IGRP: Total routes in update:
```

Example 6-12 *Scenario 6-3, **show** Commands on Router Mount Pilot*

```
MountPilot#show frame-relay pvc

PVC Statistics for interface Serial0 (Frame Relay DTE)

DLCI = 47, DLCI USAGE = LOCAL, PVC STATUS = ACTIVE, INTERFACE = Serial0

  input pkts 38          output pkts 37         in bytes 3758
  out bytes 3514         dropped pkts 0         in FECN pkts 0
  in BECN pkts 0         out FECN pkts 0        out BECN pkts 0
  in DE pkts 0           out DE pkts 0
  out bcast pkts 36       out bcast bytes 3436
  pvc create time 00:17:39, last time pvc status changed 00:17:39

DLCI = 49, DLCI USAGE = LOCAL, PVC STATUS = ACTIVE, INTERFACE = Serial0

  input pkts 31          output pkts 31         in bytes 3054
  out bytes 3076         dropped pkts 0         in FECN pkts 0
  in BECN pkts 0         out FECN pkts 0        out BECN pkts 0
  in DE pkts 0           out DE pkts 0
  out bcast pkts 31       out bcast bytes 3076
  pvc create time 00:17:40, last time pvc status changed 00:16:40

MountPilot#show frame-relay map

Serial0 (up): ip 170.1.1.1 dlci 47(0x2F,0x8F0), dynamic,
              broadcast,, status defined, active
Serial0 (up): ip 170.1.1.3 dlci 49(0x31,0xC10), dynamic,
              broadcast,, status defined, active

MountPilot#
IGRP: sending update to 255.255.255.255 via Serial0 (170.1.1.2)
      subnet 170.1.1.0, metric=8476
      subnet 170.1.103.0, metric=8539
      subnet 170.1.102.0, metric=688
      subnet 170.1.101.0, metric=8539
IGRP: Update contains 4 interior, 0 system, and 0 exterior routes.
IGRP: Total routes in update: 4
IGRP: sending update to 255.255.255.255 via Ethernet0 (170.1.102.2)
      subnet 170.1.1.0, metric=8476
      subnet 170.1.103.0, metric=8539
      subnet 170.1.101.0, metric=8539
IGRP: Update contains 3 interior, 0 system, and 0 exterior routes.
IGRP: Total routes in update: 3
IGRP: received update from 170.1.1.1 on Serial0
      subnet 170.1.1.0, metric 10476 (neighbor 8476)
      subnet 170.1.103.0, metric 10539 (neighbor 8539)
      subnet 170.1.102.0, metric 10539 (neighbor 8539)
      subnet 170.1.101.0, metric 8539 (neighbor 688)
IGRP: Update contains 4 interior, 0 system, and 0 exterior routes.
IGRP: Total routes in update: 4
```

continues

Example 6-12 *Scenario 6-3,* **show** *Commands on Router Mount Pilot (Continued)*

```
IGRP: received update from 170.1.1.3 on Serial0
      subnet 170.1.1.0, metric 10476 (neighbor 8476)
      subnet 170.1.103.0, metric 8539 (neighbor 688)
      subnet 170.1.102.0, metric 10539 (neighbor 8539)
      subnet 170.1.101.0, metric 10539 (neighbor 8539)
IGRP: Update contains 4 interior, 0 system, and 0 exterior routes.
IGRP: Total routes in update: 4

%FR-5-DLCICHANGE: Interface Serial0 - DLCI 47 state changed to DELETED
MountPilot#

IGRP: received update from 170.1.1.3 on Serial0
      subnet 170.1.1.0, metric 10476 (neighbor 8476)
      subnet 170.1.103.0, metric 8539 (neighbor 688)
      subnet 170.1.102.0, metric 10539 (neighbor 8539)
      subnet 170.1.101.0, metric 10539 (neighbor 8539)
IGRP: Update contains 4 interior, 0 system, and 0 exterior routes.
IGRP: Total routes in update: 4
```

Example 6-13 *Scenario 6-3,* **show** *Commands on Router Raleigh*

```
Raleigh#show ip route
Codes: C - connected, S - static, I - IGRP, R - RIP, M - mobile, B - BGP
       D - EIGRP, EX - EIGRP external, O - OSPF, IA - OSPF inter area
       N1 - OSPF NSSA external type 1, N2 - OSPF NSSA external type 2
       E1 - OSPF external type 1, E2 - OSPF external type 2, E - EGP
       i - IS-IS, L1 - IS-IS level-1, L2 - IS-IS level-2, * - candidate default
       U - per-user static route, o - ODR

Gateway of last resort is not set

     170.1.0.0/24 is subnetted, 4 subnets
C       170.1.1.0 is directly connected, Serial0
C       170.1.103.0 is directly connected, Ethernet0
I       170.1.102.0 [100/8539] via 170.1.1.2, 00:00:09, Serial0
I       170.1.101.0 [100/8539] via 170.1.1.1, 00:00:42, Serial0

Raleigh#show ip interface brief
Interface            IP-Address      OK? Method Status                Protocol
Serial0              170.1.1.3       YES NVRAM  up                     up
Serial1              180.1.1.253     YES NVRAM  administratively down down
Ethernet0            170.1.103.3     YES NVRAM  up                     up

Raleigh#show ip protocol
Routing Protocol is "igrp 4"
  Sending updates every 90 seconds, next due in 56 seconds
  Invalid after 270 seconds, hold down 280, flushed after 630
  Outgoing update filter list for all interfaces is not set
  Incoming update filter list for all interfaces is not set
  Default networks flagged in outgoing updates
```

Example 6-13 *Scenario 6-3,* **show** *Commands on Router Raleigh (Continued)*

```
Default networks accepted from incoming updates
IGRP metric weight K1=1, K2=0, K3=1, K4=0, K5=0
IGRP maximum hopcount 100
IGRP maximum metric variance 1
Redistributing: igrp 4
Routing for Networks:
  170.1.0.0
Routing Information Sources:
  Gateway         Distance       Last Update
  170.1.1.2            100       00:00:20
  170.1.1.1            100       00:00:53
Distance: (default is 100)

Raleigh#show frame-relay pvc

PVC Statistics for interface Serial0 (Frame Relay DTE)

DLCI = 47, DLCI USAGE = LOCAL, PVC STATUS = ACTIVE, INTERFACE = Serial0

  input pkts 36            output pkts 35           in bytes 3674
  out bytes 3436           dropped pkts 0           in FECN pkts 0
  in BECN pkts 0           out FECN pkts 0          out BECN pkts 0
  in DE pkts 0             out DE pkts 0
  out bcast pkts 34         out bcast bytes 3358
  pvc create time 00:22:07, last time pvc status changed 00:21:58

DLCI = 48, DLCI USAGE = LOCAL, PVC STATUS = ACTIVE, INTERFACE = Serial0

  input pkts 35            output pkts 35           in bytes 3444
  out bytes 3422           dropped pkts 0           in FECN pkts 0
  in BECN pkts 0           out FECN pkts 0          out BECN pkts 0
  in DE pkts 0             out DE pkts 0
  out bcast pkts 34         out bcast bytes 3358
  pvc create time 00:22:08, last time pvc status changed 00:21:58
```

Assuming the details established in Figure 6-20, Table 6-17 and Example 6-11, Example 6-12, and Example 6-13 for Scenario 6-3, complete or answer the following:

1. Examining the **show** commands on the various routers, complete Table 6-17 with the subnet numbers and broadcast addresses used in this network.

2. Describe the contents of the IGRP update from Raleigh, sent out its virtual circuit to Mount Pilot. How many routes in Raleigh's IGRP update sent to Mount Pilot? How many routes in Raleigh's routing table? Is the number different? Why?

3. Describe the contents of the routing table in Mount Pilot immediately after the VC to Mayberry was noticed to have failed.

Scenario 6-4: IPX Examination

The CCNA exam will include questions that test your recollection of the details shown in various **show** and **debug** commands. Several tasks and questions are listed after Figure 6-21, Table 6-18 and Table 6-19, and Example 6-14, Example 6-15, and Example 6-16; performing these tasks will help you solidify your recollection of what information is available in each command.

Figure 6-21   *Scenario 6-4 Network Diagram*

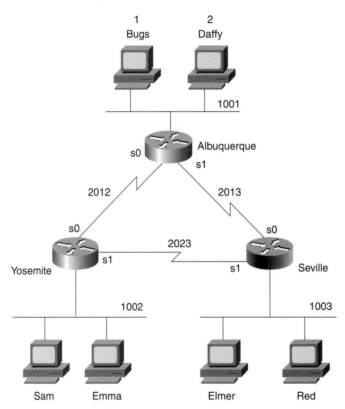

Example 6-14   *Albuquerque Command Output, Scenario 6-4*

```
Albuquerque#show ipx interface brief
Interface          IPX Network Encapsulation Status          IPX State
Serial0            2012        HDLC         up               [up]
Serial1            2013        HDLC         up               [up]
Ethernet0          1001        SAP          up               [up]

Albuquerque#show cdp neighbor detail
------------------------
Device ID: Yosemite
Entry address(es):
```

Example 6-14 *Albuquerque Command Output, Scenario 6-4 (Continued)*

```
   IP address: 10.1.12.2
   Novell address: 2012.0200.2222.2222
Platform: Cisco 2500,  Capabilities: Router
Interface: Serial0,  Port ID (outgoing port): Serial0
Holdtime : 167 sec

Version :
Cisco Internetwork Operating System Software
IOS (tm) 2500 Software (C2500-AINR-L), Version 11.2(11), RELEASE SOFTWARE (fc1)
Copyright (c) 1986-1997 by Cisco Systems, Inc.
Compiled Mon 29-Dec-97 18:47 by ckralik

-------------------------
Device ID: Seville
Entry address(es):
   IP address: 10.1.13.3
   Novell address: 2013.0200.3333.3333
Platform: Cisco 2500,  Capabilities: Router
Interface: Serial1,  Port ID (outgoing port): Serial0
Holdtime : 164 sec

Version :
Cisco Internetwork Operating System Software
IOS (tm) 2500 Software (C2500-AINR-L), Version 11.2(11), RELEASE SOFTWARE (fc1)
Copyright (c) 1986-1997 by Cisco Systems, Inc.
Compiled Mon 29-Dec-97 18:47 by ckralik

Albuquerque#debug ipx routing activity
IPX routing debugging is on
Albuquerque#
IPXRIP: positing full update to 1001.ffff.ffff.ffff via Ethernet0 (broadcast)
IPXRIP: src=1001.0000.0c35.ab12, dst=1001.ffff.ffff.ffff, packet sent
    network 1003, hops 2,  delay 8
    network 2023, hops 2,  delay 8
    network 1002, hops 2,  delay 8
    network 2013, hops 1,  delay 2
    network 2012, hops 1,  delay 2
IPXRIP: update from 2013.0200.3333.3333
    1002 in 2 hops, delay 13
    2023 in 1 hops, delay 7
    1003 in 1 hops, delay 7
IPXRIP: positing full update to 2012.ffff.ffff.ffff via Serial0 (broadcast)
IPXRIP: src=2012.0200.1111.1111, dst=2012.ffff.ffff.ffff, packet sent
    network 1, hops 3,  delay 8
    network 2, hops 3,  delay 8
    network 1003, hops 2,  delay 13
    network 2013, hops 1,  delay 7
    network 1001, hops 1,  delay 7
```

continues

Example 6-14 *Albuquerque Command Output, Scenario 6-4 (Continued)*

```
IPXRIP: positing full update to 2013.ffff.ffff.ffff via Serial1 (broadcast)
IPXRIP: src=2013.0200.1111.1111, dst=2013.ffff.ffff.ffff, packet sent
    network 1, hops 3,   delay 8
    network 2, hops 3,   delay 8
    network 2023, hops 2,   delay 13
    network 1002, hops 2,   delay 13
    network 2012, hops 1,   delay 7
    network 1001, hops 1,   delay 7
IPXRIP: update from 2012.0200.2222.2222
    1003 in 2 hops, delay 13
    2023 in 1 hops, delay 7
    1002 in 1 hops, delay 7
```

Example 6-15 *Yosemite Command Output, Scenario 6-4*

```
Yosemite#show ipx route
Codes: C - Connected primary network,    c - Connected secondary network
       S - Static, F - Floating static, L - Local (internal), W - IPXWAN
       R - RIP, E - EIGRP, N - NLSP, X - External, A - Aggregate
       s - seconds, u - uses

8 Total IPX routes. Up to 1 parallel paths and 16 hops allowed.

No default route known.

C        1002 (SAP),          To0
C        2012 (HDLC),         Se0
C        2023 (HDLC),         Se1
R           1 [08/03] via     2012.0200.1111.1111,   32s, Se0
R           2 [08/03] via     2012.0200.1111.1111,   33s, Se0
R        1001 [07/01] via     2012.0200.1111.1111,   33s, Se0
R        1003 [07/01] via     2023.0200.3333.3333,   32s, Se1
R        2013 [07/01] via     2012.0200.1111.1111,   33s, Se0

Yosemite#show ipx traffic
System Traffic for 0.0000.0000.0001 System-Name: Yosemite
Rcvd:   169 total, 0 format errors, 0 checksum errors, 0 bad hop count,
        8 packets pitched, 161 local destination, 0 multicast
Bcast:  160 received, 242 sent
Sent:   243 generated, 0 forwarded
        0 encapsulation failed, 0 no route
SAP:    2 SAP requests, 0 SAP replies, 2 servers
        0 SAP Nearest Name requests, 0 replies
        0 SAP General Name requests, 0 replies
        60 SAP advertisements received, 57 sent
        6 SAP flash updates sent, 0 SAP format errors
RIP:    1 RIP requests, 0 RIP replies, 9 routes
        98 RIP advertisements received, 120 sent
        45 RIP flash updates sent, 0 RIP format errors
Echo:   Rcvd 0 requests, 0 replies
        Sent 0 requests, 0 replies
```

Example 6-15   *Yosemite Command Output, Scenario 6-4 (Continued)*

```
                0 unknown: 0 no socket, 0 filtered, 0 no helper
                0 SAPs throttled, freed NDB len 0
Watchdog:
                0 packets received, 0 replies spoofed
Queue lengths:
                IPX input: 0, SAP 0, RIP 0, GNS 0
                SAP throttling length: 0/(no limit), 0 nets pending lost route reply
                Delayed process creation: 0
EIGRP:   Total received 0, sent 0
                Updates received 0, sent 0
                Queries received 0, sent 0
                Replies received 0, sent 0
                SAPs received 0, sent 0
NLSP:    Level-1 Hellos received 0, sent 0
                PTP Hello received 0, sent 0
                Level-1 LSPs received 0, sent 0
                LSP Retransmissions: 0
                LSP checksum errors received: 0
                LSP HT=0 checksum errors received: 0
                Level-1 CSNPs received 0, sent 0
                Level-1 PSNPs received 0, sent 0
                Level-1 DR Elections: 0
                Level-1 SPF Calculations: 0
                Level-1 Partial Route Calculations: 0

Yosemite#debug ipx routing activity
IPX routing debugging is on
Yosemite#
IPXRIP: positing full update to 1002.ffff.ffff.ffff via Ethernet0 (broadcast)
IPXRIP: src=1002.0000.0c24.7841, dst=1002.ffff.ffff.ffff, packet sent
    network 1, hops 4,   delay 9
    network 2, hops 4,   delay 9
    network 1003, hops 2,   delay 8
    network 1001, hops 2,   delay 8
    network 2013, hops 2,   delay 8
    network 2023, hops 1,   delay 2
    network 2012, hops 1,   delay 2
IPXRIP: positing full update to 2012.ffff.ffff.ffff via Serial0 (broadcast)
IPXRIP: src=2012.0200.2222.2222, dst=2012.ffff.ffff.ffff, packet sent
    network 1003, hops 2,   delay 13
    network 2023, hops 1,   delay 7
    network 1002, hops 1,   delay 7
IPXRIP: positing full update to 2023.ffff.ffff.ffff via Serial1 (broadcast)
IPXRIP: src=2023.0200.2222.2222, dst=2023.ffff.ffff.ffff, packet sent
    network 1, hops 4,   delay 14
    network 2, hops 4,   delay 14
    network 1001, hops 2,   delay 13
    network 2013, hops 2,   delay 13
    network 2012, hops 1,   delay 7
    network 1002, hops 1,   delay 7
IPXRIP: update from 2012.0200.1111.1111
```

continues

Example 6-15 *Yosemite Command Output, Scenario 6-4 (Continued)*

```
       1 in 3 hops, delay 8
       2 in 3 hops, delay 8
       1003 in 2 hops, delay 13
       2013 in 1 hops, delay 7
       1001 in 1 hops, delay 7
IPXRIP: update from 2023.0200.3333.3333
       1 in 4 hops, delay 14
       2 in 4 hops, delay 14
       1001 in 2 hops, delay 13
IPXRIP: 2012 FFFFFFFF not added, entry in table is static/connected/internal
       2012 in 2 hops, delay 13
       2013 in 1 hops, delay 7
       1003 in 1 hops, delay 7
```

Example 6-16 *Seville Command Output, Scenario 6-4*

```
Seville#show ipx interface
Serial0 is up, line protocol is up
  IPX address is 2013.0200.3333.3333 [up]
  Delay of this IPX network, in ticks is 6 throughput 0 link delay 0
  IPXWAN processing not enabled on this interface.
  IPX SAP update interval is 1 minute(s)
  IPX type 20 propagation packet forwarding is disabled
  Incoming access list is not set
  Outgoing access list is not set
  IPX helper access list is not set
  SAP GNS processing enabled, delay 0 ms, output filter list is not set
  SAP Input filter list is not set
  SAP Output filter list is not set
  SAP Router filter list is not set
  Input filter list is not set
  Output filter list is not set
  Router filter list is not set
  Netbios Input host access list is not set
  Netbios Input bytes access list is not set
  Netbios Output host access list is not set
  Netbios Output bytes access list is not set
  Updates each 60 seconds, aging multiples RIP: 3 SAP: 3
  SAP interpacket delay is 55 ms, maximum size is 480 bytes
  RIP interpacket delay is 55 ms, maximum size is 432 bytes
  Watchdog processing is disabled, SPX spoofing is disabled, idle time 60
  IPX accounting is disabled
  IPX fast switching is configured (enabled)
  RIP packets received 53, RIP packets sent 55
  SAP packets received 14, SAP packets sent 25
Serial1 is up, line protocol is up
  IPX address is 2023.0200.3333.3333 [up]
  Delay of this IPX network, in ticks is 6 throughput 0 link delay 0
  IPXWAN processing not enabled on this interface.
 IPX SAP update interval is 1 minute(s)
  IPX type 20 propagation packet forwarding is disabled
  Incoming access list is not set
  Outgoing access list is not set
```

Example 6-16 *Seville Command Output, Scenario 6-4 (Continued)*

```
 IPX helper access list is not set
 SAP GNS processing enabled, delay 0 ms, output filter list is not set
 SAP Input filter list is not set
 SAP Output filter list is not set
 SAP Router filter list is not set
 Input filter list is not set
 Output filter list is not set
 Router filter list is not set
 Netbios Input host access list is not set
 Netbios Input bytes access list is not set
 Netbios Output host access list is not set
 Netbios Output bytes access list is not set
 Updates each 60 seconds, aging multiples RIP: 3 SAP: 3
 SAP interpacket delay is 55 ms, maximum size is 480 bytes
 RIP interpacket delay is 55 ms, maximum size is 432 bytes
 Watchdog processing is disabled, SPX spoofing is disabled, idle time 60
 IPX accounting is disabled
 IPX fast switching is configured (enabled)
 RIP packets received 53, RIP packets sent 62
 SAP packets received 13, SAP packets sent 37
Ethernet0 is up, line protocol is up
 IPX address is 1003. 0000.0cac.ab41, SAP [up]
 Delay of this IPX network, in ticks is 1 throughput 0 link delay 0
 IPXWAN processing not enabled on this interface.
 IPX SAP update interval is 1 minute(s)
 IPX type 20 propagation packet forwarding is disabled
 Incoming access list is not set
 Outgoing access list is not set
 IPX helper access list is not set
 SAP GNS processing enabled, delay 0 ms, output filter list is not set
 SAP Input filter list is not set
 SAP Output filter list is not set
 SAP Router filter list is not set
 Input filter list is not set
 Output filter list is not set
 Router filter list is not set
 Netbios Input host access list is not set
 Netbios Input bytes access list is not set
 Netbios Output host access list is not set
 Netbios Output bytes access list is not set
 Updates each 60 seconds, aging multiples RIP: 3 SAP: 3
 SAP interpacket delay is 55 ms, maximum size is 480 bytes
 RIP interpacket delay is 55 ms, maximum size is 432 bytes
 IPX accounting is disabled
 IPX fast switching is configured (enabled)
 RIP packets received 20, RIP packets sent 62
 SAP packets received 18, SAP packets sent 15

Seville#show ipx servers
Codes: S - Static, P - Periodic, E - EIGRP, N - NLSP, H - Holddown, + = detail
```

continues

Example 6-16   *Seville Command Output, Scenario 6-4 (Continued)*

```
2 Total IPX Servers

Table ordering is based on routing and server info

    Type Name                    Net     Address    Port    Route Hops Itf
P    4 Bugs                      1.0000.0000.0001:0451       8/03   3  Se0
P    4 Daffy                     2.0000.0000.0001:0451       8/03   3  Se0



Seville#debug ipx sap activity
IPX service debugging is on
Seville#
IPXSAP: Response (in) type 0x2 len 160 src:2023.0200.2222.2222
dest:2023.ffff.ffff.ffff(452)
 type 0x4, "Daffy", 2.0000.0000.0001(451), 4 hops
 type 0x4, "Bugs", 1.0000.0000.0001(451), 4 hops
IPXSAP: positing update to 1003.ffff.ffff.ffff via Ethernet0 (broadcast) (full)
IPXSAP: Update type 0x2 len 160 src:1003.0000.0cac.ab41
dest:1003.ffff.ffff.ffff(452)
 type 0x4, "Daffy", 2.0000.0000.0001(451), 4 hops
 type 0x4, "Bugs", 1.0000.0000.0001(451), 4 hops
IPXSAP: positing update to 2013.ffff.ffff.ffff via Serial0 (broadcast) (full)
IPXSAP: suppressing null update to 2013.ffff.ffff.ffff
IPXSAP: positing update to 2023.ffff.ffff.ffff via Serial1 (broadcast) (full)
IPXSAP: Update type 0x2 len 160 src:2023.0200.3333.3333
dest:2023.ffff.ffff.ffff(452)
 type 0x4, "Daffy", 2.0000.0000.0001(451), 4 hops
 type 0x4, "Bugs", 1.0000.0000.0001(451), 4 hops
IPXSAP: Response (in) type 0x2 len 160 src:2013.0200.1111.1111
dest:2013.ffff.ffff.ffff(452)
 type 0x4, "Bugs", 1.0000.0000.0001(451), 3 hops
 type 0x4, "Daffy", 2.0000.0000.0001(451), 3 hops
```

Given the network in Figure 6-21 and the command output in Example 6-14, Example 6-15, and Example 6-16 for Scenario 6-4 complete or answer the following:

   1. Complete Table 6-18 with all IPX network numbers. List the command(s) you use to find these network numbers. List all commands that helped you find the network numbers.

Table 6-18   *IPX Networks in Scenario 6-4*

IPX Network	Location (for Example, "Between Albuquerque and Seville")	Command Used to Find This Information

2. Complete Table 6-19 with the IPX addresses of the three routers.

Table 6-19 *IPX Addresses on Routers in Scenario 6-4*

Router	Interface	IPX Network	IPX Node
Albuquerque	E0		
	S0		
	S1		
Yosemite	E0		
	S0		
	S1		
Seville	E0		
	S0		
	S1		

3. Describe the contents of the RIP update from Yosemite sent out its serial 0 interface. Include the numbers of routes and metrics.

4. Examine the **show ipx servers** command from Seville. How many file servers appear to be in the SAP table? What socket is Bugs using? Assuming defaults for ticks on each router, is it possible that more than one serial link exists between Seville and Daffy?

Scenario Answers

Answers to Scenario 6-1: IP Configuration 1

Refer back to the network illustrated in Figure 6-18 and Table 6-15 to establish the Scenario 6-1 design details and the context of the answers to the five tasks for this scenario.

Answers to Task 1 for Scenario 6-1

Task 1 for Scenario 6-1 asks for completed configurations, which are shown in Example 6-17, Example 6-18, and Example 6-19.

Example 6-17 *Albuquerque Configuration for Scenario 6-1*

```
hostname Albuquerque
!
enable secret 5 $1$ZvR/$Gpk5a5K5vTVpotd3KUygA1
!
interface Serial0
 ip address 148.14.4.1 255.255.255.0
!
interface Serial1
 ip address 148.14.5.1 255.255.255.0
!
Ethernet0
 ip address 148.14.1.1 255.255.255.0
```

Example 6-18 *Yosemite Configuration for Scenario 6-1*

```
hostname Yosemite
enable secret 5 $1$ZvR/$Gpk5a5K5vTVpotd3KUygA1
!
interface Serial0
 ip address 148.14.4.2 255.255.255.0
!
interface Serial1
 ip address 148.14.6.2 255.255.255.0
!
Ethernet0
 ip address 148.14.2.2 255.255.255.0
```

Example 6-19   *Seville Configuration for Scenario 6-1*

```
hostname Seville
enable secret 5 $1$ZvR/$Gpk5a5K5vTVpotd3KUygA1
!
interface Serial0
 ip address 148.14.5.3 255.255.255.0
!
interface Serial1
 ip address 148.14.6.3 255.255.255.0
!
Ethernet0
 ip address 148.14.3.3 255.255.255.0
```

Answers to Task 2 for Scenario 6-1

Task 2 for Scenario 6-1 asks for a description of the IP routing table on Seville, which is shown in Table 6-20. This table exists before static and dynamic routes are added.

Table 6-20   *Routing Table in Seville*

Group	Outgoing Interface	Next Router
148.14.3.0	e0	
148.14.5.0	s0	
148.14.6.0	s1	

The next-hop router field is always the IP address of another router and that next-router IP address must be in a directly connected subnet. For example, the route to 148.14.1.0 points to a next router of 148.14.5.1, and 148.14.5.1 is an IP address in the directly connected subnet 148.14.5.0. The Next Router field is also the source IP address in the routing update packet received from the router that advertised the route.

Answers to Task 3 for Scenario 6-1

Task 3 for Scenario 6-1 asks for static route configuration. The routes to allow users on LANs to reach each other are shown in upcoming examples. However, routes to the subnets on serial links are not shown in these examples for brevity's sake; the users should not need to send packets to IP addresses on the serial links' subnets, but rather to other hosts on the LANs. Example 6-20, Example 6-21, and Example 6-22 show the configurations on the three routers.

Example 6-20 *Albuquerque Configuration, Scenario 6-1*

```
ip route 148.14.2.0 255.255.255.0 148.14.4.2
ip route 148.14.3.0 255.255.255.0 serial1
```

Example 6-21 *Yosemite Configuration, Scenario 6-1*

```
ip route 148.14.1.0 255.255.255.0 148.14.4.1
ip route 148.14.3.0 255.255.255.0 serial1
```

Example 6-22 *Seville Configuration, Scenario 6-1*

```
ip route 148.14.1.0 255.255.255.0 148.14.5.1
ip route 148.14.2.0 255.255.255.0 serial1
```

Both valid styles of static route configuration are shown. When the next router is attached to a common point-to-point serial link, the serial interface on the router where the static **route** command is configured can be used. In any topological case, the style of static **route** command using the next router's IP address is valid.

Answers to Task 4 for Scenario 6-1

Task 4 for Scenario 6-1 asks for IGRP configuration. The same configuration is used on each router and is listed in Example 6-23. The IGRP process-id must be the same number on each router; if an IGRP update is received, but it lists a different process-id, the update will be ignored.

Example 6-23 *IGRP Configuration, Scenario 6-1*

```
router IGRP 1
network 148.14.0.0
```

Answers to Task 5 for Scenario 6-1

Task 5 for Scenario 6-1 asks for the broadcast addresses for each subnet, which are shown in Table 6-21.

Table 6-21 *Scenario 6-1 IP Addresses*

Location of Subnet Geographically	Subnet Mask	Subnet Number	Subnet Broadcast
Ethernet off router in Albuquerque	255.255.255.0	148.14.1.0	144.14.1.255
Ethernet off router in Yosemite	255.255.255.0	148.14.2.0	144.14.2.255
Ethernet off router in Seville	255.255.255.0	148.14.3.0	144.14.3.255
Serial between Albuquerque and Yosemite	255.255.255.0	148.14.4.0	144.14.4.255
Serial between Albuquerque and Seville	255.255.255.0	148.14.5.0	144.14.5.255
Serial between Seville and Yosemite	255.255.255.0	148.14.6.0	144.14.6.255

Answers to Scenario 6-2: IP Configuration 2

Refer back to the network illustrated in Figure 6-19 and Table 6-16 to establish the Scenario 6-2 design details and the context of the answers to the four tasks for this scenario.

Answers to Task 1 for Scenario 6-2

Task 1 for Scenario 6-2 asks for completed configurations, which are shown in Example 6-24, Example 6-25, Example 6-26, and Example 6-27.

Example 6-24 *Atlanta Configuration, Scenario 6-2*

```
ip subnet-zero
no ip domain-lookup
!
interface serial0
encapsulation frame-relay
interface serial 0.1
ip address 10.2.1.1 255.255.255.0
interface-dlci 41
!
interface serial 0.2
ip address 10.2.2.1 255.255.255.0
interface-dlci 42
!
interface serial 0.3
ip address 10.2.3.1 255.255.255.0
interface-dlci 43
!
interface ethernet 0
ip address 10.1.1.1 255.255.255.0
```

Example 6-25 *Charlotte Configuration, Scenario 6-2*

```
no ip domain-lookup
!
interface serial0
encapsulation frame-relay
interface serial 0.1
ip address 10.2.1.2 255.255.255.0
interface-dlci 40
!
interface ethernet 0
ip address 10.1.2.2 255.255.255.0
```

Example 6-26 *Nashville Configuration, Scenario 6-2*

```
hostname nashville
no ip domain-lookup
!
interface serial0
encapsulation frame-relay
interface serial 0.1
ip address 10.2.2.3 255.255.255.0
interface-dlci 40
!
interface ethernet 0
ip address 10.1.3.3 255.255.255.0
```

Example 6-27 *Boston Configuration, Scenario 6-2*

```
hostname boston
no ip domain-lookup
!
interface serial0
encapsulation frame-relay
interface serial 0.1
ip address 10.2.3.4 255.255.255.0
interface-dlci 40
!
interface ethernet 0
ip address 10.1.4.4 255.255.255.0
```

Answers to Task 2 for Scenario 6-2

Task 2 for Scenario 6-2 asks for RIP configuration. The same configuration is used on each router and is listed in Example 6-28.

Example 6-28 *RIP Configuration, Scenario 6-2*

```
Router rip
network 10.0.0.0
```

Answers to Task 3 for Scenario 6-2

Task 3 for Scenario 6-2 asks for the broadcast addresses for each subnet, which are shown in Table 6-22.

Table 6-22   *Scenario 6-2 IP Addresses*

Location of Subnet Geographically	Subnet Mask	Subnet Number	Subnet Broadcast
Ethernet off router in Atlanta	255.255.255.0	10.1.1.0	10.1.1.255
Ethernet off router in Charlotte	255.255.255.0	10.1.2.0	10.1.2.255
Ethernet off router in Nashville	255.255.255.0	10.1.3.0	10.1.3.255
Ethernet off router in Boston	255.255.255.0	10.1.4.0	10.1.4.255
VC between Atlanta and Charlotte	255.255.255.0	10.2.1.0	10.2.1.255
VC between Atlanta and Nashville	255.255.255.0	10.2.2.0	10.2.2.255
VC between Atlanta and Boston	255.255.255.0	10.2.3.0	10.2.3.255

Answers to Task 4 for Scenario 6-2

Task 4 for Scenario 6-2 requires consideration for the effects of split-horizon. Split-horizon logic considers subinterfaces to be separate interfaces, in spite of the fact that several subinterfaces share the same physical interface. Boston will only advertise about 10.1.4.0 in its RIP update out its subinterface 1. All other routes in Boston's routing table were learned through RIP updates from Atlanta, via updates entering that same subinterface; therefore, Boston will not advertise about those routes in updates it sends on that same subinterface.

The RIP updates from Atlanta to Charlotte, out Atlanta's subinterface 1, will advertise about all subnets not learned from RIP updates entering that same subinterface. All subnets except 10.1.2.0 (learned from Charlotte) and 10.2.1.0 (subinterface 1's subnet) will be listed in Atlanta's RIP update to Charlotte. Subnet 10.1.4.0, learned from Boston, will indeed be included in updates to Charlotte; split-horizon considers subinterfaces as separate interfaces.

Answers to Scenario 6-3: IP Addressing and Subnet Derivation

Refer back to the network illustrated in Figure 6-20 and Example 6-11, Example 6-12, and Example 6-13 to establish the Scenario 6-3 design details and the context of the answers to the three tasks for this scenario.

Answers to Task 1 for Scenario 6-3

Task 1 for Scenario 6-3 asks you to complete a table with the subnet numbers and broadcast addresses used in this scenario's network that after examining the **show** commands on the various routers in Example 6-11, Example 6-12, and Example 6-13. Table 6-23 lists the subnet numbers and broadcast addresses requested in this task.

Table 6-23 *Subnets and Broadcast Addresses*

Location of Subnet Geographically	Subnet Mask	Subnet Number	Subnet Broadcast
Ethernet off router in Mayberry	255.255.255.0	170.1.101.0	170.1.101.255
Ethernet off router in Mount Pilot	255.255.255.0	170.1.102.0	170.1.102.255
Ethernet off router in Raleigh	255.255.255.0	170.1.103.0	170.1.103.255
VC between Mayberry and Mount Pilot	255.255.255.0	170.1.1.0	170.1.1.255
VC between Mayberry and Raleigh	255.255.255.0	170.1.1.0	170.1.1.255
VC between Mount Pilot and Raleigh	255.255.255.0	170.1.1.0	170.1.1.255

Notice that the same subnet was used for all three virtual circuits; a full mesh of virtual circuits was used and a single subnet was chosen, rather than one subnet per virtual circuit.

Answers to Task 2 for Scenario 6-3

Task 2 for Scenario 6-3 asks you to describe the contents of the IGRP update from Raleigh, sent out its virtual circuit to Mount Pilot. Notice that there are four routes in the routing table and four routes in the routing update. Split-horizon is disabled on serial interfaces using Frame Relay as configured without subinterfaces. Split-horizon is disabled by the IOS if using Frame Relay multipoint subinterfaces as well.

Answers to Task 3 for Scenario 6-3

Task 3 for Scenario 6-3 asks you to describe the contents of the routing table in Mount Pilot immediately after the VC to Mayberry was noticed to have failed. The routing table is unchanged. Because split-horizon is turned off on all three routers' serial interfaces, Raleigh continues to advertise all routes in its updates to Mount Pilot. Directly connected subnet 170.1.1.0/24 remains in the routing table because serial 0 remains up. Mount Pilot can forward packets to hosts in 170.1.101.0/24, the Ethernet in Mayberry, via Raleigh.

However, Mount Pilot can no longer ping 170.1.1.1, Mayberry's Frame Relay serial interface IP address. Look back to the problem statement for Scenario 6-3, to the **show frame-relay map** command. (If this becomes confusing, consider the routing algorithm background in Chapter 3). The **icmp echo** from Mount Pilot to Mayberry's 170.1.1.1 address cannot be sent because

Mount Pilot has no map entry for 170.1.1.1 after the PVC to Mayberry has failed. Mount Pilot thinks 170.1.1.1 is in a connected network; there is no need to send the packet to any other router. But there is no way to send the packet directly to 170.1.1.1 right now. However, packets with destinations in 170.1.101.0/24 are sent to 170.1.1.2 next, based on the routing table entry for subnet 170.1.101.0. There is a map entry for 170.1.1.2 so that the packet can be forwarded by Mount Pilot to Raleigh.

Answers to Scenario 6-4: IPX Examination

Refer back to the network illustrated in Figure 6-21 and the command output in Example 6-14, Example 6-15, and Example 6-16 to establish the Scenario 6-4 design details and the context of the answers to the four tasks for this scenario.

Answers to Task 1 for Scenario 6-4

Task 1 for Scenario 6-4 asks you to complete a table with all IPX network numbers filled in. In addition, this task asks you to list the command(s) you use to find these network numbers. Table 6-24 provides the IPX network numbers for this scenario. In my opinion, the **show ipx interface brief** command and **show ipx route** commands are the best methods for learning these network numbers.

Table 6-24   *IPX Networks for Scenario 6-4*

IPX Network	Location (For Example, "Between Albuquerque and Seville")	Command Used to Find This Information
1001	Albuquerque Ethernet0	**show ipx interface brief** on Albuquerque
"	"	**debug ipx routing activity** on Albuquerque
"	"	**show ipx route** on Yosemite
1002	Yosemite Ethernet0	**show ipx route** on Yosemite
"	"	**debug ipx routing activity** on Yosemite
1003	Seville Ethernet0	**show cdp neighbor detail** on Albuquerque
		show ipx interface on Seville
2012	Albuquerque—Yosemite	**show cdp neighbor detail** on Albuquerque
		debug ipx routing activity on Albuquerque
		show ipx route on Yosemite
		debug ipx routing activity on Yosemite
2013	Albuquerque—Seville	**show cdp neighbor detail** on Albuquerque
		debug ipx routing activity on Albuquerque

Table 6-24 *IPX Networks for Scenario 6-4 (Continued)*

IPX Network	Location (For Example, "Between Albuquerque and Seville")	Command Used to Find This Information
		show ipx route on Yosemite
		debug ipx routing activity on Yosemite
2023	Yosemite - Seville	**show ipx route** on Yosemite
		show ipx interface on Seville
1	Bugs's internal network	**show ipx servers** on Seville
		show ipx route on Yosemite
2	Daffy's internal network	**show ipx servers** on Seville
		show ipx route on Yosemite

Answers to Task 2 for Scenario 6-4

Task 2 for Scenario 6-4 asks you to complete a table with the IPX addresses of the three routers. The network numbers are found from several sources as seen in Task 1. The additional requirement in Task 2 is to find the node part of the IPX addresses on each interface. The easy way to learn this information is through the **show ipx interface** command. Of course, only one such command was provided in Example 6-14, Example 6-15, and Example 6-16. The output of the RIP and SAP debugs show the source IPX addresses of the updates sent by each router, which supplies the rest of the answers to the question. Table 6-25 provides the completed answers for this task.

Table 6-25 *IPX Addresses on Routers in Scenario 6-4*

Router	Interface	IPX Network	IPX Node
Albuquerque	E0	1001	0000.0c35.ab12
	S0	2012	0200.1111.1111
	S1	2013	0200.1111.1111
Yosemite	E0	1002	0000.0c24.7841
	S0	2012	0200.2222.2222
	S1	2023	0200.2222.2222
Seville	E0	1003	0000.0cac.ab41
	S0	2013	0200.3333.3333
	S1	2023	0200.3333.3333

Answers to Task 3 for Scenario 6-4

Task 3 for Scenario 6-4 asks you to describe the contents of the RIP update from Yosemite, sent out its serial 0 interface, including the numbers of routes and metrics. First, just finding the appropriate **debug** messages takes some effort. The needed routing debug message begins with the phrase, "positing full update to 2012.ffff.ffff.ffff....". Remembering that Yosemite's S0 interface is using IPX network 2012 is a key to knowing to look for that message.

Three networks are advertised: 1003, 2023, and 1002. The hop count and delay are shown in each successive line of **debug** output. More important is what is missing—networks 1, 2, 1001, and 2013 are left out of the update due to split-horizon rules.

Answers to Task 4 for Scenario 6-4

Task 4 for Scenario 6-4 asks you to examine the **show ipx servers** command from Seville. Furthermore, this task asks you to determine how many file servers appear to be in the SAP table, what socket Bugs is using, and, assuming defaults for ticks on each router, determine if it is possible that more than one serial link exists between Seville and Daffy. There are two file servers listed in the SAP table, namely Bugs and Daffy. Both are using socket 451, as is shown under the word "port" in the SAP table. (The value is still called a socket; the heading is poorly labeled in the **show ipx servers** command.) Daffy appears to be eight ticks away, and because a serial link defaults to having six ticks, there could only be one serial link between Seville and Daffy.

The following table outlines the CCNA exam objectives that are reviewed in this chapter. The numbers shown correspond to the master list of objectives found in Chapter 1, "What Is CCNA?"

Objective	Description
38	Configure IPX access lists and SAP filters to control basic Novell traffic.
44	Configure standard and extended access lists to filter IP traffic.
45	Monitor and verify selected access list operations on the router.

CHAPTER 7

Understanding Network Security

"Understanding Network Security" is a chapter title chosen to closely relate to the Cisco CCNA exam objectives topic, "Network Security." However, an alternate title could be, "Cisco Access List Topics on the CCNA Exam." The use of IP standard and extended access lists is covered first followed by IP packet and IPX packet and SAP access lists.

These topics are covered on both the CCNA exam, and on the CCNP ACRC exam (640-403). If you are preparing for the CCNP exam as well, you may want to go ahead and get the Cisco Press title, *ACRC Exam Certification Guide* for additional access list study information (ISBN 1-57870-074-4).

How to Best Use This Chapter

By taking the following steps, you can make better use of your study time:

- Keep your notes and answers for all your work with this book in one place for easy reference.

- Take the "Do I Know This Already?" quiz and write down your answers. Studies show retention is significantly increased through writing facts and concepts down, even if you never look at the information again!

- Figure 7-1 helps guide you to the next step in preparation for this topic area on the CCNA exam.

Figure 7-1   *How To Use This Chapter*

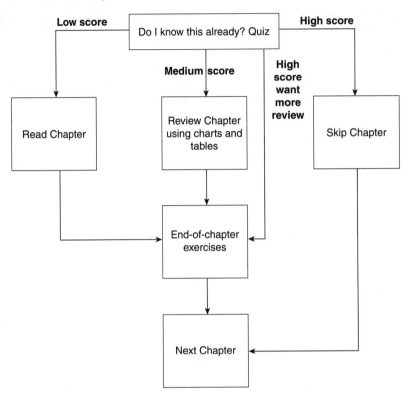

"Do I Know This Already?" Quiz

1. Configure an IP access list that would stop packets from subnet 134.141.7.0, with mask 255.255.255.0, from exiting serial 0 on some router. Allow all other packets.

    _____

    _____

    _____

2. How would a user who does not have the enable password find out what access lists have been configured and where they are enabled?

    _____

    _____

    _____

3. Configure and enable an IP access list that would stop packets from subnet 10.3.4.0/24 from getting out serial interface S0 and stop packets from 134.141.5.4 from entering S1. Permit all other traffic.

_____

_____

_____

4. Create an IPX packet filter to prevent packets from entering Serial0, except for packets from address 500.0000.0000.0001 destined for any node in network 4.

_____

_____

_____

5. What services use IPX socket 4? Socket 7?

_____

_____

_____

6. Create a configuration to add a SAP access list to filter all print services from being advertised out a router's Serial0 and Serial1 interfaces.

_____

_____

_____

7. Name all the items that a standard SAP access list can examine to make a match.

_____

_____

_____

8. Can standard IP access lists be used to check the source IP address when enabled with the **ip access-group 1 in** command and check the destination IP addresses when using the **ip access-group 1 out** command?

_____

_____

_____

9. Can a single IP extended **access-list** command be used to check a particular port number on all IP packets?

   _____

   _____

   _____

10. If all IP or IPX **access-list** statements in a particular list define the deny action, the default action is to permit all other packets. (T/F)

    _____

    _____

    _____

11. In an IPX access list with five statements, a **no** version of the third statement is issued in configuration mode. Immediately following, another access list configuration command is added for the same access list. How many statements are in the list now, and in what position is the newly added statement?

    _____

    _____

    _____

12. How many IP access lists of either type can be active on an interface at the same time?

    _____

    _____

    _____

You can find the answers to the "Do I Know this Already?" quiz in Appendix B on page 579. Review the answers, grade your quiz, and choose an appropriate next step in this chapter based on the suggestions in the "How to Best Use This Chapter" topic earlier in this chapter. Your choices for the next step are as follows:

- **5 or fewer correct**—Read this chapter.

- **6, 7, or 8 correct**—Review this chapter, looking at the charts and diagrams that summarize most of the concepts and facts in this chapter.

- **9 or more correct**—If you want more review on these topics, skip to the exercises at the end of this chapter. If you do not want more review on these topics, skip this chapter.

Foundation Topics

Filtering IP Traffic

CCNA Objectives Covered in This Section

44	Configure standard and extended access lists to filter IP traffic.
45	Monitor and verify selected access list operations on the router.

IP access lists perform a variety of functions in a Cisco router. The CCNA exam will only require you to know how to use access lists for filtering, but they can be used to filter routing updates to match packets for prioritization and for filtering packets. The CCNA exam and this book address the use of access lists for filtering only. Filtering is often used to make a network more secure, hence the name of this chapter.

Table 7-1 and Table 7-2 list the configuration commands and EXEC commands about access lists that are covered in Training Paths 1 and 2 (plus any related commands that might be on the exam).

Table 7-1 *Access List Configuration Commands in Training Paths 1 and 2*

Command	Configuration mode
access-list {1-99} {permit|deny} *source-addr [source-mask]*	Global
access-list {100-199} {permit|deny} protocol source-addr [source-mask] [operator operand] destination-addr [destination-mask] [operator operand] [established]	Global
ip access-group {*number* [**in**|**out**] }	Interface
ip access-list {standard | extended } name {permit | deny } *protocol source-addr [source-mask] [operator operand] destination-addr [destination-mask] [operator operand] [established]*	Global

Table 7-2 *Access List EXEC commands in Training Paths 1 and 2*

Command	Function
show interface	Includes reference to the access lists enabled on the interface
show access-list	Shows details of all configured access lists
show ip access-list	Shows IP access lists

The logic used for access lists can be best summarized by Figure 7-2.

Figure 7-2 *Locations Where Access List Logic Can Be Applied*

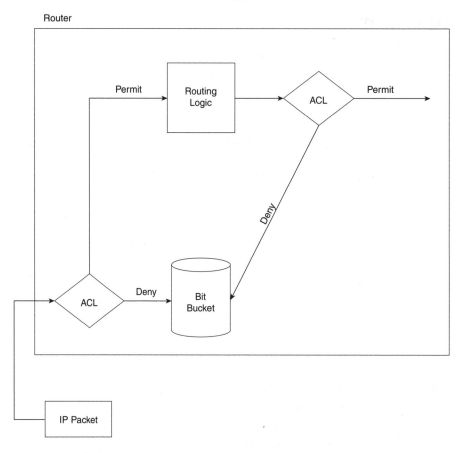

Features of the process described in Figure 7-2 are as follows:

- Packets must originate outside the router to be filtered.

- Packets can be filtered as they enter an interface, before the routing decision.

- Packets can be filtered before they exit an interface, after the routing decision.

- "Deny" is the term used in the IOS to imply that the packet will be filtered.

- "Permit" is the term used in the IOS to imply that the packet will not be filtered.

- The filtering logic is configured in the access list.

- At the end of every access list is an implied "deny all traffic" criteria statement. Therefore, if a packet does not match any of your criteria statements, the packet will be blocked.

The logic created by an access list, as shown in the diamond-shaped symbols in Figure 7-2, is best summarized by the following sequence:

1. The matching parameters of the first access list statement is compared to the packet.

2. If a match is made, the action defined in this **access-list** statement (Permit or Deny) is performed, as shown in Figure 7-2.

3. If a match is not made in Step 2, repeat Steps 1 and 2, using the next sequential **access-list** statement.

4. If no match is made with an entry in the access list, the Deny action is performed.

The logic for access lists is true whether using standard or extended access lists. The only difference is in what constitutes a match. The following sections on standard IP access lists, extended IP access lists, and named access lists outline these differences.

Standard IP Access Lists

Standard access lists can match only by examining the source IP address field in the packet's IP header. Any bit positions in the 32-bit source IP address can be compared to the **access-list** statements; for example, a subnet number can be checked. However, the matching is flexible and does not care about the subnet mask in use; it is just a math problem!

A wildcard mask is used to define the subset of the 32 bits in the IP address that must be matched. Matching is performed by comparing an **access-list** command *address* parameter and the packet's source IP address. Mask bits of value binary 0 imply that the same bit positions must be compared in the two IP addresses. Mask bits of value binary 1 are wildcards; the corresponding bit positions in the addresses are considered to match, regardless of values. In other words, binary 1s mean that these bit positions already match—hence the name *wildcard*.

Table 7-3 shows several examples of masks, packet source addresses, and addresses in **access-list** commands.

Table 7-3 *Example Access List Wildcard Masks*

Access List Mask	Source IP Address in Packet	Binary Version of Source IP Addresses	IP Address in access-list Command	Binary Version of IP Address in access-list Command	Explanation
0.0.0.0	1.55.88.111	0000 0001 0011 0111 0101 1000 0110 1111	1.55.88.4	0000 0001 0011 0111 0101 1000 0000 0100	All bits must match, and they do not.

continues

Table 7-3 *Example Access List Wildcard Masks (Continued)*

Access List Mask	Source IP Address in Packet	Binary Version of Source IP Addresses	IP Address in access-list Command	Binary Version of IP Address in access-list Command	Explanation
0.0.0.255	1.55.88.111	0000 0001 0011 0111 0101 1000 0110 1111	1.55.88.0	0000 0001 0011 0111 0101 1000 0000 0000	The first 24 bits must match, and they do.
0.0.255.255	1.55.56.7	0000 0001 0011 0111 0011 1000 0000 0111	1.55.0.0	0000 0001 0011 0111 0000 0000 0000 0000	The first 16 bits must match, and they do.
255.255.255.255	5.88.22.5	0000 0101 0101 1000 0001 0110 0000 0101	0.0.0.0	0000 0000 0000 0000 0000 0000 0000 0000	All bits match, regardless of the IP address in the packet.
32.48.0.255	33.1.1.1	0010 0001 0000 0001 0000 0001 0000 0001	1.1.1.0	0000 0001 0000 0001 0000 0001 0000 0000	All bits except the third, eleventh, twelfth, and last eight must match. The two numbers match in this case. (This is a rather impractical choice of wildcard mask and is used only to make the point that it is flexible!)

The following example, illustrated by Figure 7-3 and Example 7-1 and Example 7-2, shows a basic use of standard IP access lists, with two typical oversights in the first attempt at a complete answer. The criteria for the access list(s) are as follows:

- Sam is not allowed access to Bugs or Daffy.

- Hosts on the Seville Ethernet are not allowed access to hosts on the Yosemite Ethernet.

- All other combinations are allowed.

Figure 7-3   *Network Diagram for Standard Access List Example*

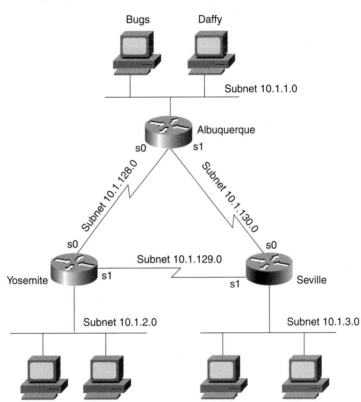

Example 7-1   *Yosemite Configuration for Standard Access List Example*

```
interface serial 0
ip access-group 3
!
access-list 3 deny host 10.1.2.1
access-list 3 permit any
```

Example 7-2   *Seville Configuration for Standard Access List Example*

```
interface serial 1
ip access-group 4
!
access-list 4 deny 10.1.3.0    0.0.0.255
access-list 4 permit any
```

These two access lists seem to perform the desired function at first glance. In Yosemite, the packets from Sam are filtering before leaving s0; in Seville, packets from 10.1.3.0/24 are filtered before leaving s1 towards Yosemite. However, should either link into Albuquerque fail, the new routes would leave an opening. For example, if the link from Albuquerque to Yosemite failed, Yosemite would learn a route to 10.1.1.0/24 through Seville. Packets from Sam would leave Yosemite's s1 without being filtered.

An alternative answer to the stated problem is in Example 7-3. The access list has been removed from Seville, and all filtering is performed on Yosemite.

Example 7-3 *Yosemite Configuration for Standard Access List Example—Alternate Solution Compared to Example 7-1*

```
interface serial 0
ip access-group 3
!
interface serial 1
ip access-group 3
!
interface ethernet 0
ip access-group 4
!
access-list 3 deny host 10.1.2.1
access-list 3 permit any
!
access-list 4 deny 10.1.3.0    0.0.0.255
access-list 4 permit any
```

Example 7-3 performs all the requested filtering, regardless of the current routing table. In many cases, the meaning of the criteria for the access lists greatly impact your configuration choices. For example, one interpretation of the criteria is that Sam is not allowed to access any host outside his local Ethernet—other interpretations are possible. Care should be taken to clearly state all criteria before configuring the access lists. On the CCNA exam, read access list questions (particularly the filtering criteria) thoroughly before selecting an answer!

Extended IP Access Lists

Extended IP access lists are almost identical to standard IP access lists in their usage; the key difference between the two types is the variety of fields in the packet that can be compared for matching by extended access lists. Extended access lists are enabled for packets entering or exiting an interface. The list is searched sequentially; the first statement matched stops the search through the list and defines the action to be taken. All of these features are true of standard access lists as well. The matching logic, however, is different than standard access lists and makes extended access lists much more complex.

Figure 7-4 describes the fields in the packet headers that can be matched.

Figure 7-4   *Extended Access List Matching Options*

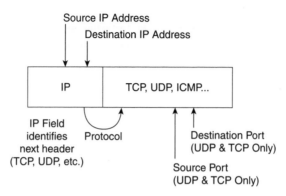

A statement is considered to match if all options in the statement match. If one option does not match, the statement is skipped, and the next entry in the list is examined. Table 7-4 provides several example **access-list** statements.

Table 7-4   *Sample **access-list** Commands and Logic Explanations*

access-list Statement	Explanation of What Matches
ip access-list 101 tcp deny any host 10.1.1.1 eq 23	Packet with any source address, destination must be 10.1.1.1, with a TCP header, with destination port 23.
ip access-list 101 tcp deny any host 10.1.1.1 eq telnet	Same as last example; **telnet** keyword used instead of port 23.
ip access-list 101 udp deny 1.0.0.0 0.255.255.255 lt 1023 any	Packet with source in network 1.0.0.0, to any destination, using UDP with source port less than 1023.
ip access-list 101 udp deny 1.0.0.0 0.255.255.255 lt 1023 44.1.2.3 0.0.255.255	Packet with source in network 1.0.0.0, to destinations beginning 44.1, using UDP with source port less than 1023.
ip access-list 101 ip deny 33.1.2.0 0.0.0.255 44.1.2.3 0.0.255.255	Packet with source in 33.1.2.0/24, to destinations beginning 44.1.
ip access-list 101 icmp deny 33.1.2.0 0.0.0.255 44.1.2.3 0.0.255.255 echo	Packet with source in 33.1.2.0/24, to destinations beginning 44.1, which are ICMP echo requests.

In Table 7-4, the keyword **any** implies that any value is matched. The keyword **host**, followed by an IP address, implies that exactly that IP address is matched. In other words, the **any** keyword implies logic like a wildcard mask of 255.255.255.255, and the **host** keyword implies logic like a wildcard mask of 0.0.0.0.

Extended IP Access Lists, Example 1

The following example, illustrated by Figure 7-3 and Example 7-4 and Example 7-5, shows the use of extended IP access lists. The criteria for this first example uses the same criteria as the standard access list example:

1. Sam is not allowed access to Bugs or Daffy.

2. Hosts on the Seville Ethernet are not allowed access to hosts on the Yosemite Ethernet.

3. All other combinations are allowed.

Example 7-4 *Yosemite Configuration for Extended Access List Example #1*

```
interface serial 0
ip access-group 110
!
interface serial 1
ip access-group 110
!
access-list 110 deny ip host 10.1.2.1 10.1.1.0 0.0.0.255
access-list 110 permit ip any any
```

Example 7-5 *Seville Configuration for Extended Access List Example #1*

```
interface serial 0
ip access-group 110
!
interface serial 1
ip access-group 110
!
access-list 110 deny ip  10.1.3.0 0.0.0.255  10.1.2.0  0.0.0.255
access-list 110 permit ip any any
```

Two important side effects occur with the configuration shown in Examples 7-4 and 7-5, compared to the standard access list configuration in Examples 7-1 and 7-2. The issue of having packets routed around the access list is already taken care of with the access lists being enabled for output packets on both serial interfaces. Also, the packets are filtered at the routers nearest the origin of the packets, which reduces network overhead.

Extended IP Access Lists, Example 2

Figure 7-5 presents the network diagram for another example on extended IP access lists.

Figure 7-5   *Network Diagram for Extended Access List Example #2*

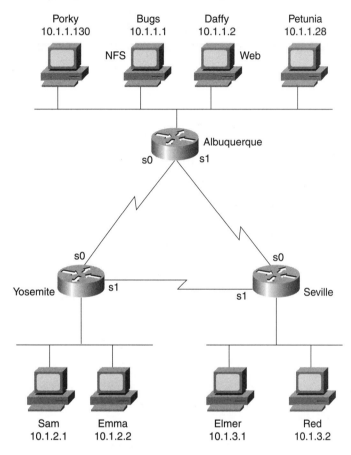

The filtering criteria for this extended access list example is more complicated:

1. The web server (Daffy) is available to all users.

2. The NFS server (Bugs), and other UDP-based servers on Bugs, are not available to hosts whose IP addresses are in the upper half of the valid IP addresses in each subnet.

3. Packets between hosts on the Yosemite Ethernet and the Seville Ethernet are only allowed if packets are routed across the direct serial link.

4. Clients Porky and Petunia can connect to all hosts except Red.

5. Any TCP client connections to servers in Albuquerque, not otherwise specified, are not allowed.

6. Any other connections are permitted.

Example 7-6, Example 7-7, and Example 7-8 show one solution to this second extended access list example.

Example 7-6 *Yosemite Configuration for Extended Access List Example #2*

```
interface serial 0
ip access-group 110
!
interface serial 1
ip access-group 111
!
access-list 110 permit TCP any host 10.1.1.2 eq www
access-list 110 deny UDP 0.0.0.128  255.255.255.127  host 10.1.1.1
access-list 110 deny IP 10.1.2.0 0.0.0.255 10.1.3.0 0.0.0.255
access-list 110 permit IP any any
!
access-list 111 permit TCP any host 10.1.1.2 eq www
access-list 1111 deny UPD 0.0.0.128  255.255.255.127  host 10.1.1.1
access-list 111 deny UDP 0.0.0.128  255.2
```

Example 7-7 *Seville Configuration for Extended Access List Example #2*

```
interface serial 0
ip access-group 110
!
interface serial 1
ip access-group 111
!
access-list 110 permit TCP any host 10.1.1.2 eq www
access-list 110 deny UDP 0.0.0.128  255.255.255.127  host 10.1.1.1
access-list 110 deny IP 10.1.3.0 0.0.0.255 10.1.2.0 0.0.0.255
access-list 110 permit IP any any
!
access-list 111 permit TCP any host 10.1.1.2 eq www
access-list 111 deny UDP 0.0.0.128  255..255.255.127  host 10.1.1.1
access-list 111 permit IP any any
```

Example 7-8 *Albuquerque Configuration for Extended Access List Example #2*

```
interface serial 0
ip access-group 112
!
interface serial 1
ip access-group 112
!
access-list 112 deny IP host 10.1.1.130  host 10.1.3.2
access-list 112 deny IP host 10.1.1.28  host 10.1.3.2
access-list 112 permit IP host 10.1.1.130  any
access-list 112 permit IP host 10.1.1.28  any
access-list 112 deny TCP 10.1.1.0 0.0.0.255 any  established
access-list 112 permit IP any any
```

The access lists on Yosemite and Seville are almost identical. The first three statements in list 110 in each router complete the first three criteria for this example; the only difference is in the source and destination addresses used in the third statement. This third statement in list 110 is missing from list 111 in each case; list 110 filters packets between hosts in Seville and Yosemite, preventing them from passing through router Albuquerque. The final statement in lists 110 and 111 in Seville and Yosemite provide coverage for the sixth point of criteria for this example.

The second **access-list** statement in list 110 and 111 on Seville and Yosemite is trickier than you will see on the CCNA exam. This example is indicative of the types of nuances that you may see on the CCNP and CCIE exams. The mask has only one binary 1 in it, in bit 25 (the first bit in the last byte). The corresponding bit in the address has value "1"; in decimal, the address and mask imply addresses whose fourth byte is between 128 and 255, inclusive. Regardless of subnet number, hosts in the upper half of the assignable addresses in each subnet are matched with this combination.

The command **access-list 112** on Albuquerque completes criteria points 4–6 for this example. The first four statements cover criteria point 4. (Clients Porky and Petunia can connect to all hosts except Red.) This specifically denies access to host Red and then explicitly allows Porky and Petunia to reach any other host. This solution implies that criteria point 4 was taken quite literally! The keyword **established** is matched for any TCP connection's flows other than the first packet; therefore, the **access-list 112** statement with the **established** keyword will match packets with TCP, from servers in Albuquerque, destined for 10.1.2.0 and 10.1.3.0, as stated in criteria point 5 for this example.

Three major problems exist when using extensive detailed criteria for access lists. First, the criteria are open to interpretation. Many people tend to create the lists to match the order that the criteria are written; no attempt at optimization is made. Finally, the lists are easy to create in such a way that the criteria is not actually accomplished, as in extended IP access-list example 2.

Figure 7-6 helps show why criteria point 1 (the web server (Daffy) is available to all users) is not accomplished with this solution.

Figure 7-6 *Extended Access List Example 2—List 112 Denies Packets, When Criteria Ask for Packets To Be Permitted*

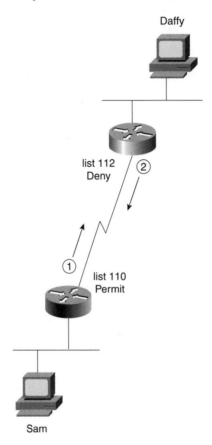

Criteria point 1 is seemingly reached with the **access-list 110** logic in Yosemite and Seville. However, any connection to the web server (Daffy) will be filtered by list 112 as packets leave router Albuquerque. Adding the statement **access-list 112 permit TCP host 10.1.1.2 eq www any** to the top of list 112 would take care of the problem. (Reminder: to add this statement to the top of **access-list 112**, the list would have to be deleted and then typed in again, in the correct order!)

Example 7-9 shows an alternative solution to the extended access-list example 2 solution, as shown in Example 7-6, Example 7-7, and Example 7-8. All access lists have been removed from Seville and Yosemite as compared with that earlier solution.

Example 7-9 *Albuquerque Configuration for Extended Access List Example #2, Second Solution*

```
ip access-group 112
!
interface serial 1
ip access-group 112
!
! next statement meets objective 1
access-list 112 permit TCP host 10.1.1.2 eq www any
! next statement meets objective 2
access-list 112 deny UDP  host 10.1.1.1   0.0.0.128  255.255.255.127
! next statements meet objective 3
access-list 112 deny IP 10.1.3.0 0.0.0.255 10.1.2.0 0.0.0.255
access-list 112 deny IP 10.1.2.0 0.0.0.255 10.1.3.0 0.0.0.255
! next statement meets objective 4
access-list 112 deny IP host 10.1.1.130  host 10.1.3.2
access-list 112 deny IP host 10.1.1.28   host 10.1.3.2
! next statement meets objective 5
access-list 112 deny TCP 10.1.1.0 0.0.0.255 any  established
! next statement meets objective 6
access-list 112 permit IP any any
```

Several differences exist between the first solution in Examples 7-6, 7-7, and 7-8, and the
second solution in Example 7-9. Web clients hitting Daffy will work because the statement with
the **established** keyword comes later. This overcomes the hole in the first solution. Criteria point
4 is completed more concisely, allowing the "permit all" final statement to allow Porky and
Petunia to talk to others hosts besides Red. No access lists are required in the other two routers,
which may seem to be less optimal. Packets are sent by Yosemite and Seville to Albuquerque
hosts, and packets sent back from servers in Albuquerque to the Albuquerque router, before
being filtered. However, the number of these packets will be small because the filter prevents
the client from sending more than the first packet used to connect to the service.

Named IP Access Lists

Named IP access lists allow the same logic to be configured as with numbered access lists, with
these three advantages:

- Names are more intuitive reminders of the function of the list.

- Names allow for more access lists than 99 standard and 100 extended, which is the
  restriction using numbered access lists.

- Named access lists allow individual statements to be deleted. Numbered lists only allow
  for deletion of the entire list. Insertion of the new statement into the list will require
  deletion and re-addition of all statements after the newly added statement.

Example 7-10 shows the configuration mode output when entering the access list used on
Albuquerque in access list 112 of Example 7-9, but as a named access list. One typo is shown,

with changes made to delete and add the statement again. (The statement that is a typo is **deny ip 10.1.2.0 0.0.0.255 10.2.3.0 0.0.0.255**. It is a typo because there is no subnet 10.2.3.0; the intent was to have configured 10.1.3.0 instead.)

Example 7-10 *Named Access List Configuration*

```
conf t
Enter configuration commands, one per line.  End with Ctrl-Z.
Router(config)#ip access-list extended barney
Router(config-ext-nacl)#permit tcp host 10.1.1.2 eq www any
Router(config-ext-nacl)#deny udp host 10.1.1.1 0.0.0.128 255.255.255.127
Router(config-ext-nacl)#deny ip 10.1.2.0 0.0.0.255 10.2.3.0 0.0.0.255
Router(config-ext-nacl)#deny ip 10.1.3.0 0.0.0.255 10.1.2.0 0.0.0.255
Router(config-ext-nacl)#deny ip host 10.1.1.130 host 10.1.3.2
Router(config-ext-nacl)#deny ip host 10.1.1.28 host 10.1.3.2
Router(config-ext-nacl)#deny tcp 10.1.1.0 0.0.0.255 any established
Router(config-ext-nacl)#permit ip any any
Router(config-ext-nacl)#^Z
Router#sh run
Building configuration...

Current configuration:

.
. (unimportant statements omitted)
.
!
ip access-list extended barney
 permit tcp host 10.1.1.2 eq www any
 deny    udp host 10.1.1.1 0.0.0.128 255.255.255.127
 deny    ip 10.1.2.0 0.0.0.255 10.2.3.0 0.0.0.255
 deny    ip 10.1.3.0 0.0.0.255 10.1.2.0 0.0.0.255
 deny    ip host 10.1.1.130 host 10.1.3.2
 deny    ip host 10.1.1.28 host 10.1.3.2
 deny    tcp 10.1.1.0 0.0.0.255 any established
 permit ip any any

Router#conf t
Enter configuration commands, one per line.  End with Ctrl-Z.
Router(config)#ip access-list extended barney
Router(config-ext-nacl)#no deny ip 10.1.2.0 0.0.0.255 10.2.3.0 0.0.0.255
Router(config-ext-nacl)#^Z
Router#show access-list

Extended IP access list barney
    permit tcp host 10.1.1.2 eq www any
    deny    udp host 10.1.1.1 0.0.0.128 255.255.255.127
    deny    ip 10.1.3.0 0.0.0.255 10.1.2.0 0.0.0.255
    deny    ip host 10.1.1.130 host 10.1.3.2
    deny    ip host 10.1.1.28 host 10.1.3.2
    deny    tcp 10.1.1.0 0.0.0.255 any established
    permit ip any any
```

Example 7-10 *Named Access List Configuration (Continued)*

```
Router#conf t
Enter configuration commands, one per line.  End with Ctrl-Z.
Router(config)#ip access-list extended barney
Router(config-ext-nacl)#no permit ip any any
Router(config-ext-nacl)#no deny tcp 10.1.1.0 0.0.0.255 any established
Router(config-ext-nacl)#deny ip 10.1.2.0 0.0.0.255 10.1.3.0 0.0.0.255
Router(config-ext-nacl)#deny tcp 10.1.1.0 0.0.0.255 any established
Router(config-ext-nacl)#permit ip any any
Router(config-ext-nacl)#^Z
Router#sh access-list

Extended IP access list barney
    permit tcp host 10.1.1.2 eq www any
    deny   udp host 10.1.1.1 0.0.0.128 255.255.255.127
    deny   ip 10.1.3.0 0.0.0.255 10.1.2.0 0.0.0.255
    deny   ip host 10.1.1.130 host 10.1.3.2
    deny   ip host 10.1.1.28 host 10.1.3.2
    deny   ip 10.1.2.0 0.0.0.255 10.1.3.0 0.0.0.255
    deny   tcp 10.1.1.0 0.0.0.255 any established
    permit ip any any
```

Notice that the final version of access list Barney is not exactly in the order of the original numbered access list (access list 112 of Example 7-9), but the function is unchanged.

If an access list is not configured but is enabled on an interface with the **ip access-group** command, no packets are filtered due to the **ip access-group** command. After the access list's first command is configured, the IOS will implement the access list's logic. This is true of IP standard access lists, as well as extended and named access lists. Access lists filtering other types of packets follow this same logic.

Access List Summary

Access lists will definitely be covered on the CCNA exam. The most important details to recall are as follows:

- The order of the list is important.

- All matching parameters must be true before a statement is "matched."

- An implied "deny all" is at the end of the list.

The philosophy of choosing the location for access lists is covered in more depth in the CCNP exam than the CCNA exam. However, generally speaking, filtering packets closer to the source of the packet is better because the soon-to-be discarded packets will waste less bandwidth than if the packets were allowed to flow over additional links before being denied.

Be particularly careful of questions relating to existing lists. In particular, if the question suggests that one more **access-list** command should be added—simply adding that command will place the statement at the end of the list, but the statement may need to be earlier in the list to accomplish the goal described in the question!

Filtering IPX Traffic and SAPs

CCNA Objectives Covered in This Section

38	Configure IPX access lists and SAP filters to control basic Novell traffic.
45	Monitor and verify selected access list operations on the router.

IPX access lists can be used to filter packets sent by clients and servers, as well as SAP updates sent by servers and routers. SAP filters are more common because they can be used to prevent clients and servers from trying to send packets.

IPX filtering is a topic that is likely to be on the CCNA exam. Although directly mentioned in objective 38, Training Path 1 does not cover IPX packet or SAP access lists. (For those of you following Training Path 1, take care to study IPX access lists.) For those of you who are studying major topics for the test only and taking a small risk on the minor topics, this topic may be a good one to spend less time on. If any single portion of this section is covered on the exam, it is most likely to be the SAP access list topic.

Table 7-5 and Table 7-6 list the IPX access list configuration and EXEC commands used in Training Paths 1 and 2.

Table 7-5 *Access List Configuration Commands in Training Paths 1 and 2*

Command	Configuration Mode
access-list {*800-899*} {**permit**|**deny**} *source-network* [.*source-node* [*source-node-mask*]] [destination-network [.*destination-node* [destination-node-mask]]]	Global
access-list {*900-999*} {**permit**|**deny**} *protocol* [*source-network*] [[[.*source-node* [*source-node-mask*]] | [.*source-node source-network-mask.source-node-mask*]] [*source-socket*] [*destination-network*] [[[.*destination-node* [*destination-node-mask*] | [.*destination-node destination-network-mask. destination-node-mask*]] [*destination-socket*] **log**	Global
access-list {*1000-1099*} {**permit**|**deny**} *network* [.*node*] [*network-mask node-mask*] [*service-type* [*service-name*]]	Global
ipx access-group {*number* [**in**|**out**] }	Interface

Table 7-5 *Access List Configuration Commands in Training Paths 1 and 2 (Continued)*

Command	Configuration Mode
ipx output-sap-filter *list-number*	Interface
ipx input-sap-filter *list-number*	Interface

Table 7-6 *Access List EXEC Commands in Training Paths 1 and 2*

Command	Function
show ipx interface	Includes reference to the access lists enabled on the interface
show access-list *number*	Shows details of all configured access lists

The **show access-list** command simply lists the logic in each access list. The **show ipx interface** command lists information about which IPX access lists are enabled on each interface.

Access lists for filtering packets are covered next. SAP filters are covered after the packet filters.

Packet filters in the Cisco IOS use the same general logic for any Layer 3 protocol. Figure 7-7 outlines the path an IPX packet can take through a router. The comments following the figure describe the basic logic behind IPX access lists.

Features of the process described in Figure 7-7 are as follows:

- Packets can be filtered as they enter an interface, before the routing decision.

- Packets can be filtered before they exit an interface, after the routing decision.

- "Deny" is the term used in the IOS to imply that the packet will be filtered.

- "Permit" is the term used in the IOS to imply that the packet will not be filtered.

- The filtering logic is configured in the access list.

Figure 7-7   *Locations Where Access List Logic Can Be Applied*

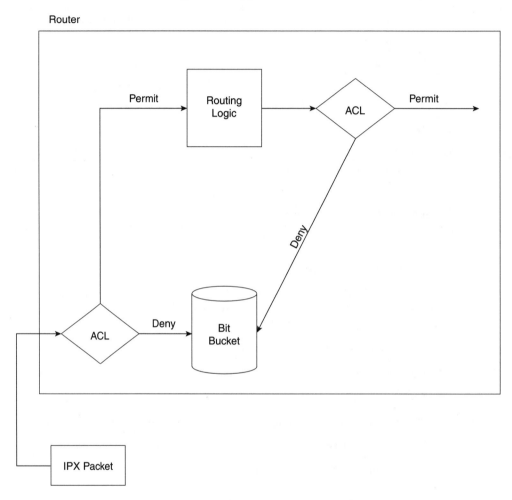

The logic created by an access list, as shown in the diamond-shaped symbols in Figure 7-7, is best summarized by the following sequence of events:

1. The matching parameters of the first **access-list** statement are compared to the packet.

2. If a match is made, the action defined in this **access-list** statement (Permit or Deny) is performed, as shown in Figure 7-7.

3. If a match is not made in Step 2, repeat Steps 1 and 2, using the next sequential **access-list** statement.

4. If no match is made with an entry in the access list, the Deny action is performed.

The logic for access lists is true whether using standard or extended access lists. The only difference is that extended access lists include more comparisons to determine a "match." These differences are outlined in the next few sections on standard IPX access lists, extended IPX access lists, and SAP access lists.

Standard IPX Access Lists

When deciding what this book should really try to accomplish, we decided that the text of the book should cover the topics in two ways. First, the voluminous details should be summarized in tables and lists whenever possible, to allow easy review if the reader already knows the topic pretty well. The explanations were to focus on topics that are less obvious from reading the manual; these are the types of tidbits that you get from the instructor in a well-taught class. When discussing IPX packet filters, I will be focusing on these tidbits! If you are new to IPX access lists, you will probably want to read the IOS documentation or get Cisco Press's *Introduction to Cisco Router Configuration,* edited by Laura Chappell (ISBN 1-57870-076-0).

Standard IPX access lists can check the source and destination network number. They can also check the node part of the source and destination addresses and use a wildcard mask to only examine parts of the node part of the addresses.

Figure 7-8 and Example 7-11 provide an example network and configuration.

Figure 7-8   *IPX Standard Access List Example*

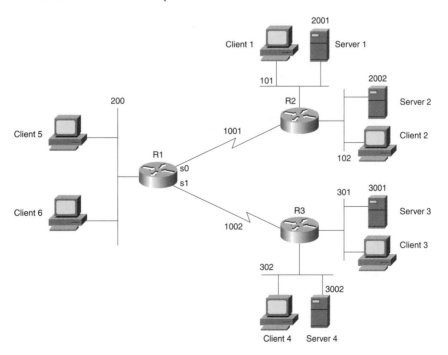

Example 7-11 *R1 Configuration for Standard Access Lists*

```
ipx routing 0200.1111.1111
!
interface serial0
ip address 10.1.1.1 255.255.255.0
ipx network 1001
!
interface serial1
ip address 10.1.2.1 255.255.255.0
ipx network 1002
ipx access-group 820 in
!
interface ethernet 0
ip address 10.1.200.1 255.255.255.0
ipx network 200
ipx access-group 810
!
access-list 810 deny 101
access-list 810 permit -1
!
access-list 820 permit 302
R2#show access-list
IPX access list 810
    deny 101
    permit FFFFFFFF
IPX access list 820
    permit 302
R2#show ipx interface s 1
Serial1 is up, line protocol is up
  IPX address is 1001.0200.1111.1111 [up]
  Delay of this IPX network, in ticks is 6 throughput 0 link delay 0
  IPXWAN processing not enabled on this interface.
  IPX SAP update interval is 1 minute(s)
  IPX type 20 propagation packet forwarding is disabled
  Incoming access list is 820
  Outgoing access list is not set
  IPX helper access list is not set
  SAP GNS processing enabled, delay 0 ms, output filter list is not set
  SAP Input filter list is not set
  SAP Output filter list is not set
  SAP Router filter list is not set
  Input filter list is not set
  Output filter list is not set
  Router filter list is not set
```

Example 7-11 *R1 Configuration for Standard Access Lists (Continued)*

```
Netbios Input host access list is not set
Netbios Input bytes access list is not set

Netbios Output host access list is not set

Netbios Output bytes access list is not set
```

The following criteria will be used in this IPX standard access list example established in Figure 7-8 and Example 7-11:

1. Packets from network 101 are not allowed onto network 200.

2. Packets from network 102 are allowed onto network 200.

3. Packets from network 301 are not allowed onto network 200, 101, or 102.

4. Packets from network 302 are allowed to go anywhere.

The example shows one way to accomplish the goals; other alternatives exist. Access list 810 implements the first two criteria for the example by filtering packets exiting Ethernet 0. Access list 820 implements the last two criteria for the example by filtering packets entering serial1. Of course, a filter allowing only packets from network 302, enabled on R3's serial0 interface, would have accomplished the same thing as access list 820 in this example, but with less overhead. However, a filter of R2 to permit all traffic except packets from network 101 could have been placed on R2's serial0 interface, but that would have stopped clients near R3 from receiving packets from network 101. The first two criteria for the example imply that clients near R3 should be able to communicate with network 101; a clear definition of the criteria is important when using any type of access lists!

None of these filters in Example 7-11 stops SAP traffic. SAP packets are not forwarded by a router, but instead the routers read and assimilate the information in the SAP updates into their own SAP tables.

Access list 810 uses the keyword **-1**, which means any-and-all network numbers. No destination networks were checked with either access list.

The optional node mask was not used and is not useful very often. For example, imagine that a requirement was added so packets from Clients 5 and 6 are not allowed to be sent to Server 4. If Client 5 and 6's IPX addresses were 200.0200.1234.0000 and 200.0200.1234.0001 and no other clients' IPX addresses began with 200.0200.1234, then the following **access-list** command could match packets from these two clients:

```
access-list 830 deny 200.0200.1234.0000 0000.0000.ffff
```

The wildcard mask works like the wildcard mask used in IP access lists; the only difference is that it is configured as a hexadecimal number. The final four "f" digits mean that the final four hex digits in the node part of the address do not need to be checked but that the first eight digits do. However, because almost everyone that uses IPX uses the burned-in MAC address for the node part of the IPX address, the IPX addresses on these clients will almost never have a convenient number to allow packets from both to be matched in the same **access-list** statement. Even if the numbers were convenient for using a wildcard mask, if the LAN adapter was ever replaced, the IPX address would change, giving undesired results from the access list. So unless you are using locally administered MAC addresses on your IPX nodes, the node mask will almost never be useful.

Finally, consider the following changes in the criteria for these access-lists. Would the currently implemented lists in Example 7-11 meet this new set of criteria?

1. Packets from Server 1 are not allowed onto network 200.

2. Packets from Server 2 are allowed onto network 200.

3. Packets from Server 3 are not allowed onto network 200, 101, or 102.

4. Packets from Server 4 are allowed to go anywhere.

The subtle difference is that packets to and from these servers use their internal IPX addresses as of NetWare 3.11 and beyond. In this case, the second and third criteria are met. **access-list 810** permits as the default, which allows packets from Server 2 onto R1's E0. **access-list 820** denies as the default, which disallows packets from Server 3 into R1's S1 interface. None of the access lists specifically match packets from the internal network numbers of any of these four servers. Example 7-12 presents the new versions of access list 810 and access list 820 to meet the new requirements.

Example 7-12 *R1 Configuration for Standard Access Lists, Modified*

```
ipx routing 0200.1111.1111
!
interface serial0
ip address 10.1.1.1 255.255.255.0
ipx network 1001
!
interface serial1
ip address 10.1.2.1 255.255.255.0
ipx network 1002
ipx access-group 820 in
!
interface ethernet 0
ip address 10.1.200.1 255.255.255.0
ipx network 200
ipx access-group 810
!
access-list 810 deny 2001
access-list 810 permit -1
!
access-list 820 permit 3002
```

Extended IPX Access Lists

Extended access lists for IPX can check the following additional items when comparing a packet to an **access-list** command:

- The source and destination socket
- The protocol type: NCP, RIP, SAP, SPX, NetBIOS, or "any"
- A wildcard mask to match multiple networks with one statement

The protocol type is not discussed in Training Path 1 and Training Path 2. Figure 7-9 shows examples packets that would be matched by the various protocol types.

Figure 7-9   *Extended Access List Protocol Types*

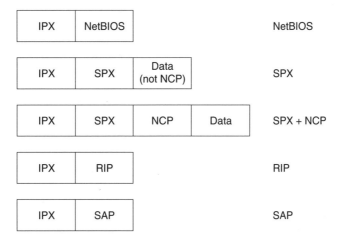

The protocol names can be misleading. Access lists for filtering SAP information use list numbers between 1000 and 1099; SAP filtering does not use extended IPX access lists with a SAP protocol type. A SAP protocol type on an extended access list would deny or permit entire SAP packets and would not be able to examine the service information inside the packet. Likewise, extended IPX access lists with protocol type RIP can allow matching of RIP packets but not the routing information in the RIP update. The most practical use of the protocol type is for NetBIOS. If NetBIOS is not an issue, most sites use the **any** keyword for the protocol type.

The socket is similar to a TCP or UDP port number, except many services can share the same socket. For example, socket 451 (hex) is used by NCP on a NetWare server. Clients dynamically assign sockets in the range of 4000–7FFF, and Novell can assign sockets to applications in the range of 8000–FFFF. Unlike IP, where each server uses a different port, the socket number does not necessarily refer to different services in the same server. So instances where the socket number is useful in an IPX access list will be somewhat rare.

NOTE   Do not confuse SAP type with socket. A server can support many unique SAPs, but multiple services can use the same socket.

The most useful extended access list feature that is not supported by standard access lists is the network wildcard mask. Figure 7-10 and Example 7-13 provide a sample where this mask is useful. The access list is configured in R2. The criteria for this packet filter is as follows:

- Clients in networks 100 and 101 are allowed access to Server 3 and Server 4.

- Clients in network 300 are not allowed to access Server 1 and Server 2.

Figure 7-10 *PX Extended Access List Example*

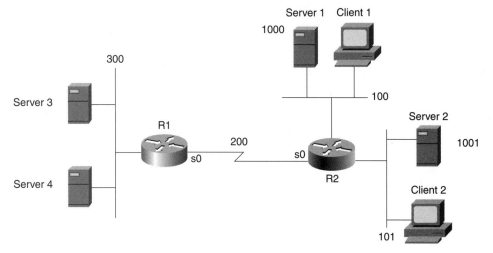

Access list 910 actually checks for packets from networks 1000-100F. The network number is eight hex digits long—the leading 0s are not shown. For the network wildcard mask, all digits are shown in the book, but the leading zeroes are omitted in an actual router configuration. The mask 0000000F means that the first seven hex digits must match 0000100, which are the first seven hex digits of the network number. The last hex digit can be any value.

To exactly match the two networks 1000 and 1001, the mask 00000001 could be used. This mask implies that all bits are checked except the one low order bit. (Feel free to convert hex 1000 and 1001 to binary, using Appendix C, and see that only the last bit is different in the two numbers.)

Example 7-13 *R2 Configuration for Extended Access Lists*

```
hostname R2
!
ipx routing 0200.2222.2222
!
interface serial0
ip address 10.1.1.2 255.255.255.0
ipx network 200
ipx access-group 910
!
interface ethernet 0
ip address 10.1.100.2 255.255.255.0
ipx network 100
!
interface ethernet 1
ip address 10.1.101.2 255.255.255.0
ipx network 101
!
access-list 910 deny any 1000 0000000F
access-list 910 permit any -1
```

SAP Access Lists

The key to understanding SAP filters is an understanding of where SAP packets flow and where they do not. The following sequence outlines what happens:

1. A router or server decides it is time to send a SAP broadcast on its attached network based on the expiration of its SAP timer.

2. That router or server creates enough SAP packets to advertise all its SAP information.

3. That router or server sends the SAP packets out into the attached network.

4. Other routers and servers are attached to the same medium; these routers and servers receive all the SAP packets.

5. The receiving routers and servers examine the information inside the SAP packets and update their SAP tables as necessary.

6. The receiving routers and servers discard the SAP packets.

7. Every server and router is using a SAP timer, which is not synchronized with the other servers and routers. When the timer expires, each server and router performs Steps 1–3, and their neighboring servers and routers perform Steps 4–6.

In other words, the SAP packets are never forwarded by a router or server. This process is effectively the same process used by distance vector routing protocols; that is why the IOS uses *distribute lists* to filter routing information, rather than packet filters.

SAP filtering provides two functions: filtering the services listed in outgoing SAP updates, and filtering services listed in received SAP updates. The first function reduces the information sent to the router's neighboring IPX servers and routers. The second function limits what a router adds to its SAP table. And unlike packet filters, SAP filters examine the data inside the packet. Figure 7-11 outlines the process.

Figure 7-11 *SAP Filter Flow Diagram*

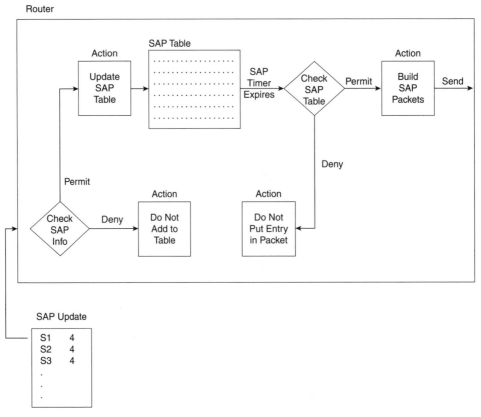

Two main reasons exist for using SAP filters. First, SAP updates can consume a large amount of bandwidth, particularly in NBMA networks. If clients in one division never need services from servers in another division, there is no need to waste bandwidth advertising the services. The second reason for SAP filters is that they can accomplish the same task as most IPX packet filters, but with less overhead. This second reason will be outlined in the SAP filtering sample in Example 7-14. SAP filters will be used to accomplish the same set of criteria that was mentioned with Example 7-13 and Figure 7-10. As a reminder, the criteria for that filter is as follows:

- Clients in networks 100 and 101 are allowed access to Server 3 and Server 4.

- Clients in network 300 are not allowed to access Server 1 and Server 2.

Example 7-14 *R1 Configuration for SAP Access Lists*

```
Hostname   R1
!

ipx routing 0200.1111.111
!
interface serial0
ip address 10.1.1.1 255.255.255.0
ipx network 200
ipx input-sap-filter 1005
!
interface ethernet 0
ip address 10.1.30.1 255.255.255.0
ipx network 300
!
access-list 1005 deny 1000 0000000F
access-list 1005 permit -1
```

The effect of the SAP filter on R1 is somewhat obvious. How the filter stops clients in network 300 from reaching Server 1 and Server 2 is not as obvious. The filter examines inbound SAP updates on serial0 from R2. Services in networks 1000–100F are filtered. All other services are not filtered; the **-1** keyword signifies "all networks." (Extended IPX access lists can use the keyword **any**. SAP filters do not currently use that keyword.)

The key to understanding what stops clients from reaching Server 1 and Server 2 is to recall the GNS process and its purpose. (Figure 6-12 in Chapter 6 outlined the process.) Either Server 3 or Server 4 will be used as the GNS server for clients in network 300. (The router will not reply to GNS requests if a real server exists on the LAN at some later IOS releases; before that, the router would delay replying so that the any local servers would send the first reply.) Neither Server 3 or Server 4 will know of Server 1 or Server 2 because they are relying on R1 to advertise SAP information, and R1 has filtered SAP in networks 1000–100F. Therefore, clients will not be able to log in to Server 1 and Server 2, because **clients can only connect to servers they find in the SAP table of the clients' GNS server**.

SAP filtering to disallow certain clients from using certain servers is more efficient than IPX packet filters. SAPs are sent once every 60 seconds, whereas packet filters cause the IOS to examine every IPX packet—a much more frequent task.

Q&A

As mentioned in Chapter 1, the questions and scenarios are more difficult than what you should experience on the actual exam. The questions do not attempt to cover more breadth or depth than the exam; however, the questions are designed to make sure you know the answer. Rather than allowing you to derive the answer from clues hidden inside the question itself, your understanding and recall of the subject will be challenged. Questions from the "Do I Know This Already?" quiz from the beginning of the chapter are repeated here to ensure that you have mastered the chapter's topic areas. Hopefully, these questions will help limit the number of exam questions on which you narrow your choices to two options, and then guess!

1. Configure an IP access list that would stop packets from subnet 134.141.7.0, 255.255.255.0, from exiting serial 0 on some router. Allow all other packets.

2. Configure an IP access list that allows only packets from subnet 193.7.6.0, 255.255.255.0, going to hosts in network 128.1.0.0, using a web server in 128.1.0.0, to enter serial 0 on some router.

3. How would a user who does not have the enable password find out what access lists have been configured and where they are enabled?

4. Configure and enable an IP access list that would stop packets from subnet 10.3.4.0/24 from getting out serial interface S0 and stop packets from 134.141.5.4 from entering S0. Permit all other traffic.

5. Configure and enable an IP access list that would allow packets from subnet 10.3.4.0/24, to any web server, to get out serial interface S0. Also, allow packets from 134.141.5.4 going to all TCP-based servers to enter serial 0. Deny all other traffic.

6. Create an IPX packet filter to prevent packets from entering Serial0, except for packets from address 500.0000.0000.0001 destined for any node in Network 4.

7. At most, three SAP filters can be enabled on a particular interface at any one time. (T/F)

8. What services use IPX socket 4? Socket 7?

9. Create a configuration to add a SAP access list to filter all print services from being advertised out a router's serial 0 and serial 1 interfaces.

10. Name all the items that a standard SAP access list can examine in order to make a match.

11. Can standard IP access lists be used to check the source IP address when enabled with the **ip access-group 1 in** command and check the destination IP addresses when using the **ip access-group 1 out** command?

12. Can a single IP extended **access-list** command be used to check a particular port number on all IP packets?

13. If all IP or IPX **access-list** statements in a particular list define the deny action, then the default action is to permit all other packets. (T/F)

14. In an IPX access list with five statements, a **no** version of the third statement is issued in configuration mode. Immediately following, another access list configuration command is added for the same access list. How many statements are in the list now, and in what position is the newly added statement?

15. How many IP access lists of either type can be active on an interface at the same time?

16. Assume all parts of the network are up and working in the network in Figure 7-12. IGRP is the IP routing protocol in use. Answer the questions following Example 7-15, which contains an additional configuration in the Mayberry router.

Figure 7-12 *Network Diagram for Question 16*

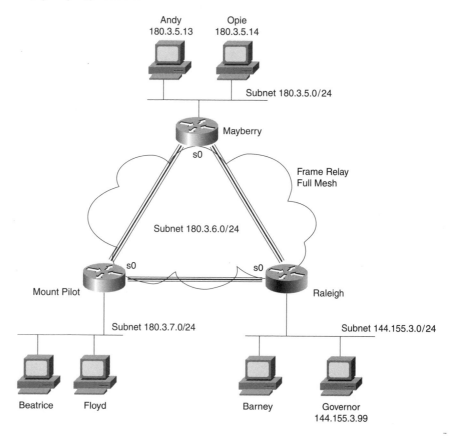

Example 7-15 *Access List at Mayberry*

```
access-list 44 permit 180.3.5.13 0.0.0.0
!
interface serial 0
ip access-group 44
```

16a. Describe the types of packets that this filter would discard, and at what point they would be discarded.

16b. Does this access list stop packets from getting to web server Governor? Why or why not?

16c. Create access lists and enable them such that access to web server Governor is allowed, but no other access to hosts in Raleigh is allowed.

Scenarios

Scenario 7-1: IP Filtering Sample 1

Scenarios 7-1–7-3 will all use Figure 7-13, each with a different set of requirements for filtering. In each case, configure a correct access list for the routers and enable the access list. Place the access list in the router that filters the unneeded packets as quickly as possible, that is, before the packets have been sent far away from the originator.

Figure 7-13 *Network Diagram for IP Filtering Scenarios 7-1, 7-2, and 7-3*

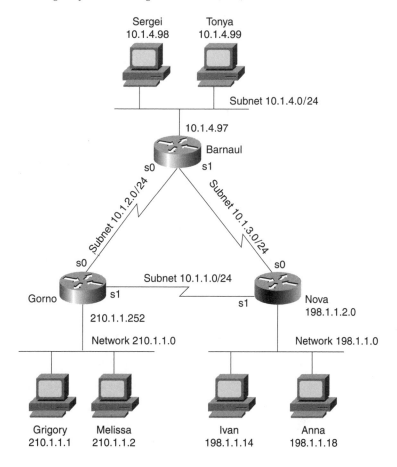

The filtering criteria for Scenario 7-1 is as follows:

- Users in Gorno cannot connect to hosts in Nova, except...

- Grigory can use the hosts on Nova's Ethernet

- All other communications are allowed.

Scenario 7-2: IP Filtering Sample 2

Again using the network diagram in Figure 7-13, create and enable access lists for a totally different set of requirements. Place the access list in the routers to filter the unneeded packets as quickly as possible, that is, before the packets have been sent far away from the originator.

The filtering criteria for Scenario 7-2 is as follows:

- Hosts on the Barnaul Ethernet cannot communicate with hosts in the Gorno Ethernet.

- Grigory and Melissa cannot communicate with hosts on the Nova Ethernet.

- Other communications between Nova Ethernet and Gorno Ethernet are allowed.

- Sergei (in Barnaul) can only communicate with other hosts in Barnaul.

- Other hosts in Barnaul can communicate with hosts in Nova.

- Any communication paths not specified are allowed.

Scenario 7-3: IP Filtering Sample 3

Again using the network diagram in Figure 7-13, create and enable access lists for a totally different set of requirements. Place the access list in the router that filters the unneeded packets as quickly as possible, that is, before the packets have been sent far away from the originator.

The filtering criteria for Scenario 7-3 is as follows:

- Grigory and Melissa can access the web server in Nova.

- Grigory and Melissa cannot access any other servers in Nova using TCP.

- Sergei (Barnaul) can only use the web server, but no other servers, in Nova.

- Hosts in Gorno can communicate with hosts in Nova, unless otherwise stated.

- Web clients in Barnaul are not allowed to connect to the web server in Nova, unless specifically mentioned elsewhere in these criteria.

- Any unspecified communication should be disallowed.

Scenario 7-4: IPX Filtering

IPX packet and SAP filtering concepts and configuration are reviewed in this scenario. Sample configurations are supplied first. Your job will be to interpret the current access lists and then create new packet access lists and SAP access lists to meet some additional criteria. The details are listed after Figure 7-14 and Example 7-16, Example 7-17, Example 7-18, and Example 7-19.

Figure 7-14 *Network Diagram for Scenario 7-4*

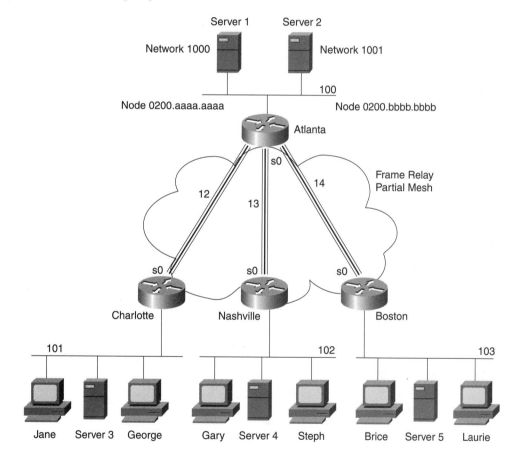

Example 7-16 *Atlanta Configuration*

```
ipx routing 0200.1111.1111
!
interface serial0
encapsulation frame-relay
!
interface serial 0.1 point-to-point
ip address 168.10.12.1  255.255.255.0
ipx network 12
ipx access-group 801 in
frame-relay interface-dlci 52
!
interface serial 0.2 point-to-point
ip address 168.10.13.1 255.255.255.0
ipx network 13
ipx access-group 903 in
frame-relay interface-dlci 53
!
interface serial 0.3 point-to-point
ip address 168.10.14.1 255.255.255.0
ipx network 14
ipx access-group 903 in
frame-relay interface-dlci 54
!
interface ethernet 0
ip address 168.10.100.1 255.255.255.0
ipx network 100
!
access-list 903 deny any 102.0000.0000.0000 1.ffff.ffff.ffff all 100
access-list 903 permit any any
access-list 801 deny 101 100.0200.bbbb.bbbb
access-list 801 permit -1
```

Example 7-17 *Charlotte Configuration*

```
ipx routing 0200.2222.2222
!
interface serial0
encapsulation frame-relay
!
interface serial 0.1 point-to-point
ip address 168.10.12.2 255.255.255.0
ipx network 12
frame-relay interface-dlci 51
!
interface ethernet 0
ip address 168.10.101.2 255.255.255.0
ipx network 101
```

Example 7-18 *Nashville Configuration*

```
ipx routing 0200.3333.3333
!
interface serial0
encapsulation frame-relay
!
interface serial 0.2 point-to-point
ip address 168.10.13.3 255.255.255.0
ipx network 13
frame-relay interface-dlci 51
!
interface ethernet 0
ip address 168.10.102.3 255.255.255.0
ipx network 102
```

Example 7-19 *Boston Configuration*

```
ipx routing 0200.4444.4444
!
interface serial0
encapsulation frame-relay
!
interface serial 0.3 point-to-point
ip address 168.10.14.4 255.255.255.0
ipx network 14
frame-relay interface-dlci 51
!
interface ethernet 0
ip address 168.10.103.4 255.255.255.0
ipx network 103
```

Given the network in Figure 7-14 and the configurations in Example 7-16, Example 7-17, Example 7-18, and Example 7-19, answer the questions and perform the tasks that follow.

1. Characterize the traffic that is discarded due to the access lists used on Atlanta. Can clients in the remote sites access the servers in Atlanta?

2. Create IPX packet filters to meet the following criteria:

   • Clients in Nashville and Boston are not allowed access to Server 1.

   • Clients in Charlotte are not allowed access to Server 2.

   • Use standard access lists if possible.

   • Place the access lists close to the source of the packets.

   • Assume all access lists from Task 1 have been disabled and deleted.

3. Create SAP filters that perform the same function as described in Task 2.

Scenario Answers

Answers to Scenario 7-1: IP Filtering Sample 1

The solution to fulfilling the criteria stipulated for this access list is straightforward. Simply matching Grigory to permit his traffic and denying packets from 210.1.1.0 is all that is needed for the first two criteria. A "permit all" needs to be explicitly configured at the end of the list. Example 7-20 provides the solution for this scenario. The access-list will be enabled on Noya, which will allow hosts in Gorno to reach Barnaul.

Example 7-20 *Solution to Scenario 7-1*

```
access-list 43 permit host 210.1.1.1
access-list 43 deny 210.1.1.0 0.0.0.255
access-list 43 permit any
!
interface serial 0
ip access-group 43 in
!
interface serial 1
ip access-group 43 in
```

Answers to Scenario 7-2: IP Filtering Sample 2

There are many solutions to fulfilling the criteria stipulated for this scenario. The solutions provided in Examples 7-21 and 7-22 attempt to filter packets as close to the source of the packet as possible. It is impossible to determine if your correct solution is better than mine, or vice versa, without more information about traffic loads and business needs in the network. Comments shown inside the configurations in Example 7-21 and Example 7-22 provide most of the detailed commentary.

Example 7-21 *Scenario 7-2 Answer—Barnaul Access List*

```
! next statement meets criteria a
access-list 101 deny ip 10.1.4.0 0.0.0.255 210.1.1.0 0.0.0.255
! next statement meets criteria D
access-list 101 deny ip host 10.1.4.98 any
! Criteria e and f met in the default
access-list 101 permit ip any any
interface serial 0
ip access-group 101
!
interface serial 1
ip access-group 101
```

Example 7-22 *Scenario 7-2 Answer—Gorno Access List*

```
! Next statements meet criteria B
access-list 101 deny ip host 210.1.1.1 198.1.1.0 0.0.0.255
access-list 101 deny ip host 210.1.1.2 198.1.1.0 0.0.0.255
! Next statement meets criteria c
access-list 101 permit ip 210.1.1.0 0.0.0.255 198.1.1.0 0.0.0.255
!Default meets criteria f
access-list 101 permit ip any any
!
interface serial 0
ip access-group 101
!
interface serial 1
ip access-group 101
```

The default action can be used to shorten the list. The only danger is that the explicitly defined statements are used first; if 90 percent of the packets match the default, a better choice would be to match those packets explicitly with an **access-list** statement early in the access list.

Answers to Scenario 7-3: IP Filtering Sample 3

There are many solutions to fulfilling the criteria stipulated for this scenario. The solutions provided in Examples 7-23 and 7-24 attempt to filter packets as close to the source of the packet as possible. It is impossible to determine if your correct solution is better than mine, or vice versa, without more information about traffic loads and business needs in the network. Comments shown inside the configurations in Example 7-23 and Example 7-24 provide most of the detailed commentary.

Example 7-23 *Scenario 7-3 Answer—Barnaul Access List*

```
! next statements meet criteria c
access-list 101 permit ip host 10.1.14.98 198.1.1.0 0.0.0.255 eq www
access-list 101 deny ip host 10.1.14.98 198.1.1.0 0.0.0.255 lt 1023
! next statement meets criteria e
access-list 101 deny ip host 10.1.4.0 0.0.0.255 198.1.1.0 0.0.0.255 eq www
! Criteria f is met in the default
!
interface serial 0
ip access-group 101
!
interface serial 1
ip access-group 101
```

Example 7-24 *Scenario 7-3 Answer—Gorno Access List*

```
! Next statements meet criteria a
access-list 101 permit tcp host 210.1.1.1 198.1.1.0 0.0.0.255 eq www
access-list 101 permit tcp host 210.1.1.2 198.1.1.0 0.0.0.255 eq www
! Next statements meet criteria b
access-list 101 deny tcp host 210.1.1.1 198.1.1.0 0.0.0.255 lt 1023
access-list 101 deny tcp host 210.1.1.2 198.1.1.0 0.0.0.255 lt 1023
! Next statement meets criteria d
access-list 101 permit ip 210.1.1.0 0.0.0.255 198.1.1.0 0.0.0.255
!Default meets criteria f
!
interface serial 0
ip access-group 101
!
interface serial 1
ip access-group 101
```

The default action can be used to shorten the list. The only danger is that the explicitly defined statements are used first; if 90 percent of the packets match the default, a better choice would be to match those packets explicitly with an **access-list** statement early in the access list.

Answers to Scenario 7-4: IPX Filtering

Refer to the network illustrated in Figure 7-14 and Example 7-16, Example 7-17, Example 7-18, and Example 7-19 to establish the Scenario 7-4 design details and the context of the answers to the three tasks for this scenario.

Answers to Task 1 for Scenario 7-4

Task 1 for Scenario 7-4 asks you to characterize the traffic that is discarded due to the access lists used on Atlanta. Furthermore, you need to determine whether clients in the remote sites can access the servers in Atlanta. The answer is not obvious in this case. The extended access list is particularly confusing, given all the options. The parameters coded in the first entry in list 903 are as follows:

- **deny**—Throw away packets that match.

- **any**—Any protocol type.

- **102.0000.0000.0000**—Source IPX address. The node part of the address will be masked, so all 0s are coded in the node part of the address. The node part of the address must be configured; otherwise, the syntax does not allow the right to use the network wildcard mask.

- **1.ffff.ffff.ffff**—Source network and node wildcard mask. With leading zeroes written in, the mask would be 00000001.ffff.ffff.ffff. This mask will match networks 102 and 103, which are identical except for the final bit in the network part of the address. The mask means, "all bits in the network must match network 102, except the last bit in the network number." (All Fs for the node mean that any node number will match.)

- **all**—All sockets.

- **100**—Destination network.

So the first entry in list 903 matches packets from Network 102 and 103, destined for Network 100, any protocol, any socket. These packets are denied. The second entry in 903 permits all protocols, all source networks, and by implication, all destination networks; in other words, this statement changes the default to be "permit all else."

By enabling list 903 for inbound packets on Atlanta's serial 0.2 and serial 0.3 interfaces, clients in Nashville and Boston cannot reach Network 100.

Access list 801 stops all packets from Network 101 from reaching Server 2's Ethernet IPX address. It also has a "permit everything else" statement at the end of the list, but because standard IPX access lists do not use the **any** keyword, **-1** is used to signify **any**.

Neither list stops access to Server 1 or Server 2 because the destination of packets to these servers will be the internal IPX addresses (1000.0000.0000.0001and 1001.0000.0000.0001).

Answers to Task 2 for Scenario 7-4

Task 2 for Scenario 7-4 asks you to create IPX packet filters to meet the following criteria:

- Clients in Nashville and Boston are not allowed access to Server 1.

- Clients in Charlotte are not allowed access to Server 2.

- Use standard access lists if possible.

- Place the access lists close to the source of the packets.

- Assume all access lists from Task 1 have been disabled and deleted.

This can be accomplished by configuring standard IPX access lists. Because the goal is to filter packets close to the source, and because the client initiates the process of connecting to a server, the filters were all placed at the remote routers and not in Atlanta. Each filter matches packets sourced in their local IPX networks and destined for Network 1000 (if filtering packets destined for Server 1), or destined for Network 1001 (if filtering packets destined for Server 2). Example 7-25, Example 7-26, and Example 7-27 show the configurations necessary to create IPX packet filters to satisfy the criteria.

Example 7-25 *Charlotte with Access List Configured, Scenario 7-4, Task 2*

```
access-list 800 deny 101 1001
access-list 800 permit -1
!
interface serial 0.1 point-to-point
ipx access-group 800
```

Example 7-26 *Nashville with Access List Configured, Scenario 7-4, Task 2*

```
access-list 800 deny 102 1000
access-list 800 permit -1
!
interface serial 0.2 point-to-point
ipx access-group 800
```

Example 7-27 *Boston with Access List Configured, Scenario 7-4, Task 2*

```
access-list 800 deny 103 1000
access-list 800 permit -1
!
interface serial 0.3 point-to-point
ipx access-group 800
```

Answers to Task 3 for Scenario 7-4

Task 3 for Scenario 7-4 asks you to create SAP filters that perform the same function as described in Task 2. Task 3 suggests a very simple solution, but the simple solution only works because there are local servers in Charlotte, Nashville, and Boston. First, the solution; then, some comments.

Because the local server in each case will be the GNS server for the remote clients, respectively, all that is needed is to stop Server 1 and Server 2 SAP information from being advertised into the remote sites. In an effort to reduce overhead, the SAP filters will be placed in Atlanta, because SAP information originates in the servers. Example 7-28 provides the solution.

Example 7-28 *Atlanta with SAP Filter Configured, Scenario 7-4, Task 3*

```
access-list 1050 deny 1000
access-list 1050 permit -1
!
access-list 1051 deny 1001
access-list 1051 permit -1
!
interface serial 0.1 point-to-point
ipx output-sap-filter 1051
!
interface serial 0.2 point-to-point
ipx output-sap-filter 1050
!
interface serial 0.3 point-to-point
ipx output-sap-filter 1050
```

SAPs about Server 1 (Network 1000) are filtered from being sent out serial 0.2 and serial 0.3 to Nashville and Boston, respectively. Likewise, SAPs about Server 2 (Network 1001) are filtered from being sent out serial 0.1. Server 3 will not know about Server 2, so it cannot tell Charlotte clients about Server 2. Likewise, Server 4 and Server 5 will not know about Server 1, so they cannot tell Nashville clients and Boston clients about Server 1.

SAP filters are also great for reducing traffic, of course. However, when using them for stopping particular clients and servers from communicating, there are some caveats. If no remote servers were in place, the remote clients would have used Server 1 or Server 2 as their GNS server. Server 1 and Server 2 have full knowledge of each other's SAP information because they are on the same Ethernet. Therefore, clients would be able to connect to the servers, in spite of our efforts.

The following table outlines the CCNA exam objectives that are reviewed in this chapter. The numbers shown correspond to the master list of objectives found in Chapter 1, "What Is CCNA?".

Objective	Description
8	Differentiate between the following WAN services: Frame Relay, ISDN/LAPD, HDLC, & PPP.
9	Recognize key Frame Relay terms and features.
10	List commands to configure Frame Relay LMIs, maps, and subinterfaces.
11	List commands to monitor Frame Relay operation in the router.
12	Identify PPP operations to encapsulate WAN data on Cisco routers.
13	State a relevant use and context for ISDN networking.
14	Identify ISDN protocols, function groups, reference points, and channels.
15	Describe Cisco's implementation of ISDN BRI.

WAN Protocols: Understanding Point-to-Point, Frame Relay, and ISDN

This chapter covers five main topic areas related to WAN protocols:

- Point-to-Point leased lines

- Frame Relay protocols

- Frame Relay configuration

- ISDN protocols and design

- ISDN configuration

The amount of coverage for PPP, Frame Relay, and ISDN is in proportion to their importance on the CCNA exam, with Frame Relay certainly being the most important of the three. All three topics are what could be characterized as *non-dial WAN connections* covered on the CCNA exam. WAN protocols on point-to-point links are covered first. Then Frame Relay is covered, with a "From the Top" section covering the nuances of mapping. The Foundation Topics section concludes with coverage of ISDN protocols and ISDN configuration.

How to Best Use This Chapter

By taking the following steps, you can make better use of your study time:

- Keep your notes and answers for all your work with this book in one place for easy reference.

- Take the "Do I Know This Already?" quiz and write down your answers. Studies show retention is significantly increased through writing facts and concepts down, even if you never look at the information again!

- Figure 8-1 helps guide you to the next step in preparation for this topic area on the CCNA exam.

Figure 8-1 *How To Use This Chapter*

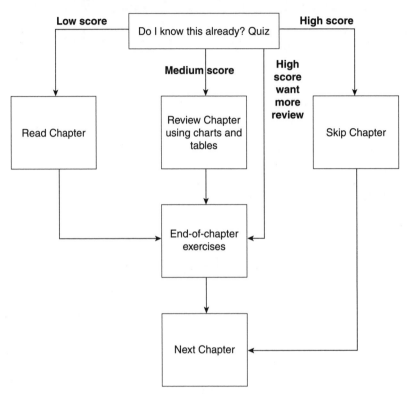

"Do I Know This Already?" Quiz

1. Name two connection-oriented Layer 2 protocols used on WANs.

_____

_____

_____

2. Name two WAN data-link protocols for which the standards define a protocol type field, which is used to define the type of header that follows after the WAN data-link header.

_____

_____

_____

3. Name two WAN data-link protocols that define a method of announcing the Layer 3 addresses of the interface to other devices attached to the WAN.

_____

_____

_____

4. The **encapsulation x25** command is seen in a configuration file immediately after the command **interface serial 0**. What command(s) would be necessary to change back to the default encapsulation on this serial link?

_____

_____

_____

5. What do the letters in ISDN represent? BRI? PRI?

_____

_____

_____

6. "Frame Relay uses source and destination DLCIs in the Frame Relay header, with length 10, 11, or 12 bits." Which parts of this statement do you agree with? Which parts do you disagree with? Why?

_____

_____

_____

7. Explain the purpose of Inverse ARP. Explain how Inverse ARP uses Frame Relay broadcasts.

_____

_____

_____

8. What does NBMA stand for? Does it apply to PPP links? Frame Relay networks?

_____

_____

_____

9. Define the term function group as used in CCNA exam objective 14. List two examples of function groups.

_____

_____

_____

10. What layer of OSI is most closely related to the functions of Frame Relay? Why?

_____

_____

_____

11. Define the attributes of a partial-mesh and full-mesh Frame Relay network.

_____

_____

_____

12. Define the terms PAP and CHAP. Which one(s) encrypt passwords before transmission?

_____

_____

_____

You can find the answers to the "Do I Know This Already?" quiz in Appendix B on page 587. Review the answers, grade your quiz, and choose an appropriate next step in this chapter based on the suggestions in the "How to Best Use This Chapter" topic earlier in this chapter. Your choices for the next step are as follows:

- **5 or fewer correct**—Read this chapter.

- **6, 7, or 8 correct**—Review this chapter, looking at the charts and diagrams that summarize most of the concepts and facts in this chapter.

- **9 or more correct**—If you want more review on these topics, skip to the exercises at the end of this chapter. If you do not want more review on these topics, skip this chapter.

Foundation Topics

Point-to-Point Leased Lines

CCNA Objectives Covered in This Section

8	Differentiate between the following WAN services: Frame Relay, ISDN/LAPD, HDLC, & PPP.
12	Identify PPP operations to encapsulate WAN data on Cisco routers.

WAN protocols used on point-to-point serial links provide the basic function of delivery of data across that one link. Most of the WAN protocols listed in objective 8 are discussed in this section. Link Access Procedure on the D channel (LAPD), High-Level Data Link Control (HDLC), and Point-to-Point Protocol (PPP) are mentioned in this section, and they all have the following functions in common:

- LAPB, HDLC, and PPP provide for delivery of data across a single point-to-point serial link.

- LAPB, HDLC, and PPP deliver data on synchronous serial links. (PPP supports asynchronous as well.)

Framing is one core feature of any synchronous serial data link protocol. Each of these protocols define framing so that receiving stations know where the beginning of the frame is, what address is in the header, and the point at which the packet begins. By doing so, the router receiving data can distinguish between idle frames and data frames and know how to process the incoming data.

Synchronous links, rather than asynchronous links, are typically used between routers. Synchronous simply means that there is an imposed time ordering at the sending and receiving ends of the link. What this really means is that the sides agree to a certain speed, but because it is very expensive to build devices that can truly operate at exactly the same speed, the devices adjust their rates to match a clock source. It's almost like in spy novels, where the spies synchronize their watches; in this case, the watches or clocks are synchronized automatically, multiple times per minute. Unlike asynchronous links, where no bits are sent during idle times, synchronous data links define idle frames. These frames do nothing more than provide plenty of signal transitions so that clocks can be adjusted on the receiving end, consequently maintaining synchronization.

Before describing the features of these data-link protocols, a brief reference to some popularly used WAN terminology is useful. These terms are not mentioned specifically as part of the CCNA objectives, but they are certainly building blocks toward a full understanding of WAN protocols. Table 8-1 lists the terms.

Table 8-1 *WAN Terminology*

Term	Definition
Synchronous	The imposition of time ordering on a bit stream. More practically speaking, a device will try to use the same speed as another on the other end of a serial link. However, by examining transitions between voltage states on the link, the device can notice slight variations in the speed on each end, so it can adjust its speed.
Asynchronous	The lack of an imposed time ordering on a bit stream. More practically speaking, both sides agree to the same speed, but there is no check or adjustment of the rates if they are slightly different. However, because only 1 byte per transfer is sent, slight differences in clock speed are not an issue. A "start bit" is used to signal the beginning of a byte.
Clock Source	The device that the other devices on the link adjust their speed to when using synchronous links.
DSU/CSU	Data Services Unit and Channel Services Unit. Used on digital links as an interface to the telephone company in the U.S. Routers typically would use a short cable from a serial link to a DSU/CSU, which is attached to the line from the Telco, with a similar configuration at the other router on the other end of the link. The routers will use their attached DSU/CSU as the clock source.
Telco	Telephone company.
4-wire circuit	A line from the Telco with 4 wires, comprised of 2 twisted pair. Each pair is used to send on one direction, so a 4-wire circuit allows full-duplex communication.
2-wire circuit	A line from the Telco with 2 wires, comprised of 1 twisted pair. The pair is used to send on one direction, so a 2-wire circuit allows only half-duplex communication.
T/1	A line from the Telco that allows transmission of data at 1.544 Mbps. Can be used with a T/1Multiplexor.
T/1 mux	A multiplexor that separates the T/1 into 24 different 64 kbps channels. In the USA, one of every eight bits in each channel is used by the Telco, so that the channels are effectively 56 kbps channels.
E/1	Like a T/1, but in Europe, using a rate of 2.048 Mbps, and 32 64 kbps channels.

Three key attributes help to differentiate between these synchronous serial data-link protocols:

- Determination of whether the protocol supports synchronous communications, asynchronous communications, or both.

- Determination of whether the protocol provides error recovery. (The LAPB, HDLC, and PPP protocols all provide error detection.)

- Determination of whether there is an architected protocol type field; in other words, the protocol specifications define a field in the header that identifies the type of packet contained in the data portion of the frame.

First, a few words about the criteria used to compare these WAN protocols are in order. Synchronous protocols allow more throughput over a serial link than do asynchronous protocols. However, asynchronous protocols require less expensive hardware because there is no need to watch transitions and adjust the clock rate. For links between routers, synchronous links are typically desired and used. All the protocols covered in this section support synchronous links.

Another comparison criteria is error recovery. Error recovery is a topic that is covered in detail in Chapter 3, "Understanding the OSI Reference Model." A brief review is in order here. All the data-link protocols described here use a field in the trailer, usually called the Frame Check Sequence (FCS), that is used to verify whether bit errors occurred during transmission of the frame. If so, the frame is discarded. Error recovery is the process that causes retransmission of the lost frame(s); error recovery may be performed by the data-link protocol, or it may be performed by a higher layer protocol. Regardless, all WAN data-link protocols perform error detection, noticing the error and discarding the frame.

Finally, the definition and use of an architected protocol type field is the final criteria for comparison. As described in more detail in Chapter 3, each data-link protocol that supports multiple network layer protocol needs a method of defining the type of packet encapsulated inside the WAN data-link frame. If such a field is part of the protocol specification, it is considered "architected," in other words, specified in the protocol. If Cisco must add some other header information to create a protocol type field, then that type field is not considered to be architected.

Table 8-2 lists these point-to-point data-link protocols and their attributes. (For a review of the protocol type field, refer to Chapter 3.)

Table 8-2 *Point-to-Point Data-Link Protocol Attributes*

Protocol	Error Correction?	Architected Type Field?	Other Attributes
SDLC (Synchronous Data Link Control)	yes	none	Supports multipoint links; assumes SNA header occurs after the SDLC header
LAPB (Link Access Procedure Balanced)	yes	none	Spec assumes single configurable protocol after LAPB. Used mainly with X.25. Cisco uses a proprietary type field to support multiprotocol traffic.
LAPD (Link Access Procedure on the D channel)	no	no	Not used between routers. Used on D channel from router to ISDN switch for signaling.
HDLC (High-Level Data Link Control)	no	no	Cisco's default on serial links. Cisco uses a proprietary type field to support multiprotocol traffic.

continues

Table 8-2 *Point-to-Point Data-Link Protocol Attributes (Continued)*

Protocol	Error Correction?	Architected Type Field?	Other Attributes
PPP (Point-to-Point Protocol)	Allows user to choose whether error correction is performed; correction uses LAPB	yes	Meant for multiprotocol interoperability from its inception, unlike all the others. PPP also supports asynchronous communication.

Be careful about confusing LAPB and LAPD. The "D" can help remind you that it is for an ISDN D channel, but don't let that make you think that the "B" is for an ISDN B channel!

HDLC and PPP Configuration

The configuration to enable most of the point-to-point data-link protocols is straightforward, with LAPB being the exception. (Make sure to configure the same WAN data-link protocol on each end of the serial link! Otherwise, the routers will misinterpret the incoming frames.) Example 8-1 lists configuration for HDLC, followed by the changed configuration for a migration to PPP. Assume Router A and Router B have a serial link attached to their serial 0 ports, respectively.

Example 8-1 *Configuration for PPP and HDLC*

```
Router A                            Router B

Interface serial 0                  Interface serial 0
encapsulation ppp                   encapsulation ppp
.                                   .
. later, changed to...              . later, changed to...
.                                   .
interface serial 0                  interface serial 0
encapsulation hdlc                  encapsulation hdlc
```

Changing serial encapsulations in configuration mode is tricky compared to some other configuration commands in a Cisco router. In Example 8-1, converting back to HDLC (the default) is done with the **encapsulation hdlc** command, not by using a command like **no encapsulation ppp**. Additionally, any other interface subcommands that are pertinent only to PPP are also removed when the **encapsulation hdlc** command is used.

PPP

PPP provides several other features in addition to synchronization and framing. The features fall into two categories: those needed regardless of the Layer 3 protocol sent across the link, and those particular to each Layer 3 protocol.

The PPP Link Control Protocol (LCP) provides the base features that are needed regardless of the Layer 3 protocol sent across the link. A series of PPP control protocols, IPCP (IP Control Protocol) for example, provide features for a particular Layer 3 protocol to function well across the link. For example, IPCP provides for IP address assignment; this feature is used extensively with Internet dial connections today.

The CCNA objectives and training paths do not focus on the control protocols. If a router is configured for IPX, AppleTalk, and IP on a PPP serial link, the router configured for PPP encapsulation will automatically try to bring up the appropriate control protocols for each Layer 3 protocol.

The CCNA Training Paths do specifically cover the features of LCP summarized in Table 8-3.

Table 8-3 *PPP LCP Features*

Function	Name	Description
Error detection	Link Quality Monitoring (LQM)	A link can be taken down by PPP based on the percentage of errors on the link. LQM exchanges statistics about lost packets versus sent packets in each direction, which when compared to packets and bytes sent, yields a percentage of errored traffic. The percentage lost that causes a link to be taken down is enabled and defined by a configuration setting.
Looped Link Detection	Magic Number	Using a "Magic Number," each router sends messages to each other with a different magic number. If you ever receive your own magic number, the link is looped. A configuration setting determines whether the link should be taken down when looped.
Authentication	PAP and CHAP	Mostly used on dial links, PAP and CHAP can be used to authenticate the device on the other end of the link.
Compression	STAC and Predictor	Software compression.
Multilink Support	Multilink PPP	Fragments of packets are load-balanced across multiple links. More often used with dial. The section "Multilink PPP" later in the chapter covers this concept in greater detail.

Error Detection and Looped Link Detection

The section "Multilink PPP" later in the chapter discusses multilink support and authentication because these topics are more typically used in a dial environment. The items in Table 8-3 called

Error Detection and Looped Link Detection are listed as a single item, called Error Detection, in Training Path 1. These two topics are covered next.

Looped Link Detection allows for faster convergence when a link fails due to being looped. Links are typically looped for testing purposes. When this occurs, a router continues to receive Cisco proprietary keepalive messages, but they are not messages from the neighboring router—they originate in this same router. Looped Link Detection defeats this problem using a PPP feature called *magic numbers*. The router sends PPP messages instead of keepalives; these messages include a magic number, which is different on each router. If a line is looped, the router receives a message with its own magic number. If configured to do so, the router can take down the interface, which will speed convergence.

Error detection (not error recovery) is accomplished by a PPP feature called *Link Quality Monitoring (LQM)*. PPP at each end of the link sends messages describing the number of correctly received packets and bytes. This is compared to the number of packets and bytes sent to calculate a percentage loss. The router can be configured to take down the link after a configured error rate has been exceeded so future packets are sent over a longer, but hopefully better, path.

Frame Relay Protocols

CCNA Objectives Covered in This Section

9	Recognize key Frame Relay terms and features.

Frame Relay provides delivery of variable-sized data frames to multiple WAN-connected sites. This section reviews the details of how Frame Relay accomplishes this goal.

Frame Relay is a well-chosen name for reminding us that it most closely relates to OSI Layer 2. The term *frame* is generally associated with a collection of data bits that includes an OSI Layer 2 equivalent header. For example, an Ethernet frame includes the Ethernet header/trailer. Frame Relay uses addresses, but that addressing does not attempt to create a logical address structure that could be used over a variety of media; therefore, addressing is closer to OSI Layer 2 addressing standards, and Frame Relay is considered to be a Layer 2 protocol. (Refer to Chapter 3 for a review of OSI layers.)

The remainder of this section summarizes the Frame Relay protocol details expected to be on the exam.

Frame Relay Features and Terminology

Frame Relay is a multi-access network, which actually means that more than two devices can attach to the medium. Multi-access is the first and most obvious difference between Frame

Relay and leased lines. However, leased lines are used as the access link component of Frame Relay networks. Consider Figure 8-2, which is a valuable resource for reviewing Frame Relay concepts.

Figure 8-2 *Frame Relay Components*

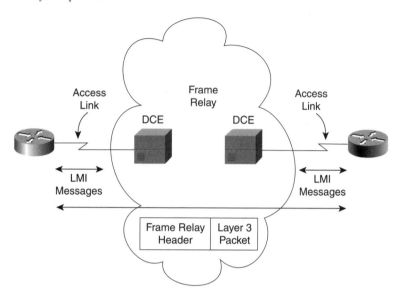

The access link between the router and the Frame Relay switch is a leased line. Both sites represented in Figure 8-2 are connected to some nearby switch via a leased line. The service provider interconnects their switches to provide connectivity.

Table 8-4 lists the components in Figure 8-2 and some associated terms.

Table 8-4 *Frame Relay Terms and Concepts*

VC (virtual circuit)	A VC is a logical concept that represents the path that frames travel between DTEs. VCs are particularly useful when comparing Frame Relay to leased physical "circuits."
PVC (permanent virtual circuit)	A PVC is a VC that is predefined. A PVC can be equated to a leased line in concept.
SVC (switched virtual circuit)	An SVC is a VC that is set up dynamically. An SVC can be equated to a dial connection in concept.
DTE (data terminal equipment)	DTEs are also known as data-circuit termination equipment. Routers, for example, are DTEs when connected to a Frame Relay service from a telecommunication company.

continues

Table 8-4 *Frame Relay Terms and Concepts (Continued)*

DCE (data communications equipment)	Frame Relay switches are DCE devices.
Access Link	The access link is the leased line between DTE and DCE.
AR (access rate)	The access rate is the speed at which the access link is clocked. This choice affects the price of the connection.
CIR (committed information rate)	The CIR is the rate at which the DTE can send data for an individual VC, for which the provider commits to deliver that amount of data. The provider will send any data in excess of this rate for this VC if its network has capacity at the time. This choice typically affects the price of each VC.
Burst Rate	The burst rate is the rate and length of time for which, for a particular VC, the DTE can send faster than the CIR, and the provider agrees to forward the data. This choice affects the price of each VC typically.
DLCI (data-link connection identifier)	A DLCI is a Frame Relay address and is used in Frame Relay headers to identify the other DTE that needs to receive this frame.
FECN (forward explicit congestion notification)	The FECN is the bit in the Frame Relay header that signals to anyone receiving the frame (switches and DTEs) that congestion is occurring in the same direction as the frame. Switches and DTEs can react by slowing the rate data is sent in that direction.
BECN (backward explicit congestion notification)	The BECN is the bit in the Frame Relay header that signals to anyone receiving the frame (switches and DTEs) that congestion is occurring in the opposite (backward) direction as the frame. Switches and DTEs can react by slowing the rate data is sent in that direction.
DE (discard eligibility)	The DE is the bit in the Frame Relay header that signals to a switch that, if frames must be discarded, to please choose this frame to discard, as opposed to another frame without the DE bit set.
NBMA (nonbroadcast multiaccess)	NBMA refers to a network in which broadcasts are not supported, but more than two devices can be connected.
LMI (Local Management Interface)	LMI is the protocol used between a DCE and DTE to manage the connection. Signaling messages for SVCs, status messages, and keepalives are all LMI messages.
LAPF (link access procedure—Frame mode bearer services)	LAPF is the basic Frame Relay header and trailer and includes DLCI, FECN, BECN, and DE bits.

The definitions for Frame Relay are contained in documents from the ITU and from ANSI. The Frame Relay Forum, a vendor consortium, also defines several Frame Relay specifications, many of which have been added to the standards body's documents. Table 8-5 lists the most important of these specifications. (Please note that the names of these specifications could be on the exam based on objective 31; however, I do not believe that these specification names are likely to be on the test.)

Table 8-5 *Frame Relay Protocol Specifications*

What the Specification Defines	ITU Document	ANSI Document
Data link specifications, including LAPF header/trailer	Q.922 Annex A	T1.618
PVC management, LMI	Q.933 Annex A	T1.617 Annex D
SVC signaling	Q.933	T1.617
Multiprotocol encapsulation (originated in RFC 1490)	Q.933 Annex E	T1.617 Annex F

LMI Messages and Types

The LMI protocols defined by the ITU and ANSI are slightly different. Q.933-A calls for use of DLCI 1023 for LMI messages, whereas T1.617-D calls for DLCI 0. Some of the messages have different fields in their information elements. The DTE simply needs to know which of the two (DLCI 1023 or DLCI 0) to use; it must match the one used by the switch. LMI autosense is supported by the IOS in version 11.2, so there is no need to code the LMI type. There is one LMI type per serial interface because the LMI is controlling the access link.

The LMI *status enquiry* message signals whether a PVC is up or down. Even though each PVC is predefined, its status can change. As with all LMI messages, these flow between the switch and the DTE.

Encapsulation

Like other data-link protocols, Frame Relay defines a header and trailer, with fields in each that allow the switches and DTEs to succeed at delivering the frame across the network. Encapsulation refers to the process of using such headers/trailers to contain data supplied by a higher layer. (Refer to Chapter 3 for additional concepts about encapsulation.)

Frame Relay uses an LAPF (link access procedure—Frame bearer services) header, defined by Q.922-A. The sparse LAPF header provides error detection with an FCS in the trailer, as well as the DLCI, DE, FECN, and BECN fields. Figure 8-3 diagrams the frame.

Figure 8-3 *LAPF Header*

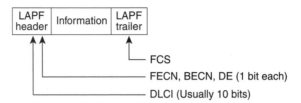

Figure 8-3 does not show the presence of a Protocol Type field. As discussed in Chapter 3, something in the header needs to define the type of header that begins the Information field. In other words, if what follows in the Information field is either an IP and IPX header, there is nothing in the LAPF header that identifies whether it is IP or IPX. If Frame Relay uses only the LAPF header, then DTEs, including routers, cannot support multiprotocol traffic because there is no way to identify the type of protocol in the Information field. (For more information about the concept of a Protocol Type field in data-link headers, refer to Chapter 3.)

Two solutions were created to compensate for the lack of a Protocol Type field. Cisco and three other companies created an additional header, which comes first in the Information field shown in Figure 8-3. It includes a 2-byte-long Protocol Type field, with values matching the same field used for HDLC by Cisco. The second solution was defined in RFC 1490, "Multiprotocol Interconnect over Frame Relay," which was written to ensure multivendor interoperability between Frame Relay DTEs. This solution includes use of a Protocol Type field and adds many options, including support for bridged frames. ITU and ANSI later incorporated RFC 1490 headers into specs Q.933 Annex E and T.617 Annex F, respectively.

Figure 8-4 provides a conceptual diagram of the two forms of encapsulation. Because the frames flow from DTE to DTE, both DTEs must agree to the encapsulation used. However, each VC can use a different encapsulation.

Figure 8-4 *Cisco and RFC 1490 Encapsulations*

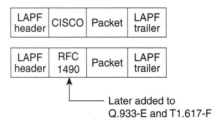

DLCI Addressing and Frame Relay Switching

The DLCI is the Frame Relay address. These addresses are used to address the virtual circuits, not the DTEs. However, when a service provider supplies a diagram of a fully-meshed network they are building for you, the DLCIs will look like they identify the DTE device. Figure 8-5 provides an example of a DLCI planning diagram.

Figure 8-5 *DLCI Planning Diagram from Service Provider*

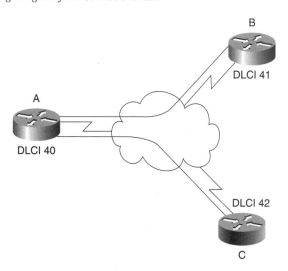

DLCI addressing as shown in Figure 8-5 shows a single DLCI for each router (DTE). Conceptually, addressing works similarly to LANs; each device has a unique address. The style of Frame Relay address assignment, in which each DTE is assigned a single DLCI, is called *Global Addressing*. The global DLCI addressing in Figure 8-5 is actually just one perception of how Frame Relay uses DLCI. This view of addressing enables you to consider that for a frame needing to be sent from Router B to Router A, the frame simply needs to be sent to DLCI 40.

But then the numbers used by a router, both inside the Frame Relay headers and the router configurations, are different than the number written beside that same router in Figure 8-5. For Router B to send a frame to Router A, B must send a frame with DLCI 40. Table 8-6 provides a better basis for explaining Frame Relay addressing nuances.

However, the DLCIs configured in the routers refer to the other routers' DLCI values. For example, Router A has a VC to both Router B and Router C; Router A will need to know each of their DLCIs. The reason for needing to refer to the other router's DLCI is that Frame Relay uses a single address field in the header. The Frame Relay switches swap the DLCI in transit. For example, Router A sends a frame with DLCI 41, hoping that it will be delivered to Router B. By the time the frame is sent over Router B's access link, the frame has a DLCI value of 40. When Router A sent the frame, the DLCI has B's DLCI in the header; when B receives the frame, it has A's DLCI in it. In fact, this feature can be summarized as follows:

From a DTE perspective, the DLCI always represents the DTE on the other end of the VC.

Figure 8-6 and Table 8-6 summarize the operation when frames are sent over the two VCs shown in Figure 8-6.

Figure 8-6 *DLCIs and Frame Flows*

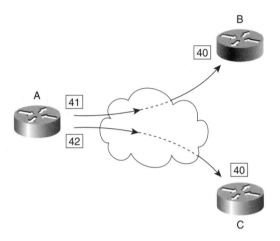

Table 8-6 *DLCI Swapping in Frame Relay Cloud*

Frame Sent by Router...	With DLCI Field	Is Delivered to Router...	With DLCI Field
A	41	B	40
A	42	C	40
B	40	A	41
B	42	C	41
C	40	A	42
C	41	B	42

Figure 8-6 shows a frame being sent from Router A to Router B in one case, and to Router C in the other case. As A sends a frame with DLCI 41, the switches send the frame toward Router B. Before being sent on the access link to Router B, the final switch changes the DLCI to be 40 so that Router B knows who sent the frame. Similarly, Router A sends a frame with DLCI 42, and it is received by Router C with DLCI 40. This style of describing DLCI addresses in Figure 8-5 is called *Global Frame Relay Addressing*. It has become popular because the planning diagram looks more like a LAN, with an address for each device attached to the network. However, configuration details in the routers require that you consider how this addressing works and configure the DLCI of the other router. For example, the configuration in Router A would refer to DLCIs 41 and 42, not to DLCI 40.

Another style of Frame Relay addressing is called *Local Frame Relay Addressing*, which describes the exact same DLCIs as Global Addressing, but instead lists the numbers from the perspective of what is configured in the DTE. Figure 8-7 shows Local Addressing, using the same DLCIs as in Figure 8-5. The configuration for Routers A, B, and C would be the same for either figure—it is just two different ways to think about Frame Relay addressing. Diagrams showing Global Addressing allow a more straightforward representation for discussing the network, and diagrams showing Local Addressing enable the person configuring the router to more easily recognize the DLCI values to be configured.

Figure 8-7 *Local Frame Relay Addressing*

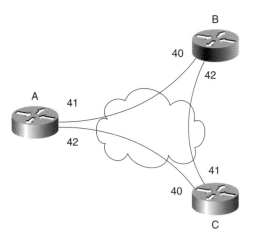

NOTE   Whether the DLCIs are shown with the Global or Local Addressing, all DLCIs are considered to be locally significant. *Locally significant* means that the number is only meaningful in one part of the network, in this case, an individual access link. For example, DLCI 41, as used by Router A to send a frame to Router B, is only used on Router A's access link. In the remainder of the Frame Relay network, DLCI 41 need not be used.

Network Layer Concerns with Frame Relay

You need to concern yourself with three key issues relating to Layer 3 flows over Frame Relay:

- Choices for Layer 3 addresses on Frame Relay interfaces
- Broadcast Handling
- Split-horizon

The sections that follow cover these issues in depth.

Layer 3 Addressing

The basic underlying concept regarding choices for Layer 3 addresses can be summed up as follows:

> All interfaces on different routers with the same Layer 3 group (such as a subnet), must have a VC between itself and all others in the group.

This section examines three cases of Layer 3 addressing in Frame Relay. Figure 8-8 starts off the first case with an illustration of a fully-meshed Frame Relay network. Because all three routers have a VC to each other, each can be considered to be in the same Layer 3 groups. Figure 8-8 also shows IPX and IP addresses. The IPX and IP addresses would be configured as subcommands on the serial interface. Table 8-7 summarizes the addresses used in Figure 8-8.

Figure 8-8 *Full Mesh with IP and IPX Addresses*

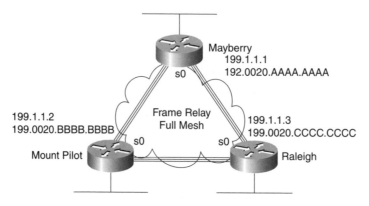

Table 8-7 *IP and IPX Addresses, No Subinterfaces*

Router	IP Address	IPX Network	IPX Address
Mayberry	199.1.1.1	199	1.0200.aaaa.aaaa
Mount Pilot	199.1.1.2	199	1.0200.bbbb.bbbb
Raleigh	199.1.1.3	199	1.0200.cccc.cccc

The second case is a partially-meshed Frame Relay network (see Figure 8-9). Because all four routers do not have VCs to each other, each VC will use a different set of Layer 3 groups. Table 8-8 shows the IPX and IP addresses for the partially-meshed Frame Relay network illustrated in Figure 8-9. The addresses would be configured as subcommands on the serial interface. (Note: The notation "/24" signifies a subnet mask with 24 binary 1s, in other words, 255.255.255.0.)

Figure 8-9 *Partial Mesh with IP and IPX Addresses*

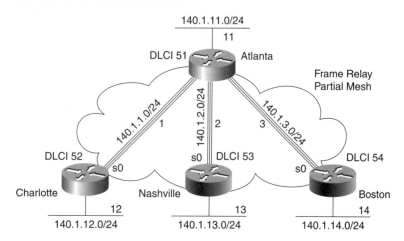

Table 8-8 *IP and IPX Addresses, Point-to-Point Subinterfaces*

Router	Subnet	IP Address	IPX Network	IPX Address
Atlanta	140.1.1.0/24	140.1.1.1	1	1.0200.aaaa.aaaa
Charlotte	140.1.1.0/24	140.1.1.2	1	1.0200.bbbb.bbbb
Atlanta	140.1.2.0/24	140.1.2.1	2	2.0200.aaaa.aaaa
Nashville	140.1.2.0/24	140.1.2.3	2	2.0200.cccc.cccc
Atlanta	140.1.3.0/24	140.1.3.1	3	3.0200.aaaa.aaaa
Boston	140.1.3.0/24	140.1.3.4	3	3.0200.dddd.dddd

Subinterfaces allow the Atlanta router to have 3 IP addresses and 3 IPX addresses associated with its serial 0 interface. Subinterfaces can treat each VC as though it were a point-to-point serial link. Each of the three subinterfaces of serial 0 on Atlanta would be assigned a different IP address and IPX address from the list in Table 8-8.

The third case of Layer 3 addressing is a hybrid between the first two illustrated in Figure 8-8 and Figure 8-9. Consider Figure 8-10, which has a trio of routers with VCs between each of them, plus two other VCs to remote sites.

Figure 8-10 *Hybrid of Full and Partial Mesh*

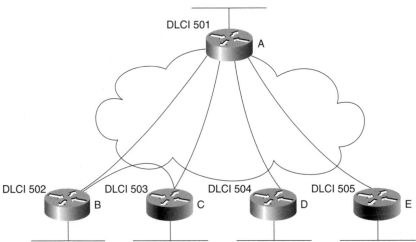

Two options exist for Layer 3 addressing in this case. The first is to treat each VC as a separate Layer 3 group; 5 subnets and 5 IPX networks would be needed for the Frame Relay network. However, if Routers A, B, and C are considered alone, they meet the criteria that each can send packets directly to each other, like a full mesh. This would allow A, B, and C to use one subnet and IPX network. The other two VCs—between A and D and between A and E—are treated as two separate Layer 3 groups. The result is a total of 3 subnets and 3 IPX network numbers.

To accomplish either style of Layer 3 addressing in this third and final case, subinterfaces are used. Point-to-point subinterfaces are used when a single VC is considered to be all that is in the group. Multipoint subinterfaces are used between Routers A, B, and C in Figure 8-10. The section "Frame Relay Configuration" later in the chapter provides full configurations for all three cases illustrated in Figure 8-8, Figure 8-9 and Figure 8-10. Table 8-9 summarizes the addresses and subinterfaces used.

Table 8-9 *IP and IPX Addresses, Point-to-Point, and Multipoint Subinterfaces*

Router	Subnet	IP Address	IPX Network	IPX Address	Subinterface Type
A	140.1.1.0/24	140.1.1.1	1	1.0200.aaaa.aaaa	Multipoint
B	140.1.1.0/24	140.1.1.2	1	1.0200.bbbb.bbbb	Multipoint
C	140.1.1.0/24	140.1.1.3	1	1.0200.cccc.cccc	Multipoint
A	140.1.2.0/24	140.1.2.1	2	2.0200.aaaa.aaaa	Point-to-point
D	140.1.2.0/24	140.1.2.4	2	2.0200.dddd.dddd	Point-to-point
A	140.1.3.0/24	140.1.3.1	3	3.0200.aaaa.aaaa	Point-to-point
E	140.1.3.0/24	140.1.3.5	3	3.0200.eeee.eeee	Point-to-point

Broadcast Handling

Broadcasts are not supported over a Frame Relay network. In other words, there is no capability for a DTE to send a frame, which is replicated and delivered across more than one VC. However, routers need to send broadcasts for several features to work. In particular, routing protocol updates and SAP updates are broadcast.

The solution to the broadcast dilemma for Frame Relay has two parts. First, the IOS will send copies of the broadcasts across each VC that you ask it to. Of course, if there are only a few VCs, this is not a big problem. However, if hundreds of VCs terminate in one router, then for each broadcast, hundreds of copies could be sent. The IOS can be configured to limit the amount of bandwidth that is used for these replicated broadcasts.

The second part of the solution is that the router will try to minimize the impact of the first part of the solution. The router will place these broadcasts into a different queue than user traffic so that the user does not experience a large spike in delay each time some broadcast is replicated and sent over each VC, for example, when the routing and SAP timers expire.

NOTE	While the CCNP exam, and not the CCNA exam, will cover such issues about dealing with overhead, a short example can show the significance of this overhead. For example, if a router knows 1000 routes, uses RIP, and has 50 DLCs, 1.072 MB of RIP updates are sent each 30 seconds. That averages to 285 kbps. (Math: 536 byte RIP packets, with 25 routes in each packet, for 40 packets per update, with copies sent over 50 VCs: 536 X 40 X 50 = 1.072 Megabytes per update interval. 1.072 X 8 / 30 seconds = 285 kpbs).

Knowing how to tell the router to forward these broadcasts out to each VC will be important on the CCNA exam. The issues relating to dealing with the volume of these updates is more likely a topic for the CCNP and CCIE exams.

Split-Horizon

Split-horizon is useful for preventing routing loops. It does this by preventing a router from advertising a particular route in a routing update on a particular interface if that route was learned via an update that earlier was received on that same interface. (Refer to Chapter 6, "Understanding Routing," for a full explanation.) However, split-horizon can cause some problems if not considered when choosing network layer addresses and subinterface types. Refer back to Figure 8-9. If split-horizon was enabled on Atlanta, it would learn about 140.1.12.0/24 from Charlotte, but Atlanta would not advertise the route to 140.1.12.0/24 in its updates to Nashville or Boston.

Split-horizon logic applies to subinterfaces if they are configured. In other words, Atlanta uses a different subinterface for each VC to the three remote sites. Split-horizon is enabled on each subinterface. However, because the routing updates from Charlotte are considered to enter Atlanta via one subinterface, and routing updates to Nashville and Boston exit two other subinterfaces, then advertising 140.1.12.0/24 to Nashville and Boston is allowed.

Split-horizon would be a problem in Figure 8-8, however. When all three VCs are up, there is no problem. However, if the VC from Mount Pilot to Raleigh went down, then split-horizon on Mayberry would be harmful. Mount Pilot will advertise routes to 199.1.11.0, and Mayberry will receive that information in a routing update. However, because no subinterfaces are used, with split-horizon enabled, Mayberry would not advertise 199.1.11.0 to Raleigh.

The multipoint subinterfaces in Figure 8-10 would experience the same problems for the same reasons as described for Figure 8-8.

The solution to the problem is to disable split-horizon when not using subinterfaces or when using multipoint subinterfaces. The IOS defaults to disable split-horizon on Frame Relay interfaces in all cases except for point-to-point subinterfaces. Table 8-10 summarizes these settings.

Table 8-10 *Split-Horizon and Frame Relay Interfaces*

Type of Configuration	Split-Horizon Is...
No subinterfaces	disabled
Point-point subinterfaces	enabled
Multipoint subinterfaces	disabled

If the default value for split-horizon is not desired, then the **ip split-horizon** interface configuration command can be used to enable split-horizon. Similarly, the **no ip split-horizon** interface configuration command disables split-horizon on that interface.

The issues with split-horizon and Frame Relay are not specifically mentioned in Training Paths 1 and 2. However, this is exactly the kind of question that is more likely to be on the exam as time passes and the CCNA exam questions focus more on the objectives and less on the words in the course books.

How Address Mapping Works

CCNA Objectives Covered in This Section

9	Recognize key Frame Relay terms and features.
10	List commands to configure Frame Relay LMIs, maps, and subinterfaces.

Frame Relay mapping is a topic you could ignore and still make Frame Relay work in a Cisco router. However, it is an important topic to cover for the CCNA exam. Why? Well, there are two main reasons. First, forcing you to understand and configure static mapping is just the kind of nasty question that is likely to crop up on the exam. Secondly, understanding mapping is a good opportunity to review the concepts behind network routing. Like most features implemented dynamically and by default, mapping can be ignored most of the time.

Mapping is required when using some other data links, but not in all. For example, with IP, the ARP process dynamically builds a mapping between an IP address and a LAN address. This section discusses the basics behind why mapping is needed for point-to-point leased lines, LAN connections, and Frame Relay, with a focus on Frame Relay.

Consider the Figure 8-11 and the routing table that follows (see Table 8-11).

Figure 8-11 *Basic Point-to-Point Network*

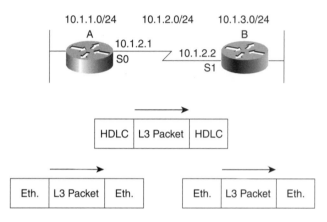

Table 8-11 *Partial Routing Table on Router A for Figure 8-11*

Subnet	Outgoing Interface	Next Router
10.1.3.0	serial 0	10.1.2.2

The core-routing logic must be considered to fully appreciate mapping. Router A receives an Ethernet frame from some host and strips the Ethernet header (and trailer). It decides to route the packet out serial 0 to 10.1.2.2 next (Router B's S1 IP address.) Router A builds the HDLC header/trailer and sends the frame.

The fact that Router B's IP address on the common serial link is 10.1.2.2 had nothing to do with the contents of the HDLC header and trailer; Router B's IP address is immaterial in this case. If Router A can get the frame across the link, there is only one possible recipient—Router B.

Now consider a diagram with Ethernet between the routers (see Figure 8-12) and the routing table that follows (see Table 8-12).

Figure 8-12 *Basic Ethernet Network*

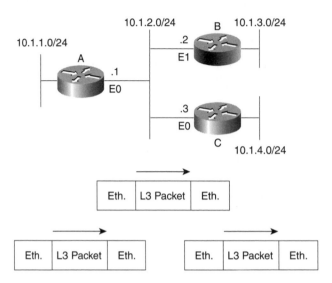

Table 8-12 *Partial Routing Table on Router A for Figure 8-12*

Subnet	Outgoing Interface	Next Router
10.1.3.0	Ethernet 0	10.1.2.2

Again consider the core-routing logic. Router A receives an Ethernet frame from some host and strips the Ethernet header (and trailer). Router A decides to route the packet out Ethernet 0 to the next router, 10.1.2.2 (Router B's E1 IP address). Router A builds the new Ethernet header/ trailer and sends the frame.

Router A builds the Ethernet header based on the next-hop router's IP address, namely 10.1.2.2 (Router B's E1 IP address). The destination Ethernet address in the header built by Router A is Router B's E1 address. Router A learns this information dynamically using the IP ARP protocol. For IPX routing, the next-hop router's IPX address has the corresponding LAN address embedded in the IPX address. (With other Layer 3 protocols, there are other processes on LANs for learning the corresponding LAN address.) The information learned by IP ARP in this case is the information that maps the next-hop IP address to the LAN address used to reach it; this is called *mapping*. A more general definition for mapping is as follows:

The information that correlates to the next-hop router's Layer 3 address, and the Layer 2 address used to reach it, is called mapping. Mapping is needed on multi-access networks.

Now consider the Frame Relay network in Figure 8-13, along with the routing table in Table 8-13.

Figure 8-13 *Basic Frame Relay Network*

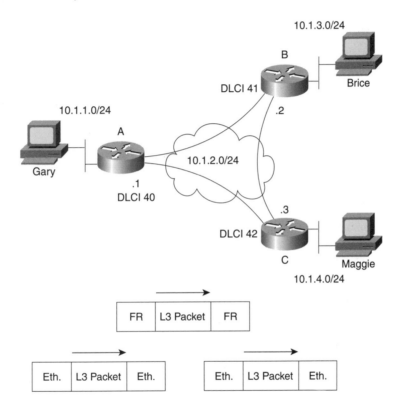

Table 8-13 *Partial Routing Table on Router A for Figure 8-13*

Subnet	Outgoing Interface	Next Router
10.1.3.0	Serial 0	10.1.2.2

Again consider the core-routing logic. Router A receives an Ethernet frame from some host and strips the Ethernet header (and trailer). It decides to route the packet out serial 0 to the next router, 10.1.2.2 (Router B's S0 IP address). Router A builds the Frame Relay header/trailer and sends the frame.

Although Router A knows which of its serial interfaces out which to forward the frame, Router A does not know the correct DLCI yet. A mapping is needed in Router A between 10.1.2.2 (Router B) and the DLCI Router A uses to reach Router B. However, the same IP ARP used on LANs will not work on Frame Relay because there is no support for broadcasts. Therefore, it cannot be used to discover that DLCI.

There are two solutions for Router A to learn the mapping between Router B's IP address and DLCI. One uses a statically configured mapping, and the other uses a dynamic process called *Inverse ARP*.

Table 8-14 lists the IP and IPX addresses of the three routers in Figure 8-13.

Table 8-14   *Layer 3 Addresses and DLCIs Used with Figure 8-13*

Router	Global DLCI	IP Address	IPX Address
A	40	10.1.2.1	2.0200.aaaa.aaaa
B	41	10.1.2.2	2.0200.bbbb.bbbb
C	42	10.1.2.3	2.0200.cccc.cccc

Example 8-2 lists the static Frame Relay **map** for the three routers in Figure 8-13. The DLCIs in Table 8-14 are the same as those used in Figure 8-13.

Example 8-2   *frame-relay map Commands*

```
Router A:

interface serial 0
frame-relay map ip 10.1.2.2 41 broadcast
frame-relay map ipx 2.0200.bbbb.bbbb 41 broadcast
frame-relay map ip 10.1.2.3 42 broadcast
frame-relay map ipx 2.0200.cccc.cccc 42 broadcast

Router B:

interface serial 0
frame-relay map ip 10.1.2.1 40 broadcast
frame-relay map ipx 2.0200.aaaa.aaaa 40 broadcast
frame-relay map ip 10.1.2.3 42 broadcast
frame-relay map ipx 2.0200.cccc.cccc 42 broadcast

Router C:

interface serial 0
frame-relay map ip 10.1.2.1 40 broadcast
```

Example 8-2 *frame-relay map* Commands (Continued)

```
frame-relay map ipx 2.0200.aaaa.aaaa 40 broadcast
frame-relay map ip 10.1.2.2 41 broadcast
frame-relay map ipx 2.0200.bbbb.bbbb 41 broadcast
```

Consider the case where Gary makes an FTP connection to Brice. The **frame-relay map** statement for Router A referencing 10.1.2.2 would be used for packets originating from Gary. Conversely, a packet sent back from Brice to Gary would cause Router B to use its map statement referring to Router A's IP address of 10.1.2.1. Mapping is needed for each next-hop Layer 3 address for each Layer 3 protocol being routed. Even with a network this small, the configuration process can be laborious. The solution is a dynamic protocol called Inverse ARP.

Inverse ARP acquires mapping information in a manner opposite of IP ARP, but the information that maps the Layer 3 and Layer 2 addresses is still found. Inverse ARP is basic; after the VC is up, each DTE announces its network layer address to the DTE on the other end of the VC. (Inverse ARP is enabled by default at IOS 11.2 and beyond, unless point-to-point subinterfaces are used.) Table 8-15 summarizes what would occur in the network in Figure 8-13.

Table 8-15 *Inverse ARP Messages for Figure 8-13*

Sending Router	Sent DLCI	Receiving Router	Received DLCI	Information in Inverse ARP
A	41	B	40	I am 10.1.2.1
A	41	B	40	I am 2.0200.aaaa.aaaa
A	42	C	40	I am 10.1.2.1
A	42	C	40	I am 2.0200.aaaa.aaaa
B	40	A	41	I am 10.1.2.2
B	40	A	41	I am 2.0200.bbbb.bbbb
B	42	C	41	I am 10.1.2.2
B	42	C	41	I am 2.0200.bbbb.bbbb
C	40	A	42	I am 10.1.2.3
C	40	A	42	I am 2.0200.cccc.cccc
C	41	B	42	I am 10.1.2.3
C	41	B	42	I am 2.0200.cccc.cccc

While Table 8-15 lists a seemingly large number of messages, no static **frame-relay map** commands are needed. All the necessary mapping information is dynamically learned.

Inverse ARP is enabled by default if there are no subinterfaces in use. Inverse ARP is also on by default for multipoint subinterfaces. However, Inverse ARP is not enabled on point-to-point subinterfaces. The reason for this is that point-to-point subinterfaces behave like a true point-to-point line in regards to routing; if the packet needs to be sent out a point-to-point subinterface, then there is only one possible next router and there is only one DLCI in use. So, Inverse ARP is not needed with point-to-point subinterfaces.

Frame Relay Configuration

CCNA Objectives Covered in This Section	
10	List commands to configure Frame Relay LMIs, maps, and subinterfaces.
11	List commands to monitor Frame Relay operation in the router.

This section covers the configuration commands needed to successfully implement Frame Relay (objective 10). Also, the EXEC commands used to monitor Frame Relay networks are covered (objective 11). Examining the **show** command output and comparing it to the configurations is a particularly useful method of exercising your memory of the subject.

Table 8-16 and Table 8-17 summarize the Frame Relay configuration commands and EXEC commands that are covered in Training Paths 1 and 2.

Table 8-16   *Frame Relay Configuration Commands in Training Paths 1 and 2*

Command	Configuration Mode	Purpose
encapsulation frame-relay [**ietf**l**cisco**]	Interface	Defines Frame Relay encapsulation is used rather than HDLC, PPP, and so on.
frame-relay lmi-type {**ansi**l**q933a**l**cisco**}	Interface	Defines the type of LMI messages sent to the switch.
bandwidth *num*	Interface	Sets the route's perceived speed of the interface. Bandwidth is used by some routing protocols to influence the metric.
frame-relay map *protocol protocol-address dlci* [**broadcast**] [**ietf**] [**cisco**]	Interface	Statically defines a mapping between a network layer address and a DLCI.

Table 8-16 *Frame Relay Configuration Commands in Training Paths 1 and 2 (Continued)*

keepalive *sec*	Interface	Defines whether, and how often, LMI status enquiry messages are sent and expected.
interface serial *num.sub [point-to-point	multipoint]*	Global	Creates a subinterface, or references a previously created subinterface.
frame-relay interface-dlci *dlci* **[ietf|cisco]**	Interface	Defines a DLCI used for a VC to another DTE.

Table 8-17 *Frame Relay Related EXEC Commands in Training Paths 1 and 2*

Command	**Function**
Show interface	Shows physical interface status.
Show frame-relay {**pvc|map|lmi**}	Shows PVC status, mapping (dynamic and static), and LMI status.

When and how to use subinterfaces for Frame Relay configuration is the most difficult part of the configuration. Subinterfaces are never required; subinterfaces can be used in any Frame Relay configuration, and most sites tend to use subinterfaces. Some general guidelines when using subinterfaces include the following:

- When the network is partially-meshed, using point-to-point subinterfaces overcomes split-horizon issues by treating each subinterface as a separate interface.

- When the network is partially-meshed, using a multipoint subinterface will work. Split-horizon issues are overcome by disabling the default setting.

- When the network is truly fully-meshed, a multipoint subinterface can be used to reduce the number of network layer groups (for example, IP subnets) that are used.

- When the network is truly fully-meshed, point-to-point subinterfaces can be used. This is typically chosen to maintain consistency with other nonfully-meshed Frame Relay networks elsewhere in the network. This choice requires a larger number of IP subnets to be used.

- When the network contains some fully-meshed portions (for example, 3 sites have VCs between each other, but the other 10 do not), a multipoint subinterface can be used for the fully-meshed portion, and point-to-point subinterfaces can be used for the rest.

- When the network contains some fully-meshed portions, (for example, 3 sites have VCs between each other, but the other 10 do not) using only point-to-point subinterfaces is another option. This requires more IP subnets, IPX networks, and so forth than when using a multipoint subinterface for the fully-meshed portion of the network.

- Many sites avoid configurations that do not use subinterfaces at all to maintain consistency.

Correlating the DLCI(s) to their subinterfaces is required when using either type of subinterface. LMI enquiry messages notify the router that PVCs are active; the router then needs to know which subinterface uses the DLCI. An individual DLCI is only used by one subinterface. For a point-to-point subinterface, only one DLCI is used; for multipoint, many DLCIs are used.

Three samples of Layer 3 addressing were used earlier in the chapter, with the networks diagrammed in Figure 8-8, Figure 8-9, and Figure 8-10. The configurations matching those networks and addresses are shown next.

Configuring Networks without Subinterfaces

The first sample network (based on the environment depicted in Figure 8-8) does not use subinterfaces. Example 8-3, Example 8-4, and Example 8-5 show the configuration for this network.

Example 8-3 *Mayberry Configuration*

```
ipx routing 0200.aaaa.aaaa
!
interface serial0
encapsulation frame-relay
ip address   199.1.1.1   255.255.255.0
ipx network   199
!
interface ethernet 0
ip address   199.1.10.1   255.255.255.0
ipx network   1
!
router igrp 1
network   199.1.1.0
network 199.1.10.0
```

Example 8-4 *Mount Pilot Configuration*

```
ipx routing 0200.bbbb.bbbb
!
interface serial0
encapsulation frame-relay
ip address  199.1.1.2  255.255.255.0
ipx network  199
!
interface ethernet 0
ip address  199.1.11.2   255.255.255.0
ipx network  2
!
router igrp 1
network  199.1.1.0
network 199.1.11.0
```

Example 8-5 *Raleigh Configuration*

```
ipx routing 0200.cccc.cccc
!
interface serial0
encapsulation frame-relay
ip address  199.1.1.3  255.255.255.0
ipx network  199
!
interface ethernet 0
ip address  199.1.12.3   255.255.255.0
ipx network  3
!
router igrp 1
network  199.1.1.0
network 199.1.12.0
```

The configuration is simple in comparison with the protocol concepts. All default settings (IOS version 11.2) were used and are as follows:

- The LMI type is automatically sensed.

- The encapsulation is Cisco instead of IETF.

- PVC DLCIs are learned via LMI enquiry messages.

- Inverse ARP is enabled and is triggered when the VC becomes active.

Suppose the following requirements were added:

- The Raleigh router requires IETF encapsulation on both VCs.

- Mayberry's LMI type should be ANSI; autosense should not be used.

Example 8-6 and Example 8-7 show the changes that would be made to Mayberry and Raleigh.

Example 8-6 *Mayberry Configuration with New Requirements*

```
ipx routing 0200.aaaa.aaaa
!
interface serial0
encapsulation frame-relay
frame-relay lmi-type ansi
frame-relay interface-dlci 42 ietf
ip address  199.1.1.1  255.255.255.0
ipx network  199
! rest of configuration unchanged from example 8-3.
```

Example 8-7 *Raleigh Configuration with New Requirements*

```
ipx routing 0200.cccc.cccc
!
interface serial0
encapsulation frame-relay ietf
ip address  199.1.1.3  255.255.255.0
ipx network  199
!
! rest of configuration unchanged from example 8-5.
```

The encapsulation was changed in two different ways. Raleigh changed its encapsulation for both its PVCs with the **ietf** keyword on the **encapsulation** command. Mayberry could not because only one of the two VCs to Mayberry were to use IETF encapsulation. So, Mayberry was forced to code the **frame-relay interface-dlci** command, coding the DLCI for the VC to Raleigh. The **ietf** keyword was needed to change from the default encapsulation of **cisco**.

The LMI configuration in Mayberry would have been fine without any changes because autosense would have recognized ANSI. However, by coding the **frame-relay lmi-type ANSI**, Mayberry is forced to use ANSI because this command disables autonegotiation of the LMI type.

Mount Pilot's configuration would need to be modified like Mayberry's for the VC from Mount Pilot to Raleigh because that encapsulation changed as well.

Configuring Networks with Point-to-Point Subinterfaces

The second sample network (based on the environment depicted in Figure 8-9) uses point-to-point subinterfaces. Example 8-8, Example 8-9, Example 8-10, and Example 8-11 show the configuration for this network.

Example 8-8 *Atlanta Configuration*

```
ipx routing 0200.aaaa.aaaa
!
interface serial0
encapsulation frame-relay
!
interface serial 0.1 point-to-point
ip address 140.1.1.1  255.255.255.0
ipx network 1
frame-relay interface-dlci 52
!
interface serial 0.2 point-to-point
ip address 140.1.2.1 255.255.255.0
ipx network 2
frame-relay interface-dlci 53
!
interface serial 0.3 point-to-point
ip address 140.1.3.1 255.255.255.0
ipx network 3
frame-relay interface-dlci 54
!
interface ethernet 0
ip address 140.1.11.1 255.255.255.0
ipx network 11
```

Example 8-9 *Charlotte Configuration*

```
ipx routing 0200.bbbb.bbbb
!
interface serial0
encapsulation frame-relay
!
interface serial 0.1 point-to-point
ip address 140.1.1.2  255.255.255.0
ipx network 1
frame-relay interface-dlci 51
!
interface ethernet 0
ip address 140.1.12.2 255.255.255.0
ipx network 12
```

Example 8-10 *Nashville Configuration*

```
ipx routing 0200.cccc.cccc
!
interface serial0
encapsulation frame-relay
!
interface serial 0.2 point-to-point
ip address 140.1.2.3 255.255.255.0
ipx network 2
frame-relay interface-dlci 51
!
interface ethernet 0
ip address 140.1.13.3 255.255.255.0
ipx network 13
```

Example 8-11 *Boston Configuration*

```
ipx routing 0200.dddd.dddd
!
interface serial0
encapsulation frame-relay
!
interface serial 0.3 point-to-point
ip address 140.1.3.4 255.255.255.0
ipx network 3
frame-relay interface-dlci 51
!
interface ethernet 0
ip address 140.1.14.4   255.255.255.0
ipx network 14
```

Point-to-point subinterfaces were used in this configuration because the network is not fully-meshed. The **interface dlci** command is needed when using subinterfaces. The subinterface numbers in the example configuration happen to match on either end of the VCs. For example, subinterface 2 was used in Atlanta for the PVC to Nashville; Nashville also uses subinterface 2. There is no requirement that these numbers be the same.

Example 8-12 shows the output from the most popular IOS Frame Relay EXEC commands for monitoring Frame Relay, as issued on router Atlanta.

Example 8-12 *Output from EXEC Commands on Atlanta*

```
Atlanta#show frame-relay pvc

PVC Statistics for interface Serial0 (Frame Relay DTE)

DLCI = 52, DLCI USAGE = LOCAL, PVC STATUS = ACTIVE, INTERFACE = Serial0.1

  input pkts 843          output pkts 876         in bytes 122723
  out bytes 134431        dropped pkts 0          in FECN pkts 0
  in BECN pkts 0          out FECN pkts 0         out BECN pkts 0
  in DE pkts 0            out DE pkts 0
  out bcast pkts 876        out bcast bytes 134431
  pvc create time 05:20:10, last time pvc status changed 05:19:31
  --More--
DLCI = 53, DLCI USAGE = LOCAL, PVC STATUS = ACTIVE, INTERFACE = Serial0.2

  input pkts 0            output pkts 875         in bytes 0
  out bytes 142417        dropped pkts 0          in FECN pkts 0
  in BECN pkts 0          out FECN pkts 0         out BECN pkts 0
  in DE pkts 0            out DE pkts 0
  out bcast pkts 875        out bcast bytes 142417
  pvc create time 05:19:51, last time pvc status changed 04:55:41
  --More--
DLCI = 54, DLCI USAGE = LOCAL, PVC STATUS = ACTIVE, INTERFACE = Serial0.3

  input pkts 10           output pkts 877         in bytes 1274
  out bytes 142069        dropped pkts 0          in FECN pkts 0
  in BECN pkts 0          out FECN pkts 0         out BECN pkts 0
  in DE pkts 0            out DE pkts 0
  out bcast pkts 877        out bcast bytes 142069
  pvc create time 05:19:52, last time pvc status changed 05:17:42

Atlanta#show frame-relay map
Serial0.3 (up): point-to-point dlci, dlci 54(0x36,0xC60), broadcast
          status defined, active
Serial0.2 (up): point-to-point dlci, dlci 53(0x35,0xC50), broadcast
          status defined, active
Serial0.1 (up): point-to-point dlci, dlci 52(0x34,0xC40), broadcast
          status defined, active

Atlanta#debug frame-relay lmi
Frame Relay LMI debugging is on
Displaying all Frame Relay LMI data

Serial0(out): StEnq, myseq 163, yourseen 161, DTE up
datagramstart = 0x45AED8, datagramsize = 13
FR encap = 0xFCF10309
00 75 01 01 01 03 02 A3 A1

Serial0(in): Status, myseq 163
RT IE 1, length 1, type 1
KA IE 3, length 2, yourseq 162, myseq 163
```

Useful management information is held in the output of the **show frame-relay pvc** command. The counters for each VC, as well as increments in the FECN and BECN counters, can be particularly useful. Likewise, comparing the packets/bytes sent versus what is received on the other end of the VC is also quite useful, as it will reflect the number of packets/bytes lost inside the Frame Relay cloud. Also, seeing a PVC as active means that it is usable (as opposed to inactive), which is a great place to start when troubleshooting. All of this information may be better gathered by an SNMP manager.

The output of the **show frame-relay map** command is surprising after the discourse about mapping. A DLCI is listed in each entry, but no mention of corresponding Layer 3 addresses is made. However, because the subinterfaces are point-to-point, this omission by IOS is intended—the subinterface acts like a point-to-point link, with two participants. Mapping is needed only when there are more than two devices attached to the link. (See the section earlier in this chapter titled, "How Address Mapping Works," for more information.)

The **debug** output shows an indication of both sending and receiving LMI inquiries. The IOS **keepalive** setting does not cause packets to flow between routers, but rather causes the router to send LMI messages to the switch. It also causes the router to expect LMI messages from the switch.

Configuring Networks with Coexisting Point-to-Point and Multipoint Subinterfaces

Finally, the last sample network (based on the environment depicted in Figure 8-10) uses both point-to-point and multipoint subinterfaces. Example 8-13, Example 8-14, Example 8-15, Example 8-16, and Example 8-17 show the configuration for this network.

Example 8-13 *Router A Configuration*

```
hostname RouterA
!
ipx routing 0200.aaaa.aaaa
!
interface serial0
encapsulation frame-relay
!
interface serial 0.1 multipoint
ip address 140.1.1.1   255.255.255.0
ipx network 1
frame-relay interface-dlci 502
frame-relay interface-dlci 503
!
interface serial 0.2 point-to-point
ip address 140.1.2.1 255.255.255.0
ipx network 2
frame-relay interface-dlci 504
!
interface serial 0.3 point-to-point
ip address 140.1.3.1 255.255.255.0
ipx network 3
frame-relay interface-dlci 505
!
interface ethernet 0
ip address 140.1.11.1 255.255.255.0
ipx network 11
```

Example 8-14 *Router B Configuration*

```
hostname RouterB
!
ipx routing 0200.bbbb.bbbb
!
interface serial0
encapsulation frame-relay
!
interface serial 0.1 multipoint
ip address 140.1.1.2   255.255.255.0
ipx network 1
frame-relay interface-dlci 501
frame-relay interface-dlci 503
!
interface ethernet 0
ip address 140.1.12.2 255.255.255.0
ipx network 12
```

Example 8-15 *Router C Configuration*

```
hostname RouterC
!
ipx routing 0200.cccc.cccc
!
interface serial0
encapsulation frame-relay
!
interface serial 0.1 multipoint
ip address 140.1.1.3  255.255.255.0
ipx network 1
frame-relay interface-dlci 501
frame-relay interface-dlci 502
!
interface ethernet 0
ip address 140.1.13.3 255.255.255.0
ipx network 13
```

Example 8-16 *Router D Configuration*

```
hostname RouterD
!
ipx routing 0200.dddd.dddd
!
interface serial0
encapsulation frame-relay
!
interface serial 0.1 point-to-point
ip address 140.1.2.4  255.255.255.0
ipx network 2
frame-relay interface-dlci 501
!
interface ethernet 0
ip address 140.1.14.4 255.255.255.0
ipx network 14
```

Example 8-17 *Router E Configuration*

```
hostname RouterE
!
ipx routing 0200.eeee.eeee
!
interface serial0
encapsulation frame-relay
!
interface serial 0.1 point-to-point
ip address 140.1.3.5 255.255.255.0
ipx network 3
frame-relay interface-dlci 501
!
interface ethernet 0
ip address 140.1.15.5 255.255.255.0
ipx network 15
```

No mapping statements were required for the configuration in Example 8-13 through Example 8-17 because Inverse ARP is enabled on the multipoint subinterfaces by default. The point-to-point subinterfaces do not require mapping statements because after the outgoing subinterface is identified, there is only one possible router to which to forward the frame.

Router A is the only router using both multipoint and point-to-point subinterfaces. On Router A's serial 0.1, multipoint is in use, with DLCIs for Router B and Router C listed. On Router A's other two subinterfaces, which are point-to-point, only a single DLCI needs to be listed. Otherwise, the configurations between the two types are similar.

Example 8-18 shows the results of the Inverse ARP and a copy of the debugs showing the contents of the Inverse ARP. Although, not specifically covered in either Training Path 1 or 2, the debug on Example 8-18 provides some insight into inverse ARP operation.

Example 8-18 *Frame Relay Maps and Inverse ARP*

```
C#sh frame map
Serial0.10 (up): ip 140.1.1.1 dlci 501(0x1F5,0x7C50), dynamic,
             broadcast,, status defined, active
Serial0.10 (up): ip 140.1.1.2 dlci 502(0x1F6,0x7C60), dynamic,
             broadcast,, status defined, active
Serial0.10 (up): ipx 1.0200.aaaa.aaaa dlci 501(0x1F5,0x7C50), dynamic,
             broadcast,, status defined, active
Serial0.10 (up): ipx 1.0200.bbbb.bbbb dlci 502(0x1F6,0x7C60), dynamic,
             broadcast,, status defined, active

C#debug frame-relay events
Frame Relay events debugging is on

C#configure terminal
Enter configuration commands, one per line.  End with Ctrl-Z.
C(config)#interface serial 0.1
C(config-subif)#no shutdown
C(config-subif)#^Z
C#

Serial0.1: FR ARP input
Serial0.1: FR ARP input
Serial0.1: FR ARP input
datagramstart = 0xE42E58, datagramsize = 30
FR encap = 0x7C510300
80 00 00 00 08 06 00 0F 08 00 02 04 00 09 00 00
8C 01 01 01 7C 51 8C 01 01 03

datagramstart = 0xE427A0, datagramsize = 46
FR encap = 0x7C510300
80 00 00 00 08 06 00 0F 81 37 02 0A 00 09 00 00
00 00 00 01 02 00 AA AA AA AA 7C 51 00 00 00 01
02 00 CC CC CC CC 1B 99 D0 CC
```

continues

Example 8-18 *Frame Relay Maps and Inverse ARP (Continued)*

```
datagramstart = 0xE420E8, datagramsize = 30
FR encap = 0x7C610300
80 00 00 00 08 06 00 0F 08 00 02 04 00 09 00 00
8C 01 01 02 7C 61 8C 01 01 03

Serial0.1: FR ARP input
datagramstart = 0xE47188, datagramsize = 46
FR encap = 0x7C610300
80 00 00 00 08 06 00 0F 81 37 02 0A 00 09 00 00
00 00 00 01 02 00 BB BB BB BB 7C 61 00 00 00 01
02 00 CC CC CC CC 1B 99 D0 CC
```

The **show frame-relay map** command provides a full insight into mapping. The neighboring routers' IP and IPX addresses correlate to the DLCIs. This is possible because the Inverse ARP messages flow over a VC; the Inverse ARP contains a Layer 3 protocol type and address. The DLCI correlates to a subinterface based on configuration.

The Inverse ARP **debug** output is not so obvious. One easy exercise is to search for the hex version of the IP and IPX addresses in the output. These addresses have been italicized in Example 8-18. For example, the first three bytes of 140.1.1.0 are 8C 01 01 in hexadecimal; this field happens to start on the left side of the output, so it is easy to recognize visually. The IPX address should be much easier to recognize because it is already in hexadecimal format in the configuration.

NOTE   Enabling debug options increases the CPU utilization of the router. Depending on how much processing is required, and how many messages are generated, it is possible to significantly degrade performance and possibly crash the router. This is a result of memory and processing used to look for the requested information and to process the messages. You may want to first type the command **no debug all** and then type your debug command. If your debug creates too much output, the **no debug all** command can be easily retrieved (Ctrl-P twice).

If Inverse ARP was not used, the following **frame-relay map** statements would have been required on Router A (see Example 8-19). Similar commands would have been required on Routers B and C.

Example 8-19 *frame-relay map Commands*

```
frame-relay map ip 140.1.1.2 502 broadcast
frame-relay map ip 140.1.1.3 503 broadcast
frame-relay map ipx 1.0200.bbbb.bbbb 502 broadcast
frame-relay map ipx 1.0200.cccc.cccc 503 broadcast
```

ISDN Protocols and Design

CCNA Objectives Covered in This Section	
8	Differentiate between the following WAN services: Frame Relay, ISDN/LAPD, HDLC, & PPP.
13	State a relevant use and context for ISDN networking.
14	Identify ISDN protocols, function groups, reference points, and channels.

This section covers all the listed objectives, but features objective 14, which could be reworded as, "Describe everything about ISDN protocols and specifications." The goal of this section is to summarize the details and to clarify complex features of ISDN and related IOS functions.

ISDN Channels

Two types of ISDN interfaces are focused on in IOS documentation: Basic Rate Interface (BRI) and Primary Rate Interface (PRI). Both BRI and PRI provide multiple digital bearer channels over which temporary connections can be made and data can be sent. The result is digital dial access to multiple sites concurrently. (Both Training Paths and the objectives do not mention PRI at all.) Table 8-18 summarizes the features of BRI and PRI.

Table 8-18 *BRI and PRI Features*

Type of Interface	Number of Bearer Channels (B Channels)	Number of Signaling Channels (D Channels)
BRI	2	1 (16 kbps)
PRI (T/1)	23	1 (64 kbps)
PRI (E/1)	30	1 (64 kbps)

B-channels are used to transport data. B-channels are called bearer channels because they "bear the burden of transporting the data." The bearer channels (B channels) operate at up to 64 kbps. The speed might be lower depending on the service provider. The section "ISDN Configuration" later in the chapter discusses configuring the correct speed for the bearer channels. D channels are used for signaling.

ISDN Protocols

Coverage of ISDN protocols and their specifications on the CCNA poses a particularly difficult problem for the CCNA candidate. The International Telecommunications Union (ITU) defines the most well-known specifications for ISDN, but there are far more specifications than anyone would want to try to memorize. The problem is choosing what to memorize and what to ignore. The approach in this section will be to list those covered in the Training Paths and to give a few hints about how to better memorize some of the meanings.

The characterizations of several key protocols made by the Cisco CRLS course are important for the exam. Table 8-19 is directly quoted from the ICRC course. Take care to remember the "Issue" column—I would call it "function" or "purpose," but the gist of what each series of specifications is about will be useful.

Table 8-19 *ISDN Protocol Table from Cisco ICRC Course (Version 11.3)*

Issue	Protocols	Key Examples
Telephone network and ISDN	E-series	E.163—International Telephone numbering plan
		E.164—International ISDN addressing
ISDN concepts, aspects, and interfaces	I-series	I.100 series—Concepts, structures, terminology
		I.400 series—User-Network Interfaces (UNI)
Switching and signaling	Q-series	Q.921—LAPD
		Q.931—ISDN network layer

The OSI layers correlating to the different ISDN specifications is also mentioned in both the ITM and ICRC courses. Memorizing the specifications in Table 8-20 and the OSI layer each specification matches is also useful.

Table 8-20 *ISDN I and Q Series Mentioned in ICRC and ITM—OSI Layer Comparison*

Layer, as Compared to OSI	I Series	Equivalent Q Series Specification	General Purpose
1	ITU-T I.430		Defines connectors, encoding, framing, and reference points.
	ITU-T I.431		
2	ITU-T I.440[1]	ITU-T Q.920	Defines the Link Access Procedure on the D channel (LAPD) protocol used on the D channel to encapsulate signaling requests.
	ITU-T I.441[1]	ITU-T Q.921	
3	ITU-T I.450	ITU-T Q.930	Defines signaling messages, for example, call setup and takedown messages.
	ITU-T I.451	ITU-T Q.931	

1. Not mentioned directly in ITM or ICRC courses.

A tool to help you remember the specifications and layers is that the second digit in the Q series matches the OSI layer. For example, in ITU-T Q.920, the second digit, 2, corresponds to OSI Layer 2. In the I series, the second digit of the specification numbers is 2 more than the corresponding OSI layer. For example, I.430, with the second digit of value 3, defines OSI Layer 1 equivalent functions.

NOTE   It is unlikely that memorizing the names of these specifications will help you in ways other than being fully prepared for the CCNA exam. Personally, if I were running out of final preparation time for the CCNA exam, this would be a topic I would consider ignoring. It is unlikely that other Cisco exams will test you on these details, and in my opinion, there are many more important topics that Cisco will want to cover on your exam. Of course, that's just my opinion!

LAPD is used to deliver signaling messages to the ISDN switch, for example, a call setup message. Figure 8-14 shows the use of LAPD versus PPP on B channels.

Figure 8-14   *LAPD and PPP on D and B channels*

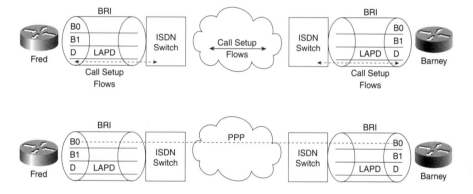

The call is established through the service provider network; PPP is used as the data-link protocol on the B channel from end-to-end. LAPD is used between the router and the ISDN switch at each local central office (CO) and remains up so that new signaling messages can be sent and received. Because the signals are sent outside the channel used for data, this is called *out-of-band signaling*.

The BRI encodes bits at 192 kbps, with most of the bandwidth (144 kbps) being used for the two B channels and the D channel. The additional bits are used for framing. The framing details and link speed could be considered to fall under CCNA objective 14. Call setup and takedown messages could also be considered to be addressed in objective 14. For further reading, refer to the ITM course, available from Cisco for a nominal fee. Also, several ISDN specifications are downloadable from http://www-library-itsi.disa.mil/org/ituccitt.html.

The service profile identifier (SPID) used in signaling is important to the configuration of ISDN and is likely to be mentioned on the exam. The SPID works like an ISDN phone number—in fact, if buying ISDN for home use, the service provider personnel will likely call it the *ISDN phone number* instead of SPID. Call setup messages refer to both the called and calling SPIDs. If a router wants to call another router, a SPID is used.

ISDN Function Groups and Reference Points

Many people are confused about the terms ISDN reference point and ISDN function group. One key reason for the confusion is that only some function groups, and therefore some reference points, are used in a single topology. In an effort to clear up these two topics, consider the following inexact but more familiar definitions of the two:

- **Function groups**—A set of functions implemented by a device and software.

- **Reference points**—The interface between two function groups; includes cabling details.

Most of us understand concepts better if we can visualize a network or actually implement the network. However, for a good understanding of function groups and reference points, keep the following facts in mind:

- Not all reference points are used in any one topology; in fact, one or two may never be used in a particular part of the world.

- After the equipment is ordered and working, there is no need to think about function groups and reference points.

- The router configuration does not refer to reference points and function groups, so many of us ignore these details.

NOTE   Function group is a term used by Cisco, but is not necessarily in popular use outside Cisco. CCNA objective 14 uses the term. Therefore, for consistency, it is used here.

A cabling diagram is helpful for examining the reference points and the function groups. Figure 8-15 shows the cabling diagram for several examples.

Figure 8-15 *ISDN Function Groups and Reference Points*

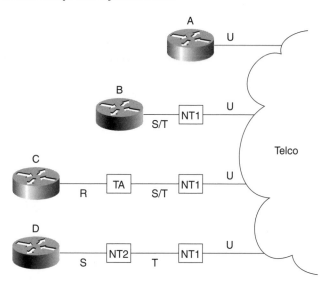

Router A was ordered with an ISDN BRI "U" reference point, referring to the I.430 reference point defining the interface between the customer premise and the telco in North America. Router B was bought with an ISDN BRI "S/T" interface, implying that it must be cabled to a function group NT1 device in North America. An NT1 function group device must be connected to the telco line (North America); the S/T interface defines the connection to Router B. Router B is called a TE1 (Terminal Equipment 1) function group device. Finally, non-ISDN equipment is called a TE2 (Terminal Equipment 2) device and is attached, using the R reference point, to a Terminal Adapter (TA) function group device.

Table 8-21 summarizes the types from Figure 8-15. Table 8-22 and Table 8-23 provide a summary of formal definitions.

Table 8-21 *Figure 8-15 Function Groups and Reference Point Summary*

Router	Function Group(s)	Connected to Reference Point(s)
A	TE1, NT1	U
B	TE1	S/T (combined S and T)
C	TE2	R
D	TE1	S

Table 8-22   *Definitions for Function Groups in Figure 8-15*

Function Group	Acronym Stands For...	Description
TE1	Terminal Equipment 1	ISDN capable. 4 wire cable. Understands signaling, 2B+D. Uses S reference point.
TE2	Terminal Equipment 2	Does not understand ISDN protocols and specifications. Uses R reference point, typically an RS-232 or V.35 cable, to connect to a TA.
TA	Terminal Adapter	Uses R reference point and S reference point. Can be thought of as the TE1 function group on behalf of a TE2.
NT1	Network Termination Type 1	CPE equipment in North America. Connects with U reference point (2 wire) to telco. Connects with T or S reference point to other customer premise equipment.
NT2	Network Termination Type 2	Uses a T reference point to the telco outside North America, or to an NT1 inside North America. Uses an S reference point to connect to other customer premise equipment.
NT1/NT2		Combined NT1 and NT2 in the same device. This is relatively common in North America.

Table 8-23   *Definitions for Reference Points in Figure 8-15*

Reference Point	Connection Between
R	TE2 and TA
S	TE1 or TA and NT2
T	NT2 and NT1
U	NT1 and telco
S/T	TE1 or TA and NT1, when no NT2 is used, or NT1/NT2 is used

Jargon definitely confuses the issue with home ISDN services. Figure 8-16 outlines the problem.

Figure 8-16 *Home ISDN User and Reference Points*

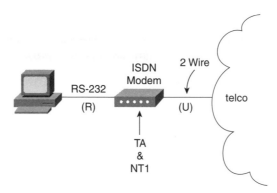

Popularly used, ISDN terminology for home-based consumers sometimes obfuscates the terminology from the ISDN specifications. The home user orders the service and the telco offers to sell the user one of several "ISDN modems." What is actually received is a TA and NT1 in one device. A PC uses a serial port to connect to the TA, which uses reference point R. But the terms reference point, TA, and NT1 are almost never used by providers; hence the confusion.

One other detail of the ISDN protocols that may be on the exam is the ISDN S-bus. The ISDN S-bus allows multiple devices to share the same BRI by sharing the S reference point. S-bus is a great idea, but it has not been deployed extensively. S-bus takes the S reference point and allows multiple TE1s to connect to the same NT1. This enables multiple TE1s to use the same BRI. If all the TE1s were data devices, then instead of using an S-bus, placing all TE1s on a LAN and using an ISDN-capable router will probably be a better solution. But to support ISDN phones, fax, video, and data TE1 devices, the S-bus can be used. Figure 8-17 shows a basic S-bus topology.

Figure 8-17 *ISDN S-Bus*

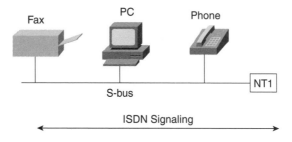

ISDN signaling can be created by the TE1s and responded to by TE1s. However, because the BRI is shared amongst the TE1s, the SPID received in a call setup request no longer uniquely identifies the TE1. Therefore, a suffix is added to the SPID, called a *subaddress*. Each TE1 on the S-Bus uses a different subaddress. The service provider connected to this NT1 and to any other NT1 from which calls are set up must support subaddressing before the user can use S-Bus.

Relevant Use of ISDN

This section is an overt attempt to address CCNA objective 13. My interpretation of that objective is, "When does it make sense to use ISDN?" For thoroughness, a few opinions about when ISDN is useful follow.

Occasional connections from a computer to a network can be accommodated by a variety of dial services, ISDN included. ISDN lines can provide access at 128 kbps, using both B channels. Compression can increase throughput, potentially getting .5 Mbps of throughput through the line. Compared to other options at the time of writing this book, ISDN, with all these options enabled, is probably the best option for fast, occasional access. In the future, *x*DSL technologies may change this environment for dial-in Internet service providers (ISPs).

Connections between routers are another relevant use of ISDN, both for backup and for occasional connection. Backup is self-explanatory. Occasional connections would include traffic for sites that do not use online applications or video conferencing and cases where additional bandwidth between sites is desired. Most of the configuration needed for these occasional connections is related to a topic called *Dial-on-Demand* routing, which is not covered on the CCNA exam, nor in this book. Figure 8-18 shows these typical scenarios.

Figure 8-18 *Typical Occasional Connections between Routers*

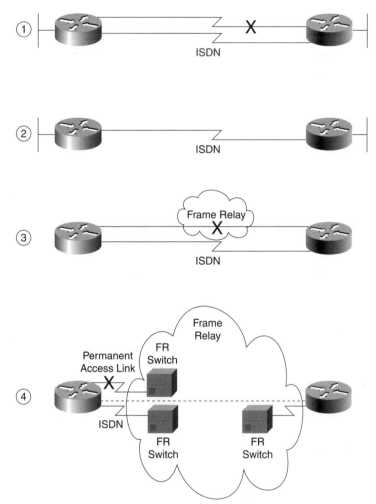

The scenarios in Figure 8-18 can be described as follows:

- Case 1 shows the typical dial-backup topology. The leased line fails, so an ISDN call is established between the same two routers.

- Case 2 shows true occasional access. Logic is configured in the routers to trigger the dial when the traffic needing to get to another site is sent by the user.

- Case 3 shows where an ISDN BRI could be used to dial into a Frame Relay switch to replace a Frame Relay access link or failed VC.

- Case 4 depicts an ISDN line that could be used to dial into the Frame Relay provider's network, replacing a failed VC or access link with a VC running over an ISDN connection to the Frame Relay switch.

PAP and CHAP

PPP and HDLC can be used on B channels, but PPP provides several features that make it the preferred choice in a dial environment. HDLC and PPP overhead per data frame is identical; however, PPP provides LQM, CHAP, and PAP authentication and Layer 3 address assignment through several of the control protocols. Each of these features is particularly important in a dial environment.

Password Authentication Protocol (PAP) and Challenge Handshake Authentication Protocol (CHAP) are used to authenticate (verify) that the endpoints on a dial connection are allowed to connect. CHAP is the preferred method today because the identifying codes flow encrypted over the link, whereas PAP identifying codes do not.

NOTE   PAP and CHAP are used for authentication over dial lines. These topics could be covered on the CCNA exam because Cisco broadly interprets objective 15.

Both PAP and CHAP require the exchange of messages between devices. The dialed-to router expects to receive a username and password from the dialing router with both PAP and CHAP. With PAP, the username and password are sent by the dialing router. With CHAP, the dialed-to router sends a message (challenge!) that asks the dialing router to send its username and password. The challenge includes a random number, which is part of the input into the encryption algorithm. The dialing router replies with an encrypted value, which is then unencrypted by the dialed-to router to yield the name and password. Figure 8-19 illustrates the message flow in PAP and CHAP environments. Example 8-20 shows the CHAP configuration for Figure 8-19.

Figure 8-19 *PAP and CHAP Messages*

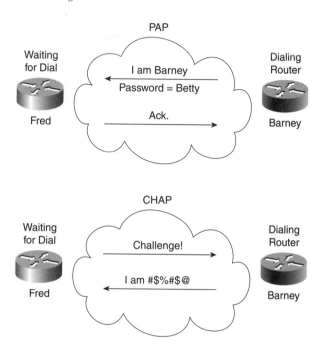

Example 8-20 *CHAP Configuration Sample*

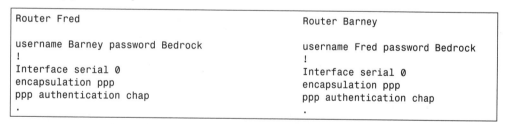

```
Router Fred                              Router Barney

username Barney password Bedrock         username Fred password Bedrock
!                                        !
Interface serial 0                       Interface serial 0
encapsulation ppp                        encapsulation ppp
ppp authentication chap                  ppp authentication chap
.                                        .
```

Notice that each router refers to the other router's hostname; each router uses its own hostname in CHAP flows unless overridden by configuration. Each codes the same password. When Router Barney receives a challenge from Router Fred, Router Barney sends an encrypted value that Router Fred can unencrypt into the name "Barney" and the password "Bedrock." Fred's username command lists both values; if these are identical matches, then CHAP authentication is completed.

Multilink PPP

Multilink PPP is a function that allows multiple links between a router and some other device, over which traffic is balanced. The need for this function is straightforward; some other considerations about when to use it are subtle. Multilink PPP is mainly included in this book because it can fall under objective 13 as a relevant use of ISDN. For the exam, focus on the concept because Training Paths 1 and 2 mention the concept; they do not cover configuration or the background concepts about routing with fast switching. These details are covered in the upcoming paragraphs and figures.

Figure 8-20 illustrates the most obvious need for Multilink PPP.

Figure 8-20 *Multilink PPP for Dial-In Device*

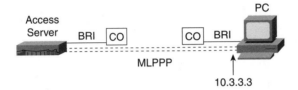

For faster service, the PC that has dialed in would want to use both B channels and use them efficiently. Figure 8-20 shows two dotted lines between the PC and access server, signifying that two B-channels are in use between the devices. Multilink PPP takes a packet, breaks it into fragments, sends some fragments across each of the two links, and reassembles them at the other end of the link. The net result is that the links are utilized approximately the same amount.

Multilink PPP is also useful between routers. For example, in Figure 8-21, video conferencing between Atlanta and Nashville uses six B channels between two routers.

Figure 8-21 *Multiple B Channels between Routers*

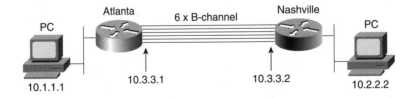

In this example, if Multilink PPP is used, the links have almost identical utilization. The negative is that the routers have to fragment and reassemble every packet. However, the 384 Kb needed for the video conference is available.

But consider the alternative—without multilink PPP, but simply PPP on each of the six links. Six routes to subnet 10.2.2.0/24 would exist in Router A's routing table. With any of the faster internal switching methods in a Cisco router (fast switching, optimum switching, NetFlow switching), the balancing effect is that *all packets to the same IP address use the same link*. The result is that router Atlanta sends some packets over one link and some over the other, but the balancing is unpredictable. But more important, all packets to the video conference system's single IP address in Nashville will use the same link—effectively limiting the video conference to 64 Kbps! An alternative is to disable the faster switching methods in the router so that multiple routes to the same subnet are used in a round-robin fashion. However, that is not recommended because it significantly slows the internal processing on the router. For that reason, multilink PPP is a better choice in this case.

Figure 8-21 shows a sample multilink PPP configuration. The Atlanta and Nashville routers will use two B channels of the same BRI.

Example 8-21 *Multilink PPP Configuration for Atlanta*

```
username Nashville password Robert
interface bri 0
ip addr 10.3.3.1 255.255.255.0
encapsulation ppp
dialer idle-timeout 300
dialer load-threshold 25 either
dialer map 10.3.3.2 name Nashville 1615555123401
dialer-group 1
ppp authentication chap
ppp multilink
```

The two key commands are the **ppp multilink** and the **dialer load-threshold** commands. **ppp multilink** enables multilink PPP; **dialer load-threshold** tells the router to dial another B channel if the utilization average on the currently used links should be more than 25 percent for either inbound or outbound utilization.

ISDN Configuration

CCNA Objectives Covered in This Section

15	Describe Cisco's implementation of ISDN BRI.

The interpretation of the CCNA objectives allows some ambiguity about whether ISDN configuration is included on the exam. Objective 15 could be interpreted to imply ISDN configuration, but I believe that ISDN configuration is unlikely to be on the exam. Of course, always check Cisco's Web site for possible changes to the objectives and then refer to the Cisco Press Web site for my comments on what additional preparation you may need!

Dial-on-demand Routing (DDR) configuration and concepts need to be understood before the ISDN configuration topics will make complete sense. DDR defines the logic behind when a router chooses to dial another site, including when ISDN is used. However, DDR is not on the

CCNA exam. This book will concentrate then on the few ISDN configuration statements needed in addition to DDR.

One detail that may more closely match the objectives is the use of certain reference points by Cisco's products. Cisco's BRI implementation includes a choice of an S/T interface or a U interface. In either case, BRI configuration in the router is identical.

The commands in this section would be used in conjunction with DDR to make the ISDN interface useful. Table 8-24 and Table 8-25 list the ISDN configuration and EXEC commands that are covered in Training Paths 1 and 2.

Table 8-24 *ISDN Configuration Commands in Training Paths 1 and 2*

Command	Configuration Mode	Purpose
isdn switch-type *switch-type*	Global	Defines to the router the type of ISDN switch that the ISDN line is connected to at the central office.
isdn spid1 *spid*	Interface	Defines the first SPID.
isdn spid2 *spid*	Interface	Defines the second SPID.
isdn caller *spid*	Interface	Defines valid SPIDs for incoming calls when using call screening.
isdn answer1 *spid:sub*	Interface	Specifies the ISDN subaddress that must be used on incoming calls for this router to answer.
isdn answer2 *spid:sub*	Interface	Specifies a second subadress that must be used on incoming calls for the router to answer.
dialer map... speed 48|56|64	Interface	Specifies the speed of a bearer channel.

Table 8-25 *ISDN Related EXEC Commands in Training Paths 1 and 2*

Command	Function
show interfaces bri *number*[*:b-channel*]	Includes reference to the access lists enabled on the interface.
show controllers bri *number*	Shows Layer 1 statistics and status for B and D channels.

Example 8-22 and Example 8-23 demonstrate the use of most of the commands listed in Table 8-24 and Table 8-25. The Smallville and Metropolis routers from the Marvel Comics network are used, and a complete configuration, including DDR configuration, is shown. Figure 8-22 provides the network diagram.

Figure 8-22 *Marvel Network ISDN Details*

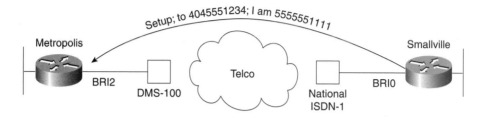

Example 8-22 *Smallville Configuration with ISDN Details Added*

```
hostname Smallville
!
ip route 172.16.3.0 255.255.255.0 172.16.2.1
ip route 172.16.4.0 255.255.255.0 172.16.2.3
!
isdn switch-type basic-ni1
!
username Metropolis password Clark
username GothamCity password Bruce
!
access-list 101 permit tcp any host 172.16.3.1 eq 80
access-list 101 permit tcp any host 172.16.4.1 eq 21
!
dialer-list 2 protocol ip list 101
!
!!!!!!!!!!!!!!!!!!!!!!!!!!!!!!!!!!!!!!!!!!!!!!!!!!!!!!!!!!!!!!!!!!!!!!!!!!!!
! ISDN Commands next
!
interface bri 0
!
! New commands here!
!
isdn spid1 555555111101
isdn spid2 555555222202
!
! end of ISDN interface subcommands. DDR, PPP, and CHAP next.
!!!!!!!!!!!!!!!!!!!!!!!!!!!!!!!!!!!!!!!!!!!!!!!!!!!!!!!!!!!!!!!!!!!!!!!!!!!!
encapsulation ppp
ppp authentication chap
dialer idle-timeout 300
dialer fast-idle 120
dialer in-band
!
! New parameter in the next statement
!
dialer map ip 172.16.2.1 broadcast speed 56 name Metropolis 1404555123401
dialer map ip 172.16.2.3 broadcast name GothamCity 1999999999901
!
dialer-group 2
!
router igrp 6
network 172.16.0.0
```

Example 8-23 *Metropolis Configuration—Receive Only, with ISDN Details Added*

```
hostname Metropolis
!
isdn switch-type basic-dms100
!
username Smallville password Clark
!
!!!!!!!!!!!!!!!!!!!!!!!!!!!!!!!!!!!!!!!!!!!!!!!!!!!!!!!!!!!!!!!!!!!!!!!!!!
! ISDN Commands next
!
interface bri 0
!
! New commands here!
!
isdn spid1 404555123401
isdn spid2 404555567802
isdn caller 555555111101
!
! end of ISDN interface subcommands. DDR, PPP, and CHAP next.
!!!!!!!!!!!!!!!!!!!!!!!!!!!!!!!!!!!!!!!!!!!!!!!!!!!!!!!!!!!!!!!!!!!!!!!!!!
!
encapsulation ppp
ppp authentication chap
dialer in-band
!
router igrp 6
network 172.16.0.0
```

The ISDN configuration commands are delineated in the examples via comment lines; those commands are described in the upcoming text. For example, the switch types are a required parameter; ask your service provider for the type of switch at each site. The SPIDs are only required for two types of switches, which happen to be the two types shown in Example 8-22 and Example 8-23, so the SPIDs are configured in each example. The **isdn caller** command establishes call screening; if Smallville's SPID is not 555555111101, then the call setup message received by Metropolis is rejected. Also, hidden in part of the DDR configuration, the speed of the B channel from Smallville to Metropolis will be 56 kbps, according to the speed parameter in the **dialer map** command on Smallville.

Q&A

As mentioned in Chapter 1, the questions and scenarios are more difficult than what you should experience on the actual exam. The questions do not attempt to cover more breadth or depth than the exam; however, the questions are designed to make sure you know the answer. Rather than allowing you to derive the answer from clues hidden inside the question itself, your understanding and recall of the subject will be challenged. Questions from the "Do I Know This Already?" quiz from the beginning of the chapter are repeated here to ensure that you have mastered the chapter's topic areas. Hopefully, these questions will help limit the number of exam questions on which you narrow your choices to two options, and then guess!

1. Name two WAN data-link protocols for which the standards define a protocol-type field, which is used to define the type of header that follows after the WAN data-link header.

2. Name two WAN data-link protocols that define a method of announcing the Layer 3 addresses of the interface to other devices attached to the WAN.

3. What does the acronym LAPD stand for? Is it used as the Layer 2 protocol on dialed ISDN bearer channels? If not, what is used?

4. "Frame Relay uses source and destination DLCIs in the Frame Relay header, with length 10, 11, or 12 bits." Which parts of this statement do you agree with? Which parts do you disagree with? Why?

5. Explain the purpose of Inverse ARP. Explain how Inverse ARP uses Frame Relay broadcasts.

6. Would a Frame Relay switch connected to a router behave differently if the IETF option were deleted from the **encapsulation frame-relay ietf** command on that attached router? Would a router on the other end of the VC behave any differently if the same change were made?

7. What does NBMA stand for? Does it apply to PPP links? X.25 networks? Frame Relay networks?

8. Define the terms DCE and DTE in the context of the physical layer and a point-to-point serial link.

9. What layer of OSI is most closely related to the functions of Frame Relay? Why?

10. When Inverse ARP is used by default, what additional configuration is needed to get IGRP routing updates to flow over each VC?

11. Define the attributes of a partial-mesh and full-mesh Frame Relay network.

12. What key pieces of information are required in the **frame-relay map** statement?

13. When creating a partial-mesh Frame Relay network, are you required to use subinterfaces?

14. What benefit related to routing protocols can be gained by using subinterfaces with a partial mesh?

15. Can PPP perform dynamic assignment of IP addresses? If so, is the feature always enabled?

16. Create a configuration to enable PPP on serial 0 for IP and IPX. Make up IP and IPX Layer 3 addresses as needed.

17. Create a configuration for Router1 that has Frame Relay VCs to Router2 and Router3 (DLCIs 202 and 203, respectively), for Frame Relay on Router1's serial 1 interface. Use any IP and IPX addresses you like. Assume the network is not fully-meshed.

18. What **show** command will tell you the time that a PVC became active? How does the router know what time the PVC came active?

19. What **show** commands list Frame Relay information about mapping? In what instances will the information displayed include the Layer 3 addresses of other routers?

20. The **no keepalive** command on a Frame Relay serial interface causes no further Cisco proprietary keepalive messages to be sent to the Frame Relay switch. (T/F)

21. What **debug** options will show Inverse ARP messages?

22. The Frame Relay **map** configuration command allows more than one Layer 3 protocol address mapping on the same configuration command. (T/F)

23. What do the letters in ISDN represent? BRI? PRI?

24. Define the term *function group* as used in CCNA exam objective 14. List two examples of function groups.

25. Define the term *reference point* as used in CCNA exam objective 14: Identify ISDN protocols, function groups, reference points, and channels. List two examples of reference points.

26. How many bearer channels are in a BRI? A PRI in North America? A PRI in Europe?

27. Is the following statement true or false: "ISDN defines protocols that can be functionally equivalent to OSI Layers 1, 2, and 3." Defend your answer.

28. What reference points are used by ISDN BRI interfaces on Cisco routers?

29. What do the letters LAPD represent? Is LAPD used on ISDN channels, and if so, which ones?

30. Name the standards body that defines ISDN protocols.

31. What ISDN functions do standards ITU-T Q.920 and Q.930 define? Does either standard correlate to an OSI layer?

32. What ISDN functions does standard ITU-T I.430 define? Does it correlate to an OSI layer?

33. What do the letters SPID represent, and what does the term mean?

34. Define the terms TE1, TE2, and TA. Which term(s) imply that one of the other two must be in use?

35. What reference point is used between the customer premise and the phone company in North America? In Europe?

36. Define the term *S-Bus* and give one example of when it would be useful.

37. What data-link (OSI Layer 2) protocols are valid on an ISDN B-channel?

38. Define the terms PAP and CHAP. Which one(s) encrypt passwords before transmission?

39. Define MLPPP. Describe the typical home or small office use of MLPPP.

40. CHAP configuration uses names and passwords. Given Routers A and B, describe what names and passwords must match in the respective CHAP configurations.

41. Configure ISDN interface BRI1 assuming that it is attached to a DMS-100 ISDN switch, it uses only one SPID of 404555121201, and you want to screen calls so that only calls from 404555999901 are accepted.

Scenarios

Scenario 8-1: Point-to-Point Verification

Use Example 8-24, Example 8-25, and Example 8-26 when completing the exercises and answering the questions that follow.

Example 8-24 *Albuquerque Command Output, Scenario 8-1*

```
Albuquerque#show ip interface brief
Interface          IP-Address      OK? Method Status              Protocol
Serial0            199.1.1.129     YES NVRAM  up                  up
Serial1            199.1.1.193     YES NVRAM  up                  up
Ethernet0          199.1.1.33      YES NVRAM  up                  up

Albuquerque#show ip route
Codes: C - connected, S - static, I - IGRP, R - RIP, M - mobile, B - BGP
       D - EIGRP, EX - EIGRP external, O - OSPF, IA - OSPF inter area
       N1 - OSPF NSSA external type 1, N2 - OSPF NSSA external type 2
       E1 - OSPF external type 1, E2 - OSPF external type 2, E - EGP
       i - IS-IS, L1 - IS-IS level-1, L2 - IS-IS level-2, * - candidate default
       U - per-user static route, o - ODR

Gateway of last resort is not set

     199.1.1.0/24 is variably subnetted, 7 subnets, 2 masks
C       199.1.1.192/27 is directly connected, Serial1
C       199.1.1.130/32 is directly connected, Serial0
C       199.1.1.128/27 is directly connected, Serial0
I       199.1.1.160/27 [100/10476] via 199.1.1.130, 00:00:01, Serial0
                       [100/10476] via 199.1.1.194, 00:00:54, Serial1
I       199.1.1.64/27 [100/8539] via 199.1.1.130, 00:00:01, Serial0
I       199.1.1.96/27 [100/8539] via 199.1.1.194, 00:00:54, Serial1
C       199.1.1.32/27 is directly connected, Ethernet0

Albuquerque#show ipx route
Codes: C - Connected primary network,    c - Connected secondary network
       S - Static, F - Floating static, L - Local (internal), W - IPXWAN
       R - RIP, E - EIGRP, N - NLSP, X - External, A - Aggregate
       s - seconds, u - uses

6 Total IPX routes. Up to 1 parallel paths and 16 hops allowed.

No default route known.

C       1001 (SAP),        E0
C       2001 (PPP),        Se0
C       2003 (HDLC),       Se1
R       1002 [07/01] via   2001.0200.bbbb.bbbb,   50s, Se0
R       1003 [07/01] via   2003.0200.cccc.cccc,   57s, Se1
```

Example 8-24 *Albuquerque Command Output, Scenario 8-1 (Continued)*

```
R        2002 [07/01] via      2001.0200.bbbb.bbbb,   51s, Se0

Albuquerque#debug ppp negotiation
PPP protocol negotiation debugging is on

%LINK-3-UPDOWN: Interface Serial0, changed state to up

Se0 PPP: Treating connection as a dedicated line
Se0 PPP: Phase is ESTABLISHING, Active Open
Se0 LCP: O CONFREQ [Closed] id 15 len 10
Se0 LCP:    MagicNumber 0x003C2A1F (0x0506003C2A1F)
Se0 LCP: I CONFREQ [REQsent] id 34 len 10
Se0 LCP:    MagicNumber 0x0648CFD3 (0x05060648CFD3)
Se0 LCP: O CONFACK [REQsent] id 34 len 10
Se0 LCP:    MagicNumber 0x0648CFD3 (0x05060648CFD3)
Se0 LCP: TIMEout: Time = 0xBA0E0 State = ACKsent
Se0 LCP: O CONFREQ [ACKsent] id 16 len 10
Se0 LCP:    MagicNumber 0x003C2A1F (0x0506003C2A1F)
Se0 LCP: I CONFACK [ACKsent] id 16 len 10
Se0 LCP:    MagicNumber 0x003C2A1F (0x0506003C2A1F)
Se0 LCP: State is Open
Se0 PPP: Phase is UP
Se0 IPCP: O CONFREQ [Closed] id 3 len 10
Se0 IPCP:    Address 199.1.1.129 (0x0306C7010181)
Se0 CDPCP: O CONFREQ [Closed] id 3 len 4
Se0 LLC2CP: O CONFREQ [Closed] id 3 len 4
Se0 IPXCP: O CONFREQ [Closed] id 3 len 18
Se0 IPXCP:    Network 0x00002001 (0x010600002001)
Se0 IPXCP:    Node 0200.aaaa.aaaa (0x02080200AAAAAAAA)
Se0 IPCP: I CONFREQ [REQsent] id 4 len 10
Se0 IPCP:    Address 199.1.1.130 (0x0306C7010182)
Se0 IPCP: O CONFACK [REQsent] id 4 len 10
Se0 IPCP:    Address 199.1.1.130 (0x0306C7010182)
Se0 CDPCP: I CONFREQ [REQsent] id 6 len 4
Se0 CDPCP: O CONFACK [REQsent] id 6 len 4
Se0 LLC2CP: I CONFREQ [REQsent] id 6 len 4
Se0 LLC2CP: O CONFACK [REQsent] id 6 len 4
Se0 IPXCP: I CONFREQ [REQsent] id 4 len 18
Se0 IPXCP:    Network 0x00002001 (0x010600002001)
Se0 IPXCP:    Node 0200.bbbb.bbbb (0x02080200BBBBBBBB)
Se0 IPXCP: O CONFACK [REQsent] id 4 len 18
Se0 IPXCP:    Network 0x00002001 (0x010600002001)
Se0 IPXCP:    Node 0200.bbbb.bbbb (0x02080200BBBBBBBB)
```

Example 8-25 *Yosemite Command Output, Scenario 8-1*

```
Yosemite#show ipx interface brief
Interface        IPX Network Encapsulation Status        IPX State
Serial0          2001        PPP           up            [up]
Serial1          2002        LAPB          up            [up]
```

continues

Example 8-25 *Yosemite Command Output, Scenario 8-1 (Continued)*

```
Ethernet0           1002        SAP             up                    [up]

Yosemite#show ipx route
Codes: C - Connected primary network,   c - Connected secondary network
       S - Static, F - Floating static, L - Local (internal), W - IPXWAN
       R - RIP, E - EIGRP, N - NLSP, X - External, A - Aggregate
       s - seconds, u - uses

6 Total IPX routes. Up to 1 parallel paths and 16 hops allowed.

No default route known.

C       1002 (SAP),          E0
C       2001 (PPP),          Se0
C       2002 (LAPB),         Se1
R       1001 [07/01] via     2001.0200.aaaa.aaaa,   46s, Se0
R       1003 [13/02] via     2001.0200.aaaa.aaaa,   47s, Se0
R       2003 [07/01] via     2001.0200.aaaa.aaaa,   47s, Se0

Yosemite#show interface serial 1 accounting
Serial1
                   Protocol   Pkts In   Chars In   Pkts Out   Chars Out
                        IP        37       2798         41        3106

Yosemite#ping ipx 2002.0200.cccc.cccc

Type escape sequence to abort.
Sending 5, 100-byte IPX Cisco Echoes to 2002.0200.cccc.cccc, timeout is 2 seconds:
.....
Success rate is 0 percent (0/5)

Yosemite#ping 199.1.1.162

Type escape sequence to abort.
Sending 5, 100-byte ICMP Echos to 199.1.1.162, timeout is 2 seconds:
!!!!!
Success rate is 100 percent (5/5), round-trip min/avg/max = 8/8/8 ms

Yosemite#ping ipx 1003.0000.30ac.70ef

Type escape sequence to abort.
Sending 5, 100-byte IPX Cisco Echoes to 1003.0000.30ac.70ef, timeout is 2 seconds:
!!!!!
Success rate is 100 percent (5/5), round-trip min/avg/max = 8/8/12 ms
```

Example 8-26 *Seville Command Output, Scenario 8-1*

```
Seville#show ip route
Codes: C - connected, S - static, I - IGRP, R - RIP, M - mobile, B - BGP
       D - EIGRP, EX - EIGRP external, O - OSPF, IA - OSPF inter area
       N1 - OSPF NSSA external type 1, N2 - OSPF NSSA external type 2
       E1 - OSPF external type 1, E2 - OSPF external type 2, E - EGP
       i - IS-IS, L1 - IS-IS level-1, L2 - IS-IS level-2, * - candidate default
       U - per-user static route, o - ODR

Gateway of last resort is not set

     199.1.1.0/27 is subnetted, 6 subnets
C       199.1.1.192 is directly connected, Serial0
I       199.1.1.128 [100/10476] via 199.1.1.161, 00:00:36, Serial1
                    [100/10476] via 199.1.1.193, 00:01:09, Serial0
C       199.1.1.160 is directly connected, Serial1
I       199.1.1.64 [100/8539] via 199.1.1.161, 00:00:36, Serial1
C       199.1.1.96 is directly connected, Ethernet0
I       199.1.1.32 [100/8539] via 199.1.1.193, 00:01:09, Serial0

Seville#show ipx route
Codes: C - Connected primary network,   c - Connected secondary network
       S - Static, F - Floating static, L - Local (internal), W - IPXWAN
       R - RIP, E - EIGRP, N - NLSP, X - External, A - Aggregate
       s - seconds, u - uses

6 Total IPX routes. Up to 1 parallel paths and 16 hops allowed.

No default route known.

C       1003 (SAP),        E0
C       2002 (LAPB),       Se1
C       2003 (HDLC),       Se0
R       1001 [07/01] via   2003.0200.aaaa.aaaa,   2s, Se0
R       1002 [13/02] via   2003.0200.aaaa.aaaa,   2s, Se0
R       2001 [07/01] via   2003.0200.aaaa.aaaa,   2s, Se0

Seville#show interface serial 0 accounting
Serial0
                Protocol   Pkts In   Chars In   Pkts Out   Chars Out
                      IP        44       3482         40        3512
                     IPX        46       3478         44        2710
                     CDP        21       6531         26        7694

Seville#debug lapb
LAPB link debugging is on

%LINK-3-UPDOWN: Interface Serial1, changed state to up

Serial1: LAPB O SABMSENT (2) SABM P
```

continues

Example 8-26 *Seville Command Output, Scenario 8-1 (Continued)*

```
Serial1: LAPB I SABMSENT (2) UA F
Serial1: LAPB I CONNECT (104) IFRAME 0 0
Serial1: LAPB O CONNECT (76) IFRAME 0 1Serial1: LAPB I CONNECT (76) IFRAME 1 1
Serial1: LAPB O CONNECT (2) RR (R) 2
Seville#
Seville#ping 199.1.1.161


Type escape sequence to abort.
Sending 5, 100-byte ICMP Echos to 199.1.1.161, timeout is 2 seconds:
!!!!!
Success rate is 100 percent (5/5), round-trip min/avg/max = 8/8/12 ms
Seville#
Serial1: LAPB O CONNECT (102) IFRAME 1 3
Serial1: LAPB I CONNECT (102) IFRAME 3 2
Serial1: LAPB O CONNECT (2) RR (R) 4
Serial1: LAPB O CONNECT (102) IFRAME 2 4
Serial1: LAPB I CONNECT (102) IFRAME 4 3
Serial1: LAPB O CONNECT (2) RR (R) 5
Serial1: LAPB O CONNECT (102) IFRAME 3 5
Serial1: LAPB I CONNECT (2) RR (R) 4
Serial1: LAPB I CONNECT (102) IFRAME 5 4
Serial1: LAPB O CONNECT (2) RR (R) 6
Serial1: LAPB O CONNECT (102) IFRAME 4 6
Serial1: LAPB I CONNECT (102) IFRAME 6 5
Serial1: LAPB O CONNECT (2) RR (R) 7
Serial1: LAPB O CONNECT (102) IFRAME 5 7
Serial1: LAPB I CONNECT (102) IFRAME 7 6
Serial1: LAPB O CONNECT (2) RR (R) 0
```

Assuming the details established in Example 8-24 through Example 8-26 for Scenario 8-1, complete or answer the following:

1. Create a diagram for the network.

2. Complete Table 8-26.

Table 8-26 *Layer 3 Addresses on the PPP Serial Links*

Router	Serial Port	Encapsulation	IP Address	IPX Address
Albuquerque	s0			
Albuquerque	s1			
Yosemite	s0			
Yosemite	s1			
Seville	s0			
Seville	s1			

3. Why are there seven IP routes in Albuquerque and Yosemite, and only six in Seville?

Scenario 8-2: Frame Relay Verification

Use Example 8-27, Example 8-28, Example 8-29, and Example 8-30 when completing the exercises and answering the questions that follow.

Example 8-27 *Atlanta Command Output, Scenario 8-2*

```
Atlanta#show interface s 0
Serial0 is up, line protocol is up
  Hardware is HD64570
  MTU 1500 bytes, BW 1544 Kbit, DLY 20000 usec, rely 255/255, load 1/255
  Encapsulation FRAME-RELAY, loopback not set, keepalive set (10 sec)
  LMI enq sent  32, LMI stat recvd 32, LMI upd recvd 0, DTE LMI up
  LMI enq recvd 0, LMI stat sent  0, LMI upd sent  0
  LMI DLCI 1023  LMI type is CISCO  frame relay DTE
  Broadcast queue 0/64, broadcasts sent/dropped 75/0, interface broadcasts 59
  Last input 00:00:00, output 00:00:07, output hang never
  Last clearing of "show interface" counters never
  Queueing strategy: fifo
  Output queue 0/40, 0 drops; input queue 0/75, 0 drops
  5 minute input rate 0 bits/sec, 0 packets/sec
  5 minute output rate 0 bits/sec, 0 packets/sec
     74 packets input, 5697 bytes, 0 no buffer
     Received 32 broadcasts, 0 runts, 0 giants, 0 throttles
     0 input errors, 0 CRC, 0 frame, 0 overrun, 0 ignored, 0 abort
     110 packets output, 9438 bytes, 0 underruns
     0 output errors, 0 collisions, 2 interface resets
     0 output buffer failures, 0 output buffers swapped out
     0 carrier transitions
     DCD=up  DSR=up  DTR=up  RTS=up  CTS=up

Atlanta#show interface s 0.1
Serial0.1 is up, line protocol is up
  Hardware is HD64570
  Internet address is 168.10.202.1/24
  MTU 1500 bytes, BW 1544 Kbit, DLY 20000 usec, rely 255/255, load 1/255
  Encapsulation FRAME-RELAY

Atlanta#show interface s 0.2
Serial0.2 is up, line protocol is up
  Hardware is HD64570
  Internet address is 168.10.203.1/24
  MTU 1500 bytes, BW 1544 Kbit, DLY 20000 usec, rely 255/255, load 1/255
  Encapsulation FRAME-RELAY

Atlanta#show interface s 0.3
Serial0.3 is up, line protocol is up
  Hardware is HD64570
  Internet address is 168.10.204.1/24
  MTU 1500 bytes, BW 1544 Kbit, DLY 20000 usec, rely 255/255, load 1/255
Encapsulation FRAME-RELAY
```

continues

Example 8-27 *Atlanta Command Output, Scenario 8-2 (Continued)*

```
Atlanta#show frame-relay map
Serial0.3 (up): point-to-point dlci, dlci 54(0x36,0xC60), broadcast, IETF
          status defined, active
Serial0.2 (up): point-to-point dlci, dlci 53(0x35,0xC50), broadcast
          status defined, active
Serial0.1 (up): point-to-point dlci, dlci 52(0x34,0xC40), broadcast
          status defined, active

Atlanta#show frame-relay lmi

LMI Statistics for interface Serial0 (Frame Relay DTE) LMI TYPE = CISCO
  Invalid Unnumbered info 0        Invalid Prot Disc 0
  Invalid dummy Call Ref 0         Invalid Msg Type 0
  Invalid Status Message 0         Invalid Lock Shift 0
  Invalid Information ID 0         Invalid Report IE Len 0
  Invalid Report Request 0         Invalid Keep IE Len 0
  Num Status Enq. Sent 43          Num Status msgs Rcvd 43
  Num Update Status Rcvd 0         Num Status Timeouts 0

Atlanta#debug frame-relay events
Frame Relay events debugging is on

Atlanta#configure terminal
Enter configuration commands, one per line.  End with Ctrl-Z.
Atlanta(config)#interface serial 0
Atlanta(config-if)#shutdown

%LINEPROTO-5-UPDOWN: Line protocol on Interface Serial0.1, changed state to down
%LINEPROTO-5-UPDOWN: Line protocol on Interface Serial0.2, changed state to down
%LINEPROTO-5-UPDOWN: Line protocol on Interface Serial0.3, changed state to down
%LINEPROTO-5-UPDOWN: Line protocol on Interface Serial0, changed state to down
%LINK-5-CHANGED: Interface Serial0, changed state to administratively down
%FR-5-DLCICHANGE: Interface Serial0 - DLCI 54 state changed to DELETED
%FR-5-DLCICHANGE: Interface Serial0 - DLCI 53 state changed to DELETED
%FR-5-DLCICHANGE: Interface Serial0 - DLCI 52 state changed to DELETED

Atlanta(config-if)#no shutdown
Atlanta(config-if)#^Z

%LINEPROTO-5-UPDOWN: Line protocol on Interface Serial0.1, changed state to up
%FR-5-DLCICHANGE: Interface Serial0 - DLCI 52 state changed to ACTIVE
%LINEPROTO-5-UPDOWN: Line protocol on Interface Serial0.2, changed state to up
%FR-5-DLCICHANGE: Interface Serial0 - DLCI 53 state changed to ACTIVE
%LINEPROTO-5-UPDOWN: Line protocol on Interface Serial0.3, changed state to up
%FR-5-DLCICHANGE: Interface Serial0 - DLCI 54 state changed to ACTIVE
%SYS-5-CONFIG_I: Configured from console by console
%LINEPROTO-5-UPDOWN: Line protocol on Interface Serial0, changed state to up
%LINK-3-UPDOWN: Interface Serial0, changed state to up
```

Example 8-27 *Atlanta Command Output, Scenario 8-2 (Continued)*

```
Atlanta#show frame map
Serial0.3 (up): point-to-point dlci, dlci 54(0x36,0xC60), broadcast, IETF
          status defined, active
Serial0.2 (up): point-to-point dlci, dlci 53(0x35,0xC50), broadcast
          status defined, active
Serial0.1 (up): point-to-point dlci, dlci 52(0x34,0xC40), broadcast
          status defined, active

Atlanta#debug frame-relay lmi
Frame Relay LMI debugging is on
Displaying all Frame Relay LMI data
Atlanta#

Serial0(out): StEnq, myseq 6, yourseen 5, DTE up
datagramstart = 0x45B25C, datagramsize = 13
FR encap = 0xFCF10309
00 75 01 01 01 03 02 06 05

Serial0(in): Status, myseq 6
RT IE 1, length 1, type 1
KA IE 3, length 2, yourseq 6 , myseq 6
```

Example 8-28 *Charlotte Command Output, Scenario 8-2*

```
Charlotte#show interface s 0.1
Serial0.1 is up, line protocol is up
  Hardware is HD64570
  Internet address is 168.10.202.2/24
  MTU 1500 bytes, BW 1544 Kbit, DLY 20000 usec, rely 255/255, load 1/255
  Encapsulation FRAME-RELAY

Charlotte#show cdp neighbor detail
-----------------------
Device ID: Atlanta
Entry address(es):
  IP address: 168.10.202.1
  Novell address: 202.0200.aaaa.aaaa
Platform: Cisco 2500,  Capabilities: Router
Interface: Serial0.1,  Port ID (outgoing port): Serial0.1
Holdtime : 164 sec

Version :
Cisco Internetwork Operating System Software
IOS (tm) 2500 Software (C2500-AINR-L), Version 11.2(11), RELEASE SOFTWARE (fc1)
Copyright (c) 1986-1997 by Cisco Systems, Inc.
Compiled Mon 29-Dec-97 18:47 by ckralik
```

continues

Example 8-28 *Charlotte Command Output, Scenario 8-2 (Continued)*

```
Charlotte#show frame-relay map
Serial0.1 (up): point-to-point dlci, dlci 51(0x33,0xC30), broadcast
          status defined, active
Charlotte#show frame-relay pvc

PVC Statistics for interface Serial0 (Frame Relay DTE)

DLCI = 51, DLCI USAGE = LOCAL, PVC STATUS = ACTIVE, INTERFACE = Serial0.1

  input pkts 36            output pkts 28           in bytes 4506
  out bytes 2862           dropped pkts 1           in FECN pkts 0
  in BECN pkts 0           out FECN pkts 0          out BECN pkts 0
  in DE pkts 0             out DE pkts 0
  out bcast pkts 26         out bcast bytes 2774
  pvc create time 00:08:54, last time pvc status changed 00:01:26

Charlotte#show frame-relay lmi

LMI Statistics for interface Serial0 (Frame Relay DTE) LMI TYPE = CCITT
  Invalid Unnumbered info 0      Invalid Prot Disc 0
  Invalid dummy Call Ref 0       Invalid Msg Type 0
  Invalid Status Message 0       Invalid Lock Shift 0
  Invalid Information ID 0       Invalid Report IE Len 0
  Invalid Report Request 0       Invalid Keep IE Len 0
  Num Status Enq. Sent 54        Num Status msgs Rcvd 37
  Num Update Status Rcvd 0       Num Status Timeouts 17
```

Example 8-29 *Nashville Command Output, Scenario 8-2*

```
Nashville#show cdp neighbor detail
-----------------------
Device ID: Atlanta
Entry address(es):
  IP address: 168.10.203.1
  Novell address: 203.0200.aaaa.aaaa
Platform: Cisco 2500,  Capabilities: Router
Interface: Serial0.1,  Port ID (outgoing port): Serial0.2
Holdtime : 139 sec

Version :
Cisco Internetwork Operating System Software
IOS (tm) 2500 Software (C2500-AINR-L), Version 11.2(11), RELEASE SOFTWARE (fc1)
Copyright (c) 1986-1997 by Cisco Systems, Inc.
Compiled Mon 29-Dec-97 18:47 by ckralik

Nashville#show frame-relay pvc

PVC Statistics for interface Serial0 (Frame Relay DTE)

DLCI = 51, DLCI USAGE = LOCAL, PVC STATUS = ACTIVE, INTERFACE = Serial0.1
```

Example 8-29 *Nashville Command Output, Scenario 8-2 (Continued)*

```
    input pkts 52          output pkts 47         in bytes 6784
    out bytes 6143         dropped pkts 0         in FECN pkts 0
    in BECN pkts 0         out FECN pkts 0        out BECN pkts 0
    in DE pkts 0           out DE pkts 0
    out bcast pkts 46        out bcast bytes 6099
    pvc create time 00:13:50, last time pvc status changed 00:06:51

Nashville#show frame-relay traffic
Frame Relay statistics:
    ARP requests sent 0, ARP replies sent 0
    ARP requests recvd 0, ARP replies recvd 0

Nashville#show frame-relay lmi

LMI Statistics for interface Serial0 (Frame Relay DTE) LMI TYPE = CISCO
    Invalid Unnumbered info 0        Invalid Prot Disc 0
    Invalid dummy Call Ref 0         Invalid Msg Type 0
    Invalid Status Message 0         Invalid Lock Shift 0
    Invalid Information ID 0         Invalid Report IE Len 0
    Invalid Report Request 0         Invalid Keep IE Len 0
    Num Status Enq. Sent 84          Num Status msgs Rcvd 84
    Num Update Status Rcvd 0         Num Status Timeouts 0
```

Example 8-30 *Boston Command Output, Scenario 8-2*

```
Boston#show interface s 0.1
Serial0.1 is up, line protocol is up
  Hardware is HD64570
  Internet address is 168.10.204.4/24
  MTU 1500 bytes, BW 1544 Kbit, DLY 20000 usec, rely 255/255, load 1/255
  Encapsulation FRAME-RELAY

Boston#show cdp neighbor detail
-----------------------
Device ID: Atlanta
Entry address(es):
  IP address: 168.10.204.1
  Novell address: 204.0200.aaaa.aaaa
Platform: Cisco 2500,  Capabilities: Router
Interface: Serial0.1,  Port ID (outgoing port): Serial0.3
Holdtime : 125 sec

Version :
Cisco Internetwork Operating System Software
IOS (tm) 2500 Software (C2500-AINR-L), Version 11.2(11), RELEASE SOFTWARE (fc1)
Copyright (c) 1986-1997 by Cisco Systems, Inc.
Compiled Mon 29-Dec-97 18:47 by ckralik
```

continues

Example 8-30 *Boston Command Output, Scenario 8-2 (Continued)*

```
Boston#show frame-relay map
Serial0.1 (up): point-to-point dlci, dlci 51(0x33,0xC30), broadcast, IETF
          status defined, active

Boston#show frame-relay pvc

PVC Statistics for interface Serial0 (Frame Relay DTE)

DLCI = 51, DLCI USAGE = LOCAL, PVC STATUS = ACTIVE, INTERFACE = Serial0.1

  input pkts 65           output pkts 54           in bytes 8475
  out bytes 6906          dropped pkts 1           in FECN pkts 0
  in BECN pkts 0          out FECN pkts 0          out BECN pkts 0
  in DE pkts 0            out DE pkts 0
  out bcast pkts 52       out bcast bytes 6792
  pvc create time 00:15:43, last time pvc status changed 00:07:54
Num Update Status Rcvd 0   Num Status Timeouts 0
```

Assuming the details established in Example 8-24 through Example 8-26 for Scenario 8-2, complete or answer the following:

1. Create a diagram for the network based on the command output in Example 8-27 through Example 8-30.

2. Complete Table 8-27 with the Layer 3 addresses on the serial links.

Table 8-27 *Layer 3 Addresses in Scenario 8-2*

Router	Port	Subinterface	IP Address	IPX Address
Atlanta	s0			
Atlanta	s0			
Atlanta	s0			
Atlanta	s0			
Charlotte	s0			
Charlotte	s0			
Nashville	s0			
Nashville	s0			
Boston	s0			
Boston	s0			

3. Complete Table 8-28 with LMI types and encapsulations used.

Table 8-28 *LMI and Encapsulations Used in Scenario 8-2*

Router	Port	Subinterface	LMI Type	Encapsulation
Atlanta	s0			
Atlanta	s0			
Atlanta	s0			
Atlanta	s0			
Charlotte	s0			
Charlotte	s0			
Nashville	s0			
Nashville	s0			
Boston	s0			
Boston	s0			

Scenario 8-3: Point-to-Point Configuration

Your job is to deploy a new network for an environmental research firm. Two main research sites are in Boston and Atlanta; a T/1 line has been ordered between those two sites. The field site in Alaska will need occasional access. The field site in the rain forest of Podunk has a digital 56 kbps link, but it has bursts of errors due to parts of the line being Microwave.

The design criteria are listed following Figure 8-23, which shows the routers and links. Note that some design criteria are contrived to force you to configure different features; these are designated with an asterisk (*).

Figure 8-23 *Scenario 8-3 Environmental Research Network*

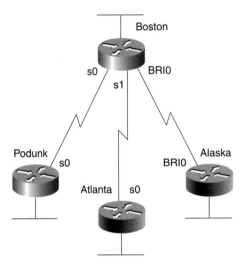

The design criteria are as follows:

- Use three different WAN data-link protocols. *

- Boston's SPID is 11155511110101; Alaska's is 22255522220101.

- Both ISDN BRIs are attached to DMS-100 switches.

- Use IP subnets and IPX networks in Table 8-29. Allocate addresses as needed.

- All IP user traffic is considered interesting for DDR.

- IPX RIP and IP IGRP are the routing protocols of choice.

Table 8-29 *Scenario 8-3 Chart of Layer 3 Groups for the Network in Figure 8-23*

Data Link	IP Subnet	IPX Network
Boston Ethernet	200.1.1.0/24	101
Podunk Ethernet	200.1.2.0/24	102
Atlanta Ethernet	200.1.3.0/24	103
Alaska Ethernet	200.1.4.0/24	104
Boston-Podunk	200.1.5.4/30	202
Boston-Atlanta	200.1.5.8/30	203
Boston-Alaska	200.1.5.12/30	204

Assuming the design criteria previously listed and the information in Table 8-29 for Scenario 8-3, complete or answer the following:

1. Create configurations for all four routers.

2. Defend your choices for the different data-link protocols.

3. Name all methods that Boston is using in your configuration to learn the Layer 3 addresses on the other end of each link.

Scenario 8-4: Frame Relay Configuration

Your job is to deploy a new network. Site A is the main site, with PVC connections to the other four sites. Sites D and E also have a PVC between them. Examine Figure 8-24 and perform the activities that follow.

Figure 8-24 *Scenario 8-4 Frame Relay Network*

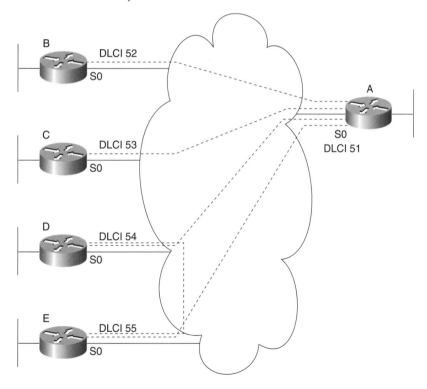

1. Plan the IP and IPX addresses to be used. Use Table 8-30 if helpful. Use IP network 168.15.0.0.

2. Using the DLCIs in Figure 8-24, create configurations for Routers A, B, and E. Use multipoint subinterfaces for the VCs between A, D, and E.

3. Create alternate configurations for Router A and Router E using point-to-point subinterfaces instead of multipoint.

4. Describe the contents of the IP and IPX routing tables on Router A, assuming the network created in Step 3 is working properly. Only LAN-based IP subnets and IPX networks need to be listed for this exercise. Use Table 8-30 and Table 8-31 if useful.

Table 8-30 *Scenario 8-4 Layer 3 Address Planning Chart*

Interface	Subinterface	IP Address	IPX Address
A's Ethernet			
B's Ethernet			
C's Ethernet			
D's Ethernet			
E's Ethernet			
A's S0			
A's S0			
A's S0			
A's S0			
A's S0			
B's S0			
C's S0			
D's S0			
D's S0			
E's S0			
E's S0			

Table 8-31 *Scenario 8-4: IP and IPX Routing Table Contents*

Layer 3 Group	Outgoing Interface	Next-Hop IP Address, or Connected	Next-Hop IPX Address, or Connected

Scenario 8-5: Frame Relay Configuration Dissection

A four-router Frame Relay network has been configured. Consider the configurations in Example 8-31, Example 8-32, Example 8-33, and Example 8-34, and answer the questions that follow.

Example 8-31 *Scenario 8-5, Router 1 Configuration*

```
Hostname Atlanta
!
ipx routing 0200.1111.1111
!
interface serial0
encapsulation frame-relay
!
interface serial 0.1
ip address 180.1.1.1 255.255.255.0
ipx network AAA1801
frame-relay interface-dlci 501
!
interface serial 0.2
ip address 180.1.2.1 255.255.255.0
ipx network AAA1802
frame-relay interface-dlci 502
!
interface serial 0.1
ip address 180.1.3.1 255.255.255.0
ipx network AAA1803
frame-relay interface-dlci 503
!
interface ethernet 0
ip address 180.1.10.1 255.255.255.0
ipx network AAA18010
!
router igrp 1
network 180.1.0.0
```

Example 8-32 *Scenario 8-5, Router 2 Configuration*

```
Hostname Charlotte
!
ipx routing 0200.2222.2222
!
interface serial0
encapsulation frame-relay
!
interface serial 0.1
ip address 180.1.1.2 255.255.255.0
ipx network AAA1801
frame-relay interface-dlci 500
!
interface ethernet 0
ip address 180.1.11.2 255.255.255.0
ipx network AAA18011
!
router igrp 1
network 180.1.0.0
```

Example 8-33 *Scenario 8-5, Router 3 Configuration*

```
Hostname Nashville
!
ipx routing 0200.3333.3333
!
interface serial0
encapsulation frame-relay
!
interface serial 0.1
ip address 180.1.2.3 255.255.255.0
ipx network AAA1802
frame-relay interface-dlci 500
!
interface ethernet 0
ip address 180.1.12.3 255.255.255.0
ipx network AAA18012
!
router igrp 1
network 180.1.0.0
```

Example 8-34 *Scenario 8-5, Router 4 Configuration*

```
Hostname Boston
!
ipx routing 0200.4444.4444
!
interface serial0
encapsulation frame-relay
!
interface serial 0.1
ip address 180.1.3.4 255.255.255.0
ipx network AAA1803
frame-relay interface-dlci 500
!
interface ethernet 0
ip address 180.1.13.4 255.255.255.0
ipx network AAA18013
!
router igrp 1
network 180.1.0.0
```

Assuming the details established in Example 8-31 through Example 8-34 for Scenario 8-5, complete or answer the following:

1. Draw a diagram of the network.

2. Is IGRP split-horizon on or off? How could you tell?

3. What type of Frame Relay encapsulation is used?

4. Create the commands on Router 1 and Router 2 to disable Inverse ARP and instead use static mapping.

Answers to Scenarios

Answers to Scenario 8-1: Point-to-Point Verification

Figure 8-25 is a diagram that matches the configuration.

Figure 8-25 *Sample Cartoon Network*

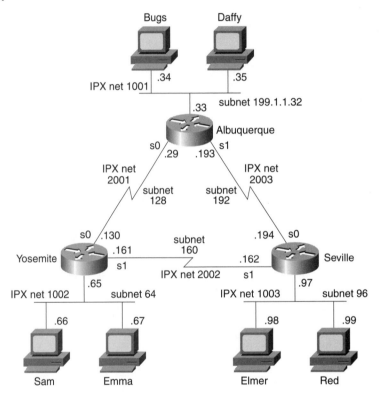

All the information needed to build the network diagram and complete Table 8-30 (Table 8-26 in Scenario 8-1) is listed in the examples in the scenario problem statement. Some of the clues are obscure, however. The best plan of attack is to find all IP addresses and masks that you can and decide which addresses are in the same subnet.

The IPX addresses are a little more difficult to find. The best method with the commands shown is via the **show ipx interface brief** command and the **show ipx route** command. In particular, the routing table lists the full IPX addresses, not just the network numbers.

The encapsulations are not easy to notice from the commands listed. The **show interface** command would have simply listed the answer. However, in this case, a few subtle reminders were included. The **debug** output on Albuquerque and Seville shows PPP output on Albuquerque's S0 interface, and LAPB output for Seville's S1 interface. The **show ipx route** commands also happen to list the encapsulation for connected networks. Table 8-32 summarizes the details.

Table 8-32   *Scenario 8-1 Layer 3 Addresses on the Point-to-Point Serial Links—Completed Table*

Router	Serial Port	Encapsulation	IP address	IPX address
Albuquerque	s0	PPP	199.1.1.129	2001.0200.aaaa.aaaa
Albuquerque	s1	HDLC	199.1.1.193	2003.0200.aaaa.aaaa
Yosemite	s0	PPP	199.1.1.130	2001.0200.bbbb.bbbb
Yosemite	s1	LAPB	199.1.1.161	2002.0200.bbbb.bbbb
Seville	s0	HDLC	199.1.1.194	2003.0200.cccc.cccc
Seville	s1	LAPB	199.1.1.162	2002.0200.cccc.cccc

An extra IP route is included in the routing tables on the PPP-connected routers. When the IPCP announces the IP addresses on each end of the link, the IOS decides to add a host route specifically to that IP address. For example, Albuquerque has a route to 199.1.1.128/27 and to 199.1.1.130/32. The "/32" signifies that the route is a host route.

Answers to Scenario 8-2: Frame Relay Verification

Figure 8-26 is a diagram that matches the configuration.

Figure 8-26   *Scenario 8-2 Network Derived from **show** and **debug** Commands*

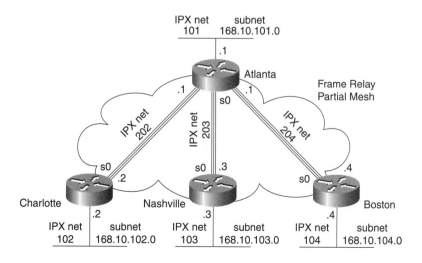

Discovering the IP addresses and subinterfaces is relatively straightforward. The **show** commands for most subinterfaces are provided, and these list the IP address and mask used. The **show cdp neighbor detail** commands also mentioned the IP address of the connected routers.

The IPX addresses were more challenging to deduce. The network numbers could be seen in the command output, but the actual addresses could only be deduced. The only command that listed the IPX addresses was the **show cdp neighbor detail** command. However, only two routers had that command output. The **show frame-relay map** command should seemingly have provided that information, but because all the subinterfaces are point-to-point, there is no true mapping needed; the subinterface acts like a point-to-point link. A **debug frame-relay events** command, which shows output for inverse ARP flows, would have identified the IPX addresses, but inverse ARP is not enabled on point-to-point subinterfaces because it is not needed. In short, there was no way to deduce all IPX addresses from the scenario. Because each IPX network number used over the Frame Relay cloud is shown, and because the node part of the IPX addresses of each router is listed at least once, the rest of the IPX addresses can be deduced.

Table 8-33 lists the answers for Layer 3 addresses and subinterface numbers (Table 8-25 in the scenario description).

Table 8-33 *Layer 3 Addresses in Scenario 8-2—Completed Table*

Router	Port	Subinterface	IP address	IPX Address
Atlanta	s0	1	168.10.202.1	202.0200.AAAA.AAAA
Atlanta	s0	2	168.10.203.1	203.0200.AAAA.AAAA
Atlanta	s0	3	168.10.204.1	204.0200.AAAA.AAAA
Atlanta	s0			
Charlotte	s0	1	168.10.202.2	202.0200.BBBB.BBBB
Charlotte	s0			
Nashville	s0	1	168.10.203.3	203.0200.CCCC.CCCC
Nashville	s0			
Boston	s0	1	168.10.204.4	204.0200.DDDD.DDDD
Boston	s0			

Note relating to Table 8-3: There was not enough information to derive the IPX addresses for Charlotte, Nashville, and Boston. The IPX network numbers are implied by the `show cdp neighbor detail` command output.

The LMI type was discovered only by examining the output of the **show frame-relay lmi** command. This command does not, however, list whether the LMI type was learned via autosensing or whether it was configured.

The encapsulation type is much more obscure. The **show frame-relay map** command output holds the answer. Table 8-34 summarizes those answers (Table 8-28 in the scenario description).

Table 8-34 *Scenario 8-2 LMI and Encapsulations Used—Completed Table*

Router	Port	Subinterface	LMI Type	Encapsulation
Atlanta	s0	N/A	cisco	
Atlanta	s0	1		cisco
Atlanta	s0	2		cisco
Atlanta	s0	3		ietf
Charlotte	s0	N/A	Q933A	
Charlotte	s0	1		cisco
Nashville	s0	N/A	cisco	
Nashville	s0	1		cisco
Boston	s0	N/A	cisco	
Boston	s0	1		ietf

Answers to Scenario 8-3: Point-to-Point Configuration

Example 8-35, Example 8-36, Example 8-37, and Example 8-38 show the configurations.

Example 8-35 *Boston Configuration for Scenario 8-3, Point-to-Point Configuration*

```
hostname Boston
ipx routing 0200.aaaa.aaaa
no ip domain-lookup
username Alaska password Larry
isdn switch-type basic-dms100
!
interface serial0
encapsulation multi-lapb-dce
ip address 200.1.5.5 255.255.255.252
ipx network 202
!
interface serial1
encapsulation hdlc
ip address 200.1.5.9 255.255.255.252
ipx network 203
!
interface bri0
encapsulation ppp
isdn spid1 11155511110101
ip address 200.1.5.13 255.255.255.252
ipx network 204
ppp authentication chap
!
interface ethernet 0
ip address 200.1.1.1 255.255.255.0
ipx network 101
!
router igrp 1
network 200.1.1.0
network 200.1.5.0
```

Example 8-36 *Podunk Configuration for Scenario 8-3, Point-to-Point Configuration*

```
hostname Podunk
ipx routing 0200.bbbb.bbbb
no ip domain-lookup
!
interface serial0
encapsulation multi-lapb
ip address 200.1.5.6 255.255.255.252
ipx network 202
!
interface ethernet 0
ip address 200.1.2.1 255.255.255.0
ipx network 102
!
router igrp 1
network 200.1.2.0
network 200.1.5.0
```

Example 8-37 *Atlanta Configuration for Scenario 8-3, Point-to-Point Configuration*

```
hostname Atlanta
ipx routing 0200.cccc.cccc
no ip domain-lookup
!
interface serial0
encapsulation hdlc
ip address 200.1.5.10 255.255.255.0
ipx network 203
!
interface ethernet 0
ip address 200.1.3.1 255.255.255.0
ipx network 103
!
router igrp 1
network 200.1.3.0
network 200.1.5.0
```

Example 8-38 *Alaska Configuration for Scenario 8-3, Frame Relay Configuration*

```
hostname Alaska
no ip domain-lookup
ipx routing 0200.dddd.dddd
!
isdn switch-type basic-dms100
username Boston password Larry
!
interface BRI 0
encapsulation ppp
ip address 200.1.5.14 255.255.255.252
ipx network 204
isdn spid1 22255522220101
ppp authentication chap
dialer-group 1
dialer idle-timeout 120
dialer map ip 200.1.5.13   name Boston 111155511110101
!
interface ethernet 0
ip address 200.1.4.1 255.255.255.0
ipx network 104
!
router igrp 1
network 200.1.4.0
network 200.1.5.0
!
dialer-list 1 protocol ip permit
```

The choices for serial encapsulation in this solution are HDLC, PPP, and LAPB. PPP was chosen on the ISDN B channel because it provides CHAP authentication. LAPB is used on the link with known continuing high error rates so that LAPB can recover data lost going across the link. And because the problem statement requests three different encapsulations, HDLC was chosen.

As you progress through your certifications, Cisco will try to ask questions that force you to deduce a fact from a limited amount of information. The final question in this scenario requires that you think beyond the topic of serial encapsulations. PPP control protocols are used by Boston on the PPP link to discern the Layer 3 addresses on the other end of the link. However, LAPB and HDLC do not perform this function. CDP is enabled on each of these links by default, and it is sending messages to discover information about Boston's neighbors. Finally, Boston examines the source address of routing updates to learn the Layer 3 addresses of its neighbors.

Answers to Scenario 8-4: Frame Relay Configuration

Check your IP and IPX address design against the ones chosen in Table 8-35. Of course, yours are most likely different. However, you should have one subnet per VC in this case, because each router is using only point-to-point subinterfaces. With the original criteria with Routers A, D, and E each using multipoint subinterfaces, those three subinterfaces should have been in the same IP subnet and IPX network. Table 8-35 gives the planned Layer 3 addresses for the configurations using multipoint.

Table 8-35 *Scenario 8-4 Layer 3 Address Planning Chart, Multipoint A-D-E*

Interface	Subinterface	IP Address	IPX Address
A's Ethernet		168.15.101.1	101.0200.AAAA.AAAA
B's Ethernet		168.15.102.1	102.0200.BBBB.BBBB
C's Ethernet		168.15.103.1	103.0200.CCCC.CCCC
D's Ethernet		168.15.104.1	104.0200.DDDD.DDDD
E's Ethernet		168.15.105.1	105.0200.EEEE.EEEE
A's S0	2	168.15.202.1	202.0200.AAAA.AAAA
A's S0	3	168.15.203.1	203.0200.AAAA.AAAA
A's S0	1	168.15.200.1	200.0200.AAAA.AAAA
B's S0	2	168.15.202.2	202.0200.BBBB.BBBB
C's S0	3	168.15.203.3	203.0200.CCCC.CCCC
D's S0	1	168.15.200.4	200.0200.DDDD.DDDD
E's S0	1	168.15.200.5	200.0200.EEEE.EEEE

Given the DLCIs in Figure 8-24, and Example 8-39, Example 8-40, and Example 8-41, show the configurations for Routers A, B, and E, using multipoint subinterfaces for the VCs between A, D, and E.

Example 8-39 *Router A Configuration, Scenario 8-4*

```
ipx routing 0200.aaaa.aaaa
!
interface serial0
encapsulation frame-relay
!
interface serial 0.2 point-to-point
ip address 168.15.202.1  255.255.255.0
ipx network 202
interface-dlci 52
!
interface serial 0.3 point-to-point
ip address 168.15.203.1  255.255.255.0
ipx network 203
interface-dlci 53
!
!
interface serial 0.1 multipoint
ip address 168.15.200.1  255.255.255.0
ipx network 200
frame-relay interface-dlci 54
frame-relay interface-dlci 55
!
interface ethernet 0
ip address 168.15.101.1 255.255.255.0
ipx network 101
!
router igrp 1
network 168.15.0.0
```

Example 8-40 *Router B Configuration, Scenario 8-4*

```
ipx routing 0200.bbbb.bbbb
!
interface serial0
encapsulation frame-relay
!
interface serial 0.2 point-to-point
ip address 168.15.202.2  255.255.255.0
ipx network 202
frame-relay interface-dlci 51
!
interface ethernet 0
ip address 168.15.102.1 255.255.255.0
ipx network 102
!
router igrp 1
network 168.15.0.0
```

Example 8-41 *Router E Configuration, Scenario 8-4*

```
ipx routing 0200.eeee.eeee
!
interface serial0
encapsulation frame-relay
!
interface serial 0.1 multipoint
ip address 168.15.200.5  255.255.255.0
ipx network 200
frame-relay interface-dlci 51
frame-relay interface-dlci 54
!
interface ethernet 0
ip address 168.15.105.1 255.255.255.0
ipx network 105
!
router igrp 1
network 168.15.0.0
```

Multipoint subinterfaces will work perfectly well in this topology. Using multipoint also conserves IP subnets, as seen in the next task in this scenario. When choosing to use only point-to-point subinterfaces, each of the three VCs in the triangle of Routers A, D, and E will require a different subnet and IPX network number. Table 8-36 shows the choices made here. Example 8-42 and Example 8-43 show alternate configurations for Router A and Router E using point-to-point subinterfaces instead of multipoint.

Table 8-36 *Scenario 8-4 Layer 3 Address Planning Chart, All Point-to-Point Subinterfaces*

Interface	Subinterface	IP Address	IPX Address
A's Ethernet		168.15.101.1	101.0200.AAAA.AAAA
B's Ethernet		168.15.102.1	102.0200.BBBB.BBBB
C's Ethernet		168.15.103.1	103.0200.CCCC.CCCC
D's Ethernet		168.15.104.1	104.0200.DDDD.DDDD
E's Ethernet		168.15.105.1	105.0200.EEEE.EEEE
A's S0	2	168.15.202.1	202.0200.AAAA.AAAA
A's S0	3	168.15.203.1	203.0200.AAAA.AAAA
A's S0	4	168.15.204.1	204.0200.AAAA.AAAA
A's S0	5	168.15.205.1	205.0200.AAAA.AAAA
B's S0	2	168.15.202.2	202.0200.BBBB.BBBB
C's S0	3	168.15.203.3	203.0200.CCCC.CCCC
D's S0	4	168.15.204.4	204.0200.DDDD.DDDD
D's S0	1	168.15.190.4	190.0200.DDDD.DDDD

Table 8-36 *Scenario 8-4 Layer 3 Address Planning Chart, All Point-to-Point Subinterfaces (Continued)*

Interface	Subinterface	IP Address	IPX Address
E's S0	5	168.15.204.5	205.0200.EEEE.EEEE
E's S0	1	168.15.190.5	190.0200.EEEE.EEEE

Example 8-42 *Router A Configuration, Scenario 8-4, All Point-to-Point Subinterfaces*

```
ipx routing 0200.aaaa.aaaa
!
interface serial0
encapsulation frame-relay
!
interface serial 0.2 point-to-point
ip address 168.15.202.1  255.255.255.0
ipx network 202
frame-relay interface-dlci 52
!
interface serial 0.3 point-to-point
ip address 168.15.203.1  255.255.255.0
ipx network 203
frame-relay interface-dlci 53
!
interface serial 0.4 point-to-point
ip address 168.15.204.1  255.255.255.0
ipx network 204
frame-relay interface-dlci 54
!
interface serial 0.5 point-to-point
ip address 168.15.205.1  255.255.255.0
ipx network 205
frame-relay interface-dlci 55
!
interface ethernet 0
ip address 168.15.101.1 255.255.255.0
ipx network 101
!
router igrp 1
network 168.15.0.0
```

Example 8-43 *Router E Configuration, Scenario 8-4, Subinterfaces*

```
ipx routing 0200.eeee.eeee
!
interface serial0
encapsulation frame-relay
!
interface serial 0.1 point-to-point
ip address 168.15.190.5  255.255.255.0
ipx network 190
interface-dlci 54
!
interface serial 0.5 point-to-point
ip address 168.15.200.5  255.255.255.0
ipx network 200
interface-dlci 51
!
interface ethernet 0
ip address 168.15.105.1 255.255.255.0
ipx network 105
!
router igrp 1
network 168.15.0.0
```

The contents of the routing table asked for in Step 4 of this scenario will be provided in shorthand in Table 8-37. The third byte of the IP address is shown in the Layer 3 group column, since the third byte (octet) fully comprises the subnet field. Not coincidentally, the IPX network number was chosen as the same number, mainly to make network operation easier.

Table 8-37 *Scenario 8-4 IP and IPX Routing Table Contents, Router A*

Layer 3 Group	Outgoing Interface	Next-Hop IP Address, or Connected	Next-Hop IPX Address, or Connected
101	E0	connected	connected
102	S0.2	168.15.202.2	202.0200.bbbb.bbbb
103	S0.3	168.15.203.3	203.0200.cccc.cccc
104	S0.4	168.15.204.4	204.0200.dddd.dddd
105	S0.5	168.15.205.5	205.0200.eeee.eeee
106	S0.2	168.15.202.2	202.0200.bbbb.bbbb

Answers to Scenario 8-5: Frame Relay Configuration Dissection

Figure 8-27 supplies the network diagram described in Scenario 8-5. The subinterfaces are all point-to-point, which is a clue that each VC has a subnet and IPX network associated with it. An examination of the IP addresses or IPX network numbers should have been enough to deduce which routers attached to each end of each VC.

Figure 8-27 *Diagram to Scenario 8-5 Frame Relay Network*

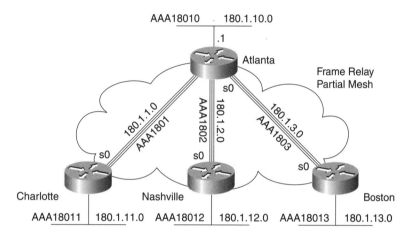

Split-horizon is turned off on all interfaces because that is the default with point-to-point subinterfaces, and no command has been configured to turn it on.

Cisco encapsulation was used in each case. The `encapsulation frame-relay` command defaults to the use of Cisco encapsulation.

Disabling inverse ARP is unlikely in real networks. However, I added this exercise so that you can be ready for the exam. Example 8-44 and Example 8-45 show the commands used to migrate not using Inverse ARP. The maps are necessary for both IP and IPX because both need to be routed across the Frame Relay network.

Example 8-44 *Scenario 8-5, Atlanta Router—Changes for Static Mapping*

```
Atlanta(config)# interface serial 0.1
Atlanta(config-subif)#no frame-relay interface-dlci 501
Atlanta(config-subif)#frame-relay map ip 180.1.1.2 501 broadcast
Atlanta(config-subif)#frame-relay map ipx aaa1801.0200.2222.2222 501 broadcast
Atlanta(config-subif)# interface serial 0.2
Atlanta(config-subif)#no frame-relay interface-dlci 502
Atlanta(config-subif)#frame-relay map ip 180.1.2.3 502 broadcast
Atlanta(config-subif)#frame-relay map ipx aaa1802.0200.3333.3333 502 broadcast
Atlanta(config-subif)# interface serial 0.3
Atlanta(config-subif)#no frame-relay interface-dlci 503
Atlanta(config-subif)#frame-relay map ip 180.1.3.4 503 broadcast
Atlanta(config-subif)#frame-relay map ipx aaa1803.0200.4444.4444 503 broadcast
```

Example 8-45 *Scenario 8-5, Charlotte Router—Changes for Static Mapping*

```
Charlotte(config)# interface serial 0.1
Charlotte(config-subif)#no frame-relay interface-dlci 500
Charlotte(config-subif)#frame-relay map ip 180.1.1.1 500 broadcast
Charlotte(config-subif)#frame-relay map ipx aaa1801.0200.1111.1111 500 broadcast
```

The **interface-dlci** settings are no longer needed because the IOS can deduce which DLCI is used by the subinterface based on the **map** command.

CHAPTER 9

Scenarios for Final Preparation

This chapter is designed to assist you in final preparation for the CCNA exam. These exercises and tasks do not cover specific topics like those presented at the end of each chapter, but require a broader perspective, which means you will need to draw on knowledge presented in each of Chapters 2, 4, 5, 6, 7, and 8. These scenarios are designed with the following assumptions in mind:

- Helping you practice your recall of many of the small details that might be covered on the exam is particularly important.

- Your understanding of the concepts at this point in your study is complete; practice and repetition is useful so you can ensure that you will have plenty of time to review your answers when taking the exam.

Chapter 9 is not the only chapter you should use when doing your final preparation for the CCNA exam. Chapter 3, "Understanding the OSI Reference Model," concepts are not covered in this chapter, mainly because Chapter 3 deals with concepts and theory; however, Chapter 3 concepts are a very important part of the CCNA exam. Review the questions at the end of that chapter, as well as look at the tables with the functions of each OSI layer and the example protocols at each layer, as a final review of OSI. Figure 9-1 describes your final preparation options with this book.

Figure 9-1 *Final CCNA Exam Preparation Study Strategy*

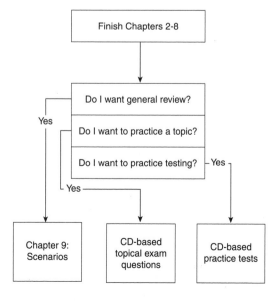

As shown, if you want even more final preparation, many practice questions are located in each chapter and on the CD. All pre-chapter quiz and chapter-ending questions, with answers, are in Appendix B, "Answers to the 'Do I Know This Already?' Quizzes and Q&A Sections." These conveniently located questions can be read and reviewed quickly, with explanations. The CD has testing software, as well as many additional questions in the format of the CCNA exam (multiple choice). These questions should be a valuable resource when performing final preparations.

How to Best Use This Chapter

The focus of these scenarios is on easily forgotten items. The first such items are **show** and **debug** commands. Their options are often ignored, mainly because we can get online help about the correct option easily when using the Cisco CLI. However, questions about the exact command options used to see a particular piece of information are scattered throughout the exam. Take care to review the output of the commands in these scenarios.

Another focus of this chapter is a review of command line tricks and acronym trivia. Like it or not, part of the preparation is memorization; hopefully, these reminders will save you a question or two on the exam!

Additional examples for IP and IPX addressing are included with each scenario. IP addressing, subnetting, and broadcast addresses will be on the exam. Also, take care to recall the Novell encapsulation options, which are also reviewed in these scenarios.

Finally, more configurations are shown for almost all options already covered in the book. If you can configure these options without online help, you should feel confident that you can choose the correct command from a list of five options in a multiple-choice question!

If you have enough time, reviewing all parts of each scenario will be helpful. However, only part of a scenario needs to be reviewed if you have limited time. For example, the answers for each scenario's part A is the background information for part B; the answers for each scenario's part B is the background information for part C. So, if you read part A or B and decide you already know those details and don't want to take the time to wade through your own answer, just look at the answer; it will lead you into the next part of the scenario.

Many of you will read this chapter as your final review before taking the exam. Let me take this opportunity to wish you success. I hope that you will be relaxed and confident for your exam, and I trust that this book has helped you build your knowledge and confidence.

Scenario 9-1

The first scenario begins with some planning guidelines that include planning IP addresses, IPX network numbers, the location of SAP filters, and the location of IP standard access lists. After it is completed, part B of the scenario asks that you configure the three routers to implement the planned design and a few other features. Finally, in part C, you are asked to examine router command output to discover details about the current operation. Also, questions relating to the user interface and protocol specifications are listed in part C.

Scenario 9-1a—Planning

Your job is to deploy a new network with three sites, as shown in Figure 9-2.

Figure 9-2   *Scenario 9-1 Network Diagram*

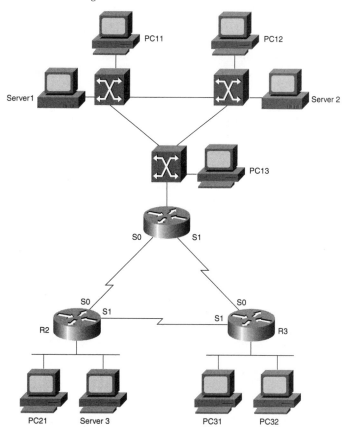

The use of point-to-point serial links, as well as the product choices, have already been made. For part A of this scenario, perform the following tasks:

1. Plan the IP addressing and subnets used in this network. Class B network 163.1.0.0 has been assigned by the NIC. The maximum number of hosts per subnet is 100. Assign IP addresses to the PCs as well.

2. Plan the IPX network numbers to be used. You can choose the internal network numbers of the servers as well.

3. Plan the location and logic of IP access lists to filter for the following criteria: hosts on the Ethernet attached to R1 are not allowed to send/receive IP traffic from hosts on the Ethernet attached to R3. (Do not code the access lists; part B will ask for that, and because the answer to part B will be based on where I chose to put the access lists, you will probably want to see the answer in part A before configuring.)

4. Plan the location and logic of SAP filters to prevent clients on the Ethernet off R2 from logging in to Server 2.

Assume a single VLAN is used on the switches near Router 1.

Table 9-1 and Table 9-2 are provided as a convenient place to record your IP subnets, IPX networks, and IP addresses when performing the planning tasks for this scenario.

Table 9-1 *Scenario 9-1a IP Subnet and IPX Network Planning Chart*

Location of Subnet/Network Geographically	Subnet Mask	Subnet Number	IPX Network
Router 1 Ethernet			
Router 2 Ethernet			
Router 3 Ethernet			
Serial between R1 and R2			
Serial between R1 and R3			
Serial between R2 and R3			
Server 1 Internal			
Server 2 Internal			

Table 9-2 *Scenario 9-1a IP Address Planning Chart*

Host	Address
PC11	
PC12	
PC13	
PC21	
PC31	
R1-E0	
R1-S0	
R1-S1	

Table 9-2 *Scenario 9-1a IP Address Planning Chart (Continued)*

Host	Address
R2-E0	
R2-S0	
R2-S1	
R3-E0	
R3-S0	
R3-S1	

Scenario 9-1a—Planning Answers

Keeping the design as simple as possible, without making it too simple to be useful as the network evolves, is a good practice. In these suggested answers, the numbering scheme is chosen to help those of us with fading memories.

The IP subnet design includes the use of mask 255.255.255.128. The design criteria left enough ambiguity that you could argue that any mask with at least seven host bits was valid; that includes the much easier mask of 255.255.255.0. However, I chose the most problematic mask just to give you more difficult practice.

The IPX network number assignment is simply a matter of choosing numbers; these are recorded, along with the IP addresses, in Table 9-3. The IP addresses are assigned in Table 9-4.

Table 9-3 *Scenario 9-1a IP Subnet and IPX Network Planning Chart Completed*

Location of Subnet/Network Geographically	Subnet Mask	Subnet Number	IPX Network
Router 1 Ethernet	255.255.255.128	163.1.1.128	1
Router 2 Ethernet	255.255.255.128	163.1.2.128	2
Router 3 Ethernet	255.255.255.128	163.1.3.128	3
Serial between R1 and R2	255.255.255.128	163.1.12.128	12
Serial between R1 and R3	255.255.255.128	163.1.13.128	13
Serial between R2 and R3	255.255.255.128	163.1.23.128	23
Server 1 Internal	N/A	N/A	101
Server 2 Internal	N/A	N/A	102

Table 9-4 *Scenario 9-1a IP Address Planning Chart Completed*

Host	Address
PC11	163.1.1.211
PC12	163.1.1.212
PC13	163.1.1.213
PC21	163.1.2.221
PC31	163.1.3.231
R1-E0	163.1.1.201
R1-S0	163.1.12.201
R1-S1	163.1.13.201
R2-E0	163.1.2.202
R2-S0	163.1.12.202
R2-S1	163.1.23.202
R3-E0	163.1.3.203
R3-S0	163.1.13.203
R3-S1	163.1.23.203

As usual, the access lists can be placed in several places to achieve the desired function. Also as usual, the criteria for the access list is subject to interpretation. The design suggested here is to just filter packets from the Ethernet off R3 and filter them as they enter R1 on either serial interface. By filtering packets in only one direction, applications that require a two-way flow will not successfully communicate. By filtering on both serial interfaces for inbound traffic, any valid route for the incoming packets will be checked.

For the SAP filter, several options also exist. By stopping R2 from adding the SAP for Server 2 to its SAP table, R2 will never advertise that server in a GNS request, nor will Server 3 learn about it in R2's SAP updates. So, the plan is to place incoming SAP filters on both serial interfaces, to filter Server 2 from being added to R2's SAP table.

Scenario 9-1b—Configuration

The next step in your job is to deploy the network designed in Scenario 9-1a. Use the answers for that scenario to direct you in regards to IP and IPX addresses, and the logic behind the access lists. For Scenario 9-1b, perform the following tasks:

1. Configure IP, IPX, IP access lists, and IPX SAP filters based on Scenario 9-1a's design.

2. Use RIP as the IP routing protocol.

3. Use PPP as the data link protocol on the link between R2 and R3.

Scenario 9-1b—Configuration Answers

The configurations are shown in Example 9-1, Example 9-2, and Example 9-3.

Example 9-1 *R1 Configuration*

```
hostname R1
!
ipx routing 0200.1111.1111
!
interface Serial0
 ip address 163.1.12.201 255.255.255.128
 ipx network 12
 ip access-group 83 in
!
interface Serial1
 ip address 163.1.13.201 255.255.255.128
 ipx network 13
 ip access-group 83 in
!
Ethernet0
 ip address 163.1.1.201 255.255.255.128
 ipx network 1
!
router rip
network 163.1.0.0
!
access-list 83 deny 163.1.3.0 0.0.0.127
access-list 83 permit any
```

Example 9-2 *R2 Configuration*

```
hostname R2
!
ipx routing 0200.2222.2222
!
interface Serial0
 ip address 163.1.12.202 255.255.255.128
 ipx network 12
 ipx input-sap-filter 1010
!
interface Serial1
 encapsulation ppp
 ip address 163.1.23.202 255.255.255.128
 ipx network 23
 ipx input-sap-filter 1010
!
Ethernet0
 ip address 163.1.2.202 255.255.255.128
 ipx network 2
!
router rip
network 163.1.0.0
!
access-list 1010 deny 102
access-list 1010 permit -1
```

Example 9-3 *R3 Configuration*

```
hostname R2
!
ipx routing 0200.3333.3333
!
interface Serial0
 ip address 163.1.13.203 255.255.255.128
 ipx network 13
!
interface Serial1
 encapsulation ppp
 ip address 163.1.23.203 255.255.255.128
 ipx network 23
!
Ethernet0
 ip address 163.1.3.203 255.255.255.128
ipx network 3
!
router rip
network 163.1.0.0
```

Scenario 9-1c—Verification and Questions

The CCNA exam will test you on your memory of the kinds of information you can find in the output of various **show** commands. Using Example 9-4, Example 9-5, and Example 9-6 as references, answer the questions following the examples.

Example 9-4 *Scenario 9-1c R1* **show** *and* **debug** *Output*

```
R1#show ip interface brief
Interface          IP-Address      OK? Method Status           Protocol
Serial0            163.1.12.201    YES NVRAM  up               up
Serial1            163.1.13.201    YES NVRAM  up               up
Ethernet0          163.1.1.201     YES NVRAM  up               up
R1#show access-lists
Standard IP access list 83
    deny   163.1.3.0, wildcard bits 0.0.0.127
    permit any
R1#
R1#debug ipx sap event
IPX service events debugging is on
R1#
IPXSAP: positing update to 1.ffff.ffff.ffff via Ethernet0 (broadcast) (full)
R1#
IPXSAP: positing update to 13.ffff.ffff.ffff via Serial1 (broadcast) (full)
IPXSAP: positing update to 12.ffff.ffff.ffff via Serial0 (broadcast) (full)

R1#
IPXSAP: positing update to 1.ffff.ffff.ffff via Ethernet0 (broadcast) (full)
R1#undebug all
All possible debugging has been turned off
R1#
```

Example 9-4 *Scenario 9-1c R1* **show** *and* **debug** *Output (Continued)*

```
R1#
R1#debug ipx sap activity
IPX service debugging is on
R1#
IPXSAP: positing update to 13.ffff.ffff.ffff via Serial1 (broadcast) (full)
IPXSAP: Update type 0x2 len 224 src:13.0200.1111.1111 dest:13.ffff.ffff.ffff(452)
 type 0x4, "Server3", 103.0000.0000.0001(451), 4 hops
 type 0x4, "Server1", 101.0000.0000.0001(451), 3 hops
 type 0x4, "Server2", 102.0000.0000.0001(451), 3 hops
IPXSAP: positing update to 12.ffff.ffff.ffff via Serial0 (broadcast) (full)
IPXSAP: Update type 0x2 len 160 src:12.0200.1111.1111 dest:12.ffff.ffff.ffff(452)
 type 0x4, "Server1", 101.0000.0000.0001(451), 3 hops
 type 0x4, "Server2", 102.0000.0000.0001(451), 3 hops
R1#undebug all
All possible debugging has been turned off
R1#
R1#
R1#debug ipx routing event
IPX routing events debugging is on
R1#
IPXRIP: positing full update to 1.ffff.ffff.ffff via Ethernet0 (broadcast)
IPXRIP: positing full update to 13.ffff.ffff.ffff via Serial1 (broadcast)
IPXRIP: positing full update to 12.ffff.ffff.ffff via Serial0 (broadcast)
IPXRIP: 13 FFFFFFFF not added, entry in table is static/connected/internal
IPXRIP: 12 FFFFFFFF not added, entry in table is static/connected/internal
IPXRIP: positing full update to 1.ffff.ffff.ffff via Ethernet0 (broadcast)
R1#undebug all
All possible debugging has been turned off
R1#
R1#
R1#debug ipx routing activity
IPX routing debugging is on
R1#
IPXRIP: update from 1.0000.0c89.b130
    102 in 2 hops, delay 2
    101 in 2 hops, delay 2
IPXRIP: positing full update to 13.ffff.ffff.ffff via Serial1 (broadcast)
IPXRIP: src=13.0200.1111.1111, dst=13.ffff.ffff.ffff, packet sent
    network 103, hops 4,  delay 14
    network 23, hops 2,  delay 13
    network 2, hops 3,  delay 8
    network 101, hops 3,  delay 8
    network 102, hops 3,  delay 8
    network 1, hops 1,  delay 7
    network 12, hops 1,  delay 7
IPXRIP: positing full update to 12.ffff.ffff.ffff via Serial0 (broadcast)
IPXRIP: src=12.0200.1111.1111, dst=12.ffff.ffff.ffff, packet sent
    network 3, hops 2,  delay 13
    network 2, hops 3,  delay 8
  network 101, hops 3,  delay 8
network 102, hops 3,  delay 8
    network 1, hops 1,  delay 7
    network 13, hops 1,  delay 7
```

continues

Example 9-4 *Scenario 9-1c R1* **show** *and* **debug** *Output (Continued)*

```
IPXRIP: update from 12.0200.2222.2222
    103 in 3 hops, delay 8
IPXRIP: 13 FFFFFFFF not added, entry in table is static/connected/internal
    13 in 2 hops, delay 13
    3 in 2 hops, delay 13
    23 in 1 hops, delay 7
    2 in 1 hops, delay 7
IPXRIP: update from 13.0200.3333.3333
    103 in 4 hops, delay 14
IPXRIP: 12 FFFFFFFF not added, entry in table is static/connected/internal
    12 in 2 hops, delay 13
    3 in 1 hops, delay 7
    2 in 2 hops, delay 13
    23 in 1 hops, delay 7
IPXRIP: positing full update to 1.ffff.ffff.ffff via Ethernet0 (broadcast)
IPXRIP: src=1.0000.0ccf.21cd, dst=1.ffff.ffff.ffff, packet sent
    network 103, hops 4,  delay 9
    network 3, hops 2,  delay 8
    network 23, hops 2,  delay 8
    network 13, hops 1,  delay 2
    network 12, hops 1,  delay 2
IPXRIP: update from 1.0000.0c89.b130
    102 in 2 hops, delay 2
    101 in 2 hops, delay 2
    2 in 2 hops, delay 2

R1#undebug all
All possible debugging has been turned off
R1#
R1#
R1#debug ip rip events
RIP event debugging is on
R1#
RIP: received v1 update from 163.1.13.203 on Serial1
RIP: Update contains 4 routes
RIP: sending v1 update to 255.255.255.255 via Serial0 (163.1.12.201)
RIP: Update contains 4 routes
RIP: Update queued
RIP: Update sent via Serial0
RIP: sending v1 update to 255.255.255.255 via Serial1 (163.1.13.201)
RIP: Update contains 4 routes
RIP: Update queued
RIP: Update sent via Serial1
RIP: sending v1 update to 255.255.255.255 via Ethernet0 (163.1.1.201)
RIP: Update contains 7 routes
RIP: Update queued
RIP: Update sent via Ethernet0

RIP: received v1 update from 163.1.12.202 on Serial0
RIP: Update contains 4 routes
R1#undebug all
All possible debugging has been turned off
R1#
R1#
```

Example 9-4 *Scenario 9-1c R1* **show** *and* **debug** *Output (Continued)*

```
R1#debug ip rip RIP protocol debugging is on
R1#
RIP: received v1 update from 163.1.12.202 on Serial0
     163.1.2.128 in 1 hops
     163.1.3.128 in 2 hops
     163.1.23.128 in 1 hops
     163.1.23.203 in 1 hops
RIP: received v1 update from 163.1.13.203 on Serial1
     163.1.2.128 in 2 hops
     163.1.3.128 in 1 hops
     163.1.23.128 in 1 hops
     163.1.23.202 in 1 hops
RIP: sending v1 update to 255.255.255.255 via Serial0 (163.1.12.201)
     subnet  163.1.3.128, metric 2
     subnet  163.1.1.128, metric 1
     subnet  163.1.13.128, metric 1
     host    163.1.23.202, metric 2
RIP: sending v1 update to 255.255.255.255 via Serial1 (163.1.13.201)
     subnet  163.1.2.128, metric 2
     subnet  163.1.1.128, metric 1
     subnet  163.1.12.128, metric 1
     host    163.1.23.203, metric 2
RIP: sending v1 update to 255.255.255.255 via Ethernet0 (163.1.1.201)
     subnet  163.1.2.128, metric 2
     subnet  163.1.3.128, metric 2
     subnet  163.1.12.128, metric 1
     subnet  163.1.13.128, metric 1
     subnet  163.1.23.128, metric 2
     host    163.1.23.203, metric 2
     host    163.1.23.202, metric 2

R1#undebug all
All possible debugging has been turned off
R1#
```

Example 9-5 *Scenario 9-1c R2* **show** *and* **debug** *Output*

```
R2#show interface
Serial0 is up, line protocol is up
  Hardware is HD64570
  Internet address is 163.1.12.202/25
  MTU 1500 bytes, BW 56 Kbit, DLY 20000 usec, rely 255/255, load 1/255
  Encapsulation HDLC, loopback not set, keepalive set (10 sec)
  Last input 00:00:04, output 00:00:00, output hang never
  Last clearing of "show interface" counters never
  Queueing strategy: fifo
  Output queue 0/40, 0 drops; input queue 0/75, 0 drops
  5 minute input rate 0 bits/sec, 0 packets/sec
  5 minute output rate 0 bits/sec, 0 packets/sec
    1242 packets input, 98477 bytes, 0 no buffer
    Received 898 broadcasts, 0 runts, 0 giants, 0 throttles
    0 input errors, 0 CRC, 0 frame, 0 overrun, 0 ignored, 0 abort
```

continues

Example 9-5 *Scenario 9-1c R2* ***show*** *and* ***debug*** *Output (Continued)*

```
         1249 packets output, 91395 bytes, 0 underruns
         0 output errors, 0 collisions, 2 interface resets
         0 output buffer failures, 0 output buffers swapped out
         12 carrier transitions
         DCD=up  DSR=up  DTR=up  RTS=up  CTS=up
 --More--
Serial1 is up, line protocol is up
  Hardware is HD64570
  Internet address is 163.1.23.202/25
  MTU 1500 bytes, BW 1544 Kbit, DLY 20000 usec, rely 255/255, load 1/255
  Encapsulation PPP, loopback not set, keepalive set (10 sec)
  LCP Open
  Open: IPCP, CDPCP, LLC2, IPXCP
  Last input 00:00:02, output 00:00:02, output hang never
  Last clearing of "show interface" counters never
  Input queue: 0/75/0 (size/max/drops); Total output drops: 0
  Queueing strategy: weighted fair
  Output queue: 0/1000/0 (size/max total/drops)
     Conversations  0/1/64 (active/max active/threshold)
     Reserved Conversations 0/0 (allocated/max allocated)
  5 minute input rate 0 bits/sec, 0 packets/sec
  5 minute output rate 0 bits/sec, 0 packets/sec
     1654 packets input, 90385 bytes, 0 no buffer
     Received 1644 broadcasts, 0 runts, 0 giants, 0 throttles
     0 input errors, 0 CRC, 0 frame, 0 overrun, 0 ignored, 0 abort
     1674 packets output, 96130 bytes, 0 underruns
     0 output errors, 0 collisions, 8 interface resets
     0 output buffer failures, 0 output buffers swapped out
     13 carrier transitions
     DCD=up  DSR=up  DTR=up  RTS=up  CTS=up
 --More--
Ethernet0 is up, line protocol is up
  Hardware is MCI Ethernet, address is 0000.0c89.b170 (bia 0000.0c89.b170)
  Internet address is 163.1.2.202, subnet mask is 255.255.255.128
  MTU 1500 bytes, BW 10000 Kbit, DLY 100000 usec, rely 255/255, load 1/255
  Encapsulation ARPA, loopback not set, keepalive set (10 sec)
  ARP type: ARPA, ARP Timeout 4:00:00
Last input 00:00:00, output 00:00:04, output hang never
   Last clearing of "show interface" counters never
   Queueing strategy: fifo
   Output queue 0/40, 0 drops; input queue 0/75, 0 drops
   5 minute input rate 0 bits/sec, 0 packets/sec
   5 minute output rate 0 bits/sec, 0 packets/sec
      2274 packets input, 112381 bytes, 0 no buffer
      Received 1913 broadcasts, 0 runts, 0 giants, 0 throttles
      0 input errors, 0 CRC, 0 frame, 0 overrun, 0 ignored, 0 abort
      863 packets output, 110146 bytes, 0 underruns
      0 output errors, 0 collisions, 2 interface resets
      0 output buffer failures, 0 output buffers swapped out
      6 transitions

R2#show ipx interface brief
Interface          IPX Network Encapsulation Status          IPX State
Serial0            12          HDLC         up               [up]
```

Example 9-5 *Scenario 9-1c R2* **show** *and* **debug** *Output (Continued)*

```
Serial1                 23          PPP           up                    [up]
Ethernet0               2           SAP           up                    [up]

R2#show ipx route
Codes: C - Connected primary network,    c - Connected secondary network
       S - Static, F - Floating static, L - Local (internal), W - IPXWAN
       R - RIP, E - EIGRP, N - NLSP, X - External, A - Aggregate
       s - seconds, u - uses

9 Total IPX routes. Up to 1 parallel paths and 16 hops allowed.

No default route known.

C          2 (SAP),        E0
C          12 (HDLC),      Se0
C          23 (PPP),       Se1
R          1 [07/01] via         12.0200.1111.1111,    59s, Se0
R          3 [07/01] via         23.0200.3333.3333,     5s, Se1
R          13 [07/01] via        23.0200.3333.3333,     5s, Se1
R          101 [08/03] via       12.0200.1111.1111,     0s, Se0
R          102 [08/03] via       12.0200.1111.1111,     0s, Se0
R          103 [02/02] via        2.0000.0cac.70ef,    21s, E0

R2#show ip protocol
Routing Protocol is "rip"
  Sending updates every 30 seconds, next due in 6 seconds
  Invalid after 180 seconds, hold down 180, flushed after 240
  Outgoing update filter list for all interfaces is not set
  Incoming update filter list for all interfaces is not set
  Redistributing: rip
   Default version control: send version 1, receive any version
    Interface      Send  Recv   Key-chain
    Serial0          1     1 2
    Serial1          1     1 2
    Ethernet0        1     1 2
  Routing for Networks:
    163.1.0.0
  Routing Information Sources:
    Gateway          Distance       Last Update
    163.1.13.201        120         00:00:02
    163.1.23.202        120         00:00:09
  Distance: (default is 120)

R2#show ipx servers
Codes: S - Static, P - Periodic, E - EIGRP, N - NLSP, H - Holddown, + = detail
3 Total IPX Servers

Table ordering is based on routing and server info

    Type Name                      Net     Address   Port     Route Hops Itf
P    4 Server3                  103.0000.0000.0001:0451     2/02   2  E0
P    4 Server1                  101.0000.0000.0001:0451     8/03   3  Se0
P    4 Server2                  102.0000.0000.0001:0451     8/03   3  Se0
```

Example 9-6 *Scenario 9-1c R3 show and debug Output*

```
R3#show running-config
Building configuration...

Current configuration:
!
version 11.2
no service password-encryption
no service udp-small-servers
no service tcp-small-servers
!
hostname R3
!
enable secret 5 $1$kI1V$NkybGlP9tzP7BYvAKYT.c1
!
no ip domain-lookup
ipx routing 0200.3333.3333
!
interface Serial0
 ip address 163.1.13.203 255.255.255.128
 ipx network 13
 no fair-queue
!
interface Serial1
 ip address 163.1.23.203 255.255.255.128
 encapsulation ppp
 ipx network 23
!
interface Ethernet0
 ip address 163.1.3.203 255.255.255.128
 ipx network 3
 ring-speed 16
!
router rip
 network 163.1.0.0
!
no ip classless
!
!
!
!
line con 0
 password cisco
 login
line aux 0
line vty 0 4
 password cisco
 login
!
end

R3#show ip arp
Protocol   Address          Age (min)  Hardware Addr   Type   Interface
Internet   163.1.3.203            -     0000.0c89.b1b0  SNAP   Ethernet0
```

Example 9-6 *Scenario 9-1c R3 show and debug Output (Continued)*

```
R3#show ip route
Codes: C - connected, S - static, I - IGRP, R - RIP, M - mobile, B - BGP
       D - EIGRP, EX - EIGRP external, O - OSPF, IA - OSPF inter area
       N1 - OSPF NSSA external type 1, N2 - OSPF NSSA external type 2
       E1 - OSPF external type 1, E2 - OSPF external type 2, E - EGP
       i - IS-IS, L1 - IS-IS level-1, L2 - IS-IS level-2, * - candidate default
       U - per-user static route, o - ODR

Gateway of last resort is not set

     163.1.0.0/16 is variably subnetted, 7 subnets, 2 masks
R       163.1.2.128/25 [120/1] via 163.1.23.202, 00:00:22, Serial1
C       163.1.3.128/25 is directly connected, Ethernet0
R       163.1.1.128/25 [120/1] via 163.1.13.201, 00:00:28, Serial0
R       163.1.12.128/25 [120/1] via 163.1.13.201, 00:00:28, Serial0
                       [120/1] via 163.1.23.202, 00:00:22, Serial1
C       163.1.13.128/25 is directly connected, Serial0
C       163.1.23.128/25 is directly connected, Serial1
C       163.1.23.202/32 is directly connected, Serial1

R3#trace 163.1.13.203


Type escape sequence to abort.
Tracing the route to 163.1.13.203

  1 163.1.13.201 16 msec 16 msec 16 msec
  2 163.1.13.203 44 msec *  32 msec

R3#ping 163.1.13.203

Type escape sequence to abort.
Sending 5, 100-byte ICMP Echos to 163.1.13.203, timeout is 2 seconds:
!!!!!
Success rate is 100 percent (5/5), round-trip min/avg/max = 64/66/68 ms

R3#ping 13.0200.3333.3333

Type escape sequence
 to abort.
Sending 5, 100-byte IPX Cisco Echoes to 13.0200.3333.3333, timeout is 2 seconds:
!!!!!
Success rate is 100 percent (5/5), round-trip min/avg/max = 68/69/72 ms
```

Using Example 9-4, Example 9-5, and Example 9-6 as references, answer the following questions:

1. Describe how the switches choose the root of the spanning tree.

2. If Switch1 becomes the root, and all interface costs are equal on all interfaces on all switches, which ports will be considered to be root ports?

3. If Switch3 blocks on port E1, and then later Switch2's E0 port fails, what notifies Switch3 so it can forward on its E1 port? What interim spanning tree states will E1 be in before it forwards?

4. Describe the contents of an IP RIP update from R1 to R3. What **debug** command options provide the details of what is in the RIP update?

5. Describe the contents of an IPX RIP update from R1 to R2. What **debug** command options provide the details of what is in the IPX RIP update?

6. What command tells you the contents of the ARP cache? Does it contain IP as well as IPX addresses?

7. What commands list the routing metrics used for IP subnets? IPX networks?

8. What command would be used to find the path a packet would take from R3 to 163.1.1.1?

9. What **show** command identifies which routes were learned with IP RIP? IPX RIP? What in the command identifies these routing protocols?

10. What **show** command lists SAP information in the router?

11. What **debug** command options create debug messages with the details of the SAP updates? Which options just provide messages referring to the fact that an update is sent, without listing the details?

12. What **debug** command options provide IP RIP update details?

13. If R3's E0 interface needed to use a new IP address and mask (10.1.1.1, 255.255.255.0), and the user is in user mode, list the steps necessary to change the IP address.

14. With the user in privileged mode, the user remembers that the IP RIP configuration should be updated, based on the change in the previous question. List the steps necessary to make this change.

15. If an EXEC command you cannot recall begins with the letter C, how can you get help to list all commands that start with C? List the steps. Assume you are in privileged mode.

16. Name the two commands to list the currently used configuration in a router.

17. Name the two commands to list the configuration that will be used the next time the router is reloaded.

18. What does CDP stand for?

19. Define the metric used by IPX RIP.

20. What does GNS stand for? What role does R2 play in the GNS process? R3?

Scenario 9-1c—Verification and Questions Answers

The answers to the questions for Scenario 9-1c are as follows:

1. Each bridge and switch sends a CBPDU claiming to be the root. The bridge or switch with the lowest bridge priority—or if a tie occurs, the bridge or switch with the lowest value for root bridge ID—is considered to be the root.

2. Because all port costs are equal, Switch2 will be getting CBPDUs with a lower cost in E0. Likewise, Switch3 will be receiving CBPDUs with lower cost on its E0 port. So, each switch will consider its E0 port to be its root port; this port is placed into a forwarding state.

3. Switch3 reacts after Switch2's MaxAge time expires and Switch2 stops sending CBPDU messages onto the Ethernet segment that Switch2 and Switch3 have in common. Switch2 then transitions its E1 port to listening state, then learning state, and finally, forwarding state.

4. The **debug ip rip** command provides the detailed RIP debug output. An example is shown in Example 9-4. It shows four routes being described in the update to R3. The routes missing in the update are 163.1.13.128, which is the subnet on the serial link between R1 and R3. The other missing route is the route to 163.1.3.128—R1's best route to that subnet is through R3. Split-horizon rules prevent either route from being advertised.

5. The command **debug IPX routing activity** is used to provide the detailed IPX RIP debug output. This output is also in Example 9-4. Two routes from R1's routing table are not included in the update, namely Networks 13 and 3. Network 13 is on the common serial link, and R1's route to Network 3 points through R3. Both networks are not included due to split-horizon rules.

6. The **show ip arp** command (refer to Example 9-6). It only contains MAC and IP addresses, not IPX, because IPX does not use a concept like ARP on LANs.

7. The **show ip route** and **show ipx route** commands (refer to Examples 9-5 and 9-6). The metric values for each subnet/network are in brackets.

8. The **trace 163.1.1.1** command (refer to Example 9-6).

9. The **show ip route** and **show ipx route** commands (refer to Examples 9-5 and 9-6). The source of the routing information is coded in a field in the left side of the output line and is based on the legend of such codes that appear at the beginning of the command output, before the actual routing table entries are listed.

10. The **show ipx servers** command (refer to Example 9-5).

11. The **debug ipx sap events** command just displays a message when an update is sent, with no details about the contents of the update. The **debug ipx sap activity** command displays the details of what is sent in the update (refer to Example 9-4).

12. The **debug ip rip** command displays the details of what is sent in the update (refer to Example 9-4).

13. Use the following steps:

```
R3> enable
password: password
R3#configure terminal
R3(config)#interface ethernet 0
R3(config-if)#ip address 10.1.1.1 255.255.255.0
R3(config)#Ctrl-Z
R3#
```

14. Use the following steps:

```
R3#configure terminal
R3(config)#router rip
R3(config-router)#network 10.0.0.0
R3(config)#Ctrl-Z
R3#
```

15. Use the following steps:

```
R3#c?
clear  clock  configure  connect  copy

R3#c
```

16. **Show running-config** and **write terminal**.

17. **Show startup-config** and **show config**.

18. Cisco Discovery Protocol.

19. The primary metric is a counter of timer ticks. If two routes to the same network tie with the ticks metric, the hop count is considered.

20. GNS stands for Get Nearest Server. Any router can respond to a GNS request, which are issued by clients. R2 will not reply as long as Server 3 is up. R3 will always reply because no other NetWare server is on the local LAN segment.

Scenario 9-2

This scenario uses the familiar Frame Relay network with three routers and a full-mesh of virtual circuits. Some planning exercises begin the scenario (Scenario 9-2a), followed by configuration (Scenario 9-2b). Finally, a series of questions, some based on **show** and **debug** command output, finish the scenario (Scenario 9-2c).

Scenario 9-2a—Planning

Your job is to deploy a new network with three sites, as shown in Figure 9-3. The choice to use Frame Relay, as well as the product choices, have already been made. For Part A of this scenario, perform the following tasks:

1. Subnet planning has been completed. Before implementation, you are responsible for providing a list for the local administrators defining the IP addresses that they can assign to hosts. Using Table 9-5, derive the subnet numbers, broadcasts addresses, and define the range of valid IP addresses. A static mask of 255.255.255.192 is used on all subnets.

2. PC11 and PC12 use different IPX encapsulations, as do PC21 and PC22. Figure 9-4 shows the types of headers used by each PC. Plan the encapsulation types to be used, including the correct keywords used in the IOS.

3. Plan the IPX network numbers to be used. Table 9-6 can be used to record the information.

Figure 9-3   *Scenario 9-2 Network Diagram*

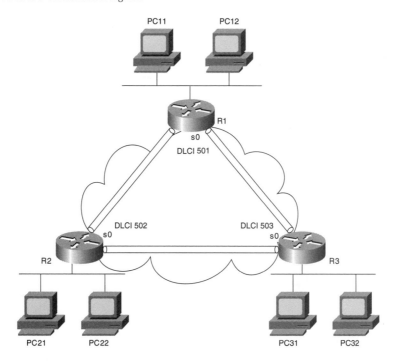

Figure 9-4 *Scenario 9-2a IPX Encapsulations*

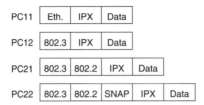

Table 9-5 *Scenario 9-2a IP Subnet and IPX Network Planning Chart; Mask 255.255.255.192*

Router Interface	IP Address	Subnet Number	Subnet Broadcast Address	Range of Valid Addresses
R1 E0	168.11.11.101			
R2 E0	168.11.12.102			
R3 E0	168.11.13.103			
R1 S0	168.11.123.201			
R2 S0	168.11.123.202			
R3 S0	168.11.123.203			

Table 9-6 *Scenario 9-2a IPX Network Number Planning Chart*

Location of Network	IPX Network
Attached to R1 E0	
Attached to R2 E0	
Attached to R3 E0	
Frame Relay	
Server 1 Internal	
Server 2 Internal	
Server 3 Internal	

Scenario 9-2a—Planning Answers

The first task was to derive the subnet numbers and broadcast addresses, so the assignable addresses in each subnet become obvious. One important item to note is that the three Frame Relay interfaces are in the same subnet, which is a clue that subinterfaces will not be used and that the Frame Relay interfaces will be treated as a single network. The answers are in Table 9-7.

Table 9-7   *Scenario 9-2a IP Subnet and IPX Network Planning Chart Completed*

Router Interface	IP Address	Subnet Number	Subnet Broadcast Address	Range of Valid Addresses
R1 E0	168.11.11.101	168.11.11.64	168.11.11.127	65-126 in last octet
R2 E0	168.11.12.102	168.11.12.64	168.11.12.127	65-126 in last octet
R3 E0	168.11.13.103	168.11.13.64	168.11.13.127	65-126 in last octet
R1 S0	168.11.123.201	168.11.123.192	168.11.123.255	193-254 in last octet
R2 S0	168.11.123.202	168.11.123.192	168.11.123.255	193-254 in last octet
R3 S0	168.11.123.203	168.11.123.192	168.11.123.255	193-254 in last octet

The second planning item requires remembering the four encapsulations for IPX on Ethernet. The important item here is to correlate the headers used by the devices to the correct name used by Cisco in the encapsulation command. Table 9-8 summarizes the encapsulations for the four PCs:

Table 9-8   *Scenario 9-2a IPX Encapsulations*

PC	Cisco IOS's Encapsulation
PC11	ARPA
PC12	Novell-ether
PC21	SAP
PC22	SNAP

Choosing IPX network numbers does not pose a particularly challenging task. However, realizing that two network numbers are needed on R1's E0 and on R2's E0 is the hidden part of the objective. As long as your network numbers are not duplicated and you planned for two IPX networks for the two aforementioned interfaces, any network numbers are fine. The ones that will be used as the basis of the configuration in Scenario 9-2b are listed in Table 9-9.

Table 9-9   *Scenario 9-2a IPX Network Number Planning Chart Completed*

Host	Address
R1 E0	110 (ARPA)
R1 E0	111 (Novell-ether)
R2 E0	120 (SAP)
R2 E0	121 (SNAP)

continues

Table 9-9 *Scenario 9-2a IPX Network Number Planning Chart Completed (Continued)*

R3 E0	130
Frame Relay	123
Server 1 Internal	101
Server 2 Internal	102
Server 3 Internal	103

Scenario 9-2b—Configuration

The next step in your job is to deploy the network designed in Scenario 9-2a. Use the answers for Scenario 9-2a to direct you in regards to IP and IPX addresses and the encapsulations to be used. For Scenario 9-2b, perform the following tasks:

1. Configure IP and IPX to be routed. Use IP IGRP and IPX RIP as routing protocols. Use IGRP process-id 1.

2. Use secondary IPX addresses to accommodate the multiple IPX encapsulation types described in Scenario 9-2a.

3. Configure Frame Relay without the use of subinterfaces. R1's attached switch uses LMI type ANSI. Cisco encapsulation should be used for all routers.

4. Assume that after you installed the network, you were forced to disable IP IGRP on R2. Define the required IP static routes to allow hosts on all three Ethernets to communicate. (This is unlikely in real life; it's just an excuse to review IP static routes!)

5. Assume that after you installed the network that you were forced to disable Inverse ARP on R2. Define static mappings as necessary for all hosts to be able to communicate.

Scenario 9-2b—Configuration Answers

The configurations for Steps 1, 2, and 3 are shown in Example 9-7, Example 9-8, and Example 9-9.

Example 9-7 *R1 Configuration*

```
ipx routing 0200.aaaa.aaaa
!
interface serial0
encapsulation frame-relay
ip address  168.11.123.201  255.255.255.192
ipx network  123
frame-relay interface-dlci 502
frame-relay interface-dlci 503
!
interface ethernet 0
ip address  168.11.11.101  255.255.255.192
```

Example 9-7 *R1 Configuration (Continued)*

```
ipx network  110 encapsulation arpa
ipx network  111 encapsulation novell-ether secondary
!
router igrp 1
network 168.11.0.0
```

Example 9-8 *R2 Configuration*

```
ipx routing 0200.bbbb.bbbb
!
interface serial0
encapsulation frame-relay
ip address  168.n.123.202  255.255.255.192
ipx network  123
frame-relay interface-dlci 501
frame-relay interface-dlci 503
!
interface ethernet 0
ip address  168.11.12.102  255.255.255.192
ipx network  120 encapsulation sap
ipx network  121 encapsulation snap secondary
!
router igrp 1
network 168.11.0.0
```

Example 9-9 *R3 Configuration*

```
ipx routing 0200.cccc.cccc
!
interface serial0
encapsulation frame-relay
ip address  168.11.11.203  255.255.255.192
ipx network  123
frame-relay interface-dlci 501
frame-relay interface-dlci 502
!
interface ethernet 0
ip address  168.11.11.103  255.255.255.192
ipx network  130
!
router igrp 1
network 168.11.0.0
```

For Step 4 in Scenario 9-2b, static routes need to be defined in all three routers. R2 will need routes to the two LAN-based subnets at the other sites. Likewise, R1 and R3 will need routes to 168.11.12.64. The routes in all three are listed in a single example, Example 9-10.

Example 9-10 *Static Routes*

```
R1(config)#ip route 168.11.12.64 255.255.255.192 168.11.123.202

R2(config)#ip route 168.11.11.64 255.255.255.192 168.11.123.201
R2(config)#ip route 168.11.13.64 255.255.255.192 168.11.123.203

R3(config)#ip route 168.11.12.64 255.255.255.192 168.11.123.202
```

Finally, Step 5 requested that static **frame-relay map** commands be configured. The **map** commands are necessary for each routed protocol. Also, the broadcast keyword is needed so packets that would normally be broadcast, like routing updates, will be sent as unicasts across each VC for each protocol. Example 9-11 lists the additional commands.

Example 9-11 *frame-relay map Commands*

```
R1(config)#frame-relay map ip 168.11.123.202 502 broadcast
R1(config)#frame-relay map ipx 123.0200.bbbb.bbbb 502 broadcast

R2(config)#frame-relay map ip 168.11.123.201 501 broadcast
R2(config)#frame-relay map ip 168.11.123.203 503 broadcast
R2(config)#frame-relay map ipx 123.0200.aaaa.aaaa 501 broadcast
R2(config)#frame-relay map ipx 123.0200.cccc.cccc 503 broadcast

R3(config)#frame-relay map ip 168.11.123.202 502 broadcast
R3(config)#frame-relay map ipx 123.0200.bbbb.bbbb 502 broadcast
```

Scenario 9-2c—Verification and Questions

The CCNA exam will test you on your memory of the kinds of information you can find in the output of various **show** commands. Using Example 9-12, Example 9-13, and Example 9-14 as references, answer the questions following the examples. Beware that the routers' Ethernet addresses are slightly different than in Scenario 9-2, Part B.

Example 9-12 *Scenario 9-2c R1 show and debug Output*

```
R1#show ipx interface brief
Interface       IPX Network  Encapsulation  Status                  IPX State
Serial0         123          FRAME-RELAY    up                      [up]
Serial1         unassigned   not config'd   administratively down   n/a
Ethernet0       110          ARPA           up                      [up]
Ethernet0       111          Novell-ether   up                      [up]

R1#show ip interface brief
Interface       IP-Address    OK? Method Status                  Protocol
Serial0         168.11.123.201  YES NVRAM  up                      up
Serial1         unassigned    YES unset  administratively down   down
Ethernet0       168.11.11.201  YES NVRAM  up                      up

R1#debug ipx sap activity
IPX service debugging is on
R1#
IPXSAP: positing update to 110.ffff.ffff.ffff via Ethernet0 (broadcast) (full)
```

Example 9-12 *Scenario 9-2c R1* ***show*** *and* ***debug*** *Output (Continued)*

```
IPXSAP: Update type 0x2 len 96 src:110.0000.0ccf.21cd dest:110.ffff.ffff.ffff(452)
 type 0x4, "Server3", 103.0000.0000.0001(451), 4 hops
IPXSAP: positing update to 111.ffff.ffff.ffff via Ethernet0 (broadcast) (full)
IPXSAP: Update type 0x2 len 224 src:111.0000.0ccf.21cd
dest:111.ffff.ffff.ffff(452)
 type 0x4, "Server3", 103.0000.0000.0001(451), 4 hops
 type 0x4, "Server1", 101.0000.0000.0001(451), 3 hops
 type 0x4, "Server2", 102.0000.0000.0001(451), 3 hops
IPXSAP: Response (in) type 0x2 len 160 src:110.0000.0c89.b130
dest:110.ffff.ffff.ffff(452)
 type 0x4, "Server2", 102.0000.0000.0001(451), 2 hops
 type 0x4, "Server1", 101.0000.0000.0001(451), 2 hops
IPXSAP: positing update to 123.ffff.ffff.ffff via Serial0 (broadcast) (full)
IPXSAP: Update type 0x2 len 160 src:123.0200.aaaa.aaaa
dest:123.ffff.ffff.ffff(452)
 type 0x4, "Server1", 101.0000.0000.0001(451), 3 hops
 type 0x4, "Server2", 102.0000.0000.0001(451), 3 hops
IPXSAP: Response (in) type 0x2 len 96 src:123.0200.bbbb.bbbb
dest:123.ffff.ffff.ffff(452)
 type 0x4, "Server3", 103.0000.0000.0001(451), 3 hops
R1#undebug all
All possible debugging has been turned off
R1#
R1#
R1#debug ipx routing activity
IPX routing debugging is on
R1#
IPXRIP: positing full update to 123.ffff.ffff.ffff via Serial0 (broadcast)
IPXRIP: src=123.0200.aaaa.aaaa, dst=123.ffff.ffff.ffff, packet sent
    network 555, hops 2,  delay 8
    network 101, hops 3,  delay 8
    network 102, hops 3,  delay 8
    network 111, hops 1,  delay 7
    network 110, hops 1,  delay 7
IPXRIP: update from 123.0200.3333.3333
    130 in 1 hops, delay 7
IPXRIP: update from 123.0200.bbbb.bbbb
    444 in 2 hops, delay 8
    103 in 3 hops, delay 8
    121 in 1 hops, delay 7
    120 in 1 hops, delay 7
IPXRIP: positing full update to 110.ffff.ffff.ffff via Ethernet0 (broadcast)
IPXRIP: src=110.0000.0ccf.21cd, dst=110.ffff.ffff.ffff, packet sent
    network 120, hops 2,  delay 8
    network 121, hops 2,  delay 8
    network 103, hops 4,  delay 9
    network 444, hops 3,  delay 9
    network 130, hops 2,  delay 8
    network 111, hops 1,  delay 2
    network 123, hops 1,  delay 2
IPXRIP: positing full update to 111.ffff.ffff.ffff via Ethernet0 (broadcast)
IPXRIP: src=111.0000.0ccf.21cd, dst=111.ffff.ffff.ffff, packet sent
    network 120, hops 2,  delay 8
```

continues

Example 9-12 *Scenario 9-2c R1 **show** and **debug** Output (Continued)*

```
       network 121, hops 2,  delay 8
       network 103, hops 4,  delay 9
       network 444, hops 3,  delay 9
       network 130, hops 2,  delay 8
       network 555, hops 2,  delay 3
       network 101, hops 3,  delay 3
       network 102, hops 3,  delay 3
       network 110, hops 1,  delay 2
       network 123, hops 1,  delay 2
IPXRIP: update from 110.0000.0c89.b130
       102 in 2 hops, delay 2
       101 in 2 hops, delay 2
       555 in 1 hops, delay 2
R1#
R1#
R1#undebug all
All possible debugging has been turned off
R1#

R1#debug ip igrp transactions
IGRP protocol debugging is on
R1#
IGRP: sending update to 255.255.255.255 via Serial0 (168.11.123.201)
       subnet 168.11.123.192, metric=180571
       subnet 168.11.11.192, metric=688
       subnet 168.11.13.192, metric=180634
       subnet 168.11.12.192, metric=180634
IGRP: sending update to 255.255.255.255 via Ethernet0 (168.11.11.201)
       subnet 168.11.123.192, metric=180571
       subnet 168.11.13.192, metric=180634
       subnet 168.11.12.192, metric=180634
IGRP: received update from 168.11.123.202 on Serial0
       subnet 168.11.123.192, metric 182571 (neighbor 180571)
       subnet 168.11.11.192, metric 182634 (neighbor 180634)
       subnet 168.11.13.192, metric 182634 (neighbor 180634)
       subnet 168.11.12.192, metric 180634 (neighbor 688)
IGRP: received update from 168.11.123.203 on Serial0
       subnet 168.11.123.192, metric 182571 (neighbor 8476)
       subnet 168.11.11.192, metric 182634 (neighbor 8539)
       subnet 168.11.13.192, metric 180634 (neighbor 688)
       subnet 168.11.12.192, metric 182634 (neighbor 8539)
IGRP: sending update to 255.255.255.255 via Serial0 (168.11.123.201)
       subnet 168.11.123.192, metric=180571
       subnet 168.11.11.192, metric=688
       subnet 168.11.13.192, metric=180634
       subnet 168.11.12.192, metric=180634
IGRP: sending update to 255.255.255.255 via Ethernet0 (168.11.11.201)
       subnet 168.11.123.192, metric=180571
       subnet 168.11.13.192, metric=180634
       subnet 168.11.12.192, metric=180634
R1#
R1#undebug all
All possible debugging has been turned off
```

Example 9-13 *Scenario 9-2c R2 **show** and **debug** Output*

```
R2#show interface
Serial0 is up, line protocol is up
  Hardware is HD64570
  Internet address is 168.11.123.202/26
  MTU 1500 bytes, BW 56 Kbit, DLY 20000 usec, rely 255/255, load 1/255
  Encapsulation FRAME-RELAY, loopback not set, keepalive set (10 sec)
  LMI enq sent  1657, LMI stat recvd 1651, LMI upd recvd 0, DTE LMI up
  LMI enq recvd 0, LMI stat sent  0, LMI upd sent  0
  LMI DLCI 0  LMI type is ANSI Annex D  frame relay DTE
  Broadcast queue 0/64, broadcasts sent/dropped 979/0, interface broadcasts 490
  Last input 00:00:01, output 00:00:01, output hang never
  Last clearing of "show interface" counters never
  Queueing strategy: fifo
  Output queue 0/40, 0 drops; input queue 0/75, 0 drops
  5 minute input rate 0 bits/sec, 0 packets/sec
  5 minute output rate 0 bits/sec, 0 packets/sec
     4479 packets input, 165584 bytes, 0 no buffer
     Received 1 broadcasts, 0 runts, 0 giants, 0 throttles
     0 input errors, 0 CRC, 0 frame, 0 overrun, 0 ignored, 0 abort
     4304 packets output, 154785 bytes, 0 underruns
     0 output errors, 0 collisions, 4 interface resets
     0 output buffer failures, 0 output buffers swapped out
     12 carrier transitions
     DCD=up  DSR=up  DTR=up  RTS=up  CTS=up
 --More--
Serial1 is administratively down, line protocol is down
  Hardware is HD64570
  MTU 1500 bytes, BW 1544 Kbit, DLY 20000 usec, rely 255/255, load 1/255
  Encapsulation PPP, loopback not set, keepalive set (10 sec)
  LCP Closed
  Closed: CDPCP, LLC2
  Last input never, output never, output hang never
  Last clearing of "show interface" counters never
  Input queue: 0/75/0 (size/max/drops); Total output drops: 0
  Queueing strategy: weighted fair
  Output queue: 0/1000/0 (size/max total/drops)
     Conversations  0/0/64 (active/max active/threshold)
     Reserved Conversations 0/0 (allocated/max allocated)
  5 minute input rate 0 bits/sec, 0 packets/sec
  5 minute output rate 0 bits/sec, 0 packets/sec
     0 packets input, 0 bytes, 0 no buffer
     Received 0 broadcasts, 0 runts, 0 giants, 0 throttles
     0 input errors, 0 CRC, 0 frame, 0 overrun, 0 ignored, 0 abort
     0 packets output, 0 bytes, 0 underruns
     0 output errors, 0 collisions, 5 interface resets
     0 output buffer failures, 0 output buffers swapped out
     0 carrier transitions
     DCD=down  DSR=down  DTR=down  RTS=down  CTS=down
 --More--
Ethernet0 is up, line protocol is up
  Hardware is MCI Ethernet, address is 0000.0c89.b170 (bia 0000.0c89.b170)
  Internet address is 168.11.12.202/26, subnet mask is 255.255.255.192
  MTU 1500 bytes, BW 10000 Kbit, DLY 100000 usec, rely 255/255, load 1/255
```

continues

Example 9-13 *Scenario 9-2c R2* **show** *and* **debug** *Output (Continued)*

```
         Encapsulation ARPA, loopback not set, keepalive set (10 sec)
         ARP type: ARPA, ARP Timeout 4:00:00
         Last input 00:00:04, output 00:00:04, output hang never
         Last clearing of "show interface" counters never
         Queueing strategy: fifo
         Output queue 0/40, 0 drops; input queue 0/75, 0 drops
         5 minute input rate 0 bits/sec, 0 packets/sec
         5 minute output rate 0 bits/sec, 0 packets/sec
            6519 packets input, 319041 bytes, 0 no buffer
            Received 5544 broadcasts, 0 runts, 0 giants, 0 throttles
            0 input errors, 0 CRC, 0 frame, 0 overrun, 0 ignored, 0 abort
            2055 packets output, 192707 bytes, 0 underruns
            0 output errors, 0 collisions, 2 interface resets
            0 output buffer failures, 0 output buffers swapped out
            6 transitions

R2#show ipx interface brief
Interface              IPX Network Encapsulation Status               IPX State
Serial0                123         FRAME-RELAY  up                    [up]
Serial1                unassigned  not config'd administratively down n/a
Ethernet0              120         SAP          up                    [up]
Ethernet0              121         SNAP         up                    [up]

R2#show ip protocol
Routing Protocol is "igrp 1"
  Sending updates every 90 seconds, next due in 6 seconds
  Invalid after 270 seconds, hold down 280, flushed after 630
  Outgoing update filter list for all interfaces is not set
  Incoming update filter list for all interfaces is not set
  Default networks flagged in outgoing updates
  Default networks accepted from incoming updates
  IGRP metric weight K1=1, K2=0, K3=1, K4=0, K5=0
  IGRP maximum hopcount 100
  IGRP maximum metric variance 1
  Redistributing: igrp 1
  Routing for Networks:
    168.11.0.0
  Routing Information Sources:
    Gateway         Distance      Last Update
    168.11.11.201       100       00:00:02
    168.11.11.203       100       00:00:09
  Distance: (default is 100)

R2#show ipx route
Codes: C - Connected primary network,    c - Connected secondary network
       S - Static, F - Floating static, L - Local (internal), W - IPXWAN
       R - RIP, E - EIGRP, N - NLSP, X - External, A - Aggregate
       s - seconds, u - uses

9 Total IPX routes. Up to 1 parallel paths and 16 hops allowed.

No default route known.
```

Example 9-13 *Scenario 9-2c R2* **show** *and* **debug** *Output (Continued)*

```
C       120 (SAP),          E0
c       121 (SNAP),         E0
C       123 (FRAME-RELAY),  Se0
R       101 [08/03] via     123.0200.aaaa.aaaa,   21s, Se0
R       102 [08/03] via     123.0200.aaaa.aaaa,   22s, Se0
R       103 [02/02] via     120.0000.0cac.70ef,   29s, E0
R       110 [07/01] via     123.0200.aaaa.aaaa,   22s, Se0
R       111 [07/01] via     123.0200.aaaa.aaaa,   22s, Se0
R       130 [07/01] via     123.0200.3333.3333,   19s, Se0

R2#show ipx servers
Codes: S - Static, P - Periodic, E - EIGRP, N - NLSP, H - Holddown, + = detail
2 Total IPX Servers

Table ordering is based on routing and server info

    Type Name                    Net      Address    Port   Route Hops Itf
P      4 Server3                 103.0000.0000.0001:0451   2/02   2 E0
P      4 Server1                 101.0000.0000.0001:0451   8/03   3 Se0

R2#show frame-relay pvc

PVC Statistics for interface Serial0 (Frame Relay DTE)

DLCI = 501, DLCI USAGE = LOCAL, PVC STATUS = ACTIVE, INTERFACE = Serial0

  input pkts 780         output pkts 529         in bytes 39602
  out bytes 29260        dropped pkts 0          in FECN pkts 0
  in BECN pkts 0         out FECN pkts 0         out BECN pkts 0
  in DE pkts 0           out DE pkts 0
  out bcast pkts 525      out bcast bytes 28924
  pvc create time 04:36:40, last time pvc status changed 04:34:54
  --More--
DLCI = 503, DLCI USAGE = LOCAL, PVC STATUS = ACTIVE, INTERFACE = Serial0

  input pkts 481         output pkts 493         in bytes 30896
  out bytes 34392        dropped pkts 0          in FECN pkts 0
  in BECN pkts 0         out FECN pkts 0         out BECN pkts 0
  in DE pkts 0           out DE pkts 0
  out bcast pkts 493      out bcast bytes 34392
  pvc create time 04:36:41, last time pvc status changed 04:34:55

R2#show frame-relay map
Serial0 (up): ipx 123.0200.aaaa.aaaa dlci 501(0x1F5,0x7C50), dynamic,
              broadcast,, status defined, active
Serial0 (up): ipx 123.0200.3333.3333 dlci 503(0x1F7,0x7C70), dynamic,
              broadcast,, status defined, active
Serial0 (up): ip 168.11.123.201 dlci 501(0x1F5,0x7C50), dynamic,
              broadcast,, status defined, active
Serial0 (up): ip 168.11.123.203 dlci 503(0x1F7,0x7C70), dynamic,
              broadcast,, status defined, active
```

Example 9-14 *Scenario 9-2c R3* ***show*** *and* ***debug*** *Output*

```
R3#show running-config
Building configuration...

Current configuration:
!
version 11.2
no service password-encryption
no service udp-small-servers
no service tcp-small-servers
!
hostname R3
!
enable secret 5 $1$kI1V$NkybGlP9tzP7BYvAKYT.c1
!
no ip domain-lookup
ipx routing 0200.3333.3333
!
interface Serial0
 ip address 168.11.123.203 255.255.255.192
 encapsulation frame-relay
 ipx network 123
 no fair-queue
 frame-relay interface-dlci 501
 frame-relay interface-dlci 502
!
interface Serial1
 no ip address
 encapsulation ppp
 shutdown
 clockrate 56000
!
interface Ethernet0
 ip address 168.11.13.203 255.255.255.192
 ipx network 130
 ring-speed 16
!
router igrp 1
 network 168.11.0.0
!
no ip classless
!
!
!
!
line con 0
 password cisco
 login
line aux 0
line vty 0 4
 password cisco
 login
!
end
```

Example 9-14 *Scenario 9-2c R3 **show** and **debug** Output (Continued)*

```
R3#show ip arp
Protocol  Address              Age (min)  Hardware Addr   Type   Interface
Internet  168.11.13.203            -      0000.0c89.b1b0  SNAP   Ethernet0

R3#show ip route
Codes: C - connected, S - static, I - IGRP, R - RIP, M - mobile, B - BGP
       D - EIGRP, EX - EIGRP external, O - OSPF, IA - OSPF inter area
       N1 - OSPF NSSA external type 1, N2 - OSPF NSSA external type 2
       E1 - OSPF external type 1, E2 - OSPF external type 2, E - EGP
       i - IS-IS, L1 - IS-IS level-1, L2 - IS-IS level-2, * - candidate default
       U - per-user static route, o - ODR

Gateway of last resort is not set

      168.11.0.0/26 is subnetted, 4 subnets
C        168.11.123.192 is directly connected, Serial0
I        168.11.11.192 [100/8539] via 168.11.123.201, 00:00:06, Serial0
C        168.11.13.192 is directly connected, Ethernet0
I        168.11.12.192 [100/8539] via 168.11.123.202, 00:00:46, Serial0

R3#ping 168.11.11.250

Type escape sequence to abort.
Sending 5, 100-byte ICMP Echos to 168.11.11.250, timeout is 2 seconds:
!!!!!
Success rate is 100 percent (5/5), round-trip min/avg/max = 76/76/76 ms

R3#trace 168.11.11.250

Type escape sequence to abort.
Tracing the route to 168.11.11.250

  1 168.11.123.201 44 msec 44 msec 44 msec
  2 168.11.11.250 44 msec *  40 msec

R3#show ipx servers
Codes: S - Static, P - Periodic, E - EIGRP, N - NLSP, H - Holddown, + = detail
3 Total IPX Servers

Table ordering is based on routing and server info

      Type Name               Net      Address    Port    Route Hops Itf
P       4 Server1             101.0000.0000.0001:0451    8/03   3  Se0
P       4 Server2             102.0000.0000.0001:0451    8/03   3  Se0
P       4 Server3             103.0000.0000.0001:0451    8/03   3  Se0

R3#show frame-relay map
Serial0 (up): ipx 123.0200.aaaa.aaaa dlci 501(0x1F5,0x7C50), dynamic,
              broadcast,, status defined, active
Serial0 (up): ipx 123.0200.bbbb.bbbb dlci 502(0x1F6,0x7C60), dynamic,
              broadcast,, status defined, active
Serial0 (up): ip 168.11.123.201 dlci 501(0x1F5,0x7C50), dynamic,
```

continues

Example 9-14 *Scenario 9-2c R3* ***show*** *and* ***debug*** *Output (Continued)*

```
                   broadcast,, status defined, active
Serial0 (up): ip 168.11.123.202 dlci 502(0x1F6,0x7C60), dynamic,
               broadcast,, status defined, active

R3#show frame-relay lmi

LMI Statistics for interface Serial0 (Frame Relay DTE) LMI TYPE = CISCO
  Invalid Unnumbered info 0        Invalid Prot Disc 0
  Invalid dummy Call Ref 0         Invalid Msg Type 0
  Invalid Status Message 0         Invalid Lock Shift 0
  Invalid Information ID 0         Invalid Report IE Len 0
  Invalid Report Request 0         Invalid Keep IE Len 0
  Num Status Enq. Sent 1677        Num Status msgs Rcvd 1677
  Num Update Status Rcvd 0         Num Status Timeouts 0
```

Using Example 9-12, Example 9-13, and Example 9-14 as references, answer the following questions:

1. What command tells you how much time must elapse before the next IP IGRP update is sent by a router?

2. What command shows you a summary of the IP addresses on that router?

3. What **show** command identifies which routes were learned with IP RIP? IPX RIP? What in the command output identifies these routing protocols?

4. What **show** command lists SAP information in the router?

5. Describe the contents of an IP IGRP update from R1 to R3. What **debug** command options provide the details of what is in the IGRP update?

6. What password is required to move from user mode to privileged mode? What configuration command(s) can be used to set the password that is required?

7. If an interface configuration subcommand you cannot recall starts with the letter D, how can you get help to list all commands that start with D? List all steps. Assume you are in privileged mode.

8. After changing the configuration and moving back to privileged mode, you want to save your configuration. Name the two commands that can be used.

9. List all characters displayed onscreen during the process of getting into configuration mode from privileged mode, changing the hostname from R1 to R2, and then getting back to privileged mode.

10. In this network, if setup mode were used to configure the IP addresses on the interface, how would the subnet mask information be entered?

11. If a routing loop occurred so that IP packets destined to 168.11.12.66 were routed between routers continually, what stops the packet from rotating forever? Are any notification messages sent when the routers notice what is happening, and if so, what is the message(s)?

12. Describe the role of R1 relating to TCP error recovery for an FTP connection between PC11 and PC21.

13. Define "Integrated Multiprotocol Routing."

14. Describe how R2 learns that R1's IP address is 168.11.123.201.

15. What does NBMA stand for?

16. When does IGRP use split-horizon rules on interfaces with Frame Relay encapsulation?

17. What effect does the **no keepalive** interface subcommand have on Frame Relay interfaces?

18. If just the VC between R1 and R3 needed to use encapsulation of **ietf**, what configuration changes would be needed?

19. What command lists the total number of Status Enquiry messages received on a Frame Relay interface?

20. List examples of two ISDN function groups.

21. What type of ISDN channel is used for signaling?

Scenario 9-2c—Verification and Questions Answers

The answers to the questions for Scenario 9-2c are as follows:

1. The **show ip protocol** command (refer to Example 9-13).

2. The **show ip interface brief** command (refer to Example 9-12).

3. The **show ip route** and **show ipx route** commands. The metric values for each subnet/network are in brackets.

4. The **show ipx servers** command (refer to Example 9-14).

5. The **debug ip igrp transaction** command provides **debug** output with details of the IGRP updates. The output is immediately following the **IGRP: sending update to 255.255.255.255 via Serial0 (168.11.123.201)** message. Notice that all four routes are advertised because split-horizon is disabled on the serial interface when no subinterfaces are used.

6. The enable password is the required password; the user is prompted after typing the **enable** EXEC command. The **enable** and **enable secret** commands define the password; if both are configured, the **enable secret** takes precedence.

7. The steps are as follows:

```
R3#configure terminal
R3(config)#interface serial 0
R3(config-if)#D?

dce-terminal-timing-enable  default          delay  description  dialer
dialer-group                down-when-looped  dspu   dxi

R3(config-if)#d#Ctrl-Z
R3#
```

8. **write memory** and **copy running-config startup-config**.

9. The answer is as follows:

```
R1#configure terminal
R1(config)#hostname R2
R2(config)Ctrl-Z
R2#
```

The most important part of this question is to realize that configuration changes are immediate. Notice that the prompt is changed immediately after the hostname command.

10. Enter the mask information as a number of subnet bits rather than simply type the mask. In this network, mask 255.255.255.192 implies six host bits. A Class B network is used, which implies 16 network bits, leaving 10 subnet bits.

11. The time-to-live field in the IP header is decremented by each router. After the number is decremented to 0, the router discards the packet. That router also sends an ICMP TTL-exceeded message to the host that sent the packet.

12. The router plays no role in TCP error recovery in this case. The endpoint hosts are responsible for the TCP processing.

13. Integrated Multiprotocol Routing means that routed protocols IP, IPX, and AppleTalk use a common routing protocol, which consolidates routing updates. EIGRP is the only such routing protocol in the IOS.

14. Inverse ARP is used by R1 to announce its IP and IPX addresses on the serial interface used for frame relay. The Inverse ARP message is sent over the VC between the two routers. R2 learns based on receiving the message.

15. Non-Broadcast Multi-Access.

16. IGRP uses split-horizon on point-to-point subinterfaces only. If multipoint subinterfaces are used, or no subinterfaces are used, split-horizon is off by default.

17. LMI keepalive messages, which flow between the router and the switch, are no longer sent.

18. The **frame-relay interface-dlci** command could be changed to include the keyword **ietf** at the end of the command, for example, **frame-relay interface-dlci 501 ietf**.

19. The **show frame-relay lmi** command (refer to Example 9-14).

20. NT1, NT2, TE1, TE2, and TA are all Function Groups.

21. D Channels are used for signaling.

Scenario 9-3

The final review scenario begins with some planning guidelines that include planning IP addresses, IPX network numbers, the location of SAP filters, and the location of IP standard access lists. After it is completed, Scenario 9-3b asks that you configure the three routers to implement the planned design and a few other features. Finally, in Scenario 9-3c, some errors have been introduced into the network, and you are asked to examine router command output to find the errors. Also, questions relating to the user interface and protocol specifications are listed in Scenario 9-3c.

Scenario 9-3a—Planning

Your job is to deploy a new network with three sites, as shown in Figure 9-5. The use of point-to-point serial links, as well as the product choices, have already been made. To complete Scenario 9-3a, perform the following tasks:

1. Plan the IP addressing and subnets used in this network. Class B network 170.1.0.0 has been assigned by the NIC. The maximum number of hosts per subnet is 300. Assign IP addresses to the PCs as well. Use Table 9-10 and Table 9-11 to record your answers.

2. Plan the IPX network numbers to be used. You can choose the internal network numbers of the servers as well. Each LAN should support both SAP and SNAP encapsulations.

3. Plan the location and logic of IP access lists to filter for the following criteria:
   - Access to servers in PC11 and PC12 is allowed for Web and FTP clients from anywhere else.
   - All other traffic to/from PC11 and PC12 is not allowed.
   - No IP traffic between the Ethernets off R2 and R3 is allowed.
   - All other IP traffic between any sites is allowed.

4. Plan the location and logic of SAP filters. Ensure that Server3 is only accessed by clients on the Ethernet off R2.

5. After your subnet numbers are chosen, calculate the broadcast addresses and the range of valid IP addresses in each subnet. Use Table 9-12 if convenient.

Figure 9-5 *Scenario 9-3 Network Diagram*

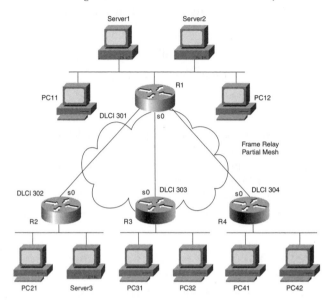

Table 9-10 *Scenario 9-3a IP Subnet and IPX Network Planning Chart*

Location of Subnet/Network Geographically	Subnet Mask	Subnet Number	IPX Network
Ethernet off Router 1			
Ethernet off Router 2			
Ethernet off Router 3			
Ethernet off Router 4			
Virtual Circuit between R1 and R2			
Virtual Circuit between R1 and R3			
Virtual Circuit between R1 and R4			
Server1 Internal			
Server2 Internal			
Server3 Internal			

Table 9-11   *Scenario 9-3a IP Address Planning Chart*

Host	Address
PC11	
PC12	
PC21	
PC31	
PC32	
AC41	
AC42	
R1-E0	
R1-S0-sub ____	
R1-S0-sub ____	
R1-S0-sub ____	
R2-E0	
R2-S0-sub ____	
R3-E0	
R3-S0-sub ____	
R4-E0	
R4-S0-sub ____	
SERVER1	
SERVER2	
SERVER3	

Table 9-12   *Scenario 9-3a IP Subnet Planning Chart*

Subnet Number	Subnet Broadcast Address	Range of Valid Addresses

Scenario 9-3a—Planning Answers

The IP subnet design includes the use of mask 255.255.254.0. If the same mask is used throughout the network, then at least nine host bits are needed because at least one subnet contains 300 hosts. Only one subnet is needed per Ethernet port on each router because the transparent bridges and switches do not separate the hosts into different subnets.

The IPX network number assignment is simple, other than remembering that two networks will be needed on each Ethernet because two encapsulations are used. Each Encapsulation type on the router requires the use of a separate IPX network. The subnets, networks, and IP addresses are recorded in Table 9-13 and Table 9-14.

Table 9-13   *Scenario 9-3a IP Subnet and IPX Network Planning Chart Completed*

Location of Subnet/Network Geographically	Subnet Mask	Subnet Number	IPX Network
Ethernet off Router 1	255.255.254.0	170.1.2.0	2,3
Ethernet off Router 2	255.255.254.0	170.1.4.0	4,5
Ethernet off Router 3	255.255.254.0	170.1.6.0	6,7
Ethernet off Router 4	255.255.254.0	170.1.8.0	8,9
Virtual Circuit between R1 and R2	255.255.254.0	170.1.10.0	10
Virtual Circuit between R1 and R3	255.255.254.0	170.1.12.0	12
Virtual Circuit between R1 and R4	255.255.254.0	170.1.14.0	14
Server1 Internal	N/A	N/A	101
Server2 Internal	N/A	N/A	102
Server3 Internal	N/A	N/A	103

The choice of IP addresses can conform to any standard you like, as long as the addresses are in the correct subnets. Refer to Table 9-15 for the list of valid addresses for the subnets chosen. In Table 9-14, the addresses chosen for the PCs reflect the number of the PC. For the routers, the addresses chosen are in the second half of the range of addresses in each subnet and are shown as a reminder of the addresses that are valid in this subnetting scheme.

Table 9-14   *Scenario 9-3a IP Address Planning Chart Completed*

Host	Address
PC11	170.1.2.11
PC12	170.1.2.12
PC21	170.1.4.21
PC22	170.1.4.22
PC31	170.1.6.31

Table 9-14 *Scenario 9-3a IP Address Planning Chart Completed (Continued)*

PC32	170.1.6.32
PC41	170.1.8.41
PC42	170.1.8.42
R1-E0	170.1.3.1
R1-S0-sub __2__	170.1.10.1
R1-S0-sub __3__	170.1.12.1
R1-S0-sub __4__	170.1.14.1
R2-E0	170.1.5.2
R2-S0-sub __2__	170.1.10.2
R3-E0	170.1.7.3
R3-S0-sub __3__	170.1.12.3
R4-E0	170.1.9.4
R4-S0-sub __4__	170.1.14.4
SERVER1	170.1.2.101
SERVER2	170.1.2.102
SERVER3	170.1.4.103

The IP access lists can be placed in several places effectively. Stopping packets in one of the two directions will succeed in stopping users from actually connecting to the servers. For the first set of criteria, an access list stopping packets from entering the serial interface of R1, stopping packets destined to PC11 and PC12, will suffice. For the second criteria, that of disallowing traffic between Site 2 and Site 3, the access lists are also placed in R1. The access lists will indeed stop the packets earlier in their life if they are placed in R2 and R3, but the traffic will be minimal because no true application traffic will ever successfully be generated between IP hosts at Sites 2 and 3.

So, the design calls for all filtered packets to be filtered via access lists enabled on subinterfaces on R1's S0 interface.

The SAP filter can be performed in one very obvious way. A SAP filter is added on R2 to filter Server 3 from the SAP table. The filter could filter incoming SAPs on R2's E0 or filter outgoing SAP updates out R2's S0 port. In this case, anticipating the day that a second Ethernet port is used on R2 and anticipating the fact that the objective probably meant that local clients should have access to Server 3, the plan in this case is to filter outbound SAPs on R2's S0 interface.

Finally, the broadcast addresses for each subnet are shown in Table 9-15. As a reminder: to calculate the broadcast address, write down the subnet number in binary. Then, copy down the network and subnet portions of the subnet number directly below it, leaving the host bit positions empty. Then, write all binary 1s in the host bit positions. Finally, convert the number back to decimal, eight bits at a time. The result is the subnet broadcast address and is the high end of the range of assignable addresses in that subnet.

The answers, which include the subnet numbers, their corresponding broadcast addresses, and the range of valid assignable IP addresses, are shown in Table 9-15.

Table 9-15 *Scenario 9-3a IP Subnet Planning Chart*

Subnet Number	Subnet Broadcast Address	Range of Valid Addresses (Last Two Bytes)
170.1.2.0	170.1.3.255	2.1 through 3.254
170.1.4.0	170.1.5.255	4.1 through 5.254
170.1.6.0	170.1.7.255	6.1 through 7.254
170.1.8.0	170.1.9.255	8.1 through 9.254
170.1.10.0	170.1.11.255	10.1 through 11.254
170.1.12.0	170.1.13.255	12.1 through 13.254
170.1.14.0	170.1.15.255	14.1 through 15.254

Scenario 9-3b—Configuration

The next step in your job is to deploy the network designed in Scenario 9-3a. Use the answers for Scenario 9-3a to direct you in regards to IP and IPX addresses, access lists, and for the encapsulations to be used. For Scenario 9-3b, perform the following tasks:

1. Configure IP and IPX to be routed. Use IP IGRP and IPX RIP as routing protocols. Use IGRP process-id 1.

2. Use secondary IPX addresses to accommodate the multiple IPX encapsulation types described in Scenario 9-3a.

3. Configure Frame Relay using point-to-point subinterfaces. R1's attached Frame Relay switch uses LMI type ANSI. Cisco encapsulation should be used for all routers, except for the VC between R1 and R4.

Scenario 9-3b—Configuration Answers

The configurations for Steps 1, 2, and 3 are shown in Example 9-15, Example 9-16, Example 9-17, and Example 9-18.

Example 9-15 *R1 Configuration*

```
ipx routing 0200.aaaa.aaaa
!
interface serial0
encapsulation frame-relay
interface serial 0.2 point-to-point
 ip address  170.1.10.1  255.255.254.0
```

Example 9-15 *R1 Configuration (Continued)*

```
 ipx network  10
 frame-relay interface-dlci 302
 ip access-group 102 in
!
interface serial 0.3 point-to-point
 ip address  170.1.12.1  255.255.254.0
 ipx network  12
 frame-relay interface-dlci 303
 ip access-group 103 in
!
interface serial 0.4 point-to-point
 ip address  170.1.14.1  255.255.254.0
 ipx network  14
 frame-relay interface-dlci 304 ietf
 ip access-group 104 in
!
interface ethernet 0
ip address  170.1.3.1  255.255.254.0
ipx network  2 encapsulation sap
ipx network  3 encapsulation snap secondary
!
router igrp 1
network 170.1.0.0

!
access-list 102 permit tcp any host 170.1.2.11 eq ftp
access-list 102 permit tcp any host 170.1.2.11 eq www
access-list 102 permit tcp any host 170.1.2.12 eq ftp
access-list 102 permit tcp any host 170.1.2.12 eq www
access-list 102 deny ip any host 170.1.2.11
access-list 102 deny ip any host 170.1.2.12
access-list 102 deny ip 170.1.4.0 0.0.1.255 170.1.6.0 0.0.1.255
access-list 102 permit ip any any

access-list 103 permit tcp any host 170.1.2.11 eq ftp
access-list 103 permit tcp any host 170.1.2.11 eq www
access-list 103 permit tcp any host 170.1.2.12 eq ftp
access-list 103 permit tcp any host 170.1.2.12 eq www
access-list 103 deny ip any host 170.1.2.11
access-list 103 deny ip any host 170.1.2.12
access-list 103 deny ip 170.1.6.0 0.0.1.255 170.1.4.0 0.0.1.255
access-list 103 permit ip any any

access-list 104 permit tcp any host 170.1.2.11 eq ftp
access-list 104 permit tcp any host 170.1.2.11 eq www
access-list 104 permit tcp any host 170.1.2.12 eq ftp
access-list 104 permit tcp any host 170.1.2.12 eq www
access-list 104 deny ip any host 170.1.2.11
access-list 104 deny ip any host 170.1.2.12
access-list 104 permit ip any any
```

Example 9-16 *R2 Configuration*

```
ipx routing 0200.bbbb.bbbb
!
interface serial0
encapsulation frame-relay
interface serial 0.2 point-to-point
 ip address  170.1.10.2  255.255.254.0
 ipx network  10
 frame-relay interface-dlci 301
 ipx output-sap-filter 1001
!
interface ethernet 0
ip address  170.1.5.2  255.255.254.0
ipx network  4 encapsulation sap
ipx network  5 encapsulation snap secondary
!
router igrp 1
network 170.1.0.0
!
access-list 1001 deny 103
access-list 1001 permit -1
```

Example 9-17 *R3 Configuration*

```
ipx routing 0200.cccc.cccc
!
interface serial0
encapsulation frame-relay
interface serial 0.3 point-to-point
 ip address  170.1.12.3  255.255.254.0
 ipx network  12
 frame-relay interface-dlci 301
!
interface ethernet 0
ip address  170.1.7.3  255.255.254.0
ipx network  6 encapsulation sap
ipx network  7 encapsulation snap secondary
!
router igrp 1
network 170.1.0.0
```

Example 9-18 *R4 Configuration*

```
ipx routing 0200.dddd.dddd
!
interface serial0
encapsulation frame-relay ietf
interface serial 0.4 point-to-point
 ip address  170.1.14.4  255.255.254.0
 ipx network  14
 frame-relay interface-dlci 301
!
interface ethernet 0
ip address  170.1.9.4  255.255.254.0
```

Example 9-18 *R4 Configuration (Continued)*

```
!
router igrp 1
network 170.1.0.0
```

Three different access lists are shown on R1. List 102 is used for packets entering subinterface 2. List 103 is used for packets entering subinterface 3, and list 104 is used for packets entering subinterface 4. Lists 102 and 103 check for packets between sites 2 and 3, as well as check for packets to PC11 and PC12. The mask used to check all hosts in subnets 170.1.4.0 and 170.1.6.0 is rather tricky. The mask represents 23 binary 0s and 9 binary 1s—meaning that the first 23 bits of the number in the access list must match the first 23 bits in the source or destination address in the packet. This matches all hosts in each subnet because there are 23 combined network and subnet bits.

Two IPX networks are used on each Ethernet because two encapsulations are used.

The Frame Relay configuration was relatively straightforward. The LMI type is autosensed. The encapsulation of **ietf** between R1 and R4 is configured in two ways. First, R1 uses the **ietf** keyword on the **frame-relay interface-dlci** command. On R4, the **encapsulation** command lists the **ietf** option, implying **ietf** encapsulation for all VCs on this serial interface.

Scenario 9-3c—Verification and Questions

The CCNA exam will test you on your memory of the kinds of information you can find in the output of various **show** commands. Using Example 9-19, Example 9-20, Example 9-21, and Example 9-22 as references, answer the questions following the examples.

Example 9-19 *Scenario 9-3c R1 **show** and **debug** Output*

```
R1#show ip interface brief
Interface          IP-Address      OK? Method Status                Protocol
Serial0            unassigned      YES unset  up                    up
Serial0.2          170.1.10.1      YES NVRAM  up                    up
Serial0.3          170.1.12.1      YES NVRAM  up                    up
Serial0.4          170.1.14.1      YES NVRAM  up                    up
Serial1            unassigned      YES unset  administratively down down
Ethernet0          170.1.3.1       YES NVRAM  up                    up

R1#show cdp neighbor detail
-------------------------
Device ID: R2
Entry address(es):
  IP address: 170.1.10.2
  Novell address: 10.0200.bbbb.bbbb
Platform: cisco 2500,  Capabilities: Router
Interface: Serial0.2,  Port ID (outgoing port): Serial0.1
Holdtime : 132 sec
```

continues

Example 9-19 *Scenario 9-3c R1* **show** *and* **debug** *Output (Continued)*

```
Version :
Cisco Internetwork Operating System Software
IOS (tm) 2500 Software (C2500-AINR-L), Version 11.2(11), RELEASE SOFTWARE (fc1)
Copyright (c) 1986-1997 by Cisco Systems, Inc.
Compiled Mon 29-Dec-97 18:47 by ckralik


-------------------------
Device ID: R3
Entry address(es):
  IP address: 170.1.12.3
  Novell address: 12.0200.cccc.cccc
Platform: Cisco 2500,  Capabilities: Router
Interface: Serial0.3,  Port ID (outgoing port): Serial0.1
Holdtime : 148 sec

Version :
Cisco Internetwork Operating System Software
IOS (tm) 2500 Software (C2500-AINR-L), Version 11.2(11), RELEASE SOFTWARE (fc1)
Copyright (c) 1986-1997 by Cisco Systems, Inc.
Compiled Mon 29-Dec-97 18:47 by ckralik


-------------------------
Device ID: R4
Entry address(es):
  IP address: 170.1.14.4
  Novell address: 14.0200.dddd.dddd
Platform: Cisco 2500,  Capabilities: Router
Interface: Serial0.4,  Port ID (outgoing port): Serial0.1
Holdtime : 149 sec

Version :
Cisco Internetwork Operating System Software
IOS (tm) 2500 Software (C2500-AINR-L), Version 11.2(11), RELEASE SOFTWARE (fc1)
Copyright (c) 1986-1997 by Cisco Systems, Inc.
Compiled Mon 29-Dec-97 18:47 by ckralik

R1#show ipx servers
Codes: S - Static, P - Periodic, E - EIGRP, N - NLSP, H - Holddown, + = detail
2 Total IPX Servers

Table ordering is based on routing and server info

     Type Name                    Net      Address      Port     Route Hops Itf
P      4 Server1                 101.0000.0000.0001:0451   2/02    2   E0
P      4 Server2                 102.0000.0000.0001:0451   2/02    2   E0
R1#
R1#debug ipx sap activity
IPX service debugging is on

R1#
IPXSAP: positing update to 2.ffff.ffff.ffff via Ethernet0 (broadcast) (full)
IPXSAP: suppressing null update to 2.ffff.ffff.ffff
IPXSAP: positing update to 3.ffff.ffff.ffff via Ethernet0 (broadcast) (full)
```

Example 9-19 *Scenario 9-3c R1 **show** and **debug** Output (Continued)*

```
IPXSAP: Update type 0x2 len 160 src:3.0000.0ccf.21cd dest:3.ffff.ffff.ffff(452)
 type 0x4, "Server2", 102.0000.0000.0001(451), 3 hops
 type 0x4, "Server1", 101.0000.0000.0001(451), 3 hops
IPXSAP: Response (in) type 0x2 len 160 src:2.0000.0c89.b130
dest:2.ffff.ffff.ffff(452)
 type 0x4, "Server1", 101.0000.0000.0001(451), 2 hops
 type 0x4, "Server2", 102.0000.0000.0001(451), 2 hops
IPXSAP: positing update to 10.ffff.ffff.ffff via Serial0.2 (broadcast) (full)
IPXSAP: Update type 0x2 len 160 src:10.0200.aaaa.aaaa dest:10.ffff.ffff.ffff(452)
 type 0x4, "Server2", 102.0000.0000.0001(451), 3 hops
 type 0x4, "Server1", 101.0000.0000.0001(451), 3 hops
IPXSAP: positing update to 14.ffff.ffff.ffff via Serial0.4 (broadcast) (full)
IPXSAP: Update type 0x2 len 160 src:14.0200.aaaa.aaaa dest:14.ffff.ffff.ffff(452)
 type 0x4, "Server2", 102.0000.0000.0001(451), 3 hops
 type 0x4, "Server1", 101.0000.0000.0001(451), 3 hops
R1#

IPXSAP: positing update to 12.ffff.ffff.ffff via Serial0.3 (broadcast) (full)
IPXSAP: Update type 0x2 len 160 src:12.0200.aaaa.aaaa dest:12.ffff.ffff.ffff(452)
 type 0x4, "Server2", 102.0000.0000.0001(451), 3 hops
 type 0x4, "Server1", 101.0000.0000.0001(451), 3 hops

R1#undebug all
All possible debugging has been turned off
R1#
R1#debug ipx routing activity

IPX routing debugging is on
R1#
IPXRIP: update from 12.0200.cccc.cccc
    7 in 1 hops, delay 7
    6 in 1 hops, delay 7
IPXRIP: positing full update to 14.ffff.ffff.ffff via Serial0.4 (broadcast)
IPXRIP: src=14.0200.aaaa.aaaa, dst=14.ffff.ffff.ffff, packet sent
    network 4, hops 2,  delay 13
    network 5, hops 2,  delay 13
    network 103, hops 4,  delay 14
    network 10, hops 1,  delay 7
    network 6, hops 2,  delay 13
    network 7, hops 2,  delay 13
    network 3, hops 1,  delay 7
    network 2, hops 1,  delay 7
    network 101, hops 3,  delay 8
    network 102, hops 3,  delay 8
    network 12, hops 1,  delay 7
IPXRIP: positing full update to 12.ffff.ffff.ffff via Serial0.3 (broadcast)
IPXRIP: src=12.0200.aaaa.aaaa, dst=12.ffff.ffff.ffff, packet sent
    network 8, hops 2,  delay 13
    network 9, hops 2,  delay 13
    network 14, hops 1,  delay 7
    network 4, hops 2,  delay 13
    network 5, hops 2,  delay 13
    network 103, hops 4,  delay 14
```

continues

Example 9-19 *Scenario 9-3c R1* **show** *and* **debug** *Output (Continued)*

```
     network 10, hops 1,  delay 7
     network 3, hops 1,  delay 7
     network 2, hops 1,  delay 7
     network 101, hops 3,  delay 8
     network 102, hops 3,  delay 8
IPXRIP: update from 14.0200.dddd.dddd
     9 in 1 hops, delay 7
     8 in 1 hops, delay 7
IPXRIP: update from 10.0200.bbbb.bbbb
     444 in 2 hops, delay 8
     103 in 3 hops, delay 8
     5 in 1 hops, delay 7
     4 in 1 hops, delay 7
IPXRIP: positing full update to 3.ffff.ffff.ffff via Ethernet0 (broadcast)
IPXRIP: src=3.0000.0ccf.21cd, dst=3.ffff.ffff.ffff, packet sent
     network 8, hops 2,  delay 8
     network 9, hops 2,  delay 8
     network 14, hops 1,  delay 2
     network 4, hops 2,  delay 8
     network 5, hops 2,  delay 8
     network 103, hops 4,  delay 9
     network 10, hops 1,  delay 2
     network 6, hops 2,  delay 8
     network 7, hops 2,  delay 8
     network 2, hops 1,  delay 2
     network 101, hops 3,  delay 3
     network 102, hops 3,  delay 3
     network 12, hops 1,  delay 2
IPXRIP: update from 2.0000.0c89.b130
     102 in 2 hops, delay 2
     101 in 2 hops, delay 2
IPXRIP: positing full update to 2.ffff.ffff.ffff via Ethernet0 (broadcast)
IPXRIP: src=2.0000.0ccf.21cd, dst=2.ffff.ffff.ffff, packet sent
     network 8, hops 2,  delay 8
     network 9, hops 2,  delay 8
     network 14, hops 1,  delay 2
     network 4, hops 2,  delay 8
     network 5, hops 2,  delay 8
     network 103, hops 4,  delay 9
     network 10, hops 1,  delay 2
     network 6, hops 2,  delay 8
     network 7, hops 2,  delay 8
     network 3, hops 1,  delay 2
     network 12, hops 1,  delay 2
IPXRIP: positing full update to 10.ffff.ffff.ffff via Serial0.2 (broadcast)
IPXRIP: src=10.0200.aaaa.aaaa, dst=10.ffff.ffff.ffff, packet sent
     network 8, hops 2,  delay 13
     network 9, hops 2,  delay 13
     network 14, hops 1,  delay 7
     network 6, hops 2,  delay 13
     network 7, hops 2,  delay 13
     network 3, hops 1,  delay 7
     network 2, hops 1,  delay 7
```

Example 9-19 *Scenario 9-3c R1* **show** *and* **debug** *Output (Continued)*

```
        network 101, hops 3,  delay 8
        network 102, hops 3,  delay 8
        network 12, hops 1,  delay 7
R1#
R1#undebug all
All possible debugging has been turned off
R1#
R1#
R1#debug ip igrp transactions
IGRP protocol debugging is on
R1#
IGRP: received update from 170.1.14.4 on Serial0.4
        subnet 170.1.8.0, metric 8539 (neighbor 688)
IGRP: sending update to 255.255.255.255 via Serial0.2 (170.1.10.1)
        subnet 170.1.8.0, metric=8539
        subnet 170.1.14.0, metric=8476
        subnet 170.1.12.0, metric=8476
        subnet 170.1.2.0, metric=688
        subnet 170.1.6.0, metric=8539
IGRP: sending update to 255.255.255.255 via Serial0.3 (170.1.12.1)
        subnet 170.1.10.0, metric=8476
        subnet 170.1.8.0, metric=8539
        subnet 170.1.14.0, metric=8476
        subnet 170.1.2.0, metric=688
        subnet 170.1.4.0, metric=8539

IGRP: sending update to 255.255.255.255 via Serial0.4 (170.1.14.1)
        subnet 170.1.10.0, metric=8476
        subnet 170.1.12.0, metric=8476
        subnet 170.1.2.0, metric=688
        subnet 170.1.6.0, metric=8539
        subnet 170.1.4.0, metric=8539
IGRP: sending update to 255.255.255.255 via Ethernet0 (170.1.3.1)
        subnet 170.1.10.0, metric=8476
        subnet 170.1.8.0, metric=8539
        subnet 170.1.14.0, metric=8476
        subnet 170.1.12.0, metric=8476
        subnet 170.1.6.0, metric=8539
        subnet 170.1.4.0, metric=8539
IGRP: received update from 170.1.10.2 on Serial0.2
        subnet 170.1.4.0, metric 8539 (neighbor 688)
IGRP: received update from 170.1.12.3 on Serial0.3
        subnet 170.1.6.0, metric 8539 (neighbor 688)
R1#
R1#undebug all
All possible debugging has been turned off
```

Example 9-20 *Scenario 9-3c R2* **show** *and* **debug** *Output*

```
R2#show interface
Serial0 is up, line protocol is up
  Hardware is HD64570
```

continues

Example 9-20 *Scenario 9-3c R2* ***show*** *and* ***debug*** *Output (Continued)*

```
  MTU 1500 bytes, BW 56 Kbit, DLY 20000 usec, rely 255/255, load 1/255
  Encapsulation FRAME-RELAY, loopback not set, keepalive set (10 sec)
  LMI enq sent  144, LMI stat recvd 138, LMI upd recvd 0, DTE LMI up
  LMI enq recvd 0, LMI stat sent  0, LMI upd sent  0
  LMI DLCI 0  LMI type is ANSI Annex D  frame relay DTE
  Broadcast queue 0/64, broadcasts sent/dropped 73/0, interface broadcasts 48
  Last input 00:00:04, output 00:00:04, output hang never
  Last clearing of "show interface" counters never
  Input queue: 0/75/0 (size/max/drops); Total output drops: 0
  Queueing strategy: weighted fair
  Output queue: 0/1000/0 (size/max total/drops)
     Conversations  0/1/64 (active/max active/threshold)
     Reserved Conversations 0/0 (allocated/max allocated)
  5 minute input rate 0 bits/sec, 0 packets/sec
  5 minute output rate 0 bits/sec, 0 packets/sec
     232 packets input, 17750 bytes, 0 no buffer
     Received 1 broadcasts, 0 runts, 0 giants, 0 throttles
     0 input errors, 0 CRC, 0 frame, 0 overrun, 0 ignored, 0 abort
     225 packets output, 12563 bytes, 0 underruns
     0 output errors, 0 collisions, 4 interface resets
     0 output buffer failures, 0 output buffers swapped out
     12 carrier transitions
     DCD=up  DSR=up  DTR=up  RTS=up  CTS=up
 --More--
Serial0.1 is up, line protocol is up
  Hardware is HD64570
  Internet address is 170.1.10.2/23
  MTU 1500 bytes, BW 56 Kbit, DLY 20000 usec, rely 255/255, load 1/255
  Encapsulation FRAME-RELAY
 --More--
Serial1 is administratively down, line protocol is down
  Hardware is HD64570
  MTU 1500 bytes, BW 1544 Kbit, DLY 20000 usec, rely 255/255, load 1/255
  Encapsulation PPP, loopback not set, keepalive set (10 sec)
  LCP Closed
  Closed: CDPCP, LLC2
  Last input never, output never, output hang never
  Last clearing of "show interface" counters never
  Input queue: 0/75/0 (size/max/drops); Total output drops: 0
  Queueing strategy: weighted fair
  Output queue: 0/1000/0 (size/max total/drops)
     Conversations  0/0/64 (active/max active/threshold)
     Reserved Conversations 0/0 (allocated/max allocated)
  5 minute input rate 0 bits/sec, 0 packets/sec
  5 minute output rate 0 bits/sec, 0 packets/sec
     0 packets input, 0 bytes, 0 no buffer
     Received 0 broadcasts, 0 runts, 0 giants, 0 throttles
     0 input errors, 0 CRC, 0 frame, 0 overrun, 0 ignored, 0 abort
     0 packets output, 0 bytes, 0 underruns
     0 output errors, 0 collisions, 5 interface resets
     0 output buffer failures, 0 output buffers swapped out
     0 carrier transitions
     DCD=down  DSR=down  DTR=down  RTS=down  CTS=down
```

Example 9-20 *Scenario 9-3c R2 show and debug Output (Continued)*

```
--More--
Ethernet0 is up, line protocol is up
  Hardware is TMS380, address is 0000.0c89.b170 (bia 0000.0c89.b170)
  Internet address is 170.1.5.2/23
  MTU 1500 bytes, BW 10000 Kbit, DLY 100000 usec, rely 255/255, load 1/255
  Encapsulation ARPA, loopback not set, keepalive set (10 sec)
  ARP type: ARPA, ARP Timeout 4:00:00
  Last input 00:00:00, output 00:00:01, output hang never
  Last clearing of "show interface" counters never
  Queueing strategy: fifo
  Output queue 0/40, 0 drops; input queue 0/75, 0 drops
  5 minute input rate 0 bits/sec, 0 packets/sec
  5 minute output rate 0 bits/sec, 0 packets/sec
     583 packets input, 28577 bytes, 0 no buffer
     Received 486 broadcasts, 0 runts, 0 giants, 0 throttles
     0 input errors, 0 CRC, 0 frame, 0 overrun, 0 ignored, 0 abort
     260 packets output, 31560 bytes, 0 underruns
     0 output errors, 0 collisions, 2 interface resets
     0 output buffer failures, 0 output buffers swapped out
     6 transitions

R2#show ipx interface brief
Interface          IPX Network Encapsulation Status              IPX State
Serial0            unassigned  not config'd  up                  n/a
Serial0.1          10          FRAME-RELAY   up                  [up]
Serial1            unassigned  not config'd  administratively down n/a
Ethernet0          4           SAP           up                  [up]
Ethernet0          5           SNAP          up                  [up]
R2#
R2#show ipx route
Codes: C - Connected primary network,    c - Connected secondary network
       S - Static, F - Floating static, L - Local (internal), W - IPXWAN
       R - RIP, E - EIGRP, N - NLSP, X - External, A - Aggregate
       s - seconds, u - uses

14 Total IPX routes. Up to 1 parallel paths and 16 hops allowed.

No default route known.

C         4 (SAP),        E0
c         5 (SNAP),       E0
C        10 (FRAME-RELAY), Se0.1
R         2 [07/01] via   10.0200.aaaa.aaaa,   47s, Se0.1
R         3 [07/01] via   10.0200.aaaa.aaaa,   48s, Se0.1
R         6 [13/02] via   10.0200.aaaa.aaaa,   48s, Se0.1
R         7 [13/02] via   10.0200.aaaa.aaaa,   48s, Se0.1
R         8 [13/02] via   10.0200.aaaa.aaaa,   48s, Se0.1
R         9 [13/02] via   10.0200.aaaa.aaaa,   48s, Se0.1
R        12 [07/01] via   10.0200.aaaa.aaaa,   48s, Se0.1
R        14 [07/01] via   10.0200.aaaa.aaaa,   48s, Se0.1
R       101 [08/03] via   10.0200.aaaa.aaaa,   48s, Se0.1
R       102 [08/03] via   10.0200.aaaa.aaaa,   48s, Se0.1
```

continues

Example 9-20 *Scenario 9-3c R2 **show** and **debug** Output (Continued)*

```
R        103 [02/02] via       4.0000.0cac.70ef,   42s, E0

R2#ping 14.0200.dddd.dddd
Translating "14.0200.dddd.dddd"

Type escape sequence to abort.
Sending 5, 100-byte IPX Cisco Echoes to 14.0200.dddd.dddd, timeout is 2 seconds:
!!!!!
Success rate is 100 percent (5/5), round-trip min/avg/max = 140/144/148 ms

R2#show ipx servers
Codes: S - Static, P - Periodic, E - EIGRP, N - NLSP, H - Holddown, + = detail
3 Total IPX Servers

Table ordering is based on routing and server info

     Type Name                  Net      Address    Port    Route Hops Itf
P    4 Server3                  103.0000.0000.0001:0451    2/02   2  E0
P    4 Server1                  101.0000.0000.0001:0451    8/03   3  Se0.1
P    4 Server2                  102.0000.0000.0001:0451    8/03   3  Se0.1

R2#show frame-relay pvc

PVC Statistics for interface Serial0 (Frame Relay DTE)

DLCI = 301, DLCI USAGE = LOCAL, PVC STATUS = ACTIVE, INTERFACE = Serial0.1

  input pkts 102          output pkts 82          in bytes 16624
  out bytes 11394         dropped pkts 0          in FECN pkts 0
  in BECN pkts 0          out FECN pkts 0         out BECN pkts 0
  in DE pkts 0            out DE pkts 0
  out bcast pkts 76        out bcast bytes 10806
  pvc create time 00:25:09, last time pvc status changed 00:23:15

R2#show frame-relay lmi

LMI Statistics for interface Serial0 (Frame Relay DTE) LMI TYPE = ANSI
  Invalid Unnumbered info 0        Invalid Prot Disc 0
  Invalid dummy Call Ref 0         Invalid Msg Type 0
  Invalid Status Message 0         Invalid Lock Shift 0
  Invalid Information ID 0         Invalid Report IE Len 0
  Invalid Report Request 0         Invalid Keep IE Len 0
  Num Status Enq. Sent 151         Num Status msgs Rcvd 145
  Num Update Status Rcvd 0         Num Status Timeouts 7
R2#
```

Example 9-21 *Scenario 9-3c R3 **show** and **debug** Output*

```
R3#show ipx servers
Codes: S - Static, P - Periodic, E - EIGRP, N - NLSP, H - Holddown, + = detail
2 Total IPX Servers

Table ordering is based on routing and server info

      Type Name                     Net      Address    Port    Route Hops Itf
P     4 Server1                     101.0000.0000.0001:0451    8/03   3  Se0.1
P     4 Server2                     102.0000.0000.0001:0451    8/03   3  Se0.1

R3#show ip arp
Protocol  Address            Age (min)  Hardware Addr   Type    Interface
Internet  170.1.7.3              -       0000.0c89.b1b0  SNAP    Ethernet0

R3#show ip route
Codes: C - connected, S - static, I - IGRP, R - RIP, M - mobile, B - BGP
       D - EIGRP, EX - EIGRP external, O - OSPF, IA - OSPF inter area
       N1 - OSPF NSSA external type 1, N2 - OSPF NSSA external type 2
       E1 - OSPF external type 1, E2 - OSPF external type 2, E - EGP
       i - IS-IS, L1 - IS-IS level-1, L2 - IS-IS level-2, * - candidate default
       U - per-user static route, o - ODR

Gateway of last resort is not set

     170.1.0.0/23 is subnetted, 7 subnets
I       170.1.10.0 [100/10476] via 170.1.12.1, 00:00:57, Serial0.1
I       170.1.8.0 [100/10539] via 170.1.12.1, 00:00:57, Serial0.1
I       170.1.14.0 [100/10476] via 170.1.12.1, 00:00:57, Serial0.1
C       170.1.12.0 is directly connected, Serial0.1
I       170.1.2.0 [100/8539] via 170.1.12.1, 00:00:57, Serial0.1
C       170.1.6.0 is directly connected, Ethernet0
I       170.1.4.0 [100/10539] via 170.1.12.1, 00:00:57, Serial0.1

R3#trace 170.1.9.4

Type escape sequence to abort.
Tracing the route to 170.1.9.4

  1 170.1.12.1 40 msec 40 msec 44 msec
  2 170.1.14.4 80 msec *  80 msec

R3#trace 170.1.5.2

Type escape sequence to abort.
Tracing the route to 170.1.5.2

  1 170.1.12.1 40 msec 40 msec 40 msec
  2 170.1.10.2 72 msec *  72 msec

R3#ping 170.1.5.2

Type escape sequence to abort.
```

continues

Example 9-21 *Scenario 9-3c R3 **show** and **debug** Output (Continued)*

```
Sending 5, 100-byte ICMP Echos to 170.1.5.2, timeout is 2 seconds:
!!!!!
Success rate is 100 percent (5/5), round-trip min/avg/max = 136/136/140 ms

R3#ping
Protocol [ip]:
Target IP address: 170.1.4.2
Repeat count [5]:
Datagram size [100]:
Timeout in seconds [2]:
Extended commands [n]: y
Source address or interface: 170.1.7.3
Type of service [0]:
Set DF bit in IP header? [no]:
Validate reply data? [no]:
Data pattern [0xABCD]:
Loose, Strict, Record, Timestamp, Verbose[none]:
Sweep range of sizes [n]:
Type escape sequence to abort.
Sending 5, 100-byte ICMP Echos to 170.1.4.2, timeout is 2 seconds:
UUUUU
Success rate is 0 percent (0/5)

R3#show ipx servers
Codes: S - Static, P - Periodic, E - EIGRP, N - NLSP, H - Holddown, + = detail
2 Total IPX Servers

Table ordering is based on routing and server info

   Type Name                     Net      Address    Port    Route Hops Itf
P     4 Server1                  101.0000.0000.0001:0451    8/03    3  Se0.1
P     4 Server2                  102.0000.0000.0001:0451    8/03    3  Se0.1

R3#show frame-relay lmi

LMI Statistics for interface Serial0 (Frame Relay DTE) LMI TYPE = CISCO
    Invalid Unnumbered info 0        Invalid Prot Disc 0
    Invalid dummy Call Ref 0         Invalid Msg Type 0
    Invalid Status Message 0         Invalid Lock Shift 0
    Invalid Information ID 0         Invalid Report IE Len 0
    Invalid Report Request 0         Invalid Keep IE Len 0
    Num Status Enq. Sent 172         Num Status msgs Rcvd 172
    Num Update Status Rcvd 0         Num Status Timeouts 0

R3#show frame-relay map
Serial0.1 (up): point-to-point dlci, dlci 301(0x12D,0x48D0), broadcast
          status defined, active
R3#
```

Example 9-22 *Scenario 9-3c R4 **show** and **debug** Output*

```
R4#show ip interface brief
Interface          IP-Address      OK? Method Status                 Protocol
Serial0            unassigned      YES unset  up                     up
Serial0.1          170.1.14.4      YES NVRAM  up                     up
Serial1            unassigned      YES unset  administratively down  down
Ethernet0          170.1.9.4       YES NVRAM  up                     up

R4#show ipx interface brief
Interface          IPX Network Encapsulation Status                 IPX State
Serial0            unassigned  not config'd  up                     n/a
Serial0.1          14          FRAME-RELAY   up                     [up]
Serial1            unassigned  not config'd  administratively down  n/a
Ethernet0          8           SAP           up                     [up]
Ethernet0          9           SNAP          up                     [up]

R4#show ipx servers
Codes: S - Static, P - Periodic, E - EIGRP, N - NLSP, H - Holddown, + = detail
2 Total IPX Servers

Table ordering is based on routing and server info

     Type Name                    Net     Address    Port    Route Hops Itf
P       4 Server1                 101.0000.0000.0001:0451    8/03    3  Se0.1
P       4 Server2                 102.0000.0000.0001:0451    8/03    3  Se0.1

R4#show ipx route
Codes: C - Connected primary network,    c - Connected secondary network
       S - Static, F - Floating static, L - Local (internal), W - IPXWAN
       R - RIP, E - EIGRP, N - NLSP, X - External, A - Aggregate
       s - seconds, u - uses

14 Total IPX routes. Up to 1 parallel paths and 16 hops allowed.

No default route known.

C        8 (SAP),        E0
c        9 (SNAP),       E0
C       14 (FRAME-RELAY), Se0.1
R        2 [07/01] via   14.0200.aaaa.aaaa,   33s, Se0.1
R        3 [07/01] via   14.0200.aaaa.aaaa,   34s, Se0.1
R        4 [13/02] via   14.0200.aaaa.aaaa,   34s, Se0.1
R        5 [13/02] via   14.0200.aaaa.aaaa,   34s, Se0.1
R        6 [13/02] via   14.0200.aaaa.aaaa,   34s, Se0.1
R        7 [13/02] via   14.0200.aaaa.aaaa,   34s, Se0.1
R       10 [07/01] via   14.0200.aaaa.aaaa,   34s, Se0.1
R       12 [07/01] via   14.0200.aaaa.aaaa,   34s, Se0.1
R      101 [08/03] via   14.0200.aaaa.aaaa,   34s, Se0.1
R      102 [08/03] via   14.0200.aaaa.aaaa,   34s, Se0.1
R      103 [14/04] via   14.0200.aaaa.aaaa,   34s, Se0.1

R4#show cdp neighbor detail
```

continues

Example 9-22 *Scenario 9-3c R4* **show** *and* **debug** *Output (Continued)*

```
-------------------------
Device ID: R1
Entry address(es):
  IP address: 170.1.14.1
  Novell address: 14.0200.aaaa.aaaa
Platform: Cisco 2500,  Capabilities: Router
Interface: Serial0.1,  Port ID (outgoing port): Serial0.4
Holdtime : 178 sec

Version :
Cisco Internetwork Operating System Software
IOS (tm) 2500 Software (C2500-AINR-L), Version 11.2(11), RELEASE SOFTWARE (fc1)
Copyright (c) 1986-1997 by Cisco Systems, Inc.
Compiled Mon 29-Dec-97 18:47 by ckralik

R4#show frame-relay pvc

PVC Statistics for interface Serial0 (Frame Relay DTE)

DLCI = 301, DLCI USAGE = LOCAL, PVC STATUS = ACTIVE, INTERFACE = Serial0.1

  input pkts 85           output pkts 63          in bytes 14086
  out bytes 8464          dropped pkts 0          in FECN pkts 0
  in BECN pkts 0          out FECN pkts 0         out BECN pkts 0
  in DE pkts 0            out DE pkts 0
  out bcast pkts 53         out bcast bytes 7614
  pvc create time 00:18:40, last time pvc status changed 00:18:40
R4#
```

Using Examples 9-19, 9-20, 9-21, and 9-22 as references, answer the following questions:

1. The ping of 170.1.5.2 (R2's E0 interface) from R3 was successful (refer to Example 9-21). Why was it successful if the access lists in R1 are enabled as shown in its configuration?

2. Describe the SAP update entering R1 over its S0.2 subinterface. How many services are described?

3. What **show** commands could be executed on R4 to display the IP and IPX addresses of R1?

4. What command lists the IP subnet numbers this router is connected to?

5. What commands list the routing metrics used for IP subnets? IPX networks?

6. What command is used to verify that IPX packets can be delivered and returned to another router?

7. If you do not know the enable password, how can you see what access lists are used?

8. You are not physically close to R2 or R3. What two methods can be used to gain access to the user mode command prompt?

9. After typing **show ip route**, you want to type **show ip route 168.11.12.64**. Describe the steps to do so, taking the least amount of keystrokes.

10. After typing **show ip route**, you want to type **show ip arp**. Describe the steps to do so, taking the least amount of keystrokes.

11. Name the editing commands (keyboard key sequences) to do the following:

    • Move to the beginning of the command line

    • Move to the end of the command line

    • Move to the beginning of the previous word

    • Move to the beginning of the next word

    • Move backward one character

    • Move forward one character

12. Describe the process of upgrading to a new version of IOS. What memory in the router is affected?

13. What do TCP and UDP stand for? Which provides error recovery?

14. What does ICMP stand for?

15. Describe how R2 learns that R1's IP address is 170.1.10.1.

16. What does DLCI stand for? How big can a DLCI be?

17. What additional configuration is needed on R3 to get routing updates to flow over the VC to R1?

18. What **show** command will list Frame Relay PVCs and the IP and IPX addresses on the other end of the PVC in this network?

19. What **show** command lists the status of the VC between R1 and R2?

20. What do ISDN, BRI, and PRI stand for?

21. List examples of two ISDN reference points.

22. What layers in the OSI model do the ISDN specifications Q.920 and Q.930 most closely match?

23. What ISDN Reference Points are supported by Cisco routers?

24. What command(s) can be used to discover details about a neighboring router without logging into that router?

Scenario 9-3c—Verification and Questions Answers

The answers to the questions for Scenario 9-3c are as follows:

1. The **ping** command uses the outgoing interface's IP address as the source address in the packet, which in this case would be 170.1.12.3. Access lists 102 and 103 check the source and destination IP addresses, looking for the subnets on the Ethernet segments. Therefore, the packet is not matched. Look further in Example 9-21 to see an extended ping, with source IP address 170.1.7.3, and see that it fails.

2. Two services are in the update, instead of the three services listed in R2's SAP table. These messages are displayed after the **debug ipx sap activity** command. This simply shows that the SAP filter on R2 is working properly.

3. The **show ip route** and **show ipx route** commands list the IP and IPX addresses of the neighboring routers. Because only point-to-point subinterfaces are in use, the **show frame-relay map** command (refer to Example 9-21) does not show details of the neighboring routers' Layer 3 addresses. The **show cdp neighbor** detail command (refer to Example 9-22) also shows information about IP and IPX addresses.

4. The **show ip route** command (refer to Example 9-6). The routes with a "C" in the left column signify connected subnets.

5. The **show ip route** and **show ipx route** commands (refer to Example 9-6). The metric values for each subnet/network are in brackets.

6. The **ping** command can be used to verify IPX and IP connectivity, as well as several other network layer (Layer 3) protocols (refer to Example 9-6).

7. The **show access-lists** command (refer to Example 9-4).

8. Dialing into a modem attached to the auxiliary port, or telnet.

9. Press the up-arrow key or press Ctrl-P to retrieve the last command. Then type the subnet number, which leaves **show ip route 168.11.12.64** on the command line. Press return.

10. Press the up-arrow key or press Ctrl-P to retrieve the last command. Then press backspace until the word "route" is erased. Then type the word "arp," which leaves **show ip arp** on the command line. Press Return.

11. The answers are as follows:

    Beginning of command line **Ctrl-A**

    End of command line **Ctrl-E**

    Beginning of previous word **Esc-B**

    Beginning of next word **Esc-F**

Forward one character **Ctrl-F**

Backward one character **Ctrl-B**

12. A file is obtained from Cisco via diskette or FTP download over the Internet. This file is the IOS. The file is placed into the default directory on some TFTP server accessible to the router that needs to be upgraded. The **copy tftp flash** command is issued on the router, and the user answers questions to tell the router the name and location of the new IOS. Flash memory is updated as a result of this process.

13. Transmission Control Protocol and User Datagram Protocol. TCP provides error recovery.

14. Internet Control Message Protocol.

15. The Inverse-ARP process is not used when the subinterface is a point-to-point subinterface; therefore, R2 can only learn of R1's IP and IPX addresses with CDP, or by looking at the source addresses of the IPX RIP and IP IGRP routing updates.

16. Data Link Connection Identifier. Lengths between 10 and 14 bits are allowed, with a 10 bit number being the most typically implemented size.

17. No other configuration is necessary; this question is a trick question. This is the kind of misdirection that you might expect to see on some of the exam questions. Read the questions slowly and read twice!

18. The **show frame-relay pvc** command will list the PVCs. When multipoint subinterfaces are used, or no subinterfaces are used, for Frame Relay configuration, then the **show frame-relay map** command will list the IP and IPX addresses. In this case, the **show ip route** and **show ipx route** commands, or the **show cdp neighbor detail** command, should be used to see the addresses.

19. The **show frame-relay pvc** command.

20. Integrated Services Digital Network, Basic Rate Interface, and Primary Rate Interface.

21. Reference Point is an interface between Function Groups. R, S, T, and U are the reference points. S and T are combined in many cases and called the S/T reference point.

22. Q.920 performs functions similar to OSI Layer 2, and Q.930 performs functions similar to OSI Layer 3.

23. Cisco routers' ISDN interfaces are either S/T or U interfaces.

24. **show cdp neighbor detail**.

Decimal to Hexadecimal and Binary Conversion Table

Decimal Value	Hexadecimal Value	Binary Value
0	00	0000 0000
1	01	0000 0001
2	02	0000 0010
3	03	0000 0011
4	04	0000 0100
5	05	0000 0101
6	06	0000 0110
7	07	0000 0111
8	08	0000 1000
9	09	0000 1001
10	0A	0000 1010
11	0B	0000 1011
12	0C	0000 1100
13	0D	0000 1101
14	0E	0000 1110
15	0F	0000 1111
16	10	0001 0000
17	11	0001 0001
18	12	0001 0010
19	13	0001 0011
20	14	0001 0100
21	15	0001 0101
22	16	0001 0110
23	17	0001 0111
24	18	0001 1000
25	19	0001 1001

Decimal Value	Hexadecimal Value	Binary Value
26	1A	0001 1010
27	1B	0001 1011
28	1C	0001 1100
29	1D	0001 1101
30	1E	0001 1110
31	1F	0001 1111
32	20	0010 0000
33	21	0010 0001
34	22	0010 0010
35	23	0010 0011
36	24	0010 0100
37	25	0010 0101
38	26	0010 0110
39	27	0010 0111
40	28	0010 1000
41	29	0010 1001
42	2A	0010 1010
43	2B	0010 1011
44	2C	0010 1100
45	2D	0010 1101
46	2E	0010 1110
47	2F	0010 1111
48	30	0011 0000
49	31	0011 0001
50	32	0011 0010
51	33	0011 0011
52	34	0011 0100
53	35	0011 0101
54	36	0011 0110
55	37	0011 0111
56	38	0011 1000

Decimal Value	Hexadecimal Value	Binary Value
57	39	0011 1001
58	3A	0011 1010
59	3B	0011 1011
60	3C	0011 1100
61	3D	0011 1101
62	3E	0011 1110
63	3F	0011 1111
64	40	0100 0000
65	41	0100 0001
66	42	0100 0010
67	43	0100 0011
68	44	0100 0100
69	45	0100 0101
70	46	0100 0110
71	47	0100 0111
72	48	0100 1000
73	49	0100 1001
74	4A	0100 1010
75	4B	0100 1011
76	4C	0100 1100
77	4D	0100 1101
78	4E	0100 1110
79	4F	0100 1111
80	50	0101 0000
81	51	0101 0001
82	52	0101 0010
83	53	0101 0011
84	54	0101 0100
85	55	0101 0101
86	56	0101 0110
87	57	0101 0111

Decimal Value	Hexadecimal Value	Binary Value
88	58	0101 1000
89	59	0101 1001
90	5A	0101 1010
91	5B	0101 1011
92	5C	0101 1100
93	5D	0101 1101
94	5E	0101 1110
95	5F	0101 1111
96	60	0110 0000
97	61	0110 0001
98	62	0110 0010
99	63	0110 0011
100	64	0110 0100
101	65	0110 0101
102	66	0110 0110
103	67	0110 0111
104	68	0110 1000
105	69	0110 1001
106	6A	0110 1010
107	6B	0110 1011
108	6C	0110 1100
109	6D	0110 1101
110	6E	0110 1110
111	6F	0110 1111
112	70	0111 0000
113	71	0111 0001
114	72	0111 0010
115	73	0111 0011
116	74	0111 0100
117	75	0111 0101
118	76	0111 0110

Decimal Value	Hexadecimal Value	Binary Value
119	77	0111 0111
120	78	0111 1000
121	79	0111 1001
122	7A	0111 1010
123	7B	0111 1011
124	7C	0111 1100
125	7D	0111 1101
126	7E	0111 1110
127	7F	0111 1111
128	80	1000 0000
129	81	1000 0001
130	82	1000 0010
131	83	1000 0011
132	84	1000 0100
133	85	1000 0101
134	86	1000 0110
135	87	1000 0111
136	88	1000 1000
137	89	1000 1001
138	8A	1000 1010
139	8B	1000 1011
140	8C	1000 1100
141	8D	1000 1101
142	8E	1000 1110
143	8F	1000 1111
144	90	1001 0000
145	91	1001 0001
146	92	1001 0010
147	93	1001 0011
148	94	1001 0100
149	95	1001 0101

Decimal Value	Hexadecimal Value	Binary Value
150	96	1001 0110
151	97	1001 0111
152	98	1001 1000
153	99	1001 1001
154	9A	1001 1010
155	9B	1001 1011
156	9C	1001 1100
157	9D	1001 1101
158	9E	1001 1110
159	9F	1001 1111
160	A0	1010 0000
161	A1	1010 0001
162	A2	1010 0010
163	A3	1010 0011
164	A4	1010 0100
165	A5	1010 0101
166	A6	1010 0110
167	A7	1010 0111
168	A8	1010 1000
169	A9	1010 1001
170	AA	1010 1010
171	AB	1010 1011
172	AC	1010 1100
173	AD	1010 1101
174	AE	1010 1110
175	AF	1010 1111
176	B0	1011 0000
177	B1	1011 0001
178	B2	1011 0010
179	B3	1011 0011
180	B4	1011 0100

Decimal Value	Hexadecimal Value	Binary Value
181	B5	1011 0101
182	B6	1011 0110
183	B7	1011 0111
184	B8	1011 1000
185	B9	1011 1001
186	BA	1011 1010
187	BB	1011 1011
188	BC	1011 1100
189	BD	1011 1101
190	BE	1011 1110
191	BF	1011 1111
192	C0	1100 0000
193	C1	1100 0001
194	C2	1100 0010
195	C3	1100 0011
196	C4	1100 0100
197	C5	1100 0101
198	C6	1100 0110
199	C7	1100 0111
200	C8	1100 1000
201	C9	1100 1001
202	CA	1100 1010
203	CB	1100 1011
204	CC	1100 1100
205	CD	1100 1101
206	CE	1100 1110
207	CF	1100 1111
208	D0	1101 0000
209	D1	1101 0001
210	D2	1101 0010
211	D3	1101 0011

Decimal Value	Hexadecimal Value	Binary Value
212	D4	1101 0100
213	D5	1101 0101
214	D6	1101 0110
215	D7	1101 0111
216	D8	1101 1000
217	D9	1101 1001
218	DA	1101 1010
219	DB	1101 1011
220	DC	1101 1100
221	DD	1101 1101
222	DE	1101 1110
223	DF	1101 1111
224	E0	1110 0000
225	E1	1110 0001
226	E2	1110 0010
227	E3	1110 0011
228	E4	1110 0100
229	E5	1110 0101
230	E6	1110 0110
231	E7	1110 0111
232	E8	1110 1000
233	E9	1110 1001
234	EA	1110 1010
235	EB	1110 1011
236	EC	1110 1100
237	ED	1110 1101
238	EE	1110 1110
239	EF	1110 1111
240	F0	1111 0000
241	F1	1111 0001
242	F2	1111 0010

Decimal Value	Hexadecimal Value	Binary Value
243	F3	1111 0011
244	F4	1111 0100
245	F5	1111 0101
246	F6	1111 0110
247	F7	1111 0111
248	F8	1111 1000
249	F9	1111 1001
250	FA	1111 1010
251	FB	1111 1011
252	FC	1111 1100
253	FD	1111 1101
254	FE	1111 1110
255	FF	1111 1111

Answers to the "Do I Know This Already?" Quizzes and Q&A Sections

Answers to the Chapter 2 "Do I Know This Already?" Quiz

1. What are the two different names for the router's mode of operation that when accessed enable you to issue commands that could be disruptive to router operations?

    Enable and privileged. Both are commonly used and found in Cisco documentation.

2. What command would you use to receive command help if you knew the **show** command option you cannot recall begins with a "C"?

    show c?. The help would appear immediately after you typed the **?** symbol. You would not need to type "return" after the **?**.

3. Instead of **show ip route**, which is the only command you typed since logging in to the router, you now want to issue a **show ip arp** command. What steps would you take to do so, without simply typing **show ip arp**?

    Up-arrow, backspace five times, type **arp**. The up-arrow retrieves the **show ip route** command. Backspace moves the cursor backward and erases the character. Typing inserts the characters into the line, but the cursor is at the end of the line.

4. What configuration command causes the router to demand a password from the console? What configuration mode "context" must you be in; that is, what command(s) must be typed before this command after entering configuration mode?

    line console 0
    login

    The **line console 0** command is a context setting command; it adds no information to the configuration in and of itself. The **login** command, which follows the **line console 0** command, tells the IOS that a password prompt is desired at the console.

5. What is the purpose of Flash memory in a Cisco router?

    To store IOS and microcode files; to allow remote loading of new versions of these files. In most routers, only an IOS is found. If microcode is upgraded, the files reside in Flash memory.

6. What is the purpose of ROM in a Cisco router?

To store a small IOS. Typically, this IOS is used only during maintenance or emergencies.

7. What configuration command would be needed to cause a router to use an IOS image named **c2500-j-l.112-14.bin** on TFTP server 128.1.1.1 when the router is reloaded? If you forgot the first parameter of this command, what steps must you take to learn the correct parameters and add the command to the configuration? (Assume you are not logged in to the router when you start.)

```
boot config 128.1.1.1 c2500-j-l.112-14.bin
```

As for the second part of the question: Log in from con/aux/telnet, **enable**, type **enable password**, **configure terminal**, type **boot ?** and help appears.

8. When using setup mode, you are prompted at the end of the process as to whether you want to use the configuration parameters you just typed in. Which type of memory is this configuration stored into if you type **yes**?

Both NVRAM and RAM. This is the only router IOS command that modifies both the active and startup configuration files as the result of one action by the user!

9. What two methods could a router administrator use to cause a router to load the IOS stored in ROM?

Setting the config register boot field to binary 0001, or adding **boot system rom** to the configuration file and copying it to the startup configuration file. To set the configuration register to hex 2101, which would yield binary 0001 in the boot field, the **config-register** *0x2101* global configuration command would be used.

10. What is the process used to update the contents of Flash memory, so a new IOS in a file called *c2500-j-l.112-14.bin* on TFTP server 128.1.1.1 is copied into Flash memory?

copy network flash. The other details, namely the IP address of the TFTP server and the filename, are requested via prompts to the user.

11. Two different IOS files are in a router's Flash memory, one called *c2500-j-l.111-3.bin* and one called *c2500-j-l.112-14.bin*. Which one does the router use when it boots up? How could you force the other IOS file to be used? Without looking at the router configuration, what command could be used to discover which file was used for the latest boot of the router?

The first IOS file listed in the **show flash** command is the one used at reload time, unless a **boot system** command is configured. Config command **boot system flash** *xyz123.bin* would override the order in Flash memory. **show version** is the command used to display the filename of the IOS for the latest reload of a router. The **show version** output tells you the version, as well as the name of the file that was used at last reload time. It is particularly difficult to find in the output of the command.

12. What does CDP stand for?

Cisco Discovery Protocol. CDP is Cisco proprietary and is not dependent on a particular Layer 3 protocol to be configured and working.

Answers to the Chapter 2 Q&A Section

1. What are the two different names for the router's mode of operation that when accessed allow you to issue commands that could be disruptive to router operations?

Enable and privileged. Both are commonly used and found in Cisco documentation.

2. What are three methods of logging on to a router?

Console, auxiliary port, Telnet. All three cause the user to enter user mode.

3. What is the name of the user interface mode of operation used when you cannot issue disruptive commands?

User mode.

4. Can the auxiliary port be used for anything besides remote modem user access to a router? If so, what other purpose can it serve?

Yes—Direct attachment of a terminal (such as the console), and dial for the purpose of routing packets. Although originally created to support remote admin access, many customers use it for dial back-up, particularly when analog lines are desired or when that is all that is available.

5. How many console ports can be installed on a Cisco 7500 router?

One. This is a purposefully strange question. You do not order the console port; every router comes with one, and only one. So, technically, you do not even order one, it is implied by ordering the router.

6. What command would you use to receive command help if you know the **show** command option that you cannot recall begins with a "C"?

show c?. The help would appear immediately after the you typed the **?** symbol. You would not need to type "return" after the **?**.

7. While you are logged in to a router, you issue the command **copy ?** and get a response of "Unknown command, computer name, or host." Offer an explanation as to why this error message appears.

User mode. The user must be in enable/privileged mode to use the **copy** command. When in user mode, the router does not provide help and treats the command as if there is no such command!

8. Is the number of retrievable commands based on the number of characters in each command, or is it simply a number of commands, regardless of their size?

Number of commands. The length (that is, number of characters) of each command does not affect the command history buffer.

9. How can you retrieve a previously used command? (Name two ways.)

Ctrl-P and "up-arrow." "Up-arrow" refers literally to the up arrow key on the keyboard. Not all terminal emulators support Ctrl-P or "up-arrow," so recalling both methods is useful.

10. Instead of **show ip route**, which is the only command you typed since logging into the router, you now want to issue a **show ip arp** command. What steps would you take to do so, without simply typing **show ip arp**?

Up-arrow, backspace five times, type **arp**. The up-arrow retrieves the **show ip route** command. Backspace moves the cursor backward and erases the character. Typing inserts the characters into the line, but the cursor is at the end of the line.

11. After typing **show ip route** *128.1.1.0*, you now want to issue the command **show ip route** *218.1.4.0*. What steps would you take to do so, without simply typing **show ip route** *218.1.4.0*?

Up-arrow, Ctrl-B (or left arrow) twice, backspace once, type **4**. The Ctrl-B and left arrow keys back up one character in the line, without deleting the character. Backspace deletes the "1" in this case. Typing inserts into the line.

12. What configuration command causes the router to demand a password from the console? What configuration mode "context" must you be in; that is, what command(s) must you type before this command?

line console 0
login

The **line console 0** command is a context setting command; it adds no information to the configuration in and of itself. The **login** command, which follows the **line console 0** command, tells the IOS that a password prompt is desired at the console.

13. What configuration command is used to tell the router the password that is required at the console? What configuration mode "context" must you be in; that is, what command(s) must you type before this command?

password *xxxxxxx*
line console 0

The **password** command tells the IOS the value that should be typed when a user wants access from the console. This value is requested of you by the IOS because of the **login** command. It must be typed while in console configuration mode, which is reached by typing **line console 0**.

14. What is the purpose of Flash memory in a Cisco router?

To store IOS and microcode files; to allow remote loading of new versions of these files. In most routers, only an IOS is found. If microcode is upgraded, the files reside in Flash memory.

15. What is the intended purpose of NVRAM memory in a Cisco router?

To store a single configuration file, used at router load time. NVRAM does not support multiple files.

16. What does the NV stand for in NVRAM?

Nonvolatile. NVRAM is battery powered if it is really RAM. In some routers, Cisco has (sneakily!) used a small portion of Flash for the purpose of NVRAM, but Cisco would not ask such trivia on the test!

17. What is the intended purpose of RAM in a Cisco router?

For storing working IOS memory (such as routing tables or packets) and for IOS code storage. In some router models, not all the IOS is copied into RAM. Some of the IOS is left in Flash memory so that more RAM is available for working memory.

18. What is the purpose of ROM in a Cisco router?

To store a small IOS. Typically, this IOS is used only during maintenance or emergencies.

19. What configuration command would be needed to cause a router to use an IOS image named **c2500-j-l.112-14.bin** on TFTP server 128.1.1.1 when the router is reloaded? If you forgot the first parameter of this command, what steps must you take to learn the correct parameters and add the command to the configuration? (Assume you are not logged in to the router when you start.)

```
boot config 128.1.1.1 c2500-j-l.112-14.bin
```

As for the second part of the question: Log in from con/aux/telnet, **enable**, type the enable password, **configure terminal**, type **boot ?** and help appears.

20. What command sets the password that would be required after typing the **enable** command? Is that password encrypted by default?

enable or **enable secret**. The password in the **enable** command is not encrypted by default. The **enable secret** password is encrypted.

21. What is missing from the configuration command **banner** *This is Ivan Denisovich's Gorno Router—Do Not Use* for it to have the correct syntax?

A delimiter character that is not part of the banner at the beginning and end of the text. For example:

```
banner # This is Ivan…. Do Not Use #
```

22. Name two commands that affect the text used as the command prompt.

    hostname and **prompt**.

23. When using setup mode, you are prompted at the end of the process as to whether you want to use the configuration parameters you just typed in. Which type of memory is this configuration stored into if you type **yes**?

    Both NVRAM and RAM. This is the only router IOS command that modifies both the active and startup configuration files as the result of one action by the user!

24. What two methods could a router administrator use to cause a router to load the IOS stored in ROM?

    Setting the configuration register boot field to binary 0001, or adding **boot system rom** to the configuration file and copying it to the startup configuration file. To set the configuration register to hex 2101, which would yield binary 0001 in the boot field, the **config-register** *0x2101* global configuration command would be used.

25. What could a router administrator do to cause a router to load file *xyz123.bin* from TFTP server 128.1.1.1 upon the next reload? Is there more than one way to accomplish this?

    ```
    boot system 128.1.1.1 xyz123.bin
    ```

    This is the only way to make the router load this file from the TFTP server.

26. What is the process used to update the contents of Flash memory so that a new IOS in a file called *c2500-j-l.112-14.bin* on TFTP server 128.1.1.1 is copied into Flash memory?

    copy tftp flash. The other details, namely the IP address of the TFTP server and the filename, are requested via prompts to the user.

27. Name three possible problems that could prevent the command **boot net** c2500-j-l.112-14.bin *128.1.1.1* from succeeding.

    The possible reasons include: 128.1.1.1 is not accessible through the network; there is no TFTP server on 128.1.1.1; the file is not in the TFTP default directory; the file is corrupted; a **boot** command could precede this **boot** command in the configuration file, and the IOS referenced in the first **boot** command would be used instead.

28. Two different IOS files are in a router's Flash memory, one called *c2500-j-l.111-3.bin* and one called *c2500-j-l.112-14.bin*. Which one does the router use when it boots up? How could you force the other IOS file to be used? Without looking at the router configuration, what command would you use to discover which file was used for the latest boot of the router?

    The first IOS file listed in the **show flash** command is the one used at reload time, unless a **boot system** command is configured. Configuration command **boot system flash** *xyz123.bin* would override the order in Flash memory. **show version** is the command used to display the filename of the IOS for the latest reload of a router. The **show version** output tells you the version, as well as the name of the file that was used at last reload time. It is particularly difficult to find in the output of the command.

29. What does CDP stand for?

Cisco Discovery Protocol. CDP is Cisco proprietary and is not dependent on a particular Layer 3 protocol to be configured and working.

30. What type of interfaces is CDP enabled on by default? (Assume IOS 11.0 and beyond.)

On all interfaces that support SNAP headers. These include LANs, Frame Relay, and ATM.

31. What command can be used to provide as much detailed information as is possible with CDP?

show cdp neighbor detail

32. Is the password required at the console the same one that is required when Telnet is used to access a router?

No. The Telnet ("virtual terminal") password is not the same password, although many installations use the same value.

33. How could a router administrator disable CDP? What command(s) would be required on a Cisco 2501 (2 serial, 1 Ethernet) router?

no cdp enable. The **cdp enable** command is an interface subcommand. So, to disable on a 2501, once in configuration mode, type: **interface ethernet 0**; then **no cdp enable**; then **interface serial 0**, **no cdp enable**; then **interface serial 1**, and finally **no cdp enable**.

34. Which IP routing protocols could be enabled using **setup**?

RIP and IGRP

35. Name two commands used to view the configuration to be used at the next reload of the router. Which one is a more recent addition to the IOS?

show config and **show startup-config**. **show startup-config** is the newer one. And, hopefully, **show startup-config** is easier to remember.

36. Name two commands used to view the configuration that is currently used in a router. Which one is a more recent addition to the IOS?

write terminal and **show running-config**. **show running-config** is the newer command. And, hopefully, **show running-config** is easier to remember.

37. The **copy startup-config running-config** command always changes the currently used configuration for this router to exactly match what is in the startup configuration file. (T/F). Why?

False. Some configuration commands do not replace an existing command, but are simply added to a list. If such a list exists, this command simply adds those to the end of the list. Many of these lists in a router configuration are order dependent.

Answers to the Chapter 3 "Do I Know This Already?" Quiz

1. Name the seven layers of the OSI model.

Application, presentation, session, transport, network, data link, and physical.

2. What is the main purpose of Layer 3?

The network layer defines logical addressing and routing as a means to deliver data across an entire network. IP and IPX are two examples.

3. What is the main purpose of Layer 2?

The data link layer defines addressing specific to a particular medium, as part of the means to provide delivery of data across that medium.

4. Describe the process of data encapsulation as data is processed from creation until it exits a physical interface to a network. Use the OSI model as an example.

Data encapsulation represents the process of a layer adding a header, and possibly a trailer, to the data as it is processed by progressively lower layers in the protocol specification. In the context of OSI, each layer could add a header so that—other than the true application data—there would be six other headers (Layers 2–7) and a trailer for Layer 2, with this L2-PDU being encoded by the physical layer onto the network interface.

5. Describe the services provided in most connection-oriented protocol services.

Error recovery is provided in most; others simply provide a pre-established path. Error recovery implies that the protocol is connection oriented. Connection oriented, however, does not necessarily imply that the protocol supplies error recovery.

6. Name three terms popularly used as synonyms to MAC addresses.

NIC address, card address, LAN address, hardware address, Ethernet address, Token Ring address, FDDI address, burned-in address. All of these names are used casually and in formal documents, and refer to the same six-byte MAC address concept as defined by IEEE.

7. What portion of a MAC address encodes an identifier representing the manufacturer of the card?

The first three bytes.

8. Name two differences between Layer 3 addresses and Layer 2 addresses.

Layer 3 addresses can be used regardless of media type, whereas Layer 2 addresses are only useful on a particular medium. Layer 3 addresses are designed to imply a minimum of two parts, the first of which creates a grouping concept. Layer 2 addresses have no such grouping concept.

9. How many bits in an IP address?

32, 8, 16, or 24 bits in the network portion of the address, and a variable number of the remaining bits comprise the subnet and then host portions of the address, based on the subnet mask.

10. Name the two main parts of an IP address. Which part identifies which "group" this address is a member of?

Subnet and host. Addresses with the same subnet number are in the same group. Technically, as described in Chapter 5, "Network Protocols: Understanding the TCP/IP Suite and Novell NetWare Protocols," there are three portions of the IP address: network, subnet, and host. However, most people think of the network and subnet portions as one portion.

11. Name at least three benefits to layering networking protocol specifications.

Reduces complexity, standardizes interfaces, facilitates modular engineering, ensures interoperable technology, accelerates evolution, and simplifies teaching and learning. This information comes directly from the ICRC course book (which is also where some of the CCNA objectives come from!).

12. Describe the differences between a routed protocol and a routing protocol.

The routed protocol defines the addressing and Layer 3 header in the packet that is actually forwarded by a router. The routing protocol defines the process of routers exchanging topology data such that the routers know how to forward the data. For example, IP is a routed protocol, and RIP is a routing protocol.

Answers to the Chapter 3 Q&A Section

1. Name the seven layers of the OSI model.

Application, presentation, session, transport, network, data link, and physical.

2. What is the main purpose of Layer 7?

Provides standardized services to applications. The definition for this layer is typically ambiguous because it varies. The key is that it does not define a user interface, but instead a toolbox used by application developers. For example, a web browser is an application that uses HTML format text, as defined by the TCP/IP application layer, to describe the graphics to be displayed on the screen.

3. What is the main purpose of Layer 6?

Defines data formats and possibly encryption.

4. What is the main purpose of Layer 5?

The session layer controls the conversation between two endpoints. Although the term used is "session," the term "conversation" more accurately describes what is accomplished. The session layer ensures that not only communication, but useful sets of communication between endpoints is accomplished.

5. What is the main purpose of Layer 4?

To provide error recovery if requested.

6. What is the main purpose of Layer 3?

The network layer defines logical addressing and routing, as a means to deliver data across an entire network.

7. What is the main purpose of Layer 2?

The data link layer defines addressing specific to a particular medium as part of the means to provide delivery of data across that medium.

8. What is the main purpose of Layer 1?

The physical layer is responsible for encoding of energy onto the medium and interpretation of a received energy signal. It also defines the connector and cabling details.

9. Describe the process of data encapsulation as data is processed from creation until it exits a physical interface to a network. Use the OSI model as an example.

Data encapsulation represents the process of a layer adding a header, and possibly a trailer, to the data as it is processed by progressively lower layers in the protocol specification. In the context of OSI, each layer could add a header so that—other than the true application data—there would be six other headers (Layers 2–7) and a trailer for Layer 2, with this L2-PDU being encoded by the physical layer onto the network interface.

10. Describe the services provided in most connectionless protocol services.

By avoiding features like error correction and windowing, connectionless protocols require fewer bytes in their headers, meaning less overhead. Also, without windowing, there is no artificial slowing of the rate at which data can be sent.

11. Name at least three connectionless protocols.

LLC type 1, UDP, IPX, IP, PPP. Remember, Frame Relay, X.25, and ATM are connection oriented, regardless of whether they define error recovery.

12. Describe the services provided in most connection-oriented protocol services.

Error recovery is provided in most; others simply provide a pre-established path. Error recovery implies that the protocol is connection oriented. Connection oriented, however, does not necessarily imply that the protocol supplies error recovery.

13. In a particular error recovering protocol, the sender sends three frames, labeled 2, 3, and 4. The receiver of these frames, on its next sent frame, sets an acknowledgment field to "4". What does this typically imply?

That frames up through number 3 were received successfully. Most windowing, error recovery protocols use forward acknowledgment.

14. Name three connection-oriented protocols.

TCP, SPX, LLC Type 2, X.25. All the protocols in the answer provide error recovery. ATM and Frame Relay are also connection oriented, but without error recovery.

15. What does MAC stand for?

Media Access Control.

16. Name three terms popularly used as a synonym for MAC Address.

NIC address, card address, LAN address, hardware address, Ethernet address, Token Ring address, FDDI address, burned-in address. All of these names are used casually and in formal documents, and refer to the same 6 byte MAC address concept as defined by IEEE.

17. Are IP addresses defined by a Layer 2 or Layer 3 protocol?

Layer 3. There is a catch. If you examine the TCP/IP protocol stack, technically, it is Layer 2. However, compared to OSI, IP most closely matches Layer 3, so the popular (and CCNA Exam) answer is Layer 3.

18. Are IPX addresses defined by a Layer 2 or Layer 3 protocols?

Layer 3. See the answer to question 17.

19. Are OSI NSAP addresses defined by a Layer 2 or a Layer 3 protocol?

Layer 3. These are, of course, truly Layer 3 because they are defined by OSI. The number of bits in the address is variable. However, I consider it highly unlikely that questions about NSAPs would be on the exam because they are not mentioned in any objective or covered in any class.

20. What portion of a MAC address encodes an identifier representing the manufacturer of the card?

The first three bytes.

21. Are MAC addresses defined by a Layer 2 or a Layer 3 protocol?

Layer 2. Ethernet and Token Ring MAC addresses are defined in the 802.3 and 802.5 specifications.

22. Are DLCI addresses defined by a Layer 2 or a Layer 3 protocol?

Layer 2. While not specifically covered in this chapter, Frame Relay protocols do not define a logical addressing structure that can usefully exist outside of a Frame Relay network; by definition, the addresses would be OSI Layer 2 equivalent.

23. Name two differences between Layer 3 addresses and Layer 2 addresses.

Layer 3 addresses can be used regardless of media type, whereas Layer 2 addresses are only useful on a particular media type. Layer 3 addresses are designed to imply a minimum of two parts, the first of which creates a grouping concept. Layer 2 MAC addresses have no grouping concept that implies that the addresses in the same group must reside on the same data link, like network addressing implies in many cases. However, all burned-in addresses from a single vendor can be considered to be "grouped," in that they all use the same value for the first three bytes of their MAC addresses.

24. How many bits in an IP address?

32 bits. A variable number in the network portion, and the rest of the 32 in the host portion. IP Version 6 uses a much larger address. Stay tuned!

25. How many bits in an IPX address?

80 bits. 32 bits in the network portion, and 48 bits in the node portion.

26. How many bits in a MAC address?

48 bits. The first 24 bits for burned-in addresses are a code that identifies the manufacturer.

27. How many bits in a DLCI address?

Typically 10, or up to 12 with extended addressing bits. Most typically 10 bits in length, for decimal 0-1023. Some are reserved for LMI and other purposes.

28. Name the two main parts of an IPX address. Which part identifies which "group" this address is a member of?

Network number and node number. Addresses with the same network number are in the same group. On LAN interfaces, the node number is made to have the same value as the LAN MAC address.

29. Name the two main parts of an IP address. Which part identifies which "group" this address is a member of?

Subnet and host. Addresses with the same subnet number are in the same group. Technically, as described in Chapter 5, there are three portions of the IP address: network, subnet, and host. However, most people think of the network and subnet portions as one portion.

30. Name the two main parts of a MAC address. Which part identifies which "group" this address is a member of?

There are no parts, and nothing defines a grouping concept. This is a trick question. While you might have guessed that the MAC address has two parts, the first part being dictated to the manufacturer, the second part being made up by the manufacturer, there is no grouping concept.

31. Name three benefits to layering networking protocol specifications.

Reduces complexity, standardizes interfaces, facilitates modular engineering, ensures interoperable technology, accelerates evolution, and simplifies teaching and learning. The answers shown here are directly from the ICRC course book.

32. What header and/or trailer does a router discard as a side effect of routing?

The data-link header and trailer. This is because the network layer, where routing is defined, is interested in delivering the network layer (Layer 3) PDU from end-to-end. Routing uses intermediate data links (Layer 2) to transport the data to the next routers and, eventually, the true destination. The data-link header and trailer is only useful to deliver the data to the next router or host; so the header and trailer are discarded by each router.

33. Describe the differences between a routed protocol and a routing protocol.

The *routed* protocol defines the addressing and Layer 3 header in the packet that is actually forwarded by a router. The *routing* protocol defines the process of routers exchanging topology data such that the routers know how to forward the data.

34. Name at least three *routed* protocols.

IP, IPX, OSI, DECNET, AppleTalk, VINES

35. Name at least three *routing* protocols.

RIP, IGRP, EIGRP, OSPF, NLSP, RTMP, VTP, IS-IS

36. How does an IP host know what router to send a packet to? In which cases does an IP host choose to send a packet to this router instead of directly to the destination host?

By configuring a default route. If the destination of the packet is in another subnet, the host sends the packet to the default router. Otherwise, the host sends the packet directly to the destination host because it is in the same subnet and by definition must be on the same data link.

37. How does an IPX host know which router to send a packet to? In which case does an IPX host choose to send a packet to this router instead of directly to the destination host?

The node will use a RIP request to locate any servers on the attached IPX network that have a route to the destination network. If the destination is an IPX address on the attached network, a router is not needed, and the node will forward the packet directly.

38. Name three items in an entry in any routing table.

The group identifier, the interface to forward the packet out, and the Layer 3 address of the next router to send this packet to.

Answers to the Chapter 4 "Do I Know This Already?" Quiz

1. Name two benefits of LAN segmentation using transparent bridges.

The main benefits are reduced collisions and more bandwidth because multiple 10 or 100 Mbps Ethernet segments are created, and unicasts between devices on the same segment are not forwarded by the bridge, which reduces overhead. The text towards the bottom of page 137 provides a more thorough reference.

2. What settings are examined by a bridge or switch to determine which bridge or switch should be elected as root of the spanning tree?

The bridge priority is first examined (lowest wins). In case of a tie, the lowest bridge ID wins. The priority is prepended to the bridge ID in the actual CBPDU message, so the combined fields can be easily compared. The bridge ID is typically a six-byte number borrowed from the MAC address value of one of the bridge's interfaces and is used to uniquely identify the bridge.

3. Assume a building has 100 devices that are attached to the same Ethernet. These devices are migrated to two different shared Ethernet segments, each with 50 devices. The two segments are connected to a Cisco LAN switch to allow communication between the two sets of users. List two benefits that would be derived for a typical user.

Two switch ports are used, which reduces the possibilities of collisions. Also, each segment has its own 10 or 100 Mbps capacity, allowing more throughput and reducing the likelihood of collisions. Also, although unlikely to be on the CCNA exam, some Cisco switches can reduce the flow of multicasts using the Cisco Group Message Protocol (CGMP).

4. Name the two methods of internal switching on typical switches today. Which provides less latency for an individual frame?

Store-and-forward and cut-through. Cut-through has less latency per frame, but does not check for bit errors in the frame, including many errors caused by collisions. Store-and-forward stores the entire received frame, verifies the FCS is correct, and then sends the frame. Cut-through sends the first bytes of the frame out before the last bytes of the incoming frame have been received.

5. Describe how a transparent bridge decides whether it should forward a frame, and how it chooses the interface out which to forward the frame.

The bridge examines the destination MAC address and looks for the address in its bridge or address table. If found, the matching entry tells the bridge which output interface to use to forward the frame. If not found, the bridge forwards the frame out all other interfaces (except for interfaces blocked by spanning tree). The bridge table is built by examining incoming frames' source MAC addresses.

6. Describe the benefits of the Spanning-Tree Protocol as used by transparent bridges and switches.

   Physically redundant paths in the network are allowed to exist and be used when other paths fail. Also, loops in the bridged network are avoided. Loops are particularly bad because bridging is using LAN headers that do not provide a mechanism to mark a frame so that its lifetime can be limited; in other words, the frame can loop forever.

7. Does a bridge/switch examine just the incoming frame's source MAC address, destination MAC address, or both? Why?

   It examines both MAC addresses. The source is examined so that entries can be added to the bridge/address table. The destination address is examined to determine which interface out which to forward the frame. Table lookup is required for both addresses for any frame that enters an interface. That is one of the reasons that LAN switches, which have a much larger number of interfaces than traditional bridges, need to have optimized hardware and logic to perform table lookup quickly.

8. When a bridge or switch using the Spanning-Tree Protocol first initializes, who does it claim should be the root of the tree?

   Each bridge/switch begins by sending CBPDUs claiming itself as the root bridge.

9. Define the difference between broadcast and multicast MAC addresses.

   Both identify more than one device on the LAN. Broadcast always implies all devices on the LAN, whereas multicast implies some subset of all devices. Multicast is not allowed on Token Ring; broadcast is allowed on all LAN types. Devices that intend to receive frames addressed to a particular multicast address must be aware of the particular multicast address(es) it should process. These addresses are dependent on the applications used. For some related information, read RFC 1112, the Internet Group Message Protocol (IGMP), for information about the use of Ethernet multicast in conjunction with IP multicast. For example, the broadcast address is FFFF.FFFF.FFFF, and one sample multicast address is 1000.5e00.0001.

10. Define the term *broadcast domain*.

    A set of LAN devices for which a broadcast sent by any one of them should be received by all others in the domain. Bridges and switches do not stop the flow of broadcasts, unlike routers. Two segments separated by a router would each be in a different broadcast domain. A switch can create multiple broadcast domains by creation of multiple VLANs, but a router must be used to route packets between the VLANs.

11. Explain the function of the loopback and collision detection features of an Ethernet NIC in relation to half-duplex and full-duplex operation.

    The loopback feature copies the transmitted frame back onto the receive pin on the NIC interface. The collision detection logic compares the received frame to the transmitted frame during transmission; if the signals do not match, then a collision is occurring. This logic implies half-duplex is being used because if collisions can occur, only one transmitter at a time is desired. With full-duplex, collisions cannot occur (because the device can transmit and listen at the same time). Therefore, the loopback and collision detection features are not needed, and concurrent transmission and reception is allowed.

12. Name the three interface states that the Spanning-Tree Protocol uses other than *forwarding*. Which of these states is transitory?

Blocking, listening, and learning. Blocking is the only stable state; the other two are transitory between blocking and forwarding. Table 4-10 on page 164 summarizes the states and their features.

Answers to the Chapter 4 Q&A Section

1. What do the letters MAC stand for? What other terms have you heard to describe the same or similar concept?

Media Access Control (MAC). Many terms are used to describe a MAC address. NIC, LAN, hardware, burned-in, UAA, LAA, Ethernet, Token Ring, FDDI, card, wire, and real are all terms used to describe this same address in different instances.

2. Name two benefits of LAN segmentation using transparent bridges.

The main benefits are reduced collisions and more bandwidth because multiple 10 or 100 Mbps Ethernet segments are created, and unicasts between devices on the same segment are not forwarded by the bridge, which reduces overhead. The text towards the bottom of page 137 provides a more thorough reference.

3. What routing protocol does a transparent bridge use to learn about Layer 3 addressing groupings?

None. Bridges do not use routing protocols. Transparent bridges do not care about Layer 3 address groupings. Devices on either side of a transparent bridge are in the same Layer 3 group, in other words, the same IP subnet or IPX network.

4. What settings are examined by a bridge or switch to determine which should be elected as root of the spanning tree?

The bridge priority is first examined (lowest wins). In case of a tie, the lowest bridge-id wins. The priority is prepended to the bridge-id in the actual CBPDU message, so the combined fields can be easily compared.

5. Define the term *VLAN*.

Virtual LAN refers to the process of treating one subset of a switch's interfaces as one broadcast domain. Broadcasts from one VLAN are not forwarded to the other VLAN; unicasts between VLANs must use a router. Advanced methods, such as Layer 3 switching in a NetFlow feature card in a Cat5000, can be used to allow the LAN switch to forward traffic between VLANs without each individual frame being routed by a router. However, for the depth of CCNA, such detail is not needed.

6. Assume a building had 100 devices that were attached to the same Ethernet. These users were then migrated onto two separate shared Ethernet segments, each with 50 devices, with a transparent bridge in between. List two benefits that would be derived for a typical user.

   Fewer collisions should occur because twice as much capacity exists. Also, fewer collisions and less waiting should occur because some unicasts will not be forwarded by the bridge.

7. What standards body owns the process of ensuring unique MAC addresses worldwide?

   IEEE. The first half of the burned-in MAC address is a value assigned to the manufacturer by the IEEE. As long as the manufacturer uses that prefix and doesn't duplicate values it assigns in the last three bytes, global uniqueness is attained.

8. Assume a building has 100 devices that are attached to the same Ethernet. These devices are migrated to two different shared Ethernet segments, each with 50 devices. The two segments are connected to a Cisco LAN switch to allow communication between the two sets of users. List two benefits that would be derived for a typical user.

   Two switch ports are used, which reduces the possibility of collisions. Also, each segment has its own 10 or 100 Mbps capacity, allowing more throughput and reducing the likelihood of collisions. Also, although unlikely to be on the CCNA exam, some Cisco switches can reduce the flow of multicasts using the Cisco Group Message Protocol (CGMP).

9. Name the two methods of internal switching on typical switches today. Which provides less latency for an individual frame?

   Store-and-forward and cut-through. Cut-through has less latency per frame, but does not check for bit errors in the frame, including many errors caused by collisions. Store-and-forward stores the entire received frame, verifies the FCS is correct, and then sends the frame. Cut-through sends the first bytes of the frame out before the last bytes of the incoming frame have been received.

10. What is the distance limitation of 10BT? 100BTX?

    10BT allows 100 meters between the device and the hub or switch, as does 100BTX. Table 4-3 on page 130 summarizes the lengths for all Ethernet LAN types.

11. Describe how a transparent bridge decides if it should forward a frame, and how it chooses the interface out which to forward the frame.

The bridge examines the destination MAC address and looks for the address in its bridge (or address) table. If found, the matching entry tells the bridge which output interface to use to forward the frame. If not found, the bridge forwards the frame out all other interfaces (except for interfaces blocked by spanning tree). The bridge table is built by examining incoming frames' source MAC addresses.

12. How fast is Fast Ethernet?

100 million bits per second (100 Mbps).

13. Describe the benefit of Spanning-Tree Protocol as used by transparent bridges and switches.

Physically redundant paths in the network are allowed to exist and be used when other paths fail. Also, loops in the bridged network are avoided. Loops are particularly bad because bridging is using LAN headers, which do not provide a mechanism to mark a frame so that its lifetime can be limited; in other words, the frame can loop forever.

14. If a switch hears three different configuration BPDUs from three different neighbors on three different interfaces, and all three specify that Bridge 1 is the root, how does it choose which interface is its root port?

The root port is the port in which the CBPDU with the lowest-cost value is received. The root port is placed into a forwarding state on all bridges.

15. How does a transparent bridge build its address table?

The bridge listens for incoming frames and examines the source MAC address. If not in the table, the source address is added, along with the port (interface) that the frame entered the bridge. The bridge also marks an entry for freshness so that entries can be removed after a period of disuse. This reduces table size and allows for easier table changes in case a spanning tree change forces more significant changes in the bridge (address) table.

16. How many bytes long is a MAC address?

6 bytes long, or 48 bits.

17. Assume a building has 100 devices that are attached to the same Ethernet. These users are then migrated onto two separate Ethernet segments, each with 50 devices, and separated by a router. List two benefits that would be derived for a typical user.

Reduces collisions by creating two collision domains. Broadcasts are reduced because the router does not forward broadcasts. Routers provide greater control and administration as well.

18. Does a bridge/switch examine just the incoming frame's source MAC, destination MAC, or both? Why does it examine the one(s) it examines?

It examines both MAC addresses. The source is examined so that entries can be added to the bridge/address table. The destination address is examined to determine which interface out which to forward the frame. Table lookup is required for both addresses for any frame that enters an interface. That is one of the reasons that LAN switches, which have a much larger number of interfaces than traditional bridges, need to have optimized hardware and logic to perform table lookup quickly.

19. Define the term *collision domain*.

A set of Ethernet devices for which concurrent transmission of a frame by any two of them will result in a collision. Bridges, switches, and routers separate LAN segments into different collision domains. Repeaters and shared hubs do not separate segments into different collision domains.

20. When a bridge or switch using Spanning-Tree Protocol first initializes, who does it assert should be the root of the tree?

Each bridge/switch begins by sending CBPDUs claiming itself as the root bridge.

21. Name the three reasons why a port is placed into a forwarding state as a result of spanning tree.

First, all ports on the root are placed into forwarding state. Second, one port on each bridge is considered its root port, which is placed into a forwarding state. Finally, on each LAN segment, one bridge is considered to be the designated bridge on that LAN—that designated bridge's interface on that LAN is placed into forwarding state. A complete definition of how a port is considered to be the root port, or how a bridge is considered to be the designated bridge, is included in the "From the Top" section on spanning tree in Chapter 4, "Understanding LANs and LAN Switching."

22. Define the difference between broadcast and multicast MAC addresses.

Both identify more than one device on the LAN. Broadcast always implies all devices on the LAN, whereas multicast implies some subset of all devices. Multicast is not allowed on Token Ring; broadcast is allowed on all LAN types. Devices that intend to receive frames addressed to a particular multicast address must be aware of the particular multicast address(es) they should process. These addresses are dependent on the applications used. Read RFC 1112, the Internet Group Message Protocol (IGMP), for related information about the use of Ethernet multicast in conjunction with IP multicast. For example, the broadcast address is FFFF.FFFF.FFFF, and one sample multicast address is 1000.5e00.0001.

23. Excluding the preamble and starting delimiter fields, but including all other Ethernet headers and trailers, what is the maximum number of bytes in an Ethernet frame?

1518 bytes. See Figure 4-2 on page 127 for more detail.

24. Define the term *broadcast domain.*

A set of Ethernet devices for which a broadcast sent by any one of them should be received by all others in the group. Bridges and switches do not stop the flow of broadcasts, unlike routers. Two segments separated by a router would each be in a different broadcast domain. A switch can create multiple broadcast domains by creation of multiple VLANs, but a router must be used to route packets between the VLANs.

25. Describe the benefits of creating three VLANs of 25 ports each versus a single VLAN of 75 ports, in each case using a single switch. Assume all ports are switched ports (each port is a different collision domain).

Three different broadcast domains are created with three VLANs, so the devices' CPU utilization should decrease due to decreased broadcast traffic. Traffic between devices in different VLANs will pass through some routing function, which can add some latency for those packets. Better management and control is gained by including a router in the path for those packets.

26. If two Cisco LAN switches are connected using Fast Ethernet, what VLAN trunking protocols could be used? If only one VLAN spanned both switches, is a VLAN trunking protocol needed?

ISL is the trunking protocol used by Cisco over Fast Ethernet. If only one VLAN spans the two switches, a trunking protocol is not needed. Trunking or tagging protocols are used to tag a frame as being in a particular VLAN; if only one VLAN is used, tagging is unnecessary.

27. Explain the function of the loopback and collision detection features of an Ethernet NIC in relation to half-duplex and full-duplex operation.

The loopback feature copies the transmitted frame back onto the receive pin on the NIC interface. The collision detection logic compares the received frame to the transmitted frame during transmission; if the signals do not match, then a collision is occurring. This logic implies half-duplex is being used because if collisions can occur, only one transmitter at a time is desired. With full-duplex, collisions cannot occur, so the loopback and collision detection features are not needed and concurrent transmission and reception is allowed.

28. Name the three interface states that the Spanning-Tree Protocol uses, other than *forwarding.* Which of these states is transitory?

Blocking, listening, and learning. Blocking is the only stable state; the other two are transitory between blocking and forwarding. Table 4-10 on page 164 summarizes the states and their features.

Answers to the Chapter 5 "Do I Know This Already?" Quiz

1. Name the parts of an IP address.

   Network, subnet, and host are the three parts of an IP address. However, many people commonly treat the network and subnet parts of an address as a single part, leaving only two parts, the subnet and host parts, with the common use of terms. On the exam, the multiple-choice format should provide extra clues as to which terminology is used.

2. Write down the subnet number, broadcast address, and range of valid IP addresses for the following address and mask: 134.141.7.11   255.255.255.0.

   For the address 134.141.7.11 with mask 255.255.255.0, the subnet number is 134.141.7.0, with broadcast address 134.141.7.255, with all numbers in between the first two being assignable to hosts in that subnet. The binary algorithm for deriving the subnet number is to Boolean AND the address and subnet mask. The broadcast address is derived by changing the subnet number to have all binary 1s in the host part of the address. Table B-1, in the following section, shows the math assuming address 134.141.7.11 with mask 255.255.255.0.

3. How many IP addresses could be assigned in the following subnet: 155.166.44.64   255.255.255.192?

   For subnet 155.166.44.64 and mask 255.255.255.192, the maximum number of assignable IP addresses is (2^6)-2=62 (6 is the number of host bits). The actual IP addresses are not needed to answer this question.

4. How many valid subnets exist if the same mask (255.255.255.0) is used on all subnets of network 134.141.0.0?

   For network 134.141.0.0 and mask 255.255.255.0, the maximum number of IP subnets is (2^8)-2=254, if avoiding the zero and broadcast subnets. The broadcast subnet is the numerically highest subnet number, and the zero subnet is the lowest. Both are allowed on a Cisco router. The **ip subnet-zero** configuration command is required to support the zero subnet. If both are used, then two more subnets are available.

5. Create a minimal configuration enabling IP on each interface, on a 2501 router (2 serial, 1 Ethernet). The NIC assigned you network 8.0.0.0. Your boss says you need at most 200 hosts per subnet. You decide against using VLSM. Your boss says to plan your subnets so you can have as many subnets as possible, rather than allow for larger subnets later. You decide to start with the lowest numerical values for subnets. Assume point-to-point serial links will be attached to this router and that RIP is the routing protocol.

   ```
   Router rip
   network 8.0.0.0
   interface ethernet 0
   ip address 8.0.1.1 255.255.255.0
   interface serial 0
   ```

```
ip address 8.0.2.1 255.255.255.0
interface serial 1
ip address 8.0.3.1 255.255.255.0
```

The zero subnet was not used in this solution. If desired, the **ip subnet-zero** global command could have been used. Subnets 8.0.0.0, 8.0.1.0, and 8.0.2.0 could also have been used in the configuration.

6. Name the three classes of unicast IP addresses and list their default masks, respectively. How many of each type could be assigned to companies and organizations by the NIC?

Class A, B, and C, with default masks 255.0.0.0, 255.255.0.0, and 255.255.255.0, respectively. 2^7 Class A networks are mathematically possible; 2^{14} Class Bs; and 2^{21} Class C addresses.

7. Define the purpose of an ICMP redirect message.

The ICMP redirect message tells a host to use a different router than itself because that other router has a better route to the subnet the host sent a packet to. The redirect also implies that the router sending the message, the host sending the original packet, and the better router all have interfaces attached to this same subnet.

8. Describe the headers used for two examples of Ethernet encapsulation when using IPX.

Ethernet_II uses Ethernet version 2 headers (destination and source address, and type field). Ethernet_802.3 uses an 802.3 header (destination and source address, and length field). Ethernet_802.2 uses an 802.3 header and an 802.2 header (802.2 adds DSAP, SSAP, and Control fields). Ethernet_snap uses an 802.3 header, an 802.2 header, and then a SNAP header (SNAP adds OUI and protocol fields). The names in the answer use Novell's names. The corresponding keywords in the IOS are arpa and novell-ether, respectively. The Novell names refer to the last header before the IPX header. See Table 5-23 and Table 5-24 on page 221 for a reference for all LAN encapsulations.

9. Create a configuration enabling IPX on each interface, with RIP and SAP enabled on each as well, for a 2501 (2 serial, 1 Ethernet) router. Use networks 100, 200, and 300 for interfaces S0, S1, and E0, respectively. Choose any node values.

```
ipx routing 0200.1111.1111
interface serial 0
ipx network 100
interface serial 1
ipx network 200
interface ethernet 0
ipx network 300
```

The node was supplied in the **ipx routing** command so that on the serial interfaces, the IPX addresses are easily recognizable. This helps troubleshooting, because it will be easier to remember the IPX addresses used when pinging.

10. How many Novell encapsulation types are valid in the IOS for Ethernet interfaces? FDDI? Token Ring?

Four encapsulations for Ethernet, three encapsulations for FDDI, two encapsulations for Token Ring. Table 5-23 and Table 5-24 on page 221 list the different encapsulations.

11. A router is attached to an Ethernet LAN. Some clients on the LAN use Novell's Ethernet_II encapsulation, and some others use Ethernet_802.3. If the only subcommand on Ethernet0 reads **ipx network 1**, which of the clients are working? (all, Ethernet_II, or Ethernet_802.3?)

Just those with Ethernet_802.3. The associated IOS keyword is **novell-ether**, and this is the default IPX encapsulation. This question is just trying to test your recall of the default encapsulation for Ethernet.

12. In the **ipx network 11** command, does the IOS assume 11 is binary, octal, decimal, or hexadecimal? What is the largest valid value that could be configured instead of 11?

All IPX network numbers are considered to be hexadecimal by the IOS. The largest value is FFFFFFFE, with FFFFFFFF being reserved as the broadcast network.

Answers to the Chapter 5 Q&A Section

1. What do TCP, UDP, IP, and ICMP stand for? Which protocol is considered to be *Layer 3 equivalent* when comparing TCP/IP to the OSI protocols?

Transmission Control Protocol, User Datagram Protocol, Internet Protocol, and Internet Control Message Protocol. Both TCP and UDP are Layer 4 protocols. ICMP is considered Layer 3 because it is used for control and management of IP. IP is the core part of the network layer of TCP/IP.

2. Name the parts of an IP address.

Network, subnet, and host are the three parts of an IP address. However, many people commonly treat the network and subnet parts of an address as a single part, leaving only two parts, the subnet and host parts, with the common use of terms. On the exam, the multiple-choice format should provide extra clues as to which terminology is used.

3. Define the term *subnet mask*. What do the bits in the mask, whose values are binary 0, tell you about the corresponding IP address(es)?

A subnet mask defines the number of host bits in an address. The bits of value 0 define which bits in the address are host bits. The mask is an important ingredient in the formula to dissect an IP address; along with knowledge of the number of network bits implied for Class A, B, and C networks, the mask provides a clear definition of the size of the network, subnet, and host parts of an address.

4. Write down the subnet numbers, broadcast addresses, and range of valid IP addresses for the following addresses and masks:

134.141.7.11	255.255.255.0
10.5.118.3	255.255.0.0
193.193.7.7	255.255.255.0
167.88.99.66	255.255.255.192

For the address 134.141.7.11 with mask 255.255.255.0, the subnet number is 134.141.7.0, with broadcast address 134.141.7.255, with all numbers in between the first two being assignable to hosts in that subnet. The binary algorithm for deriving the subnet number is to Boolean AND the address and subnet mask. The Broadcast address is derived by changing the subnet number to include all binary 1s in the host part of the address. Table B-1 shows the math assuming address 134.141.7.11 with mask 255.255.255.0.

Table B-1 *Full Example for Address 134.141.7.11 with Mask 255.255.255.192*

	Decimal Value	Binary Value
Address	134.141.7.11	1000 0110 1000 1101 0000 0111 0000 1011
Mask	255.255.255.128	1111 1111 1111 1111 1111 1111 0000 0000
Subnet (result of AND)	134.141.7.0	1000 0110 1000 1101 0000 0111 0000 0000
Broadcast (result of changing the host bits to all binary 1s)	134.141.7.255	1000 0110 1000 1101 0000 0111 *1111 1111*

The range of assignable addresses is 134.141.7.1 through 134.141.7.254, inclusive.

For the address 10.5.118.3 with mask 255.255.0.0, the subnet number is 10.5.0.0 and the broadcast address is 10.5.255.255, with all numbers in between the first two being assignable to hosts in that subnet.

For the address 193.193.7.7 with mask 255.255.255.0, the subnet number is 193.193.7.0, with broadcast address 193.193.7.255, and with all numbers in between the first two being assignable to hosts in that subnet. No subnetting is used in this case; it uses the default mask for Class C networks.

For the address 167.88.99.66 with mask 255.255.255.192, the subnet number is 167.88.99.64, with broadcast address 167.88.99.127, and with all numbers in between the first two being assignable to a host in that subnet. The binary algorithm remains the same, regardless of subnet mask used. The decimal results are not intuitive to most people when a tricky mask is used, as is the case here. There are only six subnet bits, according to the mask. Conversion from decimal to binary, and vice versa, always uses a complete byte;

the last two bits of the subnet field and the six-bit host field are used together as one eight-bit field when doing conversion back to decimal. Table B-2 shows the math assuming address 167.88.99.66 with mask 255.255.255.192.

Table B-2 *Q&A #4—Full Example for Address 167.88.99.66 with Mask 255.255.255.192*

	Decimal Value	Binary Value
Address	167.88.99.66	1010 0111 0101 1000 0110 0011 0100 0010
Mask	255.255.255.192	1111 1111 1111 1111 1111 1111 1100 0000
Subnet (result of AND)	167.88.99.64	1010 0111 0101 1000 0110 0011 0100 0000
Broadcast (result of changing host bits to binary 1s)	167.88.99.127	1010 0111 0101 1000 0110 0011 01*11 1111*

The range of assignable addresses is 167.88.99.65 through 167.88.99.126, inclusive.

5. How many IP addresses could be assigned in each of the following subnets:

134.141.7.0	255.255.255.0
155.166.44.64	255.255.255.192
10.7.8.0	255.255.255.0
128.5.0.0	255.255.0.0

   For subnet 134.141.7.0 and mask 255.255.255.0, the maximum number of assignable IP addresses is $(2^8)-2=254$. (8 is the number of host bits.) The actual IP addresses are not needed to answer this question. The mask has eight bits of value 0, implying the number of host bits in the address. The highest and lowest values are reserved.

   For subnet 155.166.44.64 and mask 255.255.255.192, the maximum number of assignable IP addresses is $(2^6)-2=62$ (6 is the number of host bits). The actual IP addresses are not needed to answer this question.

   For subnet 10.7.8.0 and mask 255.255.255.0, the maximum number of assignable IP addresses is $(2^8)-2=254$. (8 is the number of host bits.) The actual IP addresses are not needed to answer this question.

   For subnet 128.5.0.0 and mask 255.255.0.0, the maximum number of assignable IP addresses is $(2^{16})-2=65,534$ (16 is the number of host bits). The actual IP addresses are not needed to answer this question.

6. Given the list of Class A, B, and C networks, how many valid subnets exist in each case, if the subnet mask shown beside each network number is used on all subnets of that network?

Network 134.141.0.0	255.255.255.0
Network 155.166.0.0	255.255.255.192
Network 10.0.0.0	255.255.255.0
Network 199.5.0.0	255.255.255.224

For network 134.141.0.0 and mask 255.255.255.0, the maximum number of IP subnets is $(2^8)-2=254$, if avoiding the zero and broadcast subnets. The broadcast subnet is the numerically highest subnet number, and the zero subnet is the lowest. Both are allowed on a Cisco router. The **ip subnet-zero** configuration command is required to support the zero subnet. If both are used, two more subnets are available.

For network 155.166.0.0 and mask 255.255.255.192, the maximum number of IP subnets is $(2^{10})-2=1022$, if avoiding the zero and broadcast subnets.

For network 10.0.0.0 and mask 255.255.255.0, the maximum number of IP subnets is $(2^{16})-2=65,534$, if avoiding the zero and broadcast subnets.

For network 199.5.0.0 and mask 255.255.255.224, the maximum number of IP subnets is $(2^3)-2=6$, if avoiding the zero and broadcast subnets. This is a tricky one because 199.5.0.0 looks like a Class B network because it ends in two octets of decimal 0. Technically, Class C network numbers begin with binary 110, have all binary 0s for the host part of the number (the last eight bits), and any value in the remaining 21 bits, other than all binary 0s or 1s. This means that 192.0.0.0 is not allowed, and 223.255.255.0 is not allowed, but "odd" looking numbers like 199.5.0.0, 200.0.0.0, 201.255.255.0, and 210.255.255.0 are all valid Class C network numbers.

7. Create a minimal configuration enabling IP on each interface on a 2501 router (2 serial, 1 Ethernet). The NIC assigned you network 8.0.0.0. Your boss says you need at most 200 hosts per subnet. You decide against using VLSM. Your boss says to plan your subnets so you can have as many subnets as possible, rather than allow for larger subnets later. You decide to start with the lowest numerical values for subnets. Assume point-to-point serial links will be attached to this router, and that RIP is the routing protocol.

```
Router rip
network 8.0.0.0
interface ethernet 0
ip address 8.0.1.1 255.255.255.0
interface serial 0
ip address 8.0.2.1 255.255.255.0
interface serial 1
ip address 8.0.3.1 255.255.255.0
```

The zero subnet was not used in this solution. If desired, the **ip subnet-zero** global command could have been used, as well as the subnets 8.0.0.0, 8.0.1.0, and 8.0.2.0 in the configuration.

8. In question 7, what would the IP subnet of the link attached to serial 0 be? If another user came along and wanted to answer the same question, but they did not have the enable password, what command(s) might tell them this IP's addresses and subnets?

The attached subnet is 8.0.2.0, 255.255.255.0. The **show interface**, **show ip interface**, and **show ip interface brief** commands would supply this information, as well as **show ip route**. The **show ip route** command would show the actual subnet number instead of the address of the interface.

9. Describe the question and possible responses in setup mode when a router wants to know the mask used on an interface. How can the router derive the correct mask from the information supplied by the user?

The question asks for the number of subnet bits. The router creates a subnet mask with x more binary 1s than the default mask for the class of network that the interface's IP address is a member of. (x is the number in the response.) "Number of subnet bits" from the setup question uses the definition that there are three parts to an address—network, subnet, and host. The size of the network field is based on the class of address; the interface's address was typed in response to an earlier setup question. The mask simply has binary 1s in the network and subnet fields, and binary 0s in the host field.

10. Name the three classes of unicast IP addresses and list their default masks, respectively. How many of each type could be assigned to companies and organizations by the NIC?

Class A, B, and C, with default masks 255.0.0.0, 255.255.0.0, and 255.255.255.0, respectively. 2^7 Class A networks are mathematically possible; 2^{14} Class Bs; and 2^{21} Class C addresses.

11. Describe how TCP performs error recovery. What role do the routers play?

TCP numbers the first byte in each segment with a sequence number. The receiving host uses the acknowledgment field in segments it sends to acknowledge receipt of the data. If the receiver sends an acknowledgment number that is a smaller number than the sender expected, the sender believes the intervening bytes were lost, so the sender resends them. The router plays no role, unless the TCP connection ends in the router, for example, a Telnet into a router. A full explanation is in the section, "Functions at Each Layer," in Chapter 5.

12. Define the purpose of an ICMP redirect message.

An ICMP redirect message tells a host to use a different router than itself because that other router has a better route to the subnet the host sent a packet to. The redirect also implies that the router sending the message, the host sending the original packet, and the better router all have interfaces attached to this same subnet.

13. Define the purpose of the **trace** command. What type of messages is it sending, and what type of ICMP messages is it receiving?

The **trace** command learns the current route to the destination. It uses IP packets with UDP as the transport layer protocol, with TTL values beginning at 1, and then incrementing by 1. The result is that intervening routers will find TTL is exceeded and send ICMP "TTL exceeded" messages back to the originator of the packet, which is the

trace command. The source addresses of the "TTL exceeded" packets identify each router. By sending other packets with TTL=2, then 3, and so on, eventually the packet is received by the host. The host will return a "port unreachable" ICMP message, which lets the **trace** command know that the endpoint host has been reached.

14. What does IP stand for? ICMP? Which protocol is considered to be *Layer 3 equivalent* when comparing TCP/IP to the OSI protocols?

Internet Protocol and Internet Control Message Protocol. Both protocols are considered to be part of TCP/IP's protocols equivalent to OSI Layer 3. ICMP is also considered Layer 3 because it is used for control and management of IP. However, an IP header precedes an ICMP header, so it is common to treat ICMP as another Layer 4 protocol, like TCP and UDP. ICMP does not provide services to a higher layer—so it is really an adjunct part of Layer 3.

15. What causes the output from an IOS **ping** command to display "UUUUU"?

U is an indication that an unreachable message was received. The type of unreachable is not implied by the "U".

16. Describe how to view the IP ARP cache in a Cisco router. Also describe the three key elements of each entry.

show ip arp displays the IP ARP cache in a Cisco router. Each entry contains the IP address, MAC address, and the interface from which the information was learned. The encapsulation type is also in the table entry.

17. What dynamic process replaces ARP on Frame Relay networks? What command shows the equivalent of the ARP cache for Frame Relay networks? What are the three key parts to an entry in this table?

Inverse ARP is used on Frame Relay to correlate Layer 3 and Layer 2 addresses. **show frame-relay map** shows the mappings. It includes the DLCI, Layer 3 address, and interface (or subinterface). Static **frame-relay map** commands can be used instead, but there is no compelling reason to use them in place of **inverse-arp**.

18. How many hosts are allowed per subnet if the subnet mask used is 255.255.255.192? 255.255.255.252?

255.255.255.192 has six bits of value 0, giving 2^6 hosts, minus the two reserved numbers, for 62. The 255.255.255.252 mask leaves 2^2 hosts, minus the two reserved numbers, for 2 hosts. 255.255.255.252 is often used on serial links when using VLSM; point-to-point links need only two IP addresses.

19. How many subnets could be created, if using static length masks in a Class B network, when the mask is 255.255.255.224? When the mask is 255.255.252.0?

With a Class B network, the first 16 bits are network bits. With mask 255.255.255.224, there are 5 host bits, leaving 11 subnet bits. 2^{11} is 2048. If the zero and broadcast subnets are avoided, 2046 are left. For the mask 255.255.252.0, there are 10 host bits, leaving 6 subnet bits. 2^6 is 64; if avoiding the two special cases, that leaves 62 possible subnets.

20. How many bytes comprise an IPX address?

Ten bytes. The network portion is 32 bits, and the node portion is 48 bits. The node part conveniently is the same size as a LAN MAC address.

21. What do IPX and SPX stand for?

Internetwork Packet Exchange and Sequenced Packet Exchange.

22. Define encapsulation in the context of Cisco routers and Novell IPX.

Data Link encapsulation describes the details of the data-link header and trailer created by a router as the result of routing a packet out an interface. Novell allows several options on LANs. Encapsulation is used for any routed protocol on every router interface. Novell just happens to have many options that are still in use, particularly on Ethernet.

23. Give an example of an IPX network mask used when subnetting.

There is no such thing as subnetting with IPX. This is an example of a question meant to shake your confidence on the exam. Thoughts like, "I never read about subnetting IPX!" can destroy your concentration. Be prepared for unusual questions or answers like this on the exam!

24. Describe the headers used for two examples of Ethernet encapsulation when using IPX.

Ethernet_II uses Ethernet version 2 headers (destination and source address, and type field). Ethernet_802.3 uses an 802.3 header (destination and source address, and length field). Ethernet_802.2 uses an 802.3 header and an 802.2 header (802.2 adds DSAP, SSAP, and Control fields). Ethernet_snap uses an 802.3 header, an 802.2 header, and then a SNAP header (SNAP adds OUI and protocol fields). The names in the answer use Novell's names. The corresponding keywords in the IOS are arpa and novell-ether, respectively. The Novell names refer to the last header before the IPX header. See Table 5-23 and Table 5-24 on page 221 for a reference for all LAN encapsulations.

25. Name the part of the NetWare protocol specifications that, like TCP, provides end-to-end guaranteed delivery of data.

SPX (Sequenced Packet Exchange).

26. Name the command that lists all the SAP entries in a Cisco router.

show ipx servers. Many people remember that the command uses either servers, or server, or service, or sap. The exam is likely to list those four keywords as the four answers; spend a little time memorizing the commands summarized at the beginning of each configuration section in most chapters of this book!

27. How many different values are possible for IPX network numbers?

2^{32}, or around four billion. Networks 0 and FFFFFFFF are reserved. The size of the network number is one big reason that there is no need for subnetting IPX networks.

28. Create a configuration enabling IPX on each interface, with RIP and SAP enabled on each as well, for a 2501 (2 serial, 1 Ethernet) router. Use networks 100, 200, and 300 for interfaces S0, S1, and E0, respectively. Choose any node values.

```
ipx routing 0200.1111.1111
interface serial 0
ipx network 100
interface serial 1
ipx network 200
interface ethernet 0
ipx network 300
```

The node was supplied in the **ipx routing** command so that on the serial interfaces, the IPX addresses are easily recognizable. This helps troubleshooting because it will be easier to remember the IPX addresses used when pinging.

29. In the previous question, what would the IPX address of the serial 0 interface be? If another user came along and wanted to know, but they did not have the enable password, what command(s) might tell them this IPX address?

S0—100.0200.1111.1111

show ipx interface

If you left off the node parameter on the **ipx routing** command in the previous question, the IPX address would have a node number equal to the MAC address used on the Ethernet interface.

30. What **show** command lists the IPX address(es) of interfaces in a Cisco router?

show ipx interface. The other **show** commands only list the IPX network numbers, not the entire IPX addresses.

31. How many Novell encapsulation types are valid in the IOS for Ethernet interfaces? FDDI? Token Ring?

Four encapsulations for Ethernet; three encapsulations for FDDI; two encapsulations for Token Ring. Table 5-23 and Table 5-24 on page 221 list the different encapsulations.

32. A router is attached to an Ethernet LAN. Some clients on the LAN use Novell's Ethernet_II encapsulation, and some others use Ethernet_802.3. If the only subcommand on Ethernet0 reads **ipx network 1**, which of the clients are working? (all, Ethernet_II, or Ethernet_802.3?)

Just those with Ethernet_802.3. The associated IOS keyword is **novell-ether**, and this is the default IPX encapsulation. This question is just trying to test your recall of the default encapsulation for Ethernet.

33. A router is attached to an Ethernet LAN. Some clients on the LAN use Novell's Ethernet_802.2 encapsulation, and some others use Ethernet_snap. Create a configuration that allows both types of clients to send and receive packets through this router.

```
interface ethernet 0
ipx network 1 encapsulation sap
ipx network 2 encapsulation snap secondary
```

NOTE   Subinterfaces could also have been used instead of secondary IPX networks.

34. Up to 64 IPX networks can be used on the same Ethernet by using the IPX secondary address feature. (T/F) If true, describe the largest number that is practically needed. If false, what is the maximum number that is legal on an Ethernet?

False. Only one network per encapsulation is allowed. Because four Ethernet encapsulations can be used with IPX, four IPX networks are supported. With the same logic, only three networks are allowed on FDDI, and two on Token Ring.

35. In the **ipx network 11** command, does the IOS assume 11 is binary, octal, decimal, or hexadecimal? What is the largest valid value that could be configured instead of 11?

All IPX network numbers are considered to be hexadecimal by the IOS. The largest value is FFFFFFFE, with FFFFFFFF being reserved as the broadcast network.

36. What IOS IPX encapsulation keyword implies use of an 802.2 header, but no SNAP header? On what types of interfaces is type of encapsulation valid?

SAP encapsulation on the IOS implies use of the 802.2 header immediately before the IPX packet. SAP and SNAP are valid on Ethernet, FDDI, and Token Ring. SAP also refers to the field in the header that is used to identify IPX as the type of packet that follows the 802.2 header.

Answers to the Chapter 6 "Do I Know This Already?" Quiz

1. What type of routing protocol algorithm uses a holddown timer? What is its purpose?

   Distance vector. Holddown prevents counting-to-infinity problems. Holddown is explained in detail in the section titled "Distance Vector Routing Protocols." After hearing that a route has failed, a router waits for holddown time before believing any new information about the route.

2. Define what split-horizon means to the contents of a routing update. Does this apply to both the distance vector algorithm and link state algorithm?

   Routing updates sent out an interface do not contain routing information about subnets learned from updates entering the same interface. Split-horizon is only used by distance vector routing protocols.

3. How does the IOS designate a subnet in the routing table as a directly connected network? A route learned with IGRP? A route learned with RIP?

   The **show ip route** command lists routes with a designator in the left side of the command output. "C" represents connected routes, "I" is used for IGRP, and "R" represents RIP derived routes.

4. Create a configuration for IGRP on a router with these interfaces and addresses: e0 using 10.1.1.1, e1 using 224.1.2.3, s0 using 10.1.2.1, and s1 using 199.1.1.1. Use process ID 5.

   ```
   router igrp 5
   network 10.0.0.0
   network 199.1.1.1
   ```

   If you noticed that 224.1.2.3 is not a valid Class A, B, or C address, you get full credit. A new address will be needed for Ethernet 1, with a matching **network** command.

5. How often does IPX RIP send routing updates by default?

   Every 60 seconds.

6. What does GNS stand for? Who creates GNS requests, and who creates GNS replies?

   GNS stands for Get Nearest Server. Clients create the request, which is a broadcast, looking for a nearby server. Servers and routers reply, based on their SAP table, with a server whose RIP metric is low.

7. Define the term *Separate Multiprotocol Routing* in the context of the Cisco IOS and Novell IPX.

   Separate Multiprotocol Routing means that each routed protocol, like IP, IPX, or AppleTalk, uses a separate set of routing updates to advertise routing information. The term *Separate Multiprotocol Routing* is taken directly from CCNA objective 41.

8. If Serial0 has a **bandwidth 1544** interface subcommand, and Serial1 has a **bandwidth 56** interface subcommand, what metric will IPX RIP associate with each interface?

The IOS is unaffected by an interface's bandwidth when considering IPX RIP metrics; ticks will be six for any serial interface.

9. What **show** commands list IPX RIP metric values in a Cisco router?

show ipx route
show ipx servers

This is a trick question. The services listed also contain a reference to the RIP metrics, so the information is handy when looking for good servers for a GNS reply.

10. Define the term *Integrated Multiprotocol Routing* in the context of the Cisco IOS and Novell IPX.

Integrated Multiprotocol Routing means that multiple routed protocols use a common routing protocol, which consolidates routing updates. EIGRP is the only such routing protocol covered in the Training Paths; it exchanges routing information for IP, IPX, and AppleTalk. IGRP and Integrated IS-IS support both IP and OSI CLNS routable protocols. The term *Integrated Multiprotocol Routing* is taken directly from CCNA objective 41.

11. If the commands **router rip** followed by **network 10.0.0.0** with no other **network** commands were configured in a router that has an Ethernet0 interface with IP address 168.10.1.1, would RIP send updates out Ethernet0?

No. There must be a network statement for network 168.10.0.0 before RIP will advertise out that interface.

12. What routing protocols support integrated multiprotocol routing?

EIGRP supports integrated multiprotocol routing for IP, IPX, and AppleTalk. IGRP and Integrated IS-IS support integrated multiprotocol routing for IP and OSI CLNS.

Answers to the Chapter 6 Q&A Section

1. What type of routing protocol algorithm uses a holddown timer? What is its purpose?

Distance vector. Holddown prevents counting-to-infinity problems. Holddown is explained in detail in the section titled "Distance Vector Routing Protocols." After hearing that a route has failed, a router waits for holddown time before believing any new information about the route.

2. Define what split-horizon means to the contents of a routing update. Does this apply to both the distance vector algorithm and link state algorithm?

Routing updates sent out an interface do not contain routing information about subnets learned from updates entering the same interface. Split-horizon is only used by distance vector routing protocols.

3. Write down the steps you would take to migrate from RIP to IGRP in a router whose current RIP configuration includes only **router rip**, followed by a **network 10.0.0.0** command.

Issue the following commands in configuration mode:

```
no router rip
router igrp 5
network 10.0.0.0
```

If RIP were still configured, IGRP's routes would be chosen over RIP. The IOS considers IGRP to be a better source of routing information by default, as defined in the *administrative distance* setting (default 120 for RIP).

4. How does the IOS designate a subnet in the routing table as a directly connected network? A route learned with IGRP? A route learned with RIP?

The **show ip route** command lists routes with a designator in the left side of the command output. "C" represents connected routes, "I" is used for IGRP, and "R" represents RIP derived routes.

5. Create a configuration for IGRP on a router with these interfaces and addresses: e0 using 10.1.1.1, e1 using 224.1.2.3, s0 using 10.1.2.1, and s1 using 199.1.1.1. Use process ID 5.

```
router igrp 5
network 10.0.0.0
network 199.1.1.1
```

If you noticed that 224.1.2.3 is not a valid Class A, B, or C address, you get full credit. A new address will be needed for Ethernet 1, with a matching **network** command.

6. Create a configuration for IGRP on a router with these interfaces and addresses: to0 using 200.1.1.1, e0 using 128.1.3.2, s0 using 192.0.1.1, and s1 using 223.254.254.1.

```
router igrp 1
network 200.1.1.0
network 128.1.0.0
network 192.0.1.0
network 223.254.254.0
```

Because four different networks are used, four network commands are required. If you noticed that the question did not specify the process ID (1 in this sample), but configured one, you get full credit. A few of these network numbers are used in examples; memorize the range of valid A, B, and C network numbers.

7. From a router's user mode, without using debugs or privileged mode, how can you determine what routers are sending you routing updates?

The **show ip protocol** command output lists the *routing sources*—the IP addresses of routers sending updates to this router. Knowing how to determine a fact without looking at the configuration will better prepare you for the exam. Also, the **show ip route** command lists next-hop router IP addresses. Entries that are added due to a routing protocol also identify the routers that are sending routing updates.

8. How often does IPX RIP send routing updates, by default?

Every 60 seconds.

9. Describe the metric(s) used by IPX RIP in a Cisco router.

The primary metric is a counter of timer ticks. If two routes to the same network tie with the ticks metric, the hop count is considered. Ticks is a number of 1/18ths of a second. It is not measured, but administratively set.

10. Define *split-horizon*. Does IPX RIP use it?

Split-horizon means that routes learned via updates received on interface x will not be advertised about in routing updates sent out interface x. IPX RIP uses split-horizon by default. SAP also uses split-horizon concepts.

11. RIP and SAP information is sent in the same packets. (T/F) If true, can only one of the two be enabled in a router? If false, what commands enable each protocol globally in a router?

False. Only one command is used, and it enables both: **ipx routing**. Neither type of update is sent unless IPX is also enabled on the interface with the **ipx network** interface subcommand.

12. What does GNS stand for? Who creates GNS requests, and who creates GNS replies?

GNS stands for Get Nearest Server. Clients create the request, which is a broadcast, looking for a nearby server. Servers and routers reply, based on their SAP table, with a server whose RIP metric is low.

13. Define the term *Separate Multiprotocol Routing* in the context of the Cisco IOS and Novell IPX.

Separate Multiprotocol Routing means that each routed protocol, like IP, IPX, or AppleTalk, uses a separate set of routing updates to advertise routing information. The term *Separate Multiprotocol Routing* is taken directly from CCNA objective 41.

14. How often does a router send SAP updates by default?

Every 60 seconds.

15. If Serial0 has a **bandwidth 1544** interface subcommand, and Serial1 has a **bandwidth 56** interface subcommand, what metric will IPX RIP associate with each interface?

The IOS is unaffected by an interface's bandwidth when considering IPX RIP metrics; ticks will be six for any serial interface.

16. Routers forward SAP packets as they arrive, but broadcast SAP packets on interfaces in which no SAP packets have been received in the last 60 seconds. (T/F)

False. Routers never forward SAP updates, but they instead read the information in the updates, update their own SAP tables, and then discard the packets. Routers also send SAP updates every update timer (default 60 seconds), regardless of what other routers may do. This sample question is another case of tricky wording that may be used to make sure you know the topic.

17. What **show** commands list IPX RIP metric values in a Cisco router?

show ipx route
show ipx servers

This is a trick question. The services listed also contain a reference to the RIP metrics; the information is handy when looking for good servers for a GNS reply.

18. Define the term *Integrated Multiprotocol Routing* in the context of the Cisco IOS and Novell IPX.

Integrated Multiprotocol Routing means that multiple routed protocols use a common routing protocol, which consolidates routing updates. EIGRP is the only such routing protocol covered in the Training Paths; it exchanges routing information for IP, IPX, and AppleTalk. IGRP and Integrated IS-IS support both IP and OSI CLNS routable protocols. The term *Integrated Multiprotocol Routing* is taken directly from CCNA objective 41.

19. If the commands **router rip** followed by **network 10.0.0.0** with no other **network** commands were configured in a router that has an Ethernet0 interface with IP address 168.10.1.1, would RIP send updates out Ethernet0?

No. There must be a network statement for network 168.10.0.0 before RIP will advertise out that interface.

20. If the commands **router igrp 1**, followed by **network 10.0.0.0**, were configured in a router that has an Ethernet0 interface with IP address 168.10.1.1, would IGRP advertise about 168.10.0.0?

No. There must be a network statement for network 168.10.0.0 before IGRP will advertise about that directly connected subnet.

21. If the commands **router igrp 1** followed by **network 10.0.0.0** were configured in a router that has an Ethernet0 interface with IP address 168.10.1.1, would this router have a route to 168.10.0.0?

Yes. The route will be in the routing table because it is a directly connected subnet, not because of any action by IGRP.

22. What routing protocols support integrated multiprotocol routing?

EIGRP supports integrated multiprotocol routing for IP, IPX, and AppleTalk. IGRP and Integrated IS-IS support integrated multiprotocol routing for IP and OSI CLNS.

Answers to the Chapter 7 "Do I Know This Already?" Quiz

1. Configure an IP access list that would stop packets from subnet 134.141.7.0, with mask 255.255.255.0, from exiting serial 0 on some router. Allow all other packets.

   ```
   access-list 4 deny 134.141.7.0 0.0.0.255
   access-list 4 permit any
   interface serial 0
   ip access-group 4
   ```

   The first **access-list** statement denied packets from that subnet. The other statement is needed because of the default action to deny packets not explicitly matched in an access list statement.

2. How would a user who does not have the enable password find out what access lists have been configured and where they are enabled?

   The **show access-list** command lists all access lists.

3. Configure and enable an IP access list that would stop packets from subnet 10.3.4.0/24 from getting out serial interface S0 and stop packets from 134.141.5.4 from entering S1. Permit all other traffic.

   ```
   access-list 1 deny 10.3.4.0 0.0.0.255
   access-list 1 permit any
   access-list 2 deny 134.141.5.4
   access-list 2 permit any
   interface serial 0
   ip access-group 1
   interface serial 1
   ip access-group 2 in
   ```

4. Create an IPX packet filter to prevent packets from entering Serial0, except for packets from address 500.0000.0000.0001 destined for any node in network 4.

   ```
   access-list 800 permit 500.0000.0000.0001 4
   interface serial0
   ipx access-group 800 in
   ```

   A "deny all else" is implied at the end of the list.

5. What services use IPX socket 4? Socket 7?

None. This is a trick question. When I wrote it, I thought of the emotions I felt when I took the CCNA exam; I was quite irritated at the exam question writer! SAP types 4 and 7 represent file and print services, respectively. However, sockets are different, and there is no direct correlation between SAP types and sockets. The message—read ALL the words in the question!

6. Create a configuration to add a SAP access list to filter all print services from being advertised out a router's serial 0 and serial1 interfaces.

```
access-list 1000 deny -1 7
access-list 1000 permit -1
interface serial 0
ipx output-sap-filter 1000
interface serial1
ipx output-sap-filter 1000
```

In the two **access-list 1000** commands, the "-1" represents a wildcard meaning "any network." SAP type 7 is for print services; the first statement matches those services, and denies those services. However, other proprietary print solutions could use a different SAP type. This access list only matches for the standard SAP type for printers.

7. Name all the items that a standard SAP access list can examine to make a match.

Network
IPX address (network and node)
Multiples of the first two using a wildcard
Service type
Server name

Many people would consider checking the network number and checking a full IPX address as the same item. It is only listed separately here to make sure you recall that both variations are possible.

8. Can standard IP access lists be used to check the source IP address when enabled with the **ip access-group 1 in** command and check the destination IP addresses when using the **ip access-group 1 out** command?

No. Standard IP access lists check only the source IP address, regardless of whether the packets are checked on inbound or outbound packets.

9. Can a single IP extended **access-list** command be used to check a particular port number on all IP packets?

No. If the IP protocol type is configured, the port number is not allowed to be checked. The TCP or UDP protocol type must be used to check the port numbers.

10. If all IP or IPX **access-list** statements in a particular list define the deny action, the default action is to permit all other packets. (T/F)

False. The default action at the end of any IP or IPX access list is to deny all other packets.

11. In an IPX access list with five statements, a **no** version of the third statement is issued in configuration mode. Immediately following, another access list configuration command is added for the same access list. How many statements are in the list now, and in what position is the newly added statement?

Only one statement will remain in the list, namely the newly added statement. The **no access-list x** command deletes the entire access list, even if the rest of the parameters in an individual command are typed in when issuing the **no** version of the command.

12. How many IP access lists of either type can be active on an interface at the same time?

Only one IP access list per interface, per direction. In other words, one inbound and one outbound are allowed, but no more.

Answers to the Chapter 7 Q&A Section

1. Configure an IP access list that would stop packets from subnet 134.141.7.0, 255.255.255.0, from exiting serial 0 on some router. Allow all other packets.

```
access-list 4 deny 134.141.7.0 0.0.0.255
access-list 4 permit any
interface serial 0
ip access-group 4
```

The first **access-list** statement denied packets from that subnet. The other statement is needed because of the default action to deny packets not explicitly matched in an access list statement.

2. Configure an IP access list that allows only packets from subnet 193.7.6.0, 255.255.255.0, going to hosts in network 128.1.0.0 and using a web server in 128.1.0.0, to enter serial 0 on some router.

```
access-list 105 permit tcp 193.7.6.0 0.0.0.255 128.1.0.0 0.0.255.255 eq www
!
interface serial 0
ip access-group 105 in
```

A "deny all" is implied at the end of the list.

3. How would a user who does not have the enable password find out what access lists have been configured, and where they are enabled?

The **show access-list** command lists all access lists and specifies the interfaces on which they are enabled.

4. Configure and enable an IP access list that would stop packets from subnet 10.3.4.0/24 from getting out serial interface S0 and stop packets from 134.141.5.4 from entering S0. Permit all other traffic.

```
access-list 1 deny 10.3.4.0 0.0.0.255
access-list 1 permit any
access-list 2 deny 134.141.5.4
access-list 2 permit any
interface serial 0
ip access-group 1
interface serial 1
ip access-group 2 in
```

5. Configure and enable an IP access list that would allow packets from subnet 10.3.4.0/24, to any web server, to get out serial interface S0. Also, allow packets from 134.141.5.4 going to all TCP-based servers to enter serial 0. Deny all other traffic.

```
access-list 101 permit tcp 10.3.4.0 0.0.0.255 any eq www
access-list 102 permit tcp host 134.141.5.4 any lt 1023
interface serial 0
ip access-group 101 out
ip access-group 102 in
```

Two extended access lists are required. List 101 permits packets in the first of the two criteria, in which packets exiting S0 are examined. List 102 permits packets for the second criteria, in which packets entering S0 are examined.

6. Create an IPX packet filter to prevent packets from entering Serial0, except for packets from address 500.0000.0000.0001 destined for any node in network 4.

```
access-list 800 permit 500.0000.0000.0001 4
interface serial0
ipx access-group 800 in
```

A "deny all else" is implied at the end of the list.

7. At most, three SAP filters can be enabled on a particular interface at any one time. (T/F)

True. SAP filters can be enabled using three different interface subcommands: **ipx output-sap-filter**, **ipx input-sap-filter**, and **ipx router-sap-filter**. Each refers to a different SAP filter, and all can be enabled concurrently. This is probably an unfair question for CCNA preparation. However, knowing that input and output SAP filters can be enabled at the same time on the same interface is probably a topic that could be covered on the exam.

8. What services use IPX socket 4? Socket 7?

None. This is a trick question. When I wrote it, I thought of the emotions I felt when I took the CCNA exam; I was quite irritated at the exam question writer! SAP types 4 and 7 represent file and print services, respectively. However, sockets are different, and there is no direct correlation between SAP types and sockets. The message—read ALL the words in the question!

9. Create a configuration to add a SAP access list to filter all print services from being advertised out a router's serial 0 and serial1 interfaces.

```
access-list 1000 deny -1 7
access-list 1000 permit -1
interface serial 0
ipx output-sap-filter 1000
interface serial1
ipx output-sap-filter 1000
```

In the two **access-list 1000** commands, the "-1" represents the wildcard meaning "any network." SAP type 7 is for print services; the first statement matches those services, and denies those services. However, other proprietary print solutions could use a different SAP type. This access list only matches for the standard SAP type for printers.

10. Name all the items that a standard SAP access list can examine in order to make a match.

Network
IPX address (network and node)
Multiples of the first two using a wildcard
Service type
Server name

Many people would consider checking the network number and checking a full IPX address as the same item. It is only listed separately here to make sure you recall that both variations are possible.

11. Can standard IP access lists be used to check the source IP address when enabled with the **ip access-group 1 in** command and check the destination IP addresses when using the **ip access-group 1 out** command?

No. Standard IP access lists check only the source IP address, regardless of whether the packets are checked on inbound or outbound packets.

12. Can a single IP extended **access-list** command be used to check a particular port number on all IP packets?

No. If the IP protocol type is configured, the port number is not allowed to be checked. The TCP or UDP protocol type must be used to check the port numbers.

13. If all IP or IPX **access-list** statements in a particular list define the deny action, then the default action is to permit all other packets. (T/F)

False. The default action at the end of any IP or IPX access list is to deny all other packets.

14. In an IPX access list with five statements, a **no** version of the third statement is issued in configuration mode. Immediately following, another access list configuration command is added for the same access list. How many statements are in the list now, and in what position is the newly added statement?

Only one statement will remain in the list, namely the newly added statement. The **no access-list x** command deletes the entire access list, even if the rest of the parameters in an individual command are typed in when issuing the **no** version of the command.

15. How many IP access lists of either type can be active on an interface at the same time?

Only one IP access list per interface, per direction. In other words, one inbound and one outbound are allowed, but no more.

16. Assume all parts of the network are up and working in the network in Figure 7-12. IGRP is the IP routing protocol in use. Answer the questions following Example 7-15, which contains an additional configuration in the Mayberry router.

Figure B-1 *Scenario 7-5 Network Diagram*

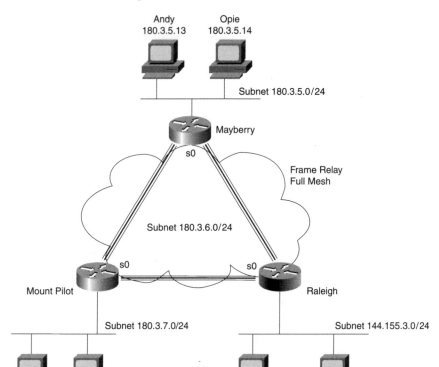

Example B-1 *Access List at Mayberry*

```
access-list 44 permit 180.3.5.13 0.0.0.0
!
interface serial 0
ip access-group 44
```

16a. Describe the types of packets that this filter would discard, and at what point they would be discarded.

Only packets coming from Andy exit Mayberry's Serial 0 interface. Packets originating inside the Mayberry router, for example a **ping** command issued from Mayberry, will work because the IOS will not filter packets originating in that router.

16b. Does this access list stop packets from getting to web server Governor? Why or why not?

Packets from Andy could get to web server Governor; packets from Mount Pilot can be delivered to Governor if the route points directly from Mount Pilot to Raleigh so that the packets do not pass through Mayberry. Therefore, the access list, as coded, stops only hosts other than Andy on the Mayberry Ethernet from reaching web server Governor.

16c. Create access lists and enable them such that access to web server Governor is allowed, but no other access to hosts in Raleigh is allowed.

```
access-list 130 permit tcp 180.3.5.0  0.0.0.255 host 144.155.3.99 eq www
access-list 130 permit tcp 180.3.7.0  0.0.0.255 host 144.155.3.99 eq www
!
interface serial 0
ip access-group 130 in
```

This access list would actually also filter IGRP updates entering Raleigh as well. That is part of the danger with inbound access lists; with outbound, the router will not filter packets originating in that router. With inbound access lists, all packets entering the interface are examined and could be filtered. An IGRP protocol type is allowed in the extended **access-list** command; therefore, IGRP updates can be easily matched. The command **access-list 130 permit igrp any any** would perform the needed matching of IGRP updates, permitting those packets. (This command would need to appear before any statements in list 130 that might match IGRP updates, and show a deny action instead of permit.)

Answers to the Chapter 8 "Do I Know This Already?" Quiz

1. Name two connection-oriented Layer 2 protocols used on WANs.

   LAPB, SDLC, Frame Relay. Frame Relay is connection oriented, but provides no error recovery. X.25 provides error recovery and is used like a Layer 2 protocol by routers, but actually more closely matches OSI Layer 3.

2. Name two WAN data-link protocols for which the standards define a protocol type field, which is used to define the type of header that follows after the WAN data-link header.

   PPP and Frame Relay. The Frame Relay protocol field was added to the standard based on efforts from the IETF.

3. Name two WAN data-link protocols that define a method of announcing the Layer 3 addresses of the interface to other devices attached to the WAN.

   PPP and Frame Relay. PPP uses control protocols specific to each Layer 3 protocol supported. Frame Relay uses Inverse ARP.

4. The **encapsulation x25** command is seen in a configuration file immediately after the command **interface serial 0**. What command(s) would be necessary to change back to the default encapsulation on this serial link?

   interface serial 0, **encapsulation hdlc**. If the user is still in configuration mode for **interface serial 0**, the **interface serial 0** command would not be necessary.

5. What do the letters in ISDN represent? BRI? PRI?

   Integrated Services Digital Network. Basic Rate Interface. Primary Rate Interface. BRI is the most likely to be on the exam.

6. "Frame Relay uses source and destination DLCIs in the Frame Relay header, with length 10, 11, or 12 bits." Which parts of this statement to you agree with? Which parts do you disagree with? Why?

   There is only one DLCI field in the Frame Relay header, but it can be 10, 11, or 12 bits in length. For further information, refer to the section titled "Frame Relay Protocols."

7. Explain the purpose of Inverse ARP. Explain how Inverse ARP uses Frame Relay broadcasts.

   A router discovers the Layer 3 address(es) of a router on the other end of a VC when that other router sends an Inverse ARP message. The message is not a broadcast. Broadcasts are not supported over Frame Relay.

8. What does NBMA stand for? Does it apply to PPP links? Frame Relay networks?

   Nonbroadcast multiaccess. PPP is nonbroadcast, but not multi-access. Frame Relay is an NBMA network. "Multi-access" really means more than two devices connected to the data link so that when one device sends data, the intended receiver is not obvious.

9. Define the term *function group* as used in CCNA exam objective 14. List two examples of function groups.

   A set of ISDN functions that need to be implemented by a device. NT1, NT2, TE1, TE2, and TA are all function groups. Cisco uses the term function groups in CCNA objective 14.

10. What layer of OSI is most closely related to the functions of Frame Relay? Why?

    OSI Layers 1 and 2. As usual, Frame Relay refers to well-known physical layer specs. Frame Relay does define headers for delivery across the Frame Relay cloud, but provides no addressing structure to allow VCs between multiple different Frame Relay networks, and therefore it is not considered to match OSI Layer 3 functions. With the advent of Frame Relay SVCs, it could be argued that Frame Relay performs some Layer 3–like functions. However, the Cisco party line (at least in the training classes in Training Paths 1 and 2) is that Frame Relay is a Layer 2 protocol.

11. Define the attributes of a partial-mesh and full-mesh Frame Relay network.

    Partial mesh means that not all DTEs are connected with a VC. Full mesh means that all DTEs are connected with a VC.

12. Define the terms PAP and CHAP. Which one(s) encrypt passwords before transmission?

    PAP stands for Password Authentication Protocol. CHAP stands for Challenge Handshake Authentication Protocol. Only CHAP encrypts the password. CHAP is the typically preferred choice.

Answers to the Chapter 8 Q&A Section

1. Name two WAN data-link protocols for which the standards define a protocol type field, which is used to define the type of header that follows after the WAN data-link header.

   PPP and Frame Relay. The Frame Relay protocol field was added to the standard based on efforts from the IETF.

2. Name two WAN data-link protocols that define a method of announcing the Layer 3 addresses of the interface to other devices attached to the WAN.

   PPP and Frame Relay. PPP uses control protocols specific to each Layer 3 protocol supported. Frame Relay uses Inverse ARP.

3. What does the acronym LAPD stand for? Is it used as the Layer 2 protocol on dialed ISDN bearer channels? If not, what is used?

   Link Access Procedure, D-channel. It is not used on bearer channels, but instead on the signaling channel. PPP is typically used on bearer channels.

4. "Frame Relay uses source and destination DLCIs in the Frame Relay header, with length 10, 11, or 12 bits." Which parts of this statement do you agree with? Which parts do you disagree with? Why?

   There is only one DLCI field in the Frame Relay header, but it can be 10, 11, or 12 bits in length. For further information, refer to the section titled "Frame Relay Protocols" in Chapter 8.

5. Explain the purpose of Inverse ARP. Explain how Inverse ARP uses Frame Relay broadcasts.

   A router discovers the Layer 3 address(es) of a router on the other end of a VC when that other router sends an Inverse ARP message. The message is not a broadcast. Broadcasts are not supported over Frame Relay.

6. Would a Frame Relay switch, connected to a router, behave differently if the IETF option were deleted from the **encapsulation frame-relay ietf** command on that attached router? Would a router on the other end of the VC behave any differently if the same change were made?

   The switch does not behave differently. The other router, however, must also use IETF encapsulation; otherwise, the routers will not be looking at the correct fields to learn the packet type. The IETF-defined headers include the protocol type field options.

7. What does NBMA stand for? Does it apply to PPP links? X.25 networks? Frame Relay networks?

   Nonbroadcast multiaccess. PPP is nonbroadcast, but not multi-access. X.25 and Frame Relay are NBMA networks. "Multi-access" really means more than two devices connected to the data link; therefore, when one device sends data, the intended receiver is not obvious.

8. Define the terms DCE and DTE in the context of the physical layer and a point-to-point serial link.

   DTE refers to the device that looks for clocking from the device on the other end of the cable on a synchronous link. The DCE supplies that clocking. An X.25 switch is a DCE in the X.25 use of the word, but probably is a DTE receiving clock from a DSU/CSU or Mux from the physical layer perspective.

9. What layer of OSI is most closely related to the functions of Frame Relay? Why?

   OSI Layers 1 and 2. As usual, Frame Relay refers to well-known physical layer specs. Frame Relay does define headers for delivery across the Frame Relay cloud, but provides no addressing structure to allow VCs between multiple different Frame Relay networks; so it is not considered to match OSI Layer 3 functions. With the advent of Frame Relay SVCs, it could be argued that Frame Relay performs some Layer 3–like functions. However, the Cisco party line (at least in the training classes in Training Paths 1 and 2) is that Frame Relay is a Layer 2 protocol.

10. When Inverse ARP is used by default, what additional configuration is needed to get IGRP routing updates to flow over each VC?

    No additional configuration is required. The forwarding of broadcasts as unicasts is enabled on each VC and protocol for which an Inverse ARP is received.

11. Define the attributes of a partial-mesh and full-mesh Frame Relay network.

    Partial mesh means that not all DTEs are connected with a VC. Full mesh means that all DTEs are connected with a VC.

12. What key pieces of information are required in the **frame-relay map** statement?

    Layer 3 protocol, next-hop router's Layer 3 address, DLCI to reach that router, and whether to forward broadcasts. Frame Relay maps are not required if Inverse ARP is in use.

13. When creating a partial-mesh Frame Relay network, are you required to use subinterfaces?

    No. Subinterfaces can be used and are preferred with a partial mesh because it removes split-horizon issues by treating each VC as its own interface. Likewise, subinterfaces are optional when the network is a full mesh. Most people tend to use subinterfaces today.

14. What benefit related to routing protocols can be gained by using subinterfaces with a partial mesh?

    Split-horizon issues are avoided by treating each VC as a separate interface. Split-horizon is still enabled; routing loops are not a risk, but all routes are learned.

15. Can PPP perform dynamic assignment of IP addresses? If so, is the feature always enabled?

    PPP's IPCP protocol can assign an IP address to the device on the other end of the link. This process is not required. PPP usually does address assignment for dial access, for example, when a user dials an Internet service provider.

16. Create a configuration to enable PPP on serial 0 for IP and IPX. Make up IP and IPX Layer 3 addresses as needed.

    ```
    interface serial 0
    ip addr 1.1.1.1 255.255.255.0
    ipx network 1
    encapsulation ppp
    ```

    encapsulation ppp is all that is needed for PPP. Having IP and IPX enabled causes PPP to enable the control protocols for each.

17. Create a configuration for Router1 that has Frame Relay VCs to Router2 and Router3 (DLCIs 202 and 203, respectively), for Frame Relay on Router1's serial 1 interface. Use any IP and IPX addresses you like. Assume the network is not fully-meshed.

```
interface serial 1
encapsulation frame-relay
interface serial 1.1 point-to-point
ip address 168.10.1.1 255.255.255.0
ipx network 1
frame-relay interface-dlci 202
interface serial 1.2 point-to-point
ip address 168.10.2.1 255.255.255.ipx network 2
ipx network 2
frame-relay interface-dlci 203
```

This is not the only valid configuration given the problem statement. However, because there is not a full-mesh, point-to-point subinterfaces are the best choice. Cisco encapsulation is used by default. The LMI type is autosensed.

18. What **show** command will tell you the time that a PVC became active? How does the router know what time the PVC came active?

The **show frame-relay pvc** command lists the time since the PVC came up. The router learns this from an LMI message.

19. What **show** commands list Frame Relay information about mapping? In what instances will the information displayed include the Layer 3 addresses of other routers?

show frame-relay map. The mapping information includes Layer 3 addresses when multipoint subinterfaces are used, or when no subinterfaces are used. The two cases where the neighboring routers' Layer 3 addresses are shown are the two cases where Frame Relay acts like a multi-access network. With point-to-point subinterfaces, the logic works like a point-to-point link, where the next router's Layer 3 address is not important to the routing process.

20. The **no keepalive** command on a Frame Relay serial interface causes no further Cisco proprietary keepalive messages to be sent to the Frame Relay switch. (T/F)

False. This command stops LMI status enquiry messages from being sent. If the switch is expecting these, the switch could take down the PVCs to this DTE. Be careful—this is exactly the type of tricky wording on the exam. The messages do not go between the two routers over Frame Relay, but it is not the Cisco keepalive message sent on true point-to-point links.

21. What **debug** options will show Inverse ARP messages?

debug frame-relay events as shown in Example 8-18 on page 419.

22. The Frame Relay **map** configuration command allows more than one Layer 3 protocol address mapping on the same configuration command. (T/F)

    False. The syntax allows only a single network-layer protocol and address to be configured.

23. What do the letters in ISDN represent? BRI? PRI?

    Integrated Services Digital Network. Basic Rate Interface. Primary Rate Interface. BRI is the most likely to be on the exam.

24. Define the term *function group* as used in CCNA exam objective 14. List two examples of function groups.

    A set of ISDN functions that need to be implemented by a device. NT1, NT2, TE1, TE2, and TA are all function groups. Cisco uses the term *function groups* in CCNA objective 14: Identify ISDN protocols, function groups, reference points, and channels.

25. Define the term *reference point* as used in CCNA exam objective 14: Identify ISDN protocols, function groups, reference points, and channels. List two examples of reference points.

    A *reference point* is an interface between function groups. R, S, T, and U are the reference points. S and T are combined in many cases and then called the S/T reference point. Reference points refer to cabling, which implies the number of wires used. In particular, the S and T points use a four-wire interface; the U interface uses a two-wire cable.

26. How many bearer channels are in a BRI? A PRI in North America? A PRI in Europe?

    BRI uses two bearer channels and one signaling channel (2B+D). PRI uses 23B+D in North America and 30B+D in Europe. The signaling channel on BRI is a 16-Kbps channel; on PRI, it is a 64-Kbps channel.

27. Is the following statement true or false: "ISDN defines protocols that can be functionally equivalent to OSI Layers 1, 2, and 3." Defend your answer.

    True. Reference points in part define the physical interfaces. LAPD, used on the signaling channel, is a data-link protocol. SPIDs define a logical addressing structure and are roughly equivalent to OSI Layer 3. Table 8-20 on page 422 summarizes ISDN protocols as compared with the OSI model.

28. What reference points are used by ISDN BRI interfaces on Cisco routers?

    A BRI interface with an S/T reference point, or a BRI with a U interface, can be bought from Cisco. With an S/T interface, an external NT1, NT2, or NT1/NT2 device is required. With the U interface, no external device is required.

29. What do the letters LAPD represent? Is LAPD used on ISDN channels, and if so, which ones?

Link Access Procedure, D-channel. It is used only on ISDN D channels to deliver signaling messages to the local ISDN switch. Many people confuse the function of LAPD, thinking it is used on the B channels after the dial is complete. The encapsulation chosen in the router configuration determines the data-link protocol on the bearer channels. There is no option on Cisco routers to turn off LAPD on the signaling channel.

30. Name the standards body that defines ISDN protocols.

International Telecommunications Union (ITU). This group was formerly the CCITT. The ITU is governed by the United Nations.

31. What ISDN functions do standards ITU-T Q.920 and Q.930 define? Does either standard correlate to an OSI layer?

Q.920 defines the ISDN data-link specifications, such as LAPD; Q.930 defines Layer 3 functions, such as call setup messages. I.440 and I.450 are equivalent to Q.920 and Q.930, respectively.

32. What ISDN functions does standard ITU-T I.430 define? Does it correlate to an OSI layer?

I.430 defines ISDN BRI physical layer specifications. It is similar to OSI Layer 1. There is no Q series equivalent specification to I.430.

33. What do the letters SPID represent, and what does the term mean?

Service profile identifier. It is the ISDN phone number used in signaling.

34. Define the terms TE1, TE2, and TA. Which term(s) imply that one of the other two must be in use?

Terminal Equipment 1, Terminal Equipment 2, and Terminal Adapter. A TE2 device requires a TA. A TE2 uses the R reference point. An S reference point is needed to perform ISDN signaling; it is provided in that case by the TA.

35. What reference point is used between the customer premise and the phone company in North America? In Europe?

The U interface is used in North America. Elsewhere, the T interface is used. The NT1 function, the dividing point between the T and U reference points, is implemented in Telco equipment outside North America.

36. Define the term *S-Bus* and give one example of when it would be useful.

S-Bus is a bus with many devices sharing the S reference point. ISDN-capable phones, faxes, and computers, wishing to share the same BRI, connect to the same NT1 using an S-Bus. The SPIDs include subaddresses to distinguish between the multiple devices when using an S-Bus.

37. What data-link (OSI Layer 2) protocols are valid on an ISDN B channel?

HDLC, PPP, and LAPB are all valid options. PPP is the preferred choice, however. If using DDR to more than one site, PAP or CHAP authentication is required. If used, PPP must be used. PPP also provides automatic IP address assignment, which is convenient for PC dial-in.

38. Define the terms PAP and CHAP. Which one(s) encrypt passwords before transmission?

Password Authentication Protocol, Challenge Handshake Authentication Protocol. Only CHAP encrypts the password. CHAP is the typically preferred choice.

39. Define MLPPP. Describe the typical home or small office use of MLPPP.

Multilink Point-to-Point Protocol. It is used to treat multiple B channels as a single link because MLPPP will fragment packets and send different fragments across the multiple links to balance the traffic. MLPPP is very useful for sharing two B channels in home or small office use. It is not restricted to home use.

40. CHAP configuration uses names and passwords. Given Routers A and B, describe what names and passwords must match in the respective CHAP configurations.

Router A has name "B" and a corresponding password configured. Router B has name "A" and the same password configured. The names used are the hostnames of the routers unless the CHAP name is configured.

41. Configure ISDN interface BRI1 assuming that it is attached to a DMS-100 ISDN switch, it uses only one SPID of 404555121201, and you want to screen calls so that only calls from 404555999901 are accepted.

```
isdn switch-type basic-dms100
interface bri1
  isdn spid1 404555121201
  isdn caller 404555999901
```

The **switch-type** command is required. The SPID(s) is required only with some switches. The **caller** command is only needed for call screening.

Numerics

A

D

O

Q

R

T

By opening this package, you are agreeing to be bound by the following agreement:

Some of the software included with this product may be copyrighted, in which case all rights are reserved by the respective copyright holder. You are licensed to use software copyrighted by the Publisher and its licensors on a single computer. You may copy and/or modify the software as needed to facilitate your use of it on a single computer. Making copies of the software for any other purpose is a violation of the United States copyright laws.

This software is sold as is without warranty of any kind, either expressed or implied, including but not limited to the implied warranties of merchantability and fitness for a particular purpose. Neither the Publisher nor its dealers or distributors assumes any liability for any alleged or actual damages arising from the use of this program. (Some states do not allow for the exclusion of implied warranties, so the exclusion may not apply to you.)